STUDIES IN
TUDOR AND STUART POLITICS
AND GOVERNMENT

VOLUME THREE

The Tudor Revolution in Government (C.U.P. 1953)

England under the Tudors, History of England, vol. 4 (Methuen 1955; 2nd edn 1974)

(ed.) *The Reformation*, New Cambridge Modern History, vol. 2 (C.U.P. 1958)

Star Chamber Stories (Methuen 1958)

The Tudor Constitution (C.U.P. 1960; 2nd edn 1982)

(ed.) *Renaissance and Reformation, 1300–1648*, Ideas and Institutions in Western Civilization (Macmillan, N.Y. 1963; 2nd edn 1968; 3rd edn 1976)

Reformation Europe, 1517–59 (Collins 1963)

The Practice of History (Sydney U.P. 1967)

The Future of the Past, Inaugural Lecture (C.U.P. 1968)

England, 1200–1640, The Sources of History (Hodder & Stoughton 1969)

Modern Historians on British History, 1485–1945 (Methuen 1970)

Political History: Principles and Practice (Basic Books 1970)

Policy and Police: Enforcement of the Reformation in the Age of Thomas Cromwell (C.U.P. 1972)

Reform and Renewal: Thomas Cromwell and the Common Weal (C.U.P. 1973)

Studies in Tudor and Stuart Politics and Government, 2 vols (C.U.P. 1974)

(ed.) *Annual Bibliography of British and Irish History* (Harvester 1976–)

Reform and Reformation: England 1509–1558 (Arnold 1977)

English Law in the Sixteenth Century: Reform in an Age of Change (Selden Society 1979)

STUDIES IN
TUDOR AND STUART POLITICS
AND GOVERNMENT

G.R. ELTON
(Geoffrey Rudolph)

VOLUME THREE

PAPERS AND REVIEWS 1973–1981

CAMBRIDGE UNIVERSITY PRESS

CAMBRIDGE

LONDON   NEW YORK   NEW ROCHELLE

MELBOURNE   SYDNEY

Published by the Press Syndicate of the University of Cambridge
The Pitt Building, Trumpington Street, Cambridge CB2 1RP
32 East 57th Street, New York, NY 10022, USA
296 Beaconsfield Parade, Middle Park, Melbourne 3206, Australia

First published 1983

Printed in Great Britain at
the University Press, Cambridge

Library of Congress catalogue card number: 73-79305

British Library Cataloguing in Publication Data
Elton, G.R.
Studies in Tudor and Stuart politics and
government.
Vol. 3
1. Great Britain — Politics and government — 1485—
I. Title
320.942   DA300
ISBN 0 521 24893 0

AL

CONTENTS

Contents

vi

PREFACE

The generous reception extended to the first two volumes of my collected papers has encouraged me to add a third, covering the productions of the last eight years. Once again the work has been sufficiently concentrated – or, as some may say, narrow – to suggest a sufficient degree of coherence in these papers, with the exception of the last, a confession of my professional faith which may help to explain the quirks of the rest. I have tried to put the papers into some sort of order, collecting two sets under general titles and arranging the remainder by subject matter rather than by year date. In editing the material I have followed the principles set out in the Preface to volume one. The text has been left untouched, even where I now know that I was in error, but notes in square brackets have been added to record repentance. I have added a small selection of reviews, chosen because they either elaborate or offer grounds for some of the views and conclusions embodied in the papers; they are arranged in rough chronological order of subjects.

In 1973 I hoped that the willingness of the Cambridge University Press to bring out the collection would not come to be thought of as quixotic. To my relief and theirs, that hope turned out to be not unjustified. Times have changed, and the world of books stands in an even worse crisis. To repeat that earlier hope would very likely bring down the whirligig's revenges, but the darkness of the day moves me to an even deeper gratitude for the Press's continued support.

Clare College, Cambridge   G.R. ELTON
January 1982

ACKNOWLEDGMENTS

The author and publisher are grateful to the following for permission to reproduce material first published by them:

The English Historical Review, and Longman Ltd, for No. 34 (i) and Review (c)
The Bulletin of the Institute of Historical Research, for No. 34 (iv)
Zeitschrift für Kirchengeschichte, for No. 43
Reviews in European History, for Review (a)
London Review of Books, for Review (b)
Times Literary Supplement, for Review (d)
History and Theory, for Review (e)
Spectator, for Reviews (g) and (h)
Journal of Modern History, for Review (i)
The Royal Historical Society, for Nos 33 and 48
The Athlone Press, for No. 34 (ii)
The University of Pennsylvania Press, for No. 36
Leicester University Press, for No. 38
Gerald Duckworth & Co. Ltd, for No. 39
The Selden Society, for No. 40
Professor J.S. Cockburn, for No. 41
The Ecclesiastical History Society, for No. 42
Wayne State University Press, for No. 44
Verlag W. Kohlhammer (Stuttgart), for No. 45 (ii)
Gütersloher Verlagshaus Gerd Mohr (Gütersloh), for No. 46
AMS Press Inc. (New York), for No. 47

ABBREVIATIONS

APC	*Acts of the Privy Council*
BIHR	*Bulletin of the Institute of Historical Research*
BL	British Library
CJ	*Journal of the House of Commons*
CS	Camden Series
CUL	Cambridge University Library
DNB	*Dictionary of National Biography*
EcHR	*Economic History Review*
EHR	*English Historical Review*
HJ	*Historical Journal*
HLRO	House of Lords Record Office
HMC	Historical Manuscripts Commission
LJ	*Journal of the House of Lords*
LP	*Letters and Papers, Foreign and Domestic, of the Reign of Henry VIII*, ed. J.S. Brewer, J. Gairdner, R.H. Brodie, 21 vols. (1862–1932)
Merriman	*The Life and Letters of Thomas Cromwell*, ed. R.B. Merriman, 2 vols. (Oxford, 1902)
Policy and Police	G.R. Elton, *Policy and Police: the Enforcement of the Reformation in the Age of Thomas Cromwell* (Cambridge, 1972)
PP	*Past and Present*
PRO	Public Record Office
Reform and Renewal	G.R. Elton, *Reform and Renewal: Thomas Cromwell and the Common Weal* (Cambridge, 1973)

RP	*Rotuli Parliamentorum ut et Peticiones et Placita in Parliamento*, 6 vols. (n.d.)
SR	*Statutes of the Realm*, 11 vols. (1810–28)
STC	*A Short-Title Catalogue of Books Printed . . . 1475–1640* (1924; new edn 1976–)
TRHS	*Transactions of the Royal Historical Society*
TRP	*Tudor Royal Proclamations*, ed. P.L. Hughes and J.F. Larkin, 3 vols. (New Haven, 1964, 1969)
Tudor Constitution	G.R. Elton, *The Tudor Constitution* (Cambridge, 1960; 2nd edn 1982)
Tudor Revolution	G.R. Elton, *The Tudor Revolution in Government: Administrative Changes in the Reign of Henry VIII* (Cambridge, 1953)

References to *LP* are to numbers of documents, elsewhere to pages. Books for which no place of publication is noted were published in London.

I

PAPERS

33

TUDOR GOVERNMENT: THE POINTS
OF CONTACT*

I. PARLIAMENT

It is one of the functions of government to preserve in contentment and balance that society which it rules. Some of the tasks involved in that general purpose are familiar enough. Government exists to maintain peace in the nation – to prevent disturbance, punish crime, and generally ensure that people can lead their lives without threats from others. Government must therefore provide the means for resolving disputes peacefully: it must administer justice and be seen to do so. In addition, since no society can ever stand absolutely still, government is charged with the task of reviewing existing relationships – relationships of rights, duties, burdens and privileges – with an eye to supplying reform, that is, changes designed to keep the general balance and contentment from deteriorating. Most discussions of problems of government revolve around these points. Analysis has concerned itself with the machinery available for discharging these tasks, and assessment has concentrated on establishing the degree of success obtained.

However, there is more to it than this. It has long been realized that the so-called realities of government involve further the social structure of the body governed. Government, we know, cannot work unless it obtains obedience and (preferably) consent from the governed and that recognition has led to a good deal of work on the power structure among the governed and its integration into the exercise of power relinquished to the ruler. With respect to the Tudor century, for instance, we have learned something about the way in which power and rule devolved outwards from a monarchy which, however hard it tried to centralize management, still depended greatly on the co-operation of the so-called rulers of the countryside, and we have increasingly come to

* [Presidential addresses to the Royal Historical Society: *TRHS*, 5th ser. 24 (1974), 183–200; 25 (1975), 195–211; 26 (1976), 211–28.]

understand the degree to which the necessary tasks of government continued to be discharged at decentralized points – in local courts and through the often spontaneous action of lesser organs of rule. The vital role of magnates, gentry and municipal oligarchies has of late been much emphasized, to a point where mistakenly low assessments of the power of the centre have unhappily become current. Arising out of this, questions have been asked about the means which help to tie peripheral authority to central; some of the lines of communication among rival interests have been traced; some patronage systems have been analysed. True, we have had rather more calls for this kind of study than performances, and such examples of revealing importance as have appeared have tended to restrict themselves territorially, to concentrate on the land market, and to go easy on the politics; but then, in the conditions set by sixteenth-century evidence, such things as political attitudes (thought, feeling and programmes), or the role and significance of patronage (the pool of favours and advantages on the one hand, the search for them on the other) are more readily apprehended in general terms than documented in working detail.[1] At any rate, we now know that Tudor government depended not only on the activities of rulers both central and local, and on the management of the machinery available, but also on the organization and rivalries of patronage systems constructed around local, familial and political foci which everywhere penetrated the visible politics of the day.

One matter, however, it seems to me, has received little attention: or rather, one particular type of question has not been asked; and since I think that that question (and if possible the answers to it) may bring us a little nearer to understanding why Tudor government remained pretty stable through a difficult century, while instability and collapse attended upon the government of the early Stuarts, it is a question I should like to look at here. Stability is the product of moderate contentment: it is preserved if the operations of government are thought to conduce to order and justice, and if they succeed in taking account of the claims to power entertained by inferior authorities. This last point has, as I have said, been largely seen in terms of local rule and ties of patronage; one element in the system is missing. We know what people wanted and can trace the contacts that put them in the way of getting it, but we have not asked whether the machinery existed to transform ambition and favour

---

[1] An interesting attempt to analyse attitudes in the north has just appeared: M. E. James, 'The concept of order and the Northern Rising of 1569', *PP* 60 (1973), 49 ff.

into achievement. To be stable, any system needs to include organized means – public structures – to provide for the ambitions at the centre of affairs of such persons as can, if those ambitions remain unsatisfied, upset that stability. The question I want to ask is really very simple: did Tudor government contain within its formal structure conventional means for the satisfaction of such people? Did it provide known and accessible instruments which enabled positive interests, demands and ambitions on the part of the politically powerful to achieve their ends? Alternatively, did the politically powerful discover in the machinery of government such means of self-satisfaction? The question is simple, but the answers, to be reasonably complete, would be very complex indeed, involving, for instance, a full study of all office-holders. All I can hope to do in this and succeeding lectures it to draw attention to unstudied problems, or perhaps to a new way of looking at problems studied often enough before, and to offer some preliminary suggestions. I also hope that others may feel encouraged to pursue these issues further.

When we think about the social organization of the sixteenth century from this point of view – when we ask ourselves whether the system of government provided obvious organization points at which the purposes of rulers and ruled (Crown and 'political nation') came into the sort of contact which could prove fruitful to the ambitions of those not yet part of the central government – we are first, and obviously, driven to look at Parliament. Parliament, after all, was thought of as the image of the nation in common political action, where, to quote Thomas Smith's familiar words once again, in the making of law the whole realm participates because 'every Englishman is intended to be there present, either in person or by procuration and attorney'.[2] The political reality of this concept needs no further discussion – or should I say that it ought to need none, though there are still some respected scholars who have their doubts about it. And yet the evidence has been accumulating, and continues to accumulate, that the sixteenth century had a clear understanding of the notion of legislative sovereignty – of the supreme power to make laws in all respects that touch the body politic; that it unquestioningly vested that power in the mixed entity called Parliament – king, Lords and Commons jointly; and that it was right to treat the operations of that mixed body as politically genuine rather than prejudged, constrained or merely formal. It seems to me that memories of royal claims in the fourteenth and fifteenth centuries, or of the more

[2] *De Republica Anglorum*, ed. L. Alston (Cambridge, 1906), 48–9.

explicit monarchic doctrines which appeared in the seventeenth, combine with misleading interpretations of the high executive authority vested in Tudor monarchs to call in doubt the reality of what Smith, and many others, regarded as the fundamental commonplace of the English constitution. One man who attended upon that constitution for half a century was quite clear on the point, and since Lord Burghley's opinion has not been often cited it may be worth producing here. He held

that their Lordships of the Upper House . . . are one member of the Parliament; and also that the Knights, Citizens and Burgesses of this House representing the whole Commons of this Realm are also another Member of the same Parliament; and her Majesty the Head; and that of these three Estates doth consist the whole Body of the Parliament able to make laws.[3]

In addition, he was quoted later as not knowing what the English Parliament could not do in the way of lawmaking. Full legislative supremacy vested in the image of the nation and politically active there: that was the basis of Tudor government. True, the full doctrine was of recent standing; in the Reformation Parliament, members of both Houses were still troubled to know whether the legislative authority of Parliament extended to the government and order of the Church, a severe limitation.[4] The years of that assembly, however, settled the matter and completed the institutional and doctrinal claims of Parliament. I repeat all this only because we are still told at intervals that institutionally Tudor Parliaments were nothing new and politically they marked a decline. The evidence will not support this double scepticism: it points to a novel recognition of the doctrine and an increased political vigour.

As the sovereign maker of laws, Parliament thus stood ideologically central to the problem of political stability; it was potentially at least useful to all who had purposes to serve, whether those purposes were national, sectional or personal, so long as they required innovation and change. On Parliament converged of necessity all ambitions to maintain or to reform the system: it was the chief organ for absorbing and satisfying the demands made upon stability in government. Even rebels regarded it in this light: the Pilgrims of Grace, for instance, while they might denounce alleged recent practices of packing and influencing,

[3] Simonds D'Ewes, *The Journals of all the Parliaments during the Reign of Queen Elizabeth* (1682), 350 (said in 1585).
[4] *Reform and Renewal*, 67; and above, no. 22.

nevertheless called for a Parliament after the old and uncorrupted sort to bring peace in the realm.[5] Yet surely to anyone raised in the traditions of English parliamentary scholarship there is something odd about the notion that the institution should be treated as an instrument of stability. Our historians have traditionally concentrated on conflict and have studied all meetings of Parliament with an eye to dispute and opposition. Sir John Neale, to take a very relevant case, found the main theme of his history of *Elizabeth I and her Parliaments* in the accumulation of unremitting political differences. The impression he leaves is that meetings of the Elizabethan Parliament were notable mainly because they set the stage for collisions between rulers and ruled and gave dissent an opportunity to disrupt the secret ways of government and policy. If James I came to think of Parliaments as like to cats that grow cursed with age or complained that his predecessors had saddled him with this tiresome burr under the tail of the body politic, it was certainly not because he distrusted stability and saw in Parliament a means for creating such political stability as might grow from participation in affairs or from the satisfaction of ambitions. It could be argued that parliamentary conflict only demonstrated the existence of disagreements which the airing they got there might even help to resolve. Parliaments might be regarded as useful safety-valves in the engine of government. However, this is a sophistical rather than a sophisticated point: months of quarrelsome debate, so far from removing the poison of disagreement, tend to increase enmity and 'polarization'. There is really no sign that in the sixteenth century disputes in either House helped to allay conflict, and from the 1590s the history of Parliament is one of increasing criticism, increasing exasperation, increasing failure to restore stability. In any case, even if Parliaments had helped to release troublesome vapours, they would still not have been serving as means for satisfying legitimate aspirations on the part of the governing nation, the role for which I am trying to cast them. So long as historians of Parliament devote themselves to the description of political disputes and rival assertions of authority, they are bound to see in Parliament not a means towards stability but an instrument of real or potential opposition.

Is this preoccupation justified — a preoccupation which (as Neale did) skates over things done by agreement, or even comes to believe that agreement could only be the result of pressure from above, subservience

[5] *LP* xi, 1182(2), 1244, 1246.

from below?[6] Did people at the time share this view? It is necessary to enquire what those concerned wanted from Parliament and why they wanted it at all. In Parliament the nation (according to contemporary experts) met to deal with its affairs. This does suggest that in the first place harmony rather than dispute was intended, and that a prevalence of opposition and conflict should be treated as a sign that the necessary stability was in danger. The monarch's purposes are reasonably clear. Mostly they called Parliament to get money: Elizabeth was the first ruler of England who let not a single session pass without obtaining supply.[7] They also wanted laws, especially in the revolutionary years between 1532 and 1559 when every session witnessed a full-scale government programme of legislation. Arguably, the Crown had less of an interest thereafter in parliamentary assemblies because, anxious now to hold a line rather than promote reform, it felt less need for continuous further legislation. As is well known, meetings grew much rarer in the second half of the century, though government legislation certainly did not come to an end in 1559. The demands of the struggle with Catholicism saw to that, and even reform, though less intense, did not terminate; not even Elizabeth could make time stand still. However, these practical needs of cash and laws do not fully explain the attitude of Tudor governments to Parliament, at least not after 1529 when all possibility ceased of ruling without the meetings of the estates. Parliaments were wanted because there the great affairs of the nation could be considered, debated and advertised: Parliament was a part of the machinery of government available to active rulers.

In its earlier days, the idea of the image of the body politic called into existence to produce the active co-operation of all its members, was the property of the Crown, even if a century later it became the weapon of an opposition. The conviction behind the royal summons was, for instance, expressed in the circular which instructed sheriffs about their duties in the elections of May 1536. Evidently it was thought desirable to offer some explanation why only a few weeks after the long Reformation Parliament had at last gone home it should be necessary to burden the country again with a Parliament.

Such matters [the king was made to say] of most high importance have chanced as for the preservation of our honour, the establishment of our succession in the

---

[6] Cf. J. Hurstfield's argument that in the sixteenth century consent only hid constraint: *TRHS*, 4th ser. 17 (1967), 99 ff.

[7] [Wrong: no supply was asked for in 1572.]

Crown of this our realm . . . have been to us and to all the lords of our Council thought necessary to be discussed and determined in our high court of Parliament to be assembled for that purpose.[8]

These delicate phrases hide the miserable business of the palace revolution which destroyed the Boleyns, and thus far the calling of Parliament seemed necessitated only by the 1534 Act of Succession, now out of date and in need of replacement. But the letter went on to explain that the business was urgent and involved both the public weal and the personal security of the monarch; a matter of high policy, very personal to the king, was described as truly the concern of the nation assembled in Parliament. As practice proved, this was more than rhetoric: Henry VIII, at least, and Thomas Cromwell treated Parliament as though they believed in this stabilizing function. We need to remember the positive note struck − the ringing assertion that public affairs of real import were the business of Parliament and justified the calling of an unexpectedly sudden one.

Henrician Parliaments unquestionably concerned themselves with affairs of state, and not necessarily only at the Crown's behest; they were freely given information on diplomatic negotiations, like those with France in 1532 which pleased both Houses;[9] in the Cromwell era, as also in the difficult years of Edward VI and Mary, no one attempted to deny (as Elizabeth was to do on occasion) that Parliaments, and indeed the House of Commons, had an active part to play in the high politics of the nation. And even Elizabeth readily conceded a political function to her Parliaments, provided she was allowed to turn the tap off when it suited her. Compelled to use Parliament for the imposition of taxes and the making of laws, Tudor monarchs also thought it necessary and desirable to involve the potentially powerful and potentially difficult in the affairs of the realm by offering the occasions of debate, discussion and support which Parliament represented. For most of the century, so far as we can judge, government certainly saw in Parliament a means of preserving stability and adjusting balances. And despite the occasions of 'conflict' (often no more than a proper exchange of views and arguments), the outcome usually produced consensus and contentment, thus justifying the theory behind the practice.

What, then, of those who came when called? We know at present far too little about the Lords, though work is in progress.[10] That people

---

[8] BL, Harl. MS 283, fo. 256 (*LP* x, 815).
[9] *LP* v, 1518. [10] Especially in the hands of Dr Michael Graves.

sought election to the Commons in the reign of Elizabeth has been sufficiently proved by Neale: I need only point to his evidence of new boroughs created by the demand for seats, or of contested elections as demonstrating the desire of rival local individuals and factions to get to the place of power and influence.[11] But similar things evidently happened in the reign of Henry VIII, too. Some of the newly enfranchised boroughs may well have anticipated the sort of purposes well vouched for in the daughter's reign, though most of the new seats were certainly added by Crown policy. Tournai, Calais, Wales and Chester owed the bestowal of the franchise to the king's desire to centralize the realm and demonstrate its unity in the visible image of the body politic. However, there are sufficient signs that individuals strove actively, and against other individuals, to get elected: the 'secret labours' made in 1534 when a by-election fell due in Warwickshire, the riotous disputes accompanying the shire election for Shropshire in 1536, the uncalled-for ambitions in Norfolk in 1539 of Sir Edmund Knyvet who managed to affront both Cromwell and the duke of Norfolk, the troublesome intervention in 1542 of one Richard Devereux at the first ever election for Carmarthenshire.[12] The beginnings of a systematic use of influence on elections which marked the Parliaments of 1536 and 1539 themselves testify to ambitions to enter the Commons, and the familiar story of the clumsy interference in Kent by Edward's Privy Council in 1547 brings out the real involvement in parliamentary affairs of both gentry and freeholders.[13] There is no reason to doubt that throughout the century the theoretical attachment to the representative institution was matched by a widespread desire to share in its operations. And it would be very rash to suppose that behind this desire was only some mildly pompous wish to enhance one's standing in the eyes of one's fellows. The people who sought election may well be presumed to have wanted to use their place for identifiable ends.

What, then, did people want from Parliament? We may assume, without question, that they were not seeking taxation, though it needs to be pointed out that from 1534 onwards Parliaments came to terms with the fact that peace-time taxation had come to stay.[14] I am not suggesting that the Tudor Commons embraced taxes with the self-sacrificing masochism displayed by twentieth-century Parliaments;

---

[11] J. E. Neale, *The Elizabethan House of Commons* (1948), esp. chs. ii–vii.

[12] *LP* vii, 1178; x, 1063; xiv (1), 672, 706, 800, 808; xvii, 48.

[13] *APC* ii, 516, 518.   [14] Cf. below, no. 37.

but I would suggest that they did not either automatically regard all taxation with the bigoted irresponsibility too readily ascribed to them by some historians. They knew as well as we do that government needed to be financed, and when persuaded that the purposes of government were sound they proved far less difficult about granting money than one might suppose. The only Parliament of the century which made really serious trouble about supply was that of 1523, a Parliament which deliberately expressed its grave disquiet about Wolsey's policies. Nor was taxation seen as a bargaining counter: apart from the session of 1566, when fears for the succession produced a real conflict, no Parliament seems ever to have attempted to use supply for the extraction of political concessions, and on that occasion no one doubted that the money grant itself was justified. Tudor Parliaments voted supply soberly and responsibly, and it should be recognized once again that the principle and practice of taxation by consent made a very real contribution to the political stability of the system. We know what happened in the next generation, as soon as serious attempts were made to tax without consent.

Still, it was not the prospect of taking money out of constituents' pockets that lured men into service in the House. Some, of course, did want to pursue political ends. Some men, well aware of the platform which Parliament provided, wished to use it to promote policies or hinder those they thought were likely to be promoted by others. This is as true of the group supporting Catherine of Aragon who organized opposition in the Reformation Parliament,[15] as it is of the 'puritan choir' of 1563 or the brothers Wentworth. But these men, seeking legitimate conflict, clearly formed a small minority of the members of the House. The main part of those who looked beyond the personal gratification and local repute which election to Parliament might bring with it seem to have had one of two ends in view: the obtaining of legislation for themselves or for groups or individuals with whom they were connected, and personal advancement. In other words, to them Parliament offered just that opportunity of fulfilling particular ambitions which are required in an instrument of political stability.

If so far I may well have seemed to be digging over well-tilled ground, I have now to confess that for the rest of this paper I can do little more than suggest lines of enquiry. That all sorts of people – indivi-

---

[15] Above, no. 8.

duals, interests, institutions, companies – wished to use Parliament in order to get their programmes and necessities embodied in legislation is, of course, a familiar point. Very little, however, has been done to see what sort of success they had in this. We need to study acts passed and failed bills, assign them to this or that initiative, and explore local and private records systematically in order to discover who attempted what and who managed to achieve what. The problems of legislative initiative are many and in the past have too often been solved by despair – by simply assuming that all reasonably general acts owed their origin to the Crown or 'the government', while those touching particular interests may safely be ascribed to those interests. This rule of thumb offers an unsafe guide. I have before this attempted to penetrate some of the jungle for the 1530s (and have disconcertingly discovered that even then we cannot be sure that king and minister worked always in mutually informed harmony),[16] while the Parliaments of 1547–57 and of 1589–1610 are being studied with such questions in mind.[17] Miss Miller's revealing study of the manner in which the city of London used Parliament needs to be followed up after 1547.[18] There are other well-organized towns to consider, as well as bodies of gentlemen in the shires. How important was it for a burgess, especially if he was what Neale has termed a carpet-bagger, or even for a knight, to serve the purposes and respond to the demands of his constituents? Can we discover anything touching the relations between electors and the man they sent to Westminster? Did re-election have to do with the successful promotion of bills? How many men in the Commons were in fact active about bills? How serious were constituencies about bills they had in the House, and can we find out anything about the cost of obtaining an act of Parliament? There are no answers at present – or only the most tenuous ones – to these and similar questions; and yet we must have answers if we are to understand what went on in Parliament and what men wanted from it. The question is the more obviously important because the existence of private act legislation is peculiar to the English Parliament, distinguishing it, for instance, from those of Scotland and Ireland. We are well advised to seek at least part of the explanation for

[16] *Reform and Renewal*, ch. 4.

[17] By Professor C. Erikson, Mr A. L. Jenkins, and Miss M. A. Randall.

[18] Helen Miller, 'London and Parliament in the reign of Henry VIII', *BIHR* 35 (1962), 128 ff.; the unsystematic remarks in Neale, *The Elizabethan House of Commons* – e.g. 336–8, 383–7 – are but a beginning.

the political differences between these assemblies in this simple fact.[19]

I cannot on this occasion attempt to fill the gap, but I can offer a few examples from the reign of Henry VIII to show how very real and active this involvement of private interests in the work of the session was. To many men, even the Reformation Parliament signified less a time of revolution in state and Church than an opportunity to advance their own business. The sheriffs and escheators of Northumberland, who for years had been paying over the profits in their charge to the chamber, in 1536 found themselves troubled with process out of the Exchequer for some seventy years' arrears; they petitioned the king for a bill of indemnity back to Edward IV, a move which yielded no result.[20] One of the king's chirurgeons did better in 1545 by getting royal approval for a bill to create a profitable monopoly in the appraising of dead men's goods; but despite the stamped royal signature the bill got nowhere, unlike four others for the settlement of various estates which were similarly approved.[21] The abbot of Conway hoped to introduce a proviso into the Dissolution bill of 1536 with which to save his house, but without success.[22] In 1539, a priest trying to help a couple who had married before learning that the lady's first husband was probably still alive, advised a private act of Parliament to resolve the embarrassment.[23] No act resulted, and it may be doubted whether Parliament would ever have entertained an indemnity bill for bigamy, however inadvertent. In the middle of the 1540 session Thomas Wyat, the poet, could not find time for social courtesies because he was in the thick of preparing his two bills for the Parliament,[24] both, incidentally, passed. The best documented seeker after useful bills in Parliament was Lord Lisle, deputy at Calais – best documented because his correspondence was confiscated and survives, but also because absence from England made statute his best hope for protecting his interests. By 1539, when he was advised that his plan to buy some woods from the earl of Bridgewater could most readily be realized by private bill legislation,[25] he had considerable experience of watching the vagaries of affairs in Parliament. With Sir Richard Whethill, a personal enemy in Calais, he had been at the receiving end: Whethill tried for legislation in 1534 to

---

[19] For Ireland see the remarks by B. Bradshaw in *The Irish Parliamentary Tradition*, ed. B. Farrell (Dublin, 1973), 71.

[20] *LP* x, 1260.

[21] *LP* xx (II), 1067, nos. 35, 37, 48–49; xxi (II), 770, no. 80.

[22] *LP* x, 1046.   [23] *LP* xiv (I), 896.   [24] *LP* xv, 783.   [25] *LP* xiv (I), 780, 877.

confirm a patent for a spear's place for his son which he had obtained in the teeth of the deputy's opposition, and two years later he attempted a similar *coup* on his own behalf.[26] On both occasions Lisle's close contacts with Cromwell enabled him to thwart his enemy. In the new Parliament of 1536 he in his turn tried to use statute to do down an opponent. Sir Robert Wingfield held the grant of a marsh in the environs of Calais which the deputy found irksome and wished to see resumed. His agents, talking to Cromwell actually in the Commons' chamber, persuaded the minister that the grant was indeed against the public interest; Cromwell there and then moved the matter in the House, obtained a vote that something be done, and commissioned the drafting of the necessary bill. But despite his repeated promises the bill, produced within twenty-four hours by William Portman of the Middle Temple (later a judge), hung in the House in which Wingfield's friends had evidently also managed to raise some support. In the end it passed, only to be held up in the Lords, but at this point Wingfield voluntarily surrendered the patent into the king's hands, rather than suffer the indignity of an act of Parliament against himself.[27] Even the haphazard evidence of the state papers demonstrates the importance of private bills, and therefore the importance of Parliament to private interests; how much more can we learn from less official archives? They need to be searched.

Though the absence of work done at present prevents a thorough discussion of these important issues, one aspect is more readily accessible and can yield some quite interesting answers even to distinctly preliminary enquiries. The acts passed which dealt with the affairs of individuals – usually but not always property matters – can safely be ascribed to their beneficiaries' initiative, and though the acts themselves are in print only down to 1539 full lists are available in the *Statutes of the Realm*. Though strictly speaking their contents need to be analysed, and though most certainly it would be desirable to consider also failed bills of a like kind, a look at mere numbers of such acts passed has its uses. Private act legislation was a well-established practice in the sixteenth century, but the pattern is far from uniform.[28] Much the biggest number of acts for private persons' concerns was passed in the reign of Henry VII whose first, third and fifth Parliaments yielded 50, 25 and 27

[26] *LP* vii, 1492; x, 580.

[27] *LP* xi, 34, 61, 94, 108; *LJ* i (12 July 1536).

[28] These calculations are based on the tables of contents in *Statutes of the Realm*, vols. ii–iv, counting as private acts those that had not previously been printed or still remained unprinted.

respectively. The average for the reign is 18.7 per session, as compared with 8.3 under Henry VIII, 9.2 under Edward VI, a mere 4.3 under Mary, and a significantly increased 13.4 under Elizabeth. However, the high figures for the first Tudor arise simply from the consequences of the civil wars: the bulk of those private acts dealt with restitutions in blood and resumptions of lands confiscated, being thus necessary products of earlier acts of attainder. This untypical activity apart, private legislation runs around a median of 4 to 5 per session down to the last session of the Reformation Parliament. Meanwhile, acts dealing with the private affairs of the royal family had also come in a steady stream – a total of 24 under the seventh Henry and 81 under the eighth. Strikingly enough, Edward and Mary each used Parliament only once for their private concerns, and Elizabeth not at all.

If one ignores the accident of the post-civil-war settlement, it becomes apparent that it actually was the Crown, under Cromwell's guidance, which first discovered and demonstrated how the machinery of Parliament could be exploited systematically for private business. The reorganization of the royal estates in the 1530s over which Cromwell and Audley presided necessitated 14, 16 and 13 private acts in the sessions of 27, 28 and 32 Henry VIII. Private interests, possibly somewhat frustrated by the massive public legislation of the Reformation Parliament, immediately picked up the idea, with 18, 16, 13 and 10 acts in the sessions 27–32 Henry VIII. The unexpected Parliament of 1536, called really to deal with the settlement of the succession, was thus very thoroughly used also for the settlement of property matters both royal and private. Detailed research is needed to discover why the Crown came to abandon the method after 1546 and why private bill legislation altogether declined thereafter until 1558, but even this superficial survey shows that in the reign of Elizabeth the landed classes came increasingly to rely on Parliament. At the same time, though public acts declined rather in political and social significance, they remained stable in numbers: the total amount of business transacted in every session – remembering that sessions themselves occurred at longer intervals of time – increased in the second half of the century.[29] The real breakthrough for private acts, whatever reason may have been behind it, came in the reign of James I whose seven sessions yielded an average of 23.3 private acts, and that despite the fact that two sessions remained totally blank. The average for the productive sessions is thus

[29] From 1529 to 1601, the average of public acts passed in each session is about 21.

15

over 32: we have entered a new era in the use of Parliament. While the import of failed bills needs to be taken into account, and though the crude figures of acts passed need to be refined by further classification, it is manifest that in the course of the sixteenth century Parliament came to be a very important instrument in the management of the political nation's private affairs. Neale's remark that while for the Crown Parliament meant money to the Commons it meant private acts,[30] does indeed, as he says, oversimplify; but the epigram displays real insight, and I could wish that its author had not in his narrative history of the Elizabethan Parliaments told us very little about the first and almost nothing about the second. People wanted Parliaments not only to make laws for church and commonwealth, not only to serve the economic and social needs of particular areas or sectional interests, but also as the major – the most conclusive – means for settling the legal problems involved in their estates policies. Here, then, is a clear way in which the institution acted to promote satisfaction and stability, and the problems caused in James's reign by sessions which failed altogether to serve this purpose need surely to be taken into account when we consider why the consensus and stability expressed in the work of the Tudor Parliaments began to disappear in the following century.

Lastly, I want to take a look at the question whether election to the House of Commons could be important in serving personal ambition and progress in a man's career. Again, this is much too big a problem to tackle thoroughly here. Some hints are scattered in Neale's book: lawyers found membership a useful way to attract the kind of attention which led to office and promotion, and some individuals actively exploited the parliamentary service they could render to patrons.[31] A systematic study must await the publication of the relevant volumes of the *History of Parliament*, which should supply all the information required. Meanwhile, let me look briefly at the tip of this particular iceberg – at the relationship, if one existed, between election to the Commons and membership of the Privy Council. We have long been familiar with the point that Tudor councillors regularly sat in the Commons and that the failure of the Stuarts to provide such a 'Treasury Bench' played its part in the collapse of co-operation between Crown and Parliament. Here I am concerned with the reverse of all this: could prominence, or even presence, in the House contribute to a man's rise into the Council? Of one man we know not only that it did but also that

---

[30] Neale, *House of Commons*, 383.   [31] E.g. ibid. 151.

he deliberately chose Parliament as a place in which to attract the monarch's attention and work his way into power. When Thomas Cromwell told George Cavendish in November 1529 that by his belated entry into the Reformation Parliament he had 'once adventured to put in his foot, where he trusted shortly to be better regarded',[32] he spoke for more than his personal fortune. He prophesied no less than the characteristic way to eminence which was to dominate English politics certainly from the Restoration onwards. Did anyone else in the sixteenth century employ it?[33]

There are, in fact, interesting hints that in this respect, once again, things changed in the 1530s — that Cromwell initiated a later practice. Information, as usual, is difficult to get for the councillors of Henry VII, a high proportion of whom, being bishops, peers, doctors of law, judges and serjeants-at-law, do not in any case come within the range of this question. In 1504 a single Council meeting included eleven men who could have sat in Parliament before becoming councillors.[34] Totally deserted by official returns, we have only the patchiest notion of their possible presence in the Commons, but the indications are against a notion that they were parliamentarians before they were councillors. Sir Thomas Lovell was Speaker in 1485 and Sir Robert Drury in 1495, but the latter had already had a full career as king's legal counsel, while the former (in company with Sir Richard Guildford, Sir Edward Poynings, Sir Gilbert Talbot, Sir Walter Hungerford and Sir Henry Wyat) had been among Henry's supporters before or at Bosworth. None of them needed to sit in the Commons to attract the king's favour, and all them almost certainly were councillors from the beginning of the reign. Sir Thomas Bourchier probably belongs to the same category; he attended the Council by 1486.[35] Nothing useful can be established about Sir Robert Litton and Sir John Risley. That leaves Edmund Dudley, Speaker in the Parliament of January 1504. It appears that the first payment to him of a councillor's fee is recorded for October that year,[36] but as a member of the Council Learned he was clearly of the Council before that year. Thus none of Henry VII's councillors can be thought of

[32] *Two Early Tudor Lives*, ed. R. S. Sylvester and D. P. Harding (New Haven, 1962), 116.
[33] For information I rely in part on such obvious sources as *DNB* and the *Official Return of M.P.s*, and in part on the biographies in the files of the History of Parliament Trust. I am grateful to the Trust for permission to use their files, and to Dr Alan Davidson for searching them in reply to my questions.
[34] *Select Cases in the Council of Henry VII*, ed. C. G. Bayne (Selden Society, 1958), 40.
[35] Ibid. p. 8.
[36] *The Tree of Commonwealth*, ed. D. M. Brodie (Cambridge, 1948), 2–3.

as using Parliament as a foundation for their careers; if they did seek election it was either as established king's men and leaders of the government, or for private reasons of status and local importance.

Much the same was true of the first half of Henry VIII's reign. The reduced Council projected in Wolsey's Eltham Ordinance of 1526 included five men of interest in this context.[37] Sir William Fitzwilliam the Younger, Sir Henry Guildford and Sir William Kingston are not known to have sat before 1529; yet the first two are vouched for as councillors by 1522 and 1516 respectively, while the last, though possibly not formally a councillor before 1533, was a well-established courtier by May 1524 when he became constable of the Tower.[38] All three, in fact, were courtiers in terms of a career-structure. Sir John Gage (vice-chamberlain) had been prominent at court for several years; he is not known ever to have sat in Parliament. As for Sir Thomas More, though he may have sat in the Parliament of 1504 (and I am very doubtful of this story of Roper's, as of some others he tells), he certainly owed neither his entry into the Council in 1517 nor his Speakership in 1523 to any species of parliamentary career.[39]

Biographical study of the first properly-listed Privy Council in August 1540, on the other hand, yields a quite dramatically changed picture.[40] Edward Seymour, never apparently elected to a Parliament, was there as the king's brother-in-law and uncle to the heir apparent. Sir John Russell, Sir Thomas Cheyney, Sir Anthony Wingfield, Sir Richard Rich and Sir John Baker had all sat in 1529 (and probably not before); all of them made it into the Council between 1531 and 1539. It would be wrong to conclude that they all owed their advancement to member-ship of the Commons; Russell and Cheyney, for instance, were courtiers first. So was Sir Anthony Brown, a burgess in 1539, the same year that (probably) he became a councillor. Still, all these men went through the Commons on their way to the Council Table, and Rich and Baker – professional civil servants – do seem to have followed in the footsteps of Cromwell by making their mark in Parliament. (Cromwell was in effect accompanied by Thomas Audley, lord chancellor by 1540: another veteran of the 1523 Parliament and Speaker in 1529, by which time as chancellor of the Duchy he was a member of the unreformed Council.) Thomas Wriothesley and Ralph Sadler, the principal secretaries of 1540, owed their promotion to Cromwell whose private

---

[37] *Tudor Constitution*, 93–4.   [38] *LP* iv, 390(28).   [39] Cf. above, no. 7.
[40] *Tudor Constitution*, 95.

secretaries they had been, but again he got them into Parliament a year before they made it into the Privy Council.[41] Naturally, one must be careful not to assume simply that temporal order (Parliament first, Council after) equals cause and effect, but it does begin to look as though by the 1530s membership of the House of Commons was something that men with political ambition could and would use as a stepping-stone in their careers.

And this situation continued and developed. The privy councillors of November 1551 included seven men who could have done what has here been postulated: all of them did.[42] Sir Robert Bowes first entered Parliament in 1539 but joined the Council only in 1551. Sir John Gates, William Cecil and Sir Edward North sat first in 1542: they were of the Privy Council by 1551, 1550 and 1547 respectively. North, incidentally, was the first clerk of the Parliaments ever to sit in the Commons afterwards. Sir John Mason and Sir Philip Hoby sat in Parliament in 1547, but in Council only in 1550 and 1551. As for Sir William Petre, that Cromwellian survival, he had passed through those stages at an earlier date: Parliament 1536, Council 1545. By this time, therefore, all the commoners on the Privy Council (and some since promoted to the peerage, like William Paget) had had a career in the Commons before they achieved membership of the government. And the same remained true for new arrivals in Elizabeth's reign when appointment to the Council often came a long time after a man had first gone into Parliament and began to attract attention there. Here are some typical examples, with the date of first election followed by the date of appointment to the Council: Sir James Croft, 1542, 1570; Sir Francis Knollys, (?)1533, 1559; Sir Walter Mildmay, 1545, 1566; Sir Thomas Smith, 1547, 1571; Sir Francis Walsingham, 1559, 1563; Sir Christopher Hatton, 1571, 1577; Thomas Wilson, 1563, 1577; Sir Henry Sidney, 1547, 1575; Robert Cecil, 1584, 1591; Sir Thomas Egerton, 1584, 1596; Sir John Fortescue, 1559, 1589; Sir William Knollys, 1571, 1596.

I am not, of course, suggesting that all these men, and others, reached councillor's status simply because they had served a political apprentice-ship in Parliament. But they had indeed served such an apprenticeship, and the only new recruit to the Council in the reign who had not was

[41] Sadler certainly sat in 1539 (A. J. Slavin, *Profit and Power* [Cambridge, 1966], 40); the History of Parliament Trust suspects a possible election in 1536.
[42] *APC* ii, 403.

apparently (*quia non potuit*) Archbishop Whitgift. I am not prepared to say that membership of the Commons had become a necessary prerequisite for elevation to the Privy Council, but it looks very much as though it had become a very useful first step. From the 1530s onwards, and not before the time that Thomas Cromwell showed the way, getting elected to Parliament was one way – and a prominent way – to get to the top. Men who wished to reach the Council, men who hoped to help govern the country, needed other means as well and other connections, but increasingly they discovered that they could lay sound foundations by seeking election to Parliament. The queen may not have consciously chosen her councillors from members of the Commons (though we do not know that she did not, and we may suppose that her advisers, a Cecil or Leicester, kept their eyes and ears open in the Parliament), but in effect she there found the necessary reservoir of talent. Once again, the point was brought out more clearly in the reign of her successor because then it ceased to be so easy to use this particular staircase to the top. Men like Sir Edwyn Sandys, Sir John Eliot, Sir Thomas Wentworth or William Noy knew perfectly well that their talents were superior to those promoted by foolish and incompetent kings dominated by favourites whose advancement had owed nothing to membership of the House. Men like these, given the opportunity, soon enough proved that their real purposes were to govern, to sit in the Privy Council. Left out in the cold, they could only agitate in a species of opposition, in the hope of attracting attention that way: and Wentworth and Noy achieved the purpose of their disruptive activities.

Thus the ineptitude of early Stuart rule produced a new political sophistication: the ambitious politician who made the life of government so difficult that it seemed best to solve the problem by giving him office. Under Elizabeth, resisters in Parliament were not men who sought high office; those who did found that an active and helpful conformity served the purpose best. So long as trouble in Parliament gathered around natural opposition men like the Wentworth brothers or around men like Norton or Fleetwood who found satisfaction in careers outside the inner rings of government, that trouble was politically insignificant. When men appeared who had hoped to use Parliament for a career leading to the Privy Council and found the road blocked, every sort of warning light went on in Parliament and Council alike. The opposition which mattered was not – then or at any other time – that of irreconcilable principle but that of frustrated political ambition.

Thus Parliament, the premier point of contact between rulers and ruled, between the Crown and the political nation, in the sixteenth century fulfilled its function as a stabilizing mechanism because it was usable and used to satisfy legitimate and potentially powerful aspirations. It mediated in the touchy area of taxation; by producing the required general and particular laws it kept necessary change in decent order; it assisted the rich in the arranging of their affairs; and it helped the ambitious to scale the heights of public power. What more could we ask of the image of the body politic? Only that it should satisfy liberal preconceptions by regularly undoing governments. But that was not a function which sixteenth-century theory ascribed to Parliament, and I can see no reason why it should have done so.

II. THE COUNCIL

The Tudor Parliament, I suggested to you a year ago, quite properly fulfilled a function of giving legitimate political ambition a chance to achieve its ends, more particularly because from the 1530s onwards, at any rate, experience in the Commons could put a man in the way of entering the royal Council. Of course, this would never be true of more than a few such knights and burgesses, nor was it either a sufficient or a necessary cause of their becoming councillors. Still, the link was there. I now want to turn to the Council itself and ask whether its history and membership similarly reflected a useful function in enabling ambition to be satisfied. Here we enter upon territory far less well known than the Houses of Parliament. The Tudor Council is not now quite so free from the attention of historians as it was even ten years ago;[43] but while we may be really well informed about it here and there, and while indeed we all think that we have a fair idea of its place in constitution and

---

[43] In 1964 I enquired 'Why the history of the early-Tudor Council remains unwritten' (above, no. 18). Since then we have had two valuable and so far unpublished Cambridge dissertations (whose use I here acknowledge with gratitude), by D. E. Hoak on 'The King's Council in the reign of Edward VI' (1970) [now a book: Cambridge, 1976], and by G. E. Lemasters on 'The Privy Council in the reign of Queen Mary I' (1971); Mr M. B. Pulman has discussed *The Elizabethan Privy Council in the 1570s* (Berkeley/Los Angeles/London, 1971); Mr D. B. McDonald is at work on the Council in the latter part of the century; and Dr J. A. Guy is pursuing further researches which have already sorted out the Court of Star Chamber in Wolsey's day [now published: *The Cardinal's Court* (Hassocks, 1977)]. Miss Margaret Condon is writing the history of Henry VII's Council.

society, it remains true that every time one asks oneself a question touching it one comes up against so far unillumined obscurities. The work of any governing body is always difficult to understand because only those there present actually know what goes on and because so much of what does go on never reaches the record; and the Tudor Privy Council made emphatically certain of preserving itself from scholarly prying by keeping no minutes of discussion at all. However, we do know who the councillors were, though even this statement needs qualifying: we know this with anything like certainty only after 1540 when the body settled down into its reformed state. It is therefore possible to enquire whether those who made the grade were the right men: right in their ability to provide for good government, and right also in the sense that those desirous of exercising influence in the body politic had a sufficient chance to get there.

Parliament, as all agreed, represented the nation; did anyone think that the Council, too, should be representative? We remember the attitudes manifest in the early fifteenth century, and before, when people talked of the rights of 'natural' councillors to advise the king and assist in making policy. Under the Lancastrians, at any rate, the composition of the Council was a matter for contention, a lively political issue in which principles that involved limiting the monarch's choice were liberally pronounced and Parliament was used to give substance to such claims. Of such things, hardly anything appears in the sixteenth century. Those chosen and those omitted seem in general to have recognized the Crown's freedom to appoint whom it wished, while the former also recognized their exclusive duty to the monarch. No dualism here – no sense that service as councillor to king or queen also involved a responsibility to the nation (except in adhering to pious platitudes about the good of the commonweal). Perhaps one may see a touch of an official sense that in a shadowy way some such responsibility did exist in the occasional attempt to associate the Council formally with the Crown in executive action, most conspicuously in the Act of Proclamations which insisted that proclamations could be issued only by the king on the advice of his Council.[44] This has a somewhat 'Lancastrian' ring about it, but there was no substance: notoriously, few Tudor proclamations cite the advice of the Council, and we know of no case in which the Council's refusal to advise prevented the publication of a proclamation. 'Our partes is to counsell,' said Cecil – seemingly no

[44] 31 Henry VIII, c. 8, sect. 1.

more and no less; what happened to the advice given was the business of the queen.[45] Characteristically, Cromwell's definition of a councillor's function was as monarchical but distinctly more dynamic; he held that the office was 'as an eye to the prince, to foresee and in time provide remedy for such abuses, enormities and inconveniences as might else with a little sufferance engender more evil in his public weal than could be after redubbed with much labour, study, diligence and travail'.[46] The contrast between Cecil's cool care and Cromwell's ardent activism helps to explain why one died in bed, full of honours, and the other dishonourably on the scaffold; it also helps to explain why Cecil's commonwealth marked time while Cromwell's went through a rebirth.

For our present purpose, however, it is more important that Cromwell's definition was in fact more accurate. The Tudor Privy Council reverberated with activity. It needs to be remembered that, unlike the Councils of France and Spain (able only to advise action which itself could never occur except on the signified authority of the king), that of England *did* things, had full executive authority, and by its own instruments (those letters signed by councillors for which there seems to have been no equivalent in the other national monarchies of the west) produced administrative results throughout the realm. Of course, it was this special capacity that gave such political weight to the privy councillor's place, and Cecil no more than Cromwell in practice ignored the active function of the body over which he presided. Playing it cool did not to him mean confining oneself to shouting advice from the terraces. And foresight – the quality Cromwell pinpointed – was Cecil's most eminent attribute. Even so, the difference between the sixteenth century's two greatest English statesmen is well illustrated by those comments.

However, one thing they were clearly agreed on: the councillor's sole duty pointed towards his sovereign, as indeed the councillor's oath itself indicated. In turn, the sovereign was supposed to confine his counsel-taking to those whom he had chosen to be his councillors, and on the whole it would seem that Tudor monarchs observed this rule, with the notable exception of Mary, whose intimacy with the emperor's ambassador at the time earned her the sort of anger and anguish that was to erupt again when James I appeared to elevate Gondomar to be his *chef du conseil*. Henry VIII may have gone behind his Council's back to the

[45] Cited Pulman, *Elizabethan Privy Council*, 52.   [46] Merriman, ii, 112–13.

friends and servants gathered in his Privy Chamber,[47] but there was no public scandal, and his Council rightly believed itself to be the real source of advice. And Elizabeth, who assuredly had plenty of non-conciliar favourites, would for once seem to have observed the constitutional rules quite faithfully.[48] Implied in this relationship, however, was one inescapable fact: the sovereign had a totally free hand in choosing his advisers, and membership of the Council depended exclusively on his will. No one had a *claim* to appointment, either social, or political, or philosophical.

Once only in the century was this convention challenged. The Pilgrims of Grace made an issue of the king's Council because they wished to be rid of Cromwell, Cranmer and Audley. True to their old-fashioned poses, they revived the sort of talk common one and two centuries before. Their first demand for the exclusion of the hated councillors was met in the king's *Answer* with some disingenuous stuff about the Council of 1536 being more aristocratic than that of 1509, and with an angry denunciation of their interference with the king's right to choose whom he wished.[49] To this they were advised to reply stoutly.[50] It was 'necessary that virtuous men that loves the commonwealth should be of his Council', and if the king insisted on a Council chosen 'at his pleasure' he should remember the entitlements of those naturally born to that position. The memorialist meant in particular the nobility and, surprisingly, pointed to France where such things were allegedly better ordered. His ideal model even led him to mention princes of the blood: did he have Courtenays and Poles in mind? Perhaps Henry was less blameworthy in the blood-bath of 1538 than we have supposed. And, the paper goes on, before Henry rested content with his deplorable choice he ought to remember that such folly had before this caused kings to be deposed, the examples cited being ominous enough – Rehoboam, Edward II, Richard II. This was one man's opinion (offered to Aske), but the attack on favourites and preference for noble councillors pervaded the whole rebellion. Mind you, the Pilgrims do not seem to have put too extravagant a value on nobility. On one occasion there was some cheering at the thought that 'as long as such noblemen of the true blood may reign or rule about the king all should

---

[47] Dr D. R. Starkey, whose completed dissertation (Cambridge, 1974) has investigated the institutional history of the Privy Chamber under the two Henries, is at work on the part it played in administration and politics.
[48] Pulman, *Elizabethan Privy Council*, 53–5.   [49] *Policy and Police*, 200.   [50] *LP* xi, no. 1244.

be well',[51] but this pious sentiment was elicited by the news that those at present of Council with Henry VIII were the duke of Norfolk (third of that creation), the earl of Oxford (the Veres really were an old house), the earl of Sussex (plain Sir Robert Radcliffe only eleven years before), the lord admiral (Sir William Fitzwilliam, a creature of Wolsey's), the comptroller of the Household (Sir William Paulet, another such), and Sir William Kingston (one of Henry's upstart courtiers). By this account, noble blood had got a bit cheap, but even so it still, of course, excluded that 'Lollard and traitor Thomas Cromwell'.

In any case, the Pilgrims lost the fight and Henry continued to choose his own Council, as did his children after him, with no more such open challenges. Our question must therefore now be whether their choice was such as to give the Council the opportunity to bring political stability by accommodating those who, dissatisfied by exclusion as the northern aristocrats had been in 1536, might possibly have upset it. And here some quite surprising conclusions emerge. Above all, it will become apparent that the reform which in the 1530s produced the Privy Council proper profoundly altered the place and function of the Council, and with it its character as a reflection of the distribution of power within the body politic. We must look at Council lists.

The most complete list extant for the unreformed King's Council — the institution built up by Henry VII and maintained in Wolsey's day — belongs to 1526–7. It survives only in a copy made for Sir Julius Caesar who found it in a book now lost.[52] Because the king's serjeants are given simply as a body, unquantified, the total is a little difficult to calculate; if we allow for an average of six of them, that Council numbered fifty-three. A further nine, at least, as we shall see, also deserved inclusion. A Council at least sixty-two strong might seem improbable, but plenty of evidence exists (for instance in the attendance lists transcribed from the lost books) to support the accuracy of Caesar's copy. The list of fifty-three includes the five categories of councillors typically found in the records down to the Council reform: seven prelates (Wolsey, five bishops, the abbot of Westminster), fourteen peers (two dukes, two marquesses, two earls, three viscounts, five barons), fifteen administrators of knightly rank, one civilian (the dean of

[51] *LP* xii, pt i, no. 1013.
[52] BL, Lansdowne MS 160, fos. 311v–12v. The list has a few errors in it: Lords Hussey and Windsor, ennobled in 1529, appear here as lords, while Windsor is listed a second time among the knights. Probably the original was carelessly amended in 1529. I have restored the position of 1526.

the Chapel), and sixteen common lawyers (all the judges of King's Bench and Common Pleas, the king's serjeants, the attorney and solicitor general). Caesar, in addition, found one more peer, three knights, and two doctors attending on other occasions who were not in the list; though he thought they had not been sworn they were in fact equally councillors in the full sense – Secretary William Knight, for instance, being thus described by February 1514, and Archdeacon Thomas Magnus by October 1520.[53] Three more names turned up in the record of a sitting on 8 June 1527: another knight, another doctor, and the lord mayor of London. This total of sixty-two is a minimum: other people still surviving bore the councillor's title before this date, and it must be pure accident that they are missing from this gathering.[54] My guess is that the total number of sworn councillors in 1527 ran to something like seventy. On the other hand, that July meeting conveniently indicates the sort of Council that could actually be got to meet: four prelates, three peers, ten knights, one doctor, and all the common lawyers – say, thirty-four heads. The Council met that day for important administrative business – an order against seditious preachers and teachers of heresy (Thomas More was present) – but the possibly surprising attendance of all the judges and lawyers, whom some scholars would already like to treat as not strictly of the Council, as regular members is well supported in other presence lists.

The working members of this Council cannot, however, be identified with any of its sections. The lawyers and civilians were office-holders, by definition, and virtually all the knights held office: these three component parts constituted the top-level civil service of the day (much of it in the Household). Of the fifteen peers named (and such expected names as Oxford and Shrewsbury are absent only because the holders of the title at the time were respectively under age and rather ancient), only four held genuine offices (Norfolk as treasurer, Suffolk as president of the Council, Lisle a deputy at Calais, and Sandys as lord chamberlain); and of the seven prelates only Wolsey (lord chancellor) and Tunstall (lord privy seal) occupied formal places in the administration. Others of these councillors had before this been involved in government office – Bishop Clerk had been dean of the Chapel and Lord Berners deputy at Calais – but the fact remains that most of the

---

[53] *LP* i, no. 2684(88); iii, no. 1036(23).

[54] E.g. John Stokesley (*LP* iii, no. 2954). Thomas Englefield, called by the title in 1524 (*LP* iv, no. 1298[8]), had certainly held it by July 1513 (PRO, E 159/292: Brevia, Trinity Term 5 Henry VIII, rot. 7d).

socially eminent councillors (the true 'lords of the Council') possessed
no such qualification at this date. We should be wrong to assume that
they were mere decorative additions to the working parts; such men as
Bishops West and Longland, or Viscounts Rochford and Fitzwalter
(soon to be the earls of Wiltshire and Sussex) were very active
councillors indeed. In fact, the whole body was real, not honorific,
though I cannot here pursue that point.

What, then was the meaning of having so large a Council, so many
and divers kinds of councillors? It included the career-men in the
Household, the law courts, and the offices of state, plus the leading
political figures in Church and nobility, plus such outliers as London's
mayor and, it seems, some gentlemen in the shires. There is evidence
that the lord mayor was habitually sworn of the Council.[55] Such things
underline a striking practice of using Council places to diffuse central
authority on the one hand, and to concentrate scattered authority on the
other. If what a man anxious to secure standing and influence required
was a place on the Council, this kind of Council offered him excellent
opportunities. The large number of peers in particular is worth
emphasis: we have here all the court nobility of the day, mixing old
families with new. The unreformed Council, in short, was well
designed to fulfil the role which I am here investigating.

The line of thought exemplified in this Council finds its ultimate end
in a well-known note of Cromwell's in the year 1534: 'to appoint the
most assured and substantial gentlemen in every shire to be sworn of the
king's Council'.[56] His intention was to provide a nation-wide body of
men in charge of internal security, a needless purpose (as it turned out)
because the substantial gentry proved active enough without taking the
Council oath. Behind this fleeting idea, however, stands a concept of the
Council as a body of all men who carried weight and as a means for

[55] Sir John Alen, lord mayor in 1525, retained the councillor's title, then acquired, for the rest of his
life, though he took no active part thereafter: *LP* v, no. 1209; vii, no. 1060; PRO, Sta. Cha.
2/34/19 (1532, 1534, 1540). The last time that I can find a current lord mayor called king's
councillor is in March 1536 (*LP Add.* no. 1053); it would appear, therefore, that the
Cromwellian reconstruction, which prevented later lord mayors from getting the appointment,
took place about the middle of that year. In 1532, Sir Thomas Denys (of Devon) is described in
an indictment taken before him as 'vnus de Concilio domini Regis ac vnus Iusticiorum dicti
domini Regis ad pacem' (PRO, KB 9/517/30).
[56] *LP* vii, no. 420. Cromwell's idea recurs in (was suggested by?) a general plan for revising the
police system (PRO, SP 1/144, fo. 211) which *LP* xiv, pt i, no. 643 places in 1539, but which
probably also belongs to 1534: three to six of the 'head commissioners' there suggested might be
admitted 'as of his grace's Council, if it so shall stand with his grace's pleasure'.

holding the social order together throughout the realm: a concept to which the unreformed Council in effect aspired. If Cromwell's proposal had been adopted it would have diluted the Council irremediably and absolutely demanded the separate creation of that real governing institution which the large Council of Wolsey's day had, despite its size, still managed to be. But to repeat: apart from being the king's instrument of rule (usable in a flexible and protean fashion, as a court, as an advisory and executive board, by way of committees), that Council was also one of those institutional answers to the need to satisfy individual ambition by permitting widespread participation which any stable system requires.

Though Cromwell did not pursue the idea of creating a nation-wide body of sworn councillors, he still did not regard the existing large Council as sufficiently concentrated and efficient. His fundamental reform, which I once dated into 1534–6 and would now venture to place in the middle of 1536,[57] created the institution which remained the government of Tudor and early-Stuart England. A look at the next relevant list of councillors shows how drastically things had changed as a result of his work. The Privy Council of August 1540, initiating its minute book as soon as the great lord privy seal was gone, is familiar enough.[58] Its total of nineteen was made up of eight knights, eight peers and three prelates, and of them all only the last (Cranmer, Tunstall, Gardiner) held no office of significance. They were there because in the age of the early Reformation no government could do without powerful ecclesiastical participation. Perhaps it would be proper to remove also the earl of Hertford, equipped with lesser sinecures but no more, from the office-holders; he was there as the king's ex-brother-in-law. But the remaining fifteen, whether noble or not, occupied the leading positions in the state and Household – those positions which, as later developments show, were to become equivalent to Cabinet rank: the lord chancellor, lord treasurer, lord steward, lord privy seal, lord great chamberlain, lord admiral, lord chamberlain of the Household, treasurer and comptroller of the Household, master of the horse, vice-chamberlain, principal secretary, chancellors of Augmentations and First Fruits. The last two disappeared in the Exchequer reforms of 1554, but most of the rest, with occasional additions, turn up again and

---

[57] On the grounds that most lord mayors before that date, and none thereafter, can be found described as king's councillors (above, n. 55).
[58] *Tudor Constitution*, 95.

again. Not all those offices involved specific duties: except on coronation day, the great chamberlain's place was one of high dignity only, and some of the other Household offices were on the way to becoming Council-worthy places rather than desk jobs. But with the judges and lawyers and civilians gone, with the old knightly element reduced to the top few office-holders, and with the peerage drastically pruned to leave only active politicians and administrators, the new Council was manifestly a working instrument of government, and no more. Membership, available now to the few and those professionals at that, could no longer be offered in hopes of satisfying private ambitions among the non-professionals, nor was there now anything remotely representative of the orders of the realm about this Council. Representation had now become exclusively the attribute of Parliament, and the emergence of the 'modern' House of Lords (as demonstrated, for instance, in the precedence act of 1539)[59] goes significantly hand in hand with the disappearance of the non-officed peerage from the king's Council. The Privy Council, as set up by its creator, was a body of politicians and departmental ministers, without any *consiliarii nati*.

Henry VIII could afford a Council entirely in his control from which he had excluded the bulk of the nobility and those men of influence around the kingdom who did not hold qualifying office. Could the notoriously weak regimes of Edward VI and Mary do as much? Tradition, of course, supposes that the desire for membership – political pressure upon the Crown – quickly restored the pre-Cromwellian situation: large and diffused Councils with factions and subdivisions. Recent research has effectively demonstrated the inaccuracy of these superficial impressions. I am grateful to Drs Hoak and Lemasters for allowing me to use their valuable dissertations,[60] and I do not propose to steal the thunder which will surely be theirs once those typescripts have become books. But a few salient points, resting upon their analyses, need to be made.

The Protector Somerset (probably guided by William Paget) made, in fact, no move away from the principles established in the second half of Henry VIII's reign. The old king bequeathed him a Council of the reformed kind, though in a few particulars it deviated from Cromwell's practice: two bishops, five peers (all office-holders), six knights, one civilian (Nicholas Wotton, dean of both Canterbury and York), and two judges. The last three mark the reintroduction of categories

[59] 31 Henry VIII, c. 10.   [60] Cf. n. 43, above.

excluded in 1536; Wotton had in fact been sworn of the Council in April 1546,[61] but no judges sat there until Henry died. It may be conjectured that Henry thought it advisable to have legal experts on a Council of regency. The knights, reduced in number to make way for the lawyers, now included leading members of the Privy Chamber, a tipping of the balance against the out-of-Household civil service which reflects the growing influence of the court in Henry's last days. This Council Somerset accepted, adding only his brother Thomas who would not be kept out and who became lord admiral (a qualifying office) when Warwick succeeded to the great chamberlaincy left vacant by Somerset's own elevation.[62]

This situation lasted for only the six weeks that Somerset required to set up his primacy, but even when he had a free hand he made no changes in principle. The Councils he appointed down to his fall fluctuated in numbers but averaged about twenty-one, well within the terms of the recent reform, and in type of membership they remained unchanged. The one civilian disappeared (though his brother Edward, treasurer of Calais, remained an ever-absent member); Cranmer and the equally absent Tunstall represented the Church; up to eight peers, all of recent creation and all but one holding the usual qualifying offices, constituted the characteristically unaristocratic noble element; the knights included not only the leading departmental officers but also always at least two gentlemen of the Privy Chamber. Lord Chief Justice Montague stayed on for a while, but was taken off when he fell out with the Protector.[63] Only the marquess of Northampton (William Parr), so far office-less, broke the pattern: he owed his appointment to his personal relationships and to his political influence. Evidently, this regime experienced no difficulty in adhering to an essentially 'royal' Council of the new kind. Remembering that Somerset's fall was engineered by his fellow councillors, we may wonder whether he would have been wiser to enlarge the Council with supporters (if he could have found any), but at any rate no such attempt was made. At the same time, it looks as though there were no men ambitious to get on the Council; as in the reign of Henry VIII, the reformed Privy Council, though not a political instrument for assuaging opposition, was also no cause of visible dissatisfaction.

No visible dissatisfaction, but what happened under Northumberland raises a question. That duke did increase the size of the Council, and

[61] *APC* i, 371.   [62] Hoak, *Council of Edward VI*, 35.   [63] Ibid. 47, 49, 51.

to some extent his additions suggest the sort of political pressure that Henry and Somerset had not experienced. By March 1552, for instance, the Privy Council numbered thirty-one, an increase which marked a serious dent in the principle of Cromwell's reform.[64] The bulk of the councillors were still holders of the normal offices, a fact which put Thomas Goodrich, bishop of Ely, there when he succeeded Rich in the chancellorship. (Tunstall had gone, now that the Reformation was striding ahead, so that the Church remained represented by two prelates.) But the number of the knights had gone up to twelve, with such relatively lesser officers as the master of the Ordnance, the master of the Rolls, and the secretary for the French tongue newly elevated to Cabinet rank. Wotton and the two judges enjoyed restoration: whether there is any special significance in this rather depends on whether councillors sworn could ever be thought of as deprived of the stigma except by death, even when for reasons of politics or personality they ceased to be councillors in anything but name. The real change had come among the fourteen peers who, for the first time since 1536, included noblemen without significant office. The single anomaly of Northampton (now regularized as great chamberlain) had blossome forth into a group of seven, one of whom – the ailing Rich – does not count, while another, Pembroke, had been a councillor since 1547 as Sir William Herbert, gentleman of the Privy Chamber. But what were the earls of Shrewsbury, Westmorland and Huntingdon, Viscount Hereford and Lord Cobham doing on the Council? Supporting Northumberland, is the short answer: that duke, unlike his predecessor, was compelled to find places on the Council for political followers. Francis Talbot, by the way, recalls one of the more curious facts about the Privy Council: for something like 180 years, almost none seems to have been reckoned complete without the current earl of Shrewsbury, very few of whom actually ever attended. Even in 1536, Henry VIII had noted that his Council included the then earl 'when he may come'.[65] One is reminded of the mid-nineteenth-century axiom that no Cabinet could survive without at least one duke in it.

Northumberland's Council thus rather makes my point for me. Having used that body to destroy his rival, he needed to strengthen his hand on it, and in order to do so he had to forsake the fundamental

---

[64] Ibid. 54 ff. Things were virtually unchanged a year later: *Tudor Constitution*, 96.

[65] *LP* xi, no. 957. Shrewsbury sat on the reformed Council as lord steward, the office held in 1540 by the duke of Suffolk.

principle of Cromwell's reform. Such freedom as he had in choosing councillors was evidently severely circumscribed by the need for a supporting faction, and this meant that men without the newly established qualifications – lesser officers and unofficial noblemen – reentered the Council. Relaxing the rules meant going back to a Council which could bring peace and temporary stability; sticking to them would have meant leaving out men who wished to join the ranks and, dissatisfied, would have been troublesome.

The Council of Edward VI's last years thus testifies to Northumberland's weakness, not the Crown's or even the boy-king's. Mary's accession brought to the throne at least a person of mature years, capable (if a woman were to turn out capable) of exercising personal rule. Yet, on the face of it, her policy towards the Council looked even more like a return to the old, unreformed institution which had worked only because it had not been a Privy Council at all – not a self-sufficient governing body but a group of governors controlled and guided by single men, Henry VII or Wolsey. Notoriously, Mary's large Council – its numbers fluctuating round about forty – provided the scene for much faction fighting, though I think that Dr Lemasters is right when he calls in question an interpretation which has too trustingly reflected the opinions of the imperial ambassador, concerned to explain his own failures. However, what matters here is the membership of that body, that seemingly very large membership which calls up memories of the 1520s. Here, too, Dr Lemasters's investigation has altered the picture by defining it more closely.[66] It would appear that Mary's councillors fall readily into three groups. The first, numerically the largest, consists of the men who attended her at Framlingham Castle at the time of Northumberland's rebellion: they were very much her personal following and friends (mostly good Catholics). Of these hardly any ever attended the Council. Secondly, there was a group of Henrician survivals or dug-outs, men who lent respectability to the body but acquired real significance only because Gardiner must be counted among them. And lastly, there were the Edwardian professionals, especially Paget and Winchester, without whom the government could not have been carried on. When one identifies the real working Council one comes up with something much more like the Cromwellian Privy Council than its unreformed predecessor: quite a small group (though, since this was no formally identified body, exact numbers cannot be

[66] 'Privy Council under Mary I', ch. 2.

given) once more consisting of the familiar office-holders. Indeed, at one point Paget (trusty guardian of the Cromwellian tradition) tried to enlist the help of King Philip in repeating his late master's achievement by turning this active sector into an institutional extraction from the swollen nominal Council, but nothing came of this.

Queen Mary's Council thus marks a peculiarly interesting stage. On the one hand it illustrates the endurance of Cromwell's reform: government remained in the hands of the type of institution he had devised for it. On the other however, it also demonstrates how the Council could be used to produce political stability – or, alternatively, how pressure upon the monarch could compel the sort of enlargement which found room for a great number of aspirants to the title who might not even intend to perform any serious conciliar duties. They were not functionless: the Framlingham group, all men of little national standing, exercised notable influence in the counties where their native weight benefited from the addition of the councillor's title. Once more, shire worthies were brought into the Council (by accident rather than policy, I think), so that some of the conciliar potential discarded in 1536 revived for a time, at the cost of weakening the singular eminence of the central body. The Framlingham men were councillors in the main because Mary believed in rewarding loyal followers, but also because she needed loyal followers on her Council: the Henrician group because a Council consisting effectively of her brother's men would have proved unmanageable, but also because they had claims upon her memory which she could not ignore. The Edwardians simply could not be spared. Mary, half pushed and half pulling, proved that the principles of the pre-reform Council had visible political advantages, but also that only the post-reform Privy Council could be trusted to govern effectively.

As is well known, Elizabeth read the lesson to mean that the second point was more important than the first. She may well have had Paget's and Cecil's advice to that effect, but she was also free from the pressures which had worked upon her sister. No group of loyalists, demonstrating their stand in a crisis, made calls upon her gratitude (not a quality anyway with which she was over-endowed); no elderly gentlemen existed, or were needed, to form a bridge to a lost past. There need be no doubt at all that throughout her reign she maintained perfect control over the choice of privy councillors; no one ever owed appointment except to her, and no one ever succeeded in forcing himself on the

Council against her will. The story of the young earl of Essex's hapless years of knocking at the door of the Council chamber is not only familiar but absolutely descriptive. And so Cromwell's Privy Council, hazardously kept alive in the troubled years by William Paget, returned unequivocally in 1558, with no further change in principle or practice till Elizabeth's death. Her Privy Council was not only small and select, but also throughout that precise instrument for royal government which Cromwell had designed. And this means not only that the body once again regarded itself as 'an eye to the prince' but also that Cromwell's other purpose was again achieved: emanation of monarchic power or not, this was a Council that governed independently, taking decisions and executive action on its own responsibility. I may remark in passing that the true Tudor Privy Council, especially when seen by the side of its French and Spanish counterparts, offers proof not so much of the existence of personal monarchy as of its limitations. There was truth in the Venetian observation that 'these lords of the Council behave like so many kings'.[67] So long as there existed the sort of Privy Council that Cromwell had established, truly monolithic kingship did not prevail in England. Michael Walzer has identified the whisper as the characteristic tone of *ancien régime* royal courts.[68] He may well be right for the monarchies of the early Stuarts and later Bourbons, but in the court of Queen Elizabeth the whisper had to compete, often unsuccessfully, with the audible noises emanating from the institutional Privy Council.

Of course, the composition of the Council did not always adhere perfectly to these principles, but the occasional departures are minimal and insignificant. Take the Privy Council of 1579.[69] Of the eight peers, six held qualifying office: Burghley (lord treasurer), Leicester (master of the Horse), Sussex (lord chamberlain), Lincoln (lord admiral), Warwick (master of the Ordnance), Bedford (president of Wales). The list of the nine knights' appointments reads familiar enough: the lord keeper, the treasurer, comptroller and vice-chamberlain of the Household, the chancellor of the Duchy, the chancellor of the Exchequer, the lord deputy of Ireland (absent, naturally), the two principal secretaries. In the reign of a female sovereign, the Privy Chamber, for obvious reasons had

[67] Cited E. P. Cheyney, *History of England from the Defeat of the Armada to the Death of Elizabeth* (1926), i, 80.

[68] *Regicide and Revolution: Speeches at the Trial of Louis XVI*, ed. Michael Walzer (Cambridge, 1974), 28.

[69] From the list of attendances in *APC* xi.

again lost its place in the Council. No civilians or lawyers (just as Cromwell had laid down), and Elizabeth, as we know, saw no reasons for burdening her government with prelates. The only two members who do not quite fit were the earl of Arundel and Lord Hunsdon. The first, who as lord steward had been a councillor at the beginning of the reign, was back after a period of disfavour, probably at Leicester's urging who wanted an ally in his perpetual sparring with Burghley; the second, soon regularized when in 1583 he succeeded to the lord chamberlaincy on Sussex's death, was the queen's cousin and the nearest thing on her Council to recall Mary's Framlingham friends. But personally he deserved the place better than those worthy nonentities. The exceptions thus were one ex-officer, already indelibly marked with the councillor's oath, and one friend and future officer – not really exceptions at all.

The last Privy Council of the reign, which was also just about the smallest (thirteen members) – perhaps because Elizabeth found it increasingly difficult to replace the departed old faithfuls by the new, young, untried, pushing men that she found troubling her grey years – really exemplified the stubborn persistence of the pattern.[70] With Whitgift and Sir John Popham, the Church and the law had penetrated into the Council, but there were good reasons of personal choice behind these appointments. Both were hard men, willing to put down disaffection and disorder with a heavy hand, and the ageing monarch, unhappy in that last decade of the century with its undercurrent of unrest produced by war and famine, liked such men. For the rest, we find the lords treasurer, admiral and chamberlain, and the master of the horse (always since Edward VI's reign a noble preserve); we find the lord keeper, the comptroller and vice-chamberlain of the Household, the chancellor of the Exchequer, the two secretaries. Only the earl of Shrewsbury, asserting the Talbot mystique, sat there – or rather, practically never sat there – without qualifying office, the one representative of relatively ancient blood.

Of course, in Elizabeth's long reign ancient blood was not much to the fore. Percies and Nevilles passed through their last eclipse, and even the Howards (ancient enough in their own estimation) suffered more than they benefited (though in the person of the earl of Nottingham, the victor of 1588, a junior branch made it into the Council). But ambitions and claims to recognition were not necessarily confined to noblemen of

[70] *Tudor Constitution*, 100–1.

lineage, and one may wonder whether a Council of thirteen, some of whom had had quite a struggle to get on, could really serve to accommodate all those who thought themselves possessed of title to be there. Indeed, one may wonder whether this reduction by one-third from Cromwell's number did not leave this Council dangerously thin and dangerously cliquey – even isolated in its narrow-based eminence. Elizabeth, we know, created a dearth of honours; did she also prove too penurious in making councillors? She may have felt no need to use councillors to keep the peace in the shires, in which indifference she was right; and she would seem to me to have been right also in denying elevation to such men of ambition as Walter Ralegh and Francis Bacon. But did she not keep out able men of proper weight, anxious to take part in the government of the realm at the highest level? For some reason she acted as though there was not enough talent around and doubled up offices, Sir John Fortescue, for instance, being chancellor of both the Exchequer and the Duchy. One would hardly expect to have any real evidence of disgruntled ambition and behind-the-scenes pressure; while the old queen lived, no one liked to question, in ways that would have left evidence behind, her right to choose as she pleased. Yet the unmistakable pressures of the next reign, when gossip grew rife, call forth doubts. Of Bacon we do know that he had aspirations before and after 1603, and we can justly suspect the same of Ralegh; thereafter such men as Cobham and even Dudley Carleton gave reasonably clear hints of their ambitions. I suspect that the court, and the country too, of Elizabeth contained more men than we know of who resented the small size of the Privy Council and wished to be on it.

More to the point, James I at once recognized the facts with his usual insight, even if with his usual bad luck and bad judgment he spoiled everything by picking the wrong men. He inherited a Council larger by one than that of 1601, Sir William Knollys having obtained the then vacant treasurership of the Household and having been succeeded as comptroller by Sir Edward Wotton. In the two weeks after 25 April 1603, James added no fewer than thirteen councillors, effectively doubling the size of the body.[71] Six of them were Scotsmen – a first step towards uniting the two kingdoms, but a step which, while it cost the king immediately some popularity, had neither administrative nor political significance for the Council itself which never saw those North Britons. As for the rest, whom do we find? The earl of Northumber-

---

[71] *APC* xxxii, 495, 496, 498.

land, 'the wizard earl', thought likely to reconcile the Catholic minority to the new regime; the earl of Cumberland, a tried and elderly courtier, remarkable only for the fact that he personally went off on the privateering expeditions which he fitted out; Lord Mountjoy, conqueror of Ireland (and of Penelope Rich); Lord Thomas Howard, another naval man in his past, but now a courtier who was to achieve the earldom of Suffolk, the lord treasurership, and prison for embezzlement; Lord Henry Howard, soon earl of Northampton, according to the *DNB* the most learned noble of the reign but more familiar as its most malicious intriguer; Lord Zouche whom James remembered as an ambassador to Scotland years before but who since 1602 had been president of the Council in the Marches; and Lord Burghley, the great Burghley's elder and stupid son, now president of the Council in the North. The last two at least held offices which before this had qualified men for the Council, but by the standards of the previous reign they were flotsam. Mountjoy, indeed, was the only man among them to have a touch of real distinction, though in the three years remaining to him he did nothing noteworthy. Still, he was only forty-three when he died, and his appointment may be thought suitable. Northumberland and Cumberland represented court nobility, though not its most useful members; the Howards did so too, but added insatiable ambition and the ability to corrupt a whole fifteen years of government.

A strange crew, *more Jacobeano*, but not without its significance in our present discussion. None, we may believe, answered the call with the reluctance (not as great as he made out) of a Thomas More; these men were looking for a place in the sun. Some – the Howards, Northumberland, possibly Zouche – were probably James's own choice, but it is hard to think that of his own free will he would have called in Burghley, Cumberland or even Mountjoy. In manner this spate of appointments suggests not only that ambition, unsatisfied, to become a privy councillor existed in sufficient magnitude at the court of Queen Elizabeth, but also once more that the strict reformed Privy Council was unsuitable for the role of creating political stability by satisfying ambition. The potential – indeed, the active principle – had been there in the unreformed Council. Its abandonment in 1536 had not then mattered much because the first task of the Privy Council was to govern the modernized state, a thing which the reformed Council was much better constructed to do; because Henry VIII and Elizabeth knew how to control unsatisfied men; and because other means existed for giving

such ambition outlets, from advancement at court through employment in war to election to Parliament. It is arguable that the expansion
of the House of Commons together with the contraction of the Council
set up one strand in that tension which was to become so manifest in the
reign of James: the increasing number of politically able and ambitious
men in the House of Commons were only too likely to start resenting
the narrow gate that led to the place of ultimate rule. James did wisely
when he enlarged his Council; if only he had continued to look to
proven ability when making his choice, he might have used both
institutions to promote stability.

In the sixteenth century, every moment of monarchic weakness
demonstrated the political disadvantages of a small Council as well as
the administrative disadvantages of a large one. It had not mattered so
much under Northumberland because his rule lasted so short a time, nor
under Mary because her leading ministers managed to preserve
efficiency in the *mêlée*. Elizabeth's determination to adhere to the
principles of a lifetime was, by the 1590s, adding to the general malaise
by leaving up-and-coming men frustrated. The dilemma was inescapable: either a Council which will give satisfaction to sufficient
individuals and interests, or a Council which will and can govern. On
balance, it is impossible to feel that Cromwell, choosing at a time when
the pressures of ambition were minimal, made the wrong choice: the
Tudor Privy Council was nearly always an impressive and remarkable
body of men, discharging very difficult tasks with genuine competence.
But their contribution to continued stability could only come from
outside – could only consist in their being the prince's vigilant eye,
foreseeing and forestalling trouble. They could never create stability by
inviting those capable of disturbing it into the charmed circle. There
were just too few places.

III. THE COURT

When on the previous two occasions I discussed Parliament and Council
as political centres, as institutions capable of assisting or undermining
stability in the nation, I had to draw attention to quite a few unanswered
questions. However, I also found a large amount of well established
knowledge on which to rely. Now, in considering the role of the king's
or queen's Court, I stand more baffled than ever, more deserted. We all
know that there was a Court, and we all use the term with frequent ease,
but we seem to have taken it so much for granted that we have done

almost nothing to investigate it seriously. Lavish descriptions abound of lavish occasions, both in the journalism of the sixteenth century and in the history books, but the sort of study which could really tell us what it was, what part it played in affairs, and even how things went there for this or that person, seems to be confined to a few important articles. At times it has all the appearance of a fully fledged institution; at others it seems to be no more than a convenient conceptual piece of shorthand, covering certain people, certain behaviour, certain attitudes. As so often, the shadows of the seventeenth century stretch back into the sixteenth, to obscure our vision. Analysts of the reigns of the first two Stuarts, endeavouring to explain the political troubles of that age, increasingly concentrate upon an alleged conflict between the Court and the Country; and so we are tempted, once again, to seek the prehistory of the ever interesting topic in the age of Elizabeth or even Henry VIII. This may do some good, but only if we know something reasonably precise about the entities we deal in. And here our mentors tend to let us down: for the historians of the early seventeenth century have not yet managed to define their terms. What is the Court? Those whom the Country dislikes. What is the Country? Those whom the Court despises. If we follow Professor Zagorin, we read the Court as embracing all office-holders, including some men in the shires who may never have set eyes on their sovereign.[72] But if we follow him, we must apparently leave our non-officed frequenters of St James's and Whitehall. I do not find this helpful.

There is often virtue in beginning at the beginning: when can we find the sort of Court that Elizabeth queened it in, that stage of all public life, social and cultural and political? I seem to sense a general conviction that its age is coeval with kingship, but I do not think this is true. Perhaps we might heed the intuition of the poet. In *Henry V*, Shakespeare takes us to the Court of France, of Charles VI, but the king of England is shown in Council, camp and battle – never in anything resembling a true Court. Is a Court such as we find under the Tudors conceivable under Henry VI? Dr Ross has suggested that there was some real novelty about Edward IV's Court, with its ceremonial detail and lavish life,[73] and it is apparent that both ceremony and display were imports from Burgundy and France whose example continued to direct the development of the Tudor Court at least down to Henry VIII's death. At present we do not

---

[72] P. Zagorin, *The Court and the Country: the Beginning of the English Revolution* (1969), 41.
[73] C. D. Ross, *Edward IV* (1974), 312.

know much about the Court of Henry VII except for the occasional – very occasional – feasts and celebrations that occurred there; and though this ignorance may reflect only the deficiencies of the evidence, I think it really springs from the fact that there is little to know. The Tudor Court as a centre of social and political life springs suddenly into existence with the accession of Henry VIII, and there are reasons why it should have done so.

The true Court of our imagining could not exist until the Crown had destroyed all alternative centres of political loyalty or (to emphasize another function of the Court) all alternative sources of worldly advancement. While there were magnates, their patronage and standing took away from the king's patronage and sovereignty, and their residences from the uniqueness of his Court. The work of raising the king upon an unattainably high platform above all his subjects was not completed until the second Tudor added the visible enjoyment of that position to the reality created by the first. Even in the sixteenth century, mini-alternatives occasionally appeared, carrying with them the phenomena of Court-like centres; Buckingham and possibly Leicester come to mind, as does that pitiful Sheffield-plate copy of the reality, the second earl of Essex. The jealousy of Tudor monarchs, who took care to sterilize such out of date endeavours, was really very well advised: their rule, their power, depended on their uniqueness, and it was their Courts that gave continuous expression to that solitary eminence. Thus the politics of the sixteenth century – personal or national, principled or merely ambitious – of necessity 'happened' in the confines of the Court. Most commonly, but not exclusively, of course; let us not forget the politics of Parliament and Council which by no means always coincided with those of the Court. But these latter were the most omnipresent, possibly the most intense, certainly the most confusing and obscure. The contrast between Court and Country ('rusticity') is in this age always one between involvement in and withdrawal from public life, never a posing of alternative public attitudes and activities. Literary convention dictated that the second should be preferred on moral and indeed on medical grounds, as in a charming and unusually lively little book by Bishop Guevara, councillor to Charles V, which that inveterate courtier Sir Francis Bryan translated a year or two before his death when old age had caused even him to tire of the Court.[74] But whether they were

[74] Antonio de Guevara, *A Dispraise of the Life of a Courtier and a Commendation of the Life of a Labouring Man*, trs. F. Bryan (1548).

sincere or not in their professed preference for the happy life and untroubled sleep of rural retirement, both Guevara and Bryan, like everybody else, took it for granted that politics equals the Court.

Thus in our search for stability-creating institutions we need to look at the people who composed the Court, no easy task because their demography has not been written, and even their population (in the natural-science sense of the term) has not been defined. There is relatively little trouble about the one formal, almost professional, component of the Court, the royal Household in its departments – the lord steward's and lord chamberlain's departments to which under the early Tudors we must now add the Privy Chamber as a separate sector.[75] Here we find bureaucratic organization – specific offices filled by knowable persons who in the sixteenth century were nearly all still personally discharging their duties, so that we only rarely need to look for obscure deputies to sinecurists. However, though this part of the Court may be accessible we still lack studies of it to compare with the work done on its Stuart successor by Professor Aylmer. The Household provided the largest single establishment of salaried and fee-earning posts in the realm, and therefore the most concentrated area for the seekers after patronage. The satisfaction of legitimate ambition ought to be readily traceable here, but this again is work that has not yet been done at all systematically. The problem is not simple or single. Take the lord steward's department. Clerks of the Kitchen and serjeants of the Pantry were men of some standing and reasonable expectation of profit: was there competition for such appointments, and could bestowal of office be influenced by the political standing of patrons? What happens as we penetrate lower down, to grooms, pages, cooks and scullions? The patronage structure of that quite teeming world needs unravelling, though a word of warning against excessive subtlety exists in the well attested fact that certain offices came to be the property, for several generations, of family dynasties like the Thynnes (exceptional only in that they rose to high eminence in the end). My general impression is that the purposes of social stability within the governing order were little affected by success or failure of job-hunting at this level, but our state of ignorance is such that I could be as readily wrong as right.

For obvious reasons one would expect to get more interesting results from a study of the Chamber where employment was offered to the

---

[75] Cf. D. R. Starkey, 'The King's Privy Chamber 1485–1547', unpublished Ph.D. dissertation (Cambridge, 1973).

offspring of the political nation, to the sons and daughters of gentlemen, esquires, and (at the top) noblemen. As Dr Starkey has begun to show, the history of the monarch's immediate entourage reflects nothing so much as the power politics of an elite. This is clearly true for the staff of Henry VIII's Privy Chamber and there are modest indications of a similar state of affairs under Henry VII; what, however, was the situation after 1547 and in particular, what was the significance of Elizabeth's changing group of attendants? One thing is clear enough: competition for appointments was at this level fierce, and the supply of places inadequate. The Privy Chamber repeatedly expanded beyond the size laid down, sometimes because the monarch might transfer his favour to new companions without wishing to cast out the old, sometimes simply because these places of honour and potential profit attracted men whose importunity was backed by influence. Any new opportunities in the Chamber establishment produced phenomena familiar, in another way, from the disposal of the confiscated property of the Church – strident appeals for the satisfaction of a share, channelled through the top agents of the royal patronage. When Henry VIII proposed in 1538 to revive the corps of gentlemen-pensioners, candidates for admission (usually on behalf of their sons) lined up in throngs that recall scenes on the mornings of rights issues in the happier days of capitalism. A pensioner's place was bound to be quite expensive to the occupier, while immediate rewards were small; but the fathers who in their dozens wrote to Thomas Cromwell rightly viewed these jobs as investments, and fairly safe investments at that. With power as well as the horn of patronage plenty now firmly monopolized by the Crown, a place at Court was the thing for anyone with ambitions to better himself. Even if a man's affairs or tastes kept him in the country he was well advised to attend the Court by proxy, that is to say, by placing a son or a nephew in a strategic position there.[76] Not that the ultimate ambition could be satisfied merely by presence at Court: membership of the Council, influence on the making of policy, power in its political guise, continued to depend only in small part on the function or place of the courtier. The statesmen of the age were no strangers to the Court, but neither were they its creatures: Christopher Hatton's career, which appeared to be an exception to that rule, caused significantly raised eyebrows. The one area of public life of which Cromwell had had no

---

[76] Wallace T. MacCaffrey, 'Place and patronage in Elizabethan politics', *Elizabethan Government and Society*, ed. S. T. Bindoff, J. Hurstfield, C. H. Williams (1961), 100–10.

experience before he embarked on his career in the king's service was the Court, and I do not think that he ever fully penetrated its essence, any more than did Sir Thomas Smith.

Nevertheless, these men and their like spent a good deal of their time in the Court, wherever it might be, and they form a group about whose role in that setting obscurity gathers most discouragingly. Some of them occupied an ambiguous place halfway between the Household officer and the politician or bureaucrat definitely not of the Household, an ambiguity which has continued to bewilder historians. The fact that, as the warrant of April 1540 puts it, the two principal secretaries were to have 'an ordinary chamber or lodging within the gates of his grace's house, in all places where the same may be', with bouge of court, has apparently persuaded a good many scholars (especially but not only those who can see no reason for accepting that major administrative changes occurred in the reign of Henry VIII) that the Elizabethan secretaries of state were still in a real sense Household officers, just like their Yorkist predecessors. Yet that same warrant clearly makes them much more specifically attendants upon the lord privy seal than the king, and no one has yet supposed that they were really members of Cromwell's household.[77] The truth is both simpler and subtler: they were part of the general machinery of the reformed state, outside the royal Household but of necessity often compelled to come to Court, a contingency for which administrative provision had to be made. But were they courtiers?

I wish we were able to confine the term courtier to its strict meaning, to the holders of specifically Court offices; but that is manifestly insufficient. There can be no sense in any interpretation which allocates Lord Treasurer Burghley to a political sphere separate and distinguishable from that in which the earl of Leicester, master of the Horse, had his being. Sir Walter Ralegh was a great figure at Court – the quintessential courtier – from 1582, but he had to wait a full seven years for an actual Court office, the captaincy of the Guard.[78] As I have suggested, the identification of offices and holders has its uses at a lower level of eminence, but it ceases to help once we come to look at the people at Court whose functions and ambitions extended to the political sphere. Here influence, even if sometimes reflected in office, really depended on personal standing with the prince; that standing might or might not be

[77] *Tudor Constitution*, 122.
[78] W. M. Wallace, *Sir Walter Raleigh* (1959), 25, 29.

embodied in office, nor need that office be Court office, nor can standing necessarily be measured by the relative importance of offices held.

Few moments in English public life carried more significance than those occupied by the monarch in signing papers – despatches, legislative proposals, the approval of private petitions: especially the last. Despite the very considerable area of activities which in England came under delegated authority – where king or queen neither acted nor necessarily knew of the action – a greater sector of public life depended upon the ruler's personal participation, usually supplied by such signatures. In particular, this was true of the dispensing of patronage, the one thing all of them reserved to themselves so long as they were of age and *compos mentis*, and far and away the thing most frequently demanded of them by their subjects. Thus, as is well enough known, the person who acted as channel between petitioner and sovereign occupied a place of singular influence and attraction. King or queen could sign only what was offered up to them, and the flow was regulated by others. Conventional doctrine holds that those others were the secretaries of state, a view shared by themselves. Robert Beale's instructions on the office of principal secretary assume without question that her highness will sign only in the presence of that officer who will do well to ease the royal labours during that painful time with 'some relation or speech whereat she may take some pleasure' (and which might distract her attention from what she was giving away?).[79] He does not forget that other people could be involved, like the various civil servants whose countersignatures, obtained in advance, will assure the queen that she could properly approve those petitions and pardons, but with respect to her immediate attendants he feels that their function is only to prepare the perspiring secretary for the reception he is likely to get: 'Learn before your access her majesty's disposition by some of her privy chamber.'[80] He is quite explicit that even the suits of those close and favoured persons must pass through the secretary's hands. Perhaps this is really what happened in Elizabeth's reign; perhaps by then the secretary had truly monopolized this vital weapon of power. But it was not always so: Cromwell faced the rivalry which ready access to the king's person gave to gentlemen of the Privy Chamber and solved the problem by staffing that department with men of his choosing, while late in Henry VIII's reign the Privy Chamber virtually drove the

---

[79] Conyers Read, *Mr Secretary Walsingham and the Policy of Queen Elizabeth* i (Oxford, 1925), 438.
[80] Ibid. 437.

secretaries from that field. Once again, it is clear that in the conduct of politically meaningful business distinctions between courtiers (holders of Court office) and administrators, real enough in terms of appointment, tenure, function and often also life-style, are less significant than the distinction between Crown officers above and below the line that divided politicians from mere civil servants.

Thus the only definition of the Court which makes sense in the sixteenth century is that it comprised all those who at any given time were within 'his grace's house'; and all those with a right to be there were courtiers to whom the fact, and the problems, of the Court constituted a central preoccupation in their official lives and in the search for personal satisfaction.

All those who had access: but how was that controlled? The Chamber bureaucracy was so organized as to ensure that sufficient gentlemen, gentlemen ushers, grooms and pages attended at Court to provide the personal services required, but this was a strictly administrative arrangement which it would be wrong to investigate for political significance reflected in presence or absence. Formal reorganization, of course, carried deeper meaning: the clean-up of the Privy Chamber in 1519, for instance, or the holocaust which struck it in the Boleyn disaster of 1536, signified upheavals which need to be read in the context of political power struggles. No such major blow seems to have fallen in the reign of Elizabeth, but the occasional removals from Court of the queen's maids of dishonour should be investigated to see whether really nothing more was involved than the queen's virginal wrath.

For the non-officed courtiers, on the other hand, the right to come to Court formed the clearest visible barometer of politics and was so used by those assiduous observers, foreign ambassadors. The test was less applicable during Wolsey's heyday when Henry several times complained about the dearth of attendants around him, a dearth which put such extra burdens on the shoulders of that reluctant courtier, Sir Thomas More, compelled to stay long into the night so that the king might be amused.[81] As Skelton pointed out, people did not come to Court because there was better profit in attending the Cardinal's rival court; and the people who stayed away included, strikingly enough, Wolsey himself whose visits to Court grew increasingly rarer and more ceremonious as time went on. Part-time courtiers like Cromwell made the effort, but Cromwell found it necessary, once his power was

[81] *Two Early Tudor Lives*, 202.

45

established, to be present by deputy, the function discharged especially by Ralph Sadler throughout the later 1530s. At least Cromwell grasped the need to keep others away; both Norfolk and Gardiner, his chief rivals, discovered the difficulty of getting permission to come during the years of the lord privy seal's ascendency. At the height of the Boleyn crisis of 1536 he even stopped Cranmer from coming to Court, apparently on the king's orders.[82] It seems that such matters were handled with relative delicacy: people were advised that there was no occasion to come or that their service might be better discharged elsewhere, rather than brutally ejected. Elizabeth on occasion practised more direct methods, publicly denying her presence to those who had fallen from grace, like her leading councillors after the execution of the queen of Scots, Essex after his mudstained return from Ireland, or Ralegh after his shotgun-marriage to Bess Throckmorton. We may suppose that this experience helped to persuade Ralegh that the Court glowed like rotten wood.

Access and exclusion mattered so much because the game of politics, unlike the government of the realm, remained so firmly fixed upon the monarch's person. It was the sight of the royal face that people needed who wished to advance their causes, a striking case of interest overcoming natural feelings as both Henry VIII and Elizabeth grew older and uglier. (It is hard to believe that anyone ever really liked looking upon Queen Mary.) And I am not sure that even now we have got these highly personal situations absolutely correct: I think we may have consistently overestimated the formality of behaviour and therefore of access. True, people knelt uncovered in the royal presence, a rule which offered well-taken opportunities for calculated graciousness. True, ceremony dominated even the meal-times of royalty. Yet there are odd indications here and there that our imaginations, nourished by accounts of the great occasions and views of the set-piece portraits, may have endowed life at the Tudor Court with a degree of coldly distant order that did not exist. I am not so much thinking of the well attested squalor of filthy kitchen-boys, accumulated garbage, stinking throngs of beggars and sightseers – all those features, inadequately covered in cloth of gold and precious stones, which regularly forced the Court to move after a few weeks from quarters which its humanity had polluted beyond bearing. Rather I have in mind the behaviour of the monarchs themselves and those who spoke to them. Of course, we know all about

[82] *LP* x, 792.

the uses of affability, and we have heard enough about the Tudor skill in preserving a necessary dignity without losing some sort of common touch, a task easier for that potential bar-room bore, King Henry, than for his daughter whose occasional escape into the aggressive masculinity of bad language and bad manners so shocked nineteenth-century historians. What I have in mind are hints that behaviour in the royal presence could be far less governed by formal respect and monarch-worshipping dread than one might suppose from reading Tudor courtiers' precepts on the subject. And if these doubts are justified, it follows that we should also have to adjust our estimate of monarchs' and courtiers' relative position in the making of careers and policy.

What looks like the surprising reality is well indicated by some of the interviews which Robert Carey, youngest son of Lord Hunsdon, had with his sovereign. When he was in disgrace for having married without the queen's approval, his father acted as intermediary and kept his courtier's laurels reasonably green. That fits the common notions of Elizabeth. When finally he managed to get access again he used very plain language to her that fits less well, replying to her reproaches for his apparent desertion of the presence that he had seen no profit in staying: 'if she had graced me with the least of her favours, I had never left her nor her court'. And some years later, when in effect he committed Essex's offence by leaving his post at Berwick without licence to rush to Theobalds for a word with Elizabeth, he was warned off, with every sign of apprehension and solicitude, by Robert Cecil, principal secretary, and by his own eldest brother, the lord chamberlain, only to find that William Killigrew, a gentleman of the Privy Chamber, could get him access and forgiveness with no trouble at all.[83] Perhaps Cecil and the second Lord Hunsdon were on that occasion acting as back-friends, but to me it looks more as though everything was so haphazard and uncertain about this business of seeing the queen that highly placed courtiers could completely misread the signs. The majesty of majesty? Rather, what a way to run a railroad.

More striking still are the improbabilities we encounter in the reign of Henry VIII. Two stories about him, neither totally unfamiliar, will bear retelling for the strange light they throw on the manners of Court life and the relations between king and courtiers. Do we not suppose that people went in fear of the king's wrath, which is death? That they had cause to expect physical blows if they did not watch their step?

[83] *The Memoirs of Robert Carey*, ed. F. H. Mares (Oxford, 1972), 29, 30–1, 43–4.

47

Surely they would not speak to him in ways that even lesser humans would find insufferably offensive. What then are we to make of the scene, some time around 1533, when Sir George Throckmorton, a knight of the Reformation Parliament who had consistently opposed the Crown's bills touching religion and the Church, was summoned to the royal presence to explain himself?[84] Being told, mildly enough, that the king was sorely troubled about his marriage to his brother's widow, Sir George riposted that marriage to Anne Boleyn would come to trouble him similarly, 'for it is thought you have meddled both with the mother and the sister' – relations which created the same canonical impediment as that alleged to exist in the Aragon marriage. Here was a man of neither standing nor significance, with a record of opposition, accusing the king to his face of multiple adultery as well as hypocrisy: surely the royal wrath struck him dead? What Henry VIII actually said, in some embarrassment, was only 'never with the mother', a reply so naively revealing as to infuriate Cromwell who, standing by, interjected, 'nor never with the sister either, and therefore put that out of your mind'. I have some difficulty in accommodating this scene to the vision of the majestic lord who broke all those bonds of man and God.

Perhaps even more significant of the realities of Court life is an occasion observed by Eustace Chapuys in April 1536.[85] Chapuys and Cromwell had for some time been negotiating over ways to reduce the Anglo-Imperial tension, and the time had come (so Cromwell thought) to bring the king into the business. Thus the ambassador went to Court where he was received with cordial kindness all round. However, either (it seems) Cromwell had miscalculated, or Henry changed his mind: he turned very cool towards the proposals worked out by ambassador and minister, and after a while withdrew into a window with Cromwell and Lord Chancellor Audley. Chapuys, who could see but not hear what was going on, noticed a dispute growing in acrimony, and after this had gone on for quite some time Cromwell came away from the window, grumbling to himself and complaining of thirst. He went out of the king's sight to sit down on a coffer and sent for a drink. Shortly after this Henry broke off his conversation and returned to the centre of the chamber; Chapuys, who first thought that the king wished to speak to him once more, then found that he was merely looking to see what had become of Cromwell. There is nothing at all odd about the core of this scene, about the display of disagreement or the failure of diplomacy.

[84] *LP* xii(II), 952.   [85] *LP* x, pp. 291–2.

But should we really have expected that Cromwell would so publicly argue with the king, would so unceremoniously leave the royal presence (making his fury plain to all), would sit down for a drink (even if out of sight), and that Henry's only reaction would be to come looking for his minister? Is that the Henry VIII of our imaginings?

The point of these doubts is relevant to the theme under discussion. If we have got the actuality of being in the royal presence out of true, if we have to think of these monarchs as far more relaxed and bewildered in their public behaviour than usually we do, it becomes difficult to maintain that Court life consisted predominantly of currying favour, of flattering or worshipping a godlike dominant person. Courtiers may have written poems to Astraea, but they talked to Queen Elizabeth and wove their webs around her. Not even she or her father, possibly the two most royal monarchs in our history, answered to the superhuman stereotype of rulers which, for instance, we find described by their latest biographers who, taking their stand with the throne, assume that everything happened as and because the monarch wished it to happen.[86] The real Henry VIII and Elizabeth lived in a setting composed of powerful people and resounding to clashing ambitions in which they had to behave with frequent circumspection if they were not (as Henry VIII and Mary frequently did) to make the most appalling mistakes under the influence of others who exploited the pretended omnipotence of royalty. But if the battle for promotion and survival did not consist simply in gaining the king's ear or catching the queen's eye and then dealing directly with the fountain of honour as supplicants to an all-powerful being, we need to know how those to whom Court air was the vital ingredient of political life really carried on their business.

Courtiers, in fact, did not constitute a gathering of individuals all individually looking towards the throne, but identifiable – and often surprisingly enduring – groupings around one or more leaders upon whom the way to the throne depended. We need to investigate faction, and perhaps this is obvious: but I would suggest that an element which we all recognize in the politics of the fifteenth century or the Stuart age has usually been left out under the Tudors, on the erroneous grounds that those monarchs governed personally, by which is meant a rule embodying direct personal action based upon personal initiative and judgment. On the contrary, like all monarchical rule that of the Tudors

---

[86] L. Baldwin Smith, *Henry VIII: the Mask of Royalty* (1971); P. Johnson, *Elizabeth I: a Study in Power and Intellect* (1974).

was both *regale* and *politicum*, but *politicum* in a sense different from Fortescue's: they were managed at worst, manoeuvred at best, by the purposeful groupings of interests that articulated the nation's politics. The idea of faction is familiar enough in Parliament, where in the sixteenth century it occurred with some regularity though only a minority of the House of Commons ever adhered to such alliances, and in the council where it existed (so far as the evidence goes) far less commonly than is usually supposed; its presence at the Court, however often asserted, has hardly been investigated at all because its vital importance has been outshone by the supposed free domination of the monarch.

The crises of Henry VIII's reign, for instance, were really all crises at Court; even the Pilgrimage of Grace fits that description when it is remembered that it was the work of noblemen who either resented exclusion from the Court (Northumberland, Hussey) or wished to transform the Court (Darcy). In particular it is true of the king's matrimonial history which so deeply influenced affairs. His last five wives were produced by Court factions in their struggles for power, but the matter has been investigated from this point of view for only one case, the fall of Anne Boleyn.[87] It is, admittedly, the clearest and most revealing episode, with an unusual number of factions interacting. There were the Boleyns themselves, with their strong hold on the Privy Chamber and their weakening hold on the king. There was the Norfolk–Suffolk group, uneasily poised for flight from alliance with the Boleyns. We can discern at least two so-to-speak conservative groupings. The remnant of the Aragonese faction, also powerful in the Privy Chamber, now concentrated on promoting the interests of the Princess Mary; while what one might call an old-nobility faction (Exeter, Pole, Darcy) adopted its anti-Boleyn stance more from resentment at innovation and centralization in general. The decline of Anne brought polarization into this *mêlée*, though it took the intervention of Cromwell, building up his own Court faction while neatly utilizing the jealousies of the rest, to precipitate the actual crisis and its solution. In the outcome, the kaleidoscope rearranged itself. The old-nobility faction remained identifiable, to be destroyed in the Pilgrimage and its aftermath in 1538; Cromwell took over the Court

[87] E. W. Ives, 'Faction at the court of Henry VIII: the fall of Anne Boleyn', *History* 47 (1972), 169 ff. In a still unpublished paper, written before Dr Ives's article appeared, Dr D. R. Starkey offers a slightly different and rather more penetrating interpretation which rightly stresses the role of the Privy Chamber in the story. I am obliged to Dr Starkey for letting me see his essay.

interest of the fallen favourite; Norfolk and Suffolk began to drift in the direction of his enemies without, however, going so far as to amalgamate with them, so that they escaped the disaster of 1538. It must be remembered that the noble leadership of the Pilgrimage had had hopes of winning Norfolk to their side. In 1538–9 Cromwell dangerously dominated the Court, as he dominated everything else, a position he used to tie Henry to Anne of Cleves and the north-European anti-papal alliance; his fall was the work of the Court faction vanquished in 1538 but enabled to revive by the fiasco of the Cleves marriage and Norfolk's change of sides. The stories of Katherine Howard and Katherine Parr similarly need to be seen less as examples of capricious despotism on the king's part and more as the effect of such factional manoeuvrings upon his supposed freedom of action.

We usually ascribe the rise of Edward Seymour to his military performances in the 1540s, and it would certainly be hard to see him as a power at Court before the last two years of the reign. Yet it was only his sister's early death that prevented the creation of a Seymour faction which could have been as troublesome to Cromwell as the Boleyns had become by 1536. And Seymour's final jump to prominence was once again a purely Court affair, the achievement of the faction war which overthrew the Howards and, at the critical moment of Henry's effective withdrawal from rule, left Hertford and Paget in command of Court, Privy Chamber and the king's dry stamp, the instrument of power. Edward VI's reign may seem a less promising age in which to study Court faction because the purpose of such groupings was, of course, to gain influence (or more) over an active king, one whose word (properly influenced) would on any given occasion generate the action desired. It is thus no wonder that the politics of the reign have usually been studied with reference to the Council rather than the Court. Yet even Northumberland's Council, enlarged (as we have seen)[88] to make room for more members of his faction, did not involve numbers large enough to show what was really going on; here, too, Court appointments and replacements should be looked at to get the politics of the age clear. This holds true even for the reign of Mary when the combination of an ecclesiastical chancellor, a foreign king, and the probably biased reporting of an imperial ambassador has firmly directed attention again to the Privy Council rather than the Court, leaving the impression that the factions were strictly conciliar. The study of the Court is here

[88] Above, p. 31.

51

complicated by the intrusion of Philip's entourage, but that makes a deeper investigation of Mary's Court only the more necessary.

One thing is clear about the situation between 1509 and 1558: factions at Court were trying to get exclusive control but never succeeded in doing so. Wolsey came nearest to triumph; or rather he may look to have been in that position because we still do not know enough about the inner history of the Court in the 1520s. The rise of Anne Boleyn assuredly demonstrated the prevalence and significance of Court factions even during the Cardinal's ascendancy: again, we need more work, though Dr Starkey's study of the Henrician Privy Chamber has covered the central ground satisfactorily. Cromwell for a brief period nearly eliminated rival factions, but partly because the role of courtier sat uneasily upon him, partly because he contented himself with keeping Gardiner and Norfolk away from Court rather than rid himself of them for good on the several occasions when with a little more Machiavellian juggling he could readily have done so, he never transmuted ascendancy into secure dominance. The chief cause of the continued faction strife lay, however, elsewhere – in the king himself. If faction enabled the politicians to use him (as it did), he also found in it the obvious means for preventing any one of them from imprisoning him. This appears to have been entirely deliberate. Unlike his father (so far as I can tell) and his elder daughter, Henry VIII purposely kept his Court divided. He had his favourites, and thanks to the existence of the Privy Chamber they played important roles in the national politics of the day; but Henry saved himself by so frequently swapping favourites that no faction ever won outright – or none, at least, until in his last decline the Seymour faction took the sceptre from his failing hands.

Notoriously this was a lesson that Elizabeth also learned, whether from him or from her own experience cannot be judged. We have grown so familiar with the notion of faction in her age that we forget how little the structure of those groupings has been studied. Even Professor MacCaffrey, for whom the first dozen years of the reign rightly revolve around the partified alliances of politicians, never specifically analyses their members or tracks the tendrils emanating from the Court.[89] Let me quote a casual aside in which Dr Neville Williams sums up the common opinion: 'Factions – the ancestors of political parties – developed round leading courtiers, and Elizabeth

[89] Wallace T. MacCaffrey, *The Shaping of the Elizabethan Regime* (Princeton, N.J., 1968).

sought to maintain a nice balance to keep the peace.'[90] I do not quarrel with this statement; I merely cannot tell whether it is really adequate. Did factions 'develop', and were their leaders always courtiers in any precise sense of the word? Did family traditions and local allegiances play a part as well as personality? Was Elizabeth really able to keep that famous balance by her own willed action; was she so much more in control of everybody than her father would seem to have been? And that parenthesis about political parties – perceptive though it is – also points to the cause of my uncertainties. The only attempts to identify factions and see them at work have concentrated on affairs, on strains in the Council, on rival advice and policy. Though everyone who looks at Ralegh or Essex is forced to consider the life of the Court, no one has yet made a proper study of Elizabeth's Court as a political centre; and the biographer of Burghley and Walsingham was able to write five large volumes without seemingly becoming aware that Court faction differed from political party, even if (possibly) one fathered the other.[91] The disastrous disappearance of Leicester's papers, together with the better survival of the *Acts of the Privy Council*, has helped to create this distortion; and I think that when Professor Hurstfield's work on Robert Cecil is before us we shall see some redressing of the balance. But so long as we are guided to regard the Court of Elizabeth as mainly a cultural centre for the English Renaissance (with Philip Sidney our paradigmatic courtier), or as merely the organization which permitted the percolation of patronage; so long as we fail to treat it as the centre of political power struggles; so long as it is held that in the affairs that mattered the queen ruled all with an even hand and a subtle mind; in short, so long as Gloriana continues to occupy that throne, I doubt whether we shall ever really get to the roots of political life in her reign. We need no more reveries on accession tilts and symbolism, no more pretty pictures of gallants and galliards; could we instead have painful studies of Acatry and Pantry, of vice-chamberlains and ladies of the Privy Chamber?

At any rate, the vital political role of the Court, and the deep significance of Court factions, are recognizable facts of Tudor life. It remains to consider their meaning – in which there also lies some sort of an answer to the question which I have tried to pose throughout this series of lectures, the question of stability. Let us return to Dr Williams's

[90] N. J. Williams, *All the Queen's Men* (1972), 14.
[91] Conyers Read, *Mr Secretary Walsingham* (three volumes); *Mr Secretary Cecil and Queen Elizabeth* (1955); *Lord Burghley and Queen Elizabeth* (1960).

definition. It is certainly true that faction gathered round leading political personalities, though before 1558 few of them were strictly one-man bands. Wolsey and Cromwell – more especially Wolsey – conducted themselves almost like modern party leaders, but the Boleyn or old-nobility factions were at the top alliances of equals. Northumberland certainly, and possibly Somerset too, were not singlehanded faction leaders; they shared temporary alliances with others to build up a following. Whether we are right to speak as plainly as we do of Burghley's faction or Leicester's, of Norfolk's or Essex's, must remain uncertain until we have been told more about them; but even at this date we should not forget men like Arundel, Sussex and Sidney early in the reign, like Ralegh, Cobham or Nottingham in the last twenty years of the century. However, the problem of leadership apart, it is evident that faction existed for the purpose of promoting individual fortunes, those of both leaders and led: it was the mechanism which, at Court, organized the satisfaction of personal ambition for wealth and power. And, though by no means everyone received what he regarded as his due and some indeed suffered total eclipse, it appears that faction sufficiently delivered the goods to prevent the build-up of resentments that could have destroyed stability. Essex alone took his resentment further than impotent grumbling – and we all know what became of Essex.

What, then, about faction being the ancestor of political party? Dr Ives would seem to think that this was indeed true of Elizabethan factions, engaged in the advocacy of rival policies and partly at least structured by religious affiliations, but he did not think that such purposes informed any of the Henrician factions except the old-nobility group of Exeter, Pole and perhaps Darcy.[92] In this I think he was too sceptical. The outward appearance of Henry's Court factions was governed by the personal rivalries which the events of the day, and the king, encouraged; and attitudes were obviously coloured by a situation in which political opposition could so easily be made to look like disloyalty or even treason. Yet nevertheless every one of the factions that one can identify cherished and promoted political ends that had nothing to do with mere personal advancement or the exploitation of patronage. Cromwell manifestly needed the backing of a faction to establish his hold on monarch and machine; as manifestly he used that control to carry out a very positive political programme. The factions

[92] Ives, *History* 47, 177–8.

that rivalled his influence unquestionably found part of their *raison d'être* in hatred of the minister, but the hatred drew more strength from opposition to his policies than from contempt for the upstart. The note thus sounded in the 1530s never died away entirely, even if at times purely personal ambition is markedly more evident than the possession of larger political purposes. (Of course, this is equally true of real political parties on frequent occasions.) Nor is the reason for this continuance of a genuine principled division between the factions at all obscure. From the moment that Henry VIII entered upon his breach with the papacy and thus opened the door to the Reformation, all political debate – all issues of domestic and foreign policy – acquired an ideological component in addition to its normal character as conflicts for power. Especially the Henrician factions subsisted on the religious split: you could no more follow Cromwell if you were a convinced papist than you could attach yourself to Norfolk and Gardiner if you thought that there had been no true religion before Luther. Of course, there were moderate men and time-servers who threaded their way between the factions, or more commonly from one to the other, but even for them every alignment and attachment to a given leader had notable political overtones. Even that supposedly most powerful faction-cement of the age, kinship, could crumble under the pressure of politics, as the vagaries of the various members of the Howard clan demonstrate throughout the century. The third duke of Norfolk remains, I think, the only uncle in our history who presided over two tribunals that condemned two nieces to death for treasonable adultery. I am not trying to make out that politics was everything – only that it always contributed, was usually ideological, and gave a purposeful backbone to those groupings of generally very self-seeking men (and women).

There are things about the Elizabethan factions which make me wonder whether the power of ideological politics was then quite as strong as it had been in the 1530s. After all, both Burghley's and Leicester's factions wished to advance the cause of the reformed religion though they differed over methods. When the debate becomes one of means rather than ends, mere personality – ambition, hatred, also affection – can prevail more easily. Still, all the Court factions of the century rested on more than personal purpose and personal attachment; they were indeed truly political groupings, though I myself would not care to try tracing their long-distance paternity to the emergence of party. And here we touch on what I suggest was the vital characteristic of Tudor Court faction. The Tudor Court was the centre of politics not only in the sense that those seeking power needed to pursue it there, but more significantly still in the sense that the battle of politics was there fought out. None of the main solutions to the problems of the day lacked advocates within the very heart of the Court itself – not even peace with Rome in the 1540s, or the puritan programme in the 1570s. Whether Elizabeth took care to maintain the factions simply to prevent herself being overwhelmed by any one of them must remain a matter for doubt; the effect, however, of her refusal to allow total victory to this or that group was to provide all political ambition with a platform at the very centre of affairs. In her reign, and in her father's too, conflict took place within the Court. When Stuart policy, whether from preference or blindness, permitted the monopolizing of the Court by single favourites and exclusive faction, conflict was forced out of Court into a public arena: but this was new. The concepts of Court and Country have their place in an analysis of Tudor politics; but in contradistinction to what happened in the seventeenth century they do not represent rival poles around which faction, or party, might gather. The factions in the Country linked to members of the Court; Court faction spread its net over the shires. The realm was one and had one centre; and the situation prevailing at Court made sure that the many political divisions within that one realm and one centre should work themselves out in the ordinary context and contests of political life, without ever threatening to divide the political nation into ins and outs. The age of Buckingham has no Tudor prehistory.

Sixteenth-century England experienced much trouble, unrest and upheaval. It was an age when true disruption and even chaos were never far away. Disaster was held off by usually strong government and the successful creation of a national selfconsciousness around the visible symbolism of a divinely appointed monarchy. These things have taken the eye, as the Tudors intended they should, but the machinery of rulership is by no means the whole story. In reality Tudor stability depended on the sharing of power, right through the structure, from monarchs to village elders; at all points there existed institutional mechanism to give reality to the principle of participation, defined by custom and law but articulated by political awareness. At the level of national affairs, Parliament offered means of advancement, the fulfilment of personal and family requirements, and a chance to the voice of both advocacy and criticism. The Privy Council, if it had not been reformed for the purpose of efficient administration, might have become a similar instrument for political stability through participation; instead its contribution lay on the side of control rather than co-operation (and a very necessary contribution it was, too). But above all, the Court – the true seat of power, profit and policy – preserved peace in the midst of strife by making certain that the strife should take place within the official centre of political life itself. No one who subscribed to a few basic loyalties needed to feel left out, and there was no occasion for a political opposition.

34

THE MATERIALS OF PARLIAMENTARY HISTORY*

I. THE EARLY JOURNALS OF THE HOUSE OF LORDS†

The early history of the Lords' Journals has been discussed several times. First came A. F. Pollard who in a well-known article debated what he called the 'authenticity' of the Journals and concluded that those beginning in 1510 started then as the clerk's private notebook and gradually underwent an 'evolution' or development towards a more formal record. He drew attention to the inadequate editing which produced the printed *Journals* and from his analysis conjectured various consequences for the history of the House, and indeed of the Parliament as a whole, especially that it was clearly still in a very unfinished state in the reign of Henry VIII.[1] Pollard's article initiated the serious study of these materials, but it was not altogether satisfactory. Its age will readily excuse not only some odd attitudinizing about authenticity and evolution but, more obviously, the fact that he could not take account of manuscripts since discovered; it is more serious that he tied himself up in certain misconceptions about the purposes and history of the manuscripts available to him. Nor is it at all clear whether he himself really made the careful study of the manuscript Journals and later copies which he succeeded in suggesting lay behind his paper.[2] A less ambitious

---

* The four papers grouped together under this head were written in an endeavour to understand the sources and grasp what their structure and history had to tell about the structure and history of the institution. While each is quite solid in respect of its particular theme, the earlier ones include necessarily premature remarks about those studied later. It would be tedious to draw frequent attention to minor inaccuracies, but it should be noted that whatever is said about the Rolls in 34 (I & II) stands to be corrected by 34 (III).

† [*EHR* 89 (1974), 481–512.]

A. F. Pollard, 'The authenticity of the the "Lords' Journals" in the sixteenth century', *TRHS* 3rd ser. 8 (1914), 17–39

[2] Doubts arise in reading the article, especially the note on p. 31 from which it appears that the study was really made by Miss Jeffries-Davis, with the great man grandly casting an eye over her

but more accurate account was given by Mr H. S. Cobb who described
the early Journals in a memorandum on the minute books of the Lords,
though he was inclined to follow Pollard more than was safe.[3]
Meanwhile, and since, scraps of Journals material for the fifteenth
century were discovered and published by Professor W. H. Dunham,
Professor A. R. Myers, and Dr R. Virgoe. These have put the whole
story on a new footing by ending the supposition that the history of the
Journals began in 1510. Odd pieces of the Journals have also been found
for the reign of Henry VIII, additional to the so-called 'official' series.[4]
However, so far no attempt has been made to gather all this material
together and to see what may be learned about the record-keeping of
the House or the work of its clerks. The materials are enough to raise all
sorts of questions but not enough to resolve them all. I propose in the
first place to describe them separately and in turn.

1

All the extant fifteenth-century material survives only in copies made in
the late sixteenth and early seventeenth centuries. There are (so far) five
pieces to note.

(A) The record of a debate in 1449, touching the finding of supplies
for the war in France.[5] This records, in Latin, a number of peers as
present and, in English, starting with the words 'the question is',
opinions expressed by various speakers. A note written on the face of the
document mentions that all this belongs to the Winchester (1449)
Parliament of Henry VI, the only indication which links the whole
document to Parliament at all; another insertion between the presence
and the debate says that the copy was made by Sir William Dethick,

labours. Some of Pollard's remarks about the MS Journal convey a less than perfect conviction
that he saw it, and his ascription of the inserted letter of 1683 to the volume beginning in 1559
(vol. 4) instead of vol. 1 is disconcerting. I have my doubts about those Speaker's copies deduced
by Pollard (23 f.) and accepted by the *Guide to the Records of Parliament*, ed. M. F. Bond, 31; it
assumes that either a current daily copy was made for the Speaker, which is impossible, or that he
was presented with a transcript at the end of the session, which seems pointless. Fortunately that
problem does not arise for the Journals covered in this paper.
[3] HLRO, *Memorandum 13* (revised 1957): 'The Journals, Minutes and Committee Books of the
House of Lords'.
[4] By Miss B. Howe (ibid. 6). They were actually discovered 150 years ago and printed by N. H.
Nicolas in his *Report on the Barony of l'Isle* (1829). I fear I was aware of neither predecessor when I
rediscovered them for myself, but I gladly acknowledge those earlier claims.
[5] BL, Harl. MS 5849, fos. 77r-v, printed and discussed by A. R. Myers, 'A parliamentary debate in
the mid-fifteenth century', *Bull. John Rylands Library*, 22 (1938), 388–404; reprinted with some
modifications in *English Historical Documents 1327–1485*, ed. A. R. Myers (1969), 468–9.

59

garter king of arms (garter 1586–1605, but knighted only in 1603), and an endorsement confirms that Dethick made the transcript for his friend, Sir Robert Cotton. There has been some debate about the reliability and import of this paper, especially as some of the peers present are not known to have reached the rank stated until after the end of this Parliament. However, Myers has satisfactorily settled most of the points. Dunham, who had studied the document independently, constructed an ingenious argument to the effect that it represents the conflation of two originals – a presence list in Parliament and a debate in Council.[6] This suggestion was doubtful from the first because the record ends, after giving the Lords' decision on the question, with an additional sentence: 'Item this day was the letter that Sir Francis Le Arragonois sent to the Duk of Suffolk red before the Lordes in the parliament the whiche was thought right notabley wryten.' It has since been entirely disproved by the discovery of the next piece which has the same structure and unquestionably deals with business in Parliament.

(*B*) The record of a debate in the same Parliament, on 20 March 1449, plus lists of the presence for 21 and 24 March. This survives in two copies. One, in English, is found in a volume of Camden's collections; it blocks the presence in a single paragraph and sets out the debate in the manner of *A*.[7] The other (in the hand of St Loe Kniveton, according to a note in the volume by Le Neve) arranges all the material in columns: the first has the presence (in Latin) for 20 March, the second the debate (in English), and the third the presence of 21 March (in Latin again), with the bishop of Norwich, noted as present in Camden's copy, missing. There is no transcript of the presence on 24 March, or of the researcher's remarks added in the Camden copy which state that in about 12 or 13 Henry VI there had been another debate touching the same matter, namely a dispute as to their precedence between the earls of Arundel and Devon.[8] Both copies have date headings, the first in English and the second in Latin. The differences between them suffice to show that they were made independently and from the lost original; Camden's is much the earlier. Concern with the Arundel earldom accounts for the survival of both copies, found in volumes which have other relevant transcripts

---

[6] W. H. Dunham, 'Notes from the Parliament at Winchester, 1449', *Speculum* 17 (1942), 402–15.

[7] BL, Lansd. MS 229, fo. 17v, first noticed by R. Virgoe in *BIHR* 34 (1961), 206, and printed in *Eng. Hist. Doc. 1327–1485*, 469.

[8] BL, Harl. MS 4840, fo. 573. I am most grateful to Dr Roger Virgoe for drawing my attention to this document, for letting me see and use an unpublished paper of his discussing *B*, and for his very helpful comments on this article.

too. The debate was on the question 'whether the Erle of Arundell in the Parliament holden Anno 12 shuld then be the Erle by the new creation or els by admission to his olde enheritaunce'. As Camden's final note indicates, the matter had been raised in the Parliament of 1444–5, but dissolution had then prevented any decision; in 1440, the judges favoured Arundel's claim but declared that it could be settled only by the king and the lords in Parliament, and after this debate an act embodying the decision was enrolled on the Parliament Roll.[9] This settles the argument whether these surviving extracts record debate in Parliament or Council in favour of the first.[10]

(C) The record of eight days' business in the Lords in the Parliament of 1461 (1 Edward IV): 28, 30 November, 1, 2, 8, 9, 10, 11 December. This is the so-called Fane Fragment.[11] The arrangement and contents of the journal are very different from *A* and *B*, though, of course, we are again dealing with a later copy. A Latin heading gives the date and notes that the lords 'subscripti et tottati [dotted]' were present. There is then a list of the peers in Parliament, in Latin, headed by the word 'Rex' which is marked off with a line. The presence list is always in the same form, in two columns. The first includes, after the king, the two archbishops; a space separates them from the bishops; after another space follow the earls; after yet another the abbots. The second column starts about halfway down the list of bishops and gives the remaining temporal lords, beginning with the prior of St John's. Some of the names are marked with a dot (as present), as the heading suggests they should be. There is thus a box formed in the top righthand corner of each page, flanked on the left by the spiritual peers and sitting upon the prior of St John's, and this box is used for recording business, which is given in English. All the business recorded is what later clerks would call by that name: that is, proceedings upon bills but no debate. Each page is devoted to one day's sitting. Dr Virgoe has pointed out that the days surviving and the present binding (which is out of date order) show that the original consisted of two sheets so folded as to record four days' sittings

[9] This information is derived from Dr Virgoe's unpublished paper.

[10] It is of mild interest to find that as late as 1610 a speech in Parliament (this time in the Commons) could automatically start with the words 'the question is' (Cambridge Univ. Library, MS Dd. II. 25, fo. 3v).

[11] BL, Add. MS 34218, fos. 100r–103v, ed. by W. H. Dunham as *The Fane Fragment of the 1461 Lords' Journal* (New Haven, 1935). There are a good many things to criticize in that edition (cf. review by K. B. McFarlane, *EHR* 58 (1938), 506–8), several of them the result of the fact that the editor apparently never saw the document or the volume in which it is found, but worked (as he explained) from a photostat supplied by Wallace Notestein.

each, and that these were preserved with the second inserted in the first; a third intervening sheet, which covered 3, 4, 5, 7 December (the 6th was a Sunday), is lost.[12] The sequence of days in the copy therefore indicates that the copyist blindly followed a misbound original. Dunham's surprising difficulty in deciding whether the Fragment is an original or a copy, doubts which fortunately he in the main resolved in the right direction,[13] is settled in any case by the volume in which it is found. The items preceding and following it, and several others too, are in the same hand. The latest piece in that hand would appear to be a copy of the king's reply to the Commons' grievances of 9 July 1610,[14] and the chances are that the Fragment was copied for Sir Francis Fane (1580–1629) in the second or third decade of the seventeenth century when he was getting ready to claim the barony of Burghersh and the earldom of Worcester in his own right, and the barony of Despenser in succession to his mother.[15]

(*D*) The copy of a record of the presence on two days of the same Parliament, 12 and 5 December (in that order).[16] The setting out is as for *C*, except that no names are dotted, though the superscription to the list for the 12th includes the word 'tottati' (the copyist writing 'totatte' by mistake). No business is transcribed. There is, of course, no telling whether these omissions were in the original or are the work of the copyist. The volume belonged to Sir Simonds D'Ewes who acquired it at the sale of Ralph Starkey's collection.[17] The chief interest leading to its compilation would seem to have been in the order of the lords in Parliament; there are many other lists of presences in it, down to the reign of Henry VIII, most of them without any dates; possibly more might belong to fifteenth-century Parliaments but only one can at present be securely identified, namely:

(*E*) A list of lords spiritual and temporal, dated 17 March, 31 Henry VI, i.e. for the Reading Parliament beginning on 6 March 1453. There are actually two copies of this list in the volume, by no means identical.[18]

[12] *BIHR* 32 (1959), 84–5.

[13] *Fane Fragment*, 34–5. Dunham obtained the odd advice that the unmistakably late-Tudor, early-Stuart hand of the copy either belonged to the end of the fifteenth century or might be that of a later calligrapher deliberately copying an older hand.

[14] Cf. *Proceedings in Parliament, 1610*, ed. Elizabeth Read Foster (New Haven, 1966), ii, 271–3.

[15] [G.E.C.], *Complete Peerage*, xii, 565 ff.

[16] BL, Harl. MS 158, fos. 129r-v. Identified and printed by R. Virgoe, 'A new fragment of the Lords' Journal of 1461', *BIHR* 32 (1959), 83–7.

[17] C. E. Wright, *Fontes Harlianae* (1972).

[18] BL, Harl. MS 158, fos. 124 and 134v–135r.

Both give the year date as 11 Henry VI but one is corrected to 31, which must be right because no Parliament sat in 1433. Neither copy transcribes the list of abbots, presumably because, by the time they were made, abbots had disappeared from the House and information about their order of sitting had ceased to be of interest. The lists were more primitive than the ones already discussed. One copy transcribes bishops, higher lords, and a few barons, but the bottom half of the sheet, like its verso, switches to the lords of the 1539 Parliament. The other, whose verso is blank, has all the bishops and lay lords of the 1453 Parliament. Nothing much can be learned from these notes, except that a record of attendance was kept by 1453.

One ghost of a fifteenth-century Lords' Journal, however, can be eliminated. In the volume of essays known as *Cottoni Postuma*, published in 1651 from Sir Robert Cotton's papers, there occurs a well known passage (pp. 53–4):

The journall Bookes [of the reign of Henry VII] are lost, except so much as preserves passages of eight dayes in the twelfth year of this Raigne, in which the King was some dayes present at all debates, and with his own hand the one and thirtieth day of the Parliament, delivered in a bill of Trade then read.

Cotton acquired this piece of information at the time that he was working on the question of the king's presence in Parliament (the subject of the essay from which this extract comes), probably early in James I's reign; a note to that effect is found in a bundle of his papers that passed through Thomas Baker's hands into the Harleian collection where they were bound up with other loose pieces.[19] Cotton's words certainly suggest that he had or saw the original. It was presumably on the authority of this statement, and just possibly after a look at the Cotton Library,[20] that a Lords' Committee of 1690 claimed to have 'examined the Journals of the House, which reach from the 12th of Hen. VII';[21] there is certainly no other evidence that the official archives ever contained any Journals before 1510. I do not think that any such fragment for Henry VII existed in the seventeenth century. As Dunham pointed out, the Fane Fragment answers so well to Cotton's descrip-

---

[19] BL, Harl. MS 6849, fo. 110; much of the volume is in Cotton's hand. Cf. Wright, *Fontes*.

[20] Nothing that answers to Cotton's description now survives in his collection at the BL, and the record of what was destroyed in the Cottonian fire (*First Series of Reports from Committees of the House of Commons*, i, 443 ff.) yields no information on the possible disappearance of a relevant MS. My own opinion is that Cotton never possessed any manuscript that would fill the bill but had seen one in someone else's possession.

[21] HLRO, *Memorandum 13*, 17.

tion — there are eight parliamentary days in it, and on 9 December, the thirty-first day of the Parliament, Edward IV is recorded as putting in a bill remedying grievances of merchandise — that surely we have here what Cotton mistakenly ascribed to 12 Henry VII. Dunham hesitated for two reasons: Cotton's date, which he argued away by conjecturing that Cotton arrived at it by working back from 1510 until he found a merchandise act that might serve, and the fact that Cotton had the king present only 'some dayes', whereas Dunham thought that the Fane Fragment showed him present every day. As to the first point, I am sure that Dunham was right: C offers no year date, and if this is what Cotton saw he was bound to conjecture one, without the aid of permanent calendars and so forth which enabled Dunham to discover the correct date of 1461. And the second point is disposed of by an examination of the original which shows (as Dunham's photograph perhaps did not) that dots were placed on the right side of the word 'Rex' (the difference from the left-hand dotting of peers presumably indicating a form of respect) on 2, 8 and possibly 11 December. This means that the king was present on 'some dayes' only, but unfortunately not, it would seem, on the day on which he personally presented a bill. However, the bill was not introduced at the start of the sitting, so that Edward presumably came in later to hand it in, even perhaps withdrawing again at once in order not to embarrass debate.

Thus the Lords' Journal for 1497 is a myth, or at least cannot be held to have survived until the later seventeenth century, and the myth owed its undue survival to Pollard who refused to accept Dunham's identification. His grounds are peculiar. In his review of Dunham's edition he grew very warm on the subject, arguing that Cotton was too good an antiquary to have confused two sessions of Parliament and not to have recognized that the peers of the Fane Fragment did not match the lords of Henry VII's day.[22] On the first point, Dunham's argument is much the more convincing. The second would be good if we could be sure that Cotton did a real job of work on those names, but the state of such aids to research as were available to him (at a time when antiquaries' notebooks were crowded with muddled and often desperate attempts to sort out noble genealogies) would have made it hard for him to discover a date for the document by that method. By

[22] *Times Literary Supplement*, 5 Sept. 1935. The anonymous notice is unmistakably by Pollard who did much reviewing for that journal. Cotton was an eager and rather credulous antiquary, the friend of much better scholars, and the most lavish and generous of collectors. Such men do make mistakes with some regularity.

1942 Pollard had persuaded himself that a small fragment of a Journal for 1497 was printed in what he called Cotton's collection in 1672, and he conjectured that Cotton had obtained the manuscript from Robert Bowyer, clerk of the Parliaments.[23] He gives no further reference. The volume of 1672 (a reprint of the first, 1651, edition of *Cottoni Postuma*) contains, of course, only a reference to that alleged Journal, no transcript. If we could link Bowyer with a lost manuscript ascribable to 1497 the case would indeed be more impressive: Bowyer, unlike Cotton, knew his Lords' Journals. But Pollard's supposition is even by him given without any evidence at all, and there is absolutely nothing to link Bowyer with any fifteenth-century Journal. It does seem manifest that what Cotton had or saw was the Journal of 1461, either the original from which the Fane Fragment was copied or the Fragment itself.

2

We turn to the sixteenth century, or rather the reign of Henry VIII.

(*F*) The 'official' Journal. Volume 1 of the MS Journals as now bound covers the reign of Henry VIII, but that binding was done in 1717.[24] What existed a century earlier were five volumes covering the following sessions:

(1) 1, 3, 6, 7 Henry VIII (1510, 1512, 1515 *bis*).
(2) 25, 35 Henry VIII (1534, 1544).
(3) 31, 32, 37, 38 Henry VIII (1539, 1540, 1545, 1546).
(4) 33, 34 Henry VIII (1542, 1543).
(5) 33 Henry VIII and 3 and 4 Edward VI (1542, 1549–50).

That was the state in which Robert Bowyer found the Journals in the Parliament Office when he became clerk on 10 January 1610.[25] That this collection was itself of very recent date is vouched for by the well-informed John Browne, clerk of the Parliaments from 1638 to

[23] *EHR* 57 (1942), 55 n. and 56.
[24] *Guide to the Records of Parliament*, 28. I shall refer to the original at the House of Lords as MS Journals, to the printed version as *LJ*.
[25] As he recorded at the beginning of his transcripts of the Tudor Journals. Those for Henry VIII are usually cited from Inner Temple, Petyt MS 537/1, but this is a copy made later in the seventeenth century. An original Bowyer transcript in that collection is Petyt MS 537/6, covering the reigns of Mary and Elizabeth, which the *Catalogue of the Manuscripts in the Inner Temple Library* (ed. J. C. Davies, Oxford, 1972), i, 45, calls 'exceptional'. The corresponding volume for Henry VIII and Edward VI (identical in size, handwriting and two-column lay-out) is BL, Tiberius D.i. Both volumes also have notes by D'Ewes. Thus Bowyer transcribed the sixteenth-century Journals into two volumes which were used by D'Ewes; one of them came to Cotton's library and one to Petyt's. The exact date of Bowyer's entry upon office is given in BL, Tiberius D.i, fo. 41v.

1644 and again from 1660 to 1691, who in 1683 explained to his underclerk, John Walker, that 'in H. 8 tyme by the Power of Cardinall Woolsey, many Journalls & Actes were taken away; and vntill Sir Tho: Smith tyme who was Clerke of the Parliament, all the recordes lay in a confused manner but he put them into that order that now they are and the same order hath ben continued euer since'.[26] Smith, Bowyer's predecessor, was clerk from 1597 to 1609. It was probably when he put the Journals in order that a note was made on the cover of the first volume, to the effect that 'ffrom this Booke which endeth with the 7 of H 8 there is no booke extant amongst the Recordes vntill the year 25'.[27] Actually, the first volume itself was deficient: the second and third sessions of Henry VIII's second Parliament (4 and 5 Henry VIII) were even then missing. Bowyer himself was responsible for adding the volume for 28 Henry VIII (1536), listed as present in the middle of the seventeenth century when a copy of the Journals was made which finished up among the Harcourt family's collections.[28] The cover-sheet of the 1536 volume is preserved in the present binding (as its dusty discoloration shows), with a note saying 'deliuered by way of loane to mee Ro. Bowyer Clerke of the parliament the 4th November 1620 by the R. Ho: the Lo: Russell'.[29] According to D'Ewes' note in Bowyer's transcript of the journals, Russell 'understood not (as it seemed) the nature of it', and Bowyer 'finding what it was, how belonging to the said office, and to his duty to preserve it, with the leave and consent of his lordship, did restore the same in the said office'.[30] There were thus six volumes of Journals for Henry VIII in existence from 1620 to 1717.

[26] Letter of 21 May 1683, now prefixed to vol. 1 of the MS Journals.

[27] Prefixed to vol. 1 of the MS Journals is a memorandum by John Walker, Browne's deputy, 'that the words abouewritten, endorsed on the couer of this Booke being become almost vnlegible I transcribed them to perpetuate the said endorsement'.

[28] HLRO, Harcourt Journal, vol. 1. The *Guide* supposes (p. 279) that the transcript was made for the first Earl Harcourt, born in 1714. Since the list of volumes shows that the copy was made before the rebinding of 1717, and since the hand seems to me to belong roughly to the middle of the seventeenth century, I incline to think that the copy was either made for an earlier Harcourt or bought in at some later date.

[29] MS Journal, i. 243. HLRO, *Memorandum 13*, 18, seems to have misread the note to mean that Bowyer lent out the volume.

[30] BL, Tiberius D.i, fo. 41v. There is a mystery about the inclusion of the Journal for 28 Henry VIII in Bowyer's transcripts. It is not a later insertion but was written out in sequence between the sessions of 1534 and 1539. A reference to it was inserted at the beginning of the volume in the list of sessions for which Journals survived, but no such correction was made immediately beneath in the list of volumes which Bowyer found in existence in 1610. Bowyer first saw the 1536 volume on 4 Nov. 1620; he was dead by 21 Mar. 1621 when Henry Elsyng was sworn in (M. F. Bond, *EHR* 73 (1958), 79). When did Bowyer make his transcripts? He presumably started

This is what survives now as the Lords' Journal for Henry VIII's reign: the present volume 1 was made up by simply binding everything found in the sequence found, so that there are some irrelevant odds and ends bound in and the accidental joining of 25 and 35 Henry VIII is preserved.[31] No Journals survived by 1600 for the sessions of 4, 5, 14 and 15, 21, 23, 24, 27 Henry VIII, but fortunately not only common sense but also positive evidence demonstrates that they had once existed. At the end of the entries for 3 Henry VIII there is a note in the hand of the clerk, John Taylor: 'Sequuntur prorogaciones huius parliamenti in alio libro De Anno R R H 8 quarto.' Evidently the record of the second and third sessions of this three-sessions Parliament was kept in a new book now lost, which would have filled the gap between 3 and 6 Henry VIII. This incidentally shows that the combination of 1, 3, 6 and 7 Henry VIII in one volume was Smith's doing. We may conjecture that Taylor either kept a separate volume for every session, or that more likely his first volume covered the first two parliamentary sessions of the reign (1510 and 1512).[32] In addition, as we shall see, there is evidence of Journal-keeping in the session of 26 Henry VIII (in the 'official' Journal) and in that of 27 Henry VIII (not in that Journal). Thomas Cromwell knew of a 'Parliament book' in 1532.[33] There need really be no doubt that a Lords' Journal was kept continually from 1510 onwards, whatever may have been true before. But except for the addition of 28

some time before 1620 but had not got beyond the first five surviving sessions when Russell showed him the missing volume. Bowyer then inserted 'vicesimo octavo' in the year dates at the start of his volume and completed the work – seven sessions of Henry VIII and three of Edward VI – in the remaining three and a half months of his life. Even if one supposes (which is likely) that the copy of Mary and Elizabeth was made at an earlier date, this still argues an astonishing performance for an ailing man. However, the evidence of the transcripts looks conclusive.

[31] The Journal for 1534 (spring session) is followed on pp. 179–238 by that for 1544. I suspect that this accidental joining accounts for John Browne's panic in 1638 when on taking over he failed to find the book for 35 Henry VIII (HLRO, *Memorandum 13*, 18). He had missed it because it was bound out of place.

[32] Something depends on whether the Journals were written up on loose quires and later bound, as Pollard believed, or in books previously bound which would run out simply when full. After all the reframing and rebinding that has befallen these records even a disbinding of the present volume would tell one nothing. As we shall see, from 1515 the Journal consisted of prepared sheets used in the House and bound up (probably sessionally). The sessions of 1 and 3 Henry VIII, and presumably the missing sessions of 4 and 5 Henry VIII, on the other hand, look to have been written up in prepared books and out of the House. Taylor's reference to another 'liber' suggests as much, and a count of the pages used supports this. 1 Henry VIII occupies 18 pages; if four-page quires had been used (as was the case with C) one would expect two blank pages to follow. But 3 Henry VIII follows straight on, on p. 19. Altogether, the first 42 pages of the MS Journals have very much the appearance of having been written up in a bound book of blanks.

[33] *LP* v, 1548.

Henry VIII, made by Bowyer in 1620, what Smith collected is all we now have;[34] all the losses occurred before, partly perhaps, as Brown supposed, because of Wolsey's highhandedness. But Wolsey could not have been responsible for the sad gaps in the 1530s; the blame must fall on Sir Brian Tuke, clerk from 1523 to 1539, or on his joint-clerk, Edward North (1531–9). They were responsible for the Journal of 28 Henry VIII which, as we have seen, was certainly out of official custody by 1600, and either Tuke or North may well have kept the books at home.[35]

Continuous the Journals were, but – as Pollard pointed out, even though I cannot accept his 'evolutionary' interpretation[36] – uniform they were not. The present volume 1 is an unholy muddle, somewhat disguised by the 'order' introduced by the editors of the printed *Journals*. While so many sessions are missing, two volumes survive for 1542, perhaps produced (as Bowyer thought) by the absence abroad of the clerk, William Paget, whose office was being executed by two deputies, though the story is more complicated than this.[37] Mr Cobb's analytical list of the contents of volume 1 makes it unnecessary for me to go through them again.[38] As for the printed version, which leaves out things without explanation, alters dates, supplies formal headings not found in the original or renders as formal what is casual there, rearranges the setting out (sometimes very confusingly), confuses original marginal notes with those added in 1717, and gives no hint of the important variations in scribal hands, only a complete new edition could really cope with its deficiencies. It seems to have led even historians who had supposedly studied the manuscript into dubious statements. Thus Pollard praised John Taylor for himself writing out the *Modus* at the start of his Journal and patronized him for 'complacently' remarking that his joint tenure of the clerkships of Convocation and Parliament

[34] J. C. Sainty, HLRO, *Memorandum 33* (1965), ii, suggests that D'Ewes must have seen pages of the Journals since lost. We know that Bowyer did. This does not apply to the reign of Henry VIII but later. It is possible that individual leaves dropped out from the dilapidated bindings noticed in 1717 (HLRO, *Memorandum 13*, 19).

[35] The records of Tuke's tenure of the treasurership of the Chamber are equally deficient.

[36] Pollard's evolutionary thesis led him to say that if we found a Journal for Henry VII's reign 'embodying the common form evolved in Henry VIII's' it would 'stand convicted of forgery' (*TRHS* 1914, 36). The Fane Fragment is not quite in the form which became standard but much more like it than to that of 1510–12; nevertheless it is a copy of a genuine original.

[37] BL, Tiberius D.i, fo. 5v. The two 1542 Journals are thoroughly discussed by M. A. R. Graves, 'The two Lords' Journals of 1542', *BIHR* 44 (1971), 182–9.

[38] HLRO, *Memorandum 13*, pp. 21–3.

was a rare thing;[39] yet neither the *Modus* nor that entry on page 126 of
the MS Journal is in Taylor's hand. These, however, are labours to be
left to the future editor who, one hopes, may one day come; here I shall
confine myself to such features of the MS Journals as throw light on the
history of the early Lords' Journals.

The first thing to note is that the 'official' Journal was not kept in
standard form throughout the reign. A virtually standard form makes
its appearance on the fourth day of the Parliament of 1515 (6 Henry
VIII). From that date the Journal gives one page to each day's sitting,
using both sides of the paper. There is a Latin heading giving the date.
Two columns on the left list the presence, in Latin, the names of those
actually present being marked with a 'p'; the very occasional absence of
such marks should be ascribed to clerical lapses, most of them readily
explained.[40] At the bottom of the third column is a note recording the
adjournment of the House to the following day, though this detail is not
present at first and not always later.[41] The appearance of the sheet makes
it plain that all this matter, the 'p's excepted, was usually written out
beforehand. The rest of the third column records the business of the day
(often in a different hand), this being confined to proceedings on bills,
with other matters appearing occasionally, as for instance the oath of
succession in 1534, transcribed on to a separate page.[42] This record is also
in Latin, though from 1542 the clerk ceased to translate the titles of bills
which in the original were, of course, in English.

This description holds good throughout the ordinary sitting days, but
the opening of a new Parliament provided additional material which
was not always so standardized. When the Journal settled down, the
preliminaries included a record of the lord chancellor's opening address,

[39] Pollard, *TRHS* 1914, 29, 36–7.
[40] There are no 'p' markings in the first two presence lists preserved, for the fourth and fifth days of
the Parliament of 6 Henry VIII. Pollard adds that none are also found on these days: 2, 6, 13 Mar.
1515; 13, 18, 19 Nov. 1515; 12 Apr. 1540; 3 Nov. 1542; 23 Nov. 1545 (*EHR* 57 (1942), 43, n. 2).
There was no Parliament in session on 3 Nov. 1542, and the House did not sit on 18 Nov. 1515 (a
Sunday); the list for the 19th has 'p' markings. On 6 and 13 Mar. 1515 the House met only to
adjourn, so that no one troubled to record the presence. There was no business done at all on 13
Nov. 1515 (the second day of a Parliament resumed after a long prorogation) and the same
explanation applies. 12 Apr. 1540 and 23 Nov. 1545 were opening days of sessions when it was
quite usual to write down who was there. Thus there remains only one of the days discovered on
which the clerk might be charged with the negligence which Pollard professed to find in him.
[41] It occurs first on the opening day of the prorogued session of 1515 (*LJ* i, 43) but is regularly
found only in the next extant sessional record, 1534 (ibid. 59).
[42] MS Journal, i, 175, followed by a blank page, which is followed by a calendar of the acts passed
that session.

the appointment of receivers and triers of petitions, the order to the Commons to elect a Speaker, the presentation of the Speaker, and probably a record of peers' proxies entered with the clerk.[43] The best example of the standard form may well be the book for the Parliament of 28 Henry VIII (1536) – the one preserved separately, out of the office, and added to the stock by Bowyer in 1620. This starts with a list of proxies, followed by the opening proceedings and a daily record in the form described; it ends with a calendar of the acts passed in the session.[44] By no means all the later sessions are covered so systematically, but it would be wise to ascribe such things as the disappearance of lists of acts to the loss of odd pages rather than poor record-keeping.[45]

The Journals for the first two Parliaments of the reign, however, look very different. That of 1510 starts with a scrambled head-note in John Taylor's hand, and he also wrote the introductory paragraph. The chancellor's speech is inserted in a proper chancery hand which cannot have been Taylor's who had no chancery training;[46] he did, however, add the date at the end, '1509, 21 Januarij', using his customary arabic numerals which the printed *Journals* elsewhere officiously expand in Latin.[47] There follow the order to the Commons to elect their Speaker, the appointment of receivers and triers (in the French customary for this entry on the Rolls of Parliament), and the record of three proxies received, all in the hand of the clerk of the Parliaments. The rest of the session's record is simply a day-book, also written by Taylor himself, which allots a block of entries to each sitting, has no presence lists, runs the date into the first entry of the day, and (apart from the day on which the Speaker presented himself) notes bill proceedings only. Daily entries run on over the pages; there are neither gaps nor blanks. The final sitting

---

[43] For proxies, cf. below, pp. 76–7.

[44] MS Journal, i, 243–78, followed by two blank pages which were probably part of the 1536 book.

[45] The first calendar of acts extant is for 25 Henry VIII, the only session of the Reformation Parliament for which there is a Journal (ibid. 133–4). This is in Latin. The sole surviving page of the Journal for the following session is an English calendar of the acts passed (ibid. 239–40). On this a later hand has added a 'Memorandum that there is one acte more than is specified here concerning the deane and Chapiter of Welles'; but I can find no such act in *Statutes of the Realm*.

[46] Cf. Pollard, *TRHS* 1914, 29.

[47] I cannot agree with Mr Cobb (HLRO, *Memorandum 13*, 20) that these numerals are in a later hand: they are in John Taylor's. Taylor was a bit of a freak in the succession of clerks of the Parliaments – a doctor of both laws and manifestly a learned man with a suggestion of clerical cultivation about him. Thus, dissatisfied with using only regnal years and those never in dating sittings (an inherited practice), he liked to scatter A.D. dates with a formula, 'secundum computationem ecclesie Anglicane', which recalls his background rather than his office. There is no reason why those dates should not be what they look like: current additions by the clerk.

is recorded at some length (more than ever again): the Speaker's address in presenting the subsidy bill, the lord chancellor's response, the ceremony of assent, and the chancellor's speech dissolving Parliament. Taylor signed under this entry, but the book contains further matter touching the enrolment of statutes the significance of which must engage us later.[48]

Essentially the same form occurs in the book for the next session, but there are some differences. The day-book was not now kept by Taylor himself but (to judge from the hands) by at least two, possibly three, underclerks; and on the first proper sitting day after the preliminaries (pp. 23–4) there is a full list of the House of Lords. It is not, as Pollard supposed, a proper presence list; there are no 'p' markings, and it is quite differently arranged from the lists that begin on page 52.[49] The underclerks introduced one innovation in the day-book: they moved the daily date from the start of the first line, where Taylor had put it, to the centre of the page above the day's entries. Since the Parliament did not end with this session, the record runs out with a brief note of the prorogation. Some dates and head-notes added show that Taylor supervised the book.

So far one might therefore think with Pollard that we have here the evolution of a record – relatively primitive at first, but formalized and with the innovation of presence lists introduced from 1515, or perhaps earlier, during the missing sessions of 4 and 5 Henry VIII. However, two facts disprove this view. One is the make-up of the book for 6 Henry VIII, as it now stands. Its first pages resemble those for 1510–12: no formal headings, continuous blocks of matter starting with the opening day on page 43. Page 44 is blank. Thus the first two-page sheet is simply a single paragraph giving an extended summary of the chancellor's speech in opening this Parliament, probably a page intended for discarding when a shorter summary was made but accidentally allowed to survive. Page 45, with a date-heading by Taylor and a summary of the speech in another hand is, however, by the standards of 1510–12 another false start: three-quarters of page 45 and all of page 46 are blank. Page 47 starts again, with yet another date-heading by Taylor and the formal opening preliminaries (order to elect a Speaker, appointment of receivers and triers). On the back of this page is the record of fifteen proxies (without the *secundo die* supplied by the printed *Journals*). The business of the third day starts at the bottom of page 48, in the manner

[48] See below, pp. 86–71.   [49] See below, pp. 89–90.

familiar from the previous two sessions' record; it runs over one third of page 49. The rest of this, and pages 50–1, are blank. Then, on page 52, which is the verso of the blank 51, we find the first example of the 'standard' record, presence and proceedings. What this tedious analysis indicates is that the book as it now stands is most unlikely to have been originally put together; rather it seems to preserve bits and pieces of two separate records linked together by the desire to produce a continuous day-by-day Journal for the session. This may have been done by Smith.

The possibility that in fact more than one type of record was kept simultaneously early in Henry VIII's reign is put beyond doubt by the next document to be considered which constitutes the second fact disproving Pollard's notion of an evolution from one form into another. We turn to the odds and ends of Henrician Journal material surviving outside the custody of the Parliament Office to this day, and never gathered in by Smith and Bowyer.

(G) An original record covering two sitting days, 2 and 3 March 1512. It consists of one large sheet and is found in D'Ewes's parliamentary collection acquired from Ralph Starkey.[50] Its form is virtually identical with what I have called the later standard version. There are two hands. One wrote the heading and the presence in Latin; the heading reads, 'Memorandum quod die Martis vicesimo quarto die parliamenti secundo die Marcij fuerunt presentes subscripti domini, videlicet'. The first column lists the spiritual peers – southern bishops and abbots. The second, starting well down the page, gives the lay peers, with the bishop of Durham (inadvertently omitted) written above them by the other hand which also wrote out the business of the day in the top half of the column remaining on the right of the sheet. This same hand also inserted the abbot of Hyde in his correct place and marked all those actually present with a 'p'. In short, one clerk prepared this sheet, while the other used it to record the day's business and found it necessary to remedy defects left by the first. Neither hand is that of the clerk of the Parliaments, but both can be found in the 'official' Journal (the day-book).

The paper contains further conclusive evidence that it was used during the actual sitting. The recording of proceedings shows traces of additions made as the House went through its bills. The recording clerk

[50] BL, Harl. MS 158, fos. 141–2. The binding of this single sheet in folded form is responsible for making the later day come first in the volume. The year-date of the document is readily established from the day of the month given and from a comparison of the business transacted with *LJ* i, 14. Its appearance leaves no doubt that it is an original.

used a small flourish to terminate each entry; in several places he wrote additions after it. Thus he noted that the bill for physicians[51] was read a third time and then added 'lecta est cum additione & assenta & missa in domum Communem', as though he had automatically put down the third reading and then found that their lordships amended the bill before agreeing to it. A bill preferred by John Burdett encountered objections raised by Edward and Anne Conway;[52] these were presented to the House, he thought, by the master of the Rolls, but he found he had erred and substituted John More, jr. A bill for the marquess of Dorset caused him more trouble.[53] He recorded the second reading, then that it was handed to the solicitor general (presumably for revision), and finally that certain provisos were annexed to it before that gentleman got it. Most remarkable of all is the fact that the clerk used this paper to write down amendments proposed to a bill. The bill in question was one for apparel and did not pass in this session of 3 Henry VIII; it was reintroduced three years later and became law as 6 Henry VIII, c.1. The Lords appear to have considered four provisos, two of which got into the act as passed (sections 4 and 6), while the other two vanished. One of these last gave trouble at the time, and the crossings out and interlineations graphically show how amendments were hammered out in debate.

The record for 3 March is much shorter. It is in the hand that wrote in the House on the 2nd. There is a standard Latin heading but no full presence; only five names appear (two earls and three barons), all marked 'p'. The business done was confined to a message from the king (recorded in Latin), conveyed by the lord treasurer (not included in the presence). This adjourned the House to the following day on the grounds that the chancellor and spiritual lords were absent in convocation. Across the bottom are the words 'hodie ex mandato Regis', the opening words of the later standard formula for adjournment at the end of each day's sitting, interesting because (as has been said) this formula is not usually found on the prepared sheets in 6 and 7 Henry VIII. Evidently the officers of the House knew that there was going to be an adjournment on 3 March and a very thin House, and so they decided not to go to the bother of writing out the usual presence list but contented themselves with a brief note actually made in the House.

A comparison of *G* with the 'official' Journal is revealing. The 'official' Journal omits all mention of 3 March, the day on which

---

[51] 3 Henry VIII, c. 11.   [52] Not passed.   [53] Not passed.

business was confined to an adjournment; it is not consistent in this, for on what is called the thirtieth day of the session, when the prior of St John's adjourned the House for the same reason, the clerk's day-book has the entry, using the same formula as that employed by G on 3 March.[54] A collation of the long entry for 2 March with the 'official' Journal demonstrates that the latter was copied from the former. In the following description I give the single sheet (G) first and the 'official' Journal (F) second. The bill for Robert Fowler was 'deliberata canc[ellario]';[55] this is properly corrected to 'per cancellarium'. The complexities of the readings of the physicians' bill are resolved by omitting 'tertia vice'. The order of two bills is reversed, probably by accident, which conveniently proves that while the sheet evidently preserves the order of business transacted the 'official' Journal cannot be trusted to do so. 'Billa concernens porpoysse' becomes better expressed as 'concernens emptionem de Porpeys et aliorum Piscium'.[56] In the entry touching Dorset's bill, the copyist omitted the mention of provisos annexed, perhaps as superfluous, perhaps because in the end none were; and he also elaborated the title of the bill for co-heirs and like tenants by adding 'pro divisione facienda',[57] a detail desirable for better identification but understandably omitted in the haste of writing currently in the House. Since the 'official' Journal ascribes the presentation of the Conways' objection only to Mr More, jr, it is useful to know from the sheet that this was John, not Thomas.[58]

Thus it can be said with some confidence that in the first two Parliaments of Henry VIII, when the 'official' Journal would seem to contradict this, the clerk had full-scale record sheets prepared, giving the presence and proceedings upon bills, very similar to those vouched for in 1461 and those extant from 1515. They were used as work-sheets and treated so casually that they were clearly not regarded as a permanent record. Afterwards, the business done was copied into day-books, running on from day to day. Not that the day-books could not be further amended, as the MS Journals show; they also were a working record, not a fair copy. On the forty-fifth day of this Parliament, a

---

[54] The 30th day should have been Sunday, 8 Mar., but though at this time the clerks tended to count every day from the opening of the session, and not only sitting days, as 'a day of the Parliament', we cannot be absolutely sure about this practice; and the day-book gives no month's dates.
[55] Not passed. [56] Not passed. [57] Not passed.
[58] John More, jr, was the judge, the father of Sir Thomas More, so called to distinguish him from his own father, an ancient worthy of Lincoln's Inn: R. W. Chambers, *Thomas More* (1935), 52.

proviso to a bill for the Merchant Taylors passed the Lords; the entry was added later, as was a note that the king had signed it on the twenty-seventh day.[59] The introduction of a bill for Dudley's heirs on the last day of the session was also a later addition.[60] Both were made by the same clerk as wrote up the book and probably reflect no more than slipshod work in the first transcribing.

Judging from Taylor's note at the end of this second session, the practice of using presence sheets in the House and copying the business transacted into day-books was followed at least in the next two sessions. But after Taylor began in 1515 in what by then was his habitual way, something happened to alter practice, and from the fourth day onwards only the prepared sheets were kept. It also looks as though these were now made out for keeping – not scribbled over, and almost certainly prepared several days ahead in batches. The day-book may still have been kept and since lost: this is possible. But the regularity with which the full record (presence and business) is thereafter preserved, and the fact that (though still evidently completed currently in the House) it was now kept clear of rough notes and memoranda, do rather suggest that the practice of copying into a day-book had ceased. We have noted that the day-book type entries in 1515 do not appear to have been made continuously in a ready-bound book, as the earlier ones certainly were. Whether Taylor was told that the Lords regarded the record of attendance as important, or whether he and his clerks found the work too much, or whether some other reason yet should be conjectured, may be left to each man's judgment. For myself I suspect that the day-book was abandoned as a laborious device which had served its purpose (a purpose discussed below). What is certain is that there was no 'evolution' from primitive record to developed; what Pollard thought primitive was in fact a deliberately abbreviated extract from what he thought developed. It is probable that Taylor innovated in 1510 by adding the day-book to the existing production of daily work-sheets.

(*H*) One sheet, very similar in appearance to *G* and also all in Latin, survives for the session of 27 Henry VIII, the last session of the Reformation Parliament, again in that invaluable volume of Simonds D'Ewes'.[61] The layout was prepared in a hand which frequently appears doing the same thing in the surviving Journal book for 25 Henry VIII; this layout is identical with that of 1534 and differs from *G* in that the

[59] MS Journal, i, 41; *LJ* i, 17b, omits the note about the king's signing.
[60] MS Journals, i, 42.   [61] BL, Harl. MS 158, fo. 143.

second column of the names starts level with the first and a clear third column is reserved for entering business. Thus this is certainly an original – a stray relic from the lost Journal for the session.[62] The recto records the business done on 4 February 1536, the first day of the new session; the verso that on 5 February. On the 4th, the lord chancellor communicated Cranmer's request that the House appoint one day of the week as reserved for Convocation. The House resolved to set Monday aside for that purpose but also that except for Mondays and, of course, Sundays, they would meet every day to attend to the 'negocia reipublice necessaria huius regni Anglie'. It is a sad comment on the steadfastness of resolutions that on the 5th, a Saturday, they met only to adjourn until Tuesday, setting an ancient precedent for a decent weekend.

(*I*) Bound together with the preceding is a list of proxies received at the Parliament Office between 4 and 26 February.[63] The hands vary, as different clerks attended to receive the documents, but all are familiar from the MS Journals. There are quite numerous additions and corrections. In this respect alone does the list differ from some bound up with the 'official' Journal which (as we have seen) should by this time normally have included a record of proxies entered at the beginning of each session's record.[64] Thus *I* confirms that both it and *H* come from the lost Journal book for 27 Henry VIII, being in fact the first two sheets of it. The most interesting aspect of these proxy lists – apart from whatever political history may be extracted from them[65] – lies in the evidence of business organization which they preserve. Not only do they demonstrate the care taken to ensure that the holders of proxies (as distinct from the givers) were officially known – which suggests that the House of Lords may have divided more often than one might suppose – but they show that the clerks collected their fees. This list of nineteen entries has four sorts of marks in the margin: fourteen are annotated 'sol' (has paid), one has a single dot against it, one has only a small circle in the margin, two have a circle and a dot, five of the 'sol'

---

[62] Not a copy, as S. E. Lehmberg supposed: *The Reformation Parliament* (1970), 218.

[63] BL, Harl. MS 158, fos. 144r-v. The note at the top of fo. 144v ('Notes of dutyes belonginge to the prevelage of Parlement') is a later addition, and meaningless.

[64] MS Journals, i, 47 (1515), 127–8 (1534), 244 (1536).

[65] The list for 27 Henry VIII was ignored by Vernon P. Snow, 'Proctorial representation and conciliar management during the reign of Henry VIII', *HJ* 9 (1966), 1–26. If he had known it he might have been less certain (p. 9) that the abbots could not be accused of absenting themselves out of existence: they gave a large number of proxies for this session which passed the first Dissolution Act. The list was used by Helen Miller in her demolition of Snow's article: 'Attendance in the House of Lords during the reign of Henry VIII', *HJ* 10 (1967), 325–51.

entries have also a cross, one has also a circle, and three have both a circle and a cross against the 'sol'. It looks as though the marks were made in the order 'sol', dot, cross and circle. Apart from the 'sol' they are obscure: presumably they indicate stages in the collection of fees, though one mark or another may hide some special favour in fees remitted. Of the other surviving lists, bound into the MS Journals, it is not possible to be sure because the binding may hide marks; but there seem to be none in the list for 28 Henry VIII, while in 6 and 25 Henry VIII all are marked 'sol'. Proxies had to be drawn by the clerk of the Crown,[66] so that the clerk of the Parliaments got only registration fees, but these were considerable. In 1621 it was laid down that each proxy paid 20s., though in 1601 apparently the clerks had managed to extract 30s.[67] We know something about these matters in the reign of Henry VIII because Lord Lisle, deputy at Calais, had trouble over his proxies for the May Parliament of 1536 and the Parliament of 1539. On the latter occasion he was first informed that registration in the Parliament Office would cost 20s., so that the ruling of 1621 would seem to have amounted to a return to ancient custom. He protested to his agent that he had been in the habit of paying 6s. 8d., but this turned out to be an antiquarian dream. In the upshot the clerk of the Parliaments demanded 23s. 4d. and his clerk 3s. 4d. for registering the proxy and making out a copy for Lisle; on top of which the gentleman usher of the Parliament came in with a request for 7s 6d. This total exceeds even the 30s. of 1601. Lisle's correspondence contributes also some indications why those marginal marks were made. Though, as his agent said in 1536, the custom was for proxies to be entered on the second day of the session, in 1539 the clerk's servant, after earlier attempts, was still seeking payments two days before the long prorogation.[68]

3

We thus find three styles of Journal before 1547. The most persistent was that later preserved as the standard form: a record of the presence obtained by marking up a prepared list of the peerage, spiritual and temporal, in a regular (though varying) order of precedence, written out in columns so placed as to leave room for taking down information on proceedings, these last being confined (apart from the opening and

[66] *LP* x, 994.
[67] Elizabeth Read Foster, *The Painful Labour of Mr. Elsyng* (Philadelphia, 1972), 106 and n. 15.
[68] *LP* x, 994, 1074; xiv, I, 1003, 1160, 1181.

closing ceremonies of sessions) to proceedings on bills. This form existed in 1453; it underwent changes in detail but not in substance; it remained as the proper form once the Journal had become the official record; fair copies, found occasionally in later periods, preserve it. During the first four sessions of Henry VIII's Parliaments, and seemingly just at the start of the fifth, a day-book was kept which was compiled by copying the proceedings part of the sheets used in the House. So far as the evidence goes, this was the first House of Lords register kept in bound form.

However, before the earliest evidence of this kind of business record we find a very different one: a record of debate. Can we reconstruct its original appearance from the Tudor–Stuart copies which alone survive? The copies differ sufficiently to show that they were not, or not all, accurate representations of the original. *A* lists the presence in columns and gives the names in Latin form; the Camden version of *B* sets them out in English and in a continuous paragraph. *B* has date headings – Camden again in English, while Kniveton uses Latin. There is no such headline in *A* which can be dated only because the copyist put 'in parliamento apud Wintoniam H. vi^{ti}' in the space between the columns of peers where assuredly it could not have appeared in the original. *A*, and *B* for the one of the three days for which transactions are copied, introduce the debate with the words 'the question is' followed by the subject to be discussed; in all versions this forms a separate paragraph heading the opinions expressed which are stated in the form 'Lord X says. . .'. The debate is given in English in all three copies.

Taking these point in turn, we may first look at the date headings in *B*. Camden's English version reads, 'Memorandum that the 20 of Marche Anno [blank] Henrici Sexti were present in the Chamber of Parlement these Lords followenge'. Kniveton's Latin says, 'Memorandum quod 20 die Martii presentes fuerunt in Camera Parliamenti domini subsequentes'. The Latin of Kniveton's version thus mentions no reign, Camden's English no year. If the original had mentioned the reign it would surely have had the year too. We may conclude that Kniveton copied a Latin original precisely, while Camden translated and added the fact that he knew which reign was in question though he could not identify the year. The presence list, too, must have been in Latin – since there can be no reason why *A* and *B* (Kniveton) should solemnly have translated an English list, and since we have already concluded that Camden did translate the headline – and presumably in the columns adopted by the two copies which adhered to the language of the original. That the record of debate was kept in English is proved not only by the fact that it is so in the two copies which adhered to the original Latin in the rest of the document, but also by a small detail in *B* (Kniveton). The opinions of the abbots of Winchcombe and Peterborough read first 'accordeth with the Lo. Cromwell'; 'with' was struck out and replaced by 'to'. This is the correct reading, as *B* (Camden) shows. By the early seventeenth century, common usage would in this phrase have employed 'with', as the copyist automatically did, before realizing that his original read differently. This shows not only that the original was in English, but also that the transcripts can be trusted to be accurate. These points are confirmed by some barely comprehensible passages in *A* which appear even to have preserved the original spelling, as 'Ane' for 'one' and 'lyvelod' and 'liveled' for 'livelihood'.[69] Thus all three papers give a sound copy of the debates. For the rest, Camden's transcript is the least accurate of the three; Kniveton is fully accurate for 20 March but deserts the original by putting the presence for 21 March side by side with the record of the preceding day; *A* is accurate enough except that it omits the headline.

The evidence is also sufficient to show that what we have is the remnant of a probably regular record kept during this Parliament – not just notes made on particular occasions. *B* (Camden) demonstrates that the original covered at least three days of the first session of the 1449 parliament (held at Westminster), while *A* shows that the clerk continued the Journal after the Parliament had resumed at Winchester on 16 June. Thus the indications are that in this Parliament John Fawkes (clerk from 1447 to 1470) kept a daily record of sittings which gave the date and the presence, the latter being taken down at the beginning of the day's sitting rather than by marking up a prepared list,[70] and which on occasion at least recorded debates in the House. There is no sign that bill proceedings reached the record. This is certainly a surprising kind of Journal to find being kept in the middle of the fifteenth century. Anything resembling semi-official minutes of debates does not occur again until the survival of scribbled books from Bowyer's time (1610) onwards, and these are quite different in form from Fawkes's entries, lacking any note of the presence and evidently meant to stand side by

[69] This passage helped to persuade Myers of the authenticity of the document (*Bull. John Rylands Library* [1938], 391).
[70] This emerges from the fact that in *A* three peers are noted as speaking who do not appear in the presence; they must have come in after the start and after the clerk had written out his list.

side with the official record kept on the prepared presence-sheets.[71] Of
course, there may nevertheless have been a tradition of writing down
this kind of thing of which no trace survives. In a well known note
prefaced to his transcripts of the Henrician Journals, Bowyer remarked
that the clerk should every day 'wright into his rough or scribbled
booke, not only the reading of billes and other proceedinges of the
howse, but, as far foorthe as he can, whatsoeuer is spoken woorthy
observacion', though only the first should go into 'the Journall booke,
which is the Record'.[72] No Lords' scribbled books remain before
Bowyer's day, but presumably he was not inventing usage when
claiming to describe it. In *A* and *B* we have either ancestors of scribbled
books or a regular Journal which then recorded that matter which was
later thought improper for inclusion. Apart from the total absence of
any record of bill proceedings in 1449 (in the state of the evidence for
that age no sort of argument at all), there is something to support the
second alternative. It has been remarked before that both in the listing of
peers and the kind of business recorded these Lords' Journals somewhat
resembled contemporary Council records. The resemblance is in
general less striking than some of the things said might lead one to
suppose,[73] but it is true that the clerk of the Council occasionally made
presence lists a little like those of our Journal, and that very occasionally
Council debates were taken down, though usually Council minutes are
confined to decisions arrived at. Thus it is not impossible that Fawkes (a
chancery clerk) borrowed the idea of such a record from Council
practice (devised by clerks of the privy seal), but it must be said that in
the formalities of his book – especially the headline – he would appear
to have invented rather than followed. It is also quite possible, though
beyond proof, that the Parliament of 1449 was the first for which such a
Journal was kept.

One thing this Journal apparently did not record was the real business
of the House, the progress of bills. There is no positive evidence of this
being done until Edward IV's first Parliament in 1461 when *C* (the Fane
Fragment) gives proof for the practice. In consequence it has been

[71] *Guide to the Records of Parliament*, 33, and Plate 2.
[72] BL, Tiberius D.i, fo. 4v.
[73] The comparison was made by Dunham, *Speculum* 17 (1942), 402–15. He gives six passages from *Proceedings of the Privy Council*, ed. N. H. Nicolas, as allegedly similar to *A*, but on inspection only one (v, 223–4) records debate, and even this differs greatly from *A* in arrangement and types of contents. The similarities are generally remote rather than close, but further work on this seems desirable.

thought possible that Fawkes may have taken note of the criticisms made of him in Pilkington's Case (1455) when the court blamed him for failing to register the date of a bill's delivery into Parliament.[74] The issue in that case turned in part on such a date. However, in the first place the judge wanted to know the day on which a bill was 'first received', a loose phrase which need not by any means signify the same thing as the date of the first reading recorded in *C*; and secondly, *E* shows that something like the Fane Fragment record was kept by Fawkes two years before Pilkington's Case. The firm evidence of our copies from a Journal for 1453 and 1461 (*C, D, E*) is this: we know that lists of the presence were prepared for one day of the former year and ten of the latter; we know that on eight days in 1461 the lists were marked up for actual presence, while on a ninth the intention to do so is shown by the word *totatti* in the headline; we know that on the eight days when the presence was marked the clerk also took note of proceedings on bills. The question is whether the extant copies reproduce the lost Journals faithfully and completely. *D* and *E*, to judge from surrounding material in the volume, were made because the copyist was interested in the order of precedence of the lords in the Parliament; he would thus have been willing to ignore marking dots and any bill proceedings he may have found in his original. On the other hand, he may have been copying sheets prepared for sittings but not used, though such things are much less likely to have survived until about 1600 than actual records of sittings. The most likely conclusion is that the deficiencies of *D* and *E* are the fault of the copyist.

Thus it looks as though by 1453 at the latest, and certainly down to 1461, the clerk kept a proper record of attendances and bill proceedings, probably during actual sittings (a point confirmed by the use made of *G*), and it is less likely that he was doing so by 1449. Remembering *G*, we may with some confidence posit the existence of a daily record of Lords' sittings in all Parliaments between 1453 and 1504. It was produced by writing out beforehand a common form which gave the date of the sitting at the head in Latin, identifying it by the day of the month and the day of the Parliament, and which noted that the actual presence would be indicated by dots placed against the names of those attending, these dots being at some date replaced by 'p's. The names

[74] Pilkington's Case is printed from the YB in Dunham's edition of the *Fane Fragment*, 99–102. The suggestion linking the judge's remarks with the production of a Journal was, I think, first made by Pollard; but I cannot now find the passage.

were set out in columns and in Latin. In the Fane Fragment the business is squeezed in above the second column. Was this done in the original, as Dunham thought?[75] The copyist's layout requires the clerk to have guessed how much space he would need, and the entries are sometimes so crammed in as to conflict with the headline: the appearance of *C* could well have been produced by the copyist's desire to save paper. He placed committees appointed between the columns of names, but while on 9 November he had no room for them in the box reserved for the record of business he could easily have got them in there on 11 December. Thus we may assume that that placing followed the original; but while the copyist left space for committees between the columns only if he had to transcribe any, the original must always have provided room there. *G*, like *C*, starts the second column of names well down the page and has business entries above it; it also, however, leaves room for continuing those entries down the right-hand third of the page. This, I suggest, was the layout already current in 1461 and standard (the order of names excepted) until replaced by the strict three-column arrangement of 8 February 1515. The Fane Fragment slightly disguises it (and saves paper) by avoiding space to the right of the presence altogether.

In all probability, the original of *C* looked exactly like *G*, with three differences. *C* and *D* include the king in the prepared presence, while neither *G* nor the standard form of the Journals from 1515 onwards does this: it appears that in the middle of the fifteenth century the king's attendance in Parliament could be presumed as likely, while by Henry VIII's reign it had become very rare. This has political and constitutional significance that cannot be pursued here. Secondly, *C* and *D* adopt an order for the presence different from that of *G*'s; of this more in a moment. And thirdly, whereas all the Henry VIII material records the business in Latin, the Fane Fragment uses English. Dunham seems to have concluded that this was the language of the original, but since he remained uncertain whether his fragment was a copy or not he never bothered to argue the case.[76] As we saw in discussing 1449, later copyists were quite capable both of transcribing accurately and of silently translating. Unlike the language of *A*, that of *C* has nothing that by 1600 would have been archaic, which in fact is surprising if *C* was originally in English; there is a 'modernity' about those notes, and especially a perfection of technical language, which seem uncommon in

---

[75] Ibid. 40, n. 28.   [76] Ibid. 41.

English-language documents of their date of composition.[77] On the
other hand, it is not easy to see that a translator of a Latin original would
have so readily produced convincing English versions of the titles of bills
and the procedural terms employed. Also, why bother to translate when
parts of the document are left in Latin? Anyone wishing to tamper with
the detail of his original would surely have reduced his labours by some
means of simplifying those long lists of names with the repetition of
Epūs and *Abbas*, and so forth. We noted that the sequence of days in the
Fane Fragment proves that the copyist blindly followed what was
before him, namely sheets out of date order.[78] All the chances, therefore,
are that he did an accurate job, and that John Fawkes, who in 1449 wrote
his English notes of debates under Latin heads and columns of names,
followed the same bilingual practice in the redesigned Journal of
1453–61. In that case, the change to Latin, vouched for by 1510 and
maintained with the occasional intrusion of English until the reign of
Mary, has to be accounted for. The evidence permits no certainty, but
the possibility that John Taylor was responsible – doctor of laws and
also clerk of Convocation where all records were in Latin – seems quite
strong.

I have said that I think it likely that the record kept in 1461 was
continued even after Fawkes ceased to be clerk. Yet for the present no
copy even of materials between 1461 and 1510 has come to light, and we
have no originals at all before the latter date, even though bits and pieces
were still around in James I's reign and their disappearance since then is a
little surprising. Would one not expect to find more such stuff if it had
ever existed? However, reasons can be adduced to account for so much
of it vanishing. Knowledge of bill proceedings mattered only during the
session itself; it ceased to be worth preserving once Parliament has risen.
Fawkes's 'record' thus served a very temporary purpose; it has neither
record-standing nor practical use in the longer run. By about 1610
Bowyer could call the Journal 'the Record', but in the fifteenth century
the only series to deserve that name were the Rolls – a record of
Parliament, not of the House of Lords. There is no evidence that the
quires on which these attendance sheets were prepared were bound up,
and the disappearance of most of them together with the fate that befell
the original quires behind the Fane Fragment powerfully supports the

---

[77] It should, however, be noted that McFarlane could see nothing in the English of C to make a
fifteenth-century composition impossible (*EHR* 53 (1938), 508).

[78] Above, p. 62.

view that at that time no regular binding took place. The few known copies together with Cotton's erroneous remarks about the alleged fragment of 1497 suggest that what Tudor and Stuart antiquaries saw was not a book or books, but loose papers. All the circumstances militated against survival. These were working papers for the clerk's use, not worth preserving in perpetuity. In this respect things changed markedly in 1510.

4

When John Taylor became clerk, he found (we may take it) that his predecessors had used prepared sheets to record attendances and the progress of bills, but he is not likely to have found any books or anything resembling a House of Lords archive. The last Parliament had met six years before, and though his predecessor Richard Hatton did not die until May 1509 he had well before that opted for clerical preferment and the provostship of King's College, Cambridge. No doubt, like others before and after him, he kept such papers as accrued in private quarters.[79] Taylor is known to have lacked one important qualification for his office in that he had no Chancery experience, and he had no predecessor or predecessor's records to guide him. The clerk's most important official function was to compile the Roll of the Parliament, a Chancery document which, moreover, had been quite drastically reformed by Thomas Hutton in 1484 and had since remained in a state of some confusion.[80] It causes no surprise to find that Taylor evidently set himself to master his new office. The day-book – his invention – was designed to help him discharge his duties.

The first volume of this book manifested his purpose in three different ways. In the first place, Taylor had the *Modus Tenendi Parliamentum* copied out, or rather, he had his clerk transcribe a version which combined two separate manuscript traditions.[81] Whether he really thought that the *Modus* gave an accurate account of parliamentary procedure is not important. The *Modus* could be relied on for those formalities that mattered to the clerk – such things as the sending out of

---

[79] The first evidence of any continuity of archives – of one clerk having papers to pass on to his successor – belongs to the reign of James I.

[80] I cannot here enlarge on this. In 1484 the Roll began to record effectively only acts passed, abandoning the old category of 'commune peticio' which had comprehended all public bills, including those vetoed. There were other changes. [See below, no. 34, III.]

[81] J. Taylor, 'The manuscripts of the "Modus Tenendi Parliamentum"', *EHR* 83 (1968), 673 ff.; esp. 686.

writs or the appointment of receivers and triers – while its extravagant and unhistorical theories concerning the popular element in Parliament did not touch the conduct of business. In any case, no other guide existed, and Taylor may have thought that by conflating the two versions he could produce a more up-to-date handbook. The *Modus* gave no advice on the processing of bills; the regular inscribing of memoranda of despatch and receipt between the Houses, as well as of the royal assent, had apparently grown up quite recently and was still in a process of development. Here Taylor was fortunate in having the original acts of the last two Parliaments at least to assist him; he may well have had a hand in preserving them for 1497 and 1504, the first sessions for which they have survived. This matter requires separate treatment some other time.

Secondly, Taylor's day-book offered a handy instrument, in bound and therefore readily accessible form, to follow bills through the sittings. Though he could have got this from the attendance-cum-proceedings sheets, the fact that instead he went to the trouble of transcribing the relevant parts into his day-book again indicates how ill kept the sheets evidently were. He took what he required for his own use, a limitation which excluded attendances, and he copied everything into a bound book of blanks – a glorified notebook.[82] Lastly, and most importantly, Taylor intended his book to assist him in the making up of the Roll at the end of the Parliament. He was careful to note the purely formal business of appointing receivers and triers of petitions, and he exceptionally used French to do so, as did the Roll which also for the rest was in Latin. These appointments were by this time so much an archaic survival without practical meaning that they cannot have appeared on the attendance-type sheets as business really done in the House; but like the other preliminaries of the session they were to survive from the day-book into the reconstituted Journal from 1515 onwards. The preliminaries from the opening address to the presentation of the Speaker had to be enrolled; they turn up in the day-book essentially in the form in which they were transcribed on the Roll; there is no earlier indication of such matters being recorded in a book. It appears, therefore, that Taylor systematized the routine of preparing the Roll, and this innovation persisted into the later regular Journal, even after these matters had been dropped from the Roll.

The clinching proof for this third purpose of the day-book is found at

[82] See above, p. 67, n. 32.

the end of the first session.[83] Here Taylor made careful record of the formula of assent to supply bills and went on to record the ceremony of assent in a degree of detail that is not found anywhere else in the 'official' Journal. The lord chancellor, we read, ordered all acts passed in the session to be recited and published. They were accordingly read by the clerk of the Crown, and the clerk of the Parliaments pronounced the formulae of assent – *le roi le veult, le roi s'avisera, soit fait comme il est desiré* – as they were endorsed on the bill 'secundum annotationes Regis voluntatis declaratione'. This was procedural information which filled some gaps in the *Modus*. The point is repeated that the proper reply to a money bill is 'le roy se remercie etc.' Against this passage we find a note:

hec responsio nostre seigneur le roy etc imponenda est immediate post tenorem cujuscunque subsidij. Item in quibusdam solet dicere soit fait come il est desyre, quod facile attendas viso originale.

There follow the record of the dissolution and Taylor's signature, effectively closing the Journal for the session. However, more matter was entered:

Sequuntur tenores horum rotulorum billarum et actuum parliamenti cum responsionibus suis in irrotulatione eorundem imponendis.

Thus there should have been at least a full list of titles with the answers to be recorded on the Roll, but this we do not find – only enough to instruct the newcomer. Taylor notes down the formula to be employed in introducing acts on the Roll, with a word on the setting out required and the concluding formula. In the margin another hand (quite probably that of the clerk of the Crown) has added that the clause recited is to be appended to every bill and to every 'restitution' and bill *formam actus in se continens* (by which he would seem to have meant private bills) –

verumtamen est advertendum quod dicta clausa non debet apponi post quemlibet actum communem sed tantum in ultimo actu quia servit pro singulis, mutatis mutandis, videlicet sic dicendo, Quibus quidem perlectis et ad plenum intellectis eisdem et eorum cuilibet cum suis provisionibus annexis per dictum regem de avisamento etc. Advertas tamen ut in fine cuiuslibet Communis actus immediate eo finito et perscripto apponas seriem verba sequentia, videlicit Regis responsio, le roy le veult.

That is, public acts are all included in a single recital of the formula

---

[83] Printed in *LJ* i, 8–9, but very confusedly; the MS Journals bear out the argument made here.

which was supposed to indicate discussion and consideration and the advice of both Houses, but each must separately carry the formula of assent.

Thus at the end of the session we find assembled in the day-book the material required for making up the Roll, with notes addressed, in the second person, to whoever was to do the actual writing: possibly an underclerk, since Taylor is most unlikely to have been able to write a chancery hand. This person is advised to use the original acts to make sure of getting the assent formulae right and to distinguish in the longer set phrases surrounding private and public acts respectively. How far all these instructions are reflected on the Roll, and whether the guidance given was not perhaps out of date, are points that require a real study of the Rolls, a separate task once more.

As for the day-book, miscalled the Journal of of the House of Lords, its overriding purpose emerges very plainly. It was the clerk's working tool for the session, enabling him to keep on top of the passage of bills and to produce a satisfactory record in the obligatory Roll. This relationship was quite misunderstood by Pollard when he noted that 'a good deal of the form of the Journal for 1510 is common to the Roll of 1504; gradually the Roll dwindles and the Journal swells. . .'.[84] There is no occasion to speak of dwindling and swelling, and the day-book has Roll material on it because it was meant to help in producing the Roll. While he was learning the business Taylor kept the book in his own hand, but thereafter he left the task to his assistants, going over the record himself only to insert the occasional point or, more commonly, dates. Nor did it ever again prove necessary to provide such careful instruction about the Roll: clerk and underclerks had learned what to do, and from the end of his first session Taylor had his office in working order. All this strongly supports the conjecture that the keeping of a day-book was an innovation introduced by him in 1510.

But so far he was not yet keeping anything truly to be described as a Journal of the House of Lords — anything that would deserve Bowyer's description of the Journal as a record. The Lords had been concerned to note attendance for decades, but hitherto neither they nor the clerk had thought this of permanent importance. However, in his second Parliament Taylor once again applied his organizing habits to the business of the office: he decided that for the purpose of preparing the work-sheets he needed to have a record of the membership of

[84] Pollard, *TRHS* 1914, 28.

the House. The entry for the first proper sitting day on 6 February 1512 begins with a columnated 'presence' which is not marked up for attendance but is a complete list of peers, the king being included as he never is on the regular sitting lists later. It is also very oddly arranged, quite differently from earlier or later such lists.[85] A word needs to be said on the layout of the various presence lists encountered.

It has been rightly noticed that in the standardized form of these lists, from 1515, the seating order of the House is observed: Canterbury on the right of the cloth of state and York on the left, southern bishops and all the abbots on the benches along the right-hand wall, northern bishops and the higher peerage opposite them, and the barons occupying the seats left there as well as the cross benches facing the throne.[86] The two columns of the lists reproduce this arrangement, thus making it easy for the clerk to note absentees. A new phase began in the history of the House on 10 May 1539 when, after the total reordering of seating precedence by the act of 31 Henry VIII, c. 10, corrections had to be made in the sheet prepared for the day to take account of the changes in placing.[87] Although there was before this sufficient uncertainty about precedence to produce minor variations in the listed order of peers, all the complete lists in the 'official' Journal and in G follow this pre-1539 pattern (e.g. in G the omission of the bishop of Durham is repaired in the correct place, at the head of the earls' bench, not among the other bishops). The pattern was also observed on the occasions when the clerk produced a list of only those present, as in H. Such abbreviated lists were made when it was certain that there would be a light House with no business, and especially at the beginning of a new session; there is evidence for this in 6, 25, 27 and 28 Henry VIII.[88] Presumably the clerks had problems in discovering the exact membership of the House when it first assembled. In 1539, with a very active and reforming deputy clerk – Thomas Soulemont, trained as Cromwell's secretary – the

[85] MS Journals, i, 23–24; cf. above, p. 71.
[86] J. E. Powell and K. Wallis, *The House of Lords in the Middle Ages* (1968), 545 ff.
[87] MS Journal, i, 318. The changes involved putting all the spiritual peers on the right-hand benches (and therefore in the first column), with the lay peers now monopolizing the remaining benches and the second column. Cromwell, as vicegerent, moved to the head of the spiritual bench – and in the Journal from his lowly place as the recently created Baron Cromwell in the second column to the top of the first. When it is noticed that the vicegerent did not appear in Parliament until these changes were made one may guess who was behind the act that made them. As Powell and Wallis say (p. 582), 1539 produced a physically different House of Lords, ending the institution's medieval appearance – and history.
[88] MS Journals, i, 47, 127–8, 244; H.

sheets from the first list the whole House.[89] Thereafter partial lists are very rare.

However, not all the lists found obey this format. In 1461, the arrangement was by rank, earls following upon bishops and barons upon abbots, as both *C* and *D* show. This cannot ever have been a picture of the House's seating order, and from the clerk's point of view the introduction of the other arrangement at some date between 1461 and 1512 marked an efficient reform. Possibly one should see in the Fane Fragment's practice some aspects of aristocratic class-consciousness which was discarded as administrative competence took charge in the House. Secondly, there is the list in Taylor's day-book for 6 February 1512, which is unique. 'H Rex' stands massively across the top. The archbishop of Canterbury (Lord Chancellor Warham) shares pride of place with the only duke (Buckingham) and marquess (Dorset) of the day. The next block lists the bishops of the southern province, not altogether in proper order: Bangor and St Asaph are placed too high, Salisbury and Ely too low, and Bath and Wells surprisingly brings up the rear. The abbots' list starts below this and runs on to the top half of the next column. Next we have a mysterious reference to *custodes spiritualium*: presumably keepers of the spiritualties *sede vacante* are meant. Still in the same column follow the prelates of the northern province, with York rightly annotated as abroad: Cardinal Bainbridge was then resident on the king's behalf in Rome. Carlisle is followed without a break by a list of the eight earls then living, and after a gap we get the barons of the Parliament, headed (as always until 1540) by the prior of St John's of Jerusalem and providing twenty-six names in all – so many that they run over into a third column. Not intended nor used for the recording of attendance,[90] this list looks like a mixture of things. The northern prelates appear in the place assigned by the parliamentary seating order, but the leading lay peers – Buckingham and Dorset – are interposed between Canterbury and London. The three-column arrangement is unique, as is the appearance of the *sede vacante* keepers. These last, however, do offer a clue: their only other

[89] MS Journals, i, 311. In 1539 the clerk started the session with what he believed to be a full members' list of the House; in 1536, his predecessor waited until the second day before he put one together. There are some hints in the daily lists for both sessions that the givers of proxies were remembered for omission, but the clerks were not consistent in this.

[90] It is true that the headline for the day says 'fuerunt presentes subscripti domini', but – quite apart from the failure to mark the list – the inclusion of the *sede vacante* custodians (never present) and the three prelates known to be in Rome disproves the superscription.

relevant appearance is in the enrolment of writs of summons to this Parliament.[91] That entry also notes that writs were sent to the archbishop of York and the bishops of Bath and Worcester though all three were acting 'in remotis', all three in fact being king's agents at Rome. The day-book list repeats the information for York but not for the other two, though the relegation of Bath (Adrian Castello) to the end of the bishops' sector probably reflects awareness that he would not be present. Though the order of persons differs in the day-book from that on the close roll, both lists include the identical body of people. Thus the so-called presence list of 6 February 1512 was in fact the total membership of the House of Lords prepared from the enrolled writs of summons and intended to assist in the preparing of genuine attendance sheets of the kind that survives in G. G omits all the prelates noted to be abroad, and in the regular lists from 1515 onwards Bath and Wells continues to appear out of his proper precedence at the end of the southern episcopal bench – evident signs that the day-book list was used in the manner suggested.[92] As for the removal of Buckingham and Dorset into the midst of the spiritualty, it has been conjectured that they stood there carrying the regalia, on the opening day of the session.[93] Even if that were so, 6 February was not the opening day but a day of proper business; that the list does not record the presence of that day is in any case clear from the inclusion of the *custodes spiritualium* and the absent bishops. On the other hand, the dividing of the prelates into southern and northern, characteristic of Lords' attendance lists and unknown to the close roll, shows that in compiling this complete membership roster the clerk prepared for its purpose by incorporating touches of the seating order principle followed in the standard lists. It looks as though on the opening day, though not on the 6th, he saw the king, the duke and the marquess in the positions indicated by his listing; but he extracted the people listed from the close roll. The resulting list has nothing to do with a particular attendance but is yet another office device of John Taylor's for improving the efficiency of the clerical organization of Parliament.

[91] *LP* i, 963. There is no reason to think that *custodes spiritualium* ever sat as such in the Lords – unless they were anyway summoned as bishops of this or that. In 1515 the Journal confusingly described Wolsey both as *custos* and as archbishop of York during the sittings of 9–16 Feb., but called him only archbishop before and after those dates. The reason for this remains unknown: Wolsey was fully enlarged into an archbishop before the Parliament met.

[92] Both Castello and Silvestro de Gigli (Worcester) are regularly included in the presence lists of 1515, though domiciled at Rome; neither of them ever appeared.

[93] Powell and Wallis, 546.

This is as far as analysis of the day-book will take us. It was started by Taylor in 1510, and its purposes were internal to the office. At the same time he and his assistants prepared and filled in the sittings papers of which evidence survives as far back as 1453 and which at this time were work-sheets, not a form of record for permanent keeping. The day-book survives for the Parliament of 1510 and for the first session of the Parliament begun in 1512. It continued in a lost book which covered the second and third sessions of that Parliament. Some sort of crisis occurred at the opening of the session of 6 Henry VIII.[94] We begin with 'day-book type' entries, but the presence of false starts and half-used blank pages indicates that Taylor was not transcribing into a ready-made book. From the fourth day of the session the day-book disappears for good. Instead the clerk began to file the work-sheets, probably by binding up the quires on which they were prepared, in readiness for them to be put in order by Thomas Smith some ninety years later. Though there are signs that for a time, and especially early in the session, the sheets were not prepared long in advance, this soon changed, as was shown dramatically in the summer of 1540. There Thomas Cromwell, vicegerent in spirituals, heads the list. He is last marked as present on 10 June, the day of his arrest, but his name is still there, eloquently without any 'p', for another six days.[95] Then it disappears. One may guess that the sheets were made up in batches of two four-page quires at a time.

Whether one calls the record that emerged in the mild confusion of 1515 an official Journal of the House of Lords must up to a point be a matter of opinion. As has already been said, losses are likely to have occurred because there was still no clear understanding that the office of the clerk of the Parliaments was an archive whose contents passed from one incumbent to another. We do not know where Smith found the material he put in order, though it looks as though it must by then have been in the clerk's office. We know that the book for 28 Henry VIII escaped custody until Bowyer recovered it. The existence of the stray opening sheets for 27 Henry VIII (*H* and *I*) proves that sessional books could fall apart. But though record-keeping did not grow perfect overnight, it remains true that Taylor's tenure of the clerkship witnessed the real inception of a continuous and proper register. He showed the way in his day-book, the purpose of which was to assist him in his work and not to record the doings of the House, and in 1515 he transformed

[94] Above, p. 71.   [95] MS Journals i, 390–6.

the traditional working papers of the clerkship into a genuine record by preserving them and having them bound up sessionally. Whether these developments should be laid solely at his door it is impossible to tell; they fit in too well with the emergence of the Lords as a separate House of Parliament to be thought of as merely administrative changes. We have no idea how the House itself regarded the Journal at this time, but it seems likely that formal recognition of it as 'the record' – especially the record of guiding principles and precedents – came only in the second half of the century. Yet well before this other clerks built on Taylor's initiatives and the House had, from 1515, a true record of its business. What happened had nothing to do with a growth from primitive to developed. The business papers of parliamentary sittings were transformed into the bound and regular Journal of the House of Lords; and this happened in the reign of Henry VIII.

However, this does not mean that all things were settled when that king's last Parliament went home. The clerks of either House have never been much bothered about following 'evolutionary trends', and as the keepers of the precedents they have been well placed to manufacture or forget them. Where parliamentary materials are concerned, experience proves the unwisdom of arguing from an earlier state of affairs to a later, and from a later to an earlier. This paper stops in 1547; what happened thereafter requires study, not extrapolation.

II. THE SESSIONAL PRINTING OF STATUTES, 1484–1547*

Once statute became accepted as the supreme form of law-making, those living under the law needed to know what Parliament had done, and lawyers in particular required copies of new statutes as quickly as possible. Such copies probably circulated even before the invention of printing, but there cannot have been many of them. The printers discovered the profitable market almost at once, and their activities came effectively to alter the very nature of parliamentary law itself: once sessional printing became the norm the product superseded the older records – the Rolls of Parliament and even the Original Acts – as the commonly used authoritative version of Parliament's output.

The first set of printed statutes ever produced was for Richard III's

---

* [*Wealth and Power in Tudor England: Essays presented to S. T. Bindoff*, ed. E. W. Ives, R. J. Knecht, J. J. Scarisbrick (1978), 68–86].

only Parliament (1484); neither of the two printers to whom the work has been ascribed could really have started earlier. William Caxton returned to England about 1476, while William de Machlinia is not found active till the later 1470s;[96] at most they missed the Parliament of 1478. This branch of printing developed rapidly. Particular acts were put out as well as the statutes of particular Parliaments and, by stages, collections of acts both ancient and recent; reprinting was frequent, dating was unknown before 1539 and far from conscientious thereafter, type was sometimes set up afresh and sometimes kept standing with new headlines supplied for successive printings. The highly successful collection of Henry VIII's statutes published by Thomas Berthelet in 1542 was reprinted in 1562, after his death, with his name still in the colophon.[97] In the course of time, such collections were often broken up and sometimes rebound in a muddle of different printings, and many libraries have holdings of seemingly well-ordered volumes that are in fact a bibliographer's nightmare. A historian who is not a bibliographer must be rash indeed to embark upon materials that can be dated only from a study of typefaces, borders and ornaments.

Though a full-scale attack on the problem ought perhaps to have involved the comparing of all extant material side by side, this was both physically impossible and quite beyond my skill. Happily, I had earlier labours to assist me. The famous introduction to *The Statutes of the Realm* provides some useful clues but also contains some confident assertions for which no grounds are given; it is a mixture of learning and imagination which is very unsafe to use and has been trusted too readily. In 1900, Robert Procter attempted to track the work of Berthelet, the most prolific pioneer of this kind of printing, in an article which relied only on the holdings of the British Museum and in fact missed some of the Berthelet statutes available there.[98] Insufficient as his effort was, it did provide the first usable chronological framework. The listings in the British Library Catalogue and the *Short-Title Catalogue of English Books 1475–1640* are of some help, though the former does not attempt to distinguish between sessional printing, parts of collections and later reprints, while the second gives only a small selection from the extant

[96] E. G. Duff, *A Century of the English Book Trade* (1948), 24, 97. The elegance of the 1484 production suggests to me that the longer-standing ascription to Caxton is correct. [Not so, according to Dr Katherine Pantzer.]

[97] Berthelet died in 1555 (*The Diary of Henry Machyn*, ed. J. G. Nichols, CS, (1848), 95).

[98] R. Procter, 'A short view of Berthelet's editions of the statutes of Henry VIII', *Trans. of the Bibliographical Soc.* 5 (1901), 255 ff.

mass.[99] Much the most important analysis is found in J. H. Beale's great bibliography, which tried to base itself on a really comprehensive survey: Beale searched twenty-four libraries in England and America. He modestly disclaimed any pretensions to completeness or total accuracy and has indeed been found wanting here and there, but his work must nevertheless form the starting-point of any enquiry.[100] With the help of these guides I have worked through a selection of the extant printed acts from Richard III's only Parliament to Henry VIII's last, and I have satisfied at least myself that I have seen all but two of the sessional prints that were produced and survive. The two absentees are listed by Beale and Anderson as found at Harvard only. If my identification of a particular statute as sessionally printed should on occasion be suspect, the error would matter the less because from a certain date the fact of sessional printing can be proved obliquely and because the reprints were scrupulous: from the first, texts were regarded as sacrosanct, and compositors seem to have exercised a care quite unusual among sixteenth-century printers, practices upon which the legal authority of those productions naturally depended.

When did the king's printer start to produce sessional acts for the public use? The first positive evidence is also utterly unambiguous. On 3 May 1510, a warrant was issued to Lord Chancellor Warham, instructing him to deliver to Richard Pynson, king's printer, a true copy of the statutes passed in the last Parliament, so that he might put them into print.[101] The first Parliament of the reign had been dissolved on 23 February, so that it was only two and a half months after it went home that Pynson got the opportunity to set about his task. He produced the desired set, a somewhat primitive affair without any title, the first act opening on page 1. The print concludes with a table of the fifteen acts printed (out of the twenty passed); the colophon explained that these were 'the Statutis holden at Westmynster [*sic*] the. xxi. daye of January in the firste yere of yᶜ most noble reygne of Kynge Henry the . viii', and claimed a two years' sales monopoly for Pynson by royal privilege.[102] We may note, for later reference, that Pynson had printed the tonnage and poundage act separately and that it was not included in the sessional set.[103]

---

[99] [The second edition, now being prepared by Dr Pantzer, will do much better].

[100] J. H. Beale, *A Bibliography of Early English Lawbooks* (Cambridge, Mass., 1926); see also the pamphlet of supplementary material by R. B. Anderson (ibid. 1943). I shall cite these works by authors' names only and printed statutes sometimes by the numbers attached in their lists.

[101] *LP* i, 485 (4).   [102] BL, C. 38. c. 2.   [103] Beale, S110a.

This fine start was not immediately followed up. The next Parliament sat for three separate sessions, and the novelty of a Parliament so prorogued seems to have bewildered both printer and clerk. No copy of any statute has been found for the session of 5 Henry VIII, but those extant for the first two sessions of this Parliament (3 and 4 Henry VIII) were printed together, being signed through and having a colophon only at the end of the double set.[104] There must be some doubt whether 5 Henry VIII ever produced a sessional printing, though the acts for that year are in the reprint collections of 1542 and 1563, and the disappearance of one sessional set among so many is much less surprising than the survival of all the rest. At any rate, while the routine of sessional printing was clearly not yet established for Henry's second Parliament, it had arrived by the time the next one met; for each of its two sessions (6 and 7 Henry VIII) a separate and sessional statute can, with some difficulty, be identified.[105] Thereafter we find sessional acts right through the reign, and from the session of 31 Henry VIII (1539) the sets carry the year date of printing.[106] From 1531 the work was done by Pynson's successor, Thomas Berthelet, who remained king's printer to the end of the reign and evidently put the whole business on a firm and regular basis. His carefulness appears, for instance, in the fact that the 'cum privilegio' in his colophon was promptly altered in 1539 to 'cum privilegio ad imprimendum solum', to accord with the order proclaimed on 16 November 1538, the full formula thereafter remaining in use:[107] this detail can help in dating stray copies. Berthelet got so efficient that he could publish (if his colophons are to be trusted which in 1543 and 1544 give the day of publication) within three to four weeks of the

---

[104] BL, C.122.f.10(2, 3).
[105] 6 Hen. VIII: Beale S117, alleged to be found at Harvard and Cambridge, has not been tracked at the former by Anderson; the CUL copy (Syn. 4.83.9) is badly mutilated and lacks everything after sig. A iv. Beale S117a seems to be a mistake, since his table gives that number to the statute for 7 Hen. VIII which his list calls S117b. Anderson S116a is probably a reprint. – 7 Hen. VIII: Anderson S117c, which from its collation appears to be a separate piece of printing.
[106] 14 & 15 Hen. VIII: Anderson S122a (Harvard). 21 Hen. VIII: BL, 506.d.31 (1) [Pynson's last]. 22 Hen. VIII: BL, 505.g.13(2) [rather than 506.d.31(2) which adds chapter numbers]. 23 Hen. VIII: BL, 506.d.31(3). 24 Hen. VIII: ibid. (4). 25 Hen. VIII: BL, C.64.e.10(1) [rather than 506.d.31(5) and 506.d.33 which look to be rushed reprints]. 26 Hen. VIII: 506.d.34 [once owned by Sir Roger Cholmeley, then recorder of London, who when chief baron of the Exchequer gave it to his nephew Ralph]. 27 Hen. VIII: BL, 506.d.31(7). 28 Hen. VIII: ibid. (8). 31 Hen. VIII: CUL, Bb*.8.31.7 [the first printing, but BL, 505.f.5(11) probably also belongs to 1539]. 32 Hen. VIII: BL, C.64.e.10(4) [subsidy and pardon, separately printed, exceptionally bound in and added to table, without chapter numbers]. 33 Hen. VIII: BL, 505.f.5(13). 34 & 35 Hen. VIII: C.64.e.10(5). 35 Hen. VIII: BL, 506.d.8 (19). 37 Hen. VIII: ibid. (20).
[107] *TRP* i, 186.

end of the session, an efficiency which did not endure; in 1555 the statutes did not become available until three months after Parliament had risen.[108]

Before Henry VIII, the situation is markedly less clear. Printed statutes exist for all but one of Henry VII's Parliaments, but the copies now found come in the main from the collection for the reign which Pynson published, probably early in the next.[109] However, he utilized earlier printings, and some of these may well have been sessional. This seems most certain for the acts of Henry VII's last Parliament (1504), printed by William Facques, the first man known to have held the title of king's printer, though the set is not dated and the elaborate production contrasts with Pynson's later rushed jobs.[110] Nothing survives for 12 Henry VII (1497); since Pynson's collection also omits this year we may suppose that no one printed anything for this Parliament.[111] 11 Henry VII yielded an elegant, even extravagant, set from Wynkyn de Worde; the only extant example of it is hand-coloured and hardly looks like print.[112] It may not have been sessional, but it was used in Pynson's collection, which follows its lay-out. Pynson's version for 7 Henry VII (no separate printing found) has no table and is altogether more primitive. The uncertainties posed by these sessions are overshadowed by the problems which the first three parliaments of the reign raise: for these we have a single printing covering all three (probably Caxton's work),[113] and Pynson's volume (by running through all three sessions before supplying tables for them which are not in Caxton's print) confirms that this collective set was all that ever appeared.

In fact, the set for the first three Tudor Parliaments must be considered together with that for Richard III's – the first for which a printed statute exists. This has always been treated as contemporary (that is, sessional), though the grounds for that conviction are not clear.

---

[108] The Parliament ended on 16 January, but it was only on 24 April that John Parkyn, who had been anxiously looking for the printed set, could despatch one to a friend in Yorkshire: A. G. Dickens, 'John Parkyn, Fellow of Trinity College, Cambridge', *Procs. of the Cambridge Antiquarian Soc.* 43 (1950), esp. 23–4.

[109] BL, C.71.ff.6, a continuous set brought out by Pynson as king's printer, an office to which he did not succeed until after May 1508 (Duff, 126–7).

[110] BL, C.122.f.9.

[111] [Dr Pantzer has now found a sessional print for this year, and I erred in missing this short statute in the collection.]

[112] BL, IB. 55195.

[113] BL, G. 6002.

The editors of *Statutes of the Realm* simply stated it as a fact that the extant print[114] appeared soon after the end of the session, and they seem to have relied on the sort of enquiries summarized in one of the record Commission's *Reports* (1806) which claims to have found copies, said to be sessional, in the Inner Temple Library and the King's Library at the British Museum.[115] But we are there given no grounds for these confident assertions which may be nothing more than the often unreliable fruits of Charles Abbot's love affair with muniments;[116] this very note calls up serious doubts when it locates copies of 31 and 37 Henry VIII at Winchester, despite the fact that, according to the same Report, 'no Originals, Records or Manuscripts were found at Winchester'. In short, the established conviction that Caxton (or Machlinia) printed the acts of Richard III immediately after the session has rested on no discoverable evidence. Nevertheless, of course, it may be correct.

Let us then look at the two productions for 1484–9 which, though they raise some tricky problems, also help to solve some of the mysteries of early statute-printing. Both look alike and differ from later prints. They are not in black-letter but in a rare cursive intended to look like handwriting; they run the acts recited into one block; and they open with a space left for an illuminated initial which in the surviving examples has not been filled in. The editors of *Statutes of the Realm* drew attention to the likeness of this format to that of the medieval Statute Roll and concluded that the Roll, now extant only to 1468, must have been continued and must have formed the original from which the printing was 'manifestly copied'.[117] This is not so. The Statute Roll has neither chapter numbers nor titles of acts: 1 Richard III has the first, and 1–4 Henry VII the second. The Statute Roll is in French, as is 1 Richard III; 1–4 Henry VII is in English. The transformation of the Roll of Parliament from its medieval into its modern form (from a record of proceedings to an enrolment of acts passed) was initiated in 1484: and it was this that made the Statute Roll superfluous. Even if any such Roll ever existed after 1468, it is much more likely that it ceased after the last Parliament of Edward IV and was never written up for 1484. Every single Statute Roll covered long periods, and even if a new one was

---

[114] BL, C.10.b.20.

[115] *SR*, ii, 477 note; *Report of Searches for Originals, Records and Manuscript Copies etc.*, 1806 (ordered to be printed by the House of Lords, 30 June 1807), App. 19, pp. 49–51.

[116] Abbot was the moving spirit behind the Record Commission and also chairman of the editorial committee for *SR*.

[117] *SR* i, p. xxxv.

started in 1472 it would only have had material from two Parliaments to enroll before the reformed Parliament Roll made the labour supererogatory: at that point the barely started Roll would likely be discarded. For practical purposes, the Statute Roll always in effect terminated at 1468.

However, this does not necessarily mean that manuscript collections of sessional statutes also ceased. The Roll consisted of transcripts – from what? The form in which the acts appear there reflects no known original. The public acts of the session could not be got from the Parliament Roll, where they appeared in the form of petitions with the king's response: the whole purpose of the Statute Roll was to enregister the positive ordinances made on this basis, and this involved turning petition into act. Moreover, since the bills and petitions in Parliament were by this time invariably in English (the Parliament Roll faithfully following suit), the acts had to be specially translated into the French of the Statute Roll. Thus the parliamentary bureaucracy had to prepare a document which could be enrolled in Chancery. We may therefore, with some confidence, posit the existence, before 1484, of sessional manuscripts of statutes put together for this purpose; and it would have really been surprising if copies of these had not become available for sale to interested parties.

The conjecture seems probable, and it can be supported by something like firm evidence. Where else but from such copies could the scribe have got his text who composed the splendid volume of statutes kept in the king's remembrancer's office in the Exchequer?[118] It is not credible that it could have been copied from the Statute Roll, kept in Chancery. *Statutes of the Realm* noted that the text of the volume 'agreed in general with those of the Printed Copies', which is the less surprising because the volume was, once printing started, quite manifestly copied from the print; before that, therefore, it would have used something like our conjectured manuscripts. Another manuscript collection favoured by *Statutes of the Realm* looks also to have been copied from such sessional

[118] E 164/11 – very handsome and with lots of illuminated initials and borders. A note inserted by Hilary Jenkinson shows that originally one volume covered the Parliaments from Edward IV to 11 Hen. VII, all written in one hand. From 1 Ric. III the book manifestly relies on the known printed statutes, reproducing some of their oddities and faithfully following their order of the acts. Like the prints, it has nothing for 12 Hen. VII. The correction of a repeated phrase in 1 Ric. III shows the copyist at work. The exception is 7 Hen. VII which, adding the royal assent and using phrases found only on the roll, evidently derived from thence. A new copyist picked up in 19 Hen. VII, and yet another added 1–7 Hen. VIII, again using the printed statutes. [The manuscripts conjectured in fact existed and some survive: see below, p. 121.]

productions. This is MS Petyt 511/6 at the Inner Temple, a volume in which the acts down to the last Parliament of Edward IV were transcribed about the end of the reign, those for Richard III and 1 and 3 Henry VII being added thereafter.[119] This manuscript uses French throughout and in both the sessions of Henry VII omits the last act included in the print, while in 1 Henry VII it added the act for the king's title which was not printed. Thus, unlike the Exchequer volume, it derived its entries for the last three Parliaments it transcribed from a source other than the prints: it offers further circumstantial evidence for the existence of our conjectured manuscripts, while its omissions indicate the advantages which were to be gained from the security of printing.

I therefore suggest that before printing began some copies at least of the sessional statutes were circulating in manuscript, that these were copies of the material prepared for the Statute Roll, and that that material continued to be put together even after copying on the Roll was abandoned. Thus when Caxton decided that there was money in the printing of statutes, he first quite simply (in the manner familiar from other areas of early printing) put an existing manuscript style into print and made the product look as like the familiar predecessor as possible. The Petyt MS indicates that a French text was still available for 1 and 3 Henry VII, but not thereafter. Consequently, when Caxton next came to produce printed statutes (for Henry VII's first three Parliaments) he no longer had the old French manuscript to work from and obtained copies of the acts in English, possibly from the Parliament Roll (with which his text agrees), though he added titles. Since, therefore, the second statute he printed differed from the first in the most important detail of all, the source of the copy used, it is indeed likely that the statute of 1484 was in effect sessionally printed – more or less at once. However, Caxton did not immediately continue to print every session; his successors played around with various formats; and before 1504 the whole business remained very haphazard.

Thus the earliest printing was not really innovatory; rather the story again demonstrates that printing did not so much produce new reading matter as give greater cheapness, celerity, distribution and reliability to already existing publications. Nor was this enterprise in any real sense official, though it is clear that once the conjectured 'Statute Roll

[119] Cf. *Catalogue of Manuscripts in the Library of the Honourable Society of the Inner Temple*, ed. J. C. Davies (Oxford, 1972), i, 217–18.

manuscripts' ceased to be prepared the printers could not have produced sessional statutes without the aid of the clerks of the Parliaments who controlled the records on which the prints depended. However, it was only in 1504, when Facques claimed the work for himself as king's printer, that the obvious association of official printer with officers of the Parliament was made patent. In 1510, the coincidence of a new printer and a new clerk, which has provided us with the first evidence of official support for the printing of statutes, opened the real history of the regular sessional practice. It is worth remembering that the clerk, John Taylor, also did much to reform the keeping of a Journal:[120] very likely the regularizing of sessional printing owed something to his tidy and organizing mind. Though the full routine of the business enterprise awaited the coming of Thomas Berthelet in 1531, it is apparent that sessional printing is yet another aspect of parliamentary record production which, on the basis of somewhat half-hearted earlier efforts, became regular from the beginning of Henry VIII's reign. What had started as the application of the new technology to the serving of a much older lawyers' market for acts of Parliament came to be a part of the government's running of parliamentary affairs.

The printers did not confine themselves to producing collections of acts either sessional or later. Some acts were printed separately. Thus supply acts, including that granting tonnage and poundage for life, were treated so from the first[121] and were not reprinted for sessional statutes, though sometimes copies of the separates were added to those publications.[122] These financial acts, which had to be distributed to all the commissioners for assessment and collection, called for immediate and numerous copies; separate printing was obviously convenient. For similar reasons, acts of general pardon received the same treatment and also do not appear in sessional sets. The 1543 statute for Wales (34 & 35 Henry VIII c. 26), not included in the sessional statute, was printed separately and is sometimes found in surviving sets where it has been bound in at the end of the year's acts.[123] Its length and the lack of general interest in it may well have counselled against putting it into the

---

[120] Cf. above, no. 34 (I).

[121] Above, p. 94.

[122] Some sets include subsidy acts and pardons in the table (printed when the set was made up) but without chapter numbers; tables were printed last.

[123] E.g. CUL, Rel.b.55.3, a collection made up from later reprints which at the end of the 1543 session inserts the original printing of c. 26. A more complete collection (Sel.3.207) achieves the same effect by using a 1547 reprint of the statute.

sessional print, but, as Berthelet's accounts show, forty copies were wanted for proclamation in Wales, so that separate printing became necessary.[124] To these practical and accidental reasons, politics from 1533 added more pressing ones.[125] The first act which is known to have been specially printed by order of the government was that in restraint of appeals to Rome which it was decided in December 1533 to publish in the form of a proclamation.[126] This must have involved a fresh setting up since the multi-page format of the sessional statute was not suitable for posting. Very soon after we come across the extraordinary possibility that acts may have been available in separate copies even before the end of a session. On 28 March 1534, two days before the prorogation, a correspondent informed Lord Lisle in Calais that he was sending him the acts passed to that day, a purpose for which he could have had nothing available except printed versions.[127] It is thus possible that Berthelet set up the acts as they passed both Houses, presumably in readiness for the sessional set, but that he was also willing to sell copies at once, before the assent was given.[128] In 1539, a well-informed observer reported the passing of the act of six articles on 13 June, a fortnight before the end of the session, and confidently expected it to be shortly published in the form of a proclamation, which would have meant 'premature' printing and publication; on the other hand, the French ambassador, markedly less well-informed, expected that printing would be done only after Parliament had risen.[129] Over a fortnight after the end of the 1545 session, the imperial ambassador reported that its acts were being kept secret;[130] while this was probably no more than an ignorant complaint that the sessional print had not yet appeared (three days after Twelfthnight) it does show that no acts had become available earlier, as had happened in 1534. All very confusing and inconclusive, but it cannot be helped that the evidence maliciously raises questions which it is then insufficient to answer.

[124] For Berthelet's accounts see below, n. 132.

[125] Sometimes with disconcerting results: for what happened to the acts posted at Coventry see *Policy and Police*, 134–5.

[126] *LP* vi, 1487 (1).

[127] *LP* vii, 384.

[128] In this period, the indispensability of the royal assent may in practice have been something of a myth, a subject too large for proper discussion here. The Original Acts of the sessions of 27 and 28 Hen. VIII have no formulae of assent inscribed on them; and the 1539 act for the seating order in the Lords (31 Hen. VIII c. 10) was carried into effect when it had passed that House, before the Commons had seen it and months before it was assented to.

[129] *LP* xiv (1), 1108, 1207.

[130] *LP* xxi (1), 37.

However, it looks as though normally separate printing, except of subsidies and pardons, was confined to the production of acts in the form of proclamations, intended for publicity throughout the realm.[131] This appears from the king's printer's accounts for work supplied to king and Council which happen to survive for 1541–3; they also show that by then such proclaiming had become commonplace and was no longer confined to matters of high political interest.[132] On 8 April 1543, in the middle of the session, Berthelet supplied 'iij little bookes of the Statutes' to the Privy Council, but this is most likely a reference to his 1542 collection of the acts of the reign. Separates he produced after the end of the session, though so promptly that printing had evidently been going on before the assent. On 20 April 1542, less than three weeks after the prorogation, he sent five hundred copies each of the first nineteen chapters of the sessional set, presumably in proclamation form; on 21 May 1543, just nine days after the prorogation, he sent five hundred copies of the first eleven acts, fifty each of two more,[133] and forty of the act for Wales, which last did not reappear in the sessional set – and this time he explicitly stated that these copies were 'made out in Proclamacions'. Further small quantities of some of them were required by 12 June. In 1542, forty-six acts passed of which thirty-nine were printed and nineteen proclaimed; in 1543 the figures were forty-eight, twenty-five and twelve (plus three separates: the act for Wales, the subsidy and the general pardon). At first sight the distinction between acts printed in the sessional sets and those printed for proclamation might appear to lie in their general significance, but though those not proclaimed included a number of distinctly local or private acts the principle does not work out consistently. Why, for instance, should the lord chancellor in 1542 have wanted five hundred copies of the act freeing Manchester from the burden of being a sanctuary town, but none of those which barred justices of assize from sitting in their county of origin or provided for the naturalization of certain kinds of children

---

[131] The suggestion in *LP* xviii (i), 67 (2, 4) that two private acts of the session were printed and then certified by the clerk of the Lords is misleading. Those documents are printed copies of certified manuscript transcripts, even the certification and the clerk's name being in print. They were most probably prepared round about 1666, as evidence in a bastardy case (HMC, *8 Report*, 102).

[132] W. H. Black and F. H. Davies, 'Thomas Berthelet's bill, as King's printer, for books sold and bound, and for statutes and proclamations furnished to the government in 1541–43', *Journal of the British Archaeological Assoc.* 7 (1853), 44–52. Cf. *LP* xviii (II), 211.

[133] cc. 12. and 13 for paving streets in London, and for knights and burgesses for Chester, both of local interest only.

born abroad? In 1543 the Crown paid for five hundred proclamations touching the manufacture of coverlets at York, but did not require any copies of the important acts amending the statutes of proclamations and fines. Perhaps temporal sequence accounted for the distinction: did the printer supply what had been got through in time? Against this is the fact that in 1542 he did not print proclamations of two acts later included in the sessional set, the attainder of Catherine Howard and that touching treason committed by lunatics, which specially received the royal assent by commission on 11 February, two months before the end of the session.[134] At any rate, the delivery dates confirm that in those years printing must have been well under way before Parliament rose.

How, then, were acts chosen for printing? Who did this, and who supplied the printer with his copy? In the absence of direct evidence something may be inferred from the printed sets themselves. The warrant of 1510, which directed the lord chancellor to supply the necessary material, might suggest a reliance on the Roll, but, if this was so, practice manifestly soon changed. The notion, recently advanced, that the Roll was not made up between 1529 and 1555 is mistaken,[135] but it does look as though none was deposited in the Chancery during those years, so that the clerk of the Crown could not have supplied copies. More conclusively, from the time (1540) that the officers ceased to enroll every act passed, it is plain that certain acts could have been printed only from the original parchment bill: thus 33 Henry VIII cc. 2, 8, 14, 15 and 21, though not on the Roll, appear in the sessional print. If the Roll was used, copies had to be made for the printer, as the warrant of 1510 envisaged; while this was supposed to be the practice also in using Original Acts, it seems only too likely that from an early date the clerk saved himself this unpaid labour by lending out the Original Acts themselves. Such improper evasion of duty perhaps accounts for the disappearance of the Original Acts of 1523 and 1529, Sir Brian Tuke's first two Parliaments. On the other hand, the original of the act of 1532 for the conditional restraint of annates (23 Henry VIII c. 20) should still

---

[134] *LJ* i, 176b.

[135] C. G. Ericson, 'Parliament as a legislative institution in the reigns of Edward VI and Mary' (London Univ. Ph.D. thesis, 1973), 154–8, misinterprets a Council order of 1556, which concerns certification into chancery, to mean that no rolls were written. For a variety of reasons it is out of the question that the rolls for the twenty-four sessions involved (all of which now exist in contemporary hands) should have been put together after 1556; but it is quite likely that the clerks of the Parliaments tried to retain the Rolls so as to keep complete control of copying and copying money. Another topic worthy of examination which awaits a study of the Rolls. [See below, pp. 133–4.]

have been available when Berthelet printed the sessional statute. It is now missing and has been so since at least Henry Elsyng's day in the 1630s: his calendar of acts at the Parliament Office, based on 'the old calendar', fails to list it and numbers through as though no such act had ever existed.[136] We know in fact what happened: on 31 August 1533, Lord Chancellor Audley (in no great hurry to execute a warrant received on 9 July) sent for the annates act in order to have it transcribed into the letters patent which were to put it into effect. Evidently it never got back into the archive.[137] But clearly it was there before this, and yet Berthelet did not include it in his sessional statute. We may suspect that someone, most probably the clerk, exercised discretion in not sending to the printer a 'public' act of general interest which was awaiting confirmation by letters patent.

In all probability, therefore, the later standard practice was followed from the first: it fell to the clerks of the Parliaments to provide the king's printer with what he was to print, and for this purpose they used the Original Acts in their keeping – either the documents themselves or copies made from them. The series of Original Acts now starts in 1497, that Parliament of Henry VII which does not seem to have resulted in sessional printing. It is not impossible that Facques's demand for copy in 1504 induced the clerk to become more careful about preserving the acts of the session even after their enrolment on the Parliament Roll had rendered them superfluous under the traditional system; master record or not, the Roll was no longer sufficient once printing became regular. What are in effect Original Acts are found scattered among the Ancient Petitions at the Public Record Office; but in view of the strong probability that no proper sets were kept before 1497 it seems unlikely that the 'unofficial' printing of those early years had such first-hand copy to rely on. I have already suggested that Caxton used a 'Statute Roll manuscript' in 1484 and switched in 1489 to a copy of entries on the Parliament Roll, presumably bought from the clerks; much the same thing may have happened in 1491 and 1495. However, it may be said with reasonable confidence that from 1504 the Original Acts always formed the foundation of sessional printing and that the printer depended on the clerk of the Lords for what he got into print. Whether the clerk was also responsible for the order in which acts were printed,

[136] Nat. Lib. of Wales, MS 17016D (cf. 'Calendar of Carew MSS', HMC, *Fourth Report*, App. 369a). The acts for 1523 and 1529 had also disappeared before that date.

[137] *LP*, vi, 1049; the patent (whose date, of course, is that on which the warrant was delivered into Chancery) is printed from the Parliament Roll in *SR* iii, 387 n.

or whether this was left to the accidents of the printing-house, cannot be determined. The point is not without interest, for the chapter numbers supplied in the print became the standard manner of legal reference to acts of Parliament, though it is very noticeable that parliamentary drafting itself (for instance in acts confirming or repealing earlier acts) studiously avoided chapter numbers and preferred the dubious precision of *ad hoc* titles. Until 1536 the numbering of the printed statute nearly always differs greatly from that on the Roll, which (except for 1529) started with private acts that were not printed; at all times even the Roll's order of acts that did get into print practically never agrees with that adopted in the sessional set.[138] Since, in their antiquarian fashion, the clerks continued to ascribe ultimate authority to the Roll, this fact may well explain why they would not use the printer's chapter numbers. But it also makes it more likely that those numbers came to be imposed as part of the printing process.

The clerk, of course, never sent all the acts to be printed; he (or whoever instructed him) made a selection. The principle of that selection is indicated by a phrase which recurs with little alteration in most of the titles of the sessional sets where it is stated that these are the acts of a given Parliament for the honour of God and Holy Church and the profit of the common weal – in other words, the acts regarded as 'public'. Whatever precise meaning this term may have had before (and the Roll for the first time, and for one time only, recognized it in 1539), it became effectively fixed once printing started: it was not so much that the printer published the public acts, but that such acts as he printed were regarded as public, especially in the important sense that they could be alleged in court without special pleading (which involved the production of a certified true copy).[139] It was print that made the acts public or private, generally knowable or knowable only upon the inspection of the unprinted original. However, though print ossified the distinction, the principle of selection preceded it: someone had always had to select the acts that were enrolled on the Statute Roll and that were grouped on the Parliament Roll as the *communes peticiones* without being transcribed. After 1484, 'public' acts, too, were enrolled in full on the Parliament Roll, at first in what was effectively a separate section of it; but before long enrolment took the acts as they came, mixing those later

---

[138] [Wrong: see below, pp. 128–9, 135–6.]

[139] The principle that public acts did not need to be specially pleaded was well established by the late fifteenth century (W. S. Holdsworth, *History of English Law*, xi, 290).

made public with those left private. At this point, the clerk's selection of what to send to the printer finally settled the difference between the two kinds.

Of course, according to the textbook theory the clerk had no choice: he ought to have separated out those acts that bore the royal assent in the form 'le roi le veult' and sent them for printing. But that rule looks better in the books than in reality, even supposing that we can rely on the assent as recorded on the Parliament Roll, a dubious supposition.[140] In 1 Richard III the Roll included among the common petitions assented to by the public formula an act touching wardship of lands held of the duchy of Lancaster; this was not printed. The important act of Henry VII's first Parliament which confirmed his title to the Crown was not printed, perhaps because it was taken to be more a declaration in, than an act of, Parliament; yet in form it was a Commons' petition to which the king gave his consent in a barely modified version of the public formula. 1 Henry VII c. 10, the repeal of an earlier act hostile to Italian merchants, was the product of a petition from the interests affected, received the assent *soit fait*, and appears on the Roll among the private acts, forty-six items before the first properly public act; yet it was printed, being for the purpose turned 'public' by various rephrasings which made the king ordain it, having considered the petition (recited) and been advised by both Houses. Two acts of 3 Henry VII (attainting certain rioters, and proclaiming certain acts of murder) have the public assent on the Roll but were not printed, which suggests that an arbitrary decision was made to the effect that their contents did not merit publicity or that they were really particular (in which case the assent was wrong). 4 Henry VII c. 5 was enrolled with a number of provisos; these did not make it into print, perhaps for no better reason than that they had become detached from the Original Act.

In the next reign, however, selection for printing does seem in general to agree with selection by assenting formula on the Roll – provided it is remembered that there is evidence (which it still needs a full study of the Roll to evaluate) that the clerk was capable of amending formulae on the Roll so as to reduce things to what he had come to regard as the proper order.[141] The Roll, of course, was by this time written at a date later than the sending of the acts to the printer; it cannot have helped to control printing but is more likely to have been adjusted

---

[140] Even in the later part of Henry VIII's reign, Roll and Original Act do not always agree.

[141] [See below, p. 137–8, for a proper discussion of formulae of assent.]

to what had been settled when the printer got his copy, and it may even (conceivably) have been copied from the print. Sometimes, however, formulae of assent were heeded with disconcerting results. It was presumably for this reason alone that the act of 1536 for the dissolution of the lesser monasteries, as palpably public and general an act as one could wish to find, which nevertheless was assented to *soit fait* (according to the Roll: none of the Original Acts of that session bears the formula of assent), was not printed in the sessional statute. According to Robert Aske, this helped to unleash the Pilgrimage of Grace. Aske told his interrogators that opposition to the Dissolution was enhanced by the discovery that the only printed act to refer to it (namely that which set up the Court of Augmentations) appeared to be so poorly phrased – it did not even define the dominions within which the houses were to be suppressed – that he and his fellows thought it void. He admitted that he had always supposed that another act, not printed, had actually authorized the confiscation.[142] In this he was right; but the argument shows the weight that a lawyer as early as this could place on the printed statutes with their general publicity.

By Henry VIII's time, therefore, the distinction between public and private acts had nothing to do with their import or the initiative behind them, nor necessarily with the formula of assent, which could be overridden or at other times adjusted to the real distinction: whether an act had been chosen for printing or not. And since the choice was made from among the parchment bills accumulating during the session in the House of Lords, the responsibility fell upon the clerk, who no doubt had his guidelines but on occasion acted independently. Once he ceased to enroll all acts, he omitted not only any private acts whose beneficiaries neglected to pay the fees, but even some acts he sent for printing and thereby defined as public. It will need a study of the Rolls and the Original Acts to discover what he was up to – if indeed he was up to anything and this can be discovered. Why, for instance, did he not enroll Catherine Howard's attainder and yet allow it to appear in print?

It should be added that at this early date no sessional statute supplied the list of acts passed but not printed which was always (or nearly always) included in the sessional statutes from 1571 onwards.[143] In a way this gave the print even more exclusive authority because it left the generality without guidance as to what other legislation might have

[142] *LP* xii (i), p. 411.
[143] Holdsworth, *History of English Law*, xi, 292.

107

passed and aware only of the matter in print. We have seen how this fact troubled Aske.

One last point about these early printed sessional statutes deserves a little attention because it throws an unexpected light on constitutional developments. The title-pages always carried some formal introductory description, and changes in this are not without significance. Pynson originally settled for a title which announced that the king at his Parliament held at a stated time and place, with the assent of the Lords and Commons, 'hath do to be ordained, made and enacted certain statutes and ordinances', and this was used down to 1523. In 1529, the title, for no obvious reason, switched to Latin and brevity, announcing simply that there were 'statuta ad rem publicam spectantia, edita in prima sessione parliamenti', etc. In the next session, Berthelet's first effort in effect adopted the same formula: 'statuta bonum publicum concernentia edita in parliamento', etc. Next year (having perhaps looked over Pynson's earlier work) he reverted to a cleaned-up version of the original phrasing according to which the king had 'ordetaned [*sic*] established and enacted certayne good statutes lawes and ordinances'; but on this occasion it was not only said that the acts had been made with the assent of Parliament but also 'by auctoritie of the same' – the full enacting clause which was coming to be customary for every individual act. From 1533 to 1536 (six sessions) the print baldly announced that these were 'Actes made in the parliament' etc., and this was also in effect the description employed in 1543 and 1546. In between, more solemn and lengthy phrases took over, according to which the king (full title) had held a session of Parliament 'wherein were established these actes folowyng' (1539, 1542, 1544, varied in 1540 by saying that the acts following were among many other acts). Thus, while originally the legislative authority was placed solely in the monarch, from 1529 onwards, with the single exception of 1533, the statutes were declared to have been made in the Parliament, there being no mention of the king ordaining them. One does not wish to place too heavy a burden on such formulations, but these title pages at first followed custom so regularly that innovations cannot be regarded as entirely meaningless. The meaning would seem to be that by the early 1530s the legislative authority had come to be seen as resting with the king, Lords and Commons as a body, a change of view which coincides notably with the clear signs that about that time the concept of Parliament (which now included the king) as a sovereign lawmaker replaced the concept of the king's high court of parliament giving authority by its consent to the laws made by the king.[144]

In this transformation of the institution the sessional printing of statutes played its part by providing a public and authoritative version of the acts produced in these sovereign Parliaments, available very soon after the end of each session. It may well be the case that so far as the courts are concerned even today 'in no case is the official print made conclusive evidence of the text of a statute'.[145] There may still be occasions when the courts might wish to ascertain the correct text of an act by looking at 'the original', but for the reigns of the first two Tudors they might have some difficulty in doing so. No Original Acts before 1497 or for 1523 and 1529, some acts printed that are not on the Roll, clear signs that allegedly independent and semi-official collections like that of the Exchequer volume were in fact copied from the print, the question marks that hang over the Rolls (especially those not signed by the clerk by way of certification into Chancery): in that state of affairs, the printed acts not only will but must become the normal evidence for the wording of an act – the version that people in general and the courts in particular will rely on. Printing made the acts rapidly known all over the realm, whether they were formally proclaimed by order of the Crown or privately sent out to the likes of Lord Lisle, Robert Aske and many others; and thus it gave equitable sense to the old principle that laws made for the commonwealth must be obeyed by all the commonwealth. For practical purposes, and virtually for all occasions of the law, printing settled the effect as well as the text of parliamentary law; it is no wonder that developments in judicial interpretation which restricted the freedom of the judges and elevated the authority of statute did not come until after the acts were regularly in print.[146] In the circumstances it was just as well that, despite his haste, his often muddled foliation, and his frequent and bewildering reprints, the king's printer took good care to print sound texts.

---

[144] Cf. above, ii, 32–6.

[145] P. H. Winfield, *The Chief Sources of English Legal History* (Cambridge, Mass., 1925), 94. There is a hint that Thomas Cromwell, that conservative radical, shared these doubts about printed copies. In 1535 he paid the clerk for certified copies of three acts (*LP* xi, 135), two of them private and not printed, but the third the Statute of Uses. Surely he had a copy of the sessional print which contained it?

[146] Cf. the discussion in S. E. Thorne's introduction to his edition of *Discourse upon the Exposicion & Understandinge of Statutes* (San Marino, Calif., 1942).

III. THE ROLLS OF PARLIAMENT, 1449–1547*

1

The Roll of Parliament, supposedly the master record of that institution, actually occupied that place until some time in the sixteenth century. Yet it has never been systematically studied for the period after Parliament had institutionally emerged in the middle of the fourteenth century. Since the rolls down to 1504 and for several of the Parliaments of Henry VIII have been in print for some 200 years, their contents have been used often enough,[147] but no one has subjected the originals to scrutiny, so that the documents themselves have not been made to tell what they can. This paper will consider the rolls for the years 1449–1547,[148] the period covered by the extant early journals of the House of Lords which have already been analysed.[149] The manuscripts reveal that the print hides many interesting features, but since the texts as printed are sound enough it will at times be convenient to use them for purposes of reference.[150]

In the course of these ninety-eight years considerable changes occurred in the contents and appearance of the roll, reflecting institutional changes of marked significance. The first point to note is that until the foundation of the Public Record Office they were not located in one archive. The person responsible for the writing of the roll was the clerk of the Parliaments who, since until the later sixteenth century there was no formal parliamentary archive,[151] was supposed to deposit them in the care of the master of the Rolls in the Rolls Chapel in Chancery Lane. At intervals, the master transferred older rolls (not only

---

* [*HJ* 22 (1979), 1–29.]

147 *RP* go down to 19 Henry VII; *LJ* vol. 1, prints the rolls for 4, 5, 14 & 15, 21, 22, 23, 24 and 27 Henry VIII for which no Journal survives.

148 PRO, C65/99–154.

149 Above, no. 34(i).

150 The only earlier attempt at an analysis of the rolls was made by H. L. Gray, *The Influence of the Commons on Early Legislation* (Cambridge, Mass., 1932), but he did not go to the manuscripts. Unfortunately even the severe critique in S. B. Chrimes, *English Constitutional Ideas in the XV Century* (Cambridge, 1936), 236–48, removes only part of the confusion created by Gray's false categories and misunderstandings, though on occasion he gets a point right. Since it seems pointless to argue with him at every turn, I have in the main avoided reference to his book.

151 Cf. M. F. Bond, 'The formation of the archives of parliament', *Journal of the Society of Archivists* i (1957), 151 ff.

those of Parliament) to the main government archive in the Tower. This transfer usually took place after quite a long time, presumably when it was thought that the material was no longer needed for immediate use by the Chancery clerks. Thus it was not until 7 October 1499 that the records for the first ten years of Edward IV, including the rolls for four Parliaments (1, 3, 4, 8 Edward IV), reached the Tower.[152] The remainder of that reign's material had certainly been deposited by the 1560s when William Bowyer, keeper of the records there, made a list of what he had in his care.[153] But no later records left the Rolls Chapel thereafter, even though Bowyer made a major effort to have them moved. His entry upon office cannot be precisely dated, but he was certainly in charge by early 1564 when he began to assert himself against the other record depositories, especially against the attempts of Henry, Lord Stafford, chamberlain of the Exchequer, to gain a foothold in the Tower on the grounds that the Exchequer records also ultimately went there.[154]

It appears from Stafford's complaints that the Tower archive was both overcrowded and dilapidated, but a few years later Bowyer could claim to have so far improved matters that he felt able to receive the records from Richard III onwards out of the Chancery. It would seem that he tried to get hold of those Rolls Chapel records in April–June 1567, at the time when his position was at last regularized by patent. He obtained the valuable support of 'the old lord treasurer', the marquess of

---

[152] *Egerton papers*, ed. J. P. Collier (CS vol. xii, 1840), 1–3.

[153] BL, Harl. MS 94, fos. 43–8, 65r–72v: 'A perfect calendar of all the records remaining in the Tower of London'; fos. 65r–72v have been misbound and really belong before fo. 44.

[154] Stafford made his move, in memorials addressed to William Cecil, in January 1564 (PRO, SP 12/33, fos. 2–3; BL, Lansd. MS 113, fos. 103–5). By this time Bowyer was in effect keeper, but his patent was dated 18 June 1567 when Edward Hales, himself appointed in April 1550 in succession to Richard Eton, surrendered his (*C[alendar of] P[atent] R[olls] Eliz.* iv, no. 496; *LP* xii (ii), 796[16]). In a letter dated only March 1, but addressed to Cecil as secretary and master of the wards (which latter office he obtained in January 1561), Bowyer explained that eight years before he had been urged by Sir Thomas Parry, lately dead, to take the office (BL, Lansd. MS 113, fos. 106–8). Parry died in 1560; before 1558 he had been no more than comptroller of Princess Elizabeth's Household, and such influence as he had therefore stood higher under Edward VI than Mary. We may therefore suppose that Bowyer's connection with the Tower began in about 1552–3, but that he did not gain formal possession of the office until much later. As he told Cecil, he had for those eight years been busy sorting and cataloguing the Tower archive, but he hinted that his proper reward had not yet come. Presumably Hales held on to the office, and Bowyer can at best have been his deputy. A further complication is introduced by Robert Bowyer's note of 3 Jan. 1605 that he in turn became keeper thirty-seven years 'and more' after his father's death (BL, Harl. MS 94, fo. 47v), a timespan which included his father's formal appointment.

Winchester,[155] and in a manner of speaking he was successful. Elizabeth signed a signet warrant to the master of the Rolls, and the resulting patent, dated 2 June 1567, ordered the transfer of all records from 1 Richard III to the last years of Mary.[156] A month earlier, on 1 May, the clerk of the Parliaments (Francis Spilman or Spelman) had been similarly instructed with respect to the parliamentary material in his keeping, an order which suggests that since 1484 there had been irregularities in the clerks' relations with the Chancery.[157] However, these orders were never executed. Bowyer seems to have been well aware of his rivals' powers of resistance even to letters under the great seal, for, surprisingly, his urgent memorials to Cecil were produced after the date on which the Chancery received the instructions supposedly embodying his victory.[158] In fact, none of the post-1484 records ever reached the Tower, being found still in the Rolls Chapel in 1732 and 1800.[159]

Thus the Rolls of Parliament ended up in two places: down to the last Parliament of Edward IV (1483) they rested in the Tower, thereafter in the Rolls Chapel. The division (even though it may have come about by accident and negligence) draws significant attention to the year 1484, and it had consequences. Later investigators habitually treated the Rolls Chapel series as different from the Tower series, frequently describing the former as statute rolls and regarding them as linked to the medieval roll correctly known by that name, whereas in fact we are dealing with one continuous series of Rolls of Parliament. And it seems probable that the failure of early seventeenth-century scholars to use the Tudor rolls – a failure which gave their researches so firmly medieval an air – owed something to the inconvenience (or worse) involved in going to the Chancery; the research was directed by people like Robert Bowyer and Henry Elsyng who as keepers of the records in the Tower naturally looked mainly to their own archives. This included not only

---

[155] SP 12/42, fo. 10, Winchester to Cecil, 11 Apr. 1567. Winchester calls Bowyer keeper of the queen's records in the Tower, two months before the delivery of the warrant for his patent into the Chancery (see previous note). This was the second letter urging Bowyer's suit upon the secretary. Winchester is now known to have been a champion of conservatism in administration.

[156] Ibid. fos. 185A–186; *CPR Eliz.* iv, no. 659.

[157] Ibid. no. 451. But cf. below, p. 133–4.

[158] SP 12/43, fos. 7–16, two appeals of 15 June 1567.

[159] *Report of the Committee Appointed to View the Cottonian Library* (First Series of Reports, i), 519–20, 525–6; *Reports from the Select Committee Appointed to Inquire into the State of the Public Records of the Kingdom* (ordered to be printed by the House of Commons, 4 July 1800), 84.

the rolls but also sessional bundles of 'petitions' (the originals of the private acts as passed) which were printed by the editors of *Rotuli Parliamentorum* but have since been broken up and distributed among the Public Record Office's 'Ancient Petitions'. Such petitions were found down to the end of Edward IV's reign, even though in January 1605, when Robert Bowyer checked his father's catalogue, he alleged that he could find none after 1442.[160] However, in 1800 the select committee of the House of Commons investigating the public records were told that the petitions stored at the Tower extended from Edward I to 1478.[161]

Apart from the change in location, one other external characteristic distinguished the later rolls from the earlier. From 1 Richard III they were rolled up from the foot instead of the head, the cover membrane now being attached to the first membrane of writing. If this was not purely an accident (a suspicion which the consistent observance of the change makes very unlikely) it suggests that the earlier rolls were written and assembled piece by piece, the cover being sewn on when the business was completed, whereas the later ones were put together in one go, rolled up, and then wrapped in the cover. This is therefore another strong indication that 1484 marked a positive change in the roll, and we shall thus first consider the last medieval rolls in the old Tower archive, those for 1449–83.

2

From the spring Parliament of 1449 (27 Henry VI) to the parliament of 22 Edward IV (1483: dissolved by the king's death) there were fourteen Parliaments comprising thirty-seven sessions.[162] On the other hand, there are fifteen rolls.[163] The discrepancy arises from the fact that the much prorogued Parliament of 1472-5 yielded three separate rolls, whereas Henry VI's 'readeption' Parliament of 1470 produced none. Normally the clerk compiled one roll for every Parliament, regardless of adjournments and prorogations which he recorded on the roll as they occurred. In all this time only two men held the office – John Fawkes down to the Parliament of 1467, and John Gunthorpe for the rest of

[160] BL, Harl. MS 94, fo. 47v.
[161] *Reports etc.* 52.
[162] *Handbook of British Chronology* ed. F. M. Powicke and E. B. Fryde; 2nd edn, 1961), 531–4. I have tried to count only actual meetings.
[163] C65/99–113.

Edward IV's reign.[164] As one would expect, Fawkes's long tenure (from 1447: eleven parliaments in all) created a standard form for the roll; Fawkes, the first clerk who can quite confidently be credited with keeping a sort of journal for the Upper House, was evidently a systematizer.[165]

As settled by him, the basic structure of the roll consisted of three parts: the opening events of the session, proceedings in the course of the session (bills and other matters, recorded in a species of narrative), and the supposedly public bills comprehended under the heading, 'Item diverse communes peticiones exhibite fuerunt in presenti parliamento in eodem existentes quarum tenores cum suis responsionibus hic inferius insequuntur'. The preliminaries recorded the opening day and meeting place, the opening address (usually given by the lord chancellor), the order to the Commons to elect and present their Speaker, the appointment of receivers and triers of petitions, and the Speaker's presentation. In 28 Henry VI (1449) and 3 Edward IV (1463), Fawkes exceptionally recorded adjournments and prorogations also on the first membrane;[166] usually these are noted (with occasional lapses) in the course of the proceedings. This second section of the roll always began with the grant of supply (if one was made) and included such private bills as were enrolled; it observed a roughly chronological order but was not written up continuously. This is proved by the many blanks left on the parchment. Thus on 16 July 1449, the Commons are recorded as petitioning for an appropriation of supply, but the note that they did so terminates well clear of the foot of the membrane, whereas the petition itself – manifestly written out separately and presumably at some earlier stage – starts on the next membrane.[167] In 1453, the record of private business is interrupted by the presentation of the duke of York's demands: this fills about three quarters of a separate membrane, the rest of which is blank, and there is a similar blank at the foot of the preceding membrane.[168] It would be tedious to multiply examples of this frequent occurrence; suffice it to say that the appearance of the roll, with its many gaps on the parchment and changes in handwriting, makes it perfectly clear that it was written out in separate parts which were then assembled and sewn together. Some of the material looks as though it had been prepared for use in Parliament and then simply incorporated instead of

---

[164] *Guide to the Records of Parliament* (1971), 303. Baldwin Hyde, who held office between Fawkes and Gunthorpe, never had a Parliament to serve.
[165] Above, pp. 78–81.   [166] C65/100, 107.   [167] C65/99, mm. 3–4.   [168] C65/102, mm. 17–19.

being copied again. Fawkes enrolled few private bills, that is petitions on behalf of an individual or a body which, when enacted, did not become part of the statute of the Parliament; only important personages or groups seem occasionally to have thought it worth their while to get their acts recorded as part of the proceedings. Bills on behalf of the Crown do seem to have got enrolled invariably. The earls of Richmond and Devon put their assented-to petitions on the roll in 1453, and so did the merchants of the Staple in 1455,[169] but most beneficiaries did without the record.[170] Especially because practice was later to change drastically, this is a not unimportant indication of the standing of Parliament in legal and in public opinion. Of course, these were the years when the main business of Parliament too often touched the political struggles of the magnates, matters which were entered in a sequence of resolutions and orders, with king's business (allocations to the Household, acts of resumption which can also appear among the public petitions) interspersed. There is a narrative structure to this record, but it is not day-by-day, even after the time (1461) that evidence for the keeping of a day-book of entries survives.

At this stage, then, the roll is in effect a current record of parliamentary business which was not, however, written up continuously. The one exception to the chronological arrangement is the third section, the *communes peticiones*, enrolled in one block at the end and including bills both assented to and vetoed. This section always starts on a new membrane and was clearly composed separately for attachment to the roll. Until 1459,[171] it always appears at the foot of the roll, even if there had been a prorogation and therefore more than one session, but in Fawkes's last two Parliaments (3 & 4 Edward IV: 1463–4; 7 & 8 Edward IV: 1467–8; C65/107–8) we find groups of *communes peticiones* entered at the end of sessions and therefore apparently in the middle of the roll.[172] The make-up of the roll somewhat disguises what happened because in both instances the *communes peticiones* of the first session, though they start on new membranes, do not run to the end of a

---

[169] *RP* v, 250–4, 295–7. Such enrolment was at the suit of the party: Chrimes, *Constitutional Ideas*, 252.

[170] The extant bills with the royal response, printed as 'Petitions' in *RP* after the sessional rolls, show that such private acts passed all right.

[171] No common petitions were presented in the Parliament of 39 Henry VI (1460) which yielded two acts. One voided the doings of the preceding Parliament: this appears on the roll as the first business, after the presentation of the Speaker (C65/105). The other, a very short law-reform measure, resulted from a private petition (*RP* v, 387–8).

[172] Below, p. 119.

membrane, the spare parchment being used for the formula introducing the forthcoming prorogued meeting, but in reality Fawkes completed the roll for the session as he had been accustomed to completing it for the Parliament and opened the business of the next session on a fresh membrane. At the end he sewed the sessional records into one roll. Here, therefore, he displays a novel recognition of the significance of sessions; perhaps we have here the first sign that business not completed in one session could not be continued after the prorogation. However, since practice soon reverted to earlier form, it is evident that if such notions began to be entertained nothing had yet been firmly settled.

In the next Parliament of Edward IV – the much prorogued meeting of 1472–5 – the roll at first sight seems to have undergone some changes. It was, of course, the work of a new clerk. In the first place, Gunthorpe devoted three rolls to this Parliament.[173] However, so far from this indicating a further recognition of the importance of sessions, it would appear to have been no more than a mechanical accident. Though the second roll happens to start with a reassembly after prorogation, the third begins in the middle of a session, and other prorogations and reconvenings are recorded currently, in the body of the rolls. The public acts of the whole seven-sessions Parliament are enrolled in one *communes peticiones* section appended at the very end, after the entry recording the dissolution of the Parliament.[174] Thus we have three rolls for seven sessions, but in the clerk's view they manifestly still formed one roll for one Parliament. It therefore appears that the division resulted from nothing more distinguished than a desire not to have too insufferably long a roll to handle.

In the second place, Gunthorpe started enrolling large numbers of private bills, describing them (as by tradition they were to be described) as petitions and recording the king's assent. In introducing these petitions he haphazardly varied the formula, using 'sub eo qui sequitur tenore', 'in hec verba', 'cuius quidem peticionis tenor sequitur in his verbis', 'hanc seriem verborum continens', 'sub his verbis sequentibus', 'sub hac serie verborum', quite without rhyme or reason. He was not the first or last clerk to use a bit of variety in these matters, but no one else employed so many and such extravagant formulae. In the later sessions Crown bills drove out private business, and of the six passed in

[173] C65/109–11.

[174] Cf. *RP* vi, 153b for the dissolution followed by the public acts (the last three of which are Crown bills, not *communes peticiones*). According to the Statute Roll, of the thirteen acts of this Parliament nine belonged to 12 Edward IV and four to 14 Edward IV.

the last session only one varies from the simplest formula – 'in hec verba' – which was to become that most commonly employed thereafter. It is not unreasonable to see in all this a reaction to a novel pressure to get private acts enrolled, with practice settling down after some experimenting, but perhaps also a case of clerical fastidiousness, an inclination to reduce the tedium of the work by a little elegant variation. But while there were many more private acts on the roll, the structure of the record remained unaltered. The reasons for this flood are extra-parliamentary: the upheavals of Edward's second capture of the throne seem to have led to an agitated search for the security of enrolment on the part of the much affected members of the ruling order. In addition one cannot rule out the possibility that the new clerk discovered the benefit of enrolment fees and therefore encouraged enrolment.[175]

The appearance of change thus misleads: on the contrary, Gunthorpe's practice testifies to the endurance of the format settled by Fawkes – preliminaries, proceedings, *communes peticiones*. Nor did Gunthorpe make any changes in his last two Parliaments (1478, 1483)[176] when again he ignored the tentative precedent set by Fawkes for treating sessions separately. Since this had not caught on in the long Parliament of 1472–5, we must suppose that in reality no one had yet arrived at the later notions which made sessions self-contained; either Fawkes did not mean as much as he seemed to do by the arrangement of his last two rolls, or he was 'ahead of his time' and out of step. The enrolment of private bills continued active, with still some variation in the formula, though 'in hec verba' now predominated. What is never found in private bills is the famous magic formula 'formam actus in se continens'; before 1484 this occurs only for bills introduced on behalf of the Crown.[177] Technically, only the king put in bills in predetermined form, and he put in a lot of them. In these Parliaments of Edward IV a

---

[175] I am not aware of any evidence for the payment of any bill fees in pre-Tudor Parliaments, but that may be only my ignorance. Seeing what happened in all government departments, it is hard to believe that the parliamentary officers served private interests for nothing.

[176] C65/112–13.

[177] Gray, *Commons' Influence*, 179–80. He made an invalid distinction between earlier 'cedule' and later 'bille' like that of 1483 for the royal Household (*RP* vi, 198). The marginal title there, 'Pro Hospicio Regis', is one of the not infrequent editorial additions in *RP* to the truth of the manuscript. Marginal titles might be worth studying, but there is too little profit to repay prolonged exposition. In general it would appear that virtually all those placed against entries before the common petitions were written by the enrolling clerk, while all those written against items in the *communes peticiones* were added later.

very large number of bills were promoted on behalf of the Crown which did not become part of the statute and were therefore regarded and treated as private bills. Where under Henry VI the roll is full of political issues, under Edward IV it enregisters the king's business and royal government. This, however, is a change too obviously produced by historical events to be treated as institutionally significant. What should not be overlooked is the formal predominance of the king whose bills are treated differently from anybody else's – described as framed in the form of the act, and regarded as passed when agreed to by Lords and Commons without formal assent from the Crown.

Thus down to 1483 the roll preserved both a meaningful function and a sameness of format. Its structure was determined by the duration of Parliament, not sessions, and its purpose was to record parliamentary business and proceedings. Though formalized, this record was still flexible enough to reflect changes in the business handled by Parliament.

3

Two aspects of this late-medieval roll require special consideration: the composition of the *communes peticiones* section, and the significance of the frequent provisos added to bills. To take the former first: how did the clerk know what bills he was to group in that section? Since it contained bills promoted in either House,[178] we cannot suppose that the selection was made at the beginning of the Parliament, nor is it conceivable that all those bills were taken together at the end of the session – never any redress of grievances until supply had been granted and the king and the great men had been satisfied! In any case, the throwing together of all the acts of the 1472–5 Parliament, passed in different sessions, disproves any such supposition. The section formed the basis of the statute (the public acts) of any given Parliament:[179] no act was included unless its bill appeared among the *communes peticiones*, though not all those bills resulted in acts.[180] There is conclusive evidence for this relationship in the covering note on a bundle of common

---

[178] E.g. Gray, *Commons' Influence*, 98. Gray's category of 'official bills' makes no sense, and his attempt to classify by 'importance' is pointless, but he has proved that bills in the *communes* section could originate in either Commons or Lords.

[179] This is what Chrimes meant (*Constitutional Ideas*, 249) when he said that statute signified 'any act of parliament of which the courts had cognizance' – the correct definition of public acts as against private (W. S. Holdsworth, *History of English Law*, xi, 290).

[180] The exception of the 1460 Parliament, whose roll misses out the section, has been noted (above, n. 117).

petitions for 1449–54, endorsed as the bills 'unde statuta sunt edita'.[181]
Only one public act is not found anywhere on the roll – 27 Henry VI,
c.3, for alien merchants. The petition, however, survives,[182] so that the
most likely explanation of this freak is that it got misplaced in the
sorting; presumably it dropped from the bundle of common petitions
from which the acts of the session had been drawn.

That covering note shows that at some stage certain bills were
gathered together to be translated into statute form. Who did this and
how? How were they chosen, how did bills become acts, and how did
the bills in question get enrolled on the Parliament Roll as *communes
peticiones?* The usual answer to these questions is that the Council made
the selection, the judges framed the statute, and the clerks of the
Parliaments then produced the formal statute (the transcript of the acts
which was sent to departments and courts, and belatedly and
inefficiently was enrolled on the Statute Roll), but this answer depends
on a single entry in the Council register of 1423.[183] This shows that on
that occasion the agreed bills of the Parliament were read to the lords of
the Council by the clerk who was then ordered to give the bills 'qui
erunt statuta' to the judges for drafting, to hand over copies of the acts
touching 'gubernacionem dominorum de consilio et regni' to the clerk
of the Council, and at the same time to enroll the lot in Chancery (that
is, write up the Parliament Roll), 'ut moris est'. But that 'ut moris est'
refers only to the making of the roll; we never hear of the Council
intervening in this fashion on any other occasion, and what happened in
the recently created Regency Council of Henry VI's minority cannot be
taken, without later evidence of which there is none, to have been the
usual practice. The Council is not known ever to have intervened again
to direct the clerk, and the judges' growing inclination to interpret the
statutes by divining the intention of legislators throws much doubt on
the supposition that they themselves were responsible for the texts.[184] In
an earlier age, when unquestionably they had done the drafting, they
did not hesitate to say so in court.[185]

---

[181] Gray, *Commons' Influence*, 399; I have amended his case endings, falsely extended from the
manuscript abbreviations.
[182] *RP* v, 155.
[183] *Proceedings of the Privy Council* (ed. N. H. Nicolas), iii, 22. See Gray, *Commons' Influence*, 389
(who invents yet another false case ending for *statuta*), and Chrimes, *Constitutional Ideas*, 228
(who mistranslates 'redigantur in mudum' – to make a fair copy – as 'rendered into clear
language', and more distortingly 'simul', at the same time, as 'as soon as').
[184] Chrimes, *Constitutional Ideas*, 293–5.
[185] As did Hengham C J in Edward I's reign, addressing counsel: 'do not gloss the statute for we

The presence among the *communes peticiones* of bills that did not appear in the statute makes plain that the defining of a bill as *communis* did not await the end of the Parliament. Those that the king vetoed explain themselves: they would obviously not become acts. They also, however, prove that the statute was not (as apparently it was in 1423) normally drawn from bills agreed to only; a vetoed bill must have been named *communis* at the start and not the end of its parliamentary career. Two bills (nos. 22–23) were in 1449 referred to the prelates; this amounts to a provisional veto or postponement, and they too naturally were not treated as enacted. Acts of resumption, which in 1449 and 1450 were enrolled among the common petitions, never became public acts, perhaps for no better reason than their inordinate length, perhaps because (exceptionally) they were not done with when the Parliament went home. The large number of provisos on behalf of individuals attached to them (which made them so long) shows that they were nevertheless sufficiently well known, though occasional belated amendments by signet letter[186] may indicate that some victims remained unaware of them uncomfortably long. The remaining omissions fall into no particular pattern, though the bills do seem to have less of a general character than was usual for public acts: bills for the abbey of Bury St Edmunds (1450), the attainder of Sir William Oldhall (1453), confirming a patent for London (1467), for named private individuals (1472). One would not expect a perfect bureaucratic order in fifteenth-century Parliaments; as it is, the coincidence between *communes peticiones* and public acts is remarkably close.

Inclusion in the special section, therefore, is the criterion that distinguishes public from private acts, not the formula of the royal assent which could be either *le roi le veult* or *soit fait comme est desire*. The selection was plainly made before the writing of the roll, and the inclusion of vetoed bills means that it was made in the course of the session. It seems obvious that public bills must have been defined as *communes* at their introduction, on the ground that they touched the common interest, a fact reinforced by the likelihood (unproven) that even at this date promoters of what became private acts had to pay fees to various officials. It follows that the decision whether a bill was private or public – whether in the end it would get enrolled in the second or

know better than you; we made it' (T. F. T. Plucknett, *Statutes and their Interpretation in the First Half of the Fourteenth Century* [Cambridge, 1922], 50).
[186] Below, p. 122.

third section of the roll — must have been arrived at at its presentation by agreement between its promoters and the clerks. So much for selection. Once passed, the common petitions had to be redrafted into acts, and this, done after the end of the Parliament, required two things. Petitioning formulae had to be removed or changed into enacting formulae, and the English petition had to be translated into the French of the statute. Both these steps were by this time quite mechanical: the act was produced not by drafting a genuine answer to a genuine request, but merely by formally rephrasing the petition. Thus anyone trained in the technical skills could do it; no question arose at this point of initiative which lay solely with the person who had drafted the bill and the promoters of amendments in the course of passage. The resulting statute — the parchment transcript of the public acts of a given Parliament — was not, as has been supposed, the work of the clerk of the Parliament; it was the responsibility of the Chancery because copies had to be made under the great seal for exemplification and distribution. On the other hand, the clerk of the Parliament knew what acts should be so transcribed. The chances therefore are that the work of producing the statute of the session was committed to him and to the responsible officer of Chancery, the clerk (master) of the Rolls.[187] The conjecture receives strength from the fact that it was these two officers that the judges in the Exchequer Chamber consulted in Pilkington's Case (1455) as the acknowledged experts on bill procedure.[188]

Once the statute had been put together, the two men went their separate ways. The clerk of the Rolls became responsible for having the statute written out and enrolled on the Statute Roll, a task notoriously carried out very inadequately in this period: as early as the 1560s, no enrolments were found of the acts for 9–23 Henry VI.[189] Negligence in enrolment does not, however, prove that the roll was little regarded; in Chancery fashion it was bound to be the master record of the statutes, especially as the Chancery apparently did not file office copies of the parchment statute except on the roll.[190] Meanwhile the clerk of the Parliaments took back the *communes peticiones*, from which he and his

---

[187] Gray, *Commons' Influence*, 396–7. My earlier failure to regard Gray led me to postulate as a likely conjecture the production of such engrossed statutes of which in fact a number survive (above, p. 98).

[188] Pilkington's Case has been twice reprinted from the Year Book: Chrimes, *Constitutional Ideas*, 360–2, and *The Fane Fragment of the 1461 Lords Journal* (ed. W. H. Dunham), 99–102.

[189] BL, Harl. MS 94, fo. 47v.

[190] Ibid.

colleague had drawn the acts, to enroll them at the end of his Parliament Roll, omitting any annotations they had received in the course of passage but noting the formulae of assent endorsed on the bill. From 1453 (29 Henry VI), but not before, the order of the common petitions follows that of the statute with great faithfulness, which indicates that the clerk kept the file of bills in the order in which they had been translated into acts.[191] Contrary to what is sometimes alleged, he did not at this time sign the roll before depositing it in the Rolls Chapel. The bills enrolled as *communes* were filed, but since an authoritative text existed on the roll they were neglected and have in the main disappeared. Unenrolled private acts the clerk kept in bundles for future reference; how many of those that had been enrolled at their promoters' suit were preserved cannot, in the present state of the archive, be established. The bundles joined the rolls in the Rolls Chapel, from whence they were ultimately transferred to the Tower.

We turn to provisos. The rolls offer some evidence on the important question of parliamentary authority. Acts, of course, were supposedly the product of a tripartite agreement and by this time, though often described as being made by the king, also usually cited the authority of the whole Parliament. However, there is irrefutable evidence that acts could be further amended after they had passed both Houses, by means of provisos added either as part of the royal assent or any time after it. It was even possible for the Crown to alter acts already enrolled. In November 1472, Edward IV modified the act of resumption passed in 1465 by signet letters exempting further individuals from its operation. These were sewn onto the membrane, a fact disguised by the printed version.[192] Another signet letter of 20 May 1478 ordered amendments in the phrasing of exceptions granted to the resumption act of 1472; these were accordingly made on the roll, and the authorizing letter was again sewn to the membrane.[193] Acts of resumption were the most common occasion for these belated interventions. In form they consisted of quite a short general cancellation of royal grants to which large numbers of excepting provisos, on separate parchment schedules, were added after

[191] Occasional lapses are only minor clerical errors. In 1453 (C65/102) one bill slipped out of sequence; in 1463–4 (C65/107) the bill for 4 Edward IV, c. 1 was entered twice, at the beginning of the *communes peticiones* for each session. The multiple sessions of Edward IV's Parliaments did lead to discrepancies in the order, presumably because the work was not done immediately after the making of the statute.
[192] C65/107, m. 15; *RP* v, 516–17. The letters were addressed jointly to the master of the rolls and the clerk of the Parliaments.
[193] C65/110, m. 17; *RP* vi, 92.

passage.[194] These exceptions were, of course, sued for by the parties concerned and added on the king's sole authority; though they did not receive agreement from either House or the formal royal assent, they were valid in law. However, there are other acts that received this treatment. Using original acts and the printed rolls, Gray satisfactorily established that enrolment of provisos after the formula of assent always signified modifications of the act made after it had passed both Houses, either in the form of an assent conditional upon those additions, or by means of separate provisos added on schedules.[195] There are numerous examples of this practice, though until 1478 all are confined to private acts. The one proviso seemingly added to a public act turns out to be a clerical mistake. On the roll, the 1461 act for sheriffs (1 Edward IV, c. 2) is followed by a surprising exception in favour of the dean and chapter of St Martin le Grand,[196] but no such proviso appears in the act itself. The enrolment of the proviso is surrounded by large areas of blank parchment, as though the clerk had left room for a longer entry. Evidently we have here one of those detached and lost provisos, written in where room could be found, for whose occasional occurrence evidence can be found elsewhere. Why there should have been room left between two of the common petitions (one agreed, the other vetoed) must remain a mystery.

There is thus no doubt about the Crown's ability unilaterally to modify acts already passed, though it needs to be remembered that such modifications extended only to the excepting of individuals from the

---

[194] The first act of resumption in our period (1450: *RP* v, 300–20) took the form of a Commons' petition assented to by the king with the reservation that his duty to his subjects called for exceptions 'contained in certain schedules' (Gray, *Commons' Influence*, 186, n. 57). Later acts, claiming to emanate from the Crown, became routine, but the assents specified that the king wished to make exceptions (e.g. *RP* v, 517). Cf. in general B. P. Wolffe, 'Acts of Resumption in Lancastrian Parliaments', *EHR* 73 (1958), 583–613.

[195] Gray, in his chapter on 'the amending of bills' (*Commons' Influence*, 164–200), makes heavy weather of allegedly earlier and later methods. Since the amendments undoubtedly represent responses to individual suits it does not matter in what manner they came to be attached to the bill: they were always signs of royal favour to suitors. Gray held (pp. 172–3) that the evidence of enrolment ceased to be reliable in 1478 when allegedly two bills treated identically at the assent were given different treatment on the roll, in that in one case the provisos followed the assent and in the other preceded it. But this seems to be wrong: the enrolment of the second bill, against unlawful games (*RP* vi, 188) notes no provisos at all. Gray's note (p. 172, n. 25) shows that though provisos at one time had been attached to the bill they are not there now; it may be that they were lost, or dropped from the bill as prematurely enacted, before enrolment.

[196] C65/107, m. 43 (*RP* v, 566–7). The proviso was in fact entered twice, being also attached to an act of the same session for the treasurer of Calais (ibid. 510). Perhaps it really belonged there, though it does not make much better sense in that place.

operation of an act. The power was never used to amend public acts until Edward IV in his last Parliament (1483) added provisos to his assent to three common bills, and these exemptions were of the same kind as those previously confined to private acts.[197] They were all, therefore, akin to later licences *non obstante*. Nevertheless, there is an important difference between provisos and licences which throws light on the development of political doctrine touching acts of Parliament. In the fifteenth century, the dispensing power operated by altering the agreed text of an act; later, that text became sacrosanct, and dispensations had to take the form of special letters patent. It should be added that the evidence of the roll occasionally helps to reveal that a proviso on a separate schedule was an amendment made in the second House. That same act for sheriffs was so amended by a proviso enrolled before the assent; it was in fact added by the Lords on 10 December 1461.[198]

4

With the roll for Richard III's only Parliament (1484) we enter a new phase of the history of this record, a transitional phase which may be said to have extended to the Parliament of 1523. There are fifteen rolls for the twelve Parliaments and eighteen sessions of these forty years.[199] The roll for 1 Henry VII is in two parts, the second being reserved for the resumption act of that year. Of the Parliaments prorogued into several sessions, only that of 1512–14 produced a separate roll for each of its three sessions; in 1523, the fact that there were two sessions is noted in the heading of the roll but otherwise ignored. Though it is possible to discover some continuous and developing principles in the making of the roll, there are also many confusions and, as it were, backslidings, not unconnected with the frequent changes in the persons responsible. No fewer than five clerks attended upon these Parliaments. Thomas Hutton served only in that of Richard III. He was succeeded by John Morgan (1485–95), Richard Hatton (1497 and 1504), John Taylor (1510–15), and Brian Tuke (from 1523 onwards). Morgan introduced the supposedly standard practice of signing the roll to certify that he had examined it, though he missed out in 1491,[200] Hatton and Taylor followed suit, but Tuke did not sign. It would, however, be rash to conclude that Morgan's predecessors and Taylor's successors did not supervise the making of the roll.

[197] *RP* vi, 221–5.   [198] Gray, *Commons' Influence*, 171; *RP* v, 494; *Fane Fragment*, 22.
[199] C65/114, 123–37. Nos. 115–22 were non-parliamentary rolls, since placed elsewhere at the PRO.   [200] C65/137.

The change that came over the roll in 1484 is approximately summed up in the contemporary endorsement on it: 'Actes of Parliament Inrolled Anno Primo Ricardi Tercij.' From now on, little appeared on the roll except the acts passed. The old narrative of proceedings had not, however, gone entirely. Thus the clerk still began with the opening ceremonies down to the presentation of the Speaker and on occasion included a note of an event in Parliament, such entries being as a rule distinguished by an introductory 'memorandum' (instead of 'item'). In Henry VII's first Parliament, the roll records, interspersed in the acts, the Commons' appearance at the bar of the House of Lords on 10 December 1485, to petition the king to marry the Lady Elizabeth of York, and the swearing of the House of Lords on 19 November to the oath against unlawful retaining.[201] The sequence of these entries suggests that there was nothing much chronological any longer about these rolls, but this impression may have been produced by a muddle in the assembling of the roll. The record for 10 December, which appears correctly on the day of prorogation, is written currently on the membrane between other matters; that for 19 November has a whole membrane to itself and may simply have been misbound. At the end of the Parliament of 1489, the Commons secured the cancellation of an unpaid part of their earlier grant of supply in exchange for a grant of a fifteenth and tenth: this is told on the roll.[202] As late as 27 June 1523, the lord chancellor's removal of the stigma of idiocy from Edward Shaa, a non-parliamentary matter apparently made public in Parliament, got onto the roll.[203] But these are now rare exceptions to the rule that the roll was really designed to record acts passed.

Even so, it is still plain that the roll was not necessarily written by one clerk, adding parchment membrane to parchment membrane; there are changes of hands and occasional blanks, though in the parsimonious reign of Henry VII these last are sometimes replaced by cut off membranes, as though the blank piece was to be used elsewhere. Furthermore, on occasion a particular section of the roll had evidently been written out independently, the resulting sheets being inserted in the roll. In 1515 this was done for the act for the general surveyors (7 Henry VIII, c. 7) which fills six membranes and just runs over into a seventh otherwise left blank; it is written in a hand very different from that of the usual writing clerk.[204] Similarly, the act of 1523 attainting the

---

[201] *RP* vi, 278, 287–8.   [202] C65/126, mm. 16–17.   [203] *LJ* i, p. cxlviii.
[204] C65/136, mm. 4–10.

late duke of Buckingham (14 & 15 Henry VIII, c. 20), filling eleven membranes and a bit of a twelfth, was evidently prepared separately, various formulae required by the roll being added later by another hand.[205] Such sensible economies of labour at any rate indicate that the roll was still 'real', not merely a formalized (and perhaps much delayed) register of acts.

Nevertheless, in the event it emerged as just that, and the transitional character of the period appears also in the manner in which acts were enrolled. In the first place, so far as we can tell, all acts passed now reached the roll, private as well as public, but vetoed bills have disappeared.[206] From 1497, when we have the original acts to compare with the roll, we know that complete enrolment was the rule, and the list of acts enrolled in 1484–95 strongly suggests that the practice had become established before. We saw that the number of private acts enrolled increased greatly in 1472–5; but since there were few in 1478 and hardly any in 1483, we must suspect a genuine innovation in 1484. One might wish to argue more confidently from the newly regular marginal headings to bills ('an act for', or simply 'pro'), which suggests a novel bureaucratic routine, but since these are by no means always contemporary with the roll they prove only that later clerks, checking the roll, thought of them as statute rolls which should bear the titles of acts.[207] If it was still true, as it had been in 1455, that enrolment of private acts happened at the suit of the party, we must suppose that parties were now in effect being constrained to sue routinely, and presumably also that the clerk thus drew a conveniently enlarged income from enrolment fees. The Original Acts – the parchment bills as passed, and the successors to the medieval files of petitions – are missing for 1484–95; preserved with a novel care from 1497 (though those for 1523 and 1529 were lost at some early stage), they never left the custody of the clerk, which is why they are now found at the Record Office of the House of Lords instead of the Public Record Office.

From 1484, when sessional printing of statutes began, there is no

---

[205] C65/137, mm. 24–35.

[206] One bill vetoed in 1510 exists among the original acts at the HLRO. It is not on the roll.

[207] These marginal titles cannot be analysed with confidence. Handwriting proves that on many rolls they were added later, one man going over a long run of them, but contemporary notes also occur. Thus the famous Star Chamber Act (3 Henry VII, c. 1) bears two – a contemporary title reading 'pro Camera Stellata' and a later addition reading 'An Acte geving the Court of Starchamber authority to punnyshe dyvers mysdemeanors'. The other public acts on that roll have only later titles. On the other hand, in 1485 the writing clerk himself added the titles of the public acts.

longer any problem in distinguishing between private and public acts: public acts were those printed.[208] The roll, too, attempted to distinguish between them, but clearly the clerks had difficulties in setting up a standard format and can be seen to be experimenting as well as being negligent. The instructions which John Taylor inserted into his day-book of 1510 are straightforward. He there provided proper introductory and concluding formulae for money grants, private acts (which he defined as bills *formam actus in se continentes*) and what he called *actus communes*.[209] Unfortunately, neither his practice nor that of his predecessors was as systematic as this suggests, but on the other hand, what they did tells something about the changing principles of parliamentary lawmaking.

At first, Hutton and Morgan endeavoured to preserve the old method of enrolling private bills (whether the king's or the subject's) each individually, while collecting the public acts in a final section of *communes peticiones*. They systematized the former, opening with acts for the king and the royal family, with the remainder in at least rough ranking order. Introductory formulae abandoned the variety common before 1484 and from 1489 settled down to two: bills were described as either petitions 'cuius tenor sequitur et est talis', or as bills 'formam actus in se continens', the distinction being based solely on the opening phrases of the document. If these were petitionary, the thing was a petition, if not it was a bill. Care was taken to adjust the formula of the royal assent which was always *soit fait* for petitions and *le roi le veult* for bills. The two forms of assent had lost all real meaning, being determined solely by the technical shape of the bill. Slips occurred, of course; thus a bill of 1495 for the earl of Surrey, which was addressed to the House of Commons, was correctly called a petition and assented to *soit fait*, but the assent was said to have been given 'cui bille'.[210] From 1487, standardization had reached the point where the royal assent was added to bills for the king, a real innovation which indicates a more settled routine for bill procedure; together with the fact that the king had lost his exclusive right to bills 'formam actus in se continentes', it underlines the growing reduction of the king's personal control of the parliamentary process. Formally, the Crown was coming to be treated like everybody else. In 1487 also we find the first clear instance of responses, and sometimes introductory formulae, being added by a second hand. This roll[211] was evidently put together as a register of acts

[208] Above, p. 106.   [209] Above, p. 86.   [210] *RP* vi, 478–9.   [211] C65/125.

127

and then turned into a Parliament Roll by the later additions. However, later rolls did not pick up this detail, until we come to 1523 when every act entered received its head and tail formulae from another hand.[212]

As for the public acts, the roll retained the old practice of gathering them in a separate section at the end. The introduction to the section underwent a change which may not be totally insignificant. The roll for Richard III's Parliament preserved the French version used in the previous reign: 'Dyuersez Comunez billes & peticions furent baillez en cest parlement les tenours des queux ouesque leur respunces cy ensuent.' Morgan changes this to a Latin version which called them 'communes peticiones . . . rem publicam concernentes', thus emphasizing their public character. It was only in 1529, when the roll went into retirement, that the printed statutes began to adopt variations of this formula.[213] The individual acts that follow the heading receive no separate introductions, whilst the assent, which is noted, again obeys the rule that bills get *le roi le veult* and bills in petitionary form get *soit fait*. Contrary to the usual belief that bills touching the generality were brought forward in the Commons, the original acts of 1497 and 1504 prove (through their formulae of transfer) that down to the end of Henry VII's reign public acts based on a Commons' petition (those starting 'prayen the Commons') began formally in the Lords, being thereafter sent to the Lower House for its assent;[214] the cessation of this archaic practice after 1510 again shows that we are in a period of transition. However, it is manifest that by this time the regular distinction on the roll between petition and bill is only a technicality of record-keeping and tells nothing about the actual legislative process.

In 1484, the printed public acts correspond entirely with the enrolled common petitions, even, with one displacement, in the order in which they appear. In 1485, the public acts are those listed as *communes peticiones* (though in a different order) but include also one taken from a bill enrolled in the private section – an act repealing a public act of 1 Richard III (for Italian merchants) which was framed out of a petition presented by those merchants themselves.[215] One can see why it should have been transferred to the public section. This was the last session, in all likelihood, for which the old French sessional statute was still prepared. The English print for 1485 was not produced until 1489 when the acts for the first three Parliaments of Henry VII appeared in one

---

[212] C65/137.   [213] Above, p. 108.   [214] See above, ii, 54.
[215] 1 Henry VII, c. 10; the bill is *RP* vi, 289.

publication covering in fact four sessions,[216] since the Parliament of 4
Henry VII had two, each graced on the roll with a *communes petitiones*
section. In 1485, 1487 and the first session of 1489, the roll's order of acts
differs wildly from the print, but in the second session of 1489 it agrees
entirely, and that agreement continues into 1491,[217] 1495 and 1497.
Thus, as soon as the print became available sessionally the roll and it
agreed, even as the roll had agreed with the old sessional manuscript of
statutes. However, for various reasons it is not likely that the clerk was
yet enrolling the public acts by simply copying the print, a practice
vouched for much later.[218] It was only in 1491 that the roll and the
statute agreed in every detail. Before that date, the roll used the petition
presented in Parliament, while the statute employed versions which (in
the old manner) revised petitions presented by the Commons or by
individuals into enacted form. From 1491 the act simply retained the
form of the bill which had passed both Houses and received the assent,
even if that form was petitionary: the roll and the print present identical
texts.[219] However, most rolls were written in entirety by one hand,
which makes copying from the parchment (which carried the assent)
more likely than use of the print which omitted it, and when, as was to
happen frequently down to 1523, the order of the roll differed
drastically from that of the print, the latter was clearly not the source of
the former. The roll still had a residue of independent reality in this
period of transition.

Unexpectedly, Richard Hatton's last roll (for 1504) drops the
separation of public acts from private.[220] Here, the twenty-four public
acts of the Parliament are enrolled all anyhow, intermixed with the
sixteen private acts, presumably just as they came to hand, and therefore
obviously from an unsorted bundle of original acts. Yet in spite of this,
membrane 22 carries the old (pre-1484) *communes petitiones* heading,

---

[216] Above, p. 96.

[217] One common petition of this session (touching the County Palatine of Lancaster) was not
printed (*RP* vi, 456). It was thus either relegated to the private sector before printing, or else
included among the *communes petitiones* by error.

[218] In 1610, Robert Bowyer recorded that the roll (which by then included only the public acts)
was written by an officer in the Parliament Office or the Petty Bag Office, at the clerk's
discretion. He copied the statutes from the sessional print, but the roll was then checked by the
clerk of the Parliaments against the original (parchment) acts. Bowyer added that he himself
preferred to use an underclerk of the Petty Bag because these were more skilful at writing the
chancery hand (Inner Temple, Petyt MS 538/12, fo. 359v).

[219] This is established by comparing the form of the following acts on the roll and in the print: 1
Richard III, c. 11; 1 Henry VII, c. 3; 3 Henry VII, cc. 10 and 12; 4 Henry VII, c. 3; 7 Henry VII,
c. 3; 11 Henry VII, cc. 4 and 19; 12 Henry VII, c. 6.   [220] C65/130.

which is followed by a continued mixture of private and public acts. This roll, from which no one could have determined what was to be printed and what left unprinted, offers belated but conclusive proof that the category to which each bill belonged must have been known throughout its parliamentary history; its general state also suggests that it was put together for form's sake rather than for the sake of orderly record-keeping.

The muddle left by Hatton would not do for John Taylor: we can see now why he took trouble in his so-called journal to lay down rules for the proper composition of the roll, rules which tried to revive the traditional practice. In 1510, the *communes peticiones*/public acts section reappears, to last down to 1523. In 1510 also Taylor presented the public acts in the order of the print.[221] But the marked difference between the old-fashioned classification of business on the roll, and the reality in which bills passed through in a continuous stream (the difference which Hatton has in effect shown up), soon led to confusion again. In the first session of the Parliament of 1512 the order of the common petitions bears no relation to the print, and – worse – two acts got printed which were enrolled just before the supposedly meaningful formula.[222] In the second session, the opposite trouble happened: once again the order is haphazard, and three bills are enrolled *communes* which did not reach the sessional statute.[223] Taylor restored perfect order in the third session of this Parliament (1514),[224] but for the last time. In his last Parliament (the two sessions of 1515) he managed to get all public acts into the *communes* section, though both times right out of the printed order, but on both occasions enrolled there some acts not printed.[225] This was also Tuke's experience in 1523, who in addition found that he had enrolled four public acts ahead of the public section; moreover, he or his clerk, going through the roll to add the assents, forgot to do so after the first two common petitions. It is hard to avoid the conclusion that the old care taken to extract a special collection of bills for transcription into the statute of the Parliament, and enrolment as *communes peticiones*, had,

[221] C65/131.   [222] C65/132.

[223] C65/133. The bills for financing the Great Wardrobe (mm. 11–12), for the general surveyors (mm. 13–17), and for the subsidy (mm. 18–27). Whether they were left out because they all touched the finances of the Crown or because they were exceptionally long cannot be determined; my guess is the latter, though some sort of precedent exists in the private king's acts of the fifteenth century. For subsidy acts see below, p. 140.

[224] C65/134. It is noteworthy that the sessional printing of these three sessions of Parliament was also confused and confusing; perhaps the difference in the sequence arose, as it had done in 1487–9, from the fact that the print appeared late.   [225] C65/135-6.

despite the pretended continuity of format, quite disappeared; the only thing that mattered was that bills previously defined as public should reach the printer, after which the roll was put together from the original acts without much effort at formal precision. This last occasion on which the medieval format was outwardly retained really proved the meaninglessness of the roll.

One further question touching this transitional phase of this record calls for comment. As we saw, the roll provides evidence that before 1484 the king could by belated proviso amend acts passed in both Houses and assented to by himself. This practice continued into the next period, but with a difference. Neither Richard III nor Henry VII used amending provisos with the lavish abandon of Edward IV, but both were more ready to apply them to public acts. 1 Richard III, c. 9 (for Italian merchants), 1 Henry VII, c. 6 (restriction of sanctuary), and four chapters (2, 5, 6, 15) of 4 Henry VII appear to have received such belated alterations. Unhappily, one cannot any longer be so sure that every proviso enrolled after the royal assent exemplified a royal intervention of this kind: yet another instance of the decline of the roll. Some provisos were unquestionably annexed before the assent and misplaced on the roll. Thus in 11 Henry VII one (king's) bill received a proviso declared to have been added by the king, while another had several declared to have been annexed; yet in both cases the transcript on the roll would suggest post-assent addition.[226] The rolls of this period frequently add schedules to the act after the assent and can treat ordinary amending provisos in the same way. However, some changes can safely be assigned to the king's intervention. He personally added a proviso to the money bill of 1497 to exempt the colleges of Oxford, Cambridge, Eton and Winchester;[227] and in December 1499 he ordered an alteration to be made on the roll to save a man out of an attainder passed in 1497.[228] Unlike Edward IV's similar missives, this one was not attached to the roll. Such belated correction could go back a long way: the resumption act of 1487 carried not only the usual immediate post-assent provisos but also one added by Richard Hatton and therefore at least ten years late.[229] The confusion created among the clerks by these out of turn amendments suggests that the practice was going out. In 1495, Morgan entered a proviso found loose, with the despairing note: 'Item quedam provisio facta est per dominum Regem in parliamento predicto pro

---

[226] *RP* vi, 462, 465.   [227] Ibid. 521.   [228] Letter in HLRO, Original Acts for 12 Henry VII.
[229] *RP* vi, 407.

David Philip armigero, set cui actu debeat affilari ignoratur'; and Hatton, in 1504, enrolled three provisos after the act punishing escapes from prison (19 Henry VII, c. 8) of which only the first was in the right place, the other two explicitly referring to 'this act of resumption'.[230] From 1510, royal action of this kind is never found again; Henry VII was the last king who felt able to amend parliamentary statutes after their passage was completed, and he was doing markedly less of it than his predecessors. His reign also provided the first clear example of a proviso treated like a bill by being read in at least one House.[231]

The disappearance of this form of prerogative discretion thus confirms what the history of the roll between 1484 and 1523 has indicated. On the one hand, the record grew by stages into a simple register of acts passed, and on the other it showed how the parliamentary process, hitherto derived from the notion that the House of Commons acted as the bringer of petitions before the king and his Great Council in Parliament to receive remedy there, turned into the passing of remedial bills ready-made in either House. More clearly than these things are usually allowed to appear, the rolls demonstrate a transition from earlier to later, from medieval to modern. The clerks' conservatism, which for instance tried to retain the section of common petitions, only underlined the facts of change. No doubt, Parliament was even before 1484 a proper lawmaking assembly, but by 1523 it exercised that function in a novel manner which signified a real change of attitude to the concepts of statute and legislation. When the statute book simply enregistered the bill as passed, without even such commonsense alterations as the turning of petitionary into enacting formulae, the triumph of parliamentary over royal legislation had arrived.

One other curious little point marks the rolls of the transition period which seems to hint at a rise in the standing of the Commons. They had always elected and presented their Speaker on the order of the Crown, and they continued to do so. Down to 1461, the roll shows that they were told when to bring him in at the same time as they were instructed

---

[230] C65/128, m. 20; 130, m. 22.

[231] In 1495: *RP* vi, 471. The original acts of 1497 and 1504 carry the king's sign manual in monogram on every bill and every scheduled proviso, except on bills vetoed, which proves that it was added after passage. Thus Henry VII, true to his nature, signified his assent in person and with his pen. No later king did so: the sign manual became a signification of royal approval before introduction, though the details of the practice remained confused in the following reign (cf. J. I. Miklovich, 'The significance of the royal sign manual in early Tudor legislative procedure', *BIHR* 52 (1979), 23–36).

to make election. In the Parliaments of Edward IV they came back to report their choice and to ask for a day on which to present him. From 1484 to 1512, they refined this procedure by reporting only that they had made their decision but mentioning no names – 'non nominando' – so that in theory the person of the Speaker came as a surprise to the monarch when the presentation was made. Since all the Speakers in question were leading king's men – Crown nominees – this piece of by-play would seem to reflect a growth of *amour propre*, a pretence at self-importance, highly characteristic of the House of Commons of later ages. No doubt it will not do to read very much into these formalities, but they can hardly have been totally without significance. From 1515, this bit of minor arrogance vanished again.

5

Before we can discuss the seventeen rolls for the sixteen sessions of the five Parliaments called between 1529 and 1545,[232] we face a new problem: we need to consider their authenticity, that is to say whether they were actually written at the conclusion of each session or at some later date. A doubt hangs over these and indeed earlier ones. As has been said, on 1 May 1567 the clerk of the Parliaments, Francis Spilman, was ordered to deliver the whole parliamentary archive in his possession (rolls, petitions, judgments, attainders and other records) from 1484 to 1553 to the Tower,[233] but this he neither did nor could have done. Much of it must by this time have been in the Rolls Chapel. Henry VII's instruction of December 1499 to amend the roll of 1497 stated that Hatton would receive the roll from the Chancery, and Taylor's certified rolls must also have gone to that office at the proper time. In fact, the Chancery in the end received all the rolls but nothing else (the Tower getting nothing); the bills and so forth remained in the clerk's hands. But did the Chancery receive the rolls after Taylor's time session by session, as it should have done? There is a somewhat mysterious Privy Council order, made in the summer of 1556 and surviving unfortunately only in a mutilated seventeenth-century copy, which complained that since

---

[232] C65/138–54. There are duplicates for the sessions of 34 & 35, and 37, Henry VIII. The roll for 27 Henry VIII, being very long, is in two parts. Although the Parliament of 1539–40 really comprised three sessions, the first two were dealt with in one roll because only one statute resulted from them, it having been agreed in Parliament that the first prorogation should not affect the passage of bills started in the first session. The second session of Henry VIII's last Parliament (1547), terminated by the king's death, produced neither acts nor a roll.

[233] *CPR Eliz.* iv, no. 451.

1529 the clerk had failed to certify 'the most part' of the acts made in Parliament into the Chancery, as had been customary, and ordered him to catch up on the backlog.[234] The order does not speak of the roll; its words would rather suggest that the Chancery expected to receive copies of individual acts, which was not the case. On the strength of this document it has been argued that none of the rolls from 1529 to 1555 was written at its alleged date,[235] and though this does not follow from an order which mentions delivery, not composition, certain peculiar features of some of these rolls call up doubts.

No doubts apply to the rolls for the Reformation Parliament and the Parliament of 1536, all of which look perfectly normal. Trouble starts with that for 1539 which adopts a new format: it is written on markedly narrower parchment and enrolls the acts of the session in two neatly presented divisions of public and private. This is effectively the format used from 1553.[236] The roll for 1540 reverts to the clearly contemporary form of the earlier rolls (wider parchment, different manner of enrolment); that for 1542 has the new style of 1539, as do those of 1544 and 1545. On the other hand, the intervening roll of 1543, while peculiar in some ways, used the wider parchment of the earlier style; its layout differs from either earlier or later. These complications are rendered the more baffling because the two sessions of 1539–40 and the three of 1542–4 belong in each case to one Parliament. One might suspect experimentation, a suspicion supported by the surprising appearance of duplicate rolls (drafts?) in 1542 and 1545, but another feature of the rolls that adopt the new format must really give pause. The old-format roll of 1540 gives the king's title in full, spelling out the supreme headship with all the rest; the new-format rolls for 1539, 1542, 1544 and 1545 replace the title of supreme head with the famous 'etc' first used by Mary to hide the intolerable stigma.[237] None of these rolls is signed by way of certification into Chancery, but though later ones

---

234 *The Manuscripts of the House of Lords,* xi (1962), 2–3. This Council order, if correctly copied, used confused and confusing language; it miscalled the clerk William Spilman; and it was signed for the Council by one Washington of whom nothing else seems to be known.

235 C. G. Ericson, 'Parliament as a legislative institution in the reign of Edward VI and Mary' (unpublished dissertation, London, 1973), 154–8.

236 E.g. C65/161, 163.

237 C65/150, the duplicate roll for 1542, mentions only the kingship of England, France and Ireland, omitting both the papal 'defender of the faith' and the anti-papal 'supreme head'. It is altogether less perfected than no. 149 and also much worse worn, so that 149 might be thought of as a replacement made before delivery into Chancery, but no interpretation of these two rolls that has occurred to me makes much sense.

again bear the clerk's signature we have seen that no clerk had signed since John Taylor, as none had signed before John Morgan, and that those earlier signatures really proved the checking of the roll, not its certification.[238]

What are we to make of all this? The format of Edward VI's reign is contemporary: the clerk's signature and the inclusion of the title of supreme head prove as much. (The Council order of 1556 thus did not mean that no rolls had been written since 1529.) The most likely explanation is that this new format was introduced by Francis Spilman who took over in 1552, and served his first new Parliament in 1553, the year which sees the restoration of the roll to soundness; in which case, he may well have been responsible for having those Henrician rolls made up to fill gaps in the series. Rolls written up in Henry VIII's lifetime, or indeed Edward VI's, could not have disguised the supreme headship, and the presence of the title in a roll not shaped to the new format establishes the point unmistakably.[239] In that case, those four rolls (1539, 1542, 1544, 1545) could have been prepared in response to the Council order of 1556, so that Spilman might be able to hand over a full tally to the Chancery. Yet the four rolls are not absolutely alike in style, and the presence of those duplicates works counter to this simple conclusion. Moreover, the two rolls differing in make-up (1540, 1543) demonstrate that rolls were still currently produced, even after 1539. All this must in part remain a puzzle. I can only suggest that the order of 1556 found the clerk possessed of some sort of record for all the sessions in question, but some of it was deficient, worn or scrappy, so that he had new rolls made in the style by then current for certification. In analysing these rolls, therefore, techniques employed in the suspect rolls cannot safely be used to reconstruct the history of practice.

This, however, matters less than it might have done because the crucial developments evidently took place in the Reformation Parliament whose rolls are sound enough. The first roll (for 1529) adopted a new heading (borrowed from the sessional statute) and for the first time entirely dropped the *communes peticiones* section. It still retained the record of the opening proceedings, but thereafter became simply a roll of bills enacted, starting with the twenty public acts (in the order of the

---

[238] Taylor ceased signing after 5 Henry VIII (1514); he always simply put his name and title. By contrast, when Spilman resumed the practice he used the formula 'examinatum et certificatum per me' (C65/161).

[239] C65/151, also more old-style than new, recorded a prorogued session and had no occasion to mention the king at the head.

print) and following with the six private acts of the session. All acts for the first time carry marginal titles supplied by the enrolling clerk; and all acts are treated alike, being given the introductory and concluding formulae hitherto reserved for private acts. Public acts are called *bille* and private ones *peticiones*. Though no one could know that this Parliament would endure for seven years and seven sessions, every session was from the start treated as a separate occasion, with a roll to itself, each headed with a formula recording the reassembly by prorogation. The rolls for 1531 to 1536 (22–27 Henry VIII) are all identical and differ from that for 1529 only in the fact that they once again enroll the private acts before the public, these latter always following the order of the sessional print. The one exception to this – 25 Henry VIII (1534) when four acts appear out of sequence[240] – resulted from a confusion in the assembling of the roll, membranes 34–40 having been sewn in in the wrong place; they should have followed on after membrane 17. This explanation receives confirmation from the appearance of membranes 30–33 which enroll the letters patent confirming the Dispensations Act. These are on parchment of a different width and in another scribal hand, the very last example of a prepared piece being inserted in the roll; evidently, the need to bind them in caused confusion. Similarly, the one failure in these rolls to enregister a public act (23 Henry VIII, c. 3) surely records only a clerical error, but one useful in demonstrating that the print, not the roll, made this a public act. Indeed, the print quite manifestly now preceded the writing of the roll which, as we shall see, now copied the public acts from it.

In 1536, the development of the roll into a mere register of acts reached completion when the introductory matter was omitted. This was now reserved for the journal which also had reached its proper form in the Reformation Parliament. Endorsements on four membranes of private acts – 'Anno xxviij^0 H viij perticular actes' – testify to the clear recognition of the separation into public and private acts (instead of *communes peticiones* and *bille formam actus etc*) which was to be explicitly made in those terms in later rolls. So far all acts continued to be enrolled, with very occasional slips that can have no significance.[241] The surrounding formulae continued to be employed even in the new

---

[240] C65/142.

[241] In 1536, the last printed act (28 Henry VIII, c. 16) was left out, unless a membrane recording it got detached and lost.

format introduced by Spilman. They caused problems which reflect upon the manner in which acts were copied. On quite a few occasions from 1531 onwards, there are corrections on the roll – erasures which indicate that *billa* has been altered to *peticio*, or vice versa, and that the formula of the royal assent has been changed to match. A comparison with the formulae actually written on the original acts, where they are available,[242] shows what happened, as an analysis of the roll for 1532 may explain.[243] The enrolling clerk originally followed the by now well established principle (on the roll) that public acts were called *bille* and assented to *le roi le veult*, while private acts were called *peticiones* and assented to *soit fait*. But this did not always agree with what had happened to the bills in Parliament where a number of acts left private received the supposedly public assent because they were in bill form. For these the clerk erased *peticio* and *soit fait*, writing in *billa* and the public formula of assent, without, of course, thereby making public acts of them. Considering the laboriousness of this procedure, it is no wonder that later on the clerk very occasionally failed to make the adjustment on the roll. The public acts, on the other hand, were not so corrected. Two of them, being cast in petitionary form, were at the assent given the so-called private formula, but on the roll they have an uncorrected *le roi le veult*. Thus the public acts were not checked against the original acts but evidently copied from the print, formulae being supplied by convention rather than inspection.

Yes, but how and when were the private acts written out? If the scribe used the assented-to bills (the original acts), why did he get any of the formulae wrong? One might suppose that he wrote the text before the end of the session and anticipated the assent, having to alter it in due course if his choice had been mistaken. This unlikely supposition is disproved by the problem of the veto (whose possible use would have removed the bill from those to be enrolled), and also by the fact that the very first act on the roll for 25 Henry VIII proves the automatic copying of the finished original act by including the transfer formulae between the Houses, placed after the assent. This copy could only have been made from a bill which had passed all stages. That leaves the mysteries of those discrepant assents. The answer lies in another mystery of the parliamentary records of those years, the absence of assent formulae

---

[242] The acts are missing at the House of Lords for 21 Henry VIII (1529); those for 27, 28 and 31 Henry VIII (1536, 1536, 1539) bear no record of the assent.

[243] C65/140.

from the original acts of three sessions when yet we know from the journal that the assent was properly granted.[244] Clearly, and contrary to the supposed rules of practice, the assent was not inscribed upon the parchment bill at the time when it was formally pronounced in the closing session; it was either added later or sometimes forgotten altogether. On the other hand, at the latest from 1534 onwards, the journal listed the acts passed (but without assenting formulae) at the end of the sessional record.[245] Thus, when the Parliament rose, the scribe knew what acts had passed and could use the text of the original acts, but he had to conjecture the assent formulae. Evidently the roll was checked later when the clerk of the Parliaments brought in the forms of assent for inscription on the acts, at which point any necessary alterations were made. The plentiful corrections in 27 and 28 Henry VIII, which prove that this was done even when the clerk omitted to put the formulae on the acts, confirm that he possessed some other record of what had been pronounced in Parliament.

In the Reformation Parliament, the roll thus came in effect to the end of its real life. Its function as a true record of the Parliament had ceased, nor was it ever replaced because instead the Journals of the two separate Houses took over. The Lords Journal was in full existence, while the Commons certainly had by 1515 a 'book of the clerk' appointed for their House, whatever may be true about earliest surviving examples.[246] Copied from printed statutes and bills passed, the roll had become entirely secondary and really superfluous. Superfluous, that is, except for one thing. Anyone wanting a copy of a private act, for his own satisfaction or for litigation, could still obtain it from two sources – from the original act or from the roll. Since fees were payable for such copies, the clerk's failure to send his roll to the Chancery becomes comprehensible; it left him in sole charge of the documents from which copies could be prepared. Since, however, he did not need two sets for this purpose, and since the original acts were a good deal more convenient to handle than the roll, it is no wonder that we find those signs of neglect, evidently hints of an intention to abandon the roll altogether. It would not have been the only series to end in that age, and

[244] Above, n. 242; for the assent in 28 Henry VIII (1536) see *LJ* i, 101.

[245] Ibid. 83.

[246] 6 Henry VIII, c. 16 (*SR* iii, 143), the act for licence of absence from the Commons. Since only the Commons were involved, it is manifest that the phrase 'clerk of the Parliament appointed or to be appointed for the Common House' refers only to the clerk of the Lower House (underclerk of the Parliament).

that other parliamentary enrolment, the Statute Roll, had long since ceased to be made because the print sufficed. However, no clear-cut decision was made in time, before bureaucratic reaction set in. In 1540, Thomas Soulemont, who in 1539 may have failed to perform, certainly produced a good roll with a resounding heading and every act except the subsidy enrolled. As was to become normal practice, he started with the public acts; once again, misbinding created the appearance of a departure from the proper order.[247] In 1543, Thomas Knight, newly appointed to the office, proved the contemporaneity of the roll, which he had redesigned, by putting his name at the head. He got some public acts out of chapter number order, in two cases inexplicably but in three because he enrolled the act for Wales and the two subsidies of the session, all of which, having been printed separately, were omitted from the printed sessional statute. He also omitted twelve of the twenty private acts: the principle of total enrolment, which had prevailed since 1484, was at last dropped. Knight's roll suggests a kind of conservative reaction, a resolve to continue the roll for the sake of keeping up the ancient functions and perquisites of the office. In view of the doubt that hangs about their authenticity, there seems no point in considering the other rolls of Henry VIII's last parliamentary sessions. The only thing worth noticing is that in these probably substituted rolls coverage became curiously patchy. All the acts are there in 1539, which may mean that it was derived from a lost predecessor still adhering to the principle of complete enrolment, but in 1542 most of the private acts as well as (surprisingly) five public ones are absent. The roll for 1544 is an absurdity: no private acts and only nine of the eighteen public ones appear on it. In 1545 we have one (draft?) roll which omits fifteen of the twenty-five acts of this Parliament, but another version which enrolls everything except the two subsidy acts in a very peculiar order, following the print but inserting private acts at random within it. Quite elegant as these substituted rolls are, they are worthless as a record and emphasize the demise of the roll.

There is another product of parliamentary activity which helps to confirm some of the conclusions reached. As has been said, on the medieval roll any money grant always appeared as the first entry after the preliminaries. From 1553, supply acts ceased to be enrolled, as did

---

[247] On the face of it, the order is confused, that of the public acts differing in places from the print, and some private ones intervening in the sequence of the public ones. However, if mm. 21–22, 25–30, and 37–40 are inserted in different places, a perfect order results.

acts of general pardon.[248] In between there was much uncertainty, probably caused by the fact that subsidy acts and pardons, though manifestly not private, were never printed as part of the sessional statute but from 1512 at the latest were available in separate printing. The medieval practice was still adopted in 1484 and 1485, but then supply acts began to wander about the roll. Morgan could not make up his mind whether to enroll them immediately before the common petitions (1487), right at the end of the roll (1489), or anywhere among the private acts (1491). Hatton put one at the end of the roll in 1497, but altogether omitted another in his mess of a roll for 1504. Taylor preferred to treat supply acts as the last item of the private section, but he enrolled one among the common petitions (1512) and another in the midst of the private acts (1515). Tuke, in 1523, all of a sudden reverted to placing it at the head of the roll, for the first time since 1485. These confusions support the view that down to 1523 the print was not employed in the making of the roll, since if it had been the sensible thing would always have been to copy the printed subsidy after copying the printed public acts – which is what happened in 1534. The 1540 roll left the subsidy out, but this was more likely a slip than the beginning of a new policy because the subsidy reappears in 1543. Interestingly enough, the suspect roll of 1545, which found room for every other act of the session, left out the clerical and lay subsidies, in the manner to become standard in the roll as reformed by Spilman, but not until then, for the money bills of 1549 are on the roll. Thus the issues raised by subsidies and general pardons strongly corroborate points already made: the start of sessional printing affected the making of the roll from 1487 and 1489 (but only in that the print was prepared as the old manuscript statute had been), public acts began to be taken from the print in 1529, the format customary in the reigns of Mary and Elizabeth was settled in 1553, and the suspect rolls of the 1540s were not put together until the reign of Mary.

6

To sum up. The accidental change of location of 1484 by chance proved a point. The middle ages were over. From one Parliament to another, the well established late-medieval format of the roll was changed, to

---

[248] In 1610, Bowyer complained that he was ordered by the attorney general (Francis Bacon) to enroll the general pardon, whereupon the lord chancellor (Ellesmere) added that he should likewise enroll the two subsidy acts of the session (Inner Temple, Petyt MS 538/12, fo. 358v). As Bowyer noted, this was contrary to the precedents.

undergo confused experimentation which did not finally settle down until the reign of Edward VI, and then only because moves to terminate the roll had failed in the face of bureaucratic conservatism. Notable stages in the process occurred in 1510–14 when Taylor appeared to have settled a slightly revised form, only to find that he himself could not adhere to it; in 1529 when copying from the print became normal practice and the pretence of a special 'common' section was dropped; and in 1536 when the introductory matter disappeared. By the time of the Reformation Parliament the roll had ceased to have any serious function, though the interests of the Chancery clerks, who needed a roll if they were to sell copies of acts, kept it in existence. In this connection, it matters greatly that after the years of total enrolment (1484–1540) the roll became increasingly incomplete, though it was only in 1593 that all enrolment of private acts ceased. This was the clerk's riposte to the Chancery who in that year once again compelled him to transmit sessional rolls: they should have their rolls but without the matter which made them profitably useful.[249]

However, the bureaucratic antiquaries of the early seventeenth century, especially Bowyer and Elsying, preserved the roll in existence, so that it was available for the attempts of the 1620s to create a record suitable for a court of record engaged, in that age of impeachments, in the trial of cases.[250] One never knows when a useless series may become useful again, but this accident must not disguise the fact that in the reign of Henry VIII the old master record became a vestigial organ of no practical value. For proceedings, the clerks looked to their Journals, and for the text of acts everybody looked to the sessional print (public acts) and the parchment bills as passed (private acts). In 1529–36, the rolls, useless at the time, become useful to the historian by demonstrating that for the first time parliamentary sessions were treated as separate parliamentary occasions and had taken on the character hitherto reserved for each particular Parliament. Earlier gropings towards that concept, in 1463–4, 1467–8 and 1512–14, were half-hearted and short-lived. So far as the records of Parliament go, the last Parliament of Edward IV was the last medieval Parliament, and the Reformation Parliament was the first modern one. In between we witness the pangs of transformation. The forms of the record, to be sure, are not

---

[249] I owe this information to Mr A. L. Jenkins.

[250] For all this see the facts collected by Elizabeth Read Foster, *The Painful Labour of Mr Elsyng* (*Transactions of the American Philosophical Society*, 1972), 29 ff.

everything in the understanding of institutions, but it would surely be unwise to pay no serious heed to them.

Lastly, the roll confirms one of the most important facts in the history of Parliament and in this transformation from medieval to modern. In the latter middle ages, the will of the whole body was still very much liable to modification by the king's sole authority, expressed in provisos added after the assent. This practice disappeared in the course of Henry VII's reign. Taken together with the evidence of the original acts, which show that after 1504 an equality developed between the two Houses as the Lords adjusted their transfer and consent formulae to those used by the Commons, this emergence of the final authority of the act agreed to by king, Lords and Commons demonstrates that in the early sixteenth century the tripartite Parliament of constitutionally equipollent partners replaced the king's High Court of Parliament in which there had been a clear gradation in status from king through Lords to Commons. This development, which must be called the emergence of the modern institution, found its consummation in the Reformation Parliament, the first body to legislate in the modern manner. Thus the record says.

IV. ENACTING CLAUSES AND LEGISLATIVE INITIATIVE, 1559–81*

Historians of the sixteenth century have for long been aware of a serious problem in judging political, social and economic action. Such action supposedly stands revealed in acts of Parliament, but since it is often impossible to know who promoted a given act it is very far from easy to deduce policy from that evidence. At one time it was customary simply to assume that all legislation reflected official thinking: pointing to the statute book to prove the case, we used to speak of kings and ministers doing this or that. But this, of course, will not do: many acts of Parliament quite certainly originated in the minds and purposes of private persons or sectional interests.[251] True, on occasion the identity of the promoter may be judged from the contents of an act, but this can be a risky business: by no means everything that advanced the Crown came from the Crown, and the needs of identifiable trades or interests might

* [*BIHR* 53 (1980), 183–91. Bad proof-reading on my part caused the second date to read 1571 in the original printing.]

251 The problem is not, of course, peculiar to the sixteenth century (cf. H. M. Cam, 'The legislators of medieval England', in *Law-Finders and Law-Makers in Medieval England* (1962), 132 ff.), but the energetic interventionism of the Tudors makes it more urgent then.

be served by official action as readily as by self-help. *Cui bono* does not prove *per quem*. The problem is particularly acute in the sixteenth century when so many laws were made for the control of manufacture and trade, while the prehistory of legislation remains obscure. The available evidence too rarely substantiates speculation about legislative initiatives: it is only occasionally that we know enough of the facts behind the making of a statute to prove who produced it. It would gain a useful advance in understanding if we could draw up a list of acts which can be assumed, with reasonable certainty, to have sprung from an official source – from Crown and Council. Can we discover some technical criterion in the form of an act which would distinguish official origin from unofficial – the bills of the Council from those put forward by individuals, by town councils, or by such groups as livery and trading companies? This article will investigate this problem for the first seven parliamentary sessions of the reign of Elizabeth I (1559–81), a period which is moderately well documented and far enough removed from the upheavals of the Reformation Parliament for practice possibly to have become settled.

The more obvious distinctions offer no help. It is well known that the casting of an act in the form of a petition by either or both Houses of Parliament proves nothing for its origins. In the very first session of the reign, the acts of supremacy and for the queen's title (1 Eliz. I, cc. 1, 3) take this form, but enough is known about their origins to make certain that in fact they came from the government. Though it is true that such pretended petitions became rare later on, they occurred on occasion – and they prove nothing. When an act cites petitionary pressure from outside the Parliament – as for instance does the act for the making of hats (8 Eliz. I, c. 11) which asks the queen 'at the lamentable suit and complaint' of the hatters that a remedy be enacted – we may accept that the ultimate initiative did come from the interest cited, but we still cannot be sure whether the complaint was taken up by the Council or by sympathizers and agents in the Commons. Furthermore, this test would at best identify as unofficial a few acts framed as petitions; the contrary supposition – that the absence of a petitionary phrase might perhaps prove an official origin – would be quite untrue. Nor is anything to be learned from establishing into which House a bill was first introduced: though Council bills were a little more likely than private bills to start in the Lords, both Houses in fact received bills of either sort. Lastly, we can get no help from the distinction between private and public acts. That between private and public bills would help: since the only useful definition of a private bill is that during its passage fees had to be paid to the officers of both houses, it is clear that no Council bill ever started as private. Unfortunately, however, only one of the many extant lists of bills passing through the Parliament distinguished between public and private, though that list does conveniently demonstrate that both kinds of bill could end up as either public or private acts – which confirms that this latter distinction offers no aid.[252] The distinction between the two kinds of acts is also straightforward: those printed in the sessional statute were public, those left unprinted were private.[253] In consequence we can always tell which category an act belonged to, but that knowledge says nothing about its origins.

There is, however, another rather less obvious difference to be found in these Elizabethan statutes, and somewhat surprisingly it leads to more helpful conclusions. This is the enacting clause (the essential link between preamble and enactment) which occurs in two basic forms. It is either long and elaborate: 'be it therefore enacted by the queen's majesty, our sovereign lady, by and with the advice and consent of the Lords spiritual and temporal, and the Commons, in the present Parliament assembled, and by the authority of the same'. Or it is very short: 'be it therefore enacted by the authority of the present Parliament'. One finds a good many verbal variations, especially for the long formula, and the very occasional further abbreviation (eight cases in seven sessions) into merely 'be it therefore enacted' may be treated as a casual form of the short formula, even though failure to mention the authority of Parliament at all displays a disconcerting looseness of constitutional attitudes. But these variations are insignificant, and the fundamental distinction between long and short holds good. The question therefore arises whether that distinction is anything more than an accident of drafting, and the table below classifies the acts passed accordingly. Subsidy acts and pardons have been omitted as they are both peculiar in all respects, including phrasing; the latter were

---

[252] PRO, SP 12/107 fos. 144–5 (5 March 1576).

[253] Cf. above, no. 34 (II). The only correct test (which is applied here) is whether the act was printed at the time. *The Statutes of the Realm*, which for this reign profess to print only public acts, include some printed at some later date but not in the sessional statute. Thus, for instance, the acts called there 1 Eliz. I, cc. 19, 22, 23, 24 were not printed in 1559 and are really private acts. A set of the sessional prints of the reign is found in Magdalene College, Cambridge, Pepys Library, vols. 1994 and 1995.

obviously always official, and so in essence were the former, though often drafted in committee. Acts are placed under 'official' if positive evidence exists to prove Council initiative or at the very least the political issues involved leave no doubt as to the originator.

Statutes classified by enacting clauses, 1559–81

	Long formula			Short formula		
	Public		Private	Public		Private
	official	uncertain		official	uncertain	
1559	2	5	16	6	6	5
1563	1	18	24	2	4	0
1566	0	8	11	3	6	4
1571	3	7	12	4	9	2
1572	1	7	4	1	0	0
1576	0	9	9	3	8	3
1581	0	8	12	4	1	2
TOTAL	7	62	88	23	34	16

These figures certainly provide some surprises. Far more acts (157) carried the long formula, but those content with the short one (73) formed nearly a third of the total, a fact which in itself argues for some meaning in the difference. However, it is the more detailed figures which really signify. Only seven acts certainly deriving from official sources used the long formula, as against twenty-three equally safely assigned to that origin which employed the other. On the other hand, among private acts – which, since most of them attended to the affairs of private individuals, assuredly exemplify an unofficial origin[254] – the long formula overwhelmingly predominates: nearly five times more acts used it than used the other. All the indications therefore are that the short formula indicates an official origin, while the long implies that the bill originated outside the government. In this period, at least, the Council's draftsmen appear to have contented themselves with merely

---

[254] E.g. the 24 private acts of 5 Eliz. I include 11 restitutions in blood. These acts were framed as petitions to the Crown, approved by the attorney general's signature, and finally authorized by the sign manual; they nearly always passed on the nod.

citing the authority of Parliament, while private draftsmen went in for the full panoply of constitutional propriety.

The point, of course, needs establishing in more detail. First of all, by what right have I called those short-formula acts certainly official? The six of 1559 are the acts of supremacy, of uniformity, for the queen's title, for the resumption of first fruits, against seditious words, and for continuing the existing act against seditious assemblies (1 Eliz. I, cc. 1–4, 6, 16), all manifestly government bills. The two of 1563 include the act of artificers (5 Eliz. I, c. 4) which, whatever its history in the Parliament, originated in official circles,[255] and the one for the sale of apparel (c. 6) which was drafted by William Cecil.[256] The three official acts of 1566 are known to have been drawn by the law officers.[257] The four assigned to this category for 1571 are less absolutely certain but still extremely likely. The treason act (13 Eliz. I, c. 1) certainly started as an official bill, though its complex passage included a lot of redrafting.[258] That prohibiting fraudulent gifts (c. 5) started with separate bills simultaneously in both Houses; the Commons' bill was dropped in favour of the Lords' whose official origin emerges from the history of this legislation, and this act carried with it the act for bankrupts (c. 7).[259] The

---

[255] Cf. S. T. Bindoff, 'The making of the statute of artificers', in *Elizabethan Government and Society*, ed. S. T. Bindoff and others (1961), 59 ff.; see esp. pp. 80–1.

[256] *Queen Elizabeth and her Times*, ed. T. Wright (2 vols., 1838), i, 126.

[257] 8 Eliz. I, c. 1 (consecration of bishops), drawn by the attorney general; c. 2 (defendants' costs) by the solicitor general; c. 4 (limiting benefit of clergy) by the lord chief justice: PRO, SP 12/107 fo. 146.

[258] J. E. Neale, *Elizabeth I and her Parliaments* (2 vols., 1953–7), i, 225.

[259] A complex story. In 1563 a bill 'to avoid fraudulent gifts of goods to deceive creditors' was defeated on its 3rd reading in the Commons (*CJ* i, 67, 69, 70, 72). Another, touching fraudulent bankruptcies, dealt with an issue that had exercised the official planners of 1559 (HMC, *Salisbury MSS* i, no. 587, item 17); the bill of 1563, however, was probably one ordered to be prepared by the London court of aldermen (Corporation of London Records Office, Repertories 15, fo. 158v). It passed both Houses but was vetoed, presumably because the Council had some objection to it (*CJ* i, 68–70, 72; *LJ* i, 615–18). The city renewed its efforts in 1566 (Repertories 16, fo. 118), but at the same time the council instructed Dyer CJCB to draw a bill against fraudulent gifts (PRO, SP 12/107, fo. 147), and in the event the issues were linked in an official bill introduced in the Lords. Though it passed there it was dashed in the Commons, on 3rd reading (*LJ* i, 627–8, 630–1, 634; *CJ* i, 74–5, 79). In 1571, the Council manifestly hoped to win through by again separating the two issues and introduced separate bills for fraudulent gifts and for bankrupts into the Upper House. That these were Council bills is shown by the fact that another one for the purpose appeared simultaneously in the Lower House. Steps were taken to ease passage: the Lords' committee on the bankruptcy bill got authority to call members of the Commons, or any other experts, to gain a better understanding. This led to a long delay, but in the end both the Lords' bills passed, the Commons substituting the official bill on fraudulent gifts for their own which was in committee when the Lords sent theirs down (*CJ* i, 84, 87, 89–92; *LJ* i, 670, 673, 675–6, 679, 685, 687, 695).

short act which validated exemplifications of lost letters patent back to
the opening day of the last session of the Reformation Parliament (c. 6)
dealt with a matter of concern to the subject but one which very
markedly involved the prerogative;[260] we may suppose that the bill, first
introduced in the Lords where it was at once committed for redrafting
to two judges, either was or immediately became an official intervention
to remedy a slightly touchy grievance.[261] In 1572, the act for fugitives
(14 Eliz. I, c. 6) explained the 'long-formula' statute of 1571 (13 Eliz. I, c.
3); its passage involved difficulties in the Commons and urgent pressure
from the Lords, points which indicate an official rather than an
unofficial origin.[262] The three acts of 1576 include two Lords' bills, one
touching the coinage (18 Eliz. I, c. 1), always a prerogative matter, and
the other again concerned with royal letters patent (c. 2). This second act
combined two matters raised earlier in the Commons: the confirmation,
by way of extra security, of all royal grants made since the beginning of
the reign, a Commons' bill for which of 1566 had been allowed to die in
the Lords,[263] and the validation of letters patent containing technical
drafting errors which had vainly exercised the Lower House in 1563.[264]
The amalgamation of both issues, so closely concerned with the
prerogative, in a Lords' bill suggests official action to remedy
long-standing grievances (that is, law reform by the Council). The act
touching fraudulent devices by the late northern rebels (c. 4) amended
the government's earlier attainder of these rebels. In 1581, the tally
comprises the act ensuring obedience to the queen (23 Eliz. I, c. 1) which
had a complex history but in the Commons was entirely handled by
privy councillors,[265] while the evidence of drafting demonstrates that
Burghley took charge of the bill,[266] the act for seditious words which
whipped through the Lords, only to run into difficulties in the
Commons,[267] the act for fortifying the Scottish border (c. 4) which
certainly did not originate with the local interests who expressed doubts
about government intentions,[268] and the act for the repair of Dover

---

[260] The act claimed to explain one of 1549 (3 & 4 Edw. VI, c. 4) whose preamble emphasized kings
and the prerogative.

[261] *LJ* i, 674.   [262] *CJ* i, 101–3; *LJ* i, 720, 722, 724, 726.

[263] *CJ* i, 77–8, 80; *LJ* i, 662–3.   [264] *CJ* i, 63, 71.   [265] Ibid. pp. 119, 123.

[266] PRO, SP 12/147, fos. 91–9; 148, fos. 10–18. If Neale's reconstruction is correct, the bill as
passed came from queen and Council (*Elizabeth I and her Parliaments*, i, 387–8).

[267] This was one of the bills which Thomas Norton had assisted in drafting, and according to
himself this was done under the direction of the Council (PRO, SP 12/148, fo. 171).

[268] HMC *3rd Rept*, Appendix, pp. 46b, 48a.

harbour (c. 6) which had been on the Privy Council's mind since the mid-1560s.[269] That makes twenty-three assuredly official acts, all using the short formula.

It should here be interpolated that one kind of act almost invariably used the short formula – any act modifying an earlier one, especially by total or partial repeal. This brings in a number of measures patently unofficial in their purport and listed in the table under 'short formula – uncertain', such as that for Essex clothiers in 1559 (1 Eliz. I, c. 14) or for the export of leather in 1566 (8 Eliz. I, c. 14). It also brings in acts reviving lapsed legislation (for instance, 13 Eliz. I, c. 8, which once again prohibited usury, and c. 11 which restored a clause of the expired 1563 navigation act). These deal with laws not about to expire but already dead; they did not follow the practice of the genuine expiring laws continuance acts which invariably used the long formula.[270] Thus it would appear that acts attending to earlier legislation in which the full formula had been employed were thought to require no more than the brief mention of parliamentary authority. It is, of course, possible that all such acts were officially drafted, but the contents of some of them and the occasional appearance of what looks like a genuine petitioning start do not make this altogether likely. It also appears, as we shall see, that the practice of using the short formula when dealing with an earlier enactment extended to the confirmation of earlier judicial decisions, but these were acts in which the participation in the drafting of the Crown's law officers would unquestionably have been helpful to the beneficiaries.

In the main, however, the short formula seems to coincide with official initiative, though there remain the questions of those seven official acts graced with the long formula and of those sixteen private acts employing the supposedly official style. Unless these can be explained, the rule here suggested would not appear to work with sufficient precision to offer general guidance. Let us therefore look first at those 'official' acts which seem to contravene it. Three of them (1 Eliz. I, c. 18; 13 Eliz. I, c. 25; 14 Eliz. I, c. 11) were expiring laws continuance acts. To the best of our knowledge, these acts at this time originated with the Council who only later handed the initiative over to the Commons, but (as we shall see) their shape had been settled before the reign of Elizabeth so that these acts simply copied an inherited standardized form which happened to use the long formula. The second

[269] *APC* vii, 310–11.　　[270] Below, p. 153.

act of 1559 listed in this category was the treason act (1 Eliz. I, c. 5) which ought to have been official; its history in Parliament is not straightforward but does not show cause why the 'unofficial' formula should have intruded. 5 Eliz. I, c. 1, touching the queen's general authority, probably started as a government bill but was replaced in the Commons by a new bill, unofficially drafted, which Cecil did not much like.[271] In 1571, expiring laws apart, I have assigned two bills as official on grounds of contents: the one against bulls from Rome (13 Eliz. I, c. 2) whose history in Parliament is full of redrafting by committees, so that even if the original bill came from the Council (which is not certain) a switch to the unofficial formula would not surprise, and the one against persons fleeing abroad (c. 3) which could very well have come from an unofficial source and stands in this column only because the paper bill, introduced in the Commons, bears an addition by Burghley (presumably therefore added before introduction).[272] Thus of these seven acts only one (the 1559 treasons act) raises doubts; in the other six cases either formal reasons account for the act's appearance in the 'long formula – official' column, or its place there is so far from certain that they need not have been listed there if the case to be established did not require the severest possible test.

We turn to the sixteen private acts which appear to break the alleged rule by using the short enacting clause.[273] There were five such in 1559. Two of them belong to the category that later got printed (and therefore now appears in *The Statutes of the Realm*) because their import was general rather than particular: 1 Eliz. I, c. 19, the notorious act which enabled the Crown to rob bishops' sees by an enforced exchange of lands, and c. 22 which empowered the Crown to make ordinances applicable in collegiate churches, corporations and schools. Both were in fact so public in their concerns that it may only have been by oversight that they did not get printed in 1559; in any case, they deal with the concerns of the Crown and are more than likely to have originated with the Council. The others are less obvious. OA no. 28, changing the laws of inheritance on certain private lands from gavelkind to primogeniture, is a petition asking the queen to grant that the step

[271] C. Read, *Mr Secretary Cecil and Queen Elizabeth* (1955), 170.
[272] PRO, SP 12/77, fos. 206–35. Neale (*Elizabeth I and her Parliaments*, i, 225) classifies both bills as government bills but does not discuss them.
[273] Private acts later printed received a chapter number in *SR* which is here used. For unpublished acts, the Original Acts at the Record Office of the House of Lords have been used; they are here referred to as OA, with the number inscribed on the document.

may be taken 'by the authority of your highness' court of Parliament'; here the form of the petition determined the framing of what is only obliquely an enacting clause at all. OA no. 29, amending the repeal of Cardinal Pole's attainder by a Marian statute, falls under the rule that modifications of earlier acts used the short formula but also involved the queen's family. Only OA no. 34, reviving a fair at King's Lynn, is manifestly a privately promoted act which yet employs the short clause – though it is true that even this made reference to an earlier act which abolished that fair. Of the four private acts in 1566, one (c. 20) repeals a clause in an earlier act, another (c. 22) confirms royal letters patent for salt-making, and a third (OA no. 30) is merely a follow-up to the gavelkind act of 1559, evidently written by the same draftsman. Only one (OA no. 32, for paving a street in Southwark) appears to fulfil none of the conditions which, on the hypothesis here advanced, would explain the use of the short formula. There are two relevant acts in 1571: one (c. 16) confirms the attainder of the northern rebels and is manifestly an official measure, while the other (c. 29, which incorporated both universities) goes out of its way to emphasize the queen's personal interest and was almost certainly also promoted by the Council. Three acts in 1576: two confirm decrees respectively of Star Chamber and Chancery (OA nos. 29, 32), which sufficiently accounts for their enacting clause, but the third (OA no. 25, for the debts of William Isley esq.) seems totally private and breaks the supposed rule. In 1581, one of the two acts relevant here (OA no. 27) arises from an earlier statute, while the other (OA no. 18) confirms an Exchequer decree. Thus three only of these sixteen private acts really do not support the hypothesis.

To sum up: in the first seven sessions of Elizabeth's reign, it looks very much as though acts that can safely be regarded as springing from official sources used the short formula, except for expiring laws continuance acts which used the long one. Only one seemingly official act breaks this rule without there being a discoverable reason for its doing so. The short formula was also employed (possibly under official influence) in acts dealing with earlier legal facts (modifications of existing legislation and the confirmation of court decrees). Private acts privately promoted used the long formula, except that three short-formula private acts appear to have no visible official connection. Checking the items listed under 'short formula–uncertain' has turned up only six acts out of thirty-four for which an official origin would be surprising, and even of these three, declared to be in response to petitions from outside the Parliament, could quite easily have been drafted for the Council.[274] On the other hand, the list of items under 'long formula–uncertain' (a total of sixty-two) contains hardly anything that one would judge should have originated with the government, the only exception being three acts in 1572 (cc. 1–3, for detaining castles, freeing prisoners and forging foreign coin). Both content and place in the list ought to imply that these were official bills. For another bill of seemingly official interest (13 Eliz. I, c. 4, for the control of receivers of revenue etc.), three *nove bille* produced during the course of passage in both Houses may well explain why the official formula disappeared.[275] A few bills, very much in the private interest, contravene the apparent rule that repeals of earlier legislation should use the short formula; just possibly these were the ones for such a purpose that the Council did not send for drafting. In the conditions of the sixteenth century, when bureaucratic practice was usually far less consistent than this, these figures are really pretty impressive: at most ten, more likely four, acts out of 96 which do not abide by the hypothesis.

Thus it would appear to be the case that the enacting clause can be used to differentiate between bills promoted officially and those promoted privately, at least during these seven sessions. It follows that acts for which no other evidence of origin exists may be cautiously assigned to one category or the other on the evidence of their enacting clauses.

One would like to know whether this rule can be safely projected forwards and more especially backwards into earlier reigns for which direct evidence of origins is generally even more slender. This article must not be burdened with a thorough investigation of these further questions, especially as I hope that before long someone else will study the later sessions of Elizabeth, but I have taken a look at the materials printed in *The Statutes of the Realm* from the institutional transformation which began in the Reformation Parliament, using that of 1523 as a minor sort of control. After 1539 that edition confines itself to public acts, but Dr M. A. R. Graves, who has studied the private acts for 1547–58, has generously supplied me with the information to be got

---

[274] These three are 5 Eliz. I, c. 22 and 8 Eliz. I, cc. 6, 11; the remainder – 18 Eliz. I, cc. 17, 20, 21 – are known to have started as private bills and deal with strictly local concerns.

[275] Neale (*Elizabeth I and her Parliaments*, i, 220, 223–4) shows that the issue was originally raised as a grievance by a private member of the Lower House, though the bill first introduced started in the Lords and may have been produced by the Council. During its passage it suffered several unrecoverable changes.

from them. In this pre-Elizabethan period we also at present know far less about the history of individual acts, but the tentative conclusions possible are nevertheless interesting.

In the reign of Henry VIII, enacting clauses varied far more in detail than they did under Elizabeth, but the distinction between short and long existed. Both styles occur regularly from 1523 onwards, with the long formula clearly predominant.[276] Before 1531 no act can with real assurance be ascribed to official initiative, and the few short-formula acts then occurring do not fit into any recognizable pattern. From 1531, we may discern the first indications that a rule may be emerging, and this is assisted by the appearance in preambles of a phrase indicating that the act arose directly out of the government's personal participation: 'the king considering that etc.' In that year, six out of sixteen public acts used the short formula,[277] and four of them also have the 'the king considering' formula. One of the remaining two deals with the export of horses which is known to have been a major concern of Henry himself.[278] Of the private acts, only one uses the short formula, but this is the only one of the session to involve the king (in an exchange of lands: c. 21). These promising beginnings carry on into 1532 when of the twelve private acts eight deal with Crown lands and seven of these alone use the short formula,[279] as do the three public acts known to have represented official initiative;[280] however, so do two more doubtfully official,[281] while the statute of sewers, certainly drafted by Cromwell, has the full formula.[282]

Cromwell, in fact, seems to have interrupted what was beginning to look like the emergence of the later rule: evidently he preferred the long formula in all his drafting, with the result that during his time no correlation can be established between official drafting and either style of clause. Usage now followed no particular rule, and those earlier beginnings had clearly lapsed when even Crown estate acts came indifferently to adopt either formula. It looks as though the Council

[276] For public acts, the figures to the end of the Reformation Parliament are: 1523 – 17, 2; 1529 – 14, 5; 1531 – 10, 6; 1532 – 15, 4; 1533 – 10, 3; 1534 (spring) – 12, 10; 1534 (autumn) – 12, 5; 1536 – 19, 11. Only in the new Parliament of 1536 (28 Hen. VIII) did the short formula triumph – 4, 13. In 1539 both recorded 7; thereafter long-formula acts again lead strongly to the end of the reign.
[277] 22 Hen. VIII, cc. 2, 7, 9, 14–16.   [278] Ibid. c. 21.
[279] 23 Hen. VIII, cc. 21–27.
[280] Ibid. cc. 16, 19, 20.
[281] Ibid. cc. 11, 13.   [282] Ibid. c. 5.

imposed no uniformity on draftsmen, while the lord privy seal himself favoured fullness of form. The first act of succession (1534) has the long formula, the second (1536) the short, and the third (1543) the long one again; and so forth. The 'king considering that' formula ceases to be associated with one particular style of enacting clause. Although from 1536 onwards more manifestly official acts got the short formula than did not, no clear-cut practice settled until after Cromwell's fall: the last five sessions of the reign produced fourteen short-clause and only three long-clause acts which can be called government-inspired. This looks like the resumption of practices first introduced before Cromwell's rise to power. Cromwell's preference for the long formula goes well with several things known about him: his liking for sonorous and forceful phrases, his interest in words and propaganda, his exaltation of both the royal majesty and the supremacy of the full tripartite Parliament. At any rate, between 1533 and 1540 the enacting clause plainly cannot be used to distinguish between official and unofficial bills, though the test may have some value for the years 1541–7. One thing that began to show some regularity even under Cromwell was the use of the short clause for acts arising out of earlier acts, and at this stage this included expiring laws continuance acts (1536, 1539, 1541).

The reign of Edward VI marked a definite interlude, perhaps because the king's minority made the short formula seem less suitable, perhaps because new draftsmen took over. That formula was never used in the first session and rarely thereafter, nor does it correlate very well with what can on other grounds be discerned as official initiatives. One result was that expiring laws continuance acts now came to adopt the long formula, a practice which persisted into the reign of Mary and was no doubt the reason why Elizabethan acts of this kind, copying established form, stayed with the long formula even though the bills came from the Council. Under Mary, the tentative beginnings of a rule applicable to official public bills which had been visible in Henry's last years reappear, though still rather tentatively. On the other hand, the evidence of the private acts passed in these two reigns fits the thesis better. In Edward's Parliaments forty-eight private acts passed, and twenty-nine in Mary's, a notable and probably significant decline, seeing that both reigns contained five sessions. Of these seventy-seven three are now missing at the House of Lords and must be left out of the account. Forty-two and eighteen respectively carried the long formula, and only five and nine the short. Of that fourteen, eight almost certainly came from the official side.[283] That leaves six unexplained – less than eight per cent – but of these a restitution in blood (1 Mary, OA no. 29) and the jointure of the countess of Sussex, at the time under arrest (4 & 5 Philip & Mary, OA no. 13), could have arisen from Council initiative. Private legislation declined in Mary's reign in which the queen's business moreover took an unusually large share of it, but nevertheless throughout this period private acts overwhelmingly used the long formula while the short occurred mostly in acts ascribable to the official side.

I must emphasize that the outcome of this enquiry is certainly surprising. I started by thinking it highly improbable that there should have been so firm a formal distinction between official and private drafting at any time in the sixteenth century, and I may say that those doubts were shared by Dr Graves. Yet both of us find the pattern presented by this analysis disconcertingly coherent and therefore persuasive. It does look as though a practice grew up from the early days of the Reformation Parliament under which Crown draftsmen adopted the short enacting formula. Before 1558 one can hardly speak of a clear-cut practice, but the evidence pointedly suggests that it was becoming more customary, and even more clearly that in measures most assuredly drafted by unofficial draftsmen (private acts) the long clause was almost invariably preferred. All reservations allowed for, we can at the very least see a move towards adopting the rule, possibly before 1532 and rather more manifestly between 1541 and 1558. On the other hand, from Elizabeth's first Parliament it would appear to have been definitely in operation, which suggests a deliberate decision to apply it consistently – a decision presumably taken by the men who controlled government drafting, that is to say especially William Cecil and Nicholas Bacon. The generality were expected to follow the preferences of Thomas Cromwell, expressing (however unconsciously) their view of the Parliament as a tripartite entity and their respect for their queen's excellent majesty. In due time, of course, the short formula

---

[283] 1 Edw. VI, OA no. 16 (establishing a deanery at Wells); 3 & 4 Edw. VI, OA no. 25 (a grant to Lord Paget); 7 Edw. VI, OA nos. 16 (the Seymour restitution in blood) and 17 (setting up two new sees in place of the bishopric of Durham); 1 Mary, OA no. 31 (the reversal of the Norfolk attainder); 1 & 2 Philip & Mary, OA nos. 20 (reversing sentences passed on Mary's Henrician supporters) and 21 (confirming the attainders of the Greys etc.); 4 & 5 Philip & Mary, OA no. 11 (Crown lands).

disappeared altogether, and today all parliamentary draftsmen are Cromwellians, at least in this formal respect.[284]

[284] A reason for the use of the short formula in official bills might be conjectured out of a surprising assertion touching the force of statute which was noted down about the beginning of Elizabeth's reign. According to *The Discourse upon the Exposicion & Understandinge of the Statutes*, ed S. E. Thorne (San Marino, 1942), 110, ascribed to Thomas Egerton's student days, an act binds the king only if he is explicitly mentioned in it, though 'he shall take advantage of the statute though he be not named'. Few acts had occasion to mention the monarch except in the enacting clause. Might it be that official opinion saw a benefit in leaving him out even there so as to increase his freedom *vis-à-vis* statute? If this was the motive, Cromwell's habitual and apparently exceptional insistence on citing the king in acts of Parliament would suggest a higher respect for 'constitutionalism' in him than in his successors.

35

PARLIAMENT IN THE SIXTEENTH CENTURY: FUNCTIONS AND FORTUNES*

Even though so much has so often been done, the study of Parliament remains active, not least so for the sixteenth century. A fresh look at the present state of the question seems appropriate on this occasion when we are assembled to commemorate Sir John Neale, the foremost historian of the Tudor House of Commons. It is now nearly twenty years since Neale completed his life's work, and those twenty years have not been without further study and thought, sometimes assisted by the discovery of new evidence.[1] No one, we may be sure, would have been better pleased than today's honorand to find that what so fully engaged his interest and his labours should continue to attract his successors – to know that he had not closed a book but opened a window.

The parliamentary studies of Sir John Neale's generation were directed by certain convictions and assumptions. This was true not only of him but also of his great friend and partner, Wallace Notestein, and it was true too of many historians engaged on the medieval predecessor to the Tudor institution. The same convictions, for instance, lay behind Professor Roskell's well-known attack on the standard Tudor accounts in which he claimed a superior status for the pre-1485 Parliaments not recovered again by that body until 1689.[2] I may summarize those assumptions under two main heads. In the first place, it was taken for granted that the real significance of the institution's history lay in its political function: its place in the constitution was defined by its ability and willingness to provide a counterbalance to monarchic rule. In consequence, interest primarily concentrated on those occasions on

* The J. E. Neale Memorial Lecture, delivered at University College, London, on 7 December 1978. [HJ 22 (1979), 255–78.]

[1] E.g. the York material edited by A. Raine (*York Civic Records*, vols. vi–viii [1948–53]) contains interesting sidelights on parliamentary procedure and the fortunes of bills.

[2] J. S. Roskell, 'Perspectives in English parliamentary history', *Bulletin of the John Rylands Library* 46 (1964), 448–75.

which the Crown came into conflict with either House or both. Secondly, historians of Parliament devoted themselves first and foremost to the fortunes of the House of Commons, seen as the natural bearer of that controlling responsibility, and – since in the end the Commons (by some date) were to become the dominant partner in the parliamentary trinity – to investigating the rise of that House, to what Notestein called the winning of the initiative. The House was treated as a corporate entity, marching to greater glory, though in fact it was some individual members who attracted attention – those who made their presence felt, could be thought to have pursued recognizable political ends, and could appear to possess independent minds and a willingness to oppose. The argument between Roskell and the Tudor historians lay just there. They held that the 'true' modern Parliament started with the constitutional developments of the reign of Henry VIII. In this they were right, but because they identified the new phase in the history of Parliament with a supposed new capacity to trench upon the powers of the Crown, instead of noting how the Reformation Parliament changed the whole concept of the institution, its records, its structure, and its impact on the law, they were vulnerable to Roskell's discovery of more successful oppositionist policies in the fourteenth and fifteenth centuries. Oppositionist policies depend on what happens in politics, not on the character of institutions. This second assumption involved the consequent notion that the sixteenth century witnessed a maturing of the House of Commons which was regarded as evolving in the course of that age from a rather primitive state into a sophisticated political instrument. In addition it was held that this development could be measured by studying parliamentary procedure: changes in procedure, described as leading to the emancipation of the Commons from the guiding control of king and Council, were thought both to reflect and to affect their standing as an element in the constitution.

Studies governed by these inner convictions gave us the Tudor and early-Stuart Parliaments which we know so well: growingly self-conscious bodies of politically aware gentlemen, engaged in promoting policies of their own and making sure that Crown policy did not offend their interests, increasingly sophisticated in their political behaviour, frequently in principled conflict with Crown and Council. The Lords stood in the wings and made their rare appearances as a body – rather like the chorus in *Iolanthe*. The making of laws and the granting of taxes were not overlooked, but of the acts made only those touching major national concerns (themselves political) received serious attention, while supply got studied only as one of the more obvious potential occasions for conflict. There was a good deal of coherence and every appearance of solidity about a picture which seemed justified even in what it relegated to secondary significance. But it did rather depend on those unspoken assumptions, and I now propose to consider them and their product, to see whether they were legitimate and whether modifications in them will alter our view of what happened in the history of the sixteenth-century Parliament. I shall in effect pay most attention to the first seven parliamentary sessions of Elizabeth's reign the problems of which at this time engage my research, but which also suffice for the present purpose because they contain enough examples of just about all the parliamentary themes identified and treated by Sir John Neale. I have often enough expressed my opinions about Parliament under Henry VIII not to want to inflict them on anyone again, and I think I should not attempt to trespass on the reigns of Edward VI and Mary, whose parliamentary history is being investigated by Dr Carl Ericson and Dr Jennifer Loach.

First, then, was the Tudor Parliament primarily a political institution – primarily concerned, that is, with matters political? It does not in itself seem probable that so intermittent a body should have been the scene of national politics, in the fashion of much later days and regular annual Parliaments; and indeed, when Neale, in a famous lecture, described 'the Elizabethan political scene' he did not mention Parliament and spoke mainly of the queen's court.[3] He was, of course, quite right: the game of continuous national politics – the struggle for policy and power – was played at court, among the individuals and factions of Privy Council and Privy Chamber. This would not necessarily mean that politics could not spill over into the meetings of Parliaments, which were obviously available instruments for such purposes, but it compels recognition of two points. Firstly, politics in Parliament are most unlikely to have been independent of the normal, court-centred politics of the day and should in all probability be studied in connection with the faction strife of the court. This necessity is beginning to be taken seriously by those younger scholars who are at present rewriting the history of early-Stuart politics and Parliaments; they are replacing the old story of a conflict between Crown and Commons by a new and complex story of interests and ambitions in which especially the

---

[3] J. E. Neale, 'The Elizabethan political scene', *Proceedings of the British Academy* 34 (1948), 97–117.

influence of various peers on individuals and groupings in the Lower House receives attention. For the reign of Elizabeth, that kind of analysis has not yet been undertaken. Secondly, it must become doubtful whether in the story of Tudor Parliaments politics should be allowed to predominate. After all, Parliament was summoned by the Crown and had no existence without the queen's decision to call it into being; and we do not suppose that she called it to give a voice to political conflict, to opposition. In fact, there is no sign that Elizabeth ever much liked calling a Parliament. She did so because she wanted money, and because her Council wanted new laws – some of them, though by no means all, possessed of political overtones because they concerned the safety of Church and state. For two at most out of the thirteen assemblies of the reign can I discern a mainly political motive in the summons or recall. In 1559, Elizabeth needed an ecclesiastical settlement, and in 1572 she wished to devolve the responsibility for the fate of the queen of Scots on to more shoulders than her own. On neither occasion can she have been particularly encouraged by the result, and throughout the reign abrupt expressions of anger and contempt are rather more common than loving talk.

Parliament was not called for political reasons. Nor was it thought of as a political assembly: it was a court, and the best contemporary opinion of its functions brings in politics only very obliquely. The long list of its competences put together by Sir Thomas Smith (choosing his order of priorities carefully, strange though it may sound to our ears) speaks of making and repealing laws, of altering rights and possessions, legitimating bastards, establishing forms of religion, altering weights and measures, settling the succession of the Crown, defining rights where the law had not settled them, granting taxes, issuing pardons, restoring in blood and condemning by attainder.[4] We should never forget that Smith knew very well what he was talking about, or that when he spoke of 'the Parliament' he did not mean the House of Commons alone. And he had nothing to say about providing a stage upon which those apprehensive of the rule of their monarch may express their opinions or push their solutions, whatever Peter Wentworth – about as unrepresentative a burgess of the House as the reign produced – may later have asserted. Smith's concept of the Parliament by no means renders impossible a use of the institution for the fulfilling of political ambitions, and in 1592 Richard Robinson could include in

---

[4] Sir Thomas Smith, *De Republica Anglorum*, ed. L. Alston (1906), 49.

the business of Parliament 'all things for the glory of God, honour of the prince and public benefit of all his good subjects, and to subversion or conversion of their adversaries' after legislation, taxation, attainders and the correction of error in lower courts.[5] But Smith's and Robinson's priorities help to call in doubt a treatment which concentrates, sometimes exclusively, on the political aspects of parliamentary history.

Concentration on politics or on what are called the large issues can readily cause us to miss the main interests of contemporaries. Take the session of 1576, which contained no major issue of conflict between Crown and Commons. Neale devoted fifty-six pages to it of which half deal with the affairs of Peter Wentworth and Arthur Hall.[6] These are both good stories and very well told, but do we get a soundly proportioned view of the session; do we see what people in Parliament saw at the time? When we look at the Commons Journal, we find that Wentworth engaged the House on three days out of the thirty-five covered by the session: he made his notorious speech on the first day, was sent to the Tower on the second, and was received back three days before the prorogation. Hall's tiresome affairs crop up on seven days, no doubt wasting more time than they were worth, but even so hardly dominating the session. And was so much time wasted? Of one of those days Neale says that 'virtually the whole morning had been spent on the debate', time being found for reading only one other bill.[7] This is not quite accurate: time also served to hear a request from the Lords for a conference and to appoint the necessary committee.[8] Besides, the bill in question was that for the subsidy which on that day received its third reading and was passed. Anyone who has ever looked at Elizabethan subsidy acts will know that reading them could take time, and their third reading in fact rarely left room over for much else on that day. In 1559 it proved possible to fit in a message from the queen; in 1563 one other bill was read; in 1571 two short bills got read and a third was passed on the question. Only in 1566 did the Commons get through substantial other business on the day of the third reading of the subsidy bill – nine additional bills, an achievement which in the circumstances seems remarkable and might merit a closer look.[9] Thus the day in question usually saw little else done, and Hall did not really cut all that much into the Commons' time. Altogether, then, the Journal must cast

---

[5] R. Robinson, 'A brief collection of the queen's majesty's high and most honourable courts of record', *Camden Miscellany* 20 (1963), 2–3.

[6] J. E. Neale, *Elizabeth I and her Parliaments*, i (1953), 313–68.

[7] Ibid. 339.   [8] *CJ* i, 108.   [9] Ibid. 54, 66, 79, 88.

some doubt on an account of the session (a session which handled more bills than many a longer one) which leaves out the bulk of what happened in those five weeks: the ordering of priorities does not really reflect the facts of the record.

Indeed, what do the records of Parliament tell us about its function? I mean the records produced by the institution itself which need to be properly analysed and understood before other evidence of a more private sort — letters and diaries — is brought into play. Technically, the master record was still the Roll of Parliament, but this had ceased to have any real significance. After attempts to maintain its usefulness in the changes which came over the institution during the transitional period 1484–1523, it was nearly abandoned during the 1540s but in the end survived, mainly for the enrolment and copying fees obtainable from the beneficiaries of private acts.[10] It had by stages become no more than a list of acts passed, and from 1529 the public acts were always copied on the Roll from the sessional print. Its decay meant that the Parliament as a whole lost the only record it has ever possessed. Instead — and the fact, of course, reflected institutional changes — each House now kept a Journal. That of the Lords was fully established and made official in the course of the Reformation Parliament; it recorded proxies, presences, formal occasions (especially the opening and close of each session), and bill proceedings — nothing else. The Commons Journal, on which more in a moment, also in essence confined itself to the formal business arising out of the legislative process (readings, committees, conferences and divisions), but in addition it recorded orders (some of them), licences for absence, and matters of privilege. Next there are the Original Acts, the bills as passed, which form the most manifest deposit of parliamentary activity. A last record, also in effect official, was the sessional print of the public acts, produced by the queen's printer under the guidance of the parliamentary bureaucracy.

Thus the records of Parliament concentrated very evidently on one kind of thing — the making of statutes. Bills and acts of all kinds, not political issues, were the business of Parliament, of all the three partners in the process. When one considers the amount of business handled in these usually very short sessions, that conclusion ceases to be surprising. It is not, I think, generally known how much was dealt with in Parliament. The first seven sessions of Elizabeth's reign passed 144 public and 107 private acts; in addition (this calculation cannot be

---

[10] See above, no. 34 (III).

absolutely precise) at least 514 bills were introduced which failed to pass. Of these 514, thirty-four passed both Houses but did not receive the royal assent. Further, we occasionally hear by accident of more bills put into the Parliament which were not read even once. An average of about thirty-five bills passed and another seventy-three considered in sessions which averaged just under ten weeks in length implies a lot of work, especially as a good many bills of less than world-shaking importance took a great deal of time. In the picture presented by the Journal for 1576, for instance, the private act settling a dispute over the lands bequeathed by Sir Richard Wenman of Carswell (Oxon.), which necessitated nine entries as well as a lengthy arbitration, with parties and counsel present, before the bill committee,[11] loomed rather larger than the shenanigans of Peter Wentworth. The Lords went to further trouble to amend the bill.

So far as the nation was concerned, therefore, the function of Parliament was to make laws, public and private, a recognition which calls for a prolonged investigation that obviously cannot be pursued here. It does, however, lend some support to the conventional concentration on the House of Commons, which was the first House to see much the greater number of these bills. Mind you, the Lords' House enjoyed a notable share of the legislative initiative. In the productive long session of 1563, nineteen of the acts passed started in the Commons but thirty-two in the Lords, a disproportion which owed something to the many repeals of attainders which by custom were supposed to be introduced (graced with the sign manual) into the Upper House. However, in 1576 when no such special reason intervened, the Commons' twenty acts are still matched by the Lords' seventeen, and the Commons won this competition only because the session produced a number of private estate acts, habitually introduced into the Lower House. Thus even the business of lawmaking, not to mention influence or social superiority, draws more attention to their lordships than they have received from historians. Council bills very often started in the Lords, if only because the lord chancellor always sat there, and from 1571 Lord Treasurer Burghley too.

Unfinished bills nearly all started in the Commons; theirs was the House in which the generality – individuals, communities, pressure groups and lobbies – sought remedy for their particular and general grievances. This might suggest that they were indeed the right

[11] HLRO, Original Acts, 18 Eliz. 1, no. 30; *CJ* i, 110–13, 115; *LJ* i, 746–9.

instrument for opposition, for opposition, of course, might grow out of grievances. But the grievances we here speak of were not of a kind to produce political opposition to the Crown: they touched people's real problems such as matters of agriculture and trade and manufacture, law reform, the settlement of property rights, naturalization and denization, the almost invariable concerns of most of the acts passed and nearly all failed bills. Nor can the Lords be forgotten even when we consider unfinished business; very ordinary failed bills could start there too, as one for uniting parish churches in Winchester in 1563, or one touching the limitation of fees for 'counsellors and others towards the law' in 1571.[12] This last one is actually an odd case – the sort of case which emphasizes that individual bills must be studied with some care if we are ever to understand what those Parliaments were like and what went on there. The subject was first brought up in the Privy Council's preparations for the session of 1563 (two sessions back). The bill passed the Lords with ease and reached the Commons with a special recommendation from the queen. A short hold-up occasioned by the failure of the Lords' clerk to inscribe the transfer formula (the Commons refusing to look at the bill until it was properly presented) meant nothing; the bill passed within three days. Both Houses had passed it, the queen had urged it on the Commons, the Privy Council had long since wanted it, it did not receive the royal assent. Why?[13]

The evidence of the parliamentary record thus suggests that bills and acts – the making of every sort of law – should be treated as the first business of the Elizabethan Parliament if the institution is to be seen in the correct light; only then should occasions of political importance – debates over great causes and the making of parties, matters which (as diaries show) often greatly interested individual members – find their place in the story. That brings me to the second underlying assumption, namely that the chief theme of parliamentary history revolved around the fortunes of the Lower House as the instrument for restraining the power of the Crown. Important and neglected though the Lords have been, it might still be that historians' preoccupation with the Commons and their 'rise' is justified, if rise there was. Some might see a pointer in the behaviour of the city of London. Though the court of aldermen proved its understanding of parliamentary realities when, in 1563, it advised the brewers to amend a bill rejected in the Commons and

[12] *LJ* i, 597, 696.
[13] PRO, SP 12/40, fo. 149; *LJ* i, 696, 698; *CJ* i, 93.

reintroduce it that same session in the Lords,[14] it also in Mary's reign began to fee the clerk of the Lower House where in Henry VIII's reign it had voted money to the clerk of the Upper,[15] and it habitually spoke of the Parliament, or the Parliament House, when it meant the Commons. But London's bills naturally started in the Lower House where its four members sat; put to it, the city knew quite well how to lobby the Lords, some of whose more influential members had in any case incurred a sizable debt of gratitude by their frequent requests (not always successful) on behalf of clients who wished to obtain the freedom of London without paying for it. The notion that the Commons 'rose' does not depend on such casual evidence but rather on three substantial arguments: that their Journals demonstrate a development from 'primitive' to 'mature', that the history of procedure confirms this maturing, and that the House proved itself increasingly capable of political intervention against the Crown and its policies. I propose to look at these arguments in turn.

The notion that the Journal demonstrates the institutional growth of the House was first put forward by Sir John Neale in his famous paper on the Journals, written at a time when, under Pollard's influence, evolutionary theories dominated Tudor constitutional history.[16] He inferred it from the fact that while John Seymour, clerk from 1548 to 1566, kept a book in which only bill proceedings and other formal matters were briefly entered, his successor, Fulk Onslow, produced one cast in more extended prose and with formal entries expanded to include messages and reports which threw light on opinion. The view assumes that a Journal 'evolves' in step with the inclusion of non-formal matters, especially speeches, and it does so because what interests us is debate in the House. However, it does not follow that the makers of the Journal necessarily shared a predilection which is not apparent in the thoroughly 'mature' Journal after 1660, or indeed in practice before 1640. The well-matured record of the Lords always omitted all the casual matter − more especially debate − which yet the clerk, as Robert

[14] Corporation of London Records Office, Repertories 15, fo. 188.
[15] Ibid. 13(1), fo. 251; Helen Miller, 'London and Parliament in the reign of Henry VIII', *BIHR* 35 (1962), at p. 139. Most sessions under Elizabeth seem to have yielded no reward for either clerk.
[16] J. E. Neale, 'The Commons Journals of the Tudor period', *TRHS* 4th ser. 3 (1920), 136–70. This contains the most charming howler in Neale's whole corpus: he read the clerk's addition of the conventional JHS (Jesus Hominum Salvator) to the year date as an inscription of the clerk's first name, Johannes.

Bowyer told us, entered in his scribbled book.[17] Onslow himself put in no speeches except set pieces on formal occasions, as the opening of Parliament or a report from a conference with the Lords. It was the discovery that Ralph Ewens, his successor, inserted the names of contributors to debate that caused the Commons in 1607 to appoint the first committee for the control of his book, and when they came again to reform their Journal in 1628 they excluded from it (partly for fear of giving a handle to such an enemy as the king) all except the formal proceedings that Seymour, though he had far fewer to note, thought it proper to put in. Of course, Seymour's book was different from John Wright's in 1628 – less full in its entries, detailing no reports, omitting full committee lists – but, given its purpose, his book was just that: different, not more primitive. Thus it seems to have been held in general that the Journal ought to be confined to a precise and impersonal record of business, though different clerks interpreted that principle differently. Throughout the period, the Journals remained very much the clerk's own record and reflect individual practice, insecure grounds for estimating evolution.

While, nevertheless, it might be the case that these clerks' changing practices described changes in the institutional character of the House of Commons, a study of the Journal in the reign of Elizabeth does not bear out this possibility. For Seymour's predecessor, Richard Urmeston, very little survives, though he must have kept records enabling him to control the passage of bills and the work of committees. He certainly recorded the former, for the first extant Journal – the volume we know as 'the book called Seymour' – starts with 'a note of the bills, when they were read in the Commons House' for the first session of Edward VI's first parliament, which was Urmeston's last session. The note is a fair transcript made by a scribe; it indicates that by accident or design a new book was opened for the reign, and we may safely conjecture the existence of earlier records of a like kind now lost. We may also allow that to all appearances Urmeston did not believe in preserving an archive, but we cannot deduce from this that the House was not perfectly well run and sufficiently served by the records available to the clerk during sessions. Seymour, who became clerk in the second session of that Parliament, later proved his faith in rather more careful

<hr />

[17] BL, Cotton MSS, Tiberius, D. i, fo. 4v. This is the original of Bowyer's transcript of the Lords Journals for Henry VIII and Edward VI; the volume at the Inner Temple, Petyt MS 537/1, from which this passage is usually cited, is a later copy [above, p. 65, n. 25].

record-keeping when he personally added the Speaker's name at the beginning of the Parliament, but for the remaining sessions the same scribe copied out Seymour's working papers, which included bill proceedings, orders of the House and matters of privilege – always the essential contents of the Journal. In particular Seymour noted licences for absence, as the act of 1515 (6 Henry VIII, c. 16) required him to do; to him at least the daily record sufficed to do duty for 'the clerk's book' mentioned in the statute. From Edward's second Parliament (1553) to the session of 1566 Seymour himself wrote up the record and manifestly did so during actual sittings;[18] he added opening and closing procedures and chairmen of committees. He thus put all the business of the House into his Journal: in effect complete, it reflected this clerk's desire for a concise and easily used record, uncluttered by matter not belonging to business. 'The book called Seymour' is as much a proper Journal as what followed, only more spare.

Fulk Onslow took over in 1571. His Journal does look different, but the difference can deceive. What now survives is the record for 1571–81, in a fair transcript made at the time. Thanks to Simonds D'Ewes' description of the materials he used in composing his collection, we know that Onslow continued the practice of entering business during sittings in a 'scribbled book', though the chances are that at first this was not a bound book but a collection of quires. He planned to copy these often messy notes fair and did so for the first four sessions of his tenure, presumably discarding the quires as he went. A fragment for 1581, however, escaped the discard, for D'Ewes found it bound in with the 'scribbled book' for 1584–1601 which he used for that period; that book still existed in 1633 but has since disappeared.[19] We may suppose that the quires were bound up because no 'perfected' transcript was ever made for those sessions, quite possibly because Onslow declined in health as the reign wore on,[20] but that a remnant of the last session to be copied fair survived by accident to be bound in with the rest.

Thus, when comparisons are to be made, we have a 'scribbled book' for Seymour, but for Onslow a perfected book whose earlier scribbled stage is lost. The crucial question, therefore, is whether the fair copy accurately represents the contents of the record kept during sittings.

---

[18] This becomes clear from an inspection of the MS. That the hand that wrote the book is Seymour's is confirmed from his annotations on bills in the Original Acts.

[19] For all this cf. Sheila Lambert, 'The clerks and records of the House of Commons, 1600–1640', *BIHR* 43 (1970), 215–31.

[20] The suggestion is A. F. Pollard's: ibid. 17 (1940), 78–85.

Neale convincingly argued that when Onslow made his transcript he added material from other papers in his keeping, as for instance reports and speeches.[21] This means that the real difference between 'the book called Seymour' and 'the book called Onslow' does lie predominantly in the fact that the former is a scribbled and the latter a perfected book. A comparison of the use made by D'Ewes of the two different Onslow manuscripts available to him (one fair, one scribbled) bears this out: the matter included in the last six sessions does not differ in character or completeness from that of the first four, the only apparent differences (apart from the use of other records) resulting from the insertion of material at the time of copying. It is true that Seymour and Onslow seem to have treated committee lists differently. These are absent from Seymour's book (where only the chairman is mentioned) and present in Onslow's perfected Journal; D'Ewes' manuscript shows that he found them also in Onslow's scribbled book, at least on many occasions.[22] However, Seymour must have had lists of committees taken down as they were named but presumably kept on separate slips, so that Onslow's innovation consists only in his use of his scribbled book for that purpose. In all essentials, therefore, the two clerks regarded their daily journals in much the same light, as a record of business transacted, minor differences arising from personality or temperament. Onslow looks to have been more voluble and less businesslike, perhaps just less austere. But the move from Seymour to Onslow is a move from one clerk's preferred habits to another's; it is not at all a large move, and certainly not one up some evolutionary ladder. In fact, bills can be tracked more conveniently in the earlier Journal than the later.

Though the Journal is the matter really at issue here, we must note that Onslow left traces of other records kept by him for which no evidence survives for Seymour. In 1633, among the clerk's papers confiscated by Mr Secretary Windebank, there was a 'book of originals' running from 1571 to 1610. This has long since vanished and its purpose can only be conjectured. At a later date, many orders of the House are known to have been entered in a separate book; one such survives effectively from 1610 onwards, of which the lost book could have been the predecessor.[23] The House, or rather the clerk, increasingly came to register such routine orders as the addition of a member to a committee,

---

[21] *TRHS* 1920, 146–8.
[22] I am grateful to Miss Norah Fuidge for this information.
[23] Inner Temple, Petyt MS 537/18, contains the remnants of this book.

a sign of innovations in bureaucratic habits but not of developments in institutional stature; the initiation of an additional record series demonstrates changes in office practice that could easily be matched, for instance, with similar endeavours among the clerks of the Privy Council, who also complicated their record-keeping without altering the status of their institution. Alternatively, it has been suggested that the book may have formed an intermediate stage (containing record of debate) in the preparation of the Journal, between scribbled book and perfected copy, a practice vouched for in the making of the Lords Journal.[24] However, to judge from the size of the fair transcript (without debate) for four of Onslow's sessions, one volume covering all ten would have had to be enormous; and in any case, if the book belonged to the making of the Journal it cannot affect our earlier conclusion that the completed Journals will not support evolutionary theories about the House.

The suggestion that the lost book contained a record of debate takes some comfort from the fact that Onslow, unlike his predecessors, is known to have at least on occasions noted down remarks: if the lost book was a scribbled book for this purpose only, it might at least satisfy the test of size. Of Onslow's notes we can now trace only three fragments. One is in his own hand: found among the Braye Manuscripts, it covers part of the 1572 session.[25] A second was detected by Sir John Neale hidden in D'Ewes' account of the earlier sittings of 1581; the deposit left there fits accurately in style with the Braye Manuscript.[26] And a third would appear to be the alternative version for 1586–7 which D'Ewes said he used in composing his account of that session, for here again we find named speakers in the fashion characteristic of these notes but not of Onslow's finished Journal.[27] Perhaps these were excerpts from that lost book. Nevertheless, among all these conjectures I would tentatively opt for a book of orders, as most likely for practical reasons and least incredible on grounds of size.

However, the fact remains that Onslow at least sometimes took notes of debate, and the one example still physically in existence indicates his

[24] Lambert, 'Clerks and records of the House of Commons', 221–2: on the supposition, quite plausible in itself, that the date 1610 is a scribe's error for 1601.

[25] HLRO, MS 3186, printed in *Manuscripts of the House of Lords*, xi, 6–15.

[26] Neale, *Elizabeth I and her Parliaments*, i, 379, referring to Simonds d'Ewes, *The Journals of all the Parliaments during the Reign of Queen Elizabeth* (1682), 282–3, where we find details of debate otherwise absent from both *CJ* and D'Ewes.

[27] Cf. Neale, *TRHS* 1920, 120; unaware of the then unknown Braye MS, he was unable to make the identification.

method. It is a fair copy which could never have been written during a sitting and must derive from a scribbled original. The copy gives the titles of the bills in question (and in the process clears up a confusion in the Journal for 1572),[28] before adding remarks for and against. Those titles, of course, were entered in the scribbled book and could have been obtained from there. The notes of debate, on the other hand, cannot have been entered in that same book because otherwise we should find them reflected in D'Ewes' account of the later sessions. It would thus appear that Onslow wrote up his Journal (possibly on prepared sheets, to reduce the immediate labour) during sittings, while at the same time jotting down notes on speeches on separate sheets, either on occasions or quite regularly. He meant to perfect the former into a fair transcript and to produce neat copies of the latter – and of these one survives while D'Ewes encountered and used two more.

Why, then, was Onslow taking notes of speeches, a practice of which there is no sign before him? For whom did he transcribe them? He did not ever insert such material into the Journal proper;[29] it was only after his day, under the far-from-competent Ralph Ewens, that proceedings and debate got mixed up in one scribbled book, with the result that historians can be tempted to speak of even more 'developed' or 'evolved' Journals in the reign of James I. We know that in 1628 the Commons sensibly insisted on restoring the earlier practice by removing all record of debate, though by then the clerk had been in the habit of noting details for nearly sixty years. So for what purpose did Onslow embark on these additional labours? When we remember how the Council used later clerks as sources of information on what went on in the Commons, when we recall that Onslow took office in the first session during which Sir William Cecil, now Lord Burghley, no longer in person attended the Lower House, and when we reflect that in 1572 the notes spread themselves in greatest detail on the highly delicate subject of the queen of Scots, we may conjecture their ultimate destination without undue rashness. It must be conjecture because none of Onslow's transcripts now survives among what is left of Burghley's papers, though the lord treasurer certainly got such information on

[28] On 29 May, *CJ* i, 99, lists two bills against vagabonds, one rejected on second reading and the other read a third time; the Braye MS (*Manuscripts of the House of Lords*, xi, 7) shows that the first was really one for building cottages on wastes and commons.
[29] The statement, ibid. p. x, that Onslow began to insert speeches in 1581 is mistaken. Though his extant Journals show some increase in longwindedness, they never altered in the principles which governed what was included.

occasion, as in the detailed report on speeches sent to him in 1584–5, written in an unidentified hand, perhaps that of a burgess but equally perhaps that of some assistant clerk.[30] The conjecture at least makes good sense – really the only good sense – out of the evidence that the clerk at times briefly recorded what was said. One can certainly think of occasions when Burghley would have been glad to know how members stood to some issue or other; the soul-searching touching Mary Stuart is one such. Who better than the clerk, a man appointed by the Council, to act as informant? Those notes would have fully equipped him for the purpose, and that purpose is much the most likely reason for their having been taken.

Thus the most notable innovation or 'development' in the Commons' records during the reign of Elizabeth had nothing to do with any growth in the standing or self-esteem of the House; rather the most convincing interpretation of it is that it testified to a new form of conciliar control, called into existence by the departure to the House of Lords of the manager-in-chief. When so much material is lost, when the changes in the Journal (in 1548, 1571 and 1604) so manifestly arise from the changing practices of new clerks, and when the main effect of change is to assist the management of business, I think it inadvisable to read institutional, let alone constitutional significance into what happened. Indeed, what to us might seem a less developed Journal by no means describes a House properly to be called primitive. Instead we discern in the much worse documented reigns of Elizabeth's three predecessors a sufficiently sophisticated body going competently about its business, dealing with bills, attending to supply (the most contentious debate over which in this century occurred in 1523), and on suitable occasions taking issue with some government proposal. *Nil novi ex Westmonasterio.*

Similar conclusions emerge from a look at procedural developments: they occurred but they do not signify what has been read into them. Historians have been tempted to treat procedure as an active agent, bringing about material change in the standing and purposes of Parliament, whereas, of course, it is simply the agreed method of getting through business in known ways which can be stated for all to learn. A knowledge of procedure remains very important because ignorance of it is perhaps the most frequent cause of the misinterpretation of the evidence, more frequent even than preconceived ideas; Sir John Neale

[30] BL, Lansdowne MS 43, fos. 164–75.

was quite right to give so much attention to it and to stimulate us into pursuing the problems further. But as a temperature chart for political or constitutional developments the history of procedure is suspect, especially in a body which so readily invented or ignored precedent, when convenience or interest dictated, as that House of Commons was capable of doing.[31] Its way with bills and the behaviour of members settled early (probably well before the sixteenth century) into a reasonably ordered pattern because this was one of the aspects of businesslike efficiency which the House derived from its close association with the Council, the managers of the king's affairs. The details got more refined and more precise. The problem is whether one can deduce institutional growth or an advance in public standing from such changes; for instance, does listening to new rules being laid down by such assertive Speakers as Edward Coke or Christopher Yelverton really demonstrate some increase in maturity – that 'adolescence was over' in 1597?[32] If that was so, we may wonder when senility set in. Very often changes of practice look only like minor cleaning-up operations which in no way altered the principles of parliamentary business methods. Thus it is true that the number of bill-readings steadied to a regular three from an earlier willingness to record more than that number, but I do not think that this proves some sort of advance on the part of the Commons, the more so because the change was in fact more apparent than real. It is not the case that 'between 1547 and 1558 there were many instances of a fourth, fifth, or even a sixth reading': I can find only about ten reasonably certain examples in those eleven sessions.[33] Others turn out to be the product of erroneous numbering in the Journal,[34] or of other clerical confusions.[35] Most of those genuine multiple readings are explained by the occasion: they occur in the passage of very contentious and much revised bills. What changed later

---

[31] Cf. the remarks made in 1584 (Northants. Record Office, MS F(M), P.2, fo. 35v): 'It was by one said that as precedents were necessary to instruct the House what had been done and thereby did give the better light how to proceed in matters adoing, so were they in no sort binding the House what should be done: for, being a free council, it cannot be concluded but hath still a power remaining in it . . . according to the necessity of the causes in handling, either to alter, make new or continue any precedent'.

[32] J. E. Neale, *The Elizabethan House of Commons* (1948), 376.

[33] Ibid. 370; *CJ* 1, 3, 4, 19, 21, 23, 30, 31, 38, 41.

[34] Ibid. 5, 7, 10, 16, 22, 39, 41, 45.

[35] Ibid. 25 and 26 (a committal numbered as a separate reading); 15 (a repeat reading on the same day, probably to facilitate understanding, counted as a formal reading); 22, 41, 45 (where the confusion seems to hide replacement bills).

was not so much the actual facts of readings as the conventional notion touching the number they were expected to reach, so that a reading followed on another day by an order to engross, which earlier would have counted twice, is later liable to be given *secunda* on both occasions. Once again, such changes illustrate clerical practice, not an advance in institutional perfection.

However, the big issues cluster around the history of committees, the growth of large committees, the appearance of grand committees, ultimately the arrival of the committee of the whole. Ever since Notestein tied a whole set of constitutional theories to the committee of the whole, by claiming that it was a device of opposition, the so-called growth of independence in the House of Commons has supposedly been measurable by its history. Sir John Neale, discussing committees, was a deal more cautious than the impression that people took from his words might suggest; he made no extravagant claims, but neither did he contradict the Notestein thesis.[36] He recognized that the chief purpose of large or standing committees was to shift debate away from the floor of the House and streamline business, not to gain 'freedom' or 'initiative'. Similarly, though he suggested some sort of institutional advance in the occasional practice of arranging for more frequent sittings, he also showed that such reforms were pressed upon the House by the Council and its men;[37] this bit of procedure, if that is what it was, represented no maturing but only a willingness to work harder at the bidding of the queen who hated long sessions, and in the interests of constituents who were promoting bills. All these devices for getting more work out of the House and reducing tactics of delay in fact originated with the official side. Throughout it was the Council's men who chaired the important committees; and the councillors rather than any dissidents took advantage of the opportunity offered in committee to speak repeatedly to the same matter. Thus even the famous committee of the whole really sprang from the managerial devices of the Council and should no longer be treated as the ultimate in opposition tactics.[38]

After all, if it were the truth that in the course of the reign the House in some sort grew up, one would surely expect to see it gaining specific powers in its own right. Yet what did it gain? There was no increase in its control over its own existence, or even over the contents and order of

---

[36] Neale, *House of Commons*, 377–81.   [37] Ibid. 380.

[38] This discussion of committees rests on the work of Miss Sheila Lambert, forthcoming in the *English Historical Review*. [See now *EHR* 95 (1980), 753–81.]

the business before it; and when something new turned up in its functions, as when consideration of expiring laws was in 1593 transferred to a Commons committee, this again happened at the choice of the Council who had hitherto attended to that matter through a committee of its own. Occasional attempts to link grievances to supply never produced a remedy for the first and never prevented the ready granting of the second. The House could never secure the presence of persons or records without the willing compliance of the parties affected, showing itself thus bereft of a power that vested in every court of record in the realm. Elizabeth's invention of a distinction between matters of state and matters of the commonwealth seems to me to have restrained free speech in the House below the level of what Sir Thomas More had asked for in 1523, but despite occasional protests the restraint was successfully maintained. It is true that the House always jealously protected its own, especially in cases of arrest at a private suit; though Arthur Hall's much disliked exploitation of that privilege might have taught them to reform themselves into respectability they never even thought of doing anything about it. The privilege of freedom from arrest signifies private advantages, not public responsibility. The only occasions on which I can discern a sign of corporate selfconsciousness were those on which the House showed a certain schoolboyish tetchiness with the Lords. Above all, perhaps, the House never succeeded in forcing the queen to refrain from arresting members after or even during sessions, a fundamental failure which was to have serious consequences when Stuart kings came to exploit the precedents.

I do not doubt that long parliamentary experience could produce complacent assumptions of importance and excellence, or that desire for action could lead to high-flown assertions of the institution's capacities, but these are not matched by an evidence of positive power. Nor need this surprise us, for on the whole the House had little occasion in this reign to seek such power. Perhaps we have heard too much of the spats that now and again interrupted what was in general an even tenor of co-operative labours. Institutions do not grow in assertive strength unless there is something to assert oneself against, and a Parliament whose three parts could be made to work in reasonable harmony was a poor soil for such ambitions. If the House of Commons did not in fact acquire the characteristics of an independent and independence-conscious part of the body politic, this was because in this age it felt no impulse to free itself from conciliar management and did not contemplate the pursuit of a pointless independence. The people who controlled parliamentary sessions at the beginning of the reign were the royal element in the House — councillors, officials, Speakers, clerks — and despite the occasional tussle the same people still stood in the same position at the end of it.

Yet does not this description, which seems to me to be well justified by the record of events, by procedural developments, and by the history of privilege, conflict with the famous account of tensions and disagreements that fills Sir John Neale's two narrative volumes? Indeed it does, and the conflict demands a closer look at those occasions of trouble. I have already suggested that they need to be studied more broadly, with due account taken of all the work done in Parliament, however routine it may appear to us, and of the parts played by Lords and Council. We need to distinguish more precisely between the activities of isolated individuals who failed to elicit any response from the House, and more concerted efforts possibly stage-managed by the official element. Particular events must be considered in their particular circumstances: we cannot assume that a continuous body of opposition produced those apprehensions and confrontations of which we hear. Certainly, there were dramatic moments and some serious clashes, though I cannot recall one such clash that did not end in the victory of the managerial side, but a very flexible approach is required if those interruptions of the more normal harmony are to be properly understood. The accepted story supposes that differences in policy were thrashed out in the Commons where opposition was maintained by a selfconscious and cohesive body of men. The queen could rely on the Lords to protect her interests, but in the Lower House, at least down to 1589, a powerful and singleminded pressure group rendered control very difficult and achieved notable conflicts with the representatives of the government, conflicts which really involved the queen. Sir John Neale considered that pressure group to have consisted of puritans, of men driven by their extremer religious views into opposition to the Crown; he found them active in all sorts of ways, but particularly in matters touching religion, the Church, and the queen's marriage and succession, always against the official interest. In another place he demonstrated how often the queen's displeasure with her Parliaments arose at such times as she herself stood almost alone against the desires of Council, Lords and Commons all together,[39] but when he wrote his

[39] E.g. *Essays in Elizabethan History* (1958) 118–19.

narrative account he placed the emphasis on the presence of a puritan party in the Lower House.

Puritanism is not quite what it was twenty years ago when Neale inclined to treat it as a subversive conspiracy which he sometimes compared with communism in the 1940s and 1950s.[40] After the work of Professor Collinson and others, which has revealed the numerical weakness of genuine presbyterianism and the fact that what is often called puritanism by historians was to contemporaries just zealous protestantism and a sensible fear of Rome, we need to reconsider an interpretation of Parliament which involves a repeated and consistent use of the Commons for the advancement of oppositionist ambitions. I must emphasize that while I feel compelled to raise doubts about the general theory of a puritan opposition I do not mean to fall into the opposite extreme of pretending that there were no parliamentary moves at all that deserve to be ascribed to puritan agitation. We can always find some members of the Commons who hoped to use Parliament for the achievement of even drastic ecclesiastical reform. Moves associated with *The Admonition to the Parliament* or Cope's Bill and Book reveal the existence of purposeful pressure groups, though not very large ones. In the 1580s the subversive organization of the 'platform' in the Church found co-operative allies in the Commons. But the claim that session after session the House of Commons was led in opposition to queen and Council by a determined band of puritan members, forerunners of all the so-called great parliamentarians, depends on judging every instance of political debate from the conviction that this is what happened: that such a continuous group existed, that it followed consistent lines, that it was held together primarily by religious opinions hostile to the settlement of 1559, and that it often manoeuvred successfully against the management of the Privy Council. And this, I think, cannot be maintained.

Neale really built his interpretation upon two foundations which determined the shape of the structure that rose thereafter. First, he discovered the extremists at work in 1559, forcing Elizabeth to accept a more protestant settlement than she had intended. His ingenious argument, widely but never completely accepted, has recently been reviewed in a Cambridge dissertation which restudied the session by dint of taking all its business into account. It came to the conclusion (which I find compelling) that the settlement emerged virtually in the

[40] Ibid. 121.

175

shape designed beforehand by queen and Council; the notorious prolongation of the session became necessary because important bills touching bishops' lands remained unfinished and because time was needed to reduce the opposition in the House of Lords which really did threaten the uniformity statute; there was no effective forcing of the pace by zealous protestants in the Commons.[41] Neale's second foundation stemmed from the accidental survival of a 'lewd pasquil' which in 1566 made fun of some forty-odd members of the Commons by attaching to them rather subtle Latin tags and rather unsubtle one-word descriptions in English.[42] He took that 'choir' to represent the puritan hard-core in Parliament, but the lampoon says no such thing; it is a skit on the people who in that session made all the noise in the House but who might hold all sorts of views, and it ought to be read with particular reference to the succession debate of 1566 which inspired its author. It implies no permanent faction building and defines no future political attitudes. Indeed, it is hard to see what Francis Alford the conservative ('fortune favours the brave'), William Winter the admiral ('by land, by sea'), Richard Grafton the printer ('cum privilegio regali') or William Bowyer the keeper of records ('concordat cum originali') should be doing in a puritan pressure group.

Once, however, the existence of this known group is accepted, every appearance by one of its members is bound to suggest the intervention of oppositionist tactics, even on occasions which at the very least can be read another way. Was Alexander Nowell's opening sermon on the succession in 1563 really an unexpected incendiary *faux pas*?[43] Could it not as easily have been arranged with the Council who in that session were as anxious as anyone to get the queen to attend to the future of the throne? A lot depends on one's view of Thomas Norton, seen by Neale as the puritan parliamentary leader *par excellence*, a man so active in the House that his purposes must indeed be understood. I do not want to deal at length with him here because Dr Michael Graves has a paper in the press which strongly suggests that Norton was throughout his career something like the Council's man.[44] That is what he himself vigorously

---

[41] N. L. Jones, 'Faith by statute: the politics of religion in the parliament of 1559', unpublished dissertation (Cambridge, 1978).

[42] CUL, MS Ff. 5.14, fos. 81v–84v. Neale made the 'choir' puritan by selective citation; the Latin jokes would repay more attention than he gave them.

[43] Neale, *Elizabeth I and her Parliaments*, i, 95.

[44] [M. A. R. Graves, 'Thomas Norton, the Parliament Man: an Elizabethan M.P., 1559–1581', *HJ* 23 (1980), 17–35.]

maintained in a conversation in 1581 when challenged about his activities in the recent session. He admitted a hand in the drafting of a large number of bills but claimed that he had been the original deviser of none: 'all that I have done I did by commandment of the House and especially of the queen's Council there, and my chiefest care was in all things both to be directed by the Council and to move them first to understand her majesty's pleasure in any great matter'.[45] If Norton looked to the Council for his instructions, many things in the story come to look differently; for instance, it would cease to be curious to find him in 1571 in possession of the sleeping bills for religion of 1566.[46] It must be allowed that a hatred of popery and an occasional distrust of bishops do not make a man a consistent leader of a puritan opposition. All told, we cannot (to speak no more strongly) rule out the possibility that much of what happened in the House was managed from above rather than promoted by such an opposition: the agitations over the succession or the Church may very well have represented a use of Parliament by the Privy Council — all or part of it — to push forward policies which they could not get the queen to accept. All this calls for further work, and a lot of it. As I have already suggested, we need to study the links between Council, Lords and Commons, and the factions in all three, rather than structure the House by a simple division between government men and men in opposition.

The bill for coming to church and receiving communion, which made much stir in 1571, provides an example of the difficulties created by the conviction that in the Commons the government faced an active group of skilled oppositionists and trouble-makers. At the second reading a conflict of advice arose which puzzled Neale.[47] He several times expressed a feeling, which I believe to have been correct, that the bill had support from both bishops and councillors, but he thought that a motion by a councillor, Sir Thomas Smith, that the bishops be consulted ruled out any official origin for the bill. Yet surely Smith could easily have been carrying out a prearranged tactical move designed to bring all interests into accord on the bill. The rival and successful motion, that the bill be immediately committed, came from Recorder Fleetwood and, since Fleetwood appeared in the pasquil, was read as an opposition move to by-pass the bishops. In that case, the committee appointed — all officials except Fleetwood himself who, we should note, was throughout his traceable career a faithful client of

[45] SP 12/148, fo. 171. [46] Neale, *Elizabeth I and her Parliaments*, i, 196. [47] Ibid. 192 ff., 212 ff.

William Cecil's[48] – hardly supports the oppositionist purpose conjectured behind the motion. Both proposals seem, in fact, to have come from conciliar sources, which suggests that there were two minds among councillors, some anxious to prepare the ground further, some looking for immediate action. Though the latter won, Smith seems to have had better sense on his side, for the bill proved difficult to draft and occupied much time; it was not done with until 25 March, having been in the making in both Houses virtually throughout the session. However, it did pass both Houses. The queen vetoed it, in the teeth – as Neale rightly said – of its popularity with Commons, Privy Council and at least some bishops.[49] As Neale correctly noted, Archbishop Grindal with some colleagues tried to revive the issue in the 1572 session by appealing directly to the queen, without success.[50] What he did not remark is that nevertheless the bill was reintroduced in 1576 and 1581, both times in the Lords; a draft of it, annotated by Burghley, also survives.[51] It did not prosper much on either occasion, the queen's views being known. However, it must surely now look like a bill which the bishops wanted and for which they mobilized Council support. Bishops, too, care about religion, and there are plenty of signs that in the early 1570s they were much exercised over the failure of too many people to attend the services of the established Church. The fact is that activism in religion cannot be equated with puritan subversion. When, in the same 1571 session, an attempt was made to bring back the bills for religion lost in 1566, the committee appointed followed the course advocated by Sir Thomas Smith on the other occasion: they asked for a deputation to the bishops 'to know their pleasures concerning the motions to be made to them in matters of religion'.[52] Yet they were talking of bills which had come straight out of what has been seen as a puritan and anti-episcopal agitation in the previous session.[53]

As I have said, one important thing now to be done involves studying

[48] As his letters show: e.g. T. Wright (ed.), *Queen Elizabeth and her Times* (1838), ii, 17–21, 244.

[49] Neale, *Elizabeth I and her Parliaments*, i, 216.

[50] Ibid. 304.

[51] *LJ* i, 731; ii, 29. SP 12/147, fos. 121–2. John Strype (*Life of Grindal* [Oxford, 1821], 478–81; *Annals of the Reformation* [Oxford, 1824], i, 460–1) printed an early draft which he claimed was in the hand of Bishop Aylmer. He found it in William Petyt's collections, but I have been unable to trace it either at Inner Temple or in the Public Record Office, the two locations where Petyt material is now to be found.

[52] *CJ* i, 83.

[53] My doubts about Neale's interpretation are shared by P. L. Ward, *William Lambarde's notes on the procedures and privileges of the House of Commons* (House of Commons Library Document no. 10, 1977), 10.

the interaction between the three parts of the Parliament – of queen, Lords and Commons – if we wish to understand the political as well as the normal business of this institution. The Lords, we are commonly told, were a means for keeping the Commons in check. Were they? In the very disturbed session of 1566, ten bills approved by the lower House did not pass the Upper. Five of them simply ran out of time – touching fines and recoveries, a monopoly of armour plate, record depositories in Wales, confirmation of letters patent since the beginning of the reign, and almshouses in Plymouth; two of these became statutes in later sessions.[54] The Lords did not proceed with bills touching demurrers after verdicts and ex-chantry lands, or with one modifying the 1563 act against the sale of apparel on credit;[55] they explicitly dashed only one, a bill promoted by the London Vintners but disliked by Cecil. Commonplace occurrences, with no political overtones and matched by the four Lords bills defeated or lost in the Commons.[56] Three bills suggest a little more possibility of deliberate manoeuvring because the Lords passed them but with conditions which the Commons found unacceptable. A sumptuary bill came back to the Lower House in a new form and was there defeated.[57] One for certain imports the Lords amended to a point where the Commons preferred to abandon it. And the expiring laws bill of this session – here at last we touch on matters of concern for the Crown – was lost because the Commons refused the Lords' demand that they remove certain tacked-on extraneous matter. Neale maintained that this was done in revenge for the Lords' failure to proceed with the only one of the bills for religion which had managed to get through the Commons, by way of protest against government management through the Lords.[58] However, there is only conjecture to support that conclusion, and since we do not know what tack the Commons had attempted we cannot overlook the possibility that their action sprang simply from chagrin at losing those additions. Besides, the arrest of the bill for religion was not

---

[54] 18 Eliz. I, c. 2 (letters patent) and 23 Eliz. I, c. 3 (fines).

[55] 5 Eliz. I, c. 6, a very brief act drawn by Cecil himself. If the 1566 bill went counter to his intention, why did Cecil let it pass so readily in the Lower House? The bill was said to be in explanation of the act, no more; the Lords' refusal to proceed is, in the circumstances, likely to reflect a superfluity rather than an unwanted purpose in it.

[56] Dashed: bankrupts, ironworks at Wonersh (Surrey), assizes in Lancashire and Durham. Lost: engraving of ulnagers' seals.

[57] There is nothing in the evidence to support Conyers Read's conjecture (*Mr Secretary Cecil and Queen Elizabeth* [1955], 359) that this bill was connected with the vestiarian controversy.

[58] Neale, *Elizabeth I and her Parliaments*, i, 169.

Papers

strictly the work of the Upper House; it was done by the explicit command of the queen and against vocal opposition at least from fifteen bishops who protested against the destruction of a bill they much wanted – a bill which nevertheless has been treated as part of a puritan programme.[59]

It really does not appear that it was the foremost function of the Lords to stop the Commons from misbehaving in matters of great moment; the real relations between the two Houses cannot be deduced from that doubtful axiom. Like so much else, the events of 1566 rather hint that when things went wrong between Elizabeth and her Parliaments it commonly was because she found herself in isolation, opposed not by an eager unofficial group in the Commons but by both Houses in harmony and on issues promoted by her own Privy Council. (Parliament, we might say, was the continuation of politics by other means.) That leaves her last defence, her veto. Did she find herself using it to maintain policy, or was its employment governed by other motives? We rarely hear of vetoing in so many words, but we may suppose that a bill which had passed all stages and yet did not become an act had in fact been vetoed. This is the criterion applied by Neale, and it seems sensible to me.[60] In the first seven sessions of the reign Elizabeth disallowed thirty-four bills. Only four of them even begin to suggest a parliamentary defeat for the queen which she had to use the veto to overcome: a bill for purveyors (1563), the bill for coming to church (1571), and – less likely to belong here – a bill touching presentation to benefices, vetoed twice (1572 and 1576). Why then were those other thirty also quashed? Why did both Houses three times pass a bill to separate the shrievalties of Buckinghamshire and Bedfordshire, and twice pass a like bill for Cambridgeshire and Huntingdonshire, only to see them thrice and twice vetoed, a question the more puzzling because

[59] SP 12/41, fo. 100. Cf. Neale, *Elizabeth I and her Parliaments*, i, 168.
[60] The supposition is supported by a piece of evidence which at first sight seems to contradict it. In September 1573, writing to Burghley, Lord Keeper Bacon reported that the clerk of the Parliament had the failed bills of the last session in his keeping, a session in which seven bills appear to have been vetoed (HMC *Calendar of Salisbury MSS*, ii, 58). Yet Bacon went on to say that only one of them might justify the recalling of Parliament – the one concerning which the queen had said she would be advised of. Since *la reine s'avisera* was the formula of the veto one might suppose that Bacon knew of only one bill vetoed in 1572. However, what he had in mind was the bill against the queen of Scots. When refusing it, Elizabeth went out of her way to appear conciliatory by explaining that on this occasion she would take the words of the formula seriously: she claimed that she really wanted further advice in the matter (Neale, *Elizabeth I and her Parliaments*, i, 309–10). Thus Bacon was distinguishing between the bills truly vetoed and the one ostensibly reserved for future action.

180

a bill doing the same thing for other joined counties passed readily on the first occasion?[61] Why did the veto protect rooks from being exterminated and safeguard abuses of the writ of latitat? Several of those vetoed bills passed without comment in later sessions. At present I do not pretend to be able to answer all these questions, but a notion seems to be forming. It does look as though the veto was most commonly used not for political reasons, or to protect the Crown, but because it had become apparent that some act proposed might damage legitimate or powerful interests. I would suggest that sometimes people affected by intended legislation, having perhaps failed to stop the bill in Parliament, managed to register a protest in the right quarter which secured at least the postponement, more commonly the abandonment, of a measure until the matter had been investigated and perhaps compromised. In 1576 Burghley put crosses against those items on a list of 'the acts passed in both Houses' which 'her majesty is thought will not assent to'.[62] He did well with his crosses: they mark the seven bills vetoed that year. But had the queen told the lord treasurer that she could not in conscience consent to having Cringleford in Norfolk, lately destroyed by fire, rebuilt by act of Parliament? Who had even let her know that such a place existed? In the next Parliament Cringleford got its private act.[63]

We are, in a manner, back where we started. Even in these relations between the partners of the High Court of Parliament, bills and acts – the business of legislation – seem to matter more than the occasional disputes of a high political sort. The function of this Parliament was, in the first place, to resolve the problems of the subject – the whole nation, part of it, individuals – by legislation, and the problems of the Crown by granting money and making laws. Its history tends to reveal a continuous dominant management emanating from the government, rather than the influence of a rising opposition, though some men and groups of men could at times use the platform offered by parliamentary meetings to promote their policies and ideals as well as their ambitions. Such men did not have to be 'puritans' or confine themselves to the House of Commons. Conflict, when it occurred, cannot be assumed to have been ideological; very often it reflected disagreements within the governing group as much as between that group and the Commons, and difficulties arose over many issues reckoned material at the time in which it was the pressure of private

[61] 8 Eliz. I, c. 16, made permanent by 13 Eliz. I, c. 22.   [62] SP 12/107, fos. 207–8.
[63] HLRO, Original Acts, 23 Eliz. I, no. 19.

interest that counted. In the fortunes of Parliament no significant development occurred to take either the whole body or the Commons further along the road to new initiatives or a new independence – further, that is, from the position attained in the Reformation Parliament when the subjection of the spiritualty conveyed full legislative sovereignty to the Parliament, and when the guided experience of seven very active sessions turned it, so far as we can tell, into the body familiar from the better documented second half of the century.

Thus after twenty years we need to rethink and rework much history. We need to take heed of the fact that the once dominant reconstruction of the early-Stuart Parliaments, associated with Wallace Notestein and his school, is crumbling before the onslaughts of scholars concerned to gain a better grasp of the institution itself, to investigate the relationship between identifiable individuals and interests, to unravel the effect of faction, and above all to avoid the teleological structure which related all events to the ultimate breakdown in civil war and revolution. The new insights emerging there cannot help reflecting backwards upon a history of Tudor Parliaments which assumed that it knew from Notestein what happened after the death of Queen Elizabeth. Much of Sir John Neale's work, more firmly based on comprehension from within, still stands up to the test of advancing study, but no more than any historian's contribution can it claim eternal life. Thanks to him – and it is heartfelt thanks – we know where we must start in order to go further.

36

POLITICS AND THE PILGRIMAGE
OF GRACE*

Few scholars these days like to be called political or constitutional historians: it is widely held that those have ceased to be useful occupations. Especially in the United States, a preoccupation with social analysis and the study of ideas and ideologies has become not only predominant but arrogant. It is, I suppose, quite just that political historians, who have for long derided the work of even earlier annalists, should now in turn suffer the contempt of the modern *Annalistes*, but neither these debates nor the prevalent attitudes are especially beneficial to the study of history. Contempt for political history arises from a sometimes justified conviction that its practitioners have in the past been too ready to rest content with surface history – with the lives and doings of kings, bishops, soldiers, politicians and diplomats; they have ignored the great mass of the dead, allowed a few individuals much too great an influence on events, and by-passed the operation of impersonal 'forces'. On top of this we have the beliefs of those to whom no history is worth writing unless it fits a framework of general theory and contributes something to the search for predictable developments. The result has been to replace the political historian's simplifications with the vast simplicities of dehumanized generalization: events have given way to circumstances and men to movements. Yet, as any historian knows who has really looked at the materials of historical study, those great structures and their lesser offspring can be maintained only if the many inconvenient facts – deeds and thoughts and reactions, unpredictable outcomes and accidental stirrings – are left out. And among these inconvenient facts the constant irruption of politics, understood in its fullest sense, stands out above the rest.

Politics are the activities of men in political society, and though they

* [*After the Reformation: Essays in honor of J. H. Hexter*, ed. Barbara Malament (University of Pennsylvania Press, 1980), 25–56.]

may be the active concern of the few, their effects spare none. To study the history of any society without seeking to know what its government was doing is even more inadequate than to study government without reference to social structure or intellectual climate, those vague vogues that at present attract so much devoted and often misguided labour. No one means to defend inadequate forms of political history, and a concern with all that the analysers of 'function' and 'structure' and indeed of ideas and ideologies can tell him is the particular duty of the political historian who wants to tell the fullest story possible about the past, a story through time and space. No more than any other human activity does political history stand still, and its critics ought not to look at long-past performances and attitudes if they really wish to know what it is doing today. The fact is that without a history of public affairs there tends to be no history at all; instead we are likely to get a rather dubious sociology of the past, unrealistically static, devoid of a sense of time passing, often devoid of humanity. I have set out the case at sufficient length elsewhere and do not mean to repeat myself.[1] But in true historical fashion, the case should be proved by example, and this is what I should like to attempt here. The example I propose to study is too large to be fully investigated in an essay, and this paper is in part designed to show the need for further research. However, I hope also to demonstrate that even in the less obvious areas of the past we cannot safely ignore the methods and concerns of political history.

There are few important things that raise our problem in more acute form than large-scale movements against the existing governmental order. They often have political programmes, and their behaviour involves political action; yet the springs of action, the reasons for adherence, the composition of such movements (what is often called their inner reality) cannot as a rule be illuminated by political history as such. Political descriptions of such events, the word goes, stay on the

---

[1] In *Political History: Principles and Practice* (New York, 1970), the one of my books which practically nobody seems to have read. Even Professor Hexter, whose *History Primer* shows (as indeed we know) that he and I agree very widely on the true character of historical study, has never referred to it. No doubt the book justifies that neglect, but I confess to an affection for this runt of the litter, and I was delighted to find my opinion shared by the editor of this volume, who encouraged me to reinforce my assertions by a practical demonstration. I should add that the appearance of an exclusive narrow-mindedness which some have seen in the book is misleading. It was intended to be one of a series on various forms of history; my assignment to consider political history was to be matched by similar studies of economic, social, military history, and so forth. It is a mistake to produce a first volume in a series when in the end there turns out to be no series.

surface; a real understanding depends on economic and social analysis, on the investigation of personal and familial and regional relationships, perhaps above all on theories and typologies of revolution – on all those techniques and interests of which political history remains innocent. Of course, there is some truth in this, but it is also true that when the politics of such events are forgotten the whole thing becomes unexplained and mysterious. To see whether this is so, let us once more consider the largest revolt ever mounted against the rule of the Tudor monarchy in sixteenth-century England – the northern rebellions of the autumn of 1536. Conscious as I am of the effrontery involved in attempting a reconsideration of so vast a subject in a short essay, I am quite prepared to be rapidly overtaken by the progress of research; nevertheless, the time seems ripe to take a comprehensive look.

The fullest account of these risings was provided in the magnificent two volumes which Margaret and Ruth Dodds devoted to them some sixty years ago.[2] Their narrative of events has stood unchallenged and is, indeed, in the main beyond challenge: using all the available evidence (and incidentally using the manuscripts rather than calendar versions), the Misses Dodds told the story in massive and fascinating detail. As they saw it, a spontaneous outburst of protests against Henry VIII's policies began in Lincolnshire on 1 October; within a few days, that shire was convulsed, and very soon the rising spread to the East Riding of Yorkshire, from where it travelled rapidly over all the six northern counties. Everywhere the initiative lay with 'the commons', that it to say, mainly the yeomanry, husbandmen and craftsmen; many of the gentry, compelled by threats, took the pilgrims' oath reluctantly but accepted invitations backed by force to become the leaders of the rebels. The book lays out the full story of negotiations, collapse, betrayal and aftermath – a magnificent tale and a true drama. Though the Misses Dodds recognized some diversity in the various centres of rebellion, and though they provided some analysis of the leadership which should have cast doubt upon their conviction that the upper classes only followed the lead of the commonalty, they confined themselves essentially to an 'old-fashioned' political description of events. They accepted the various sets of demands as trustworthy evidence for the desires of the rebellious body: the whole north was delineated as having risen spontaneously in defence of the old Church, for the Princess Mary's

---

[2] M. E. and R. Dodds, *The Pilgrimage of Grace, 1536–7; and the Exeter Conspiracy, 1538*, 2 vols. (Cambridge, 1915).

right to the throne, for the restoration of the monasteries, for much else, and in particular against the low-born heretical councillors who had perverted the king's policy and brought the realm to ruin. Above all, their exhaustive account gave lasting substance to the figure of a great and uncorrupted leader in Robert Aske. The Doddses' volumes, so dramatic in themselves, provided the material for an influential fictitious treatment which for many has settled the holiness of the Pilgrimage and the saintliness of its leader.[3]

This magisterial discussion held the field quite undisputed for some fifty years, during which little work was done on the history of the Pilgrimage and its aftermath except for some articles by A. G. Dickens, who gradually came to work out his conviction that Yorkshire at least was less devotedly Catholic than had been supposed, a conviction finally elaborated in a work on northern heresy that undermined many of the inherited notions about the Pilgrimage.[4] But by and large the Misses Dodds were supposed to have done it all. In one of the curious notes which Conyers Read occasionally appended to entries in his *Bibliography of British History: the Tudor Period*, their work was summed up as 'impartial, wealth of detail, co-ordination of materials, but little new in conclusions. Valuable.'[5] Certainly it was valuable and provided a wealth of well-co-ordinated detail, but Read might have noticed that its conclusions, though not utterly new, became orthodoxy just because of its apparently total coverage and mastery of the evidence. But impartial it was not: from first to last the book breathes an animus against Henry, Cromwell and the reformers, something like devotion to the cause of Catherine of Aragon, and a profound conviction that what was at stake in the Pilgrimage was 'liberty', a term never defined but frequently employed. On one of the rare ocasions on which they allowed emotion to overtake them, they said of the pilgrims' oath that there was 'a ring in the words that, even today, sets a calm Protestant heart beating to the tune of the Pilgrims' March'.[6] The not necessarily calm heart of a later agnostic finds that oath, well written though it is, a good deal more resistible; but, in any case, the phrase gives the game away. The Misses Dodds were not impartial, nor was there any reason why they should have been. What gave their patently biased account such authority and long life, however, was the fact that it did seem to be entirely in accord

---

[3] Hilda Prescott, *The Man on the Donkey* (1952).
[4] *Lollards and Protestants in the Diocese of York* (Oxford, 1958).
[5] 2nd edn (Oxford, 1959), no. 489.   [6] Dodds, *Pilgrimage of Grace*, i, 182.

with discoverable facts. Even the sceptic, rereading the evidence on which they relied, must admit that to all appearance their story of a truly popular movement which coerced the upper sort into compliance and promoted the restoration of the old Church against the innovators – a movement in which (as they said) such other motives as feudal allegiances, economic grievances and local distrust of interference from the centre played their subsidiary parts – truthfully reflected what had happened.

To all appearance: and it is here that the rub lies. This was a political story handled by the conventional methods of political history, answering the question 'what happened' with the aid of the genre's established and recognized techniques. Was this the truth of events or the truth of the surface? For a long time no one troubled himself further to seek behind the carapace of the tale for the quivering live body, but by the mid-1960s interest revived in the Pilgrimage. The rebellion has never been subjected to the full treatment of structural or quantifying methods, partly because the evidence does not permit much of this and partly because the established orthodoxy suited a historiography which preferred to take its stand with the victims of Henry VIII. Nevertheless, the effects of those novel forms of enquiry were felt here and there, at some remove, and in due course more searching studies of what actually went on, who rebelled, and why they did so have begun to appear. Although no one has yet attempted a comprehensive reassessment, much recent work has made it impossible to agree any longer with any of the major interpretations offered by the Misses Dodds. This new evaluation owes much to a move away from strictly political history and thus bears out the claims of those who campaign against those old-fashioned ways: so far so good. Yet, as I hope to show, undue disregard of politics has also prevented the revisers from seeing what went on and thus from restoring the coherence of explanation that the older account possessed.

The first returns to the problem did not seriously affect the general issues. In 1940 Garrett Mattingly gave renewed currency to the idea that the Pilgrimage was associated with a 'neo-feudal conspiracy' hatched around the imperial ambassador; his highly speculative account, which nevertheless grasped some important connections too readily neglected since, accepted a false sociological concept which has proved persistent.[7] In 1967 A. G. Dickens daringly suggested that the role of religion in the

---

[7] G. Mattingly, *Catherine of Aragon* (1940), 286–90.

insurrections had been greatly exaggerated; especially he could not find that love for the monastic orders was as fervent as the conventional story alleged, and he suggested that the real grievances behind the risings – the grievances of peasants and weavers – stood rooted in economic discontent and apprehensions of further exactions. He still, however, believed that nobles and gentry assumed the leadership under duress; to him the risings were still truly popular movements.[8] A year later, C. S. L. Davies took issue with his argument: he pointed out that the economic circumstances of 1536 were markedly better than those of 1535, that the risings were in no sense a peasants' or class war against the gentry, and that the event required an ideology which it had found in religion – in the defence of the monasteries and the protection of clergy and laity against doctrinal innovation as well as fiscal exaction.[9] These papers usefully reopened the closed subject and presented some helpful insights, but they did not begin to touch the hard core of the Dodds version. At about this time, J. J. Scarisbrick was able to sum up the accepted interpretation by calling the Pilgrimage

a large-scale, spontaneous, authentic indictment of all that Henry most obviously stood for; and it passed judgment against him as surely and comprehensively as *Magna Carta* condemned John or the *Grand Remonstrance* the government of Charles I.[10]

I now mean to show that none of those three adjectives will stand the test of deeper investigation, for even as Scarisbrick wrote, the old view was being thoroughly undermined by studies on the ground – studies that owed much to the preferences and advice of the social historian and that forced upon us a new, but so far incoherent, view of the event. Let us therefore begin by considering how completely this recent work (plus some additional investigations of my own) may have demolished the opinion that the rebellions were large-scale, spontaneous and authentic.[11]

[8] A. G. Dickens, 'Secular and religious motivation in the Pilgrimage of Grace', *Studies in Church History*, vol. 4, ed. G. J. Cuming (1967), 39 ff.
[9] C. S. L. Davies, 'The Pilgrimage of Grace reconsidered', *PP* 41 (1968), 54 ff.
[10] J. J. Scarisbrick, *Henry VIII* (1968), 338 ff.
[11] For the discussion underlying the revision see the following works, which will not be cited at every point. M. E. James, 'Obedience and dissent in Henrician England: the Lincolnshire Rebellion of 1536', *PP* 48 (1970), 3 ff.; and also his *Change and Continuity in the Tudor North: the Rise of Thomas First Lord Wharton*, Borthwick Papers no. 27 (York, 1965), and 'The first earl of Cumberland (1493–1542) and the decline of northern feudalism', *Northern History* 1 (1966), 43 ff. Margaret Bowker, 'Lincolnshire 1536: heresy, schism and religious discontent?', *Schism, Heresy and Religious Protest – Studies in Church History*, vol. 9, ed. D. Baker (1972), 198 ff. R. B.

At first sight, the risings were certainly large-scale – altogether seven counties, about one-third of England, were up in arms in the last months of 1536. This appearance, however, hides much of the reality. Despite the great hosts of 'commons' (and gentry) moving about the countryside, they never roused the whole region. In Lincolnshire, the rebels made little impact south of Lincoln; in Lancashire they dominated only north of the Ribble; in the northern counties the border regions proper remained quiet; Skipton, Carlisle and Scarborough never surrendered; in Clifford country most of the gentry remained loyal; everywhere, and especially in the West Riding, rebellious patches mingled with loyal ones, often depending on the line taken by the lords of different fiefs.[12] Moreover, by no means all the troubled areas formed parts of one single movement. There was interaction but no proper liaison between the Lincolnshire rising and the Pilgrimage of Grace. Lancashire stirred before Aske transferred some of his influence there and remained very uneasy after Aske had called off his proceedings.[13] Northumberland always stood aside from the main rising, and the Middle March (Tynedale and Redesdale) behaved in its traditional lawless fashion rather than joining in the true rebellion. Above all, the disturbances in the Craven district of the West Riding, around Kendal, and in Cumberland, a peasant protest against exploiting landlords, had little more than a chronological coincidence with the Pilgrimage. Though delegates from all parts met at Pontefract, the great host at Doncaster did not include companies from all 'the north', but was really drawn only from Yorkshire and Durham. The troubles comprehended a variety of variously motivated small-scale risings, given a spurious coherence by the one great upheaval in Yorkshire and the purposeful leadership that emerged there. This is not to deny that, especially from the point of view of Henry's government, these various rebellions naturally coalesced into the semblance of one vast disaffected region; but it is important to remember that they never confronted seven counties all united on a single programme and purpose.

I turn to spontaneity. What does one mean by saying that a rebellion is spontaneous? No sizable movement of this sort can occur without some degree of inducement, management and influence: people do not

Smith, *Land and Politics in the England of Henry VIII: The West Riding of Yorkshire, 1530–46* (1970), Ch. 5. C. A. Haigh, *The Last Days of the Lancashire Monasteries and the Pilgrimage of Grace* (Manchester, 1969), esp. ch. 6; also his *Reform and Resistance in Tudor Lancashire* (Cambridge, 1975), ch. 9.

[12] See esp. Smith, *Land and Politics*.   [13] Haigh, *Lancashire Monasteries*.

suddenly, of their own minds, rise up in thousands to march in protest about the countryside or riot through the streets of towns and villages. Somebody will have persuaded them to do so. Of course, there has to be a readiness to be persuaded, though we know enough by now about the psychology of crowds and in-groups to understand something about the way in which a willingness to protest or rebel can be generated among people who had not thought of doing any such thing. In discussing spontaneity we shall therefore be content with that limited sense applicable in such cases – the sense that the outward appearance of an unprepared and unmanaged uprising represents the essential truth of the event. That was what Cromwell's investigators were told had happened in 1536. According to the examinees, the spontaneous outburst at Louth rapidly drew in sympathizers elsewhere in Lincolnshire; what at first were potentially isolated riots quickly formed a co-ordinated movement; the people of Yorkshire and the rest joined in of their own volition as the spark fled down the line; and the Pilgrimage was carried on by self-risen bands of the commons marching from place to place, compelling their betters to come in by threats of violence to life and property, and forcing towns to open their gates and join the rebellion. The demand for action came, so the story went, from below; it originated in the volatile dissatisfaction and distress of the generality, which the upper classes, traditionally rulers and controllers of the people, were powerless to resist.

That some such spontaneous events occurred need not be doubted. The dissolution of the smaller houses of religion provoked positive and self-generated resistance at Hexham in Northumberland and Norton in Cheshire, and at both places the monks received ready assistance from the neighbourhood. However, neither Hexham nor Norton played any part in the Pilgrimage, which never even involved Cheshire at all. It looks likely that the peasant uprising at Kendal, in Craven and around Carlisle was truly spontaneous – a continuation of earlier rioting against enclosing and rack-renting landlords, especially the earl of Cumberland. This, too, however, must be thought pretty marginal to the Pilgrimage proper: Aske experienced real difficulties in incorporating the northwest into his own movement, and the last flicker of rebellion was defeated at Carlisle early in 1537 by just those gentry-led forces that in Yorkshire and Durham constituted the pilgrims' host. Lancashire north of the Ribble also witnessed some independently spontaneous rebellion, which again had to be specifically integrated into the main rising by the despatch there of pilgrims' leaders (Sir Stephen Hamerton and Nicholas Tempest) and which continued in existence after Aske had accepted the duke of Norfolk's promises in December. There was possibly also something sufficiently spontaneous about the activities of the Lincolnshire clergy who first set light to the tinder: the vicar of Louth may possibly have preached his fatal sermon on 1 October without co-ordinating things with anyone else, and the reaction of threatened monks and disaffected parish clergy elsewhere in the shire may have owed little to organization. We cannot be sure (and await further investigation), but quite likely these men were truly and thoroughly worked up by the religious policy of the government – by the break with Rome, by the threat of the Dissolution, and even more by the ban on traditional devotional practices (not to mention taxation).

Or so it might seem: but there must be serious doubts about all this in the light of researches which have left in shreds the story as it was told by those involved. We may look at three aspects of these events which make the notion of spontaneity look less than convincing: the role of the gentry, the manner in which the crowds were set in motion and the evidence of premeditation.

The gentry, nobility and higher clergy who got involved all without exception later claimed to have been coerced: the initiative had never come from them. That, of course, is what they were bound to say if they wished to save their lives, and it is clear that the government accepted these excuses more generally than it believed them: no one wanted a holocaust which would leave six counties without settled order or leadership. But it is also evident that the tale rings very false. The gentry not only joined the rebellion in considerable numbers but invariably acted as its leaders; except among the peasant rioters of the northwest, the commons are always represented as calling for gentlemen to take charge. Such deferential unanimity is in itself not too probable in the midst of a rebellion, and very occasionally even our distorted evidence allows glimpses of a more class-structured conflict: some of the Lincolnshire rebels expressed the desire for noble blood of which one would expect to hear in a peasant uprising and which, for instance, was prominent in the inept plotting inspired by the northern events that occurred in Norfolk in 1537.[14] The usual story is really very odd: everywhere leading gentlemen of ancient authority are shown quivering in their shoes at threats to themselves, their families, their houses and

---

[14] *LP* xi, 972. *Policy and Police*, 142–51.

livestock, and the next moment they are seen taking a most active lead, gathering their tenantry to march to assembly points, debating the purposes and demands of the rising, imposing the terms of negotiation and treating 'the commons' as cannon fodder. No doubt there were popular stirrings here and there, but that the Pilgrimage came to be entirely commanded by supposedly coerced members of the ruling classes is beyond all dispute, and Cromwell had good reason to ask why they should all have been so frightened into positive action when they could point to no single case in which a gentleman had suffered in life or limb for resisting the rebels.[15] Determined 'loyalty' was indeed possible, even though it seems quite often to have been grounded in feuds between gentlemen; thus Sir Brian Hastings, an enemy of Darcy's and hostile to the Percies, never wavered even though it cost him some heads of cattle. One may believe that the crowds of riotous husbandmen and artisans scared some people, and Aske on occasion used threats to extract money and victual from reluctant monks and assistance from reluctant towns; but the overwhelming impression must be that the Pilgrimage originated among the better sort, who brought out the people, leading at first from behind and soon enough from the front. The point has been thoroughly established for Lincolnshire, while the pervasive influence of the Percy connection has been elucidated for Yorkshire, Durham and Northumberland.[16] The government knew the truth from the first, expressing concern to find out 'what personages had in deed the rule of all things whosoever bare the name thereof'.[17] It is no longer possible to avoid the conclusion that in the main the northern risings were not the spontaneous work of the commons but owed far more to the activities of 'alienated' members of the ruling sort, who managed and guided the outbreak from first to last – from causing it to happen to bringing it to a close. Who they were and what caused them to be so disaffected shall be discussed later.

There were real rebels among the commons, and their behaviour confirms that the events of October 1536 did not come about spontaneously. Some people quite evidently accepted the gentry's leadership with a reluctance not shown by the vast majority, watched their betters' doings with deep suspicion, and felt betrayed when the gentry came to terms with the king. Hallom was only the most prominent man of this type. These differences within the commonalty

---

[15] *LP* xii, I, 900, Article 67.   [16] James, 'Obedience and dissent'; Smith, *Land and Politics*.
[17] *LP* xi, 944.

need a lot more working out, but the fact remains that the 'true rebels' emerged in the course of events, adopted their position as the rebellion progressed, and never succeeded in dominating it. Thus, they seem to have tried to profit from proceedings which owed their origin to the activities of others.

The fact of upper-class guidance is further confirmed by the manner in which the rebellion was spread through the north. Right from the start trouble was stirred by means of wild rumours and stories – stories of new taxes, loss of church plate, licences for the eating of better food (white bread and capons) – and it was upon the wings of such rumours, carefully designed to disturb the common people and reinforced by subversive prophecies and ballads, that the rising spread. The idea that the commons took up arms to defend the Church or be rid of Cromwell will not stand up to the evidence: they rose because, already much unsettled by what had in fact been happening to familiar practices of daily piety, they were led to believe often extravagant tales of further doings which would touch their pockets. Money, not the faith, caused the people to stir, if the stories spread are any indication; and the government showed itself aware of this truth in its constant efforts to kill the rumours and to point out that the recent tax touched hardly anyone among the protesters.[18] Furthermore, there were specialists in this task of rumour-spreading: the job was committed to the clergy, both regular and secular, who did their work well, always to the fore in every new hearth of disturbance and for ever prophesying dire threats to people's pockets.[19] At Knaresborough the friars went so far as to post bills all over the place proclaiming the false stories of new imposi-tions – plough money, cattle taxes, heavy charges for baptisms.[20] The clergy, and especially the monks, had assuredly most to lose and could be expected to be active; the wonder is that so many stayed aside while others really submitted to threats. But of the many who enthusiastically threw themselves into the fray and carried disaffection across the north, the important point is that they were agents, not originators. Even the apparently spontaneous action of the Lincolnshire clergy, deeply upset by episcopal pressure to conform to the 1536 Injunctions,[21] looks to have

---

[18] The subsidy of 1534, levied only on those worth over £20 p.a., was the lowest assessed since the beginning of the reign.
[19] The role of the clergy in the rising has been well summarized in Susan Brigden's Manchester B.A. thesis (1973), 'The northern clergy in the Pilgrimage of Grace: a study in resistance'. I am grateful to Miss Brigden for allowing me to use that essay.
[20] *LP* xi, 1047.   [21] Bowker, 'Lincolnshire 1536'.

been staged. Rumours of the characteristic kind ran about the county a good month before the vicar of Louth's sermon,[22] and when the outbreak came, organized agitators who even paid to rent their crowds made their appearance.[23] In fact, the clergy most active in the business would seem to have been the clients of the disaffected gentry: Mrs Bowker tells me that she finds convincing links between ecclesiastical patronage and involvement in rebellion in Lincolnshire, while Miss Brigden can document the use of their clergy by the Yorkshire gentry. Behind the carriers of the infection we again find the normal ruling order of the region.

The same conclusion emerges from a study of the manner in which the pilgrims' host was gathered together. Though many groups of armed rebels assembled in their parishes, and though Lancashire and the northwest relied in the main on this method (the signal being the ringing of bells), the gentry quickly took over and applied their traditional methods – the calling out of the tenantry in formal musters at assembly points.[24] When he decided to come into the open, Darcy used a convenient priest to convey his orders for the mustering of the southern West Riding, and he did so as constable of Pontefract and king's deputy for the region.[25] The essentially independent and unorganized stirrings in Lancashire did not satisfy Aske who in late October sent orders for the systematic raising of that country.[26] Though everybody – the king as well as the rebel leaders – talked as though wild mobs were roaming the countryside with no leadership or organization (and though there were some such excesses here and there), the truth was very different. Aske from the first commanded a reasonably well founded army, to which he added further gentry-led contingents as the rebellion advanced. Anyone doubting this might care to look at the proclamation calling out Marshland and Howdenshire – which started the whole business north of the Humber – or read the account of the great captain's lordly and military bearing at Pontefract, where Lancaster herald found him holding a sort of court in a camp of war.[27]

The best argument, of course, against genuine spontaneity lies in the evidence of planning. It has already been said that the riot at Louth did not come out of the blue, and (as Mr James has shown) the fact that what

---

[22] *LP* xii, I, 70 (xi).   [23] James, 'Obedience and dissent', 12 ff., 20 ff.
[24] See the description of the Yorkshire assembly in *LP* xii, I, 191.   [25] *LP* xi, 1402.
[26] Haigh, *Lancashire Monasteries*, 70–1.   [27] *LP* xi, 622, 826.

was in Tudor terms a commonplace bit of trouble should have rapidly
been enlarged into a general rising demonstrates the existence of careful
preparation. Rumours that by Michaelmas any common man might
find it to his advantage to be in Lincolnshire were current in Norfolk by
the beginning of September.[28] It is therefore important that we should
know as much as possible about the preparatory activities of those who
ultimately emerged as leaders, but much of this will forever remain
obscure. Still, a strictly preliminary look at some of them will be useful
here, if only because it at once throws a very different light upon them
than that cast in the conventional account. Aske apart, about whom
more in a moment, the three key figures were Lord Hussey in
Lincolnshire, Lord Darcy in the West Riding, and Sir Robert Constable
in the East Riding. They are key figures not only because they so
obviously commanded much of the trouble, but also because they stand
well aside from the so-called feudal structure of the north, which itself
requires particular consideration.[29] All three claimed to have been
forced into the ranks of the rebels against their will; all three were
executed for treason. Did their behaviour through the rising bear out
their claims: were they innocent victims? All three were old men in their
seventies who had spent most of their lives in active service under the
Tudor monarchy, and only Constable (the one of them who belonged
to an old-established county family) had failed to profit massively from
his service. According to Hussey himself, they had as early as 1534
agreed among themselves that they 'would not be heretics, but die
Christian men'.[30]

Virtually nothing can be discovered about Constable, for whom no
examination or incriminating letters survive. There are hints of
disaffection: by late 1534 Cromwell received advice from Yorkshire
that Constable ought to be removed from the Commission of the Peace
because he was not carrying out his duties properly.[31] His attachment to
the old religion is in no doubt,[32] but his tracks remain well covered in the
autumn of 1536. Thus, his guilt in planning the revolt can only be
inferred from his old association with the others, against whom the
evidence is clearer. It may also be guessed at from the fact that he was
condemned for treason when other gentlemen of the East Riding whose
actions must raise suspicion (for instance Sir Ralph Ellerker the younger)
remained untroubled. But those are circular arguments of little weight:
let Constable's case stand unproven. Hussey's is clearer and has been

[28] Ibid., 543.   [29] Below, p. 207–9.   [30] *LP* xii, i, 899.   [31] *LP* vii, 1669.   [32] *LP* xii, i, 851.

sufficiently worked out by Mr James, who concludes that he 'was the central figure around whom the Lincolnshire movement both gathered momentum and eventually collapsed'.[33] Hussey certainly played an equivocal part during the rising (I shall offer an explanation of his behaviour later), but the man who, among much dithering, advised the rebels to take Lincoln (which they did) cannot readily be absolved from having foreknowledge of the event. His first reaction to the news of the rioting in the northern part of the county – a letter enquiring whether what had happened involved the gentry – strongly suggests the difficulties of a man who, having planned for just such an event, now needs to discover whether his plans are taking effect or he has been upstaged by an interloper.[34]

Darcy, on the other hand, leaves no doubt. He helps the historian because, in spite of his often tedious pose as the bluff and honest soldier (gruffly referring to himself in the third person – 'old Tom'), he kept a careful and ordered office whose archives came to the Crown at his arrest. Thus, we know that by 1 October he had organized his military following in a long array of knights, esquires and gentlemen (with their retinues) 'promised to serve the king's grace' under his command 'as he appoints upon an hour's warning'. This is an outline of the West Riding's military system, wapentake by wapentake.[35] Thereafter he certainly pretended to be opposed to the rising and to be keeping an eye on it, but Henry justly complained that he was not sending the right or the full information. Having sent his second son, Arthur, on a mission to the earl of Shrewsbury, he then tried to get him back to Pontefract in an effort to avoid leaving a hostage in royalist hands, warned York of the approach of Aske's army in terms which can only be read as an encouragement to surrender, and refused to proceed against Aske or (later) to hand him over because to do so would offend his honour.[36] The speed with which he surrendered Pontefract told most urgently against him, and no wonder; but the point is that the moment the rebels entered the castle Darcy emerged as Aske's chief fellow commander, very much the second man in charge of the proceedings. So rapid a conversion makes sense only on the assumption that Darcy had been in the plot from the first. What perhaps tells most forcefully against him, as Cromwell realized who pressed him hard on the point,[37] was the famous badge of the five wounds of Christ under which the pilgrims marched.

[33] James, 'Obedience and dissent', 52 ff.   [34] *LP* xi, 532.   [35] Ibid. 522.
[36] Ibid. 605–6, 627, 1045.   [37] *LP* xii, I, 900, Articles 73–87.

It had been Darcy's badge over twenty years before when he took his retinue to southern France in the disastrous expedition led by the marquess of Dorset in support of Ferdinand of Aragon. Its use in 1536 was lamely explained by a story that the accidental killing of a man among the rebels had suggested the need for a distinguishing badge. Well and good: but how did thousands of badges get made in one night? Or had he dug out that ancient store? The implication that Darcy had fully prepared for the rebellion is overwhelming and, as we shall see, there is in fact plenty of evidence for a conspiracy with Darcy at the centre. Darcy and Hussey were in close contact in November 1536, and though the particular messenger used denied that he had ever carried messages to Constable, the very manner of his denial hints that somebody else did.[38] The chances that in early October 1536 these three men were taken totally by surprise are too slight to be seriously considered.

The most formidable case, however, lies against Aske, whose emergence as the chief leader, the great captain, is rather astounding. Unlike the others he carried no natural authority; a minor gentleman of good family and, of all things, a lawyer (the bogey-man most hated among the common people), he really makes an odd choice for the command of rebellious shires. The fact has, of course, been read as evidence of true spontaneity: driven into rebellion, the commons found an idealist deeply disturbed by the king's policy and got him to take upon himself the organizing of the protest. But that is not what really happened. Aske's own story of how he came to be involved has always been accepted without question, mainly because we have learned to believe in the axiom of his saintly uprightness.[39] Yet it hardly makes sense. As Aske told it, he was visiting the Ellerkers in the East Riding for a weekend's hunting when Sir Ralph had to go off to attend to his duties as a subsidy commissioner. This broke up the party, and Aske decided to go to London for the start of the law term. This innocent purpose was interrupted when a band of Lincolnshire rebels captured him after he crossed the Humber and made him swear the rebel's oath. Even by his own account he immediately acquired some authority among them, and he took it upon himself to ride to Caistor (even though he took care to emphasize that leaving the band put him in danger of being regarded as a treacherous turncoat) in order to find out what was going on there. In fact, as he admitted, he went over to confer with Thomas Moigne,

---

[38] Ibid. 1013.
[39] His narrative was printed by Mary Bateson in *EHR* 5(1890), 330 ff.; summary in *LP* xii, i, 6.

one of the leaders of the Lincolnshire rising. He then returned to Yorkshire, allegedly to prevent any spontaneous outbreak there, but found on his rejoining the rebels south of the Humber that he was now unable to travel further toward London because, on account of his brief departure, he was threatened with assassination if he should reach Lincoln. There was nothing for it, therefore, but to cross back into Howdenshire once more; the weather delayed him, and meanwhile a forged letter pretending to run in his name raised Beverley – and so the trouble started.

It is a story full of improbabilities. The king knew of the rebellion early on 4 October;[40] yet Aske started his journey that day in alleged ignorance that anything had happened. Even when the ferryman at Barton-on-Humber told him that Caistor was up he continued his journey. His talking to Moigne (a fellow lawyer) is deeply suspicious. Having once got away from the rebels who had forced him to take the oath, he yet rejoined them. His excuse for not pursuing his professed original intention of going to London is surely unbelievably thin. Even if it was true that he had reason to fear for his life – and I do not find this credible – the alternative he chose to getting to Westminster Hall, namely the transmission of the rebellion to Yorkshire, leaves his real mind very much exposed. And even if the proclamation in his name was forged, why should Marshland and Howdenshire have risen in response to it unless they were expecting it; and why should a forger have used his name unless it was known that he was preparing the East Riding for an uprising? Aske's whole conduct in that first October week makes sense only on the assumption that he was involved in a conspiracy but was taken by surprise when Lincolnshire burst out before he was ready in Yorkshire. He then, I suggest, went to see what was going on and made some efforts to prevent premature and ill-co-ordinated stirrings; indeed, the speed with which the Lincolnshire rising collapsed testifies to his good sense in wanting to be convinced that the operation was being properly conducted. He managed to hold the East Riding back long enough to make sure that when he unleashed rebellion it would sweep immediately and successfully through Marshland and Howdenshire, thus at once providing the means of power which made possible the rapid march to York and the speedy link-up with Darcy and Sir Thomas Percy in the West Riding. Success here enabled Lord Latimer to mobilize the North Riding, Sir Ingram Percy to do the same in

[40] Dodds, i, 107.

Durham, and a general rebellion to spread through the north. That Aske knew nothing of plans to rebel until he encountered those Lincolnshire men on 4 October simply cannot be believed, and the manner in which Yorkshire joined testifies impressively to the preparations that he and others had made – preparations good enough even to overcome the handicap of what must now look like a premature outbreak in Lincolnshire that came close to jeopardizing the whole enterprise.

Spontaneous, therefore, is the wrong word to apply to the northern rebellions of 1536. Nearly all of them were planned in advance and organized from above, though without any doubt at all planning and organization were effective because the materials of disaffection and protest lay thick upon the ground. These materials have usually provided the arguments for thinking the rebellion 'authentic' – that the protests embodied in the pilgrims' demands represented the general and genuine grievances of those into whose mouths they were put. Is this true?

Of course, one accepts that such sets of demands – a programme – cannot emerge spontaneously in any case; someone must do the drafting, and in so mixed and muddled a rising as that of 1536 the outcome is bound to include notions put forward by various sections as well as compromises between them. Such things do not deny 'authenticity', but there are features about the rebels' programmes that raise serious doubts. They emerged in ways that hint at total control by a small group, and they contain items that do not fit the generally projected image. The various sets of demands put up in Lincolnshire appear to have run to eight items: no taxation except for war, the restoration of the Church's ancient liberties and the abolition of first fruits and tenths, an end to the Dissolution, an end to heresy and the punishment of Cranmer, Latimer and Longland, reliance on noble councillors and the destruction of Cromwell, Rich, Legh and Layton, a pardon for the rebels, and the repeal of the Statute of Uses.[41] At first sight they seem both comprehensive and representative of the various elements in the insurrection – poor commons, religious houses, the ordinary clergy, conservatives in religion and politics, the landowning and conservative gentry. However, we know that they were effectively put together by one man – George Stones or Staines – who most energetically made propaganda for them; we know that they were agreed by gentlemen only, at a meeting held while the commons were busy killing one of their victims; and we know that they had to be

[41] Ibid. 114, plus the last one, well vouched for elsewhere and strangely omitted by Dodds.

explained in detail to the multitude who were later alleged to have put them forward.[42] Not only were many people puzzled to know what the Statute of Uses might be, but they even had to be told who Cromwell was and why removing him should help. No doubt the houses still standing supported the call for no more suppressions, but the fact remains that no attempt was made in Lincolnshire to restore a single one of those already dissolved.[43] The list of men named as enemies of the people is surely strange. If the commons wanted heretical prelates, Cranmer, as archbishop, would readily come to mind; but was Latimer, who had never been active in the north, really known there? His fame ran in the west country and at court, a point of significance. As for Longland, whatever his position toward the reform, he was no heretic in the Latimer mould, but he happened to be the local man and had been exceptionally active in enforcing the government's orders touching the innovations. Stranger still is the roll call of offending ministers. Cromwell: well, yes; but the commons did not know him for an enemy, and he was pointed out by the gentlemen, and especially by Stones. The mention of Legh and Layton again reflects the feelings of those troubled by the Dissolution, but no one could possibly have regarded these non-councillors as leading members of the government. As for Rich, he had been active as chancellor of Augmentations since April 1536[44] and thus may have collected the hatred of the defenders of monasticism; he was certainly not a prominent man in the realm at large. However, he had sworn away Sir Thomas More's life: and George Stones had a strong connection with the late lord chancellor's family circle.[45] At one point, the master of the Rolls (Christopher Hales) joined the proscription list, a man who had never shown the slightest leaning towards heresy; on the other hand, he had been Stones's master, which might be a better reason for his pointless inclusion. Thus, there are at least strong hints here that the demands embodied not only a confusion of local grievances, many of them sold to the rebels rather than produced by them, but also a bundle of London-based court grievances which had nothing to do with Lincolnshire at all.

[42] James, 'Obedience and dissent', 24, 37. And cf. Dodds, *Pilgrimage of Grace*, i, 102–3.

[43] Dodds, i, 112.

[44] W. C. Richardson, *History of the Court of Augmentations* (Baton Rouge, 1961), 65. Rich was also Speaker (elected with unusual difficulty) in the 1536 Parliament, which passed the Second Act of Succession, a measure that again ignored Mary's claims; this may well have been the reason for his appearing in the rebels' grievances.

[45] James, 'Obedience and dissent', 26.

The demands of the Pilgrimage of Grace, better recorded and far better worked out, pose very similar problems. Aske's first proclamation, a very incendiary document claiming to speak in the name of 'the barony and communalty' of 'the conventual assembly or pilgrimage', listed six: the Dissolution, the Act of Uses, payment of first fruits, general taxation, the 'base council about the King', the new bishops (which excludes Longland, that Lincolnshire speciality, who had held his see since 1521).[46] Elaborated and added unto, these remained the basis of the programme. It was admitted that this foundation did not originate in Yorkshire but simply took over the Lincolnshire articles, which Aske brought with him when, with two Lincolnshire messengers, he transferred the rising to Yorkshire, and one of the more reluctantly involved gentlemen later stated that he had never heard any of these grievances discussed before the insurrection.[47] Thus, for instance, Aske's admission that the Statute of Uses would never have been mentioned if Stones had not with some difficulty forced it into the Lincolnshire articles must at once call in question the seriousness of that particular complaint.[48]

The final comprehensive statement of demands, worked out at Pontefract, was composed by Aske in consultation with Darcy and other leaders; though based on grievances contributed by the representatives of various parts of the north, it underwent careful recension at a very few hands; it was then agreed, article by article, with the delegation sent to Doncaster, where they were to present it to the duke of Norfolk; finally it received approval from the full assembly of leaders – that is, gentry and clergy – at Pontefract.[49] This careful procedure must not disguise the fact that Aske (with perhaps Darcy) remained personally in charge of production throughout: the Articles were very much one man's work, but they also offer some manifest clues concerning the influences behind their composition.

Following the Misses Dodds, we may discuss them under four headings: religious, constitutional, legal and economic. The last category needs no more than a glance. The recent subsidy was widely resented, partly because all taxes annoyed but especially because this one

[46] *State Papers of Henry VIII* (1830), i, 466–7.
[47] *LP* xi, 808; xii, I, 29 (2).
[48] *LP* xii, I, 901 (2).
[49] Dodds, i, 346 ff. I base my discussion on the usefully classified summary of the grievances set out there, though it should be noted that the authors' comments reveal some bias and some ignorance, especially of the law.

called expressly for contributions to peacetime government;[50] on the other hand, the protest against enclosures and high 'gressums' (entry fines) was, as is well known, a specialist grievance of the tenantry in Cumberland, Westmorland and the upper Yorkshire dales. Here we seek no hidden hand. Similarly, there are some points among the religious complaints which we can readily concede as authentic, not only in the sense that certain obvious groups would sincerely (and selfishly) maintain them, but also on the grounds that many of the commons and the bulk of the gentle no doubt were genuinely attached to traditional rights, practices and beliefs. Resentments at attacks on the clerical privileges of sanctuary and benefit of clergy were nothing new; the whole southern Convocation had demonstrated its feelings in 1515, and those of the north evidently still continued to hold much the same opinion. We may also believe without question that the clergy assembled at Pontefract wished to recover the liberties of the north (Durham, Beverley, Ripon, St Peter of York) against the recent act which had abolished all such. After all, Archbishop Lee, owner of Ripon and Beverley, was there, though Tunstal of Durham throughout prudently hid himself from everybody. The articles attacked first fruits and tenths, as had the Lincolnshire demands, but at Pontefract they sought to protect only monasteries; again no doubt a genuine point of ordinary selfishness.

But these were not the crucial matters under the head of religion. Three issues predominated: the royal supremacy, the fate of the abbeys and the spread of heresy. It is on the basis of those articles that the Pilgrimage has generally been regarded as primarily a movement of religious protest. Touching the first, the leaders of the rising, who throughout claimed to be loyal subjects of Henry VIII, were in a cleft stick, and the only point they dared include was one which reasserted the pope's supremacy in matters spiritual (*cura animarum*) and in the consecration of bishops. Even this, in the year that saw the culmination of the government's campaign against Rome, was to tread on very dangerous ground. It was also a demand, as he confirmed, that owed its inclusion mainly to Aske, who admitted that it had hardly been discussed by the leaders and was put in when he thought he heard no objections.[51] So far as the evidence goes, the Pilgrimage produced no general enthusiasm for the pope or against the royal supremacy; in the many letters describing the grievances of the people, the political

[50] See below, no. 37.   [51] *LP* xii, I, 909 (44).

revolution in the Church remains resoundingly unmentioned. The fate of the religious houses excited more interest, but again Aske's very exceptional concern emerges from his testimony. The familiar song of praise about the great good done by the monks of the north occurs solely in what he told his interrogators and is there described as his own opinion.[52] One need not take scepticism to excess: the monastic institution had undoubtedly retained more respect in the north than elsewhere. Nevertheless, the only evidence of spontaneous support for the religious comes from Lancashire; Professor Dickens has drawn attention to manifestations of a well-entrenched hostility to monasteries in parts of Yorkshire; though Aske very early in the rising ordered the restoration of dissolved houses, at most sixteen of the fifty-five affected experienced the return of the inmates, the only safely documented case once again belonging to Lancashire; the religious themselves displayed so remarkable a reluctance to grasp the helpful hand offered by rebellion that they have drawn stern censure from their foremost historian.[53] We have really been far too ready to accept the view that the whole uprising was unleashed by conservatism in religion, even if it is conceded that conservatism in religion existed and helped to create the unsettled atmosphere. Aske said that that issue alone would have caused rebellion even if there had been no other; and this has well suited a variety of historians' attitudes ranging from personal convictions about the Reformation to methodological convictions concerning the primacy of socioeconomic and ideological explanations. The evidence for Aske's statement is very meagre and mostly derived from his other remarks. At most we can say that many of the clergy, especially the seculars, expressed their dislike of the innovations and indoctrinated many of their parishioners, and that Aske deliberately from the first gave to the movement that air of a spiritual protest (a pilgrimage) which correctly reflected his own convictions but which he had difficulty in keeping alive among the mass of his followers. The moderate ease with which 'the north' (Lancashire excepted) settled thereafter to the Reformation should sufficiently indicate that the religious purposes of the Pilgrimage had shallow roots, except among the few who dominated its ideology, eloquence and propaganda.[54]

[52] Ibid. (23).

[53] Dickens, 'Secular and religious motivation'; G. O. Woodward, *The Dissolution of the Monasteries* (1966), 93–7; D. Knowles, *The Religious Orders in England*, vol. 3 (Cambridge, 1959), ch. 25.

[54] This is a tricky business, and further research may well renovate the opinion that profound attachment to the old religion was widespread through the north. Davies, 'Pilgrimage of Grace

But were the pilgrims not dead set against heresy, as three of the leaders (Darcy, Hussey and Constable) had agreed they were a full two years earlier? The articles speak strongly on the subject, but in tones that are far from clear. They mention a general demand for the punishment, by burning or otherwise, of all heretics, episcopal (no names) and lay, and they charge Cromwell, Audley and Rich with being supporters of heresy who merit condign punishment. Even the Lincolnshire rebels had been more specific about which bishops they wanted done away with, but then the pilgrims at Pontefract could not even make up their minds as to what constituted heresy.[55] They inclined to accepting the Ten Articles (which had so much troubled the parish clergy ordered to proclaim them), and the curious Rump Convocation that met at Pontefract broke up without a usable answer to the question.[56] Aske reckoned that Cranmer, Latimer, Hilsey and Barlow were heretics, and another document added Brown of Dublin:[57] quite a reasonable list, which proves that someone in the know supplied names, though the omission of these or any names from the articles themselves argues that the general assembly had insufficient grasp to become specific. Even more mysterious is the list of heretical writings whose suppression was demanded, a list which (it is supposed without much evidence) may have derived from a memorial put up by Robert Bowyer, a citizen and lawyer of York.[58] The continent supplied Luther, Hus, Melanchthon, Oecolampadius, Bucer, the Augsburg Confession, Melanchthon's *Apology*, 'and such other heresies of Anibaptist' (did they really suppose there was a heresiarch of that name?). England added Wycliffe, Tyndale, Barnes, (William) Marshall, (John) Rastell, (Christopher) St German. One must wonder at the inclusion of Oecolampadius and Bucer, neither of whom appeared in English translation till many years later: here one smells a degree of sophisticated, even esoteric, information. But if the rebels were so well informed about heresy, why did they include Rastell, recently dead, who had published only on the common law and common morality, and St German, whose lay criticism of clerical abuses only Thomas More had ever thought remotely heretical? How

reconsidered', makes a good case for the part played by religion as the ideology necessary to turn a series of conventional riots into a major uprising. But for the present it looks to me as though the ideology was there because Aske injected it, not because it authentically represented the views of the multitude.

55 The Doddses' index says, charmingly and revealingly: 'Heresy, see New Learning'. It is some sort of definition, and one shared by the more obscurantist conservatives of the day, but hardly one to put before a spiritual court.

56 Dodds, i, 382–6.   57 *LP* xii, i, 901 (31); xi, 1182 (2).   58 Dodds, i, 346.

did the men of the north even come to think of them? In fact, More supplies the missing link: he had campaigned against St German, and Rastell was a renegade from his circle who had turned to work for Cromwell. Furthermore, these men were prominent London lawyers, a point that deserves to be remembered. This idiosyncratic list of heretics lends no support to the notion that the risings took their origin from a widespread resistance to the religious side of the Reformation. Altogether, then, the rebels' demands fail to substantiate the authenticity of the religious protest, though it is clear that there was much vague discontent concerning the reform and that some of the participants – Aske in particular – put religion first. It can be believed that without the religious shape given to the rising it would probably have lacked cohesion, drive and endurance; whatever raised 'the commons' in the first place, they found companionship and fervour under the banner with the cross and the five wounds. But the positive positions expressed in the demands were held by a group of leaders, not by 'the north'.

The real problems that concern us are raised by the so-called constitutional and legal articles, hardly any of which can be said to have risen from general or spontaneous demand. Perhaps the pilgrims generally abominated the 1534 Act of Treasons, and no doubt the rather blatant request that all debts incurred during the rebellion should be cancelled by act of Parliament met with sober acclaim. But the Statute of Uses, so obviously offensive to the landed classes, would, as we have seen, have been forgotten except that it was in the pronouncements transferred from Lincolnshire. Aske admitted that he disliked it because it disturbed the settled land law, but the possible legal effects he mentioned were marked more by perverse ingenuity than sense: he was never more the lawyer than when he tried to persuade his interrogators that the statute worked against the king's feudal rights.[59] Whether such minor grievances as the act against handguns (resented by hunting squires and poachers)[60] or complaints about escheators' false inquisitions *post mortem* (an ancient and conventional theme) reflected a general or a very particular opinion cannot be settled and does not matter. The real issues under this head were four: the restoration of the Princess Mary, the freeing of Parliament from royal influence, dislike of the Succession

[59] *LP* xii, i, 407–8. No one has ever explained what his rigmarole meant, and I do not believe that he understood the statute.
[60] The act was intended to improve, not to hamper, the arming of the nation; the Misses Dodds here talk liberal rubbish (*Pilgrimage of Grace*, i, 346).

Act because it empowered Henry to bequeath the Crown by his last will and testament, and the defence of the common law against recent innovatory practices. Taken together, these four clearly reveal who and what stood behind the real leadership of the Pilgrimage, though I can here only summarize a provisional but compelling conclusion.

The first and third points both arose from the consequences of Henry's Divorce and constitute a demand that the king's first marriage be held legitimate and its issue be recognized as the true heir to the Crown; the complaints about Parliament combine the strangely antiquarian grumbles of Lord Darcy with an already well established 'country' (backbench) dislike of influence which was to have a long history thereafter (after all, the first place bill was introduced in Mary's reign), while the last constitutes the professional protest of one faction among common lawyers against the recent growth in the power of Chancery – against the work of Wolsey. An Aragonese-Marian faction, 'country' independents in the Commons resentful of aggressive royal policies, conservative lawyers: these particular interests were also, as has already been suggested, responsible for the personal attack on Cromwell, Audley and Rich, hated far less by 'the commons' than by disappointed courtiers and certain London lawyers. It was Aske who hated Audley, as he said, because of the chancellor's use of injunctions,[61] though Wolsey had been more lavish with them and More no less convinced of their usefulness; it was St German who in his best known book (*Doctor and Student*) had defended the powers of equity. Quite manifestly his so doing offers a more convincing reason why he should have joined the list of enemies of the commonwealth than his alleged heresy. The significance of the More connection, and therefore of Sir Thomas's death as one of the causes of violent hostility especially to Cromwell, peeps through obscurely, and so does the leading role of lawyers and their disputes. Their influence in the rising is manifest but has not yet been studied: Aske and Moigne were only the most prominent of an Inns of Court group who lent their support and leadership to the Pilgrimage and in return appear to have expected the pilgrims to endorse their professional griefs. However, until more work has been done on connections and attitudes it is not possible to do more than suggest that one of the positive origins of the risings should be tracked back to the Inns of Court and Westminster Hall.

As for Cromwell and Rich, it must be doubted whether they were so

[61] *LP* xii, I, 6:9.

universally hated as has been alleged. Quite certainly they had their enemies, and some efficient propaganda was conducted, in songs and prophetic utterances, especially against the lord privy seal, but Aske himself said that he knew of no cause to consider him a destroyer of the commonweal.[62] The case against him was put, with much violent abuse, in a memorial submitted by (probably) Sir Thomas Tempest, who sat for Newcastle in the Reformation Parliament: here we find, most usefully, a plain expression of the state of mind of a country backbencher who resented conciliar management in the Commons (and it says something for the isolation of historians one from another that this typical complaint, matchable over the centuries, should regularly have been regarded as a convincing indictment of Henry's and Cromwell's relations with Parliament).[63] It was Tempest who introduced the furious complaint about influence over elections and influence in the House, because of the result: 'Whatsoever Cromwell says is right, and none other.' The other thing that stuck in Tempest's throat was Cromwell's severe action the year before against the grand jury of Yorkshire, who had discovered that gentle status and country independence were no protection against Star Chamber. Perhaps some really hated Cromwell as a heretic – the charge which in the end destroyed him – but quite manifestly the real complaint of the northern gentry against him in 1536 was his government of the realm and especially his competent management of the king's affairs in Parliament. Tempest, like Darcy, was objecting to political defeat – to the victory, in and out of Parliament, of religious reform and administrative centralization – and here lies the vital clue.

It is now plain that the conventional view of the northern rebellions will not stand up. All in all, the affair was not large-scale, spontaneous and authentic. It drew in many quite real grievances and dissatisfactions, and it mobilized resentments of all kinds – social, economic, religious. It was dominated, and to all appearance instigated, not by the commons who were induced to make the running, but by the gentry who, to use Mr James's phrase, were 'alienated from the court': this was as true of Yorkshire, Durham and Northumberland as it was of Lincolnshire. Moreover, there is plain evidence of preparation, indeed of conspiracy. Who conspired, and why?

The usual answer – of those, that is, who admit the conspiracy – is the answer of the social historian: the rebellion was a feudal or

[62] Ibid.   [63] *LP* xi, 1244.

Papers

(sometimes) neo-feudal phenomenon, a typically northern reaction to
Tudor centralization and a hangover from the fifteenth century. This
view is found well embedded in the literature and requires no lengthy
demonstration here. The one man who really tried to dissect the
conspiracy thought that it should be called feudal.[64] The feudal north has
so well settled in the historical consciousness that even those scholars
whose social analysis underlies so much of the revision attempted here
have not escaped from the compulsion of the tag.[65] Yet what was so
feudal about the Pilgrimage (for even the convention will allow that the
adjective does not fit Lincolnshire)? Of the great northern families,
Clifford supported the king, and Dacre, contrary to expectations, never
moved at all either way. Nevill, sadly in decline, supplied a leader of
sorts in Lord Latimer, offspring of a cadet branch and a member of that
anti-feudal institution, the Council of the North; the earl of Westmorland kept his distance. Only the Percies behaved in a possibly feudal
way, for certainly Percy influence explains many of the alignments in
Yorkshire and Northumberland. But the earl of Northumberland, head
of the family, took every step he could to avoid involvement; he was the
only man of standing whom the pilgrims inspected as a possible
conscript and left alone. His brothers, Thomas and Ingram, so
prominent in the rising, were fighting not for the 'Percy interest' but for
their inheritance, lost to them by the earl's bequest of his possessions to
the Crown; they were trying not to recreate the Percy lordship but to
keep the Percy lands, in a very unfeudal and totally gentlemanlike way.
When the cry of Percy was raised, as it was at York, effectively against
the earl, feudalism seems a long way off. The rising did not even reveal
much clannishness; families were far from standing together. Lord
Darcy's two sons resolutely abstained from rebellion and never thought
to avenge his death; Robert Aske's brother defended Skipton for the earl
of Cumberland; Constables and Ellerkers are found on opposing sides.[66]

Thus, the two things absent from the troubles were feudalism of any
convincing sort and dynasticism. The political structure of the northern
shires, particularly of Yorkshire and Lincolnshire, the real heart of the

[64] Mattingly, *Catherine of Aragon*, 286–90; Scarisbrick, *Henry VIII*, 340, accepts his definition of
the conspiracy as neo-feudal.
[65] In his *Faculty, Lineage and Civil Society* (Oxford, 1974), M. E. James places the transformation
from a feudal to a normal, gentry-dominated, society in the generation *after* the Pilgrimage.
[66] Cf. the duke of Norfolk's cry (*LP* xi, 909): 'Fie, fie upon the lord Darcy, the most arrant traitor
that ever was living, and yet both his sons true knights; old Sir Robert Constable as ill as he is,
and all his blood true men.'

rebellion, already looks much like that of the south. The relationships of various gentry groupings, involving also the members of the northern Council, themselves local gentlemen and higher clergy, dominated county politics, but the groups could be readily 'polarized' by the arrival of new men within the inner circle, by the workings of Crown patronage, and by the intrusion of government, producing the sort of 'court and country' situation so characteristic, for instance, of Elizabethan Norfolk.[67] This is much too large a theme to be worked out in detail here, and one must be careful of overlarge generalizations: but to my mind the situation in the north in 1536 resembled much more the structure which produced the civil wars of the seventeenth century than that which accounts for the civil wars of the fifteenth.

It was upon this situation that the actual conspiracy which did occur impinged. It itself was even less 'feudal'. Who were the real leaders of rebellion? Darcy and Hussey stood out among them, and they were no feudatories. Though they persuaded the often gullible Eustace Chapuys, Charles V's ambassador, that they were 'great magnates on the border', a view too trustingly accepted by the historian,[68] they were nothing of the sort. Both owed their elevation to the Tudor monarchy, and both were primarily courtiers, as incidentally Constable had been before he inherited his lands and retired north. Darcy had been prominent in the court faction which overthrew Wolsey,[69] and in retrospect it must seem that one of his motives on that occasion had been his belief that Wolsey bore the responsibility for Henry's break with his first wife. For Darcy was soon an equally prominent activist in the Aragonese court faction which from 1530 or a little later attempted to arrest the Divorce and the attack on the Church's independence that went with it. Hussey, Mary's chamberlain, naturally stood always in the thick of this group. In September 1534 both men came very close to plotting violence as their only hope, though at that time they did not wish to move without assurance of at least token military support from the emperor. Hussey himself sought out Chapuys and mentioned Darcy as his closest associate and the one who would professionally handle the military side, but it was he who really gave the game away when he

---

[67] Cf. A. Hassell Smith, *County and Court: Government and Politics in Norfolk, 1558–1603* (Oxford, 1974).

[68] *LP* vii, 1206; Mattingly, *Catherine of Aragon*, 287.

[69] Curiously enough, at the head of the charges against Darcy one of Cromwell's men added a reference to Darcy's part in Wolsey's fall (*LP* xii, I, 848). Was Cromwell thinking of avenging his old master, to whom he alone had ever shown any loyalty?

advised a manner of proceeding which would first organize an insurrection of the people and then bring in the nobility and the clergy.[70] Darcy also told Chapuys that he kept his real mind secret even from his sons: evidently their loyalty in 1536 derived from their ignorance of the conspiracy. What happened in October 1536 was plainly contemplated some two years earlier, and Hussey's remark (which has unaccountably been overlooked by the historians) clinches the case for the interpretation of the Pilgrimage here advanced.

The conspirators assured Chapuys that they had good hopes of several noblemen; they mentioned Derby, Rutland, Shrewsbury, and, more doubtfully, Norfolk, all by the way court peers. It is on this slender basis that the whole business has been called feudal. Perhaps the addition of Stanleys, Manners, Talbots and Howards might have created a true feudal array against Henry, but conspirators' hopes do not equal the truth, and however much these noblemen may have disliked Cromwell or innovation in the Church, they never deserted their duty to the king and in the event were largely responsible for the failure of the rising to spread. And no wonder: with the possible exception of Shrewsbury, they were all Tudor creatures who owed their local ascendancies to the favour of the Crown, not to feudal roots. In 1534 nothing further happened, perhaps because (as has been suggested) Darcy was kept in London at the time, but also, no doubt, because Charles V never responded to the various attempts to involve him actively in the defence of his aunt. The death of that aunt in January 1536 deprived the Aragonese faction (strong in the Privy Chamber) of an impressive figurehead and turned its attentions to two political ambitions: the overthrow of the Boleyns, vulnerable since Anne had lost her hold on the king, and the restoration of the succession to the Princess Mary. The first was achieved in April, when a court line-up against the Boleyns received the accession of Cromwell, who had his own reasons for wishing to be rid of what had become highly embarrassing allies.[71] But he also had his plans for his new and highly temporary allies at court. No sooner were Anne and her associates out of the way than Cromwell used the new Succession Act (hostile to Mary) and the princess's obstinate refusal to submit unreservedly to the royal supremacy to discredit the remnant of the Aragonese faction, who in July stood in fear of execution themselves. Hussey lost his office in Mary's household, and his wife spent a spell in the Tower for allegedly

[70] *LP* vii, 1206.   [71] For this complex story cf. above, p. 50, n. 87.

encouraging the princess's obstinacy. The conservatives discovered that all they had achieved by their attack on the Boleyns was the final elevation of Cromwell to complete power under the king. Darcy, back in Yorkshire since mid-1535, played no direct part in these court battles, but it would be absurd to suppose that he did not know what was going on. The events of April–July 1536 provide ample explanation for the virulent hatred of Cromwell displayed by Darcy and other members of the faction, a hatred of which there had been no sign in the days when they concentrated their venom on Anne Boleyn.

Thus, it would appear that these events – the defeat of a court faction in one of the typical political struggles of the age – convinced the leadership that drastic measures were needed both to save themselves from destruction and to overthrow Cromwell, and they therefore resolved to put the old plans for raising the country into effect. No doubt the further disturbance caused by the dissolution of the lesser monasteries encouraged hopes of success and certainly provided useful agents for a rising, but the decisive events to bring about the northern rebellions happened at court, not in the country. On this occasion a court faction transferred its power base to the country, a step most unusual in the sixteenth century. It had to do so because it had lost all hope of victory by conventional means, and it was able to do so because the country – or at least Lincolnshire and Yorkshire – were ready to be so politicized. Widespread consternation at Cromwell's revolution in the Church laid the foundations. In Lincolnshire the leading gentry were deeply suspicious of the growing intrusion of court interests (especially the Brandon duke of Suffolk and the Blounts, ambitious newcomers in the county);[72] in Yorkshire, the king's forthcoming inheritance of the Percy estates reinforced deep apprehensions about the extension of central power through Cromwell's policy and men. Sir Thomas Tempest left explicit record of this typically 'country' reaction to the advancing tentacles of the court, but that he was not the only one is clear, for instance, from the behaviour of such men as Sir Ralph Ellerker and Sir Robert Bowes, local men in the royal service who saw in the rebellion a means of preserving their local power against invasion from yet newer men in the royal service. There was, therefore, a rebellion to be unleashed, but it was actually unleashed by the specific political ends of one of the age's political parties, namely the restoration of Mary and the undoing of Cromwell, both intended to change the

[72] James, 'Obedience and dissent'.

king's proceedings from revolution to reaction. That is why these 'demands' figured so prominently in the pilgrims' programme; that is why the Statute of Treasons (which had made little impact in the north before October 1536) and the Second Succession Act made their appearance in the articles. Among the political motives present, the desire to avenge Sir Thomas More's death and resistance to equitable interference with the common law may also have played their part, but these purposes were themselves germane to the main programme of the faction and, as it were, entertained by its fringe members.

Of course, the plans of the faction soon ran into major complications. The troubles of Sir Thomas and Sir Ingram Percy offered fertile ground for exploitation and greatly assisted the rapid spread of rebellion, but they also reduced the singlemindedness of the movement. The Dissolution and the cause of the Church also provided ready material for rebellion, and fears of Reformation and heresy stood high among the reasons for the faction's opposition to Cromwell; but the passions roused also allowed the original protest to get out of hand to a point where Henry could not concede anything without total loss of authority. The intrusion of grievances touching the law and lawyers may also have been confusing: their effect was to extend the range of the demands well beyond what the main part of the rebels cared about or even understood. Darcy's tactics were basically simple: he wished to overthrow the dominant faction at court and procure a reversal of policy by persuading the king that a change of minister would lead to loyal peace. But he came to command a movement sworn to ends which could be obtained only by total victory over the king, and that was never on the cards.[73] However, in the main the northern risings represent the effort of a defeated court faction to create a power base in the country for the purpose of achieving a political victory at court.

This fact explains many puzzling features of the troubles. It explains the constant affirmation of loyalty to the king – the sincerely meant assertion that the rising was for him, not against him. This was the necessary stance of a party intent upon ruling about the king – a stance very different, incidentally, from the truly feudal attitudes of defiance leading to the overthrow of the dynasty which had characterized the fifteenth-century civil wars. It was the leaders' perfectly honest belief

[73] I have my doubts about the conventional view that the pilgrims could easily have won a decisive military victory. Once it was clear that the south, though much disturbed, would not rise, and once Lincolnshire was quiet again, a campaign launched across the Don in mid-November or later could not seem a very promising enterprise – as Aske clearly recognized.

that they were only continuing the power struggle of the court by novel means that enabled Darcy to believe that he was no traitor and enabled so many prominent government men to take their share in shaping the course of the rebellion. Darcy's early letters, which have been read either as demonstrating his sincere desire to prevent rebellion or as hypocrisy, in reality show him trying to get the necessary 'remedies' out of Henry by the mere threat of major trouble, so as to render unnecessary 'the hasty follies' planned by the hotheads.[74] The activities of a court faction explain, as I have said, the appearance of some of the demands, especially the concentration upon the succession to the throne. They explain much about the initial behaviour of the leading conspirators, who evidently had not given up their old hopes of attracting important conservative court peers to their faction. Both Darcy and Hussey kept an anxious eye on the earl of Shrewsbury, for if he had come in, so assuredly would Derby have done, and the political situation would have been transformed. Both waited for the earl's decision before declaring themselves, though when he refused to move they reacted with characteristic difference. While Hussey at once threw in the towel and fled from Lincolnshire, Darcy resolved to go it without the earl and to resort to force.

The crucial significance of the court faction, of course, helps to explain the concentrated attack on Cromwell and his ministerial colleagues, enemies to the faction, not to the commons: Audley's and Rich's real offence was not their supposed favour to heresy but their role as leading members of Cromwell's own faction. Another odd little problem also becomes clearer when the realities of the situation are understood. On one occasion the pilgrims expressed great satisfaction at hearing that the king was now surrounded by councillors of noble blood and not by those despised upstarts.[75] But those allegedly noble councillors included only three peers, one of them (Sussex) of very recent making (though not quite as recent as the Lord Cromwell); the other three – Sir William Fitzwilliam, Sir William Paulet and Sir William Kingston – were all respectable gentlemen, administrators transferred from Wolsey's stable. However, Fitzwilliam and Kingston were certainly never real friends to Cromwell and appear in the

---

[74] *LP* xi, 563, 566. It has sometimes been suggested that Darcy remembered Henry's surrender to the taxpayers' strike of 1526. If he did, he allowed the north to get out of hand much too quickly, for by the time Aske entered York the situation no longer permitted Henry any such tactical withdrawal.

[75] *LP* xii, 1, 1013.

reconstruction of an anti-Cromwellian faction late in 1539;[76] they may be presumed at least to have been acceptable to the anti-Cromwellian faction of 1536. No one has ever discovered any political side-taking in Paulet (the later Lord Treasurer Winchester), but I suggest that his inclusion among this group of Cromwell's opponents does hint at something more than aloofness from faction strife.

The whole course of the rebellion — its inception, its spread, its avowed and secret purposes, its end — becomes clearer when it is recognized that it was at heart the work of a political faction which utilized the social, economic and religious grievances to be found in the disaffected north, grievances linked not to feudal or popular uproar but to the increasing distrust felt by the regional gentry towards a thrusting and revolutionary court policy. A common interest joined the defeated court faction with the anti-court 'country' and offered an opportunity for forcing Henry to change course. In this way, the Pilgrimage, so far from being the last manifestation of 'medievalism', accurately fore-shadowed the political mechanism of the next two centuries, though in the reign of Henry VIII the mechanism was still so novel that its use had to take the form of a treasonable conspiracy.

In Lincolnshire the conspiracy proved rather incompetent, perhaps because Hussey, old and dithery, was not up to it: he never controlled the rising which evidently started before everything was ready, and his intended allies among the gentry lost the taste for politics when they began to fear that they had set loose the elements of social rebellion. Hence the rapid termination there. Darcy and Aske were sterner metal and, mainly thanks to the younger Percy brothers, had a much better developed power base from which to operate, but they too failed to manage the northwest (where social rebellion did start, only to be put down by Darcy's hoped-for allies among the border gentry) or really even Lancashire, which went its own way. Whether the fatal revival of trouble by Bigod's outburst had links with the court, of which he had certainly once been a member, I do not know; probably not, because Bigod evidently fell victim to simple and genuine fanaticism, but the possibility might be investigated. The bad timing of the vicar of Louth very likely prevented the wider dissemination of factional action in the south, of which we hear hints here and there; this, too, could profitably be studied further.[77]

---

[76] *LP* viii, ɪɪ, 279–81.

[77] The 'Exeter conspiracy' did exist, after a fashion, but failed to co-ordinate with the north; Exeter

Obviously, this paper cannot discuss all the questions or settle all the details of so massive a historical event as the northern rebellions of 1536. Its purpose has been to consider the received view of that event, to assess the effect upon that view of recent analysis (mostly social and structural in kind), and to show that what happened cannot be properly comprehended from a study of the north alone and by means of currently fashionable methods. Why rebellion happened at all, and why it happened the way it did, are questions, as it turns out, that receive their answers from an understanding of the central politics of the day; baffled by the event, the social historian still needs to call upon his political brother for aid.

later blamed Darcy for mismanaging the insurrection. The hopes Darcy had of Derby in Cheshire and Rutland in Kent may not have been entirely self-delusive. Miss Susan Brigden has shown me evidence from the London archives which suggests that the mayoral elections of 1536 were affected by factionalism connected with the northern rising.

37

TAXATION FOR WAR AND PEACE
IN EARLY-TUDOR ENGLAND*

The effect of war upon any country's economy always poses difficult problems for the historian, but in early-sixteenth-century England one point immediately stands out. War was the time of taxation: direct taxes were imposed on the nation only when war or the likely prospect of it could justify such exceptional burdens. It was, indeed, something very like a constitutional principle that the king had no right to call for special supply on any other grounds; extraordinary revenue – that is, revenue granted in Parliament – could be refused unless it were demanded by the purposes of war. Quite possibly this principle had a less ancient history behind it than was once supposed,[1] but it clearly existed by the reign of Edward IV. Henry VII's taxation observed it faithfully.[2] So did Henry VIII's in the first half of his reign. Every one of the seven Parliaments that met between 1510 and 1523 was called to grant money, and every grant of a fifteenth and tenth, or of the new subsidy, explained in its preamble that it arose from the special needs of war, even though on occasion the money was required to cover martial expenses already incurred.[3] Even the life-grant of tonnage and poundage in 1510 was (as convention dictated) 'for the defence of this your said realm and in especial for the safeguard and keeping of the sea.'[4] At times the preambles amounted to quite a lengthy historical

---

* [*War and Economic Development: Essays in Memory of David Joslin*, ed. J. M. Winter (Cambridge, 1975), 33–48. My arguments were attacked by G. L. Harriss in *EHR* 93 (1978), 721–38, but my own conviction that the attack misses its point is supported in a forthcoming article by J. D. Alsop. See now *EHR* 97 (1982), 1 ff.]

[1] Cf. B. P. Wolffe, *The Royal Demesne in English History* (1971), 40 ff. He argues that the English Crown financed its work mainly from taxation until the notion that the king should 'live of his own' emerged in the fourteenth century.

[2] 7 Henry VII, c. 11; 11 Henry VII, c. 10; 12 Henry VII, c. 12.

[3] 3 Henry VIII, c. 22; 4 Henry VIII, c. 19; 5 Henry VIII, c. 17; 6 Henry VIII, c. 26; 7 Henry VIII, c. 9; 14 & 15 Henry VIII, c. 16.

[4] 1 Henry VIII, c. 20.

exposition of foreign affairs, as when Parliament was made to inform the king in 1511 and 1512 how well it knew the recent machinations of France – encouraging the duke of Gueldres against the king's ally, the prince of Castile, or organizing a schism in the Universal Church. The preamble of the Subsidy Act of 1523 reviewed the international scene from the war of 1513 onwards. Evidently great care was taken to make sure that the Crown's extraordinary claims should rest securely on grounds conventionally accepted as proper.

Thus down to the meeting of the Reformation Parliament war always affected the national purse in the most direct and obvious manner, and conversely the economic consequences of national taxation were felt only in times of actual or impending war. No other aspect of government policy had any comparable effect upon the economy. Yet one of the side-effects of the major reorganization which began in the 1530s was to end this simple correlation. As the king pulled together the national identity of his dominions, his subjects were to discover that they would in future find themselves more regularly called upon to contribute to the cost of government. Very soon, attempts were made to secure supply in times of peace, and new justifications emerged for these unpopular calls on people's pockets. The government managers thus found it necessary to frame a different formula to explain the demand for direct taxation and conciliate opinion in Parliament.[5]

The Parliament of 1529 was called for several reasons, but financial need played its part, too. Immediately, however, no one felt able to attempt a new taxation, especially since that of 1523, when actual war had provided a legitimate excuse, had met sufficient resistance. All that the king secured in the first session was a cancellation of the repayment of money raised by means of forced loans.[6] In effect, this act constituted a concealed and retrospective grant, and it is interesting to note that it was justified – in highly coloured and rather emotional language – on the grounds that the king had incurred great expenses in helping to stamp out disunity in Christ's Church and in preserving the realm in safety. Although there had been no war and none looked likely to come, the preamble almost managed to suggest that English armies had taken the field against heretics and schismatics: it is among the most specious and insincere statements to be found even in the preambles of Tudor

[5] For the general setting of the problems here treated cf. R. S. Schofield, 'Parliamentary lay taxation 1485–1547' (unpublished Ph.D. dissertation, Cambridge, 1963). I am grateful to Dr Schofield, who kindly commented on this paper, for many discussions on the subject.
[6] 21 Henry VIII, c. 24.

taxation statutes. But by that very fact it demonstrates that so far the Crown remained anxious to preserve the constitutional principle which governed the granting of taxes.

However, the needs of government even in times of peace could hardly any longer be covered by 'the king's own', and the diplomatic proceedings touching the Divorce were exceptionally expensive. The need to conciliate France if the emperor should turn actively hostile put the French pension (renewed in 1526) in jeopardy; though in fact it was duly paid down to 1534, planning had to proceed on the assumption that it would cease. The fall of Wolsey and the rise of Cromwell were accompanied by signs that the ordinary sources of revenue would be more energetically exploited,[7] but these would never yield enough and certainly were not sufficiently elastic. From 1531 the government turned to the wealth of the Church, but the first attack – the *praemunire* fine of £118,000 of which less than two-thirds were ever collected – secured only an unrepeatable windfall. Before Cromwell obtained a more permanent addition to the king's income by means of the transfers, in 1534, of the clerical first fruits and tenths, he was thus driven to consider the possibility of parliamentary taxation to fill empty coffers at a time of likely national crisis. National crisis, yes, but not the crisis of a war: for the whole success of the break with Rome depended on avoiding war. If war came, supply could be demanded; but if war came, or was even officially admitted to threaten, the chance of establishing the royal supremacy without major internal disruption would be gone. The simple fact was that Tudor government had reached the point where traditional financing would no longer do, and so Cromwell was driven to finding a way of imposing taxation at a time when the maintenance of peace was one of the government's most effective propaganda claims. The resort to specious pretences about war, as employed in 1529, was out from 1532 onwards.

If the imperial ambassador was correctly informed (and in this case there is no reason why he should not have been) an attempt was made, and the difficulties were brought home, in 1532. It appears that the Crown tried for a fifteenth and tenth on the grounds that the Scots were threatening an attack, an unconvincing allegation at the time and exposed in the Commons where some bold men pointed out that all danger from the Scots could be avoided if the king would stop pursuing his present policy and thus remove all occasion of trouble. The

[7] Cf. *Tudor Revolution*, 145–7.

ambassador heard that the allegedly subservient House had nevertheless agreed to the grant, but here he was wrong; nothing came of these negotiations, and Cromwell had to make do without direct taxation at this stage.[8] (1532 was the last session in which he was not yet the king's leading councillor.) He next tried in 1534, by which time Parliament had been more firmly subjected to his managerial influence and the drastic new policy had fully proclaimed itself, and this time he succeeded in getting an act whose preamble discovered quite a new line of justification.[9]

Certainly, the grounds on which this grant rested were in part traditional. They spoke of the late wars against Scotland, which could hardly mean real war but only border skirmishing since no war had been fought since 1513 while the manoeuvres of 1522 had already done duty in the money bills of 1523 and 1529. They mentioned the present troubles in Ireland which had unquestionably involved reinforcing the garrison there. References to expenses incurred in building defence works – especially repairs at Calais and Dover – might just be accepted as falling within the traditional categories of reasons. But the main justification was put first: the king 'by the space of twenty-five years' has so effectively governed and guarded the realm and kept it 'in wealth, unity, rest and quietness, to the high pleasure of Almighty God, the great glory praise honour and merit of our said sovereign lord the King', that his most loving subjects felt obliged to assist. This was the first time that the Almighty made his appearance as the backer of a subsidy bill. A very fulsome paragraph committed the Parliament to a fruitful love and admiration for this most marvellous of monarchs; more, it explained that in making the grant the Commons had considered not only past burdens but also the great national benefits to be gained in the future from the repair of Dover and Calais (not by any means yet completed, after all) and 'the reformation of the said land of Ireland'. The whole lengthy preamble, very different from the sober and precise factual recitals that characterized Wolsey's subsidy acts, breathed a new spirit: a commitment of the nation to the national policy of the Crown and its readiness to support government with money now and in future. Such actual occasions of expense as were cited were turned into examples of a general policy and the extraordinary start, acknowledging the splendour of twenty-five years of Henry's rule as grounds for taxation, coloured all the detail that followed.

[8] *LP* v, 762, 941, 989.   [9] 26 Henry VIII, c. 19.

Cromwell knew that he was innovating, and moreover doing so on exceptionally touchy territory. After all, he had sat in the House of Commons which proved so refractory to Wolsey's demands in 1523 and had himself there delivered a powerful speech in which he had attacked the kind of foreign policy habitually used to justify taxation.[10] Moreover, there are signs that in 1534 he was not primarily interested in raising money. The details of the act which concerned its administration were loosely drafted,[11] and the sum asked for was modest – one fifteenth and tenth and one subsidy rated on the wealthier members of the nation only. Even so it proved hard to raise; collectors met with quite unusual resistance and underassessment.[12] As a money-raiser, the act was not a patch on the subsidy acts promoted by Wolsey between 1512 and 1523. It looks as though the reluctant taxpayers recognized Cromwell's real purpose, a purpose plain from three things. This was taxation in peace-time, and effectively admitted to be so. It introduced the principle that national government needed financial support for extraordinary expenses not incurred by war. And the lavish gratitude to the king expressed in the preamble, together with two technical points – the royal assent was given in the 'public act' formula *le roi le veult*, and the commissioners for the subsidy were to be appointed by letters patent, not as hitherto in Parliament – underlined Cromwell's conviction that the king should be entitled to call for such contributions however little tradition sanctioned them.

However, from the purely financial point of view this first step towards reorganizing the royal finances on the basis of national, and possibly regular, taxation proved rather a failure, and Cromwell fell back on the expropriation of the Church. The Parliament of 1536 encountered no request for supply. In 1539, however, Cromwell felt both able and compelled to try again. The suppression of the rebellions in the north had been expensive, and the cost of modernizing the country's defences, a task which he comprehensively tackled from 1538 onwards, threatened ruin to the Exchequer. (The king's mania for building did not help, but this could hardly be used as an argument in public.) It looks as though Cromwell tried for a subsidy in the 1539 session, though none was granted. On 20 May 1539, the twelfth day of the session, his enemy the duke of Norfolk delivered a curious speech in the House of Lords the inwardness of which cannot be wholly explained but from which it appears that proposals for raising a tax may by that

---

[10] Merriman, i, 30–44. [11] Schofield, 'Lay taxation', 215. [12] Ibid. 328–9.

date have reached the Upper House from the Lower.[13] Norfolk agreed that the king's expenses and labours had been very great and hoped that their lordships would give serious consideration to them: no doubt each man would wish to give according to his ability. However, pressure of time made it impossible to do anything about this just then, and he therefore moved for a petition to the king that, inasmuch as Parliament was about to be prorogued, the decision on supply might be deferred to that later time. This representation was debated in the Privy Council on the same day, and on the 23rd the House was prorogued for a week;[14] but though it sat thereafter for another four weeks, the question of supply never came up again. Instead, the debates over the Six Articles took precedence in the Lords. It looks very much as though Norfolk, who had been a firm supporter of that reactionary measure from the start, may have used the prorogation to clear the road for his preferred subject by ending discussion of a subsidy. In that way he would score a double victory over Cromwell: he forced on a settlement of religion deeply distasteful to the lord privy seal, and he lowered the minister's credit as the man who could get money from Parliament.

It is in fact apparent that Norfolk throughout this session out-manoeuvred Cromwell who was in an impossible position. On 5 May, a committee consisting of Cromwell and a mixture of radical and conservative bishops had been appointed to consider the problem of diversity in religion. The vicegerent in spirituals could hardly avoid appointment to it, but since he was saddled with irreconcilable opponents and knew that the king would accept only a solution repulsive to himself he was sure to lose face and credit. He tried to save something by inaction, but here, too, Norfolk got the better of him. On the 16th, the duke, protesting at the committee's failure to achieve anything, himself introduced the Six Articles (agreed with the king) as a basis for a definition of the faith and asked for a penal act.[15] Possibly Cromwell blocked him for a few days by getting the money bill brought up from the Commons. However, as we have seen, on the 20th the duke intervened to stop that debate, his private knowledge of the forthcoming prorogation and evident assurance that a postponement of supply would not be resented showing where at this point the ascendancy in the Council lay. And the Whitsun prorogation does seem to have been decisive: on reassembling the Lords at once received a royal message supporting the demand for a penal statute on religion, and

[13] *LJ* i, 111a. [14] Ibid. i, 111b, 112b. [15] Ibid. i, 105b, 109a.

thereafter the Six Articles Act took shape while no more was heard of money.

Before this Parliament met for its third session in the spring of 1540, Cromwell had recovered much ground, and he made very careful preparations to secure the subsidy upon which his political standing now depended. Fortunately some important evidence survives to show the workings of his mind. He was engaged upon the act by February 1540, and on the eve of the session (which opened on 12 April) he reminded himself to inform the king 'what hath been done touching the grant to be made in the Parliament'.[16] This was to be unmistakably *his* subsidy bill. In the drafting he paid particular heed to the arguments used to justify the demand. A long roll was compiled giving a very detailed list of reasons to be advanced: the costs of suppressing the northern rebellions; the expenses of reorganizing the local councils in the north, the Welsh marches and the west (advertised as offering swifter justice and greater safety to the people); the charges for putting the navy on a war footing during the previous year's invasion scare; the garrisoning of towns and fortresses in the Pale of Calais and against Scotland, as well as the heavy building programme of forts around the south and southeast coasts; the repairing of Dover harbour which had turned out to be unexpectedly expensive; the maintenance of an army in Ireland; general rearmament (casting of guns, stockpiling of bows, arrows, gunpowder and so forth); repairs to Westminster Hall; and the unbelievable costs sustained by the king in carrying through the break with Rome and the Reformation which had meant such a saving to the nation.[17] All these points, except the minor ones touching rearmament and Westminster Hall, appeared concisely stated in the preamble of the statute, except also that the last point was here put first.[18]

The statute in fact followed the precedent of 1534 by first of all reminding the nation of the excellent government they had enjoyed since 1509 and then enlarged upon this by particularizing. Special gratitude was owed to the king for bringing his people 'out of all blindness and ignorance into the true and perfect knowledge of Almighty God'. This point was made separately from the more practical reminder that the abolition of papal authority had saved the nation such vast sums of money in payments to Rome, and it needs a closer look. To the drafters of the act it was a serious point, not a mere

[16] *LP* xx, 195, 332, 438.
[17] PRO SP 1/159, fos. 37–46 (*LP* xv, 502[2]).   [18] 32 Henry VIII, c. 50.

flourish: they really wished to emphasize the Reformation as the basis of all that the government had done. This becomes clear in an alternative preamble, ready drafted but in the end not used.[19] This concentrated exclusively on the glories of the Reformation in discussing which it adopted quite an exalted tone. The Commons are made to describe themselves as 'members of the same Church [of England], men selected to utter and express the voices and minds of the whole realm'. They have before their eyes 'the manifest commodities and high benefits that it hath pleased Almighty God to pour on us through the opening and showing of his most holy Word to the salvation of our souls, the prosperity and wealth of our bodies, and the most high advancement and benefit of the common wealth of this our most dear and beloved country'. They remember the 'errors and blindness that we and our forefathers have long slept in', deceived by 'the subtle serpent, the bishop of Rome – enemy to Christ and his gospel'. They therefore think it right 'to bestow not only our goods and all that we have but also to spend our lives' in protecting the reform and destroying the old evil. The preamble deviates into Scripture, citing Christ's promise to those who will leave all to follow him. True Christians (it goes on) have ever suffered persecution; wherefore they 'look for none other but for the extreme persecution and devilish hatred of the bishop of Rome and his adherents'. True, they trust in God's protection: 'yet we ought to put our aiding hands to our power in the defence of our wives, children and proper persons'. It is necessary, in fact, to prepare for the defence of the realm, an expensive business. The Commons, 'having perfect confidence and affiance in the said pardon of our Saviour, most heartily and above all things desiring to be partakers thereof', determined to show that they have fully renounced the papacy, and also resolved 'to prefer, set forth and glorify Christ and his gospel', therefore offer the necessary money.

This passionate preamble would certainly have looked pretty odd on the statute book, and it is no wonder that in the event it was replaced by a more conventional statement of needs. However, it remains highly significant. The language is that usual in the circle of humanist and reformist commonwealth-men who surrounded Cromwell; but the language also reflects the minister's own convictions concerning the nature of the reforms he had carried through, the rule of Scripture and

---

[19] PRO SP 1/159, fos. 33–6 (*LP* xv, 501[1]), endorsed by Cromwell's 'for a subsidy'.

the social regeneration involved in the Reformation.[20] The document is in a hand that may well be Ralph Sadler's (Cromwell's confidential secretary), and Cromwell showed that he had read it by endorsing its purpose on it; it represents a considered, not a cranky, view of what taxation should be justified by. It was Cromwell's point that the renewal of the common weal was the financial business of the nation. He took up the hints of 1534: the nation owes such special benefits to the king's rule that it must do all it can to respond to his call for money. There had been no war nor, by the time that the subsidy bill was introduced, could anyone any longer pretend that the danger of war existed; Cardinal Pole's mission of 1539 had clearly collapsed, and there was no immediate threat.[21] Nor does the preamble try to present a case based on war. The most it can say is that papal hostility will continue and demand future investment in defence. Its real purpose is to commit Parliament to the achievements of Cromwell's decade and express a free willingness to support the Reformation by paying taxes.

In the event, these sentiments were boiled down into a perfectly sober recognition of the gains made – spiritually and materially – in the wake of the rejection of the papacy, and care was taken to append the other more usual justifications listed in the résumé prepared beforehand. Cromwell indicated his order of priorities when he took the benefits of good government from the end of the list and put them at the head. The other grounds may indeed have been more usual, but they were still unusual enough. Certainly much play was made with the costs of military preparedness, but no one suggested that there had been a war or was going to be one. Pre-Cromwellian subsidy acts had always been able to tie even mere preparations to proven bellicose events. Items like the benefits of local councils or the repair of Dover harbour (for trade) did not even profess to be linked to the possibilities of war, and the repetition of the general gratitude for the king's now thirty-one years of rule plainly restated the fact that taxation could be demanded to support government in general, not only the extraordinary expenses incurred through war.

What is more, Cromwell took care to have these novel ideas pressed

---

[20] Cf. *Reform and Renewal*.

[21] The bill reached the Lords on 3 May, the twelfth day of the session (*LJ* i, 134b). The foreign threat that started with the Truce of Nice of June 1538 had led to an apparent danger of invasion in the spring of 1539, but by April that year Charles V had plainly abandoned all such purposes. In February 1540, Norfolk's embassy to France announced that normal relations with that country had been resumed.

home in the House. Himself unable to speak there, he used Richard Morison, a member of his secretariat for whom he had obtained a seat in 1539 explicitly that he might act as a government spokesman.[22] Morison's draft of the speech which (presumably) he delivered survives, with some interesting corrections by Cromwell.[23]

Significantly the speech opens with a sonorous passage stressing the king's charges but saying not a word of war:

Forasmuch as reason, honesty and duty bind all subjects that will be counted loving both oft to consider the manifold benefits that they receive of their prince's politic governance, and also the excessive charges that those princes are called unto, which pass little of money where either the wealth or safety of their subjects require the expense of it, we assembled here in Parliament, men chosen to utter the voice, to express the mind, of the whole realm, have thought it our bounden duties, whereas the King's majesty's charges have been of late wonderful great and are now like to be greater than ever they have been in his highness' time, to show unto his majesty, though we be not able fully to satisfy his grace's innumerable benefits towards us his loving subjects, that yet according to the true profession of obedient subjects we are body, soul and goods all whole at his grace's commendment.

The king, says Morison, has found us ready to aid him in times past; the issues are greater than ever (still no word of war), and should we refuse now to prove our good will to his face 'and this our most dear country'? He admits that there have been payments before: but look how well they were spent, and you will have to think rather we gave too little. 'His highness well declareth that a private person had it not of us, but one that remembereth still both in what place God hath set him and also for what purpose God hath given him more than a great many, which would serve his highness if the tender love he beareth to this his empire, to us his subjects, did not enforce him daily to new charges.' In 1540, after all, any talk of taxation was bound to encounter the obvious argument: the king's revenues had of late been so much augmented that a demand for more subsidies seemed thoroughly unjustified. Morison foresaw and blocked that line of thought. He went on to elaborate on the costs of military preparations, with an impassioned reference to Pole's mission but again with no pretence that there might still be any danger of war. All Morison can say is that the Parliament must do

[22] Merriman, ii, 199.
[23] Cotton MSS, Titus B, I, fos. 109–16 (*LP* xiv, I, 869). The *LP* dating to 1539 is purely conjectural; 1540 answers much better. The document is a speech drafted for delivery, not (as *LP* has it) a memorial: this becomes plain in the reading of it.

everything possible to forestall any move that might restore the pope in England — and the papists, he warns, 'care not what charges they be at, so usurped power may run again'. There follows an appeal for support for the Reformation, rather along the lines of the discarded preamble which altogether had left its mark on this speech. If the enemy will risk their all to advance 'error and idolatry', are we to refuse to give our property or even our lives 'for the defence of God's Word, for the maintenance of his glory, for the keeping with us rightly restored religion'? Victory depends on God, but he will only help those who prove their worth by helping themselves. The women of ancient Rome are called in to aid, for sacrificing their jewels ('which, ye know, women love little worse than life') to defend their country. A merchant travelling in a tempest-tossed ship would rightly be thought mad if he refused to cast overboard his merchandise at the behest of the master, and thus to save some piece of property be fully cast away. Morison goes to some lengths to paint the horrors of papal rule.

This tyrant of Rome is not content with the thraldom of bodies except souls brought from light and liberty be hurled into the deep dungels of errors. The Turk compelling no man to forsake his faith, this tyrant resteth not while Christ be forsaken and his baggage in Christ's place taken.

Dangers like these cannot be dealt with afterwards: they must be provided against beforehand. And the king is doing just that. Here Morison takes up the points of the preamble and drives them home rhetorically. Any of you who used to know Calais or Guisnes should see them now! The charges the king has incurred at Dover! Ireland, the maintenance of Berwick and Carlisle — you have no idea how expensive it all is! The king cannot for ever pay for all this himself, and when his money runs out where shall we be?

Lastly the speaker turned to argue that the nation could well afford to tighten its belt — if indeed to do so was necessary for a people given to indulging themselves. We live much too well in England: 'might we not think honesty would we left the love of our bellies for a season and gave that we foolishly spend in our exceeding fare to our country, being in need of it?'

Let us lay up our sweet lips for a three or four months, giving the overplus of our accustomed monthly charges to the present necessity of the common-wealth, to the maintenance of Christ's religion and pure doctrine, to the utter confusion of our enemies and perpetual establishment of God's honour. Let us spend it thus awhile, and if any man think it evil spent so he may imagine it is spent in belly cheer, as it was wont to be. After this sort we shall not only highly serve God, maintain the prosperous wealth of our country, abash the brags of our utter enemies, without the abating of our bags and coffers, but also hereby much enrich ourselves and make our bodies, which commonly now are with superfluities of meat in danger of many diseases, very lusty and healthy. More might be said, but where they will not serve, of like more would little move.

A powerful speech, though Morison's draft did not entirely satisfy his master. Some of Cromwell's corrections remind one of his attested concern for the English language, though it is of interest to note that, being an older man, he disapproved on occasion of Morison's modernized spelling.[24] Most of his changes make the devotion to Henry even more fulsome. In the last passage quoted, Cromwell added several phrases to give greater weight to the good prospects to be expected from the use of the tax-money; after his revision it read:

giving with good will not only the overplus of our accustomed monthly charges to the present necessity of the commonwealth, to the maintenance of Christ's religion and pure doctrine, but also liberally and with good heart to depart with our goods worldly, lent to us but for a time, to our good King and protector, which shall be spent to the utter confusion of our enemies, the assurance of ourselves and posterity, and the perpetual establishment of God's honour.

We see how anxious he was to emphasize the general purposes of taxation and the general need for it. Two of his corrections, however, display a careful realism. The dangerous, because obviously nonsensical, phrase 'without the abating of our bags and coffers' he crossed out: he was not fool enough to pretend to the House of Commons that paying taxes left people as well off as they had been. And Morison's 'three or four months' during which self-restraint should be applied became 'years': the burden on the country of the money asked for – four fifteenths and tenths and a subsidy spread over two years – would be heavier than Morison's airy phrase pretended.

In Morison's speech, therefore, we hear the voice of Cromwell. And

---

[24] Cf. *Reform and Renewal*, 10. Morison wrote that 'reason, honesty and duty bind all subjects'; Cromwell changed this to 'bindeth'. His insertion of 'duty' into 'benevolence, gratitude and love' no doubt makes a substantive point but also achieves a more sonorous balance. Where Morison spelled fetched 'fecched', Cromwell substituted the old-fashioned 'fett'. Morison's 'leaue' becomes 'leue'. Morison's 'what charges hath his grace been at Dover' rightly seemed to Cromwell to lack an 'in' before 'Dover'. Evidently the great man could be a pedant at times.

once again in 1540, the arguments put forward for raising a tax concentrated on the general benefits of government and the particular benefits of the reform in the Church. It is to support these and to protect them from possible (but so far by no means actual) attack that the nation is to pay. The preliminary memorial, the preamble of the act itself, this supporting speech in the House all revolve around the same complex of ideas. The act of 1540 abandoned some of the less fortunate features of its predecessor. The formula of assent returned to tradition inasmuch as the Parliament once again formally presented the grant and the king thanked his loyal subjects for their generosity.[25] It is just possible that the failure to observe these ancient forms had been an oversight in 1534, but there could also have been purpose behind it – the purpose of stressing some sort of right to tax possessed by the Crown. The 1540 act, nicely constitutional in this respect, nevertheless preserved the new principle that commissioners for the subsidy were not appointed by Parliament; it empowered a Council committee to see to this. The important clauses dealing with assessment and collection were much more carefully drafted. This time Cromwell really wanted money quite as much as he needed to assert his novel principle, and indeed, the country was to pay much more readily and completely than it had done in 1535–6. But 1540 was very careful to continue the real innovation of 1534, namely that extraordinary contributions could be levied for reasons other than war.

It should be emphasized what it was that Cromwell really wanted. There is no sign at all that he either meant to free taxation from the need for parliamentary consent or to make parliamentary supply a regular feature of every session. The first could not be contemplated by a government which always operated within the confines of law and custom; the second, which, thanks to all those wars, had been virtually achieved in the first half of Henry's reign, was both less necessary and less desirable in these later days of political upheaval when Crown revenue had gained so much from the Church. Cromwell's point was rather that the whole concept of extraordinary expenditure needed enlarging. No doubt there had been a time when only war demanded outlays from the Crown for which its customary and prerogative revenues were insufficient. The money grants of Henry VII's day and Wolsey's had accepted that principle: Henry VII had managed his government satisfactorily inside it, but by Wolsey's time inflation and

[25] Schofield, 'Lay taxation', 58.

the consequences of an active policy had rendered it highly doubtful. The great expansion of government activity since 1529, and especially since 1533, had really brought its inadequacy into the open. There had, of course, been particular expenses like those occasioned by the northern rebellions or the Irish unrest, but most of the arguments but forward centred on the making good of past neglect, and on the general reform of Church and commonwealth. Thomas Cromwell conceived himself to be presiding, under the king, over a national government engaged upon the reconstruction of the polity, a government which could fairly demand support for all its work when this involved so much beneficial innovation and reconstruction. His attitude is revealed in every aspect of his work; not surprisingly it also comes out in his readiness to tax in peace-time and in the justifications he offered for doing so.

The renewal of war soon after Cromwell's fall allowed the new principle to retreat. Henry VIII secured two more grants, in 1543 and 1545.[26] The first could point to the victorious war against Scotland and explain how the king's lawful claim to that crown had led to hostilities; the second referred to the unhappy necessity of war imposed on a peaceful king by those 'ancient enemies', Scotland and France. The basic justification thus reverted to traditional grounds. However, Cromwell's work left important residue behind. The acts continued to appeal to memories of the king's prosperous reign, in the formula first introduced in 1534. That of 1543 made the bad mistake of interpreting the Cromwellian principle much too crudely:

And forasmuch as among other considerations and respects the civil and politic bodies ought to have in all commonwealths they should most principally and specially regard study and devise for the conservation and increase of the royal estate honour and dignity and estimation of their chief head and sovereign lord by whom they be stayed and governed, and for the preservation and surety of his person and of his succession, and with all their powers might and substance to resist and stand against all such which by violence force fraud deceit or otherwise would attempt to decrease diminish appair or hurt the same, in body dignity title or honour: We therefore . . .

Here the king was claiming financial support as of right, by virtue of his kingship. Where Cromwell had alleged that royal government, being for the good of the nation, could rightly call for support when policy could be shown to be yielding benefit, his successors tried to assert that every call for money from the Crown demanded loyal obedience as a

[26] 34 & 35 Henry VIII, c. 27; 37 Henry VIII, c. 25.

matter of course. This extravagant and dangerous idea had disappeared by 1545 when the preamble turned quite exceptionally humble, even smarmy, with absurd touches which one may be well advised in ascribing to Henry himself, but said nothing about a generalized duty to pay.[27] The Byzantinism of these later acts was assuredly initiated in Cromwell's preambles which, anxious to hammer home feelings of gratitude and duty convenient in smoothing acceptance of a new and disconcerting principle in taxation, had deserted the factual sobriety of earlier drafting. But Cromwell was not responsible for the absurdities to which this sort of thing came to descend after his time. He was responsible for successfully reminding the nation that even without war government now cost more money than the personal revenue of the king could support, and when war again came to make the justifying of taxes easier that reminder survived in the phrasing of preambles.

The initiative of Cromwell's day was not forgotten when again it became desirable to raise money in peace-time. Edward VI's sole tax-grant, obtained in 1552, did refer to the financial consequences of the Protector Somerset's disastrous war policy, but the tax was justified on grounds of ordinary government: gratitude for the preservation of the realm in peace, gratitude for the restoration of a decayed commonwealth (a likely story), gratitude for the establishment of the true religion, and desire to demonstrate a proper loyalty to the king.[28] Mary also raised money only once, in 1555, before she got involved in the Habsburg–Valois wars; her statute is peculiar in that the grant came jointly from both Houses instead of being moved by the Commons alone, and in that the preamble abruptly returned to concise brevity.[29] The grounds stated were exclusively of the new type: appreciation for the general benefits of the queen's rule, the great debts she had inherited from the previous reign, and the large present burdens of government. This act in a way consummated the changes introduced by Cromwell: not a word about war or even preparation for defence, nor any attempt to make the brief statement of motives more convincing or more palatable by elaboration. Peace-time taxation had become accepted.

The crunch came in the reign of Elizabeth – the first reign in English

---

[27] Despite the storms of war, Englishmen, like 'small fishes of the sea' who in tempests hide under rocks and banks, had, thanks to the king, lived in peace; it is hoped that the king will accept the Commons' poor gift, 'as it pleased the great King Alexander to receive thankfully a cup of water of a poor man by the highway-side'. Ugh.

[28] 7 Edward VI, c. 12.

[29] 2 & 3 Philip and Mary, c. 23.

history in which money was asked for and granted in every session of
Parliament, whether the sessions came at long intervals or more closely
together.[30] Indeed, it looks very much as though the queen called
Parliament only when she wanted money, a fact which made the rarity
of meetings a matter of propagandist pride to her. Despite the political
developments in Parliament during those forty-five years, Elizabeth's
insistence on supply is likely to have evoked a general appreciation for
her kindness in calling so few. Nor did she make any bones about the
justification of taxation. In 1559, 1563, 1571 and 1576 the grounds stated
circle around such non-extraordinary needs as the Crown's penury,
thanks for the restoration of a prostestant Church, the preservation of
peace and the restoration of the coinage.[31] Even in 1563 when she had
just been involved in a species of warlike operations in Scotland, with
undoubted military expenditure, the Subsidy Act alluded delicately to a
'provident and seasonable enterprise' successful in preventing war.
Instead of thankfully accepting the chance of using the ancient grounds,
she deliberately pretended that none such existed. The act of 1566 is a
singular exception in the century: its preamble was drafted in and by the
Commons. That session witnessed a major political battle between the
queen and a patriotic opposition, and the latter, much to her fury,
succeeded in forcing a preamble into the Subsidy Act which offered
money in return for her alleged promise to marry and settle the
succession.[32] She never again allowed Parliament any such paper
victory.

War, however, was not permanently avoided in the reign, and the
later subsidy acts reflected the fact. The three grants of 1581–7, using a
virtually standardized formula, spoke of rebellion in Ireland and threats
from Rome.[33] The last four grants were made after the outbreak of war
with Spain, and all of them naturally stressed that event in justifying
themselves.[34] Even so, the last two spread themselves on the general
splendour and beneficial virtue of the queen's long rule and do not use
the war alone to explain the need for money. As in her father's reign so
in Elizabeth's, the renewal of war brought heavier taxation which not
surprisingly was claimed to be necessary to pay for the war. But even as
Henry VIII's later acts spoke of other general grounds as well, so did his

[30] [Wrong: no tax was raised in 1572.]
[31] 1 Eliz. I, c. 21; 5 Eliz. I, c. 31; 13 Eliz. I, c. 27; 18 Eliz. I, c. 23.
[32] 8 Eliz. I, c. 18; cf. J. E. Neale, *Elizabeth and her Parliaments 1559–1581* (1953), 161–4.
[33] 23 Eliz. I, c. 15; 27 Eliz. I, c. 29; 29 Eliz. I, c. 8.
[34] 31 Eliz. I, c. 15; 35 Eliz. I, c. 13; 39 Eliz. I, c. 27; 43 Eliz. I, c. 18.

daughter's. In any case, the practice of the years 1555–76 had settled it: the Crown could now legitimately claim to tax in peace-time, for purposes other than war or the threat of war. From 1534 it became accepted that government finance would at all times depend in part at least on direct taxation, and Parliament from that time forward made grants of a kind that had been neither necessary nor strictly constitutional in the first half-century of Tudor rule.

Thanks to Cromwell, therefore, constitutional theory had by mid-century caught up with the inescapable facts of the situation: in an age of inflation and increasing commitments, the Crown could no longer live of its own. Until 1601 at least, the Crown nevertheless managed to maintain independence. It retained control of the administration of tax money; until 1624, there was no return to pre-Yorkist practices of parliamentary supervision (which had never worked well). Subsidy bills were regularly introduced early in the session: thus the famous notion of redress of grievances before granting of supply did not become part of the English constitution,[35] although it had long been established in other Parliaments, especially the Cortes of Aragon, and although it was brought up in the remarkable session of 1566. But that one occasion when the Commons used supply to exert political pressure upon government proved a flash in the pan because Elizabeth showed that she could learn lessons in management. However, the comfortable situation in which the Crown could hope to obtain parliamentary assistance in the financing of government without having to concede anything to parliamentary opposition, would not necessarily endure, as events were soon to prove under the Stuarts. Probably Elizabeth avoided her successor's troubles in this respect because she used her rights sparingly

[35] Though 'everybody knows' that the principle existed in the medieval history of the English Parliament, it is in fact hard to discover it there. It could operate in practice, as apparently it did in Henry IV's reign, and it was certainly affirmed in the *Modus tenendi parliamentum* (cf. K. B. McFarlane, *Lancastrian Kings and Lollard Knights* [Oxford, 1972], 96–7). However, Henry himself successfully refused to admit that any such principle existed, and the *Modus* notoriously embodied the views of a radical reformer, not the constitutional practice of the realm. Of course, the idea of using the power of the purse to put pressure on governments that failed to please was too obvious never to occur; what matters is that it was never established as a parliamentary right and that taxation was usually passed early in the session. In the middle ages, the Commons did not try to force legislative concessions from the Crown by threatening to withhold supply; they confined themselves to asking that the money be spent on the purpose for which it had been granted (A. Rogers, 'Henry IV, the Commons and taxation', *Medieval Studies* 31 (1969), 44–70, esp. pp. 49, 68). Even in the early-Stuart period, when the difficulties between king and Commons brought the alleged principle back again, it did not operate: thus the very disturbed sessions of 1621 witnessed the passing of subsidy acts and nothing else, a manifest indication that grievances did not have to be satisfied before money was granted.

and her explanations rang true. Taxation in peace-time had come to stay, but political sense suggested that it should not be too frequent or too obviously unproductive of benefit to the realm. As it turned out, the taxation most vocally resented in the queen's reign was that of the 1590s, even though that could appeal to the full force of traditional justifications – resented because it was so heavy, not because it was thought wrong in principle. No Parliament after 1534 questioned the Crown's right to ask for supply on whatever grounds of need could be put forward.

The historian concerned to understand the effects of war upon the economy in the sixteenth century therefore needs to be careful in the use of his most obvious indicator. Down to 1529, he can treat all taxation (and its effects) as the product of war; thereafter he needs to distinguish. It then becomes desirable to follow up the collection of revenue by an investigation of expenditure, in order to ascertain whether the impact of government on the economy through direct taxation may be ascribed to actual war, impending war, or much more ordinary peace-time needs. That task waits to be done.

38

REFORM AND THE 'COMMONWEALTH-MEN' OF EDWARD VI'S REIGN*

Amongst the received truths of Tudor history, the existence in the reign of Edward VI of a group of reformers called the commonwealth-men occupies an apparently secure place. I have myself before this called them a party,[1] as has W. K. Jordan even more firmly.[2] That party stands at the centre of the standard work on the Tudor common weal.[3] Others, though less persuaded of quite such a formal coherence, still accept that a body of people, likeminded and active, surrounded Somerset's government, offering criticism and advice on the problems of the day and their solution. A collection of concerned and vocal individuals are supposed to have been working inside government circles in the age of Somerset, more articulate and influential even than their predecessors in the age of Cromwell whose existence has more recently been demonstrated.[4] Only Michael Bush, casting a critical eye on all the traditional views of Somerset's regime, finds that if there were commonwealth-men they did not work together, formulated no agreed programme, and constituted no 'group or party'.[5] He comes very close to discovering this particular emperor totally devoid of clothes.

Where, indeed, did the notion originate? If we look to the nineteenth-century historians we find no mention of commonwealth or commonwealth-men. Dixon managed to discuss John Hales and the movement against enclosures at some length without ever using the

---

* [*The English Commonwealth 1547–1640: Essays in Politics and Society presented to Joel Hurstfield*, ed. P. Clark, A. G. R. Smith, N. Tyack (Leicester, 1979), 23–38.]

[1] *England under the Tudors* (2nd edn, 1974), 206.

[2] W. K. Jordan (ed.), *The Chronicle and Political Papers of King Edward VI* (Ithaca, 1966), p. xxv.

[3] W. R. D. Jones, *The Tudor Commonwealth 1529–1559* (1970), 24 ff., 27, 32.

[4] S. T. Bindoff, *Tudor England* (1950), 129 f.; D. M. Loades, *Politics and the Nation* (1974), 209; C. S. L. Davies, *Peace, Print and Protestantism* (1976), 272 ff. (who denies that they said anything very new but accepts their influence). For the Cromwellian group see *Reform and Renewal*.

[5] M. L. Bush, *The Government Policy of Protector Somerset* (1976), 61 ff.

234

shibboleth, and Froude, recognizing that what he calls the 'sincere and upright among the Reformers' concentrated on the social evils produced by human greed rather than on theological dispute, also had never heard of this party.[6] But as the twentieth century opened the whole concept sprang fully armed from one man's head. 'Under Edward VI', said Pollard, 'a small but able party, including divines and politicians, began to form.' What is more, 'it was called the "Commonwealth" party'; and he cited among its followers the threesome who have dominated that scene ever since – Latimer, Lever and Hales.[7] Such a categoric description, alleging even a contemporary use of the term party, must surely have rested on solid evidence. In fact, Pollard had only one quotation to offer: a letter from Sir Anthony Auchar to William Cecil, written on 10 September 1549 to complain of those who by their critical attacks on the practices of the upper classes had helped to stir up the commons.[8] Auchar did not use the word party, but he did refer to 'these men called commonwealths' and 'that commonwealth called Latimer'. Though we may, therefore, believe that some critics of society had been nicknamed after one of their favourite catchwords, Pollard would seem to have erected his party structure on somewhat narrow foundations. He certainly made that letter work hard for himself, citing it again and again in his book on Somerset so as to create an impression of multiple support.[9] When some years later he came to write his general history of the period, Auchar had suffered multiplication or subdivision, and his men 'called commonwealths' had become the fully fledged concept; 'staid officials', we are told, 'wrote in alarm about the new commonwealth party'.[10] It is necessary to remember that we still depend solely on that one letter with its brief reference to undefined possessors of a soubriquet and its mention of only one name. In due course Tawney (who in *The Agrarian Problem in the Sixteenth Century*, published in 1912, appeared never to have heard of these people whose concerns were so very close to his own) added his authority to the story when he spoke of a group 'known

---

[6] R. W. Dixon, *History of the Church of England* (1895), ii, 505 ff.; J. A. Froude, *History of England* (Standard edn, n.d.), iv, 354 ff.

[7] A. F. Pollard, *England under the Protector Somerset* (1900), 215 f.

[8] PRO, SP 10/8, no. 56. [Since this paper was written, it has been discovered that the Latimer mentioned in this letter was not the famous preacher and martyr: B. L. Beer & R. J. Nash in *BIHR* 52 (1979), 175–8.]

[9] Pollard, *Somerset*, 256, 268, 281 n.

[10] A. F. Pollard, *Political History of England*, vi: 1547–1603 (1910), 31.

to their enemies as the "Commonwealth men"' whose prophet was Latimer and whose man of action was Hales.[11]

Thus, blessed by the twin stars of the Tudor heaven, the commonwealth party of Edward VI's reign entered the general consciousness of historians: a body of likeminded men, including preachers and administrators, devoted to a programme of social reform, and attached to the Protector Somerset who espoused their policies and attempted to put them into effect. As we have seen, not everybody since then has accepted this view in every detail, but the historiography of the reign has nevertheless been marked by their alleged existence (with the maverick and honourable exception of Dr Bush). And yet, anything like a closer look must at once call up doubt. The very name 'commonwealth men' is nowhere vouched in the record: Pollard's sole piece of evidence does not use it but instead gives us the much more attractive, if contemptuous, term 'the commonwealths'. If the concept of the commonwealth – which, as is now well accepted, did not originate in the 1540s and in any case meant no more than 'the common good'[12] – had really been such a hallmark of reform one would expect to see it freely used in the reforming legislation of the day; but it occurs there much more rarely than in the statutes of Thomas Cromwell's time. I have found only nine mentions of it. On five occasions it is used to advocate a measure beneficial to the common weal;[13] three acts attack vagabondage and such like as dangerous to the common weal;[14] once only does it seem to carry the meaning of 'body politic' which has generally been regarded as its primary significance.[15] Of Somerset's proclamations only six contain the word, four of them using it to mean the state;[16] why, even the famous enclosure proclamation of 1 June 1548 has no hint of it.[17] Similarly it rates no mention in acts which one might think would call for it, such as those against price-fixing arrangements, or the codifying acts for tillage, cloth manufacture and usury.[18] What is more, of those nine statutory occurrences only four could conceivably be associated with Somerset's administration; the rest came too late.

[11] R. H. Tawney, *Religion and the Rise of Capitalism* (1926), 145.
[12] *Reform and Renewal*, 7.
[13] Acts touching the Iceland fishery, the making of malt, the tanning of leather, commons and wastes, and sewers (2 & 3 Edward VI, cc. 6, 10, 11; 3 & 4 Edward VI, cc. 3, 8).
[14] Acts touching vagabonds, tinkers and alehouses (1 Edward VI, c. 3; 5 & 6 Edward VI, cc. 21, 25).
[15] Unlawful assemblies (3 & 4 Edward VI, c. 5).
[16] *TRP* i, nos. 328, 331, 334, 336, 337, 341.
[17] Ibid. no. 309.
[18] 2 & 3 Edward VI, c. 15; 5 & 6 Edward VI, cc. 5, 6, 20.

(Northumberland's proclamations use the word nine times.)[19] Of course, the term may have been more freely used in the many failed bills of the reign, but at any rate it has left no convincing signs of being any sort of party slogan.

Worse doubts arise as one looks at the people whose pronouncements and actions have been used to define the programme of this 'party' and who were active in 1548–9, until the rebellions of the latter year provoked a reaction which allegedly swallowed up Somerset and commonwealth alike. Four names recur with convincing regularity: Hugh Latimer, Thomas Lever, Robert Crowley and John Hales. Professor Bindoff almost alone draws attention to Thomas Smith, the most remarkable economic theorist of the day, while Dr Jones adds a list of eminent divines (Bradford, Ridley, Becon and Hooper) who, however, cannot really be said to have written seriously about the social ills of the common weal. That first quartet deserve a closer look: they all unquestionably addressed themselves to such problems, they left behind plenty of evidence for their views, and it need not be denied that they approached the issues with much the same preconceived convictions touching the miseries of the poor. However, even a first glance, before the look becomes closer, raises a striking fundamental difficulty. If these 'commonwealth-men' influenced the policy of 1548–9, one must surely find them expressing their views in those years, not later. Yet there survives no sermon of Lever's from before 1550, and most of Crowley's relevant writings – including that cited most often – belong to that year and the next. Pollard's treatment of Latimer reinforces apprehensions first raised by his treatment of Auchar. Latimer did preach two series of sermons before Somerset's fall – one before Edward VI in Lent 1549, and one at Paul's Cross ('On the Plough') a few months earlier. It is this second series on which Pollard relies in claiming that Latimer attacked enclosure.[20] Since there is not one word on enclosure in the one sermon extant from the series, one must suppose that Pollard had intuitive knowledge of what was in the three that are lost. Only Hales unquestionably and entirely devoted himself to these commonwealth matters at the right time, in the years 1548–9, and only Hales can be proved to have established direct contact with Somerset; the rest, no

---

[19] *TRP* i, nos. 366, 367, 371, 377–81.

[20] *Political History*, vi, 32. On the same page another of Latimer's sermons is used to support the statement that 'fraud was employed to supplement intimidation'. On the page cited I can find nothing to justify the allegation.

doubt at times in favour at court, never entered the inner circles of government.

This analysis has so far been entirely negative, to clear the ground. It has really become manifest that there was no such thing as a commonwealth movement or party in the days of Somerset; those that have failed to find a programme devised by thinkers and applied by government (the sort of thing that happened in the 1530s) arc quite right. But that does not necessarily dispose of certain other aspects of that mistaken interpretation. Doing away with the commonwealth-men does not deny the existence of the economic crisis – inflation and destitution – or the antisocial practices of landlords and middlemen. No one would wish to shut his eye to the crisis; and while the alleged malpractices deserve rather more searching discussion than they usually receive from those for whom the sermons of the day contain the whole truth, they cannot here be considered at length. This essay will confine itself to an examination of the actual views expressed by those who, whether a party or not, have so strongly influenced posterity's notions of that age. Now that we have disposed of the commonwealth party it does not matter whether Lever preached and Crowley wrote before or after the upheavals of 1549; it matters greatly that we should be sure we know what in fact they said if we are to understand them and their age correctly. Here again, it seems to me, the established consensus of historians rests on at best a partial reading of their works, and a reading moreover blinkered by the sort of convictions which Pollard and Tawney brought to their investigations.

Hugh Latimer deserves his place of primacy as a champion of the poor: age, authority and the passion of his discourse make him a leader. Even Auchar, as we have seen, singled him out as a chief instigator of discontent and also a protector at court for others who thought like him. It is not certain that we really know what he said in his preaching: he worked without scripts, and we possess no texts written or passed for printing by himself, but only reports taken down at the time and printed without his assistance. In all public addresses, the best bits are always likely to survive such treatment; duller passages will vanish from the memory. Still, what we have looks sufficiently of one piece and the product of one voice to overcome nihilist scepticism: it is very probable that Latimer said approximately what has been preserved as his sermons. What then did he say?[21] Of the four Paul's Cross sermons on the plough

[21] All references are to *Sermons of Hugh Latimer*, ed. G. L. Corrie (Parker Soc., 1844).

only the last survives,[22] but it sufficiently indicates the burden of his message, especially as it begins by recalling the preacher's theme for the series. The traditional title easily misleads one into thinking that he was preoccupied with the agrarian problems of the nation, but his plough was a metaphor and had nothing to do with husbandry. He was talking of preparing the ground for the sowing of true religion, and the main targets for his displeasure were not the enclosing landlords but the inadequate clergy, especially the bishops. The prelates, he charged, were neglecting their duty to preach the word: 'They are otherwise occupied, some in the king's matters, some are ambassadors, some of the privy council, some to furnish the court, some are lords of the parliament, some are presidents and controllers of mints.'[23] The last especially seems to have rankled: 'The saying is, that since priests have been minters, money hath been worse than it was before. And they say that the evilness of money hath made all things dearer.'[24] In this sermon, this is really the only reference to the economic problems of the day, and while what 'they' said rightly pointed to debasement as the cause of inflation it was hardly sensible to lay the blame exclusively on the Durham mint. What we really hear in these charges are Latimer's reasons for refusing to resume the episcopal office he had held in the 1530s: preaching, not government service, he regarded as the first duty of the clergy, and this is the overriding burden of his sermon. A secondary line called for educational reforms, to make all the laity more useful to the community, a commonplace inherited from the reformers (humanist as well as protestant) of Latimer's old acquaintance. He also observed the rules of popular preaching by attacking a decline in charity: Londoners, especially, were blamed for no longer supporting learning with bequests for scholarships.[25] In this address to a public audience, the preacher said nothing at all about the miseries of the peasantry or the wickedness of landlords — and this even though it was only a few months since the enclosure commissions had gone forth to do battle with those alleged abuses. There is no sign here that such things interested him.

On the other hand, they did on occasion engage him in the seven sermons he preached at court between 3 March and 19 April 1549. The first of them contained those famous passages which have been quoted over and over again to prove the depravity of the Edwardian

[22] pp. 59 ff.   [23] p. 67.   [24] p. 68.

[25] Latimer was quite right: charitable bequests began to decline in the 1530s. See the recalculation of W. K. Jordan's figures by W. G. Bittle and R. Todd Lane in *EcHR*, n.s. 29 (1976), 203 ff.

regime – his splendid threnody on the yeomen of Old England and his crack about the 'pretty little shilling' which he had nearly mistaken for a groat. It also included some brief references to the agrarian problem. He spoke of 'graziers, enclosers and rent-rearers' who were causing depopulation;[26] covetous landlords, he cried, by their enhancing of rents had produced 'this monstrous and portentous dearth made by man' at a time of plentiful harvests (what had become of the Durham mint?). Throughout, of course, he showed himself concerned for the poor who, he repeatedly said, could get no justice: he urged the Protector to hear their suits in person and charged the lord chancellor with needlessly delaying poor men's causes by refusing to attend every day to his sealing duties.[27] However, it would be quite wrong to treat those Lent sermons as primarily directed against the oppressors of the poor. For one thing, all the really stinging things were said in the first, which caused offence; in the third, Latimer defended himself and others against charges of preaching sedition but thereafter noticeably avoided such contentious themes. His famous lament on the decline of the yeomanry reveals what his real grievance was. He was not primarily concerned with bettering the peasant's lot: what troubled him was that impoverishing that rank of society would bar them from educating their sons and marrying their daughters: the universities would collapse and whoredom increase. 'I say, ye pluck salvation from the people and utterly destroy the realm.' The remark about the new shilling, which reads very much like an impromptu preacher's joke, will hardly bear the burden of economic criticism so often placed upon it by historians, though at the time some of his hearers, against whose pompous resentment Latimer unleashed some of his best irony, displayed the same humourlessness at the other end of the spectrum.[28] Other themes certainly got far more thorough treatment than economic grievances: insufficient preaching by the clergy, the general decline of university studies, the prevalence of prostitution in no way arrested by the closing of the stews in 1546. He gave almost more time to his advocacy of archery as a cure for lechery than to enclosing landlords.[29] Above all, the last three of those seven sermons are astonishingly dominated by the preacher's defence of the destruction inflicted upon Thomas Seymour, the Protector's brother, a defence which gradually drove all other matters from his mind. Interesting though his words are, and important in that they reveal some of the activities of court faction, they gravely call in doubt his genuine

[26] pp. 95, 98–9, 100, 101–2.   [27] pp. 127, 211.   [28] pp. 134–6.   [29] pp. 196–7.

independence and his real role. To me at least, these quite intemperate, even hysterical, attacks on a man already lost deprive Latimer of a claim to which his preaching otherwise entitles him – the claim to have bravely confronted the mighty with the immorality of their worldly dealings. But even if a more charitable view is taken of one who thus used the pulpit for the benefit of faction, it must be plain that the confused heaping up of delinquencies seen in the body politic constitutes at best only a general outburst of grieved spleen, devoid of either a reforming programme or any rational understanding of what had gone wrong. As one might expect, Latimer was not analysing the ills of the common weal but denouncing sin and blaming those who permitted it to flourish.

This truth is brought out more clearly still in the last of his court sermons, delivered in the Lent of 1550. After the upheavals of the previous year one might have expected him to devote his time to the causes of unrest, and we do indeed hear scathing remarks touching those who rob the ploughman of his pasture – almost the only passage surviving from Latimer which shows a positive understanding of peasant life.[30] Latimer also once more defended his preaching against the charge that it caused sedition. But the real subject of the sermon is once again sin, the sin of covetousness, and he charges everybody with it, the rebellious peasantry as much as the exploiting lords: 'both parties had covetousness, as well the gentlemen as the commons'.[31] His insistence that the greed of the supposedly dispossessed, and not the misdeeds of the possessioners, had led to rebellion is worth remembering; Latimer gives no comfort to those who would regard an uprising as a legitimate response to misery. What really must startle the reader, however, is the manner in which he leads into the subject of greed. He begins by demanding the death penalty for adultery and involves himself at length in a diatribe against lechery, a diatribe which clearly amused his hearers so that, indignantly, he was forced to cry out that it was no laughing matter. Lechery, he argues, leads to covetousness because lechers need cash.[32] So that was what was wrong with England. And what is Latimer's proposed remedy? The sermon ends with a passionate appeal to the king to use all means to enforce the law against all who take profit at other people's expense: 'For God's sake, make some promoters. There

---

[30] p. 249. [31] p. 247.
[32] pp. 244–5. Coming back later to the same theme, he asks that lechers be excommunicated (p. 258): why if they had already been hanged?

lack promoters, such as were in king Henry the Seventh's day, your grandfather.'[33] Promoters – professional informers – had been among Henry VII's most disliked expedients. In this appeal Latimer fully demonstrated his inability to think constructively rather than emotionally about the common weal. Harking back to a strangely glorified past, he stuck to that past's sole conviction about the human condition: that man's covetousness caused all his troubles. That had been the message of Colet's preaching;[34] it had been the message of More's *Utopia*; and it was no doubt valid enough in any display of virtuous indignation. But what was the practical use of such declaiming? If all, poor and rich alike, were sinful greedy men, what did Latimer propose to do about it? He proposed to hang some and fine the rest, searching them out by means of entrepreneurs who made a profit out of prosecuting breaches of the law.

Latimer, of course, was an old man, an old man with memories though still full of passion. Thomas Lever, on the other hand, was only 29 in 1550 when he preached three powerful sermons about the evils of the commonwealth, and from him we might expect a much more direct involvement in the problems of the day. Since we have these sermons in a printed version published under the preacher's own oversight, we can be sure that we hear his authentic voice. We also, in consequence, have magnificently composed and tightly structured discourses in splendid prose, in place of the run-about and knock-about flood which Latimer was recorded as delivering.[35] Lever's three relevant sermons were preached early in 1550 in the shrouds at St Paul's, on 16 March 1550 before the king and Privy Council, and on 1 December 1550 at Paul's Cross: all, therefore, after the rebellions of 1549, which in fact constitute the main theme of his discourses. We have not one word of Lever's from before those troubles, and since all he has left us was said after Somerset's fall it is not possible to associate him with the reforming activities of the duke's regime.

However, though Lever cannot be supposed to have had any influence on the policies of the so-called commonwealth-men, his preaching fits the conventional notions of that group a little better than

[33] p. 279.
[34] H. C. Porter, 'The gloomy dean and the law: John Colet, 1466–1519', *Essays in Modern English Church History in Memory of Norman Sykes*, ed. G. V. Bennett and J. D. Walsh (1966), 18 ff.; see esp. p. 19.
[35] Thomas Lever, *Sermons* (1550). Reference to this unpaginated original printing has to be by signatures. I have modernized spelling and punctuation.

does Latimer's. At least he did attack the behaviour of the upper classes in some detail, and to their faces, crying out at landlords who forced tenants to surrender their leases by sharp practices, thus increasing the numbers of the starving and homeless poor who earned his special compassion, at traders who were more anxious to make money than to provide cheap goods, at impropriators of livings and those who bought offices for money. It has, however, to be said that he sounds most convincing when he weighs in with complaints against the clergy[36] and about the decline of education. Nothing in his sermons exceeds in sincerity his bitter conviction that the English nation, rescued so lately from the darkness of popery, has utterly failed to benefit from that reformation: 'it is not virtue and honesty but very vice and hypocrisy whereof England at this day doth most glory'.[37] 'Papistry is not banished out of England by pure religion, but overrun, suppressed and kept under within this realm by covetous ambition.'[38] Lever, predictably, was a Christian preacher, concerned with the wrath that God has in store for the reprobate; he too is more concerned with reproving sin than with improving the economy. This is not to overlook the positive suggestions he makes – more and better schools financed from the monastic lands, as was first intended, or the use of the profits enjoyed by unfaithful office-holders in state and Church for the relief of the poor – but it is to put the emphasis where he thought it belonged.

To treat Lever's concern for the poor as though he had been a premature Fabian pamphleteer is to misjudge both him and his century. In the first place, he is quite as much concerned to denounce rebellion as he is to condemn oppression, and his words on this point sound fully as sincere as anything he says: he was assuredly not just pandering to his audience. That 'generation of vipers, the ungracious rebels' who in his opinion had been treated much too mercifully the previous year,[39] get an equal share of his anger with the gentlemen whose practices impoverish the realm for private gain. Almost in one breath he upbraids his noble audience for abusing the gifts of the reform ('the fault is not in the things to be set forth but in you that have set them forth') and calls for the destruction of all rebellion.[40] The tenets of communism – he is

---

[36] Witness the splendid outburst against inadequate incumbents (sig. E.viii): 'Yes, forsooth, he ministreth God's sacraments, he saith his service, and he readeth the Homilies, as you fine flattering courtiers . . . term it; but the rude lobs of the country, which be too simple to paint a lie, speak foul and truly as they find it, and say: he minishes God's sacraments, he flubbers up his service, and he cannot read his Humbles.'

[37] Sig. A.iii.   [38] Sig. I.i.   [39] Sig. E.vi[v].   [40] Sigs. F.i–G.i.

thinking of Anabaptists and similar sectaries – get very short shrift: they encourage only greed. He agrees that no one should be left in need and that the rich must use their surplus to relieve the poor, but that, he says, is a very different thing from demanding that all things should be owned in common.[41] Like Colet, Latimer and all good moral preachers since the dawn of time, he identifies covetousness as the ultimate cause of all trouble, 'the root of all evil', and wants to see it pulled from everybody's heart – not only from those of gentlemen who exact high rents and fines but also from those of husbandmen only too willing to pay what was demanded in order to take other men's lands.[42] The one thing he denies to the oppressed without any qualification at all is the right to help themselves even against unjust treatment: 'As the people can have no remedy against evil rulers by rebellion, so can the rulers have no redress of rebellious people by oppression.'[43] And while it is assuredly wrong for rich men to 'make strait laws to save their own goods', it is worse to rebel and thus wreak greater havoc than that produced by the most tyrannical of laws.[44] How very serious he could wax about the duties of subjects: they must even pay all taxes as demanded – though the government should demand only what is just – 'and not to be curious to know for what cause it is asked'.[45] The doctrine of obedience could go no further. After all that convincing denunciation of exploiting gentlemen and corrupt clergy, the commons are left with no chance of redress except through the voluntary amendment of the upper classes instructed by the preacher's moral exhortation.

Those who have seen in Lever a social reformer and a fiery champion of the poor should really have noticed what lies at the heart of his system: not the redistribution of wealth to relieve poverty, but the exercise of voluntary charity. While communism is evil, it is the duty of the rich to distribute largesse. If they, too, fall on hard times and have no surplus to give away they must liquidate resources to fill the coffers of charity: 'yea, if there be great necessity he must sell both lands and goods to maintain charity'.[46] This is not a prescription that displays much understanding of economic problems or was likely to lead to a better maintained common weal. When all is said and done, Lever's complaint against the gentry may be summed up in his own words:

[41] Sig. A.vi[v].   [42] Sigs. B.viii[v]–C.i.   [43] Sig. B.vi.
[44] Sig. C.i. We recall Somerset's appeal to the Cornish rebels: 'And dareth any of you with the name of a subject stand against an act of Parliament, a law of the realm? What is our power if laws should be thus neglected, or what is your surety if laws be not kept?' (*Grafton's Chronicle*, repr. 1809, ii, 518).   [45] Sigs. D.i–ii.   [46] Sig. A.vi[v].

For a gentleman will say that he loveth his tenants as well as his father did, but he keepeth not so good house to make them cheer as his father did, and yet he taketh more fines and greater rents to make them needy than his father had.[47]

The good gentleman will not only avoid squeezing his tenants but he will in particular provide them with hot dinners.

Of course, Lever denounced the covetousness which ruined the peasantry and had diverted the wealth of the secularized estates from the good social and educational purposes at first intended. But his remedies remain unconstructive, backward-looking and moralistic, and through all his sermons his devotion to a conservative, hierarchic society in which active protest equals foul rebellion shines through. Lever was a very powerful and very attractive preacher, readily angered by the doings of sinful men, but he was neither a liberal nor a socialist. Nor was he a commonwealth-man, and the court at which he preached was dominated by the duke of Northumberland who willingly let him have his say.

Latimer and Lever were divines, in holy orders and closely tied to the universities: Latimer's repeated complaint of the lack and poor quality of matriculands shows this as plainly as does Lever's affecting description of the frugal life led by Cambridge scholars. With Robert Crowley, even though he took a degree at Oxford and in 1551 got ordained, we are in a different company – that of the London-based printers and pamphleteers who put forth books of topical concern. He assuredly belongs to the long tradition of social protest, and it is no wonder that those who believe in the 'commonwealth party' are likely to mention the two preachers with respect but to cite from Crowley. True, such quotations are not always as well considered as they might be. Crowley's splendid invective against the rich – 'men that have no name because they are doers in all things that any gain hangeth upon; men without conscience; men utterly void of God's fear; yea, men that live as though there was no God at all', and so on – naturally attracted Tawney's attention, and his use of it has firmly established this diatribe in the reservoir of useful quotations.[48] But what Tawney failed to say, and what those who take their Crowley at second hand do not know, is

---

[47] Sigs. B.v^v–vi. Cf. also sigs. H.iv^v–v: 'The chief cause why the commons do not love, trust or obey the gentlemen and officers is because the gentlemen and officers build many fair houses and keep few good houses . . .'.

[48] Tawney, *Religion and the Rise of Capitalism*, 145; followed blindly by Jones, *Tudor Commonwealth*, 53.

that Crowley does not here profess to speak for himself: this is the sort of thing, he explains, which a poor man will say if asked for the cause of his troubles. Later on he similarly puts picturesque abuse of the commons into the mouth of a notional rich man. On the whole Crowley was certainly on the side of the poor, but he did not assert that he personally endorsed all that colourful abuse.

Two works of Crowley's are relevant here, one written in 1548 and as part of a campaign to get action from Somerset in aid of the distressed (*An Information and Petition against the Oppressors of the Poor Commons of this Realm*), and one written in 1550, after the experience of rebellion (*The Way to Wealth*).[49] They display interesting differences arising from circumstances as well as a reasonably coherent standpoint. The first was addressed to the Lords and Commons of the Parliament then sitting; it was 'compiled and imprinted for this only purpose that amongst them that have to do in the Parliament some godly-minded men may thereat take occasion to speak more in the matter than the author was able to write'. The pamphlet offers a programme of reform by legislation. The second claimed that it 'taught a most present remedy for sedition' and outlined ways for restoring harmony. Both, however have no doubt that the condition of the people of England left a great deal to be desired and that the cause of all the misery are certain greedy exploiters.

Crowley's advice to Parliament started by taking it for granted that the oppression of the poor 'by the possessioners as well of the clergy as of the laity' was the main issue to be discussed, even more than the settlement of religion which nevertheless also called for debate. He sets out grievances on both scores. The poor suffer because the rich act on the principle, 'it is mine own: who shall warn me to do with mine as myself listeth?' This attitude might serve if there were no God, but 'we have a God' who has told us that he will hold all those who possess wealth to account for their stewardship. Crowley certainly operated on a very different assumption: all men have an equal right to wealth, that is to say what they can earn by their sweat, and 'the whole earth therefore, by right of birth, belongeth to the children of men. They are all inheritors thereof indifferently by nature.'[50] One sees why he felt it necessary to defend himself against any suspicion of communist views,[51] though in the light of such principles his defence does not sound terribly

---

[49] *The Select Works of Robert Crowley*, ed. J. M. Cowper (Early English Text Soc., 1872), 153 ff. and 132 ff.; spelling and punctuation here modernized.
[50] pp. 163–4.   [51] p. 156.

convincing. The main trouble, according to him, is that landlords
squeeze every penny out of their lands and the poorer sort can get no
property of their own. In consequence, the children of the poor perish:
boys quite capable of following the liberal arts ('whereof the realm hath
great need') instead must resign themselves to menial work in support
of their impoverished parents, good girls are forced to stay unmarried or
to marry for money against their inclination, and 'immodest and
wanton girls have hereby been made sisters of the Bank'. It is quite an
original line (though one that echoes Latimer) which finds the worst
consequences of the gentlemen's greed in foregone scholarly careers,
enforced virginities and the filling of the brothels. More particularly
Crowley lists two abuses: leasemongering which piles rent upon rent on
each piece of property, and inflationary valuations by land surveyors.
Both these drive men of modest means out of the land market. The
former is particularly prevalent in London where nine-tenths of all
houses are sub-let down a chain of tenants, so that rents rise sky-high.
Since, however, neither touches 'the wealth of the nobility' – 'yea, it is
rather hindrance to many of them to have these things redressed than
any increase of their wealth' – these evils will not be mentioned in
Parliament unless the pamphleteer draws attention to them.[52] The only
other secular grievance listed concerns usury, Crowley wanting to see
the statutory permission (of 1545) repealed. As a programme of social
reform it strikes one as both limited and idiosyncratic, especially in its
manifest concentration upon London. London also looms large in
Crowley's notions of what is wrong with the spiritual realm: the only
matter he specifically complains of is the tithe as levied in London under
arrangements settled by statute.[53] Even the standard charge against the
clergy, that they do not discharge their true function properly, drags in
London: when 'our ministers . . . apply themselves to priesting because
they like well the idleness of the life', they behave like craftsmen seeking
the freedom of the city for their own ends. There is a good deal of
passion, backed by scriptural citation, in this pamphlet, but the
substantive content remains pretty slight, especially after the expectations aroused by its title. Crowley is manifestly very angry, but as a
promoter of reform he prefers cutting phrases to comprehensive
analysis.

When two years later this champion of the underdog came to offer
his 'present remedy for sedition', he turned out to be yet another broken

[52] pp. 166–7.   [53] p. 171.

reed, though his gift of language had not deserted him. Professing to find a way to root out the causes of rebellion, he addressed himself in turn to three sorts of men – the poor, the clergy, and the possessioners. The poor, he knows, will readily identify the source of their distress: 'Cormorants, greedy gulls: yea, men that would eat up men, women and children are the causes of sedition!'[54] It is exploitation that men say rouses them to rebellion – which, of course, is true enough. Does Crowley agree? He feels very sorry for a poor man, oppressed by those who should be his natural protectors, and he accepts that without such provocation the false prophets that urged rebellion would have found no following. But 'no cause can be so great to make it lawful for thee to do against God's ordinance', and the poor are urged to search their hearts: are not their sufferings perhaps caused by their failure to obey God's commands? 'Submit thyself wholly to the will of God; do thy labour truly; call upon God continuously.'[55] Humble submission and prayer – those are Crowley's advice to men who suffer from the ruthlessness of their betters. As for those betters, they too have no difficulty in identifying the cause of sedition: in their opinion 'the peasant knaves be too wealthy, provender pricketh them'. And so the knaves wish to do away with rank and 'have all men like themselves, they would have all things common'.[56] Crowley, who for some reason calls the rich 'churl's chickens', has an answer for them too: by your unlawful enclosing, rack-renting and so forth you taught the poor disobedience: you failed to obey the king's proclamation, and rebellion came upon you as God's punishment. They too, therefore, are told to practise humility and (presumably) obedience to the laws which limit their power to do with their wealth as they please – wealth which is really 'the public wealth of England'.[57] The clergy receive advice which mingles the commonplace with the baffling. Noting that 'a great number of your unworthy curates have been the stirrers up of the simple people in the late tumults', he enjoins their spiritual duty upon them in unexceptionable but also unmemorable terms; secondly he demands that they make their extravagant wives behave themselves. Crowley was noticeably obsessed with female extravagance, but even so it is odd that he should have singled out ministers' wives for special condemnation. The point has value, however, because it helps us to understand the man: cranky, prejudiced, without vision but readily moved to

[54] pp. 132–3 (part of the passage cited above, p. 245).   [55] pp. 133–4, 141.
[56] pp. 142–3.   [57] p. 149.

indignation, Crowley was the archetypal pamphleteer and a poor peg on which to hang notions of a powerful and deeply concerned reform movement. Also, by the way, a poor peg on which to hang a real understanding of the state of the realm: citing Crowley proves nothing about the economic crisis.

That leaves John Hales – John Hales of Coventry, clerk of the hanaper, an enthusiast for causes who under Edward devoted himself to abolishing enclosures and under Elizabeth promoted the claims to the throne of the Seymour family, getting into trouble on both occasions. There is no need to review at length his ideas touching enclosure which have been sufficiently studied before, except to remark that he has now clearly been deprived of the authorship of *The Discourse of the Common Weal* which is in fact the work of Sir Thomas Smith.[58] What matters here is that unlike the other propagandists discussed Hales was without doubt in close touch with the duke of Somerset and his government: if there was a commonwealth party active in the reform of the realm, he was it. When after the troubles of 1549 Hales heard that he was accused of being the sole begetter of the agrarian policy which took the blame for the uprisings, he defended himself vigorously by alleging that he had but been the agent of a group of likeminded men. This, if true, is the best evidence for the existence of a body of commonwealth-men; is Hales right? He names no names, but those he calls to witness are a strange company of bedfellows. It was not he at all who had sued out the enclosure commission of 1548, but partly certain poor men protesting against landlords' practices 'and partly . . . some of those that now be most against it', the latter apparently including the king, the Protector and 'many of the Council'.[59] One may well believe that protests from the commons drew the government's attention to the need to do something, and it is possible – though less likely – that the first commission had the support of a large part of the government, even though its outcome was so null that their sincerity must stand in much doubt. At any rate, Hales's description excludes the likes of Latimer, Lever or Crowley who even after 1549, while deploring rebellion, charged the gentry with agrarian malpractices including enclosure. In

---

[58] For Hales's activities see the introduction to the *Discourse of the Common Weal*, ed. E. Lamond (1893), hereafter cited as Lamond; Smith's paternity of that impressive treatise has been convincingly proved by Mary Dewar, e.g. in her new edition of the work (1969). One economic measure – the sheep tax of 1549 – needs further study; for the present there is no convincing evidence that Hales was responsible for it.

[59] Lamond, p. liv.

September 1549 Hales presented himself simply as a servant whom it ill became 'to reason with his master': he did as instructed.[60] But in the summer of 1548 Hales, as is well enough known, took an energetic initiative on the commission to which he belonged, and which alone of those appointed attempted to carry out the policy; and his report to Somerset also suggests that it was he who had pushed on that policy. On 22 July he wrote urging the continuance of the commission and reminding the Protector of his own words, spoken when they were discussing the state of the realm: 'that maugre the Devil, private profit, self-love, money and such like the Devil's instruments, it shall go forward'.[61] That sounds much more like an enthusiastic convert's response to his mentor than like the speech of a master instructing his servant in the action to be taken. As for Somerset's motives in espousing Hales's programme, Dr Bush has rightly found them in the duke's eagerness to appear a friend to the common weal without stopping the flow of money required by his Scottish war and supplied by the disastrous debasement of the coinage.[62]

Whatever may be true about the enclosure commission – and the chances are that Hales instigated the policy and attracted official support for it – he really proved his personal responsibility for the agrarian measures of this government by the initiatives he took in the Parliament of 1548–9 for which he prepared three bills of his own devising.[63] What he says about their fate cannot fully be reconciled with the evidence of the Journals of either House, but that difficulty probably reflects only the known defects of those records. Two of his bills Hales rather surprisingly channelled through the Lords. The first was yet another bill for the maintenance of tillage which he says was rejected on first reading. It is not mentioned at all in the *Lords Journal.*[64] The second (which attacked regraters of foodstuffs and especially graziers) passed the Lords after being amended by a small committee (Lord Chancellor Rich and James Hales, serjeant-at-law);[65] John Hales says that it was much debated in the Commons where it was committed and killed by delays, but the *Commons Journal* has no mention of it, even though the

---

[60] Ibid.
[61] P. F. Tytler, *England under the Reigns of Edward VI and Mary* (1839), i, 115–16.
[62] Bush, *Protector Somerset*, 40–3.
[63] Lamond, pp. lxii–iii.
[64] Lamond (pp. xlv–lii) prints a draft which very probably was this bill. Its long and impassioned preamble makes no mention of the commonwealth.
[65] *LJ* i, 318b, 333b, 334b.

clerk noted many bills as introduced which failed. Hales's third bill, introduced (he says) in the Lower House and there defeated after much opposition both to its substantive provisions and to its enforcement clauses, is probably the 'bill for the common weal' which received a first reading on 27 February 1549 and was not mentioned again. It aimed to improve the supply of meat, milk, butter and cheese by compelling sheep farmers to maintain two cows and rear one calf for every 100 sheep they had over 120; and it committed enforcement to the parson and 'two honest men' of the parish who were yearly to survey all pastures and present both breakers and observers of the law.[66] We may (with Hales, if he plays fair to his opponents) think little enough of the arguments allegedly advanced against the main sections of the bill – that scarcity of cattle was better remedied by the tried expedient of temporary bans on the slaughtering of calves, and that supplies would in any case be sufficient if the modern habit of eating butter and cheese in Lent were suppressed – but it is hard to share his contempt for the resistance to the introduction of yet another piece of snooping into village life. So far as their tenor can be reconstructed from his brief remarks, Hales's bills were not, as a matter of fact, particularly sensible or likely to produce that improvement in the common weal that he expected from them. And the reason for his inadequacy is, once again, plain enough: driven to defend his proposals, he can only launch forth into the familiar declamations against greed and covetousness. Something, he cries, must be devised 'to quench this insatiable thirst . . . for it is the destruction of all good things'. The one thing that really links Hales to the preachers is this dedication to a reform of man's nature, but Utopia has never yet been constructed by laws which command no consent among the agencies of enforcement.[67]

Besides, the question remains whether the realm really suffered so exclusively from the covetousness of the possessioners. The diagnosis offered by Latimer, Lever, Crowley and Hales – no 'group or 'party' but certainly men exercised over social distress and trying to do something about it – has until recently been accepted without question, and the authority of Tawney in particular established the orthodox opinion on the subject. Jordan's lengthy discourses also simply endorse

---

[66] Lamond, pp. lxiii–v.

[67] As Crowley once echoed Latimer (above, p. 247), so a phrase of Hales's – 'it may not be lawful for any man to use his own wealth as him listeth' (Lamond, p. lxiii) – recalls Crowley (above, p. 246). Those who want to make them into a 'party' on the strength of such possible borrowings are welcome to do so.

those contemporary criticisms, uncritically rehearsing what was said at the time.[68] It has been firmly taken for granted that inflation and pauperization arose from the economic ruthlessness of gentlemen landlords and grasping middlemen, exploiting their advantage without regard for the rights and needs of the labouring poor. A 'new' type of landlord ruined yeomen and husbandmen by the manner in which he maximized his profits; capitalist agriculture revolutionized the rural scene by destroying a happily ordered society in which greed was restrained by the recognition of mutual obligations. We are no longer so well convinced of all this. We are better aware that the purchasers of Crown lands were rarely new and more rarely still of a new type among landowners; we recall the very similar complaints raised against their predecessors; we know rather more now about the agrarian improvements of the age, about the benefits accruing to a tenantry in the main well protected by the customary and common laws, and about the effect of changing conditions which, for instance, reduced sheep farming through the collapse of the wool boom more successfully than anti-enclosure laws ever could have done.[69] There will, of course, be those who see in such historical revisions merely an alternative form of bias, and one more disagreeable than the old one because it seems lacking in compassion and indignation. However, apart from the fact that the newer views rest on better, and better understood, evidence, it should not be forgotten that similar opinions were also advanced in the reign of Edward VI itself. In the most notable piece of economic analysis produced in the century, Sir Thomas Smith's *Discourse of the Common Weal*, we find a much more balanced and penetrating discussion than in all the sermons of Latimer and Lever, the singleminded obsessions of Hales, or the other likeminded writings which have not been discussed here. Smith recognized the weight of many contemporary complaints but showed how they often cancelled one another out and how none of the sectional grievances really explained the crisis; his preferred answer, that a restoration of the coinage alone would lead to the sort of improvement in which the other defects would right themselves naturally, was proved correct when government policy finally abandoned unprofitable moralizing and ill-considered unenforceable

---

[68] W. K. Jordan, *Edward VI the Young King* (1968), esp. 416–38.

[69] These large issues obviously require more research, freed from traditional preconceptions and able to see that conditions and behaviour were uniform neither through the governing classes nor through the whole age; for the present see in particular the work of E. Kerridge: *The Agricultural Revolution* (1967) and *Agrarian Problems of the Sixteenth Century and After* (1969).

legislation in favour of recoinage. And Smith gave the classic answer to the worthy men who wished to root covetousness out of men's hearts:

> But can we devise that all covetousness may be taken from men? No, no more than we can make men without ire, without gladness, without fear, and without all affections. What then? We must take away from men the occasion of their covetousness in this part.[70]

The right answer, he maintained, was to make those activities which benefited the common weal more profitable than those which harmed it. He called not for repressive laws or moral exhortations but for a wise manipulation of the means of gain available, so that men's natural desire to better themselves should redound to the good of all.

A sane prescription, no doubt, but also not one easy to follow, as mankind has discovered often enough. Still, there was wisdom in such counsel beyond the worth of the appalled complaints and bitterness of preachers, pamphleteers and enthusiasts. This spirit of constructive encouragement rather than mere repression had guided the activities of Thomas Cromwell's reform administration and was to make itself felt again in the early years of Elizabeth's reign when William Cecil got his hands on the reins of state. Cecil knew Smith intimately – fellow secretaries both first to Somerset and then to the king – and he possessed a copy of the *Discourse*.[71] Both men were products of that Cambridge in which Cromwell had found many recruits for his administration and which he had endeavoured to turn into a nursery for servants of the state. It is this line of thought and action that now merits better attention: the succession of men who thought coolly, secularly and constructively about the problems of the common weal and who faced the practical tasks involved in turning aspiration into action. They, rather than the laudators of a glorious past that had never been and the lamenters over man's fallen nature, were the true reform party of the sixteenth century.

[70] *Discourse* (ed. Dewar), 118.
[71] HMC, Salisbury MSS, i, no. 225.

39

ARTHUR HALL, LORD BURGHLEY
AND THE ANTIQUITY OF
PARLIAMENT*

The sad story of the conflicts, in 1576 and 1581, between Arthur Hall, burgess in Parliament for the Lincolnshire borough of Grantham, and the House of Commons is not unfamiliar, but especially Hall's downfall on the second occasion has not yet been properly investigated. At first sight it might seem to be no more than the minor tale of personal misfortune and thin-skinned members of the House which has been told before.[1] However, as one looks more closely, some hitherto unnoticed details emerge which by throwing light on Elizabethan politics and political notions justify another account of the case.

Hall first drew adverse attention to himself in the session of 1572 when, contrary to the temper of the House, he opposed the petition for the execution of the duke of Norfolk and thus became something of a marked man, especially for that busy parliamentary hand, Thomas Norton. In the next session (1576) he added to his offence by trying to use the parliamentary privilege of freedom from arrest for his private advantage. An old quarrel between himself and one Melchisedech Mallory had involved an assault as a result of which his servant Edward Smalley was assessed for damages, to the tune of £100, in the court of London's recorder, William Fleetwood. To escape payment, Smalley got himself arrested and then released by privilege, in order to bar the judgment. The House outmanoeuvred Hall by recommitting Smalley to the Tower, an action which protected the privilege but nullified its effect. In the end Hall had to find the £100 to free Smalley and, furiously angry at what he regarded as biased proceedings, put the

* [*History and Imagination: Essays in honour of H. R. Trevor-Roper*, ed. H. Lloyd-Jones, V. Pearl, B. Worden (1981), 88–103.]

[1] H. G. Wright, *The Life and Works of Arthur Hall of Grantham, Member of Parliament, Courtier and first Translator of Homer into English* (1919), 68–75; J. E. Neale, *Elizabeth I and Her Parliaments, 1559–1581* (1953), 407–10; S. E. Lehmberg, *Sir Walter Mildmay and Tudor Government* (1964), 183–5.

whole affair on record in a tract written some time after the end of the 1576 session and sent to the printer. It was this product of let-off steam that provoked the troubles of 1581.

Hall's pamphlet[2] consisted of two really separate pieces:

A letter sent by F.A. touching the proceedings in a priuate quarrel and vnkindnesse, betweene Arthur Hall and Melchisedeche Mallerie Gentlemen, to his very friende L.B. being in Italy. VVith an admonition to[3] the Father of F.A. to him being a Burgess of the Parliament, for his better behauiour therin.

Though the two parts were signed through separately, there is no doubt that they were printed and published together, as contemporary comment, for instance in the rebuttal drafted in the circle of Sir Walter Mildmay,[4] confirms. Yet the two 'letters' concerned themselves with very different issues. The first is an account – vigorous and fascinating, with much splendid use of language – of the whole Mallory–Smalley affair: Hall's side of the story, though not quite as partisan as this sounds. The second essay contains reflections on the nature and antiquity of Parliament, with a long and not always courteous analysis of the qualities requisite in a member of the House of Commons. It makes no reference at all to the business of 1576.

As the Commons later pointed out, the book carries the name of neither author nor printer. The printer, in fact, was one Henry Bynneman, a member of the Stationers' Company who held various printing privileges.[5] The book also bears no date, but the first part, pretending to be a real letter, is dated 19 May 1576, two months after the end of the session it describes. This therefore will be the genuine date for the composition of part one, the other being written later; and there is no doubt that the pamphlet was printed later still. In his testimony before the Commons' committee Bynneman mentioned that Hall had received six copies of it in the last Michaelmas term (1580) and six in the Michaelmas term before that,[6] but those copies of 1579 were produced

---

[2] Only one copy survives, in the Grenville Library now in the British Library (G.5524). The tract was reprinted in *Miscellanea Antiqua Anglicana* (for Richard Triphook, 1816), and since this reprint is more readily available it will here be used for the text. In all subsequent citations of this or any other document I have modernized the spelling.

[3] *Sic.* The reprint silently and convincingly emends to 'by'.

[4] Northamptonshire Record Office, MS.F(M)P.112; see below, p. 259.

[5] W. W. Greg (ed.), *A Companion to Arber* (1967), 22, 26, 34, 44. Bynneman's responsibility was discovered by the House of Commons (*CJ* i, 122–3).

[6] Thomas Cromwell's Parliamentary Diary (Trinity College Dublin, MS N.2.12; hereafter Cromwell Diary), fo. 104. The testimony of the scrivener and his man (*CJ* i, 122–3) throws light on the complex processes involved in book production.

only after Hall had told his printer that the Privy Council raised no objection to the copies already printed.[7] Hall engaged the Council's attention in September–November 1579, and although the matter then at issue arose out of a different quarrel (with the bishop of Lincoln) mention was made of a book of Hall's on which a little earlier the Council had pronounced.[8] Thus most probably the Council had the *Letter to F.A.* before them in the middle of 1579, and most probably it was printed in the spring of that year.

The Parliament, of course, could not turn its attention to the affair until it met again, on 16 January 1581, and even then it took more than two weeks before the blow fell. On 2 February, Thomas Norton reported the allegedly libellous book to the House and offered the conjecture that it had been written by Hall. Two councillors joined in. Mr Secretary Wilson conveyed the information that Hall had admitted his authorship before the Council, and Sir Walter Mildmay, chancellor of the Exchequer, described the book's contents as 'dangerous and lewd'. It was resolved that the serjeant-at-arms should arrest Hall, and a committee was appointed to examine the printer.[9] On the 6th, when both the printer and Hall were examined at the bar, Hall's behaviour was insufficiently subdued to please his adversaries. The Commons greatly enlarged the committee of enquiry which sat on the 13th; on the 14th, its chairman, Sir Christopher Hatton, vicechamberlain, reported its findings. Hall was declared guilty of a serious breach of both privilege and decorum, and his punishment was pronounced in several resolutions. He was to be imprisoned in the Tower for at least six months until he had made a full and acceptable submission to the House, was to be fined 500 marks (the money going to the queen), and was to be expelled the House for the duration of the present Parliament. Hall appeared once more in the record: on 18 March, the day of the prorogation, it was agreed that, since Hall had not yet submitted, further action should be left to a committee of privy councillors who were to report in the next session.[10]

On the face of it, therefore, the case appears to be precisely what it has usually been taken to be. Angered by a publication which had revealed the secret proceedings of Parliament, had criticized a number of members (especially Speaker Bell, since dead) for their activities in 1576,

[7] *CJ* i, 125.   [8] *APC* xi, 293, 306, 313, 326–7.
[9] None of the committees appointed in this affair appears to reflect any significant selection or bias.
[10] *CJ* i, 122–3, 125–7, 136; Cromwell Diary, fo. 104.

had questioned the antiquity of the Commons' share in the authority of Parliament, and had by implication suggested that many members were less than fit to sit in the House, the Commons had spontaneously and unanimously quashed the offender, creating in the process some valuable precedents for their own juridical power over their members. The lead had been taken by that notoriously independent, indeed oppositionist, burgess, Thomas Norton, who disliked Hall on grounds of religion, but even some who in 1572 had stood up for Hall now joined in the hunt against him. Few cases in the reign of Elizabeth display a more unitedly affronted and determined House of Commons, acting by its own will and from within its own precinct: and that is the impression left by Neale's account.

Yet there are some fairly obvious puzzles in it all. If Norton really felt that the dignity of the House had been so badly affronted by a book published nearly two years earlier (if indeed it was ever actually published in more than a technical sense), why did he allow more than two weeks to elapse before he raised the matter? This delay contradicts Neale's conviction that both Norton and the Commons were anxious to get at Hall. Those two weeks witnessed a quarrel with the queen over the Commons' proposal for a political fast,[11] and it would have been well in accord with Tudor managerial practices if Arthur Hall had been used tactically to take the House's mind off its defeat in that business. If this is what happened, the appearance of spontaneous anger becomes less convincing.

The record in the Commons Journal also raises difficulties. The entry on 14 February narrates the day's proceedings, from Hatton's speech to the last resolution of the House, ending with the words: 'And so it was afterwards drawn into form, read to the House, and entered by the clerk, in haec verba, viz.'[12] There follows exactly the same matter once more, in the form of a report (the information laid before the House, the details of the investigation, finally the resolutions) which repeats much of the first part verbatim. Probably this formal record, though placed on the right day in the fair copy of the Journal, was not put before the House until the last day of the session (18 March) when a member recorded that 'this day was an order penned read in the House concerning Mr Arthur Hall and allowed of the House'.[13] To judge by appearances, therefore, the House on 14 February arrived unprompted at the orders for Hall's conviction and punishment, the clerk then

---

[11] Neale, 378–82.　　[12] *CJ* i, 125–7.　　[13] Cromwell Diary fo. 114v.

257

drawing up the record and presenting it for approval at a later date. However, there exists a perfect draft of that record, now found among the Burghley papers and headed with the date 13 February, the day on which the committee investigated Hall.[14] Who then drew up the decisions of the House? Did the resolutions of the 14th first get formulated that day or were they in fact produced in the committee? Burghley's possession of the draft, while it does not necessarily indicate any responsibility in the lord treasurer himself, assuredly implies an involvement of the Privy Council. Thus the location of the draft tentatively suggests that the councillors on the committee rather than the Commons as a House were responsible for the decisions taken, while its date strongly suggests that on the 14th the House received not only a report on what had happened but also in effect instructions on what to do about it. Who was after Hall?

The Council's activity throughout the business calls for investigation. As we have seen, they had probably examined the book in the summer of 1579 but the order then issued cannot have been hostile to it. After it had been made, Hall told his printer that he could go ahead, and copies were produced about which no one troubled himself for some eighteen months. Bynneman printed a small stock and distributed some of it, before stopping because he wanted to see payment first.[15] Thus, whatever may have been said at the Council Table when Hall admitted his authorship, and despite the fact that the investigation by itself proves some objections to book and author, no action resulted: in 1579 the Council did not home in on Hall. Yet when the matter came up in Parliament in 1581, councillors quickly took the lead, with Wilson in effect putting the case against Hall, Mildmay backing him up, and Hatton chairing the committee which attended to him. Were these councillors acting simply as conscientious members of the House?

There was certainly some personal animus involved. According to Hall himself, he and Wilson had at one time been on good terms, but this ended in 1576 when Wilson voted for Smalley's committal to the Tower.[16] Mildmay, so far as the evidence goes, took the most trouble over the affair. Among his papers there survives a long analysis and

---

[14] BL, Lansdowne MS 31, fos. 41v–52r. The date as given reads Tuesday, 13 February, though the day was actually a Monday.

[15] *CJ* i, 122–3. There was some conflict over numbers printed. Bynneman said that he produced some eighty or a hundred of which twelve had been sent to Hall; Hall claimed that he had only ever received one, knew nothing of the stock, but was willing to have it destroyed if the House demanded that.   [16] *Letter to F.A.*, 34–5.

confutation of Hall's discourse on the antiquity of Parliament, written in the hand of his secretary (his son-in-law William Fitzwilliam).[17] It is most unlikely that this paper could have been produced in the middle of a busy session; surely it was written earlier, probably when Mildmay first encountered Hall's pamphlet during the Council's investigation of 1579. The dating is supported by the fact that Mildmay's counterblast ignored those offensive revelations about the 1576 session which became the burden of the charge against Hall in the Commons. Apparently, therefore, he had at once, in 1579, taken exception to Hall's scepticism touching the antiquity of Parliament, but, finding himself frustrated by the Council's unwillingness to take action, had to wait until the next Parliament to demonstrate his disgust.

However, Wilson and Mildmay had not been the first movers: that role belonged to Thomas Norton. Norton and Hall were certainly enemies: even the *Letter to F.A.* makes this plain. It may be (as has been held) that Norton, supposedly a puritan, resented one who according to himself respected the old religion,[18] but this would not appear to have been the reason most obvious to Hall himself. As he told the story, he discovered during Smalley's troubles that he had run foul of a much more easily identified interest: after the jury's verdict against his man he used strong language 'of his trusty and well spoken friends the Londoners' and regretted 'the defences to his ability he hath made in all places where anything was spoken to their rebuke'.[19] It is certainly the case that right through these conflicts he found himself running up against Norton, the lord mayor's remembrancer, and Fleetwood, the city's recorder in whose court Smalley had been tried. When first the possibility was mentioned that Smalley had behaved deviously, Norton started hot on the trail and Fleetwood promptly joined in; and it was Fleetwood who in 1576 introduced an abortive bill to confirm the judgment against Smalley and to expel Hall from the House for his share in the deceit — five years before this was actually done.[20] Thus there are some broad hints that the hunting of Arthur Hall sprang from motives linked to the obscure politics of the city.

[17] Northants Record Office, MS F(M)P.112 (unfoliated). For Fitzwilliam's role see Lehmberg, *Mildmay*, 313.
[18] Norton was passionately anti-papist, whether or not that makes him the puritan partisan Neale held him to be. As for Hall, he explained that his enemy Mallory died 'leaning to the old father of Rome, a dad whom I have heard some say Mr. Hall doth not hate'; he also admitted to liking Father William Peto, that implacable opponent of Henry VIII's Divorce and later cardinal, though, as he put it, he doubted his cloth (*Letter to F.A.*, 21, 105).
[19] Ibid. 19.   [20] Ibid. 31, 41.

City politics, however, do not adequately explain Norton's role, any more than does his personal dislike of one who perhaps leant to Rome. In Neale's picture of these Parliaments, Norton appeared as an independent, a puritan, and a frequent leader of opposition to queen and Council. However, we now know that he was really one of the Council's most important men of business in the House and that his initiatives are always likely to have reflected the desires of the Council.[21] Thus his behaviour again draws attention to the reality behind the pretence. The whole affair was set up in the Commons by three interventions: Norton's first report of the book opened the campaign, Wilson's lengthy description firmly tied Hall into the story, and Mildmay's measured indignation defined the tone of the attack. This looks like the execution of a well-rehearsed plan. Hall's troubles must now look to have been manufactured for him in the Council, with his enemies there using the Commons against him after the Privy Council itself had failed to act on first seeing the book.

One further puzzle turns up a significant answer when resolved. Even though at the start of the Commons' investigation Hall shared the stage with Henry Bynneman, the printer, with Henry Shurland, the scrivener responsible for writing the fair copy delivered to the printer, and with one Welles, Shurland's man, who had scurried about between the other three, thereafter nothing more is heard of anyone except Hall himself. In the conditions of Elizabethan pamphleteering, a determined pursuit of an author which absolutely ignored his printer strikes one as very surprising. However: Norton, as counsel to the Stationers' Company and employed against unlicensed printers, had long been well versed in the politics of the printing trade. While the whole complex story is still being unravelled, a few relevant points have already emerged.[22] Thus in October 1582, in the course of his activities against John Wolf, a member of the Fishmongers' Company who was moonlighting as a printer, Norton included Bynneman in a list of those properly licensed to print.[23] He was unlikely to persecute a member of the trade of whom he expressly approved. More revealing still is a letter of the following January, from Norton to Hatton, in which Bynneman is described as

---

[21] M. A. R. Graves, 'Thomas Norton the Parliament Man: an Elizabethan M.P., 1559–1581', *HJ* 23 (1980), 17–35.

[22] I am most grateful to M. A. R. Graves, who is investigating these matters as part of his study of Thomas Norton, for drawing my attention to this side of the story.

[23] Greg, *Companion to Arber*, 24.

Hatton's servant.[24] If the printer was a protégé of the chairman of the committee which dealt with Hall, his disappearance from the action becomes very explicable. The difference of treatment meted out also puts Hatton, with Wilson and Mildmay, among Hall's enemies on the Council, while the whole tenor of these proceedings confirms that we should look to Council politics if we wish to understand the truth about the assault on Hall.

Thus the Privy Council appears to have contained influential men who took the first opportunity to raise the Commons' hackles against Hall, yet it had done nothing itself in 1579. For Hall had his friend on the Council too, and that no less a person than Lord Treasurer Burghley. Their association went back to 1552 when William Cecil acquired the wardship of young Arthur Hall,[25] and true to his conscientious style he seems thereafter to have kept a soft spot in his heart for his difficult ward and a protective eye on his doings. Burghley's friendship is quite enough to account for Hall's immunity in the investigation of 1579, but the behaviour of those other councillors in 1581 — in the Commons, where Burghley no longer sat — calls for a look at their relations with the lord treasurer. Wilson, an older man who was to die soon after the end of the 1581 session, belonged to the earl of Leicester's faction on the Council and favoured the earl's forward Protestant policy in the Low Countries, against Burghley.[26] Mildmay, the lord treasurer's professional assistant in Exchequer matters and his loyal ally in the faction struggles of the 1560s, had yet risen in office under Burghley's predecessor, was never really a Cecilian, and because of his puritan sympathies came to oppose the Alençon match, the chief issue dividing the Council in the years under consideration. Thus he stood with Leicester against Burghley.[27] Hatton, whose rise at court had not been exactly agreeable to the lord treasurer though their relations usually remained amicable on the surface, in 1579–81 also resented the queen's dalliance with French suitors and favoured an aggressive foreign policy;[28] whether of

24 BL, Add. MS 15891, fo. 42. I owe this reference to Dr Graves.
25 Hall was described as Cecil's ward as early as October 1552 (*Calendar of State Papers Domestic 1547–1580*, 46), though the patent did not issue until 12 May 1553 (*Calendar of Patent Rolls, Edward VI*, v, 136–7). The wardship yielded Cecil an annuity of £50.
26 Thomas Wilson, *A Discourse upon Usury*, ed. R. H. Tawney (1925), 8–9.
27 Lehmberg, *Mildmay*, esp. pp. 157 ff. For earlier relations see Wallace T. MacCaffrey, *The Shaping of the Elizabethan Regime* (Princeton, 1968), esp. 182, 200.
28 E. St J. Brooks, *Sir Christopher Hatton* (1946), 167 ff. Cf. esp. Hatton's letter to Burghley, 26 Sept. 1580: H. Nicolas, *Memoirs of the Life and Times of Sir Christopher Hatton K.G.* (1847), 158–61.

Leicester's faction or not, he certainly at this time strengthened it on the Council. That is to say, all these three councillors at this juncture opposed Burghley's support of the queen's policy. As for Norton, who ordinarily had good relations with several councillors, his closest tie at this point was to Hatton: unlike his formal letters to Burghley, his correspondence with the vicechamberlain breathes an air of familiar friendship.[29] On the other hand Fleetwood, so eagerly active against Hall in 1576, took no part in the campaign of 1581 — and Fleetwood was very definitely Burghley's man. This would seem to clinch it: the real target for the Council group in pursuit of Hall was Hall's sole friend in high places, Burghley himself.

Burghley's friendly assistance came into the open in the later stages of the affair. The attack on Hall through the Commons had been sufficiently successful to get him imprisoned in the Tower and condemned to severe penalties. However, Parliaments came and went, and (as we have seen) the impending prorogation caused the enforcement of the condemnation to be remitted to a committee of all the privy councillors in the House. When they were appointed the Parliament was about to be prorogued, so that the demand for a report back made sense, but since that Parliament never met again, being after eighteen more prorogations finally dissolved in April 1583,[30] it proved easy to substitute for that committee of councillors the Council itself in full session — with Burghley at the head of it. On 10 March 1581, after four weeks in the Tower, Hall decided to mobilize his patron.[31] Opening with the characteristic reflection that 'to the afflicted and wronged mind without remedy, complaint is some ease', he explained he was writing because he understood that Burghley was to be 'judge between the late dealings of the Lower House of Parliament and me'. Thus he knew of the remission to the Council eight days before the Commons formally ordered it, a detail which once again indicates who was really running things there. The chances are that it was Burghley himself who had decided to get the case thus transferred once the inconvenient Parliament was out of the way; certainly no one would have known the date of the coming prorogation sooner than he.

It would seem that Burghley had first hoped for an accommodation with the House, but this had proved impossible. In his letter, Hall related

[29] Cf. e.g., ibid. 161–2, 234–5, 242–3.
[30] Symonds D'Ewes, *The Journals of all the Parliaments during the Reign of Queen Elizabeth* (1682), 310.   [31] BL, Lansdowne MS 31, fo. 114.

that after his imprisonment he had with difficulty obtained from the
Speaker a copy of the articles compiled against himself and had at first
intended to answer them in writing, no doubt in his customary
unrepentant spirit. Reflecting, however, 'how my answers, my excuses
and submission hath been always hitherto accepted of the House', he
decided to wait 'till I might be heard by a more favourable judge'.
Nevertheless, on the advice of 'my great and good friends (of the which
your lordship is chief)', he had against his better judgment written 'a
few lines' to the Speaker to test the opinion of the House, 'whether it
remained as hardly bent towards me as it began'. That note the Speaker
had on the 8th read to the House, at which point (so Hall had heard)
'there was some appearance of favour'. The House appointed a
committee who, as he understood it, were to come to discuss those
articles with him, though according to the Journal this new committee
was left entirely free to do as they pleased about Hall's letter.[32] The
message that in the end reached the prisoner testified to no relaxation of
hostility: the House 'willed me to look to myself, for I should receive no
such favour [of an interview to explain and answer the articles], and that
I that made the book might find out what urged against me'. He felt
sure that he could show that his alleged offence did not merit 'any such
censure as they lay on me', but Burghley could see 'what profit I should
have reaped if I had liberally submitted myself to them in writing when
upon such a preparative as I have written so small fruit follows'. With
this letter he sent a draft reply to the articles which does not survive.

So Hall would have to make his explanation to the Council, at which
point Burghley took over: it was now he who guided Hall's mind, and
indeed his pen, in preparing his submission. The draft, in Hall's own
hand, was plentifully corrected and enlarged by Burghley in person, and
the fair copy accepted all his emendations.[33] Many of these represented
only verbal improvements, several of them tending to made Hall sound
a little more respectful than at first he appeared. For instance, he had
admitted that 'I did, being in some passion for mine own private cause,
touch the Speaker and some other parties by name'; after Burghley's
revision this emerged as 'use some speeches of the Speaker, whom

[32] *CJ* i, 132.
[33] The draft is BL, Lansdowne MS 31, fos. 54–55v; the fair copy (ibid., fos. 56–7) was written out
by Hall's secretary (the scribe of the letter of 10 March). The interesting drafting history of the
document was inexplicably muddled by Wright who claimed that Hall's draft had 'corrections
in another hand' and that the copy was 'in Burghley's own handwriting' (Wright, *Arthur Hall*,
190, n. 1). Perhaps he misread his own notes.

263

otherwise I reverenced, and some other persons by name to whom I have no malice, though I was somewhat offended'. There are several such mollifing additions, but it is not they that mark the interest of Burghley's recension.

For what must strike one on reading the draft is that in effect Burghley made no real attempt to alter Hall's tone and general stance – the tone of an honest man carried by justified grievance into slightly over-hasty and unfortunate speech and action, and the stance of one whose very particular allegations and complaints, arising out of his private affairs, had been unfairly interpreted as a general attack on the claims and doings of the Commons, or even on the validity of the law made in Parliament. On the contrary (Burghley's additions in brackets):

I do from the bottom of my heart reverence the laws and proceedings in the Parliament (in both Houses and Council) and do allow of the ancient authority of that (Common) House wherein the third estate of the (whole) realm is duly represented.

Thus Burghley fully agreed with Hall that the Commons had exaggerated what had happened, an opinion supported by an actual reading of the pamphlet which is nothing like as provocative as had been pretended. The lord treasurer's longer additions enlarge rather than diminish Hall's claims to righteousness and show clearly on whose side Burghley was. One such inserted passage explains that Hall's mistakes were entirely venial: Hall was made to confess his fault only 'as far forth as in my conscience any ways I can be moved, knowing that to be true that the wisest may say, *hominis est errare*'. And where Hall had ended by asking that his words be ascribed 'rather to the passion of myself being grieved than to any intent of slander or infamy to any of them all', Burghley added a long and powerful peroration:

And I require them and every of them to consider how easily many very wise men, yea men of age and experience, may err in speeches and writings uttered whilst their minds are grieved with their particular conceits touching themselves in credit and profit. Aye, though I know that my coming hither is not to pronounce anything against any person but against myself, yet in acknowledging mine own faults I do hope that some others, though very few, will not so condemn me as that they will not be content to enter into their own hearts or conscience to consider whether by some sharp speeches against me, as I did take them, I had not some cause to think hardly of them. But yet, howsoever any other might so seem to give me cause, yet I confess that I did not well in such a public sort to tax any for the same, but I know I ought to remember the saying of Almighty God, which says, *Mihi vindiciam.*

Thus the most defiant words in the submission as prepared came from Burghley, not from Hall, and it may not be fanciful to read in them the lord treasurer's answer to those fellow councillors who had used Hall against him. However, further thoughts seem to have counselled caution: before the Council saw the document the whole passage after 'credit or profit' had disappeared, to be replaced by a few colourlessly conventional phrases:

By him who is most willingly ready to spend his ability and life in her majesty's service, and to his uttermost to maintain and pray for the prosperity of all her Highness' most honourable councillors and others the makers and judges of the laws of this realm.[34]

These words, too, have more of a ring of Burghley than of Hall.

The Council accepted the submission on 2 April, and Hall went free, long before the six months' minimum imposed by the House had elapsed. His fine, too, was remitted by the queen, and since that Parliament never met again his expulsion had no consequences. Indeed, he was again elected for Grantham to the next Parliament, in 1584, though he delayed turning up (if ever in the end he came) and grew apprehensive that his enemies might reopen the whole affair by enquiring whether the earlier sentence had been carried out – and if not, why not.[35] No such move was made, and if it had been it would have failed, as one of Hall's enemies noted in due course – Thomas Cromwell the diarist, a member of every committee appointed in the business and chairman of the one which returned so dusty an answer to Hall's attempt to make peace. In 1587, collecting precedents for the arrest and release of members of the House, Cromwell listed 'Mr. Hall, committed to the Tower by order of the House and delivered by force of the general pardon'.[36] That is to say, Hall was allowed the benefit of the statute 23 Elizabeth I, c. 16, a benefit which effectively barred any further action against him for any alleged offence committed before the date of his pardon. We may well suppose that Burghley had procured this for him.

The Council had been the first to see the offending pamphlet;

---

[34] *APC* xiii, 8–11. [35] Hall to Burghley, 13 Dec. 1584 (Wright, 193–4).

[36] P. L. Ward (ed.), *William Lambarde's Notes on the Procedures and Privileges of the House of Commons, 1584* (House of Commons Library Document no. 10), 90.

councillors and their chief assistant had led the hunt in the Commons;
the Council brought the affair to an end, and factious favour there
rescued Hall, even as factious hostility had first got him into trouble.
Even though obscure conflicts within the city of London and the readily
roused *amour propre* of the House of Commons played their undoubted
part in the story, the real origin of Hall's troubles evidently lay in the
Privy Council. Like so many other parliamentary events in the reign of
Elizabeth, the demolition and restoration of Arthur Hall reflected the
politics of Council factions rather than strictly House of Commons
matters. In the rash folly of Burghley's client, his opponents in the
Council saw an opportunity to get at Burghley himself, for if Hall had
had to suffer the punishment imposed by the House the loss of face
would certainly have extended to his patron. Very possibly the fact that
by attacking Hall the conciliar managers of the Commons got
themselves out of an awkward situation at the start of a session which
looked likely to turn difficult gave them their chance; Burghley could
not well oppose a move, however tiresome to himself, which might
bring peace between queen and Commons. With admirable dexterity
he had then saved Hall without causing positive offence in the
Commons or exacerbating the feelings of his conciliar opponents.

The councillors got their chance also because the anger excited by
Hall's book was not unreal. In 1601, Francis Bacon recalled that Hall
was sent to the Tower because he had alleged 'that the Lower House was
a new person in the Trinity',[37] and that vivid phrase — which was indeed
Hall's[38] — has stuck in the memory. Neale held that of all the counts
against Hall this was the one 'that stung deepest'.[39] Perhaps it did, and it
is certainly true that when Norton opened the attack he complained not
only of animadversions on the individual members (which are to be
found in the first part of Hall's pamphlet) but of general doubts cast on
the authority of the House, a theme of the second part.[40] However, it
looks as though he emphasized the former far more, and the articles
which Hall extracted from the Speaker, as well as the formal record
entered in the Journal, also concentrate on the offence committed in
revealing the secrets of Parliament and in making personal attacks on
members there. What therefore really stirred things up was Hall's
reckless (though at this distance rather delightful) description of all that

[37] *The Letters and Life of Francis Bacon*, iii, ed. J. Spedding (1868), 37.
[38] *Letter to F.A.*, 78: a study of past legislation 'will dissuade the antiquity of our third voices, which many defend, and also will show a light of the admitting the third person in this trinity'.
[39] Neale, 407.   [40] *CJ* i, 122a.

had happened over Smalley's Case in 1576. In his hostile analysis, Mildmay disallowed Hall's professions of good intent and concluded that it was the denial of antiquity to the Commons that constituted 'this lewd purpose and perilous practice thus maliciously published in print',[41] words which he repeated in the House; but in actual fact the attack concentrated more on the personal issues.

That first part of the book does indeed include a certain amount of angry disrespect directed at personal enemies, though – contrary to the allegations – it is hard to see that Hall had been particularly cutting about Robert Bell who at worst emerges as a man capable of bungling and changing his mind: a bit inefficient in executing his managerial role. Norton and Wilson come in for worse swipes. What that section does not display is enmity to the Parliament as such. Hall knew himself well enough and was capable of admitting his faults. The device of a fictitious author permitted a description of the real one: Hall, we are told, was possessed of 'a sensible tongue at will to utter his mind, no want of audacity, of sufficient courage, well disposed to liberality, loving and sure to his friend, secret where he is trusted', but also 'overweening of himself . . . furious when he is contraried, without patience to take time to judge or doubt the danger of the sequel . . . so implacable if he conceive an injury'.[42] His enemies might have wished to adjust the balance of this appraisal, but it was not a bemused one, nor does the tale of the quarrel with Mallory disguise the absurdities and follies of Hall's own behaviour. The tone of the pamphlet inclines one to its author – a frank and rather wry tone. As for Parliament, Hall opens with an earnest avowal of his pride in his place in the House ('I am a member of the grave, great and considerate council of the Parliament') and concludes with a special complaint that Mallory's behaviour had contemptuously impeded 'the judgment of that High Court of Parliament': and both points were sincerely made.[43]

Hall thus did not despise Parliament; the charge was false. That makes the second part of his book, in some ways the less entrancing, the more profoundly important one. In it he considered the institution, its history and authority. In form an address of advice to a new member of the House – 'Son, forasmuch as I now have obtained for you my place in the Common House of Parliament' – it professes to teach him his proper bearing there and introduces that subject quite logically with a discussion of the kind of institution of which this tyro has now become a

[41] Northants. Record Office, MS F(M)P.112, at end.   [42] *Letter to F.A.*, 3.   [43] Ibid. 2, 45.

member. Whatever hidden purposes may be read into the analysis, the writer appears only anxious to understand the reasons for certain claims to political power which he himself accepts as rightly maintained in his own day, and he therefore considers the antiquity of Parliament's authority and the date from which he can demonstrate the Commons' share in it. With a precision exceptional in these debates, Hall had seized on the crucial point: he defined Parliament as a body that makes laws, and in tracking its antiquity he thus pursued the making of laws through English history. A survey of that history from Brutus to Henry III firmly disposes of any notion that something properly called a Parliament existed before the thirteenth century. While Hall admits to finding the term used in the chronicles, he rightly points out that these 'do rather use the word (as indeed it is proper where any conference is) than that it carries with it, where it comes, the same to be understood to be the great court of Parliament' as it has existed from Henry III's day to the present.[44] Such laws as were made before that time were made by kings, and if they took advice they got it from assemblies very different from genuine Parliaments. Even the assembly at Merton (1236), which he recognizes as 'the first Parliament of name and record', should not be regarded as identical with 'a Parliament as now we use ours'.[45]

Hall thus evinced a grasp of historical context unusual among Elizabethan historians, let alone parliamentarians. Moreover, even after something really to be called a Parliament can at last be found, distinctions, he insists, must not be fudged. Though he accepts the existence of the institution from the reign of Henry III, he points out (correctly) that throughout the thirteenth century all laws continued to be enacted by the king's authority alone.[46] Like others since his time, he finds the presence of the commonalty first properly documented in the Statute of York (1322). Again in tune with more recent research, he emphasizes that under Edward III parliamentary consent applied more particularly to taxation, but he is perhaps a little more strict than some modern successors when he argues that, whatever may be said about request or consent or advice, the documents clearly show that the lawmaking authority remained with the king alone. While he agrees that the authority of the whole Parliament is recorded by the time of Henry VII, he maintains that a real change to the present condition came only with the assembly of the Reformation Parliament in 1529; from

---

[44] Ibid. 61.   [45] Ibid. 63.   [46] Ibid. 63–7.

that point he has no difficulty in recognizing his own kind of Parliament 'held of the three estates, wherein the Commons were one'.[47]

Hall's history was really very good. He was right in holding that the making of laws 'by the authority of this present Parliament' (instead of by the king's authority, though made in the present Parliament) came about during the fifteenth century, though he postdated the event a little;[48] and he was right about the change which came over the institution in the 1530s when it assumed its Elizabethan – indeed, its modern – guise. Standing so near to the event, he could not properly work out what had happened under Henry VIII, but he pinpointed the critical date with surprising accuracy.

The rest of this second part of the pamphlet discusses the function of the Commons in a modern Parliament and deduces the qualities required for service in the House. In both respects Hall could hardly be faulted. He firmly rejected the possible charge that his historical review intended 'to disgrace that noble, grave and necessary third state of Parliament (which if I were so lewdly disposed I never were able to touch)', and he took care to demonstrate his loyalty to the queen by praising her regard for Parliament. One of his most perceptive remarks touched the policy of the Tudors in this respect: 'What contented minds of late ages the kings and queens of this realm have carried in matters of Parliament, when things have not fallen out current to their expectations, I think not only all Parliament-men but the whole country knows.'[49] He demanded exceptional qualities in a member of the House, though his violent onslaught on any willing to serve outside interests there for a fee set standards of austerity beyond the possibilities of the scene.[50] No doubt it caused offence where it was intended to.[51] Otherwise, however, nothing that he said about the nature of the Elizabethan Parliament and the Commons' function in it could possibly distress the most slavish admirer of the institution. This song of praise sufficiently accounts for the fact that in trying to convict him of contempt his enemies had to concentrate on his report of Smalley's Case and exaggerate the offensiveness of his remarks there. Still, none of that

[47] Ibid. 74.
[48] Cf. above, no. 22 (esp. p. 29) for an analysis of these problems written long before I had occasion to read *Letter to F.A.* and based on the same principle that the constitutional position of Parliament needs to be assessed from an analysis of its lawmaking power.
[49] *Letters to F.A.*, 78–9. [50] Ibid. 93–4.
[51] Dr Graves has rightly pointed out to me that in 1572 Norton was much attacked in the House precisely over this issue. Hall had his wicked moments.

praise could disguise the manner in which he had denied remote antiquity to the Parliament (dating it from about 1250 instead of the mists of time) and had reassessed the Commons' share in the legislative process (refusing to accept it as surely proven before the reign of Henry VII).

With these arguments Hall had entered into a current debate among scholars which had important meaning for the sense of self-importance common in Parliament, not to mention practical implications for anyone wanting to use the institution as an instrument for political action. The history of Parliament could not be confined to the concerns of pedants, and the debate about 'origins', active in Elizabeth's reign, was to endure for some time. Most contributors professed to find something justly called a Parliament almost as far back as they could reach. They usually achieved this by looking for assemblies called to give advice and naming every such meeting, however selective, a Parliament; what they entirely ignored was Hall's important emphasis on the making of laws and the authority behind them.[52] Hall was aware of the antiquaries: 'In reading, I have gathered many flowers out of Mr William Lambarde's garden, a gentleman, after my verdict, though unknown to me, for his painful, rare and learned collection worthy to be known.'[53] It is interesting that he should have seen Lambarde's notes on Parliament, which later appeared in his *Archeion* (1591), before 1579; since he had no acquaintance with the author and advised readers to look for themselves at what Lambarde had to say, we must suppose that those collections were generally available much earlier than is usually thought.[54]

Mildmay knew them too: he used them in trying to demolish Hall's attack on the ancient authority of Parliament. In the main his treatise was a point-by-point refutation of Hall's texts and arguments from the

[52] Cf. the essays printed in T. Hearne, *Curious Discourses* (1771), i, 281–309, which show such views being expressed by eminent antiquaries like Francis Tate, Arthur Agard, and even William Camden. John Hooker, in 1572, reprinted the medieval *Modus Tenendi Parliamentum* under the impression that it described Parliament in the days of Edward the Confessor. *Parliament in Elizabethan England: John Hooker's 'Order and Usage'*, ed. Vernon F. Snow (New Haven, 1977), 125.

[53] *Letter to F.A.*, 75.

[54] His biographer, citing no evidence, says that Lambarde began to work on the *Archeion* 'at least as early as 1579' (Retha M. Warnicke, *William Lambarde – Elizabethan Antiquary* [1973], 84). Hall's testimony would support this conjecture and even permit thoughts of a markedly earlier date since by 1579 at the latest Lambarde's notes on Parliament must have been circulating in a reasonably finished form.

reign of Henry III onwards.[55] He convicted Hall of some over-rapid citation and of occasional tendentious compression; but because of his refusal to give weight to Hall's discovery of a principled line of argument (the authority by which laws are made), his attack missed its target and testified more to the rage of injured pride than the disagreements of scholars. Though he promised to consider the chronicle evidence for the existence of Parliament before the beginning of the statute book, evidence which Hall had comprehensively discarded, he never did so, contenting himself with a few rude remarks to the effect that Hall's analysis was too vague to merit examination. Mildmay added a hint that Hall's authority, Lambarde, in fact did not support him. Up to a point, this was true: in the *Archeion* Lambarde allows various pre-Conquest assemblies back to the days of Ine to have been lawmaking Parliaments.[56] On the other hand, being an honest antiquary, he could not discover any indication of the three estates before the days of King John and felt much happier once he could rely on the statute book; it was manifestly this section, from the Statute of Merton onwards, that was used by Hall.[57]

Hall's achievement, hidden because buried in a virtually vanished polemical tract, must be accounted notable. Rather than piling up cases of general assemblies back to Lucius or even Brutus in a desire to give the Parliament the desirable accolade of immemorial existence, he endeavoured to establish criteria by which to define the institution and then to trace back their historical existence; and he set them out. Perhaps he was moved by considerations less worthy than scholarly truth – a mischievous desire to puncture the pretensions of self-important men who had ill-treated him – but this hardly matters, except to show that dubious motives can produce good learning. As he saw it, the Parliament of his day was to be defined by three characteristics. It consisted of the three estates of prince, lords and commons – a very important definition which had only recently displaced the opinion that the king was no part of Parliament whose three estates comprised the spiritualty, the nobility and the commons.[58] Secondly, only Parliament had

---

[55] Northants. Record Office, MS.F(M)P.112.

[56] William Lambarde, *Archeion*, ed. C. H. McIlwain and P. L. Ward (Cambridge, Mass., 1957), 129–33.   [57] Ibid. 136–40.

[58] Cf. above, ii, 32–5. This opinion, the modern commonplace, was accepted by Mildmay in F(M)P.112, at the start ('our Parliament is a public assembly of the three estates, viz. the prince, nobility and commons of the realm') and endorsed in 1584 by Burghley who declared that the

power to deprive the subjects of this land of life, lawful inheritance, or goods. The authority thereof doth stretch to them all, to take away life, inheritance, yea of the crown of this realm, and every man's chattels, and hath full power to make and alter laws.

Thirdly, therefore, the authority of Parliament consists in its exclusive power to make law.[59] By tracing back these characteristics – the three estates, omnicompetence, and the authority behind the laws made – the proper antiquity of Parliament could be discovered.

That still remains the sole sound method for solving this particular historical question, and it still produces very much the answer pronounced by Hall. He made his mistakes: even allowing for the limited materials available to him – chronicles and the statutes from Magna Carta onwards – one may accuse him of hasty and sometimes slipshod research, though one must be impressed by the consistency with which he applied his defined criteria to the evidence he used. In the result, he dated both the parliamentary authority of lawmaking and the arrival of the Commons' House a little too late, as Mildmay was not slow to point out, though Hall certainly came much nearer the truth than did Mildmay and all the other believers in immemorial antiquity. Hall made his minor mistakes partly, no doubt, because they suited his polemical purpose, but partly because he so well realized the importance of the ultimate emergence, in the reign of Henry VIII, of the kind of Parliament familiar to him at first hand that he discounted partial moves in that direction during the previous century and a half. Conscious of a revolutionary moment in the 1530s, he underplayed the prehistory of the revolution. Well, that can happen to us all, and in all essentials Hall was right.

Thus Arthur Hall, difficult, choleric and often tiresome, was not just an 'egregious' person given to wonted pigheadedness – a man (it has been claimed) who, even though his history may have been better than his opponents', deserved his fate because he crossed the men whose devotion to Parliament heralded the future.[60] He did get into trouble with needless ease and, as he himself recognized, once in it would not again extricate himself while any sense of grievance remained. Like

---

Commons and Lords were two members of the Parliament, and the Queen, its head, the third: 'of these three estates doth consist the whole body of the Parliament able to make laws' (D'Ewes, *Journals*, 350).

[59] *Letters to F.A.*, 80–1.

[60] Cf. esp. Neale, *Elizabeth I and her Parliaments*, i, 253, 408. See also ibid. ii, 437–8, for the apostolic succession of 'great parliamentarians'.

others of Burghley's wards he must have been a sore trial to that father of his country. At a later date, further soured by his experiences in a truly ridiculous pursuit of the widowed countess of Sussex, Hall was to turn against his patron,[61] but in 1581 he relied on him and had cause to thank him. In his conflicts with the House of Commons, the most important of which originated in conflicts quite extraneous to the House, Hall had much justice on his side, and as an historian of Parliament he stood high above his contemporaries because he understood the need to allow for change through time. For an Elizabethan, he avoided anachronism with exceptional success. It is good to know that Lord Burghley, engaged in once more saving him from the consequences of his ready temper, agreed with him about the antiquity as well as the current authority of Parliament.

[61] Wright, *Hall*, 88–9.

40

ENGLISH LAW IN THE SIXTEENTH CENTURY: REFORM IN AN AGE OF CHANGE*

I am not a legal historian, I am not a lawyer; to address a body so eminent in those particular ways is something of an excitement, a strain, an embarrassment, a pleasure; at least I can talk history, perhaps teach history, to lawyers. Because what I would like to talk about today is not really the history of the law so much as how the changes that happened in sixteenth-century law may be seen to fit into a larger historical framework – an interpretation of the sixteenth century which takes account of the dynamics of that age and gives us some way of understanding initiatives and the proceedings that also affected the history of the law. It is a well-known fact that the sixteenth century witnessed a major transformation in the history of the common law, though it is also a well-known fact that we face here one of the 'dark ages', as Dr Baker has called them, in the history of that law.

In other words, we know that things were transformed but we have not very much idea of what they were transformed from or into, and least of all do we yet know exactly what transformations happened in the course of that major change; nor can I give you much detail of that kind. We are waiting for a legal specialist to tell us more. But we do know that the land law was profoundly altered by the legislation of Henry VIII's reign and subsequent practices. We know that mercantile law developed. We know a great deal, I suppose, about changes in the criminal law though not as much as we would like to know. We know that the old forms of action died to the point where at one time we thought that all the forms of action had become ossified, until trespass on the case crept from its hiding and hit us all over the head with its multiple details. We know a great deal, I suppose we know most of all in this respect, about changes in the courts that administered the law. We

---

* [The Selden Society Lecture, delivered 5 July 1978 and published by the Society in 1979.] The lecture was delivered unscripted, and this is a slightly modified version of the taped recording.

know about the great new growth of equity in its various aspects, in its various courts, Star Chamber and Requests, as well as Chancery. We are learning more about those things every day, for this is indeed where historians, institutional historians, have been most active. The great revival of legal history which has been happening in the last ten years or so and is beginning to show the signs of a runaway conjuncture is, I think, now really hitting the sixteenth century, and that is one reason why I should like today to discuss not the changes in the law themselves but how those changes might be approached.

So we know that these things happened; we know, for instance, that if we look up my lord Coke's work we find there something like a summing-up of a hundred years of transformation. After all, *Coke on Littleton* really amounts to Coke saying, 'don't bother to read *Littleton*, it has all changed'. That is in fact what happened in that area as in so many others. People usually ask why it happened, rather than the first question which I think we ought to ask, which is how it happened. What were the stages of transformation, what were the stimuli and drives, what were the reasons for all this that altered the ancient law of England so drastically? People talk about the interests of lawyers and their clients, they talk about the pressures of the courts, they will talk about the effects of the dissolution of the monasteries which indeed must have had profound effects as title all over the realm came to be called in question or had to be freshly established. All sorts of things were hunted out; all sorts of things had to be resolved, or failed to get resolved, with even more dire consequences. People will talk learnedly about the great effects of social transformation. That is a good traditional explanation: the sixteenth century — an age of social transformation, all social classes rising. Do you remember the gentry that used to rise upon its pink clouds for ever and ever until it hit the ceiling and had to come down again? We now know that the gentry never rose; it was always there at the top anyway. There is the decline of the aristocracy, 'the crisis of the aristocracy', as Professor Stone has termed it in a book which conclusively proves that there was an aristocracy and conclusively fails to prove that there was a crisis. Was there, in fact, any social change at all? I am inclined to think there was not. And if there was no social change, no change really in the structure of the nation, with the sole exception of the decline of the Church (a very separate problem from the point of view of the law), then I think we need to start thinking more precisely and not use these rather happy general terms and generalizations to get ourselves out of the task of explanation and understanding.

What, therefore, I want to discuss is the how, rather than the why. It seems to me there were two major mechanisms changing the law: one was internal, the other external. Internal: by this I mean the effect that the practices of the law had upon the law itself, the work of the courts and of the lawyers; and here the chief instrument of change, I would suggest to you, was legal fiction. Fictitious forms of action, fictitious practices, fictitious arrangements which, by pretending to preserve established and well-known practices, in effect produced total innovation. While this is not what I am going to talk about today, I would leave this thought with those who can pursue it more learnedly than I can: we need to know a great deal about the manner in which the courts themselves by their inventions affected the substantive law.[1] The external changes are essentially embodied in the work of Parliament and statute. Legislation alters the law most obviously, most drastically and perhaps most completely, though it may do so more on the surface than in reality. We know often enough that a law may be made and a law may even be observed, and yet it will not have the effect that it appears to have or that it was intended to have, and many Tudor laws were very poorly if ever enforced. Nevertheless, legislation, the work of statute, is what I should like to look at today. Reform by legislation is really the main theme of this discourse. Now here it seems to me that if you read the standard authorities – and I use that term with some reluctance; I would not use it amongst historians who, in my opinion, neither are nor have authorities, but I am willing to use it amongst lawyers who, I think, believe that they both are and have such authority – if you read the standard works on this you are liable to suppose that statutory law reform, the work of Parliament, went on all the time in essentially undifferentiated fashion all through the period we are considering, say the years from about 1500 to perhaps the civil war, or at any rate down to the end of Elizabeth's reign, and that there is no real chronological structure to this. Holdsworth, for instance, is capable of saying in one place that 'after the passing of the Acts of 1540 and 1623' something ought to have happened.[2] Two acts touching limitation of actions, 1540, 1623: eighty-three years between. A longer life span than most of us are

---

[1] Soon after the lecture was delivered the answer appeared: cf. J. H. Baker's 'Introduction' to his edition of *The Reports of Sir John Spelman* (Selden Soc., 1978), ii, *23–396*.

[2] W. S. Holdsworth, *History of English Law*, iv, 485. The correct date of the session is 1624.

likely to enjoy! From the historian's point of view this is a really disastrous remark; it is the sort of thing that makes one shudder – this running together of all the events that happened to have some kind of family resemblance into a single sentence. What in fact we must try to get at is the phasing of these changes and of possible movements for reform through the hundred years we are concerned with and in that way, looking at Parliament, we may, I would suggest to you, have a better chance of understanding both the motives that underlay action and the pressures that affected these changes; we may possibly thus get at the reality behind them and the effects they had.

In order to do this, I would like to put before you now a theory about the reform movements of the sixteenth century which is general and does not apply to the law alone. Was the sixteenth century in fact an age of reform? What do we mean by an age of reform, a term commonly applied to it, as it can be applied to other ages? In trying to understand this question, I overstepped the bounds of proper historical method and decided to build a model of an age of reform in the crudest possible sociological fashion. I came to the conclusion, basing myself upon two well-known ages of reform, that a model of this kind has five components. Those two well-known ages were the first quarter or so of the nineteenth century which, after all, is described in the *Oxford History of England* as the 'age of reform', so that that must be true; and the last thirty years or so, which we are all liable to agree at least were an age of massive change, whether or not we like and approve the changes that we have witnessed. There are five components to my model. There must, in the first place, be a recognition of the need for reform, a consciousness that things are inadequate or wrong. Now that's not a universal though it is very commonly found. In the second place, there must be a recognition of the possibility of self-help. Men must be willing to suppose that they by their own efforts can alter the inadequacies of their society and make them better. That again is not always found throughout most of what we call rather crudely the 'middle ages'; the notion that the common fate of mankind was God's will, and that the only improvement was to be found in another life, was widely held. In the third place, there must be, I think, a programme of reform, a reasonably consistent, coherent, diffuse and diverse set of notions of what specifically should be done. In the fourth place there must be what I would call a public opinion in favour of reform. Now by public opinion I here mean that those who are involved or potentially involved in the necessary action should be by and large of the same mind; should feel about the social structure which they are trying to reform in much the same way; should have a common view of the lines along which reform should proceed. In our present age, for instance, this task, this particular need, must be fulfilled by an effectively democratic electorate. The sort of milk-and-water socialism or corporatism which has dictated all the reforms since 1945, no matter which party was in power, represents the common consensus which is the kind of public opinion that I have in mind. Whichever party rules us, the lines upon which action is taken are very much the same because people are very much agreed on the function of the reforming agency and on the remedy for deficiencies. In the 1830s Benthamism supplied a similar common element right through all the areas of government: the forming of opinion, the shaping of analysis, in journalism and the like, so that there was a common ground, a consensus, upon which action could rest. In the sixteenth century that area needs to be smaller but it needs still to be there. Those who are active in government – active in the shaping of measures, as well as in formulating views – need, in my opinion, to be found to possess a common public opinion of this sort. And lastly, there has to be leadership from those who can translate ambition and aspiration into action – those, in other words, who have the means of power under their hand. If you have a consciousness of the need, a willingness to act, a common opinion and a programme, but there is no co-operation from those who take the lead in action, you do not get an age of reform but you get a potentially very explosive, potentially revolutionary situation, because here you have people wanting reform and being frustrated. Therefore, perhaps most importantly, a true age of reform can exist only if those who control power co-operate with those who plan reform.

Now, if you take this five-part model (it is not much of a model, but it will do for our purposes) and look at the sixteenth century in the light of it, quite interesting things emerge. It emerges, for instance, that the reign of Henry VII was in no sense an age of reform. This is testified to us by his last and perhaps his most distinguished minister, Edmund Dudley who, in 1510, under sentence of death in the Tower, wrote a treatise in which he explained that the realm was badly conducted, that the state of affairs that he found was poor, and that, therefore, something should be done; and this experienced statesman, this very practical and very competent man, offers for a diagnosis only that men are not sufficiently moral, that they are not as good as God would wish them to be; and for a remedy he maintains only that they should, in consequence, be as good as God would wish them to be.[3] That is no programme of reform. That is loose, moralistic preaching talk and does not get you anywhere. It pains me to hear it from a man of this quality. In fact, there are other reasons for writing Henry VII out of the story. I myself am inclined to think that very few of the things that ever since Francis Bacon we have said Henry VII did were actually done by the king, and certainly most of the legislation of his reign, I strongly suspect, never came before Court or Crown or Council.

We then pass on into ages that were more conscious of the reality of social deficiencies and more capable of propounding remedies along reasonable and rational lines. In 1516 Thomas More's *Utopia* supposedly put before us a reform programme which first analysed the deficiencies of the realm in considerable detail and then proposed an ideal society or at least a society apparently in good order, which, some people have supposed, More would ask us to substitute for that of England. I do not think More really meant that. He would not have called this island Nowhere (*Utopia*) if he had supposed that it could be anywhere in reality. More certainly did not suppose that you should take England and twist it over into Utopia, and it is very fortunate that no one has ever attempted to do so, because Utopia would be a disastrous country to live in: grey, uninspired, unchanging, undynamic, devoid even of the most basic accumulation of wealth on behalf of the community and, therefore, forever the same, final and finite. I think we should all be horrified to live in it; a living death but no doubt very good and proper, and nobody there is greedy, or so More tells us. In effect, More was telling the reform movement of the 1510s, the Christian humanist reform movement, which is usually given the name of Erasmianism, that their dreams of a better society were only their dreams and not reality. The true and good society cannot exist in this fallen world: it exists Nowhere.

The Christian humanists, however, were joined very soon after by a new stream of reform notions associated with the Protestant Reformation, the continental Reformation and Martin Luther; it was in fact protestantism that gave to the large and, on the whole, rather woolly ambitions of the Erasmians the positive drive and the very precise and fierce passion which were required if reality was to take note of reform.

[3] Edmund Dudley, *The Tree of Commonwealth*, ed. D. M. Brodie (Cambridge, 1948).

It is the alliance of the next generation of Christian humanists with the new continental religion that, it seems to me, produced the great outburst of genuine reforming which we witness in the 1530s. Here in the 1530s we have all the details of my model in existence. You only have to read someone like Thomas Starkey, one of Thomas Cromwell's leading advisers or leading writers, to see how many deficiencies were discerned in the body politic and how willing these people were to think in terms of a reform done by human hand. Cromwell's papers included a very large number of very specific reform proposals: interestingly enough, many of them cast in the form of bills for the Parliament, ready for action, some sensible, some senseless. You find a major poor law reform side by side with the proposal that a law should be made to prevent lusty young men from marrying worn-out old widows because it was bad for the stock. They were always doing that, you see, these lusty young men, because that was where the money was. The reasons for which the old widows married young men I will not go into. A common public opinion is also available in that group of humanistically trained men with Protestant inclinations who gathered around Cromwell, not only from the universities but also from the city of London, from the trading community, men who thought about the needs of the community and the society along very similar lines and were forming, therefore, a pressure group right at the centre of affairs, ready and able to put up these reforming ideas in specific and positive and pragmatic form. And, of course, above all, we find a lead from the top. In Thomas Cromwell this movement received not only support but leadership as well as participation in the planning of ideas and details. Here we have all the details of the model assembled, and we have indeed in the 1530s a consequent outburst of reforming activity.[4]

To keep this long story short, that activity goes on thereafter in a declining fashion. Cromwell's fall was the end of a true age of reform. After Cromwell, for the rest of Henry's reign, there is no leadership from the top. Yes, certainly reforms of one kind and another are still visible. Cromwell's activity had been so explosive, so all-embracing, affecting so many things, that there had to be an aftermath, there had to be a follow-up. Things done had to be in part undone, or to be taken further. The effect of the turmoil that the 1530s started in Church and state, in society, in people's private lives, these effects were to be seen there for a good many years but they were no longer carried along by an

[4] For all this cf. *Reform and Renewal*.

active movement for reform. These are people now tinkering with the after-effects as need arises. And that is true, too, of the supposed age of reform which marks the era of the Protector Somerset. You will probably all have heard, or many of you will have heard, of the commonwealth movement of the reign of Edward VI, when a group of thinkers and divines allegedly put together various notions about the true common weal, tried to put them into practice and got the active leadership of Protector Somerset, acting on behalf of the young King Edward. It, therefore, comes as something of a grief to me to have to explain that the reform movement called the Commonwealth party was invented by A. F. Pollard in the year 1900 out of one single letter; it never existed. This would take too long to explain and there is, in fact, a paper in the press which explains it, and in which, in due course, you may find support for this rather drastic revision.[5] The so-called reformers of 1547–9 were not reformers, they were preachers – men like Latimer who preached against sin, as he was entitled and indeed as he was obliged to do. His remedy for sin was, of course, an end to sinful feelings; we are back with the level of analysis and remedy that we found in Edmund Dudley. One other of these supposed reform preachers, Thomas Lever, who in fact never preached a word before the fall of the Protector Somerset, similarly advocated that sin be terminated and the world would then be better. These are not reform movements of a genuine kind and certainly not useful to anyone interested in what was happening to the law.

In fact, right down to the accession of Elizabeth, all you can see is the occasional continuation of the Cromwellian impetus following through and following up where the 1530s had led. There is one exception to this, the work of Sir Thomas Smith, *The Discourse of the Common Weal*, the most remarkable analytical treatise, I think, of the sixteenth century, which really does take the problems of the common weal to pieces and propounds sensible and practical reforms as well as things that no one has ever yet achieved: it is a serious, secular treatment of serious and secular problems. And Smith, I think, had his effects on the first decade of Elizabeth's reign when we see a last echo of a genuine reform movement in the work of the young William Cecil, trying to use the power of the state for the betterment of society. Cecil had given up by the end of the decade; Elizabeth never started. Elizabeth's chief purpose throughout her reign was to make time stand still. Change was at an end

[5] Above, no. 38.

with her accession. In 1580 she even succeeded in making her face stand still. Her portraits were fixed from that point and no more changes permitted: only the wrinkles of the first forty-seven years and none thereafter. And so the administration of the reign of Elizabeth largely stood under the leadership of a regime which believed in holding a line but not in changing anything, not in advancing. Of course, there were still changes and reforms under Elizabeth, but they were not those that we can associate with a genuine age of reform when the whole force of the state and the community is directing itself towards its basic problems, trying to revise and review what needs doing and attempting to provide those things that need doing. The one exception to this that might be cited in fact proves my point: you will remember that towards the end of Elizabeth's reign the so-called great Elizabethan Poor Law emerged in the acts of 1597 and 1601, the basis of poor relief for the next two hundred years or so. Was this not the product of a great social reform movement? The answer is no: it certainly is nothing of the sort. In 1593 the House of Commons petitioned the Crown that all the existing poor law acts be repealed, on the grounds that they were now superfluous. The realm was in such a splendid state that there was no need for these provisions. With the usual skill in such matters, peculiar to politicians, the House made this plea on the eve of the worst economic disaster of the century. The next three harvests failed disastrously, the war destroyed trade, the country was full of maimed soldiers and seamen. The problems of poverty and plague suddenly exploded, in the 1590s, right in the face of this complacent assertion of 1593. The acts of 1597 and 1601 were specific and pragmatic answers, based on earlier experience, and had nothing to do with a major reform movement. They also, because they were passed just before the end of Elizabeth's reign, became ineffective through the reign of James I, a reign which was marked even more than any other you could name in our history as an age in which nothing happened, in which nothing was done, in which government neglected all its duties. Even the administrations from 1964 onwards, I think, were not quite so disastrous as the reign of James I – but it is touch and go, touch and go.

Thus, the chronology of reform in general, was something like this. Nothing much at all until about 1510 when we begin to get a movement for reform which we call Erasmian for shorthand purposes. This, however, achieves very little, mainly because such co-operation from government as you could wish to find would mean the co-operation of Cardinal Wolsey, who produced a great deal of interest and a good many initiatives but never actually seriously applied his mind to this particular task, mainly because his preoccupations were too many. Mainly; I think there were other reasons as well. I do not think Wolsey ever would have really made a reforming minister. And in Thomas More's view, real reform on earth was out of the question anyway, and More was the most distinguished member of that group. Then in the late 1520s, and spilling over into the 1530s, a great pressure for reform builds up amongst intellectual and practical circles at the universities and in London, and receives from Thomas Cromwell the accolade of an age of reform, when action is really very powerful. Of course, the break-up in the Church is the most important aspect of it, but there are a great many other things as well. 1540 marks the end of the last genuine age of reform in Tudor history. Yes, reform continued to be undertaken. Changes occurred, most of them in some way deduced from the explosion of the 1530s with many others that were simple responses to immediate need, but there are no more ages of reform.

Now, does this chronology help us in looking at the transformation of the law which, after all, I am supposed to be talking about? There is here, first of all, a very serious problem of evidence. If we are talking about legislation as the means of changing the law, we look in the first place, of course, to the statutes passed. But it would be a sad mistake to confine our attention to them; we need to look very much at the bills introduced that never passed. It may not be widely known that in the reign of Elizabeth, for instance, the average number of acts passed in a session was about twenty to twenty-two public acts; about ten to twelve or fifteen private acts. The average number of bills introduced that failed ran around about eighty per session. There is an enormous area here of activity which must not be ignored; which fact is vital to an understanding of Parliament, and which has been consistently ignored in the history of Parliament so far. Unfortunately, however, we know about these failed bills only from 1547 when the Commons Journals begin. Before that we are effectively ignorant of what bills were introduced in the House and never got through. Now and again we know of one, by accident, but we do not get that systematic knowledge which we gain thereafter. Though we do not always know the content of those bills, we know at least the titles, or those titles that the clerk in his wisdom ascribed to them. But even allowing for this deficiency, which is liable to distort the picture, we can nevertheless, I think, look at law reform from the point of view of the model I have put before you and of the consequences that the model has for an understanding of the sixteenth century; and we shall see that indeed things fit. I am concerned here, of course, with the reform of the substantive law. I am not concerned here with changes in law courts, nor am I concerned with the simple fact that all legislation deals with law; I am talking about changes in the private law and civil matters in the main.

If you look at the history of legislation in the sixteenth century from about 1510 onwards, the first thing you notice is that for practical purposes there is no law reform passed at all before the Reformation Parliament. In the first Parliaments of Henry VIII, the reaction against Henry VII does produce a few acts which would come within the meaning of this particular term. We have, for instance, acts touching false offices, touching traverse of lands and one, you may remember, which repealed the act touching information laid before justices of the peace. But these were all reactions against Henry VII's activities; incidentally, bogus reactions, pretending things that had never happened. They were largely designed to start the new reign off in a glory of popularity. They did not really affect the law seriously at all. And thereafter I can find no law reform acts in the Parliaments of Henry VIII down to and including the Parliament of 1523. There is one touching exigents in 4 Henry VIII. Thereafter in the Reformation Parliament, however, we do find law reform coming in. At first the main concern is with the reform of the criminal law: benefit of clergy, sanctuary, the trial of felonies; especially the various acts touching the trial of felonies in Wales and the marches, and a number of things of that kind. It is quite clear that if there was a reforming movement going on under Cromwell's control from 1532 onwards, its first concern is with law and order and it is active in that respect, though the main act touching sanctuaries was not passed until 1540 in Cromwell's last Parliament.

But there are two sessions of the Cromwellian era which fully bear out the notion that we have here an age of reform in the law as well. The last session of the Reformation Parliament in a relatively minor way was a great law reform Parliament: the Piracy Act; the Statute of Uses, of course (especially that); and the Statute of Enrolments; an act touching criminous servants; touching tithe; and the great Act of Franchises, ostensibly 're-continuing' them, as it said, but really putting an end to them. So we have here major law reform, especially in Uses and Enrolments, government-inspired and based upon Council planning.

How many bills may have failed in this Parliament, we do not know. And then, in Cromwell's last Parliament in 1540 (32 Henry VIII), law reform really took over. Dr Abbott has described it as the age of Cromwellian law reform and compared it with the activities of Edward I and his reforms,[6] and, I think, not without reason because, as you will probably know, by the middle of Elizabeth's reign it was these acts of Henry VIII's reign that formed the substance of teaching at the Inns, whereas the Edwardian acts, hitherto the main pabulum of the young student, lay forgotten and mouldering. The law had been changed totally in so many respects by these acts of Henry VIII's reign that the old laws were already no longer worth teaching. Let me just read you the relevant acts that were passed in 32 Henry VIII: Statute of Wills; touching limitation of prescription; debts on executions; embracery and the buying of titles; sanctuaries; the liberties and franchises of dissolved religious houses; an act protecting lessees; collusive recoveries; mispleading and jeofails; joint tenants for life or years; wrongful disseisin to be no descent in law; grantees of reversions; an exposition of the Statute of Fines; recovery of arrears by executors; touching marriages and pre-contracts. Piecemeal, of course, no doubt; not comprehensive in the manner of modern law reform (which never happens) but massive in its extent; a large number of acts, most of them, I think (although this still needs a lot of work on it) officially inspired; pushed through in what Thomas Cromwell would almost appear to have foreseen was his last Parliament – in the middle of which he was taken in Council and committed to the Tower. That was the end of him and the end, virtually, of the reign of Henry VIII.

The Parliament of 1540 is above all else a law reform Parliament. It was introduced in a speech by the lord chancellor who proposed exactly that: that there should be law reform, though some of the reforms he proposed never got anywhere while others did. It was for that purpose and for no other almost, except a subsidy, that that session met. So here we have the triumph, if you like, of a true age of reform in Tudor times, expressing itself in terms of law reform. Attention, hitherto preoccupied with the Church and the economy, turns to the law, attacking the problems of the law.

The rest of the story demonstrates that it also follows the same pattern as the general phasing of reform movements. In the remainder of Henry VIII's reign there is nothing in the way of law reform except

[6] L. W. Abbott, *Law Reporting in England 1485–1585* (1973), 67.

follow-ups upon the Cromwellian initiative. Then under Edward VI and thereafter we are at long last able to compare what was done with what was intended and proposed, because we have those failed bills; and here we come to some very interesting results. If you will, for instance, take the first Parliament of Edward VI, no law reform act of significance was passed: none. But the bills that were introduced include again an act touching exigents; for proclamations; averment of fines and recoveries; putting distresses in several pounds; touching copyhold leases and grants; reform of divers laws and process in the laws of this realm. (That must have been a nice, comprehensive bill if only we knew its detail!) To appear by attorney in writs of subpoena and privy seal; farmers and lessees to enjoy the leases and copies. These were the law reforms that reformers of one kind and another thought necessary. They got nowhere. And the same is true of later Parliaments. Take the Parliaments of Elizabeth, not yet properly studied from the point of view of legislation, though a lot of work is going forward in that direction; certainly there were some reforms but very few in her early years. For instance, in 1566 three acts passed: one awarded costs to a wrongfully vexed defendant; another deprived cut-purses of benefit of clergy (I don't think I can really count that in very much), and a third touched appeals in civil and marine causes. It had been tried twice before and finally got through in 1566. Not very much achieved in the matter of law reform, but eight failed bills touched the bill of fines and recoveries, which finally got through in 1581; one for fraudulent gifts by bankrupts which got through in 1571; demurrer after verdicts; confirmation of the queen's letters patent; exemplifications under the Augmentation seal to be accepted; vexation by latitat; delays in real actions; general reform of execution of statutes and the reformation of certain disorders of the law – another of those comprehensive titles of which we do not know the contents. Once more we see a number of things that people want to do and yet nothing much happens, unlike 1540. In 1576 again we have five acts: confirmation of letters patent finally got through; there is an act touching the suppression of common informers; benefit of clergy is removed from rape and burglary. There is an act for *nisi prius* in Middlesex, which really hardly comes within a general law reform, and there was one for jeofails. But fifteen bills failed: traverse in cases of slander; stealing away children by privy contracts; errors in fines and recoveries; bastardy; assurance of lands without covin; common of estovers; fines and recoveries in Chester and the same in Wales; trials by jury, although I don't know what that implied; attornment of tenants; collateral warranties; defeasances of statutes staple; costs for defendants in vexatious slander suits; avowry and incest; plaintiff to swear to the Bill as the defendant is to swear to his answer. Law reform of all sorts is still in the air, but nothing is getting done. In fact, in 27 Elizabeth, in 1584, a number of the bills that had been appearing in Parliament after Parliament did finally achieve statutory enactment. That was a law reform Parliament of sorts in 1584 when six such acts passed.

Now one interesting thing that emerges when you look at the acts that passed (and I am now speaking a little prematurely because we still need to do the work on this) suggests that they derived from bills promoted by the Council. I am concluding this, perhaps rashly, from the enacting clause which presents a very odd and interesting phenomenon in the reign of Elizabeth. You all know the enacting clause: 'Be it therefore enacted by the Queen's most Excellent Majesty, our sovereign lady, and the Lords spiritual and temporal, and the Commons in this present Parliament assembled, and by authority of the same.' That is the full enacting clause which you occasionally get in Elizabeth's reign. A number of acts have an enacting clause which leaves out 'the Queen, the Lords, the Commons' and merely says: 'Be it therefore enacted by the authority of Parliament.' There is reason to think that those are the ones that were drafted by the Council or for the Council.[7] This, I repeat, is for the present a rash statement, but they do curiously hang together: official bills, bills that must be official, touching treason for instance and so on, do not have the full resonant formula; and little things like mending somebody's weir, or preventing somebody from erecting an iron mill, those will have it. Now if that is any guide at all, then it appears that in the reign of Elizabeth, the only law reform bills that stood a chance really were those rare bills promoted on behalf of the government. And yet there is law reform of one kind or another propounded in these Parliaments, in bill upon bill upon bill; sometimes, as I say, with attempts to get it through time after time. In many cases a bill lapses after the first reading, getting no further; no one is willing to promote it actively except one man.

What is going on, what do we conclude from all this? I think we must conclude that the cause of law reform by statute, the attempt to amend the law from outside by the action of the legislature, depends essentially

[7] Above, no. 34(IV).

on whether we are in an age of true reform or not. It could happen only if the active co-operation of government backed the ambitions of reformers, many or few. It depended very much, therefore, on the full model of an age of reform that I put before you, being actually in existence. Law reform stood no chance, or very little chance, if it was promoted by individual or non-governmental interests in the Parliament. Why this should be so remains still to be discovered. For the present I can only say that this conclusion follows pretty clearly from these facts and figures. In fact, law reform depended on a lead from above, however much pressure there was from below.

None of this sixteenth-century reform, however, amounted to the kind of comprehensive transformation that we associate with the term 'law reform'. We can now have sitting and standing commissions reforming the law. We talk about law reform in the Commonwealth era under Oliver Cromwell and in the age of Matthew Hale, always supposing that the whole of the law must be taken under review and churned up from the bottom upwards and then settled down again. Well, that way it never happens. We all know that it is not the way in which the common law can be reformed, or perhaps even the way in which it should be reformed. Destroying from the ground up merely leaves you with something hanging in mid-air, and I think the sixteenth and seventeenth centuries were perhaps better aware of this basic fact than sometimes we are today. But law reform of a sufficiently important kind, which witnessed and realized so many deficiencies, so many particular details as well as large issues in need of treatment – *that* we do find in the sixteenth century and that underlay that transformation the details of which we still search for. But when we search we should remember that we cannot expect to find the same kind of law reform, the same kind of transformation, the same kind of pressure, the same kind of success at all stages of this hundred years' process; that we need to look specifically to those ages, or perhaps only that age which really self-consciously, deliberately and with leadership from the top set about the remaking of its own society, whereas at other times we witness the partial and rarely successful activities of interested parties, or parties sufficiently concerned, or men of sense, or men of thought, or merely men of self-interest; but we cannot then expect, and we shall not probably find anything in the nature of that sort of reform which produced that ultimate transformation of the law in the sixteenth century that we so urgently need to study in all its details.

41

CRIME AND THE HISTORIAN*

Crime and the criminal eternally fascinate; they rather than politics supply the journalist's daily bread, nor is this a particularly modern order of preference. Our popular newspapers fill their pages with crime because that is what sells copies, and even a mildly sensational case fills the court with spectators; the eighteenth century avidly read the *Newgate Calendar* (as sordid a publication as ever was the *Daily Thingummy* or the London *Moon*), gaped at prisoners through bars and attended executions; the sixteenth enjoyed on the stage nothing better than criminals whether contemporary (*Arden of Feversham*) or historical (*Timon of Athens*). Since at least until the eighteenth century the accident of record survival biases the weight of the evidence towards the work of law courts, the people of whom we are most likely to know – at least below the level of the great and powerful – are those that came into conflict with the law. And yet, the present outburst of social history has been slow to turn its attention to crime, leaving that matter still to the kind of writer whose books bear titles like *Olden Days Punishments* or *Highwaymen I have Known*. The dearth of serious studies forces the historian to rely on Sir Leon Radzinowicz's massive *History of English Criminal Law and its Administration from 1750*, for his purposes much too much a lawyer's book, with its deferential attitude to 'the authorities' and its rather uncritical treatment of sources. Perhaps the fact that crime has been little studied owes something to so many lawyers' contempt for the criminal law and its practice, thought to be intellectually undemanding and professionally unrewarding.

Very recently, however, the real historical investigation of the subject would seem at last to have begun.[1] This book explores some of the possible lines. As the frequent signals of doubt, uncertainty and

* ['Introduction' to *Crime in England, 1550–1800*, ed. J. S. Cockburn (1977), 1–14.]

[1] E.g. J. S. Cockburn, *A History of English Assizes 1558–1714* (Cambridge, 1972); J. Samaha, *Law*

cautious reserve indicate, the essays here assembled are the work of scholars still pioneering in something like a wilderness. They approach crime and the criminal from a concern with social relationships and their effect upon the individual, a worthy and potentially fruitful reason for their studies but also one with hidden dangers, because it is liable to throw back upon the past distinctly present-day preoccupations and concepts. Despite his reliance on some doubtful generalizations of Lawrence Stone's, Mr Sharpe (pp. 96–7) sees the difficulties, and his warnings on the point are well taken. However, since these are early days and since some of the snags are at present only dimly discerned, there may be virtue in taking a look – no doubt a look that could be better informed – at the problems facing the historian of crime.

The issues resolve themselves into three: the identification of the subject matter, the machinery used for coping with crime, and the analysis of the criminal material discovered. It is the last that really has attracted the new interest: most of our authors ask questions about the amount of crime committed, the proportions ascribable to different kinds of offences, the people committing crimes (analysed by sex, social standing, age and ultimate fate): crime as a social phenomenon, pursued through time, is the topic of concern. In the present volume only Dr Baker thoroughly attends to the second issue, though several other contributors – and especially Dr Beattie – realize that only a precise knowledge of the machinery can really unlock the meaning of the record. But none of the contributors asks the first and fundamental question, mainly because their acquaintance with modern theory makes them suppose that the answer is obvious.

1

Historians anxious to study crime in the sixteenth, seventeenth and eighteenth centuries must first realize that their subject was not known then by that name. The word was current, but it lacked precise meaning, especially in the law; it rates no entry in Giles Jacob's *Law Dictionary*, an excellent guide. In studying crime we therefore study something like an artificial construct, a compound comprising breaches of the law which at the time of being committed were regarded as diverse and separate. What Jacob knew were felonies and trespasses, the

and Order in Historical Perspective: The Case of Elizabethan Essex (New York, 1974); Albion's Fatal Tree: Crime and Society in Eighteenth-Century England, ed. D. Hay, P. Linebaugh and E. P. Thompson (1975).

former identifiable by the simple fact that they involved capital punishment. His definitions therefore depended on the identification of penalties, on the possibility of conviction in a court with predictable consequences. This is not the definition present to the writers of these essays who – as a rule tacitly – equate crime with breaches of social norms. A social criterion in place of a legal one has its attractions: it provides a comprehensive category, it turns 'crime' into a tool for analysing social standards and behaviour, and it offers opportunities for moral disapproval. But it does have the disadvantage of using a category unfamiliar to the people studied: it thus introduces occasions for confusion. While most of our contributors confine themselves to offences punishable by the secular law, Mr Sharpe and Dr Ingram reach out to include the work of the archdeacons' courts. Yet it is unwise to throw theft and adultery into one bag because contemporaries did not regard them as of one kind at all: the search for social disapproval as the common element in 'crime' is misdirected from the start when it is assumed that all discoverable offences are descriptive of a single stance. The society in question treated the protection of property and the prevention of illicit sexual relationships very differently, expressing its beliefs by showing respect for the king's courts and contempt for those of the Church. Dr Macfarlane's familiar analysis of witchcraft in Essex stretches the category 'crime' beyond what it can safely bear; the fabric tears, and in that essay we are a long way from the themes studied by the rest.

There is a mildly anachronistic confusion here. It is taken for granted that laws are intended to provide against misdeeds which carry social disapproval. In fact, the law of that age provided against misdeeds thought to be unlawful – contrary to principles at least believed to be eternal and not socially conditioned – and even though, no doubt, that belief at times embodied a measure of self-deception it had consequences: it sometimes led to the prohibition of actions which carried at least partial social approval, such as common immoralities, theft occasioned by hunger, killing in self-defence – approval which could extend so far as biased acquittals of those indubitably guilty in the law. The case of John Ayly cited by Mr Sharpe (p. 98), for twenty-three years regularly denounced in the archdeacon's court and yet never effectively punished and in no way socially ostracized, should act as a warning: offenders of his kind cannot be lumped together with vagabonds and thieves of whom authority disposed in short order and with general approval. Treating crime as a social rather than a legal phenomenon further leads the historian to mishandle the problem of enforcement; he can come to see social significance in laws which were applied very haphazardly or even allowed to fall into desuetude. More particularly, it makes impossible a serious study of pardoning, a study which, partly for that reason, no one has yet undertaken for our period; and yet pardoning lies at the heart of the question of enforcement and itself bears heavily upon the question of social attitudes.

The legal criterion, therefore, will distinguish between systems of law as well as systems of courts operating in the realm, producing clearer results. Offences against the law of the Church are not crimes, even though they may constitute disruptive or antisocial activity. In the thinking of the day they were sins – offences against God not man. Sin lacked the strictly criminal element of deliberate and malicious intent against another person's rights which, so far as a principle can be discovered, underlay the common-law definition of the various activities which deserve to be called criminal. It also lacked human enforceability, the appointment of tangible punishment in body or purse, especially as penances imposed ceased to be done. Defamation (one of the archdeacon's main preoccupations) lies on the borderline between sin and crime, as the Star Chamber recognized when it extended its competence over it; its renewed relegation, after 1640, to the spiritual courts left the law of slander in an unsatisfactorily primitive condition, very poorly defined in a few relevant statutes. Defamation was on the point of becoming a crime, so to speak. Strictly, however, the term crime – doubtful though it must remain – should be reserved for offences punishable in the secular courts, though it would be too restrictive to confine it to pleas at the king's suit, a definition applicable only to 'major crimes' – another otherwise uncertain category. In fact, even if we omit sins from the calendar, we still need to make important distinctions because the various types of offence recognized by contemporaries received different treatment, were subject to different processes and ended in different ways, with the result (among other things) that some may be readily studied and some tend to escape historical investigation altogether. All of them, however, still call for investigation not of their occurrence or incidence but of their very nature.

The first category of criminal offences – the real crimes, as it were – comprised treasons and felonies, punishable by death. In the lists of triable misbehaviours found in pardons or charges to juries, murder was usually mentioned separately, but it really constituted a felony at common law. Because these capital crimes pose relatively few problems to the historian, they have been taken for well understood, but some real difficulties remain. Statute often added to and sometimes took away from them, especially in the reign of Henry VIII and in the eighteenth century. That fact is well enough known, but no one seems to have asked why this should have been so and exactly what it meant; it is taken for granted that 'society' was savagely inclined and its rulers sufficiently frightened, for some reason or other, to pile on the felonies. In actual fact, these outbursts of felony-making by act of Parliament are much less straightforward, especially that of the eighteenth century, and before conclusions are drawn from them they need to be very particularly investigated, without those ready-made assumptions about class interest which bedevil these discussions. The unsolved questions multiply. If the ruling classes really wanted more frightful laws against thieves and robbers, why did they not secure a higher percentage of convictions and why did they suffer – indeed, in the persons of the judges, encourage – contrived acquittals and the substitution of penalties well short of what the law could exact? A good many of those statutory crimes would appear to have been punishable at law anyway: why were arsonists constructively tried under the Waltham Black Act when arson was an ancient common law felony? Why did the new laws add crimes in so piecemeal and specific a fashion – and again crimes which do not look new at all? 15 George II, c. 34, which made stealing from shipwrecks a felony, would seem to have singled out a special case already comprehended in the law concerning larceny; the act in fact referred to good laws already in existence. Why were so few of those many laws apparently ever applied in court? Legislating about theft could reduce the effectiveness of the common law. Thus it was grand larceny to steal linen and other materials, but when this felony was made statutory by 4 George II, c. 16 strict interpretation reduced the possibility of conviction; an amending act (18 George II, c. 27) explained the need for further legislation on the ground that 'the respective goods and wares, the stealing whereof from the respective places therein mentioned and described is by the said Act intended to be prevented' had not been listed 'with sufficient certainty'. Stealing sheep and cattle was a felony at law; yet Parliament passed the act 14 George II, c. 6 against sheepstealing, only to find it necessary next year to extend it to cattle, doubts having arisen over the limitation of the statute (15 George II, c. 34). It would seem necessary to look at every one of these statutory felonies – at the way they came into existence and the manner in which they were applied. I suspect that a proper investigation would reveal a story commonplace in eighteenth-century legislation when individuals or very small pressure groups proved regularly able to put their pet projects onto the statute book.[2] If that was the case, there is manifestly a danger in using that statute book to discover general social attitudes or even the attitudes of the often falsely classified upper classes.

Still, the problems of felonies are open to successful investigation; things get worse as one moves down the scale to lesser offences. Trespass started as a genuine form of crime but by the time in question had in the main become a means for resolving the civil disputes of private parties: it should be left out of the count, at least from about the middle of the sixteenth century onwards. Yet the kind of deed which it originally described had not ceased just because the action for trespass had moved into the realm of useful fictions. Breaches of the peace, that mainstay of both quarter sessions and petty sessions, never received proper classification. There is a whole series of illicit acts – let us call them misdemeanours, a term known to the age but never given precise content – which at least in the sixteenth and early seventeenth centuries were largely left to the discretion of magistrates, with very little guidance from law and statute alike; and since subversion short of treason fell into this category (rumour-mongering, for instance, or *scandalum magnatum*, very inadequately legislated for in the reign of Elizabeth) it is evident that any analysis of crime must seriously concern itself with this sort of thing. It is at least possible that the prevalence of offences against property, unsurprisingly discovered in the records of assizes and quarter sessions, springs from the fact that those were the main offences triable there whereas a good deal of lesser criminal activity (beatings, assaults, various forms of cheating, creation of nuisances) were dealt with in manorial courts, municipal courts, or by single justices acting informally. Summary jurisdiction poses very great problems because it so often left little record and cannot be presumed to have followed a common form. Among all these offences, indictability ought perhaps to offer a good means of distinction, being precise and well understood at the time; unfortunately indictment applied to

---

[2] Cf. *House of Commons Sessional Papers of the Eighteenth Century*, ed. S. Lambert (Wilmington, 1975–6), introduction, i, *35*.

varieties of offences, and presenting juries included dung-heaps left in streets together with larceny and homicide.

The question may also be raised whether 'crime' should not include offences like fraud, extortion or embezzlement, none of them felonies and ill provided for in the procedural law of the usual commissions (oyer and terminer, and of the peace). Many cases in Star Chamber (incapable of dealing with felonies and treasons) and Chancery involved what would now be called crimes, left out in current studies. Jacob treated fraud as the business of equity, extortion as defined in statutory expositions of the common law and confined to offences by office-holders, and embezzlement as non-existent. On the other hand, I am inclined to omit *qui tam* actions on the so-called statutes penal or popular.[3] Though they had something of the character of near-criminal legislation and set fines and forfeitures, their purpose was to regulate manufacture and commerce: and if breaches of such regulations are to be accounted criminal the theme loses its last chance of cohesion. Certainly no seventeenth-century lawyer would have understood a single category which comprised both felonies and these kinds of statutes. Yet, if they are left out, what do we do about smuggling?

Lastly, we must return to sins punished – or rather, rarely punished with any effect – by the Church courts. Once they have been distinguished in order not to confuse the issue, they must be brought back into the picture because they did concern conduct against which legal action was possible and which did carry potential penalties, however spiritual.

Thus the task – the primary task – of defining the subject matter of a history of crime involves two steps. First, it is necessary to abandon modern categories based on the concepts of social norms, social justice and antisocial behaviour, in order to identify contemporary categories based on legal definition or the absence of it, to analyse the distinctions to be made here, and to resolve their many technical problems (through time, as well). Secondly, one needs to reintroduce those modern concepts in order to discover what possibly criminal activities the strict analysis may have eliminated and whether they should be added to the area of inquiry. Once this is done it is possible to study criminality in the early modern period.

2

The problems of the machinery of repression are, on the face of them, less daunting. Much of it is well known. Dr Baker's chapter in this

[3] Ingram (p. 113 below) includes these.

volume quite admirably delineates the procedural law of trials upon indictment, and the operations of the ecclesiastical courts (where especially cases *ex officio* come within our purview) have been adequately described more than once.[4] As Dr Baker shows, we are much better informed about the trial of felonies than of misdemeanours (even when indictable), but so long as offenders were indicted we know reasonably well how their cases were meant to be handled. Two questions nevertheless remain: how accurately did actual trials follow the rules of process, and what happened to persons accused outside the machinery of indictment and *ex officio* proceedings?

Dr Baker himself raises the question of whether the evidence of cases supports the notion that criminal process at common law was governed by strict rules. This must at present await investigation, though the indications in general are that the answer is yes – with exceptions; we want to learn how serious and frequent those were. As late as the reign of Henry VIII (perhaps later?) juries sometimes behaved in ways contrary to the supposed rules; they could take on tasks proper to prosecution or defence, and they were assuredly not free from pressures and corruptions. A good history of the post-medieval jury, derived from what actually happened, is urgently needed. How careful were the courts of their own principles in interpreting penal (i.e. crime-creating) statutes? They held, we are told, that such acts must be interpreted strictly, that is as applicable only to offences indubitably intended in them. Yet throughout the eighteenth century the judges would appear to have used the notorious Waltham Black Act against alleged criminals whose misdeeds had absolutely nothing to do with the origins or original purposes of the act: a singular, possibly unique, case of their enlarging the effects of a penal statute which has misled historians into ill-considered views of eighteenth-century Parliaments and supposed class legislation.[5] Real mysteries continue to hang about an important stage in every trial, namely about what happened after the jury's verdict. How did some convicted persons secure the calling up of the case into King's Bench (by *certiorari* or *mandamus*), to have their indictments declared invalid or to plead a pardon? Why did others fail to

[4] E.g. B. Woodcock, *Medieval Ecclesiastical Courts in the Diocese of Canterbury* (Oxford, 1952); *An Episcopal Court Book for the Diocese of Lincoln 1514–1520*, ed. M. Bowker (Lincs. Rec. Soc., lxi 1967), introduction.

[5] The history and purposes of the act are very inadequately handled by Radzinowicz whose erroneous interpretation distorts parts of E. P. Thompson's *Whigs and Hunters: the Origins of the Black Act* (1975). Cf. *House of Commons Sessional Papers*, ed. Lambert, 37–8.

do so? What part did the judges play in this? How regular was the
practice of binding persons acquitted in sureties of good behaviour or
for appearance? I am familiar with such things happening in the
sixteenth century: did practice change? All these are questions that need
to be resolved from a study of actual trials, whereas actual trials can be
successfully studied only with a clear understanding of the procedure
which ruled what went on: a circular problem not incapable of solution,
but at any rate enjoining caution upon the operator.

The biggest procedural problem, at best quarter solved, concerns the
initiation of prosecutions: how was it that people found themselves
facing a court? The king's courts relied on presentment by jury; the
Church courts upon presentment at visitations. Both thus originally
thrust the responsibility upon the community and relied on 'common
knowledge', not on detection. By our period the situation had certainly
altered quite a lot as indictments came increasingly to be drawn on
behalf of the Crown, with the presenting jury reduced to an opinion on
the evidence offered; but that merely raises the question of how offences
came to the notice of those responsible for putting bills of indictment
before the jury. We need to learn a lot more about how information
came to be gathered, processed and introduced. Thanks to Thomas
Cromwell, we know a good deal of the manner in which trials for
treason originated, but for ordinary felonies we have only a beginning
of an understanding, especially as Dr Langbein is inclined to take the
words of statutes as describing actual practice.[6] Since we urgently need
to comprehend why some people were sucked into the machinery of
criminal process while others, who had committed the same offences,
were not, we want more searching concentration on that first stage in
the process.

For offences outside the strictly criminal machinery, the dark areas of
the unknown are larger. Much 'antisocial behaviour' escaped the
clutches of indicting juries and archdeacons' visitations, and yet (as we
have seen) it needs to be taken into account if a study of crime and
criminality is to be complete and balanced. In this respect the studies in
the present volume are deficient because they concentrate on a
particular layer of the phenomenon – the layer defined by local
enforcement in superior courts. By concentrating – as following the
obvious evidence rightly leads them to – on assizes, quarter sessions and
archdeacons' courts, the investigators miss levels that may be called both

[6] *Policy and Police*; J. H. Langbein, *Prosecuting Crime in the Renaissance* (Cambridge, Mass., 1974).

higher and lower. On the one hand, they omit the work of the conciliar courts, of the King's Bench itself, and of special commission of oyer and terminer; on the other they stop short of courts leet. As for the Church, episcopal courts tend to get ignored. Now in some of these omitted regions the regular procedural machinery described applied in theory: special commissions relied on indictment (though one still needs to know something about who the commissioners were), and consistory courts used the same methods as archdeacons', only more so. But what happened in Star Chamber and manors differed in principle; this needs to be allowed for and, where not yet known, clarified. When it comes to summary procedure and arbitration, we have just about everything still to learn. The specific questions asked by students of crime depend for their answers on a really instructed understanding of what went on.

3

That brings us to the real concerns of our contributors who all, in various ways, want to know not what constituted crime or how crimes were dealt with but what crimes predominated and why, who committed crimes and what happened to criminals. All these essays, pursuing such themes from various approaches and in different contexts, stress the uncertainties and insufficiencies of their findings. In particular, it is conceded over and over again that no reliable statistics can be compiled because the evidence does not permit any satisfactory use of quantifying techniques. I must emphasize that I am in no way criticizing the authors for this: on the contrary, they deserve every praise for avoiding spurious certainties and the easy road of ready-made opinions leading to influential but unproven conclusions. All I should like to do here is to identify the source of this lack of positive results and to see whether it is not possible to find at least partial remedies. The exercise seems the more desirable because such conclusions as do get established tend to be somewhat unsurprising. Dr Cockburn (p. 57) tells us that homicide was rare and most murderous violence occurred within families. Though it is satisfactory to have the more lurid notions of a people forever battering one another disproved, this remains what one would have expected. Similarly Dr Curtis finds that violence was usually casual and unpremeditated: were we to think that the realm was full of professional hit-men? Dr Cockburn (p. 63) also notes that many thefts punished at assizes were committed by vagrants, and his conclusion that 'outsiders' were more likely to be brought to court is supported by Dr Ingram (p. 133). Perhaps this really reveals respective attitudes to familiars and strangers, but it would seem as likely that men without possessions or a means of livelihood would do most of the stealing as that people readily blamed their losses on the conventional tramp. Dr Ingram (p. 117) seems surprised that men accused of crime could be very bitter about their fate; perhaps this requires no comment. Dr Beattie's careful compilations of statistics leads to the less than surprising conclusion that repression of crime grew more severe as criminal activity increased. Certainly there are other less obvious findings in this volume; in particular Dr Munsche's analysis of poaching most refreshingly departs from the stereotype and revives its subject very satisfactorily. In general, however, the mixture of honestly admitted uncertainty and rather expected answers must raise the question whether the enterprise is bound to remain so inconclusive.

It appears to me that there are two kinds of obstacles to a more formidable attack on the history of crime: the state of the evidence, and some unacknowledged preconceptions with which the task is approached. The first creates the limitations which trouble all our writers, but perhaps these need not be so unyielding. The second inhibits the asking of unprejudiced questions and tends to produce those expected answers.

Of the insufficiencies of evidence the foremost and least remediable is total absence. As everyone knows, assize and quarter sessions records start late because before the end of the sixteenth century the statutory demand for returns into King's Bench was very poorly obeyed. It is really only from about 1660 that we again get the sort of continuous record which the cessation of the great eyre terminated in the middle of the fourteenth century.[7] The Great Fire of London is likely to have closed the books pretty conclusively on the criminal history of the capital before that date, which – since capitals, being populous, are notoriously interesting in the study of crime – is unfortunate. The records of the ecclesiastical courts, too, do not survive in perfect series, though in this area so far the chief problem has lain in their technical difficulty and illegibility; they call for more urgent exploitation. Losses apart, there is the further difficulty of records never kept. We shall never know much about the inmates of jails, for instance, because few jailers cared to provide us with the evidence. All this needs no labouring: the

[7] See e.g. Cockburn, *Assizes*, especially the revealing bibliography of manuscript sources.

student of crime works with necessarily very patchy and incomplete materials. One result, as this volume shows, is that the work will concentrate on the eighteenth rather than the seventeenth century, the seventeenth rather the sixteenth, a commonplace experience in all social history. However, in view of these deficiencies it is a pity that what does exist should not be used more comprehensively. Historians of crime will have to remember that the central government records contain material for them which, while not so immediately the product of criminal activity as are the local records of assizes, sessions, borough courts and manors, can help to narrow the blank areas. I have in mind not only the proceedings of Star Chamber and Requests, but also the records of the Exchequer, the Admiralty and perhaps the Court of Wards in all of which offences against property rights and persons leave some deposit. There may be others. This sort of material is unlikely to improve the opportunities for quantification, but it can still tell us much about breaches of the peace, forcible dispossession, fraud, assault and larceny.

Dr Macfarlane interestingly raises the possibility of yet another source of information when he argues (pp. 77–8) that accounts of witchcraft cases in pamphlets show up the inadequacies of the court records. It is probably true that for the spectacular crime, which includes murder, this sort of evidence adds a dimension, but it needs to be used with much scepticism; the history of the 'Elizabethan underworld', for so long too readily written out of the imaginative literature of the day, should stand as a warning. Certainly it is necessary to search chronicles and diaries, though here again the historian will uncover only a very unsystematic collection of cases biased towards the sensational.

There is, in fact, little one can do about missing evidence, except to recognize, as our contributors do, that some questions must remain unanswered while some can be answered only for particular periods and regions. The uncertainties emphasized in these essays come more commonly from the nature of the evidence extant.[8] The most systematic materials are the records of courts, central and local, and it is a characteristic of these that their formality hides as much as it reveals. In a trial for felony, for instance, it is usually easy to discover the court that tried the case, the names and descriptions of accused and victims, the type of crime alleged, the names of the jurors, the fact of conviction or acquittal. We cannot learn from the record the particulars of the crime,

[8] See especially Cockburn (pp. 50–1 below); Dr Ingram's essay, too, is pervaded by a recognition of these problems.

the details of what went on in court, or – more surprisingly – quite often whether the sentence was carried out. It is this stifling formality that renders supporting materials so valuable, especially recognizances for appearances, for keeping the peace and for other purposes, such as those which Dr Samaha is at present editing from the Colchester archives.[9] Generally speaking, if investigation is to achieve a reasonable degree of objectivity and completeness, it will be necessary in the first place to concentrate on areas which provide both a more or less continuous record and a variety of unsystematic supporting evidence; and it should be said again that the second will often be found in the Public Record Office rather than the local archive. (I must, however, add what a pleasure it was to find Dr Curtis take one away from ever-present Essex, to the historian the one county equipped with criminals).

Next there is the urgent problem how far we can trust the information provided in the extant records. Dr Cockburn has thrown grave doubts on the accuracy of indictments: he has found strong indications that especially the description of the accused, their status and domicile, could be frequently mis-stated.[10] This is not only a disconcerting but also a somewhat surprising discovery, for there is good evidence (in the 'ancient indictments' and the King's Bench plea rolls) that such mistakes were readily used to get convictions quashed. It is possible that the little people involved in those assize indictments did not know their rights or were overwhelmed by the speed of events, but a good many of those known to have used legal technicalities to escape the consequences of their deeds were insignificant and poor enough. It would appear that among the first tasks to be now performed the critical appraisal of the evidence must stand very high. Before we use these materials to answer questions not of legal but of social history – the social status of alleged criminals, the places whence they came, the relationship between social classes, the attitudes manifested and so forth – we had better be sure that the facts taken from the record can be trusted. Here again recognizances may be more reliable than indictments. At any rate, the discussion initiated by Dr Cockburn needs to be continued.

A peculiar difficulty of this kind is raised by the discovery that so

[9] [See now J. B. Samaha, 'The recognisance in Elizabethan law enforcement', *American Journal of Legal History*, 25 (1981), 189–204.]

[10] J. S. Cockburn, 'Early-Modern assize records as historical evidence', *Journal of the Society of Archivists*, 5 (1975), 215–31.

many persons indicted by grand juries got off at their trial. Dr Beattie (pp. 175 ff.), after describing a system far from considerate to the accused and in which especially trial juries were forced to come to snap decisions, finds that of those brought to trial at eighteenth-century assizes and quarter sessions about a third left the court freed from the threat of rope or transportation. The fact in itself is certainly interesting, but what does it mean? Do we suppose that so large a proportion were falsely accused, or that juries acquitted in the teeth of the evidence, either from compassion or under some kind of pressure? Star Chamber often enough attended to delinquent juries (without being able to reverse the false verdicts rendered); did its abolition free juries for what in law must be called misbehaviour? Most accounts do seem to assume that the savagery of the law was countered by juries' refusal to heed it, but is it certain that presenting juries were more accurate in their findings? The system, after all, rested on the assumption that presentment would inevitably gather in some false allegations; it did not even begin to hold that *billa vera* equalled guilt. Since I am not persuaded that even the indiscriminate savagery of the law has been satisfactorily established – one hears too much of a few bad cases, and tracking back the general statements in the books too often ends up with one of the impassioned parliamentary speeches of certain notoriously unreliable law-reformers of the early nineteenth century – I should like to see the issue of acquittals and convictions tackled without the commonplace preconceptions long enshrined in the literature and sanctified by Radzinowicz.[11] Once again, we need a critical study of sources from the record outwards. This may be pointlessly bland advice from someone who does not know the records in question. I am very willing to be so convicted by any historian who has actually asked such questions of his evidence.

There is, however, one area of possible criminal activity which will escape even the best instructed investigation, however careful of complete coverage and however critical of its sources it may be. What do we do about crime unreported – crime that never reached even the lost records? It is possible to make estimates of offences known but not tried; and though Hext's statement (p. 50) that in 1596 these constituted four-fifths of all such occurrences seems astonishingly high, this means

---

[11] Also by Douglas Hay whose remarkable essay on 'Property, authority and the criminal law' (*Albion's Fatal Tree*, 17 ff.) at times falls into the error of relying on assumptions taken to be axiomatic.

only that one's instinctive beliefs need adjustment in the light of the evidence. If his proportion is approximately right over the whole period, one wants to know why so much detected thieving went untroubled and how that society coped with such a prevalence of tolerated criminality. Beyond this lie breaches of the law of which no one told. Experience suggests that there must have been such, and experience (as any policeman will confirm) also says that there is nothing the investigator can do about it. However, Edward Hext's estimate here offers some consolation. If only every fifth known breach got to trial, the chances that beyond this there were still considerable quantities of crime lost to view are not great. Obviously it would be folly to rely on trials only for statistics of crime, but perhaps more could be done, along the lines mapped out by Dr Cockburn, to establish better totals of offences by investigating pre-trial stages. In all these issues – crimes untried and criminals acquitted – one needs to be more continuously aware of the possibilities of false accusations and mere malice than Mr Sharpe, for instance, shows himself to be (pp. 107–8). I may misunderstand him, but he seems to be saying that the charges conditioned by the predilections of 'a society attempting to control religious belief and most aspects of sexual morality', while peculiar, were in their own terms truthful. It is as likely that in such a society personal animosities invented accusations of the kind acceptable to the authorities in order to get at a private enemy.

All this amounts to no more than saying that now, with the pioneers half settled in their difficult territory, the time has come to consolidate, and that consolidation calls for a more systematic and more critical analysis of the available sources than has yet been attempted. In this way, the deficiencies of the material will be properly pinpointed but they will also receive such remedy as can be got. The conclusion that the attraction of arriving at substantive answers to the social historian's questions must for the present be resisted, so that ground-clearing operations can be carried out, is also supported by the signs of unconscious, or premature, assumptions which do appear here and there in these essays. This is tricky, even touchy, ground, and I do not mean to be offensive. Yet a brief word should be said. Most of the historians who study this kind of history – history from below – are concerned to redress a balance not only in historiography but also in the fortunes of the men they study. One result is to make them work from preconceptions about class relationships; these essays share certain implicit convictions about the effect of the interests entertained by the possessing classes upon determinations of crime and who shall suffer for it. In consequence the fact that the law protected all property, not only that of the rich, escapes attention, and in consequence we are likely to miss one of the most telling features of the scene, namely that the poorer sort seem to have suffered most at the hands of thieves who yet got tried, convicted and often executed. Dr Beattie (p. 182) contributes a peculiar variant of the distorting preconception when he ascribes the relatively lenient treatment of female offenders to the alleged fact that they were regarded as less of a social threat. This allows nothing for an often instinctive chivalry, or if you like embarrassment, which was a common reaction of that day when confronted with women who broke the rules. There are several examples in these papers of answer by jargon – the solemnities of the sociologist overcoming the instructed frivolity of the historian. Crime is no joke, either for the victim or the offender, but nothing is gained by pulling long-worded faces.

It would be utterly unfair to end on such a note. The essays in this volume have much to teach, and if this introductory piece has concentrated on the warnings they contain that is because my assignment constrained me to criticize. Our authors can be trusted to speak for themselves and to deal faithfully with the devil and his advocate. I am sure that they can readily convict me of crass error and possibly of complacency. The latter I repudiate; to the former we are all liable. It is by isolating and correcting error that progress comes, and in the very difficult region of historical enquiry exemplified here the practitioner need not object to having traps and pitfalls pointed out to him, even if some of them turn out to have already been sprung or filled in.

42

ENGLAND AND THE CONTINENT
IN THE SIXTEENTH CENTURY*

There are those who would deny a distinction between England and the continent of Europe, alleging that the island is in every respect – politically, socially, culturally – a part of Europe. This is an opinion that could be held only by those whose knowledge of the continent is derived from books and from visits; anyone who has actually ever lived there knows how fundamental those differences are. Or perhaps one should say, how fundamental they were; possibly they have in the last thirty years been disappearing together with an England that was real, and apparently unchangeable, at any rate down to 1939. It may also be argued that those differences have not always existed, time out of memory: medieval England, part of one European Church, may have displayed more likeness to the rest of Christendom than difference. An island ruled for so many centuries by Danish, Norman and Angevin princes perhaps demands to be treated as part of those continental dominions. I am certainly familiar with arguments of this kind from historians concerned to understand the medieval English Church or the Norman Conquest and its consequences. Yet even then there were real differences, and if the novel (and very persuasive) thesis that England never knew a 'true' peasantry survives detailed scrutiny those differences may well come to matter more throughout English history than any superficial resemblances in religion, in language, or in the social habits of the upper classes.[1]

In the history of this intriguing question, the sixteenth century occupies a special place because it seems to present the observer with a complex paradox. On the one hand, Tudor England witnessed a manifest withdrawal from continental links, with the separation from

---

* [Introducing *Reform and Reformation: England and the Continent*, ed. Derek Baker (Oxford, 1979), 1–16.]

[1] A. J. Macfarlane, *The Origins of English Individualism* (1978).

305

Rome and the completion of a centralized unitary state structure. On the other hand, it became deeply involved in the Reformation which on the face of it was a very continental movement. In both respects, it is true, one can also point to contraries: the separation from the continental Church and the consolidation of the realm did not (as used to be supposed) lead to an immediate turning away to oceanic enterprise or the termination of political ambitions centred upon involvement and even conquest in Europe, while the English Reformation had its own antecedents which the recent rediscovery of Lollard survival into the sixteenth century has made appear very important. Just where did the England of that day stand in relation to the neighbouring landmass?[2]

In the first place it should be noted that sixteenth-century England was an ex-imperial power. Until 1558, Calais preserved both memories and illusions which had really left the realm of reality a century earlier. None of the Tudor monarchs ever fully abandoned ambitions and convictions arising out of that imperial past, and the notion that England's 'destiny' turned in that age towards new worlds belongs to historical hindsight. Foreign policy, whether aggressive or defensive, remained fixed inexorably on the European centres of power – on Rome and Brussels, Madrid, Paris and Vienna. Indeed, in the course of the century English interests grew geographically, to embrace central and eastern areas of no concern to pre-Tudor governments. Down to the accession of Henry VII, Europe had really meant France, Burgundy and Italy; when Elizabeth died it included also Germany, Scandinavia, Poland and (supposing that it belongs to Europe) Russia. So far as the interests of monarchy and realm are concerned, it would be hard to avoid calling Tudor England a European power. But unlike the realities of that imperial past, in the sixteenth century those concerns were the accompaniments of diplomacy – involvement from outside, not participation from within. Not that this relationship – connection rather than integration – was absolutely new; it is important to remember what the imperial position of the later middle ages really meant. Duke William's England is no doubt rightly to be regarded as a Norman dependency, and the Angevin empire's centre of gravity presumably lay somewhere in France, even though only England supplied the coveted royal title to all those rulers. But the empires of Edward III and Henry V

[2] In my view, the differences, real as they were, between the various component parts of Europe are far less considerable than those between Europe and England, so that it becomes legitimate to treat the continent as an entity and contrast it with what the Germans like to call 'the island realm'.

were really English – extensions of the kingdom's sway over foreign territories, promoted for dynastic interests which exploited nationalist sentiment and in the end were combated as an alien intrusion. Thus the imperial past of which Tudor kings and writers dreamed was an English past, the past of a separate and different realm which had temporarily embraced dependent regions outside itself. The Tudor withdrawal into the boundaries set by the sea confirmed rather than contradicted the reality of that past; it made the separateness, the difference, of England more manifest but did not create it out of its opposite.

That difference appeared in all sorts of ways, none entirely new but all now given a vigour and sometimes a subtle transformation which made something new out of inherited facts. The political institutions of England were peculiar. In a manner quite unknown elsewhere, its monarchy combined high prerogative claims and exceptionally effective government with the absence of coercive power and an instinctive regard for the supremacy of the law. Its Parliament uniquely combined co-operation in government with the satisfaction of the subject's needs: no other representative institution in Europe was so firmly integrated into the monarchical system of government, so thoroughly organized for routine business, so flexibly able to accommodate all interests. In England taxes fell most heavily on the wealthier part of the nation, an oddity which provides perhaps the most striking contrast of all to European custom – which in this respect was to grant exemption to the powerful. English law, notoriously, was very different indeed, reflecting and creating differences right through the social structure which it would take volumes to expound. And these, and other, distinctions appear not only to the eye of the historian; they were very visible also to observers of the day. By the side of the often bemused and rarely commendatory reports of visitors from abroad there grew among Englishmen a strident selfconsciousness of separateness, from Richard Morison's 'English hands and English hearts' peculiarly able to win against all odds, through John Aylmer's God who is English, to John Foxe's elect nation.

Of course, none of this once again was absolutely new in the sixteenth century. Monarchy, Parliament and law derived from what had been developed before, to such a degree that current opinion among scholars is more likely to underestimate than overrate the differences produced in all these respects by the years of Tudor rule. Even the peculiar English conviction that they alone lived on good red meat whereas miserable foreigners had to make do with vegetables is found already held by Sir John Fortescue. (Salads reached England from Italy in the sixteenth century.) However, all these institutional and conscious differences were built on and up in the aftermath of the great demonstration that 'this realm of England is an empire': the upheavals of the 1530s, successful just because they drew upon existing and inherited phenomena, produced such a heightening in those phenomena that they drastically altered the terms of the equation. Pre-Reformation England was indeed different from the continent, but those were differences inside a complex of family likenesses. Post-Reformation England was just different, and everybody at home and abroad came to see this. Nothing perhaps underlines the point more forcefully than the vain attempts of Elizabethan Catholic exiles to remain Englishmen, an endeavour in which, for instance, neither William Allen nor Robert Persons was ultimately successful. The court of Henry VIII, that aggressively English king, always looked to the example of France; that of Queen Elizabeth looked only to itself. The Church of Cardinals Morton and Wolsey had its special features but was unmistakably a part of the Church of Rome; that of archbishops Parker and Whitgift was like no other Church anywhere else. The absolute differentiation of England from the continent was achieved in the aftermath of the great transformation which we call the Henrician Reformation, and it was in the end achieved with conscious recognition and even deliberation.

So much appears to be plain; but am I in danger of overstating a case? Perhaps there should be a note of warning in the fact that the architect of that revolution in the 1530s, Thomas Cromwell, was of all the English statesmen in the century the one least obviously raised in English traditions and had the widest personal knowledge of the European continent. Cromwell, in fact, might be said to exemplify the paradox of the age in the way in which he brought non-English experience to bear upon the inherited facts of England's social and political structure. The outcome produced a heightening of Englishness as the non-English influences came to be absorbed. The real story of England and the continent in the sixteenth century presents a complex interplay of contacts between a selfconsciously separate national entity and massive cross-currents of continent-wide cultural explosions. Sixteenth-century England, so distinct in its politics and its society, had in matters of the mind no independence to speak of: culturally and intellectually it was, to all appearance, very much a part of Europe.

This truth emerges in all sorts of ways. Englishmen trying to learn about the conduct of war romanced about longbows and Agincourt but actually looked to the continent for instruction; in the sixteenth century, Machiavelli was better known as the author of *The Art of War* than for his political treatises. English political thinkers, from More, Elyot and Starkey onwards, needed the stimulus of European writers to set them thinking at all. English poetry, stuck in the debased aftermath of the Chaucerian tradition, notoriously went to Italy and France to renew itself; and some of the borrowing, even at its best as in Wyatt's adaptations of Petrarch, was pretty slavish. English biblical scholarship derived from Erasmus, and classical scholarship leant on Budé and Scaliger. The new history of the century took its origin with the study of the ancients and more particularly with Polydore Vergil's demonstration of its effectiveness. The most striking example, perhaps, is provided by the law, just because this was beyond all doubt a peculiarly English thing. Even though we no longer agree with Maitland, who supposed that in the reign of Henry VIII the common law faced a very real danger of being replaced by the civil law of the Italian jurists, we should note that respect for that law, and resort to its advice, marked all the more intelligent common lawyers of the century. This held true not only in case of necessity, as when problems of international contact rendered the custom of England inadequate – in diplomatic and commercial relations – but also in concerns with specifically native problems. Christopher St German used the principles of various 'foreign' laws to elucidate the function of equity in the English system and could quote Baldus.[3] John Parkyns demonstrated his acquaintance with the civil law when he isolated the special characteristics of the English land law.[4] Early in James I's reign, Sir John Davies found the Roman law useful when he was faced with the task of acclimatizing Irish customs to the law of England, and even the great Edward Coke, despite all his tub-thumping, knew the law of Rome and could employ its principles when reducing the common law to some sort of system after that century of upheaval which historians are only just beginning to understand.[5] For all these aggressively chauvinistic Englishmen, the

---

[3] *Doctor and Student*, ed. T. F. T. Plucknett and J. L. Barton (Selden Society, 1974).

[4] John Parkyns, *A profitable book teaching of the laws of England* (1555: the first English edition of a book originally published in law French in 1528).

[5] Cf. J. H. Baker's introduction, in vol. 2, to his edition of *The Reports of Sir John Spelman* (Selden Society, 1978), for the fullest demonstration of the revolution in the law. For the points touching Davies and Coke I owe much thanks to discussions with Mr H. Pawlish whose researches are

fountains of learning and the best examples lay outside England: they were all, in varying degrees, Europeans.

But they were Europeans with a difference: if their dependence on continental skills and systems is plain, so is the fact that in their use of these preceptors they invariably produced a specifically English result, unimaginable anywhere else. Even as they eagerly sought and acknowledged those foreign influences, they regularly transmuted them by native traditions of great force and effectiveness, creating (and I think this was really new) originality out of borrowing. No amount of reading continental political writers could unseat the English notion of the common weal represented in Parliament: here medieval precedents were made, often by the use of continental systematizers, to turn into quite novel principles serving the unitary state.[6] The poets might learn about the sonnet from Italy, and Sidney's *Art of Poesy* despised much that nowadays passes for the native tradition, but the outcome – especially but not only in Shakespeare – witnessed a total transformation of the model into a vigorously native production much assisted by the revolution in language which (again aided by foreign influences) occurred between 1530 and 1580. The historians might learn from Polydore how to escape from the chronicle tradition, but the modes that dominated their work in Elizabeth's reign – the uses of topography and genealogy, the concentration on 'origins', and the hunt for a specifically English line of development – owed more to John Leland, John Bale and Matthew Parker, all driven forward by insular and practical, rather than continental and philosophical, concerns. As for the lawyers, they might indeed resort to the civilians for the organization of their law, but its renovation developed strictly from the old common law itself which remained as different from the law of the continent as it had been for centuries. Though the English genius of the sixteenth century seems to have lacked strictly independent generative powers, it was very far from lacking ultimate originality. Leaders of thought were noticeably English Europeans, and in the outcome their Englishness showed up much more clearly than did the sources of inspiration and the guiding models they had employed.

The same fruitful (and very confusing) mixture of continental

refuting the doctrine of English legal insularity set up by J. G. A. Pocock, *The Ancient Constitution and the Feudal Law* (1957) esp. ch. 2, and Donald R. Kelley, 'History, English law, and the Renaissance', *PP* 65 (1974) 24 ff.

[6] Cf. William Marshall's translation (1535) of Marsiglio of Padua's *Defensor Pacis* which kept emphasizing the sovereignty of a Parliament quite unknown to the author translated.

inspiration and English artefact marked the country's participation in the two outstanding intellectual movements of the age – humanism and the Reformation. The so-called early humanism of the fifteenth century (sometimes pursued by historians as eager about origins as were the antiquaries of Elizabeth's reign) amounted to nothing more than a feeble transplanting of Italian models, and to see originality in Grocyn or Linacre testifies to misplaced patriotism. The powerful Thomas More lobby, with its highly developed public-relations machine, has created the impression that More was one of the great original and originating figures in the humanist movement, but this is some way from the facts. Even John Colet – though his so-called humanism really extended little beyond a specific point of bible study – has a better claim to have started something; after all, Erasmus, who thought himself indebted to More for the stimulus of friendship, always acknowledged an intellectual debt to Colet. There is no question that More certainly contributed that genius for friendship and a gift for drawing others out, but his own intellectual development derived from foreign influences and did not turn him into an influence upon others. He himself knew his sources well: he regarded himself as a follower (of Pico della Mirandola and of Erasmus) but not as a leader. One need only compare his correspondence with that of Erasmus to recognize the difference: the difference between an outstanding man of the world and an original scholar.

Even *Utopia*, with its ancestral echoes from Plato and the Benedictine rule, offers no originality in analysis or prescription: its analysis accepts all the commonplaces of the day, and its prescription consists of a logical working out of the ancient conviction that mankind suffers from the consequences of original sin. What is original about *Utopia* are its very shape, its fantasy, and its living passion, all of which makes it a remarkable work of literature but does not bestow any weight of philosophical initiative upon it. This is not to denigrate More, a man who needs no one's adulation to make him great, but to define his correct place and function. Though he contributed little or nothing to the scholarly content of the humanist movement, he supported and accommodated many of its leading aims: he gave it a home in England, even as he gave a home to Erasmus. Significantly, he really did not provide any particular direction even to English humanism, and that despite the enormous regard in which he was held at the time. More had neither disciples nor followers among the men of learning, a fact quite plain even before political disaster terminated his influence. So far as the evidence goes, the next generation of humanists derived very little, perhaps nothing, from him; even *Utopia* made hardly any immediate impact at home, very much in contrast to the attention it attracted on the continent.[7] Despite More, English humanism remained rooted abroad. His posthumous career began in the reign of Mary, under the management of his family, and because it was built upon his martyr's death rather than his real intellectual career it both exaggerated and distorted his originality. Even so, it is in Europe, not in England, that More has been treated as the fountainhead of a moralistic political philosophy based on law and constitutionalism, making him the natural counterpoint to Machiavelli.[8] The fact that he was not very well suited to that role matters only to this extent that his failure to live up to the part created for him stemmed, once again, from his essential lack of originality. If More can be made to stand for a concept of the law-governed commonwealth it is only because he accepted the conventions inherited by any early-sixteenth-century English lawyer; in these matters he seems to me to have displayed less capacity for original thought than did St German.

The humanism of the post-More generation, in many ways more inventive and progressive mainly because it came to be linked with the reformation of the Church, similarly derived from foreign inspiration. It was Italy and Erasmus, not Oxford, that turned Thomas Starkey and Richard Morison humanist and taught them the problems and the solutions which they espoused. From that point, however, the transmutation began. From the 1530s onwards, we may discern a distinctively English form of the movement, more especially in educational concerns – which turned out to be its major preoccupation. More than any other humanist community, the English contingent picked up the pedagogic message preached by Erasmus, so that teaching rather than scholarship became the hallmark of the English humanist tradition. Its notables are men like John Cheke and Roger Ascham, Nicholas Udall and Richard Mulcaster, pedagogues all. I know of no other country that makes heroes of its headmasters, nor of any other which knows its scholars only if they ignore Ralph Hythloday's warning and take up public office. Sir Thomas Smith is the prototype

[7] D. B. Fenlon, 'England and Europe: *Utopia* and its aftermath', *TRHS*, 5th ser. 25 (1975), 115 ff.

[8] The juxtaposition of More and Machiavelli is the theme of Gerhard Ritter's *Die Dämonie der Macht* (1947): it appears to have become widely accepted among German commentators.

here: that brilliant man of learning who would have been readily forgotten if he had not also become a somewhat indifferent secretary of state. The striking gulf between English schools and universities on the one hand, and those of the continent on the other – a gulf much remarked in the last century and this – opened in the reign of Elizabeth as English education, absorbing humanist and protestant instruction, set out on a road of its own. Once again, the borrowed and derived preoccupations came to be turned into a highly unusual and really very original complex of ideas and practices.

How does this pattern apply to the history of Church and religion in the sixteenth century? The question is not exactly new, but it remains important, and the more searching enquiries of the present generation, untroubled by denominational or patriotic pressures, have made more satisfactory answers possible. No one has ever doubted that the English Reformation owed much to that of protestant Europe, though from the first – from John Foxe's virtual neglect of Luther and his belief in Wycliff as the morning star[9] – the search for native roots has been relentless. It would, I think, be fair to say that at present few people would like to offer any sort of straightforward answer, and that no doubt is sensible. Still, without attempting to classify native and imported influences, or worse still to quantify their contributions, one would like to assess – because it is desirable to arrive at some assessment – the real inspirations behind so overwhelming a pheno-menon as the creation of English protestantism and a protestant England, and our authors here offer all of them helpful assistance. James Cargill Thompson goes a long way to determine the debate which has gone on over Tyndale's originality: he very clearly owed his first conversion and conviction to Luther's influence, though by 1530 he was emerging as an independent mind, no longer the carrier of other people's ideas. Claire Cross shows how in the second half of the century the debts to continental centres of reform were being repaid (though perhaps rather in penny packets) by the English universities' hospitality to young continental students, an unexpected continuance of the close links that marked the earlier stages. David Loades helps to explain the late arrival of true sectarianism in England when he integrates the Lollard tradition into mainstream rather than deviationist protestantism and discounts the influence of continental Anabaptism. Patrick Collinson's elegant demonstration of the manner in which those

[9] [Untrue: Foxe admired Luther and sought to reintroduce him to the English.]

unassimilable gobbets, the strangers' churches of London, both highlighted and reduced the peculiarity of Elizabethan Anglicanism underlines the international solidarity present in the protestantism of the age without abolishing the differences. Basil Hall usefully elaborates the differences between the native (Lollard) and imported (Lutheran) beginnings, though he probably overestimates the length of time during which Luther provided the continental inspiration for English protestants. James Cameron has more to say about Scotland than England, a very different story not here at issue, but he, too, emphasizes the continental dimensions of protestantism in Britain without disallowing its native guise and special character.

As our authors demonstrate, the interaction continued into the next century, with this difference that the established English Church could become an example to the continent as much as a humble disciple. Continental influences still made themselves felt in unexpected places: that self-willed character, Richard Baxter, drew strength from Hugo Grotius, as Geoffrey Nuttall demonstrates, while C. de Jonge shows how sects who refused to admit virtue in all not of their persuasion could yet seek the approval of Dutch theologians. More typical, however, are the continental promoters of peace who found the English compromise congenial: Jean Hotman, son of a more famous father, approached Grotius and reconciliation after years of living in England (G. H. M. Postumus Meyjes), and Adrianus Saravia's views derived in great part from an instructed preference for the English middle way (W. Nijenhuis). In a way the synod of Dortrecht terminated a phase in the relations between England and the continent by bringing these eirenic ambitions to an end: John Platt commiserates with those Anglicans who lost their hope of seeing accommodation prevail abroad as well as at home, while C. Grayson deprecates James I's pleasure at finding Calvinism triumphant with his assistance in view of the manifest fact that his diplomacy was really a failure. Nevertheless, tenuous echoes of the earlier intense relationship can be heard in the exchanges between English evangelicals and Switzerland in the early eighteenth century, chronicled by Eamon Duffy, or in the unexpected influence of English puritanism upon German pietism discovered by W. R. Ward.

The question is: did the English Reformation derive from that of the continent, or did it grow upon its own inherited stock, or rather – since such a stark distinction is not only patently wrong but inherently highly improbable – was it really part of the continental movement or essentially a thing of its own? At first sight, it appears to fit the pattern we have discerned behind other events in the realm of ideas. The first inspiration came from Europe when Luther's message reached an England prepared both by the survival there of Lollard heresy and by the powerful sweep of Erasmian evangelism which had penetrated the Church, the Court, the universities and the upper ranks of society. Tyndale not only listened to Luther; he also wrote books which often incorporated translations from the master and followed his example by providing a vernacular version of the scriptures. That first generation of English protestants lived of necessity in exile and therefore stood firmly under the influence of its hosts; this appears to have been true as much of George Joye and John Frith, Robert Barnes and Simon Fish, as of Tyndale himself.[10] Meanwhile, the attraction of the Lutheran reform caught up people at home where, under the guidance of Cromwell and Cranmer (who after all learned much about the faith from his father-in-law, Andreas Osiander of Nuremberg), Lutheran ideas were permitted expression in the press and came to affect such reforming measures as the Ten Articles and the Royal Injunctions of 1536.

By 1538 at the latest, however, a new continental influence had replaced the charms of Wittenberg, and from thenceforward 'Upper German' protestantism – the voices of Bucer, Zwingli, ultimately (no longer German) Calvin – assumed the role of mentor.[11] That role it retained to the end of the century. The Reformation of Edward VI's reign benefited from the guidance of continental exiles who to a man were more radical than Luther, and in the reign of Elizabeth English protestants maintained the links they had established with Bullinger's Zurich and Calvin's (ultimately Beza's) Geneva during their renewed exiles in the 1540s and 1550s. Elizabethan puritanism drew sustenance from its contacts with the Calvinist leadership, and even the new sectarians of the reign owed more to such continental imports as the Family of Love and to such continental examples as were found in the Netherlands than to any native tradition. At the same time, however, the English predilection for naturalizing foreign imports operated on the Reformation, and the protestant Church of England, established in 1559 and thereafter maintained through the modifications imposed by debate, emerged by the end of the century as a distinguishable form of Christianity, different not only in a structure inherited from the medieval past but also in a theology in which the doctrine of adiaphora

[10] W. Clebsch, *England's Earliest Protestants, 1520–1535* (1964).   [11] Below, no. 43.

modified demands for uniformity, while doctrines of the covenant as
well as beliefs in the validity of traditions communicated by the Church
modified the predestinarian and strictly scriptural foundations of what
was in the main a Calvinist faith. Men as diverse as Richard Hooker,
John Whitgift, William Perkins and Peter Baro, all members of the
Church of England, held to a protestantism which is manifestly
Anglican, and which by the same token is neither purely 'evangelical'
nor purely 'reformed', to use the terminology appropriate on the
continent.

This, I think, is not an unfair summary of what would usually be said,
especially now that we have finally learned to regard puritanism as a
variant of the Anglican faith rather than a Geneva-oriented enemy to it.
Nor would I myself wish to dispute the essential acceptability of such a
summary, with two rather serious reservations which in their different
ways contradict the thesis derived from the other intellectual experiences of the age. In the first place, I now think that the usual description
seriously underestimates the native roots of the reform, and in the
second I think that it passes a little too readily over the continuing
continental impact on the late-Elizabethan Church.

Touching the first, the most detailed study yet made of pre-Reformation heresy in England has discovered a powerful strain of reviving
Lollardy which rivalled rather than assisted the Lutheran impact and
made its own distinctive contribution to the history of the English
Reformation.[12] These were the 'Christian brethren' who drew the
attention and the wrath of Thomas More. They differed from the
original continental reform as it reached England not so much (as has
been supposed) by being the religion of the poor, for their influence can
certainly be traced among the beneficed clergy and prominent
townsmen; they differed in matters theological. In particular this
Lollardy held to a characteristically sceptical opinion of the real presence
in the eucharist which went counter to Luther's inmost beliefs. In
consequence, however, it set up a sympathy for the 'sacramentarian'
tenets of the Zwinglians and of continental sectaries, links which moved
Henry VIII himself to oppose such developments with the utmost
determination but which, operating together with common Erasmian
antecedents and a common preoccupation with social problems, assured
the triumph in England of the Helvetic over the Saxon centre of the

[12] J. F. Davis, 'Heresy and Reformation in the south-east of England, 1520–59', unpubl. D.Phil.
diss. (Oxford, 1968).

reform. At the same time, this triumph did not eliminate the continuing conscious influence of the native tradition itself.

Sacramentarianism, derived from Lollardy, coloured the English Reformation throughout. It played its role in settling Henry VIII's policies. It assisted in the reforming career, and less justly in the destruction, of Thomas Cromwell. It assisted in the turns taken by the Edwardian reformers, in the distribution of emphases which character-ized the Elizabethan settlement, and in the anti-sacerdotal tenets of puritanism which throughout appeared markedly less attached to the role of the sacraments and the rule of the ministry than were either Geneva or such Genevan offsprings as the presbyterianism of Scotland or the Calvinism of France. The growth of sects also drew upon that native source: the gathered churches of Elizabeth's reign and their successors in the next century owed little (as Dr Loades says) to continental Anabaptism but probably more than he allows (this needs more work) to the brethren of Henrician London and Essex. Of all the protestant communities of the sixteenth century, the reformed English would seem to have been least impressed by clerical claims and pretensions: and this lasting contempt for the priesthood, often resented very vocally by its victims, was one of the bequests which medieval Lollardy left to English protestantism. One wonders whether Queen Elizabeth ever realized how much her own treatment of her bishops owed to what her ancestors had always abominated as an insidiously subversive movement. At any rate, some of the essential peculiarities of English protestantism did not so much develop in the course of the Reformation; rather they were present from the first.

On the other hand, an interpretation which stresses the Lollard ancestry of Elizabethan puritanism and recognizes its continuous influence on Anglican reform can come to underestimate the theologi-cal dependence of protestant Englishmen on the teachings of the continent. As we learn more about the importance of covenant doctrines from Tyndale onwards – doctrines which inescapably weaken the concentration on God's unpurchasable grace from which Luther and Calvin alike started – we are liable to forget that the only official theology of Elizabethan England was professedly Calvinist. This was as true of Whitgift (who proved the point in the Lambeth Articles of 1595) as of Cartwright and the small band of true presbyterians. But it was also true of what is usually called moderate puritanism which in matters theological was not moderate at all. An essentially conforming

cleric like Laurence Chaderton – a world removed from thoughts of
separation or revolution – held firmly to the full panoply of Calvinist
doctrine, in which stance he was typical enough of the large number of
clergy whose dissatisfaction with the state of the Church made them
look for further reform without leading them to a religion which might
pose an obstacle to loyal adherence to that Church.[13] The popes of
Zurich and Geneva continued throughout to provide a lead to their
faithful followers in a Church of England that organizationally and in
many details of observance looked very suspect from the perspectives of
Switzerland. It was only in the age of Bancroft that those loyalties began
to come into conflict, and only in the age of John Preston (when
covenant theology became openly dominant) that the native traditions
began to undermine official Calvinism even among the self-professed
Calvinists. Elizabethan uniformity rested not only upon the law and the
queen's determination to see it enforced; it also depended on an almost
general agreement touching the essentials of the faith. The point might
be best pursued (though not here) in a study of what official champions
would regard as heresy and where they found it; concentration so far on
the politicized disagreements of the day has stopped historians from
following up leads given by scholars attending to the earlier days of the
Reformation. One result of this wide agreement was that nonconfor-
mity always tended to deal in issues of lesser moment and surrendered
quite readily. What matters here is that that agreement looked to the
continent for its authority as well as for the resolution of problems that
the royal demand for uniformity created in a Church dedicated to
maintaining *multa in uno*.[14]

These matters, as I have said, need much further thought and study.
The more we come to realize that such traditional pairs of dichotomy as
Anglican and puritan. Calvinist and anti-calvinist, conformist and
separatist, even perhaps protestant and catholic, do not really describe
the truth of the Elizabethan religious scene, the more impossible is it
becoming to describe that scene at all. But perhaps a clue may be found
in the continuing coexistence of the two quite different midwives who
assisted at the birth of the English Reformation: the pragmatism of
native sacramentarian and anticlerical traditions on the one hand, and on
the other the theological and ecclesiological systems imported from

[13] P. G. Lake, 'Laurence Chaderton and the Cambridge moderate puritan tradition, 1570–1604',
unpubl. Ph.D. diss. (Cambridge, 1978).

[14] A good example is provided by the efforts made to devolve the decision in the vestiarian
controversy upon Henry Bullinger.

abroad. Unlike humanism, the Reformation did not come purely from
abroad and achieve naturalization, nor did it ever entirely relinquish
debate with that abroad and dependence upon it.

Yet there is one thing missing in that conclusion, a thought that
brings us back to the other dominant phenomenon of the sixteenth
century, namely the creation of a self-contained political identity in the
unitary realm of England. It is a thought that helps to resolve the
original paradox which appeared to lie in a simultaneous political
separation from the continent and an intellectual (and spiritual) deep
involvement with it. One feature, after all, above all others distinguishes
the Reformation in England and sets it apart from its fellows in the
protestant camp, even in such regions of monarchical reform as
Denmark and Sweden, and that is its political structure. The newly
established royal supremacy and the preservation of an old system of
episcopal government are the most notable hallmarks of the Church of
England in the sixteenth century and after. They came first, before the
genuine Reformation had even begun, and they were the deliberate
achievement of the founders, Henry VIII and Thomas Cromwell. That
those two begetters did not see things in quite the same light, and that as
things developed Cromwell's parliamentary concept triumphed over
the king's caesaro-papism,[15] are important considerations but less
important than that they both rested their vision of the Church upon
this political rather than any spiritual foundation. One of the two
hallmarks was truly novel and the other as truly conservative, but
between them they amounted to a revolution in the state by causing it to
incorporate the Church, a Church moreover of ultimately unique
character. It was within this framework of royal rule plus an adopted
and adapted system of administration that the religious and spiritual
history of post-Reformation England was to take place, and inevitably
the framework conditioned what happened. The specifically English
Church which emerged by the end of the century owed much to
continental roots and influences: it was a part of a European movement.
But its shape and inner reality it owed much more to the measures taken
in the process of separating England from the continent. In the last
analysis, and despite the recurrent dependence on European inspiration,
the reformed Church of England confirmed the foremost truth about
the sixteenth century. Unlike the medieval kingdom, so closely linked
to its neighbours across the Channel, the modern realm stood by itself

[15] G. R. Elton, *Reform and Reformation: England 1509–1558* (1977), 196–200.

upon its island base. Whatever antecedents may be discovered are no more than that: they do not do away with the fact that before Henry VIII England was recognizably part of a general European system and culture, while after him it had acquired a visibly different political and cultural style of its own. The difference of England stemmed from the revolutionary steps taken in the 1530s; if that difference is indeed now gone, the counter-revolution of the 1960s, which has at last drawn the line beneath the effect of Thomas Cromwell's work, must be held responsible.

43

ENGLAND UND DIE OBERDEUTSCHE REFORM*

Daß die englische Reformation sehr eigener Art gewesen sei, gehört zu den Gemeinplätzen der Geschichtsschreibung; oft wird hinzugesetzt, daß sie einzig und allein einer Aktion des Staates entsprungen sei. Eine in ihrer Struktur und in vielen Zeremonien traditionelle Staatskirche gilt als einzigartig, und einzigartig auch darin, daß angeblich nur ein Machtkalkül und realpolitische Umstände an Stelle einer religiösen Revolution sie hervorgebracht haben. Obwohl die jüngere Forschung davon viel in Frage gestellt hat, bleiben die allgemeineren Darstellungen besonders außerhalb Englands noch bei der alten Deutung. Andererseits dominiert selbst in Deutschland heute nicht mehr die Überzeugung, daß die deutsche Reformation sich einfach von Luther und vom geistigen Aufruhr herleiten lasse: man anerkennt besser die Bedeutung der oberdeutschen und schweizerischen Reformation und kommt allmählich dazu, die Erklärung nur in den sozialen Umständen und Spannungen zu suchen. Die Entdeckung, daß in dem Abschied von Rom die Städte eine nicht weniger wichtige Rolle als die Fürsten gespielt haben, hat schon zu einer Version geführt, in der Straßburg als bedeutender denn Wittenberg erscheint und die Gesellschaftsprobleme den theologischen Streit in den Hintergrund drängen. Ich darf vielleicht bemerken, daß diese Neuansichten gewiß schon nach England gelangt sind (im Gegensatz zu der revidierten Geschichte Englands in Deutschland); meiner Ansicht nach hat man sogar das Neue zu eifrig geschluckt. Eine Interpretation der Reformation, bei der es sich rein um Luther und den Glauben handelt, ist ebenso unzureichend wie eine, in der nur von Zwingli und der Stadtpolitik die Rede ist. Die Interaktion zwischen England und Süddeutschland in der ersten Hälfte des 16. Jahrhunderts bietet die Möglichkeit, diese einerseits etwas veralteten und andererseits

* [Zeitschrift für Kirchengeschichte (1978), 3–11.]

etwas zu neugeprägten Theorien der Geschichtsschreibung einer hoffentlich nüchternen Prüfung zu unterziehen.

Als sich zunächst in England der Drang zum Bruch mit Rom bemerkbar machte, bestand an sich die Wahrscheinlichkeit, daß das Königreich die Reformation Luthers annehmen oder sich ihr doch wenigstens weitgehend annähern würde. In den zwanziger Jahren des Jahrhunderts erwarb sich Luther eine Anzahl Schüler an den englischen Universitäten. Besonders gewann seine Lehre Gewicht durch den Einfluß von Tyndale, der ihr den Großteil seiner reformatorischen Ideen verdankte. Und Tyndale war ein tätiger und geschickter Propagandist. Selbst nachdem seine Schriften verdammt und ihr Lesen verboten worden war, konnte man ihn doch mittels der endlosen Zitate kennenlernen, die sich bei Thomas More in seinen Gegenschriften finden. Seine Glaubensgenossen – besonders George Joye und John Frith – blickten auch nach Wittenberg, und selbst die von More geleitete Verfolgung der Jahre 1530–2, in der auch Frith umkam, vermochte die ansteigende Flut nicht einzudämmen. Es ist natürlich wahr, daß der Ehestreit des Königs und dessen autonome Lösung – die Aufrichtung des königlichen Supremats in der Kirche – der protestantischen Propaganda wertvollen Boden vorbereitete; aber wir sind uns jetzt doch sicher, daß diese Ausbreitung der Ideen einen starken Antrieb aus geistiger Unzufriedenheit darstellte, wie sie überall die Tradition untergraben hat. In England kam noch hinzu, daß die neue Lehre aus dem Ausland mit einer einheimischen Ketzerei – Lollardy – gemeinsame Sache machen konnte.

Die politischen Führer der dreißiger Jahre, besonders Thomas Cranmer und Thomas Cromwell, neigten Sachsen zu. Cranmer fand dort den ersten Anlaß zu seiner immer protestantischer werdenden Theologie, und Cromwell erklärte ausdrücklich, er sei in Sachen des Glaubens der lutherischen Meinung, abgesehen davon, was ihm die Politik und der Dienst seines Königs aufzwinge. Man denke auch daran, daß die lutherische Reformation schon hinreichend bewiesen hatte, wie nützlich sie für die Landesfürsten sein konnte, die ihre Territorien zu konsolidieren, ihre Kirchen der weltlichen Obrigkeit zu unterwerfen und die finanziellen Vorteile der Säkularisation auszubeuten bestrebe waren. Dem Beispiel, das Sachsen und Hessen in den zwanziger Jahren geboten hatten, folgten in den Dreißigern Brandenburg, die Braunschweiger und Kleve-Jülich in verschiedener Weise. Auch Skandinavien bewegte sich bereits in dieselbe Richtung. Unter dem Einfluß

Cromwells knüpfte Heinrich VIII. die Verbindung nicht nur mit der bürgerlichen Regierung Jürgen Wullenwevers in Lübeck an, sondern besonders mit Sachsen, Dänemark und Kleve: landesfürstliche Verbündete haben ihn mehr angezogen als städtische. Viele der Voraussetzungen, vom religiösen Eifer bis zur Herrscheridee, die allmählich in Norddeutschland und im Baltikum zum Luthertum führten, waren auch in England vorhanden.

Und dennoch erreichte das Luthertum nie einen schlagkräftigen Einfluß in England; im Gegentiel, es war dort bald im Abstieg begriffen. Was auch immer sein Minister, sein Erzbischof und seine Prediger sagen mochten, der König selber blieb der unerbittliche Gegner von Wittenberg. Natürlich stand er dabei nicht allein. Die Partei der Reform, die in sich auch selbst uneins war, weil sich die Rivalität protestantischer und erasmischer Einflüsse bemerkbar machte, blieb zu jener Zeit zahlenmäßig auch in Regierungskreisen in der Minderheit; und das Weiterbestehen einer Kirche, die nach außen hin die alten Züge von Bischöfen, Kirchengerichten und ausgedehntem Landbesitz behielt, verhinderte auch den einwandfreien Bruch mit der Vergangenheit. Den englischen Theologen war es nicht möglich, in allen Dingen mit der Wittenberger Reform übereinzustimmen, besonders, da doch die Lutheraner gerade zu der Zeit miteinander und mit anderen Reformatoren im Streite lagen. Um sich mit Luther zu verständigen, mußte man ja immer seine ganze Lehre ohne Zögern annehmen: vom freien Verhandeln konnte nicht die Rede sein. Doch alle Hindernisse wären schon mit der Zeit und mit der Art von Entschlossenheit, die Cromwell eigen war, überwunden worden, wenn der König nicht absolut die Annäherung zurückgewiesen hätte. Einmal hieß es, er sei bis zum Ende seines Lebens orthodox katholisch geblieben, aber die Neuuntersuchung seiner Ansichten läßt diesen Schluß nicht mehr zu. Heinrich ist in Wirklichkeit sein eigener Theologe gewesen, der sich sehr eklektisch einen eigenen Glauben aus Tradition, Erneuerung und Selbstsucht zusammengestellt hat. Die Bedeutung der Laienrolle in der Kirche nahm er zum Beispiel bereitwillig an, so daß die Lehre vom Priestertum aller Gläubigen ihn nicht gestört hat, und obwohl er eine vorsichtige Einstellung gegenüber der Abschaffung des Aberglaubens und der heilbringenden Werke bevorzugte, hatte er im Grundsatz nichts gegen den Begriff 'sola fide'. Hingegen mißtraute er der volkssprachlichen Bibel und haßte die Priesterehe, zwei Schnörkel, die in den Verhandlungen von 1538 dem Übereinkommen mit den

323

Lutheranern im Wege standen. Diese seltsame Konzentration auf weniger wichtige Einzelheiten, obwohl sich doch die beiden Seiten im wesentlichen ganz nahestanden, deutet auf die Wahrheit hin. Wie es bei diesem König immer der Fall war, beruhten seine öffentlichen und politischen Entscheidungen auf höchst persönlichen Grundlagen. Weder hatte er Luther die heftige und verächtliche Antwort auf sein Buch über die Sakramente verziehen, noch hatte er das Wittenberger Urteil gegen seine erste Ehescheidung vergessen. Auch hat er nicht recht einer Richtlinie getraut, die durch die Betonung der Laienrechte sein eigenes Monopol von Gottes Gnaden über die Kirche beeinträchtigen konnte; sein Zwist mit Cromwell entsprang dessen Wunsch, das weltliche Recht und das Parlamentsgesetz über die Ansprüche einer Kirchenidee jure-divino triumphieren zu lassen. Also ist es effektiv Heinrich VIII. gewesen, der in den dreißiger Jahren Luther aus England ferngehalten hat, gerade zu der Zeit, als an sich die Rezeption der norddeutschen Reformation die besten Chancen hatte. Trotz des vorhandenen Willens, dieses Ziel zu erreichen, fehlte es an der Macht, das einzige entscheidende Hindernis, den Widerstand des Königs, aus dem Wege zu räumen.

Heinrich hatte aber noch einen weiteren Grund für seine Weigerung, auf dem wohl approbierten Schisma nun noch eine wahre Reformation aufzubauen, und hier sah er deutlicher als Cromwell, dessen Fall seinem Mangel, die Gefährlichkeit gewisser Tendenzen einzusehen, zuzuschreiben ist. Selbst in den dreißiger Jahren stand der Einfluß Luthers (ob direkt oder durch die Nachfolger von Tyndale vermittelt) nicht mehr allein da. Den wirklich extremen Radikalen brauchen wir hier nicht nachzugehen. Von ungefähr 1536 an gab es in England schon Wiedertäufer, aber sie machten keine Fortschritte und bekehrten fast niemanden; die wenigen, die man gefunden und entweder vertrieben oder verbrannt hat, waren Deutsche und Niederländer. Die Rivalen, um die es sich hier handelt, gehörten auch zu den großen Reformatoren, aber an Stelle der Stimme von Wittenberg hören wir immer mehr die der städtischen Vertreter. Schon 1536 ließen sich die Aufrührer in Nordengland dazu überreden, Butzer und Oekolampad zusammen mit Luther und Melanchthon anzuprangern – zu einer Zeit, da von ihren Schriften noch nichts ins Englische übersetzt worden war. Die öffentliche Politik wendete sich besonders gegen die sogenannten Sakramentarier, ein Schimpfwort, das wohl auch Täufersekten einbegriff, hauptsächlich aber gegen die angeblichen Anhänger Zwinglis gerichtet war. Man warf ihnen vor, sie hätten die Idee der Realpräsenz im Abendmahl vollkommen aufgegeben, was sie für Heinrich VIII. zu den unerträglichsten aller Ketzer machte. Daneben verwechselte man sie noch mit den wahren Subversiven, die vom Gemeinbesitz allen Eigentums und aller Frauen redeten: auch in England hatte das Königreich von Münster seinen Eindruck hinterlassen. Ob er nun auf Rom oder Wittenberg oder seine einheimischen Konservativen hörte, Heinrich war überzeugt, daß Butzer, Zwingli und ihresgleichen gefährliche soziale und religiöse Revolutionäre seien, die alle gute Ordnung und Tradition zu vernichten suchten. Und so kam er zu dem Schluß, er könne seine reine und orthodoxe Kirche nur dadurch vor diesen letzten Abscheulichkeiten retten, daß er jeder Art von Reformation Widerstand leistete. Daher die Reaktion von 1539–40, die die Messe, den Zölibat und die Ohrenbeichte wiederherstellte; daher das Ende Cromwells, von dem der König zwar kurz nur – doch lang genug – zu glauben bereit war, daß sein Vizegerent Zwinglianer und Sakramentarier sei. Obwohl er die Anfänge der Reformation auszutilgen nicht gewillt war, verhinderte Heinrich bis zum Ende seines Lebens jeden weiteren Fortschritt; und als er endlich verschwand, war Luther schon vor ihm gestorben, und der Schmalkaldische Bund stand am Vorabend seines Zusammenbruches. Die Möglichkeit einer lutherischen Reformation in England war vorbei.

Durch einen historischen Zufall, ein persönliches Mißverständnis, haben also die oberdeutschen Reformatoren zu Luthers Niederlage in einem Reich beigetragen, das an sich für dessen Erfolg vielversprechend ausgesehen hatte. Und sowie einmal die schwere Hand Heinrichs VIII. das Ruder freigab, pflückten sie auch die Siegesfrüchte. Die von Cranmer während der Zeit Eduards VI. geleitete protestantische Reformation fand ja ihre religiöse Inspiration bekanntlich bei festländischen Theologen, von denen allein Melanchthon sich zum Luthertum bekannte. Und der reiste nie nach England, wohingegen wohlbekannte Oberdeutsche voller Eifer nach London, Oxford und Cambridge eilten. Die Mühlberger Schlacht deutete das Ende von Straßburg als einer Zufluchtsstätte an, so daß der Ruf aus Canterbury gerade zur rechten Zeit kam, um Martin Butzer, Peter Martyr Vermigli, John a Lasco usw. vor dem Sieg Karls V. zu schützen. An der Spitze derer, die zu Hause blieben und ihre englischen Kollegen aus der Ferne berieten, stand von nun an der Zürcher Heinrich Bullinger. Diese Verbindungen hatte man während der katholischen Reaktion der vierziger Jahre angeknüpft, als exilierte Protestanten in Straßburg, Basel und Zürich Zuflucht nahmen. Geradezu ostentativ hatten sie Wittenberg und Antwerpen, die Heilsstätten der zwanziger Jahre, beiseite gelassen, und bei der Rückkehr brachten sie ihre neuen Überzeugungen mit. Obwohl die Forschung noch diskutiert, wie weit das Ergebnis aus einheimischen Traditionen oder unter fremdem Einfluß hervorgegangen ist, kann man doch nicht bezweifeln, daß die theologische Grundlage der protestantischen Kirche Englands mit Ziegelsteinen aus oberdeutscher Manufaktur gebaut worden ist. Am deutlichsten erscheint das in der anglikanischen Abendmahlslehre, drückt sich aber auch anderswo aus: z.B. in der Prädestinationsdoktrin, in der Stellungnahme zu den Zeremonien, allmählich auch in der Ekklesiologie, und besonders in der Betonung des Unterschiedes zwischen dem zum Heil Essentiellen oder Indifferenten – in der Lehre von den Adiaphora. Keinem der Zentren der Reformation ist es geglückt, England ausschließlich für sich zu erobern, und die erneuerte Landeskirche behielt markant manches bei, das ihr eigen war. Die 39 Artikel, auf denen der Glaube dieser Kirche ruht, sind ja bekanntlich so allumfassend, daß es wohl nur dem Teufel und dem Türken – und unter Christen nur den Täufern – unmöglich gewesen wäre, sie anzunehmen. Will man jedoch die anglikanische Staatskirche in eine der Kategorien einordnen, die aus dem Durcheinander der Reformation hervorgingen, dann stehen Zürich, Basel und Straßburg am nächsten und Wittenberg sehr fern. All dies wurde bei der Wiedererneuerung durch Elisabeth I. bestätigt. Das Settlement von 1559 stellte eine im Glauben hauptsächlich oberdeutsche Kirche her, die für den Einfluß Calvins offen war. Es ist hoffentlich klar, daß ich hier an die Theologie denke, aber wenn man von der Kirche redet, soll die Theologie nicht immer vergessen sein, was auch im Bereich von Disziplin und Besitztum vorgehen mag. Unter Elisabeth blieben auch weiter die Verbindungen mit Zürich sehr rege; in der Achtung, die englische Geistliche der Belehrung vom Kontinent her widmeten, wurde selbst Beza nie von Bullinger übertroffen.

Aber erscheint dies Resultat nicht sehr merkwürdig? Wenn es wahr ist, daß die englische Reformation die Ziele der weltlichen Obrigkeit verköpert hat – besonders die einer machtgierigen Krone und einer landbesitzgierigen Oberschicht – dann muß man sich fragen, warum von diesen Interessen her eine Religion angenommen wurde, die in den Städten und für städtische Zustände entwickelt worden war, und die gewisse, gegen jede Kontrolle von oben her eingestellte Prinzipien des

Glaubens und der Kirchenordnung in sich barg. Daß der Einfluß von Zwingli und Calvin, der sich in dem sogenannten puritanischen Flügel der elisabethanischen Kirche bemerkbar machen sollte, zur Forderung nach einem presbyterianischen Klerus und einer jedenfalls ein wenig demokratisierten Kirchenordnung führen würde, war schon vor 1559 vorauszusehen; gewiß bereitete es denen keine Überraschung, die Süddeutschland als Exulanten unter Heinrich VIII. und der Königin Maria besucht hatten. Wenn andererseits die oberdeutsche Reformation so eindeutig eine städtische Bewegung war, die man nur im Zeichen des Bürgertums verstehen kann, dann läßt sich kaum erklären, wieso ihre Religion auf eine nationalterritoriale Kirche, wo der Monarch regierte, der Landadel die große Politik betrieb, und die Kanzel konsequent den Obrigkeitsgehorsam predigte, eine solche Anziehungskraft ausüben konnte.

Zur Erklärung kann man vielleicht auf reine Zufälle hinweisen. Wären Melanchthon und Bugenhagen anstelle oder an der Seite Butzers nach England gekommen, dann wäre Cranmer möglicherweise zu seiner ersten Liebe, zum Luthertum, zurückgekehrt. Als ein Mensch, der zeit seines Lebens nach Aufklärung und Zusicherung suchte, war er ja immer jedem direkten Einfluß ausgesetzt. Der reine Zufall erklärt aber nicht die Bereitwilligkeit, auf die Botschaft von Straßburg und Zürich (und schließlich von Genf) zu hören, die man bei zuversichtlichen Menschen wie Nicholas Ridley, John Hooper und Richard Cox findet. Tatsächlich erscheinen die konventionellen Theorien über das Zeitalter als unzureichend und irreführend. Gewiß wurde die Reformation in England durch die Mitarbeit der weltlichen Macht möglich gemacht. Ohne Heinrichs VIII. Eheproblem hätte sie nicht so früh angefangen; ohne Cromwell hätte der Zwist mit dem Papst nicht sofort zur Förderung des Protestantismus geführt, der spontane Unterstützung nur von einer kleinen Gruppe reformgesinnter Geistlicher und sympathisierender Laien erhielt; wenn die Herzöge von Somerset und Northumberland der totalen Reformation feindlich gegenübergestanden hätten, würde selbst die Gegenwart einer nun stark gewordenen Anzahl von reformierten Pastoren den Umsturz unter Eduard VI. nicht erzwungen haben. Doch hat die unabkömmliche Mitarbeit der Regierung, die man überall, wo es zur Reformation kam, vorfindet, den englischen Anteil an der großen Veränderung nicht speziell zu einer Staatsaktion gemacht. Ihren Kurs bestimmten die gewöhnlichen Sachverständigen, die Theologen. Gewiß brachte England im 16.

Jahrhundert keinen großen und erneuernden Theologen hervor, doch gab es im Lande eine rechte Anzahl gut gelahrter Herren, die für die von der anderen Seite des Ärmelkanals herüberspringende Botschaft von der Erneuerung genügend ausgebildet waren. Und nur aus dem Grunde, weil die religiösen Führer fast von Anfang an die oberdeutschen Lehren für überzeugender hielten als die Luthers, bewegte sich England sogleich mehr in die radikale Richtung, die Zwingli zuerst angedeutet hatte.

Zweitens sieht es nun so aus, als ob jede Analyse, die die Unterschiede zwischen Luther und Zwingli und ihren Kirchen einzig und allein auf die sozialpolitischen Umstände ihrer Tätigkeit zu schieben sucht, auch unzureichend und irreführend ist. Da die wesentlichen Bestandteile des in der Helvetischen Konfession niedergelegten Glaubens sich auch in dem sehr verschiedenen Klima und in der sehr andersartigen Gesellschaft Englands zu Hause fühlen konnten, läßt sich ihre Eignung zur unabhängigen Existenz nicht verleugnen. Die verschiedenen Vorkämpfer in diesem Ringen um das Wort Gottes dachten doch, daß es um die Wahrheit der Schrift ging; obwohl wir als Historiker das Recht haben, die sie bildenden zeitbedingten Zustände zu studieren, dürfen wir doch nicht vergessen, wie die Sache für sie selber aussah. Die gründliche Untersuchung von Städten und Sozialschichten, von Gesellschaftsstruktur und Klassenkampf, von Wirtschaftsinteressen und politischem Ehrgeiz, so wichtig und aufhellend sie auch sein mögen, erklären uns nichts über die Reformation, wenn wir es uns nicht gestatten, die geistigen und glaubensbedingten Angelegenheiten der daran Beteiligten zu überblicken. Zwingli hat Zürich nicht etwa reformiert, weil seine Art Kirche der dortigen Obrigkeit paßte oder weil er den Imperialismus der Stadt unterstützen wollte (gewiß zwei seine Reform fördernde Umstände), sondern weil er überzeugt war, er wisse, wie die rechte Kirche gestaltet und der rechte Gottesdienst gehalten werden sollte. Eine gewisse Ironie liegt in der Tatsache, daß die Zürcher Reformation steckenblieb und die territoriale Ausdehnung der Stadt aufhörte, während andererseits der Glaube Zwinglis in weiter Ferne eine neue Kolonie gründete. Ich bin wahrhaftig nicht geneigt anzunehmen, daß die Ideen immer mächtiger und ausdauernder sein müssen als die materiellen Interessen der Menschheit, aber ihre Kraft zu verleugnen, wenn sie so deutlich auftritt, wäre doch eine Dummheit.

Warum aber erwiesen sich die Ideen der oberdeutschen Reform in England als so besonders anziehend? Wie schon gesagt, standen dort die zur Reform geneigten Geister früh mit Luther in Verbindung und schienen ein Jahrzehnt lang hauptsächlich auf ihn zu hören, aber von 1538 an gingen sie fast einstimmig und auf Dauer zu der Art Reformation über, die Luther für falsch und verderblich hielt. Die Antwort auf diese Frage liegt in den Einflüssen, die auf diese englischen Empfänger ausländischer Lehren gewirkt haben. Canterbury und die Städte Süddeutschlands, die in der Sozialstruktur, den Verwaltungs-methoden und den volkswirtschaftlichen Bedingungen nichts miteinander gemein hatten, stammten von denselben intellektuellen Vorfahren ab und hatten daher bei der Auseinandersetzung wenig Schwierigkeiten. Diese gemeinsame Grundlage läßt sich in drei Teilen analysieren.

Zunächst einmal standen alle englischen Reformatoren stark unter dem humanistischen Einfluß des Erasmus. In Cambridge, wo er von 1511 bis 1514 untergekommen war, galt sein Ruf ebensoviel wie in Basel, wo er sich in den zwanziger Jahren niederließ. Zwingli, Oekolampad und Capito waren nicht weniger in das Netz seines Briefwechsels einbezogen als seine Freunde in England. Weil die treuesten dieser Freunde – Thomas More und John Fisher – der Reformation Heinrichs VIII. zum Opfer gefallen sind, lassen sich diese engen Beziehungen leicht verdunkeln; man hat erst vor kurzem wiederentdeckt, daß die jüngere Gelehrtengeneration, die Cromwell und Cranmer bei der Kirchenreform Beistand leistete, auch weiter von Erasmus viele Anregungen bezogen hat. Cromwell selbst hielt nicht nur viel von Erasmus, sondern gab ihm auch ein schönes Stück Geld – eine Art der Anerkennung, die Erasmus besonders gewürdigt hat. Anderer-seits, wie ja bekannt ist, haben sich Luther und Erasmus schon 1525 getrennt. Es kommt noch hinzu, daß die englischen Reformatoren, die konventionell bei den Scholastikern zur Schule gegangen waren, die Verachtung der Humanisten für die zwei traditionellen Wege – die via antiqua wie die via moderna – geteilt haben. Daher fanden sie bei Luther, dessen Denken (wie wir es ja neuerdings besonders von Herrn Professor Oberman erfahren haben) stark unter dem Einfluß des Nominalismus stand, vieles, was ihnen letzten Endes kaum verständlich und sogar unsympathisch war. Das tritt besonders in der wichtigsten Debatte der Frühreformation hervor – in dem Streit über die Abend-mahlslehre. Zwingli und Butzer gebrauchten dabei manches, was auf Erasmus weist: In ihrem Denken über das Mysterium des Willens Gottes steckte z. B. mehr an humanistischem Rationalismus als es später Calvin angenehm war. Daher fanden sie Anklang in England, wo die

Achtung für Erasmus nie vor Luthers Donnergewitter gewichen war und wo man Luthers komplizierte Lehre von einer Korporealpräsenz ohne Transsubstantiation philosophisch nicht akzeptieren konnte. Diese Verehrung der humanistischen Tradition hielt auch während der dunklen Jahre am Ende von Heinrichs Regierungszeit die Flamme der Reform am Leben, besonders in dem Kreis, der sich um seine letzte Königin gebildet hat. Auch bei der Reformation Eduards VI. und 1559 spielten die humanistischen Neigungen eine wichtige Rolle.

Zweitens zog die oberdeutsche Reformation die Engländer durch ihre Betonung von friedlichen und versöhnlichen Prinzipien an. Auch in England gab es Fanatiker (obwohl der mächtigst von ihnen, John Knox, sorgfältig in sein heimatliches Schottland abgelenkt wurde), aber die Haltung der Führenden suchte immer nach Mäßigung und hielt an der Idee fest, daß gute Christen in einer Kirche miteinander existieren können, selbst wenn sie sich nicht in allen Einzelheiten einig sind. Die allumfassende Kirche Englands, wie sie 1559 hervortrat, stand auf zwei Säulen. Sie wählte den Mittelweg zwischen den Extremen, und sie bestand auf dem Unterschied zwischen den zum Heil unabdingbaren ewigen Dingen einerseits und den indifferenten Dingen andererseits, die man verschieden beurteilen darf und die zeitlich und örtlich gebunden sind. Via media, adiaphora: Dies waren die Losungen, ohne die der Anglikanismus nie bestanden hätte. Beide traten von Anfang an in den Auseinandersetzungen auf, besonders bei Thomas Starkey, Cromwells wertvollstem Mitarbeiter, obwohl auch er einmal von Cromwell persönlich angewiesen werden mußte, ein noch stärkeres Gewicht auf den Mittelweg zu legen. Diese Losungsworte hatten aber auch für die Oberdeutschen, besonders für Butzer, bei ihren Bestrebungen große Bedeutung, die verschiedenen Reformparteien zur Einigkeit zu bringen. Es handelt sich hier nicht um einen direkten Einfluß oder etwa ein Ausleihen von Ideen. Das gleiche Streben nach Frieden, Einverständnis und Mäßigung fand man in England und Straßburg, so daß sich das Tor leicht für den Einzug der süddeutschen und schweizerischen Reform öffnen ließ. Andererseits aber paßten diese beiden Grundlagen den kalvinistischen Nachfolgern Calvins recht wenig, so daß sich auch in der elisabethanischen Kirche eine kompromißfeindliche und fanatische Partei bildete. Doch benahm sich immer nur eine Minderheit der englischen Kalvinisten und der Puritaner jeweils in so extremer Façon; im wesentlichen blieben alle Strömungen in der Kirche der Suche nach dem Mittelweg treu.

Zum Dritten schließlich enthielten die oberdeutschen Ideen einen starken sozialen Aktivismus, der auch wieder in England einen einheimischen Anklang finden konnte. Schon Tyndale und seine Mitarbeiter beschäftigten sich sowohl mit den praktischen Problemen der allgemeinen Erneuerung als auch mit den feineren Punkten der theologischen Debatte. Von vornherein waren sie mehr an der Ethik als an der Dogmatik interessiert, und dieser Vorzug wurde in vieler Hinsicht typisch. Gewiß hatte auch Luther das tägliche Dasein keineswegs vergessen, aber er kümmerte sich doch sehr viel weniger als die süddeutschen Städte und ihre religiösen Führer um die Probleme der sozialen Kontrolle, um die Einmischung in Wirtschaftsangelegenheiten, um die Organisation der Armenfürsorge. Für seinen eschatologischen Geist war dies alles im Vergleich zum transzendentalen Heil nicht nur unwichtig, sondern geradezu Zeitverschwendung. Ein Buch wie Butzers 'De Regno Christi' konnte man aus seiner Feder nicht erwarten. In England gewann die praktische Rechts- und Lebensreform von Anfang an ebenso große Bedeutung wie das Abschaffen der Messe oder die Übersetzung der Schrift in die Landessprache. Und bei dieser Tätigkeit verfolgte Cromwell nur Ziele, die auch den geistlichen Führern als wichtig und richtig erschienen.

In dieser Weise erwies sich die städtische Reformation des Südens für die Fürstenreformation Englands brauchbarer als die Fürstenreformation des Nordens. Die Ideengemeinschaft wirkte entscheidender also irgendwelche politischen Ähnlichkeiten oder Verschiedenheiten. Einerseits war die englische Reformation nicht einfach eine Staatsaktion, andererseits aber sollte man bei den Oberdeutschen nicht weniger die Reformation als den städtischen Hintergrund in Betracht ziehen.

44

CONTENTMENT AND DISCONTENT
ON THE EVE OF COLONIZATION*

My purpose is to set out the background to early English colonization in the North American continent, to the way in which the English moved into the continent and began to settle it. I therefore propose to say a little about the society from which these settlers came and the impulses which drove them forth. In all history there are many open questions, and this sad truth certainly applies to the problems considered here. Though much has been written about these issues, much still remains obscure; in addition, much of what has been written arises from certain convictions that I must regard as doubtful, especially the conviction that among the early English settlers those who mattered were fleeing from oppression and were seeking liberty to live and worship according to their preferences. While I do not pretend that I can really close any of these open questions, I hope at least to indicate what they might be.

Why, in fact, did a part of a small nation on the edge of Europe decide to go out into the unknown and start new lives in new and strange worlds? As I have already said, it is a widely accepted view that the colonizing activity of the English in the sixteenth and seventeenth centuries owed most to discontent, to a profound dissatisfaction with the manner in which things were arranged in the home country. These emigrants were sick and tired of the way in which they were being treated and in particular were driven forth by religious intolerance, which compelled them to seek a way of managing their relationships with God in a country that was new, empty and free of government. There is of course some truth in this – it applies to a small section of the colonists concerned to set up intolerant regimes of their own – but I

---

* Abbreviated and modified text of a lecture delivered and tape-recorded at St Mary's College of Maryland, 16 November 1977. [Published in *Early Maryland in a Wider World*, ed. D. B. Quinn (Detroit, 1982), 105–18.]

should like to suggest to you now that it is nothing like the whole truth, or indeed anything like the important part of the truth.

Let me begin by asking what life was really like in Elizabethan and early-Stuart England. What moved people? What were their ultimate ambitions? What, in the life they led, contented or discontented them? Well, in the first place, we need to grasp how miserable and indeed horrible by our standards (the standards of a generation determined to regard itself as the most ill-used ever) life then really was. You may at times have come to wonder – and if you haven't, I wish you would – how it was that human beings of a not unfamiliar kind, people like ourselves, could tolerate, for instance, the manner in which their law dealt with its victims. Have you considered the true meaning of that sentence of execution for treason: hanging, drawing and quartering? I will not spell it out in detail here, merely remarking that those three words by no means describe everything that was done to such a traitor, because I like sparing finer feelings. Have you ever considered what the death sentence for heresy really meant: burning alive at the stake? What it meant when, as the books so calmly and smugly tell us, Thomas Cranmer, archbishop of Canterbury, pitifully and painfully degraded from that status, was led out and tied to the stake and, because he had signed recantations which now he wished to with-draw, put his hand into the flames until – to cite those books – it was consumed?

What sort of people are we dealing with, who can do such things and do them in public? You could not help supposing them to have been inhuman, inhumane and insufferable, unless you grasped that in the conditions of the time what man could do to man was as nothing compared to what God was forever doing to man. Men's lives were governed (beyond our experience, perhaps beyond our comprehension) by pain, by physical pain and the proximity of death. Ever since painkillers and anaesthetics came to our aid, we have lost a ready means towards an understanding of the past, but just contemplate what it was like to live in an age in which you could not reduce the pain inflicted upon the human body by the things that naturally happen to it. If you can make that effort, you should begin to understand how these people could do those things to one another and could suffer them, as well as what sort of lives they were really leading. If you survived the first year after birth, average expectation of life in Elizabethan England was in the neighbourhood of thirty-five years. That is a rough average: many people died much younger, but if you reached sixty or so your expectation of life became approximately what it is now. But most people lived short and suddenly terminated lives. The killer diseases with which we are familiar did not much trouble them, because those are the diseases of old age and not commonplace before thirty-five. People died of injuries, many of them minor, and of the many infectious diseases that were running around, most of them painful. Try to think (but not for too long) what cutting for the stone really meant, and then try to think (even more briefly) what people suffered when the stone was not so treated. We are speaking of an age when pain was ever present and nasty forms of death encompassed all, quite unassisted by human agents except those well-meaning practitioners who pretended to be able to cure the one and stave off the other. Doctors caused a lot of agony.

Yet people of course lived, and often lived happily, but if they were to be able to face the miseries of life created by the frailty of the human body they had to observe the two conditions which make contentment possible in such circumstances. In the first place, they accepted the promise of better things to come after death: religion was required to carry a man through his troubles in order to achieve the potential ultimate bliss which was promised to him and which faith alone could guarantee. Secondly, they developed a degree of stoicism and resistance to the effects of pain and misery which we in our present state find hard to imagine, but which in fact accounts for much about the age, including its casual cruelty. Let me make myself plain. I am not saying that theirs was a good life and ours is bad; I am not saying that I wish to go back to the days before aspirin, anaesthetics, painkillers, and so forth. But I wish to emphasize that in that very different age, despite all the miseries that we would regard as intolerable, people still managed to live perfectly contented lives. Much of what to you may seem strange and alien about the sixteenth and seventeenth centuries comes out of those basic human experiences, fundamentally different from ours and yet experienced by people in many ways recognizably like ourselves. There is something of a problem here. To treat the past as real is not as common a practice, even among historians, as you might think. Even those professionally concerned with it do not as fully and regularly open themselves to the reality of the past as they should, and for that reason so much history is dead as you read it. Do, when you think about the past, remember that you may now be alive, but so were they; that you may now be suffering, but so were they; that you may now be rejoicing, but so were they.

Therefore: those real people in that somewhat remote society underwent those debilitating experiences and coped with them, in part because they felt sure that they could, if only they did things right, achieve bliss in another world, and in part because they had schooled themselves to face the inescapable adversities decreed by God. It is out of this matrix, with its cure for helpless discontent, that the men and women came who transferred their existence to a new world. It is, of course, quite difficult to establish exactly why people started colonizing. It is even quite difficult to establish when people started colonizing, especially as the tally must not include voyages of exploration or of trade and plunder. Settlement in the North American continent is what concerns us. Let us, however, take the years from the first Virginia foundation of 1585, temporary though this was, as defining our era. It so happens that in this era the English people experienced the return of several difficulties and problems that had been temporarily absent. After a relatively prolonged peace they found themselves at war; plague returned to England;[1] and economic depression came in the wake of both. One of the problems to make itself felt was overpopulation, or so at least contemporaries thought. There were supposed to be too many people in late Elizabethan and early-Stuart England, and though historians have by and large concluded that the supposition was mistaken — the country could readily accommodate the extra numbers — what matters is that such views were current at the time and did have some support from what was happening.

The reign of Elizabeth had opened in a very peculiar fashion. Population had been growing in England from the middle of the fifteenth century or even earlier. When a total population runs at about two and a half million, it takes some time for increases to produce large absolute figures, but the rate of increase was considerable — probably something like 50 per cent over the whole of the sixteenth century — which means that the impact was strongly felt. That increase had been effectively uninterrupted down to the 1550s, raising notable problems of unemployment and food supply much discussed at the time. But 1557 and 1558, the last two years of Mary's reign, witnessed really major epidemics: plague struck, as did the famous sweating sickness, a virus disease which remains unidentified. (John Shrewsbury, the historian of

[1] See J. F. D. Shrewsbury, *A History of Bubonic Plague in the British Isles* (Cambridge, 1970), passim.

plagues, thought it was the same as the trench fever of the First World War, but that does not help because nobody knows what caused trench fever.) In addition, England was visited in those years by a devastating influenza epidemic. In consequence, I would suggest, the reign of Elizabeth started with the population suddenly reduced by probably something like one-fifth, which meant a marked reduction in the hitherto prominent problems of employment, food supply and poor relief. Thus one reason why that reign started in a cloud of glory lay in the deaths of the superfluous. I don't think that those who lived through the experience were particularly pleased by it, but from the point of view of the great queen, who after all had a quite superb skill at exploiting the benefits that God scattered about here and there, it was a very interesting start.

Divine favour freed the realm from plague for thirty years, so that by the 1580s the population was again outgrowing the country's resources, with the result that some began entertaining thoughts of finding overseas outlets for excess people. On the other hand, in the 1590s plague, war and economic depression combined to create the second most serious crisis in the whole of the century, so that suddenly life became very unpleasant indeed for a large number of people. Despite the peace of 1604, adverse conditions (combining alleged overpopulation and chronic economic difficulties) continued into the reign of James I. Thus the first age of colonization was one in which the conflicting pressures of general distress and apprehensions touching overpopulation created a patchy but widespread discontent. People had become unhappy about their condition in ways which previously had not been prominent, and the empty New World stood beckoning.

In addition, we can find in the years between 1590 and 1620 (or 1640) another form of discontent – political disaffection. Here I am in some difficulty. The accepted interpretation of the prehistory of the English Civil War, with its alleged constitutional conflicts between Parliament and the Crown and its emphasis on the problems associated with the supposed rise of puritanism, seems to me to be totally at variance with the facts. Until 1642 there was no struggle between Parliament and the king. All those familiar earlier occasions of conflict turn out (as the closer inspection of recent years is beginning to show) to be struggles between various court factions of politicians using Parliament for their own purposes. There is no battle over sovereignty, no rise to power of the House of Commons. I apologize for striking all these things into the discard in a few sentences, but on this occasion I have no time to elaborate: I must ask you for the present to accept this revision of hoary error on trust. Nor can I believe in puritanism as a revolutionary movement. All that had been genuinely revolutionary in puritanism had gone by 1590, and in the early seventeenth century puritanism simply describes the attitude of convincedly Calvinist members of the Church of England, content to live within it, ambitious to reform it, but in no way anxious to seek some other region in which to develop possibly disruptive forms of religion. Such discontent, in other words, as appeared in politics and religion in late-Elizabethan and Jacobean England did not make for colonization, did not make for emigration, did not advance the spread of the English people over the western world; these are facts despite the attempts of a few very small groups of true dissidents who did set up some settlements of minimal survival value. The heart of English colonization at this time lay not in New England but in Virginia, where settlement owed nothing to any flight from those political or religious discontents.

What, then, of contentment, of which there was certainly a good deal around, despite the miseries of life? One of the things that you have to grasp about the English of the sixteenth century is that they were a confident nation. It would be an error to suppose that they were uncertain of themselves. Of course, they had no reason to be overconfident in the face of God, but I think I have said enough about this. Though quite sure that life was short and miserable and dangerous, by and large they faced those dangers and those miseries often with pessimism, but rarely with despair. I will not say that despair did not exist – some aspects of Tudor religious life were markedly morbid – but I will say that a more universal reaction was to accept man's fate and to confront it firmly. This made for confidence. In fact, the reign of Elizabeth was notable for chauvinistic arrogance, a fact which by itself must cast some doubt on the notion that what happened in the colonizing activities of the sixteenth and seventeenth centuries was a flight from England, a flight from home, a flight from familiar and no longer tolerable circumstances. You will, I think, have heard of Milton's famous remark about God's Englishman – that creature to whom God always first reveals his will. You may not have heard of John Aylmer, who in 1559 wrote a treatise exalting the English, who, possessed of the best system of government, could triumph over all adversities. A marginal note says why: 'God is English.'[2]

Something like this conviction was widely held throughout the century. God was English, though – since God was not always kind – this did not mean that everything was always going well. But ill fortune did not affect the national conviction of the superiority of the English, a visible hallmark of the century. It is found, for instance, in Richard Morison's writings in the 1530s, perhaps the first sign of this kind of thing; it is fully ripe in John Foxe and in similar writers of the Elizabethan era. God has singled out the English for his own, as the true elect nation. Morison, for instance, pointed out that the English ate beef while the French lived on broth and vegetables, a plain proof of English superiority. And this was the view of a man who, I ought to emphasize, had lived many years abroad. We are not talking about ignorant men; we are talking about men who, having seen both sides, were (and I do not know that they were necessarily wrong) content to believe that the country they had been born into was especially blessed. That conviction is very marked among the Elizabethans and Jacobeans. It needs stressing because attention to the deeper and finer spirits of the age – to a Walter Ralegh or John Donne – will miss it. Deeper and finer spirits are always pessimists and rarely chauvinists. The convictions I speak of are found widely diffused in popular consciousness, among the aristocracy, the gentry and the people at large, whether travellers or stay-at-homes. They might dislike one another, trouble one another, and be discontented with one another, but relative to the foreigner, relative to the poor and depressed subjects of supposedly despotic powers, they knew themselves specially favoured. The objective truth of the situation is here irrelevant. What matters is not whether life and conditions in this demiparadise really surpassed anything to be found elsewhere, but only what it felt like to live in England in that age, on the eve of colonization. The English thought England was good and elsewhere was inferior. Thus, if they went forth from home it was not because they despaired of life there or dreaded it; with a very few exceptions, it was not even because they were driven thence. Let me repeat that emigration for causes religious was, before the age of Laud, the 1630s, a most uncommon event. The tiny sects that left England for the Netherlands and from there took ship for the New World kept moving on because they could not coexist with anyone. They could not even live together

[2] John Aylmer, *A harborowe for faithfull and trewe subjects* (1559), sig. D4v.

among themselves. As colonizers they were the freaks, not a main force. Discontent existed, but it did not drive people overseas. Contentment, more widespread and prominent, positively operated against emigration. Why then did the English begin to found more and more colonies in the century after about 1580? This sort of venturing forth to settle in unknown lands is not, after all, an unremarkable thing to do. It requires a special sort of courage, or perhaps of recklessness. You will remember the moon capsule, now to be seen in the Air and Space Museum in Washington. A truly ramshackle construction it appears to be, of no particular shape (because apparently out in space there is no need for proper shapes), all stuck over with bits of foil, like a roasting chicken whose wrapping has come unstuck. And yet men could be found to enter this peculiar container and have themselves shot to the moon. So men boarded their cockleshells to cross the wild Atlantic. The conditions are not very alike: for one thing, we knew more about the surface of the moon when we sent men there than the Elizabethans knew about the hinterland of Chesapeake Bay when they set sail for it. Our moon-men also had a good chance of remaining in touch with base, unlike those voyagers who were quite on their own once England had disappeared over the horizon. Yet the comparison may help a little to make us understand how those early settlers felt. Admittedly, they thought they knew something about the lands they meant to colonize, for over the years a good many ships had explored those regions and had returned with reports – always graphic and very often highly imaginative ones. Exploring, however, is one thing and settling another; we still have not colonized the moon. Very special inducements, stronger than mere discontent and more lasting than a passion for adventure, were surely needed before people would transfer themselves for good to barely known territories, inhabited by possibly hostile natives and equipped with a certainly hostile environment. (The prospectuses of the day tried to disguise these facts.) Of course, emigrants had before them the example of Spanish success in settling the Indies, but they also had the example of the French who had already failed to settle in Florida. A cool assessment probably would have determined that the risks clearly outweighed the advantages. I therefore think it matters greatly that before ever the Elizabethans thought of America they had already had experience of colonization. They had been trying their hand in Ireland.

Ireland was not an unknown country, and it was not very far away. Perhaps symbolically, one of the earliest English attempts to take part in the great voyaging movement, John Rastell's expedition of 1517, ended up at Waterford and never got further. Really it was Ireland that the English were about to colonize, not the North American continent. So what drove them to settle colonies in Ireland – those plantations of Leix and Offaly in the reign of Queen Mary, of the Desmond lands in Munster in the reign of Queen Elizabeth, of Ulster in the reign of King James? Did those moves represent a great urge to expand, an intention to enlarge the realm of English power and to conquer the world for one small nation? Or were they produced by discontent and persecution at home? Not either of these, I fear: they demonstrated a drive for land and for fortune. What stirred people into these extraordinary activities were the common and acceptable human emotions of greed and the search for greater wealth. Ireland, I may say, as regularly disappointed such hopes as did later colonies.

Insofar as a desire to better oneself represents dissatisfaction with one's present lot, we might conclude that discontent rather than contentment lay behind the colonizing activity. But the term is much too strong and just possibly too noble. The colonists were attracted – deliberately so, in the advertising of the organizers – by promises of riches, not by visions of liberty. And here the expansion of population does play its part, even if contemporaries overestimated its effect, because it reduced a man's chances to improve his lot at home.

Let us remember one essential characteristic in the structure of this society. Where did its economic centre of gravity lie? It was a landed society, a society which regarded only land and landed wealth as ultimately acceptable in creating status. True, there was wealth of other kinds. Mercantile and banking fortunes are found in Elizabethan England. Lawyers' incomes – a fact familiar to twentieth-century America – were considerable. There were – another familiar fact – far too many lawyers, busy creating a great deal of law upon which they could live. Money was being made and wealth created in other ways than by landed possessions, but the only form of wealth which could gain you social recognition was land, possession of land. However, the land law of England operated on the principle of primogeniture. By and large, unless you were the eldest son of a landowner, you inherited little or nothing in the way of that status-breeding wealth. You had to seek your own; you had to find land elsewhere. It so happened that down to the 1560s there was an available resource of landed property in England. The confiscation of Church lands, from the dissolution of the monasteries onward, and their redistribution because of the Crown's need for ready cash had created a very active land market in which many younger sons, cadet branches of gentle and aristocratic families who would normally have been driven out of landed ownership, found it possible to reestablish themselves in that society into which they had been born and whose acceptance they sought. But in the 1560s that supply was cut off as the Crown resolved to stop selling. Free gifts in particular ceased totally. It is true that Crown lands, though no longer sold, were readily being leased for terms of years, but that (while helping the queen's coffers) could not create the new estates which landless men wanted. You could not found status upon leaseholds, though you could add to your wealth by acquiring them; you needed freehold property before you could gain the position of a landed gentleman, or even of a man of weight in your county. Only freehold, for instance, qualified you for the parliamentary franchise.

Thus, from about the 1560s onward, this preferred way of improving yourself was no longer open at home, but there were other lands to which the English Crown extended its sway and where so far the possibilities of acquiring real property had not been exhausted. Ireland here quite evidently formed an experimental ground. Compared with the North American continent, Ireland was not empty, though it was rendered a good deal more empty than it should have been by internal strife and the warfare involved in the English reconquest of the semi-independent Irish. Ireland also posed legal problems because it was not 'new land', but the lawyers soon developed some ingenious ways of eradicating the native arrangements and acclimatizing landholding in Ireland to English laws and social requirements. These were valuable experiments which could readily be extended into emptier and more extensive lands. In many ways, the expansion overseas, the colonizing activity of this society, can really best be understood by studying what was going on in Ireland from the 1570s to the 1600s. The prehistory of exploration, and of those intrepid voyagers seeking trade or piracy, is by comparison almost irrelevant, except inasmuch as it familiarized people with the notion of oceans and America. Settlement is something quite different; it is not expatriation but an extension of the *patria*, of that region in which the normal existence of the English landed gentleman and the yeoman farmer could be satisfactorily recreated. Here Ireland led the way and set the example; Virginia (in particular) and Maryland soon followed. What confronts us here is not a truly popular movement, a great rush of individuals all somehow taking off for the New World and settling down there; rather we are dealing with organized, controlled and licensed transfers of the English existence to the American continent. When the organizing agents settled the North American continent, they were not cutting loose or turning their backs on Europe; they were simply finding new areas for the exercise of their entrepreneurial qualities of which they had given sufficient evidence in England and Ireland for years before that. The colonizing activity of the English in the early seventeenth century resulted predominantly from an expansion of that sort of commercial (in this case, land-buying) enterprise for which the northern part of the North American seaboard has become more famous than the southern, but it started in the south. I may add that even those puritan dissidents who settled Massachusetts and Rhode Island remained firmly in touch with the mother country. Colonization never meant separation, and thus it really testified to an energetic contentment with things English rather than to discontent.

The dominant theme of English colonization in the seventeenth century was that it was English, by licence, enterprise and continued connection, and not American, by conquest and the cutting of ties. If I am right about this, a rather important consequence follows. This conclusion must cast doubt on the conventional view that the ultimate disruption of this first British empire in the War of Independence and the Revolution of 1776 sprang as a natural outcome from the fact that the colonists were essentially freedom-seeking separatists, a bunch of especially inspired (and justly discontented) idealists who wished to be free of the ancient system and its constraints. Those who have seen it that way have, I think, committed the fundamental error of casting back later history upon the earlier. This history of the American Revolution continues to be written (on both sides of the Atlantic) by those who are on its side, as indeed the history of the English Civil War continues to be written by those who are very glad it happened. The historians of the English Civil War forget how very nearly there never was a war. Similarly, historians of the American Revolution tend to forget how large the number of loyalists was who, had they won as they so very nearly did, would certainly have put the black spot on all those rebels who have ever since been sainted founding fathers.

That entrenched explanation of 1776 therefore owes a good deal to a certain notion about the years between 1580 and 1640 or 1650: that colonies were founded by dissent and discontent. Actually, they were founded by enterprise directed from above; by good and solid greed, and by the quite normal expansion of generally accepted attitudes and purposes prevalent in the governing order in the realm of England. That period of activity witnessed an expansion of the English Crown, not a separation from it. If later there came, as indeed there did come, a breakdown in relationships, we must not seek its cause in their origins. We must remember that throughout the seventeenth and early eighteenth centuries contact between mother country and colonists was current, constant and straightforward. There was no question of disruption, none of rebellion. Those colonists, leaders or followers, wanted one main thing from their enterprise: to better themselves by adding to the wealth they had and the wealth they could create for others. Such constraints as they escaped from were the mere accidents of home – shortage of land, too many people, economic distress, some details of the law – and not the essence of England, with which they were well content and which they endeavoured to recreate across the ocean. They were seventeenth-century Englishmen, most of whom went to the colonies because a sense of adventure, a willingness to take risks, and hopes of profit made them ready material for those enterprising companies and individuals who were organizing the spread of English settlement throughout the western continent.

45

THOMAS MORE

I. THE REAL THOMAS MORE?*

How well do we really know Thomas More? Directed to one of the most familiar figures of the sixteenth century, the question must appear absurd. Even without the aid of stage and screen, surely everyone has a clear idea of England's leading humanist, great wit, friend of Erasmus and other continental humanists, author of *Utopia*, family man, man of convictions, ultimately martyr. The familiar Holbein portrait seems to sum it all up, as does at greater length the much admired biography of R. W. Chambers. Chambers, in fact, completed the picture when, to his own satisfaction and that of others, he disposed of 'inconsistencies' discerned by earlier observers between the cheerful reformer and 'liberal' of 1516 on the one hand, and the fierce opponent of Lutheran reform and savage polemicist of 1528–33 on the other. No man's personality in that age, not even King Henry's, seems more fully explored and more generally agreed than More's.

If nevertheless I cannot accept that we yet can be sure of knowing Thomas More it is in part because of the way in which his portrait has been created. All modern assessments start axiomatically from an image constructed out of two sorts of evidence and brought to perfection in those famous last scenes – imprisonment, trial and death. More's life has in effect become a preliminary to his end and is written with that end in view. The evidence mentioned consists of Roper's *Life* and the descriptions left by More's friends, good sources indeed but like even the best sources in need of critical inspection. Roper's book – which permeates all the early lives and indeed still dominates in tone and structure even Chambers's book – was written with two motives in mind: filial affection, and a desire to prove his great father-in-law

* [*Reformation Principle and Practice: Essays in Honour of A. G. Dickens*, ed. P. N. Brooks (1980), 23–31; reprinted in *Psychological Medicine*, 10 (1980), 611–17.]

worthy of canonization. The words of Erasmus or Vives, all of them incidentally about the early More, the More of the Erasmian heyday, tell us why they were More's good friends and assuredly present a truth about the man, but again they do not form dispassionate or rounded appraisals. And even when the other massive evidence is employed – the evidence especially of More's own writings and deeds – it is always, no doubt unconsciously, adjusted to the figure first created out of Roper and those letters. Chambers in particular, while seeming to weigh judiciously the difficulties posed by some of More's books, really works hard at bringing them within the limits defined by the stereotype of the great and good Sir Thomas. Of course, I acknowledge that More so appeared to many who knew him, though even among his acquaintance other opinions could at times be found, and I know that the traditional More existed; but is he the whole, the real More?

My difficulty in accepting that he might be can be stated simply. I do not find More inconsistent, or hard to understand on given occasions, or improbably described by those who knew him. I find him consistently ambiguous: at all sorts of points, his mind, his views, his actions, his person seem to me to tend in more than one direction, withdrawing from observation into consecutive layers of indeterminacy. Like any adept user of the ironical front, he hides his self behind vaguely transparent curtains; as the light flickers over him, so his face changes, subtly and strangely. His wit, which so enchanted his friends, nearly always had a sharp edge to it: he often, and knowingly, wounded his targets. We are told that his temper was exceptionally equable and his manner ever courteous; yet through nearly all his life he displayed restlessly combative moods and in his controversies lost his temper, dealing ruthless and often unfair blows. His famous merry tales pose some manifest psychological problems. Is it not strange that when this man, who created such a happy family life, wished to amuse he constantly resorted to strikingly anti-feminist tales? I can recall no single story that shows a woman in a favourable light; that world of parables is peopled by shrews and much-oppressed males – almost the world of James Thurber's cartoons, and certainly the world of one well-estab-lished medieval tradition, but also a world presented by More with manifest enjoyment. His attitude to his second wife, Dame Alice, leaves me bewildered. He is supposed to have treated her with affection; yet the conviction that she was foolish and tiresome rests in great part on the sly allusions to female deficiencies scattered through his works which, as family tradition knew, were directed at her. More in office – flexible, diplomatic, at times accommodating – differs visibly from More the scholar and More at home. Some of his public attitudes can be called lawyer-like, in the pejorative sense of that term. The persecutor of heretics cannot really be buried in the sophistical arguments deployed by Chambers: he did in practice deny those forms of toleration which he had incorporated in *Utopia*. His part in the parliamentary opposition to Henry VIII's proceedings and his contacts with the Imperial ambassador's intrigues were not straightforward; his refusal to accept a friendly letter from Charles V, on the grounds that without it he could be of better use to their common cause, must be called ambiguous. And what did he really think of the papacy? He never properly explained his position, and the hints tend more than one way; I can well understand why Rome hesitated for four hundred years before bestowing the saint's halo.

I once spent half an hour before that splendid fireplace in the Frick Museum in New York above which Thomas Cromwell and Thomas More for ever stare past one another, with St Jerome in the middle keeping the peace. In the end I thought that I understood the plain, solid, straightforward man on the right, but the other man, with that subtle Machiavellian smile, whose looks and look kept altering before one's eyes, left a sense of unplumbable ambiguity. And I then did not even know what an X-ray investigation has since discovered: that the famous portrait is painted over an earlier attempt which reveals a much less refined, less humanist, Thomas More. Why, even the man's year of birth is uncertain because his father in recording it contrived to puzzle posterity: the year date first put down was rendered dubious by the addition of a weekday which does not fit the year. Ambiguity, wherever one touches him, in matters weighty and indifferent.

In one sense, of course, the ambiguity of Thomas More does not matter; his ability to present a kaleidoscope of aspects even helps to make him more interesting and attractive, especially as those variations quite clearly inhere in the man and are not merely reflections of the observer. They are of his essence and of his choosing. Yet anyone concerned to understand the early sixteenth century, the age of the Reformation, and the character of a powerful intellectual movement with far-reaching influences upon later generations, needs to come to terms with Thomas More. Once one ceases to be satisfied with the plaster saint created by the worshippers, one is cast loose upon an uncharted ocean where there lurk too many rocks and whirlpools to permit complacency. If More was not simply the finest, kindest, wisest of men foully done to death by wicked enemies who could not bear his saintliness, many things about that age need reconsidering. If he was not really that steadfast figure of tradition, we would want to know what exactly he died for – though that is a question I shall not pursue here. His ambiguity, if he was ambiguous, also makes his own actions harder to understand: why, for instance, did this man, who all his life had avoided the simplicities of a total and unmistakable public commitment, suddenly harden his conscience on an issue which on the face of it was itself ambiguous enough? I feel convinced that we need to understand Thomas More, or at least to make every effort to do so, even though in the end he may well escape us. Especially for someone who sees him so characterized by ambiguity as I do, the ambition to penetrate to his inner core may well be foolish, but it is worth the attempt. Where is the real Thomas More?

The best way to go about this search would seem to lie in ignoring what others said about him and in trying to grasp More's relation to mankind from what he himself said to those among whom he lived, from his books. I propose to look at three of his works which at first sight seem to have little enough in common, in order to see whether they can nonetheless reveal that common element which must be there if there is a real Thomas More to be fetched forth from the veils in which he hid himself. *Utopia*, not without reason always his most famous work, appears as an exciting intellectual exercise, a critique of the world of his day, a dream of better things, lively and sunny in manner, the product of true wit. *The Confutation of Tyndale's Answer*, endless, nearly always tedious, passionate, devoid of humour and markedly obsessive, was, of course, written in very different circumstances and for a very different purpose, but it was still written by the same man. *The Dialogue of Comfort*, too, in which passion is left behind and serenity deals sovereignly with some of the most frightful of human problems, breathes an air which is quite different again – but air from the same pair of lungs. Who is this Thomas More who held three such diverse manifestoes together in one single mind, however capacious?

The essence of *Utopia* is nowadays usually sought in More's condemnatory analysis of the political and social structure which he wished to reform, but that seems to me the wrong approach. Surely the ideal commonwealth of his devising can tell us more about him. His description is detailed enough to give us a very vivid sense of life in the island of Nowhere – ordered and orderly, hierarchically structured through a system of interlocked authorities, permanent and apparently not only incapable of change but not interested in any. Life in *Utopia* was comfortable and worthy enough, so long as no one resented its lack of diversity, lack of colour, indeed lack of anything dynamic. This is, as no one has ever doubted, a very restrictive commonwealth, subduing the individual to the common purpose and setting each man's life in predetermined, unalterable grooves. Whether More really thought such a commonwealth to be feasible, or whether he was perhaps hinting that the only good polity was also one unattainable on earth, is not the issue here, though the likelihood that the second alternative more correctly defines his intent bears on the object of our search. The fundamental question is this: why did More think it necessary to erect so rigid and oppressive a system for the sake of preserving his supreme good – peace and justice? And the answer lies in his identification of the wrong at the heart of all existing human communities. This wrong is the nature of man, fallen man, whom he regarded as incurably tainted with the sin of covetousness. Greed, he argued, underlay everything that troubled mankind. Wealth, and the search for it, ruined the human existence and all possibility of human contentment; the only cure that could work must remove all opportunity of acquiring wealth by prohibiting all private property and allowing to each man his sufficient subsistence at the hands of an all-wise, and despotic, ruling order. To judge from *Utopia*, that 'sunny' book written by a man in the fullness of his powers and before his world collapsed in a welter of contending ideologies, More from the first held a deeply pessimistic view of mankind whose natural instincts were, he maintained, totally selfish, anarchic and sinful.

By the time he came to do battle with Tyndale he had, of course, reason to think that the sinfulness of man had found a new and vastly more dangerous area of operations. The *Confutation* is really a distressing book to read – an interminable, high-pitched scream of rage and disgust which at times borders on hysteria. Even allowing for the conventions of sixteenth-century polemics, it is hard to feel that More had retained any sort of balance when confronted with the consequences of Luther's rebellion. Even among the opponents of Lutheran heresy More stands out for the violence of his explosion, as Erasmus was to note in his last remarks on his old friend, by then dead. The helpless fury of the

Confutation is not convention; it is the very personal reaction of a very specific man. Yet this is the man who had always impressed his circle by the evenness of his temper, the man of whom William Roper alleged that in fourteen years of close acquaintance he had never known him to be in a fume.

Why did More lose all sense of proportion when faced with the new heresies, to the point of making his book vastly less effective than it might have been? The very passion of his involvement diminished the success of his assault. Surely we are once again in the presence of More's fundamental conviction about human nature. If man was by his nature so incapable of living the good life, it followed that only the outward restraints imposed by organized and institutional structures saved his world from falling into chaos; only obedience to the order decreed by God preserved the chance of salvation. If the Utopians, with all their advantages, could maintain their orderly commonwealth only by submitting to exceptional restraints, how much more necessary was it for real people, ever driven on by the pressures of sinful desires, to adhere to the established order? Because he thought that he understood the dark heart of man, More, it would seem, was exceptionally conscious of the thinness of the crust upon which civilization rests, a conclusion which our age has no cause to doubt. In consequence he held that in attacking the Church the Lutheran heretics had pierced that crust. There is no need to suppose that he wished to withdraw any of the criticisms of the Church that he had so freely uttered in earlier days; even when, in the *Dialogue of Comfort*, he regretted that he and Erasmus had in their time published critical views of what now stood in mortal danger, he wished only that they had not made those views public, not that they had never held them. More's defence of the Church arose not from a change of mind but from the same ultimate convictions which had earlier led him to attack it. It, too, was a human institution and therefore inexorably tainted with original sin, but it was also the instrument chosen by God to restrain and guide men towards their only hope, salvation through faith in Christ. Just because the protestants made that hope the centre of their message, while destroying and denouncing the chosen instrument, More had to defend the Church with such immoderate commitment, such furious rage.

Thus whether he was planning the good commonwealth of humanist devising, or fighting off the threat to the divine order on earth in his war with the Lutherans, More rested all his argument on an inexorably pessimistic view of fallen man. In the extent of his Augustinianism he seems to me to have had only one equal among the major figures of the day – Martin Luther himself – however different the conclusions were that these two prophets drew from their identical premise. More (unlike Luther) was evidently of an essentially conservative temperament, concerned to preserve existing institutions because – man being what he is – all change is at the very least risky, while such revolutionary change as he discerned in the heretics' demand must certainly lead to the dissolution of all good order. Man simply could not be trusted to command his own fate, and a beneficent deity had recognized this fact when he provided institutional means for channelling the anarchic instinct into the restraints of enforced obedience. And those institutional instruments must therefore be allowed to preserve themselves at all costs, which meant enforcing the law with prison and the stake. The alternative was certain chaos here and now, and all hope gone for salvation in the hereafter. Sitting as he was on an eggshell beneath which raged the fires of hell, man could be permitted to dream and talk about how nice it would be to paint that shell in splendid colours, so long as he kept his feet still. But when he started dancing upon his fragile earthly habitation he must at once be stopped by the most drastic means available. The danger was simply too overwhelming to be tolerated.

If it is objected that the More I am describing – the deep pessimist about man and his nature – cannot be reconciled with the More we have heard so much about (a man full of human kindness and friendship), I reply that on the contrary this supposed contradiction supports my interpretation. Anyone so deeply conscious of the unhappy state of mankind in the mass is always likely to do what he can for particular specimens of it. Believing that man has cast away grace does not necessarily make the believer into a misanthrope; and in his courteous and considerate behaviour towards all and sundry More was only testifying to the compassion of his conservative instincts. Genuine conservatives despair of humanity but cherish individuals, even as true radicals, believing in man's capacity to better himself unaided, love mankind and express that love in hatred of particular individuals. To avoid any rash inferences touching the author of these remarks, I had better add that most of us oscillate between those extremes most of the time. More was more consistent.

The *Dialogue of Comfort* does not breathe quite so pervasive an air of despair about the human condition, for the interesting reason (in part at least) that it confronted genuine and real tribulations instead of the intellectual challenge of *Utopia* or the wild apprehensions of the *Confutation*. This is not the place to discuss it at length, though it matters that its chief purpose was not, I should assert, to discover a way in which man can overcome the miseries of his life, but rather to offer instructed guidance to this end. More was not seeking comfort but giving it, having himself long since found it in his meditations on the Passion. In consequence, the keynote of the work is a kind of hortatory and pedagogic serenity – that address to the individual human being who must be cherished, rather than to the whole of fallen mankind who must be despaired of, which was so noticeably absent from the other two works considered. However, the *Dialogue* also provides one specific clue helpful in the present search. Concerned with imminent death, More needs to attend to the problem of hell and does so several times, in the process making his views very plain. Hell to him was a physical place – 'the very pit and dungeon of the devil of hell' sited at 'the centre of the earth' – where the souls of sinners suffered 'torment world without end'. Not for More those modern evasions. Hell was to him not other people, or eternal ice, or eternal loneliness, or a state of mind, or any of the devices for expressing merely human despair. It was yet another of the creator's chosen instruments for the control of his creation, with a real location, where real devils inflicted real pain on real souls. Hell was there to take care of the consequences of the Fall for those who refused to admit those consequences and thus despised the means of redemption. Even more, perhaps, than his vision of the blessed in heaven, More's matter-of-fact description of hell defines him as a man of his day: the world he saw here and beyond was the medieval world in every physical detail, ascribed to the purposeful creation of God.

Of course, there was nothing original in More's 'medieval' world-view, in his pessimism about mankind. Conventional Christianity in his day (and after) entirely agreed with it, indeed demanded it. The last thing More would wish to display was originality in religion. Only those who have tried to make him an improbable saint all his life, or (perhaps worse) some sort of a star in the liberal firmament (between, as it were, Socrates and John Stuart Mill), can be put out by discovering that More believed in hell and damnation. Nevertheless, a question arises. More's faith in the conventional doctrine of his day does seem to have been particularly complete and passionate, much more so than was found in the men with whom he shared his life, his thought and his death. I do not know that Erasmus spoke of hell in More's terms, any more than that he opposed the manifestations of covetous sin with More's horrified intensity. There is here a strong hint that More's acceptance of conventional teaching on the Fall was exceptionally personal. He does seem to have been exceptionally conscious of sin, with the result that not humanism but anti-humanism – the relentlessly unoptimistic conception of human nature – stood at the heart of all his serious writing. Such a powerful consciousness of sin argues a personal experience of it: envisaging sin in a very special, very personal way, More talks like a man who has found and fought sin in himself.

At this point we begin to tread on dangerous ground. Entering into a dead man's mind and private experiences (especially one so concerned to hide himself) is at best a speculative enterprise, and the line I shall take will in addition cause displeasure. However, I mean to do no more than follow the signposts which More himself has left behind. Let me list some of them. For four years in his youth More tried to find out whether he had a vocation for the monastic life, and he did so in the strictest order of the day, the Charterhouse. Even after he decided that he could not abandon the world, he wore a hairshirt. There are strong echoes of the monastic principle in the organization of Utopia, though the Utopians knew nothing of that heart of the monastic existence, the vow of chastity. In fact, they are unmistakably concerned with sex and procreation, their attitudes including both the rule that engaged couples shall see each other naked before they have taken the irrevocable decision to marry, and an off-hand likening of the carnal act to an easing of an itch, or of the bowels – both common sense and a mild distaste. In his private existence, too, More notoriously worked hard at combining some of the monastic practices with a transformation of the sexual instinct into a family life pleasing to God. At the same time his merry tales evince a notable strain of distrust of women, at times rising to positive dislike. One main thread in the *Confutation* is provided by Luther's special vileness in breaking his vow of chastity, a theme that is treated with obsessional frequency, nor is Luther the only heretic whose special heinousness lies in this particular sin. In the *Dialogue of Comfort*, so generally compassionate, the kindness of God is illustrated with a very odd parable about a beautiful young woman who is saved from adultery by a heaven-sent fever which destroys her beauty – 'beautifieth her fair fell with the colour of the kite's claw' – and so entirely destroys her lust that the close presence of her lover would make her vomit at the very thought of desire. It is a strangely disgusted, and rather disgusting, passage; and it is really not possible to deny that More, attentive to humanity, was more frequently than most preoccupied with the problems of sexuality, with what he would have called 'the flesh'.

Such a preoccupation was bound to come to one so deeply concerned about the human condition, about the future of mankind, the injunctions of religion and the life eternal, but once again one feels that in More the preoccupation was sharpened by personal experience. His youthful attraction to the life religious, and the manner in which echoes of that life resound throughout his later years, argue powerfully that here lay his true ambition. In that case he was bound to regard celibacy as the only condition really acceptable to God, and of celibacy he had proved incapable. More, after all, throughout his life proved himself to be a passionate man – passionate in his beliefs, passionate in his friendships, passionate in his reactions to insults and contumely, passionate in his attacks upon heresy. It would have been strange if he had not also known the passions of the flesh: and what were hairshirts for except for the mortifying of it? But his inmost convictions about the true claims of God and religion made his inability to renounce the world and live celibate into a sin, into his personal experience of the Fall of man. Being a man of sense and wisdom, he had for all practical purposes come to terms with his failure in the face of the monastic challenge: the least he could do, and the most, if he could not live in a cloistered chastity, was to beautify the consequences of his carnal nature by building a family life which transcended the original impulse of mere desire, and for the rest to come as close as possible in life and in thought to his monastic ideal. But none of these compensations can have altered a conviction that he had failed to live up to what he (that very medieval man) regarded as God's ultimate demand on man, and had thus found in himself a plain case of original sin. What indeed was the Fall all about, and what had been the fruit of the tree of knowledge? He knew about the Fall with that special intensity that came from experience and self-knowledge. He must have held that he had seen the right way and had proved incapable of it: for a man of his integrity and conscience, that knowledge could never cease to torment. If this passionate man was really never seen 'in a fume', his powers of self-control were indeed formidable: and all his life, especially his last three years, show how formidable they were. But it is to do him almost an injustice to suppose him always serene and equable, effortlessly kind and considerate, a man of ever-undisturbed balance. Such qualities had to be worked for, and outbursts had to be guarded against. The guard did slip at times – in the argument with Germain de Brie, in his often cutting remarks at the expense of inferior beings, most of all in the reckless and often untruthful vituperation of his polemics. More, I suggest, knew demons – demons whom he could subdue and tame but never exorcise. Grounds enough for withdrawing into privacy and ambiguity.

More, then, understood the problems of man's unregenerate nature because he shared them, and his deep consciousness of the implications at times overrode his sympathy. So long as he lived an active and public life he remained determined to apply coercion and judgment to dangerous sinners rather than compassion and comprehension. But we can now understand why he appeared to change so notably after he resigned the chancellorship, and especially after he began his imprisonment. The Thomas More of the 'Tower works', and of those last letters to Margaret Roper is, on the face of it, a very different person from the persecutor of protestants, and the hammer of poor Christopher St German – even from the More who translated Lucian with Erasmus and dreamed up the island of Nowhere. No more aggression or combativeness; no more sarcasm, no more savagery; even the censoriousness of the loving father, who was also a judge, had gone. But he was, of course, not really a different man. He had displayed those qualities of calm good sense and gentle kindness often enough throughout his life, as he was to display them so remarkably at the end. Before this, however, they had cost him self-control and discipline; now, they came easily. He had found peace; the demons were gone at last. In the most splendid passage of the *Dialogue of Comfort*, perhaps the most splendid passage he ever wrote, More asked why men should so much dread imprisonment and the prospect of death. The life to which man's disobedience to God had condemned him was itself a prison, with death at the end its only certainty. What could others do to a man to aggravate that inescapable fate? 'There is no more difference between your grace and me but that I shall die today and you tomorrow.' He spoke these words to Norfolk on the eve of his imprisonment, and before the end of 1534, he knew that he meant them exactly. The Tower liberated him, because here, at last, he had reached his only possible cloister, out of the world. What others thought of as a good man's prison was to him his monk's cell. He had found the tonsure in the Tower.

II*

Thomas More – berühmter Humanist, Kanzler von England und Opfer der Reformation – wurde am 6. Februar 1478 in London geboren. Sein Vater John war Jurist; im Laufe der Zeit brachte er es zu Richterstellungen an den zentralen königlichen Gerichtshöfen. Thomas erhielt eine gute Erziehung an einer Londoner Lateinschule und als Page im Haushalt des Kardinal Erzbischofs John Morton. Mit 14 Jahren ging er auf die Universität Oxford, wo er jedoch weniger als zwei Jahre verbrachte. Unter dem Einfluß seines Vaters verlegte er sein Studium an die sogenannte Rechtsuniversität in London, die Inns of Court. Er studierte das englische Gemeinrecht als Mitglied von Lincoln's Inn, wo ihm Familienbeziehungen zu Hilfe kamen, und erhielt um 1500 den Rang eines Rechtsanwalts (barrister). Ehe er aber die vom Vater vorgeschriebene Karriere anfangen konnte, geriet er in eine Gewissenskrise; er dachte daran, in ein Kloster einzutreten. Vier Jahre lang lebte er zeitweise als eine Art Laienbruder in der Londoner Kartause, um festzustellen, ob er eine Berufung habe und ihrer würdig sei. Am Ende siegte die Welt. 1504 verheiratete er sich mit Jane Colt, der Tochter eines kleinen Landedelmannes, und zeugte rasch hintereinander vier Kinder. Als seine Frau 1511 starb, nahm er sofort eine Nachfolgerin ins Haus: angeblich, weil die Kinder eine Mutter brauchten. Seine zweite Frau war Alice Myddleton, eine Londoner Witwe und eine gute Hausfrau, die aber anscheinend dem Gatten geistig nicht gewachsen war und auch seine Freunde nicht besonders schätzte.

Da das Klosterleben sich als unerreichbar erwiesen hatte, verfolgte More nun eine weltliche Karriere. 1509 wurde er Unter-Sheriff von London. In dieser kleineren, aber nicht unwichtigen Richterstelle erwarb er sich schnell den Ruf eines billigen und weisen Mannes. Die Verbindungen mit der Kaufmannswelt der Hauptstadt führten dazu, daß er die Aufmerksamkeit einer höheren Instanz auf sich zog. Zwischen 1515 und 1518 nahm More an drei königlichen Gesandtschaften teil, die mit den Niederlanden und der Hanse Handelsverträge abzuschließen versuchten. Er war dabei so erfolgreich, daß König Heinrich VIII. ihm alsbald den Eintritt in den königlichen Rat

* [*Gestalten der Kirchengeschichte, Reformation I*, ed. M. Greschat (Stuttgart, 1981), 89–103; included here because it elaborates and complements the argument of the previous piece.]

aufdrängte, und im Sommer 1517 nahm er, ein wenig zögernd, an. More hatte genug Erfahrung zu wissen, daß er damit die Freiheit einbüßen mußte, seinen eigenen literarischen und philosophischen Interessen nachzugehen, doch empfand er es als Pflicht, der Allgemeinheit zu dienen. Trotz der Gunst des Königs stieg er nur langsam auf: 1521 erhielt er den wohlbezahlten Posten des Unterschatzmeisters im königlichen Schatzamt, 1526 wurde er Kanzler des Herzogtums Lancaster – ein Richterposten in der königlichen Verwaltung – und 1529, nach dem Sturze des allmächtigen Kardinals Thomas Wolsey, ernannte Heinrich ihn zum Lordkanzler. Im Parlament von 1523 diente er auch als Sprecher des Unterhauses, was zu der Zeit eine offizielle Stellung war. Während der zwanziger Jahre war More ständig im königlichen Dienst tätig, vor allem als inoffizieller Sekretär des Königs, der ihn wegen seiner Klugheit, seiner Besonnenheit und seines Witzes bewunderte. Viel hatte er auch mit diplomatischen Verhandlungen zu tun, bei denen seine Sprachkenntnisse und sein europäisches Renommee nützlich waren. Dennoch scheint es ihm in den Jahren der Vormacht Wolseys nicht gelungen zu sein, erheblichen Einfluß auf die Politik auszuüben. Im Lande wurde seiner Meinung nach nicht genug getan, um die religiöse Einheit aufrechtzuerhalten, und die Außenpolitik brachte zu oft Krieg statt Frieden. Seine geringe Meinung von Wolsey brachte More auch 1529 bei seiner Antrittsrede im Parlament zum Ausdruck. Man sollte, so erklärte er, nunmehr die richtigen Maßnahmen treffen, obwohl er bei dieser Gelegenheit nicht klarmachte, was er damit meinte. Immerhin stand er nun an der Spitze der Regierung – eine eindrucksvolle Krönung seiner Karriere.

Seinen Weltruf jedoch verdankte er dieser Karriere nicht. Die Grundlage seines Ruhms als eines der bekanntesten Denker und Schriftsteller der Zeit war bereits vor seinem Eintritt in den öffentlichen Dienst gelegt worden. 1499 hatte More die Bekanntschaft des Desiderius Erasmus gemacht, und bald entwickelte sich zwischen den beiden eine wirklich enge Freundschaft. Mit Erasmus teilte der amüsante und scharfsinnige Engländer die Sehnsucht nach der Wiederherstellung der guten Bildung und der Erneuerung von Kirche und Staat, wobei für More der letztere, praktische Zweck doch wohl die größere Rolle gespielt hat. Er machte sich Mühe, ein echter Gelehrter zu werden, und lernte z. B. die griechische Sprache im Privatstudium. Sein tiefes Interesse an der Philosophie der italienischen Renaissance bewies er, als er die Biographie des Giovanni Pico della Mirandola ins Englische übersetzte. Andererseits führte das griechische Studium zur Zusammenarbeit mit Erasmus an der Übersetzung von Lukians Gesprächen ins Lateinische. Getreu der Mode dieser humanistischen Sucher nach der wahren Antike war More auch Dichter: d. h. er verfaßte nach den besten Mustern satirische und panegyrische Verse, die wohl ein gewisses Geschick beweisen, im allgemeinen jedoch keinen besonderen Wert haben. Bei alledem herrschte eine gewisse Tändelei – ein Spielen mit Ideen und auch mit den technischen Sprachproblemen. More besaß Witz und Humor, doch seine Gedanken waren meist recht konventionell. Sein gutes Latein war kompliziert und verglichen mit dem des Erasmus fast schwerfällig. Ein spezielles und originelles Interesse hatte More am Drama: er schrieb kleine Bühnenspiele und scheint auch selber im Privatkreis als Schauspieler aufgetreten zu sein.

Diese Neigung zum Dramatischen trat ebenfalls in zwei viel wichtigeren Werken seiner Jugend hervor. 1513 fing More eine historische Arbeit über die Usurpation König Richards III. an, aber obwohl er gleichzeitig eine englische und eine lateinische Fassung schrieb, vollendete er das Werk nie. Das ist an sich bedauerlich, denn was er hinterlassen hat, deutet an, daß er eine ganz neuartige Mischung von Historie und dramatischem Roman hätte schaffen können. Selbst unvollendet übte dieser Torso großen Einfluß aus. Der Historiker Edward Hall druckte die englische Fassung in seinem Buch über 'Die Vereinigung der Häuser Lancaster und York' (1548) ab und durch ihn erfuhr Shakespeare von dem König, der 'ein entschlossener Schurke' bleiben wollte – eine Figur, die zwar Mores Darstellung entspricht, jedoch nicht der geschichtlichen Wahrheit. Dieselben dramatischen Gaben kamen auch Mores bekanntestem Werk zugute, das ihn in ganz Europa berühmt machte und auf dem auch heute noch sein allgemeiner Ruhm in erster Linie beruht. Im Jahre 1516 erschien in Löwen, angeblich wider seinen Willen, Mores lateinisches Buch Utopia – die Darstellung eines idealen Staates. Auf der Insel 'Nirgendwo' war alles richtig, wenn auch streng geregelt, so daß die Fehler und Unzulänglichkeiten der wirklichen Welt vermieden werden konnten. Insbesondere gehörte dort aller Besitz der ganzen Gemeinschaft, die dafür sorgte, daß jedermann das ihm Notwendige zugewiesen bekam. Die Kritik an dem zeitgenössischen England und Europa, die man im ersten Band vorfindet, ist zum Teil recht scharfsinnig, zum Teil auch konventionell, stets jedoch in denkwürdiger Weise ausgedrückt. Sie umschließt fast alle Beschwerden über die Sünden der Menschheit, die in Mores Kreisen

(d. h. bei den sogenannten christlichen Humanisten) im Umlauf waren, was das Buch fast zum Manifest einer Gruppe machte.

Der Idealstaat bereitete More viel Vergnügen. Er erfand für ihn die Geographie, die Geschichte, das Gesetzbuch, sogar die Sprache. Die Nachwelt hat er allerdings in manche Schwierigkeiten versetzt. Mores Kunstgriff war es nämlich, die Beschreibung im Rahmen einer Diskussion darzustellen, in der ein allwissender Weltreisender namens Raphael Hythlodaeus unter anderem über die neuentdeckte Insel berichtete, auf der das Dasein so erfolgreich reguliert sei. Da auch überall Mores Neigung zur Ironie durchklingt, kann man nie sicher sein, wie weit die Beschreibung die Ansichten des Verfassers wiedergibt. Bejahte er zum Beispiel die Idee des Gemeinbesitzes oder kritisierte er sie? Die Debatte über die Utopia wird wohl nie zu Ende gehen. Man hat More verschiedentlich als Vorkämpfer eines bereits veralteten Christentums und des marxistischen Kommunismus der Zukunft ausgelegt. Da auf der Insel Glaubensverschiedenheiten nicht zur Verfolgung führten, sehen manche in ihm einen Freund der toleranten Gewissensfreiheit; andere betonen die sehr autoritären Züge eines Systems, in dem jedem Menschen seine Rolle zugeteilt und der Fortschritt unbekannt ist. War das ganze Werk ein Witz oder meinte es der Autor ernst? Er selber hat uns darüber keine Auskunft hinterlassen. Es läßt sich annehmen, daß More diese Meinungsverschiedenheiten nur Freude bereitet hätten, denn vor die Öffentlichkeit trat er nie unverschleiert. M. E. hat er es ernst gemeint und das utopische System für das beste gehalten. Es sei betont, daß er zu jener Zeit vornehmlich unter zwei Einflüssen stand. Platon und der italienische Neuplatonismus waren wohl für die Darstellungsweise und die untergelegte Philosophie verantwortlich; andererseits trug der spätmittelalterliche Katholizismus mit seinem Ideal der regulierten Orden und der Bettelmönche mehr als vielleicht ein verfrühter Glaube an den Sozialismus zu dem kommunistischen Grundprinzip bei. More führte die Probleme der Menschheit auf die allgemeine Gier zurück, der alle schlimmen Folgen entsprangen; er schlug vor, sie wie bei Mönchen zu kurieren, indem man den Privatbesitz abschaffte. Nur in einer Beziehung waren die Utopier keine Mönche: ebensowenig wie der Verfasser konnten sie sich mit der Keuschheit abfinden. Das Sexuelle interessierte und amüsierte sie, und ihrer Sozialordnung lag die Familie zugrunde.

Obwohl ihm später die Feder kaum jemals aus der Hand kam, blieb die Utopia das einzige Buch, das More zum eigenen Vergnügen geschrieben hat. Im Gegensatz zu seinen Freunden, von denen besonders Erasmus oft sein Bedauern über die Verstrickung in das öffentliche Leben bekundete, war More ja Beamter, 'regi a secretis'. Zwölf Jahre verbrachte er im inneren Kreis der englischen Politik und am Ende trat er an die Spitze. Reiner Wissenschaftler oder Literat war er nie. Seine Tätigkeit und sein Schicksal hingen unentrinnbar mit der großen Welt zusammen, und die machte sich gerade jetzt bereit, die fröhliche Stimmung der Humanistenzeit zu Ende zu bringen. Ein Jahr nach dem Erscheinen von Mores humanistischem Reformprogramm, worin die christliche Religion nur flüchtig erwähnt worden war, brach die Reformation Luthers aus. Zunächst hat sie More scheinbar gar nicht berührt, aber innerhalb weniger Jahre machte er ihre Bekanntschaft, 1521 schrieb sein König eine Streitschrift gegen Luther, die von dem Reformator die gewohnte grobe Antwort erhielt. Im folgenden Jahr beauftragte Heinrich daher den hervorragendsten Schriftsteller in seinem Rat, darauf zu reagieren. Damit fing Mores neue Karriere als Erzfeind des Protestantismus an. Er spielte diese Rolle mit derart unermüdlicher und verbissener Energie, daß er seinen Verehrern große Verlegenheit bereitet hat. Oft hat man versucht, die Tatsachen zu verhüllen oder doch abzuschwächen. Daher muß gesagt sein, daß More selber solche Entschuldigungsversuche nicht verstanden hätte, denn seiner eigenen Ansicht nach tat er nur seine unumgängliche Pflicht im Dienste Gottes.

Die Antwort auf Luther – recht langweilig und schwerfällig lateinisch geschrieben – ist schon längst vergessen. Aber sie sagt doch etwas über den geistigen Zustand Mores aus, als er sich zum erstenmal der neuen Häresie entgegenstellte. Von Anfang an war er maßlos entsetzt und zur Gegenwehr entschlossen. Er nahm sofort aktiv teil an den Bemühungen, die Einfuhr lutherischer Schriften zu verhindern und die von diesen vergifteten Geister vor die Bischofsgerichte zu bringen. Damit wurde er der einzige Laie im Lande, der sich konsequent und rücksichtslos der Ketzerjagd widmete. Vor allem hat er diskutiert – endlos gelesen und schäumend geschrieben. Seine polemischen Werke gegen William Tyndale, John Frith, Christopher St German und andere (1528–34) umfassen Tausende von Druckseiten und sind zum Teil kaum lesbar. Dabei war seine Polemik wenig erfolgreich, allein schon deshalb, weil More den Gegner immer ausführlich zitierte, um ihn in allen Einzelheiten zu widerlegen. Dadurch ermöglichte er dem Leser die Lektüre der an sich verbotenen Schriften. Seine Bücher wurden viel zu lang und machten müde. Jede kleinste Abweichung von der Orthodoxie wurde verfolgt. Weil er zu viel, zu schnell und zu leidenschaftlich schrieb, verschlechterte sich sein englischer Stil. Hinzu kommt, daß More sogar im Zeitalter der Reformation als ein ungewöhnlich schmähsüchtiger Polemiker hervorragt. Die Meinung, er habe nur die üblichen Methoden angewandt, trifft nicht zu; jedenfalls im Rahmen der Auseinandersetzungen in England waren seine Kampfmanieren besonders schlecht. Ab und zu einmal zeigte er noch Humor; manchmal erfreut einen noch sein scharfer Witz und einige (keineswegs alle) der sogenannten 'fröhlichen Geschichtchen' beleben die Diskussion über Glaube und Theologie. Doch im allgemeinen erwies er sich als grob und derb, rücksichtslos und maßlos; oft wurde er geradezu hysterisch und sein Ketzerhaß erlaubte ihm nicht die kleinsten menschlichen Zugeständnisse. Daß ein Mensch ehrlich dem Irrtum verfallen könnte, hielt More für unmöglich: an Ketzern ist alles verdorben! In der Person und in der Gesellschaft sind sie einfach Hunde – wilde Hunde, die man ausrotten muß. Jeder von ihnen werde, wie er mehrmals sagte, 'am besten verbrannt'. In dieser Polemik scheint More vollkommen die Balance verloren zu haben und an der Unmenge überflüssiger Streitschriften, die sechs Jahre lang seine geistige Welt und schriftstellerische Tätigkeit ausgefüllt haben, ist für den Leser etwas Peinliches.

Als Lordkanzler war More vom November 1529 an in der Lage, die Verfolgung von der Druckschrift in die Wirklichkeit zu übertragen, und zwei Jahre lang gab er sich hierin ehrliche Mühe. Doch befand er sich auch von Anfang an in einer schiefen Lage. Wolsey war gestürzt worden, weil er Heinrichs erste Ehescheidung (von Katharina von Aragon, der Tante Kaiser Karls V.) nicht durchzuführen vermochte. Dieser Scheidung widersetzte sich More jedoch sofort und prinzipiell. Obwohl Heinrich wußte, daß das Gewissen es seinem Kanzler nicht erlaubte, die königliche Politik zu approbieren, riskierte er die Ernennung, weil kein besser geeigneter Laie vorhanden war. Das bedeutete aber, daß Mores Rolle als Diener des Königs mit seiner Pflicht als Diener Gottes in Konflikt geriet. Dazu kam noch, daß der Streit mit dem Papst zu voraussehbaren Angriffen auf die Einheit und Freiheit der Kirche führen mußte, also gerade zu derartigen Entwicklungen, die More zum Ketzerverfolger gemacht hatten. Trotzdem faßte er den Vorsatz, seine Stellung dazu zu verwenden, Kirche und Glauben so lange wie möglich zu schützen, und er wurde politisch aktiv. Betreffs des Königs hegte More keine Illusionen; er verstand das Schicksal, das ihn erreichen mußte, wenn er nicht nachgab. Nachgeben konnte er aber nicht, da es sich für ihn um das ewige Heil handelte. Als Kanzler nahm More Verbindungen mit den kaiserlich Gesinnten zu Hause wie im Ausland auf. Dabei kam er dem Hochverrat nahe, obwohl ihn seine wohlbekannte Sorgfalt vor wirklich gefährlichen Schritten, wie sie bei anderen vorkamen, bewahrt hat. Doch in den Jahren 1529–32 wuchs trotz aller Bemühungen der Einfluß radikaler Räte unter der Führung von Thomas Cromwell immer mehr an, seitdem es klar geworden war, daß sie allein dem König eine Lösung seiner Probleme anbieten konnten – und daß diese Lösung die Trennung Englands von der allgemeinen Kirche einschließen würde. Nach einem letzten Rückschlag trat More im Mai 1532 aus dem Amt und dem öffentlichen Leben. Er war entschlossen, niemals wieder etwas mit der Politik zu tun zu haben und sich fortan nur noch auf sein irdisches Ende vorzubereiten. Für die Regierung Heinrichs und Cromwells war es jedoch nicht so einfach, den großen Mann mit seinem starken und ihnen feindlichen Einfluß zu vergessen. Der König haßte jetzt seinen ehemaligen Günstling und lehnte es ab, ihn in Ruhe zu lassen. Verschiedene Versuche, ihn in das Schicksal einiger Oppositionsmitglieder zu verstricken, schlugen fehl. Im April 1534 jedoch weigerte More sich, den verlangten Eid auf die Sukzessionsakte, die Heinrichs zweite Ehe mit Anna Boleyn bestätigte, abzulegen. Er wurde festgenommen und dann im Parlament zu lebenslänglicher Haft im Londoner Tower verurteilt; sein Eigentum konfiszierte man, wie das üblich war. Nichts hiervon bereitete More Überraschung; im Gegenteil, er hatte schon längere Zeit darauf gewartet. Trotz des Ruins seiner Familie gewann er ganz plötzlich eine neue Abgeklärtheit, die in den im Tower verfaßten Schriften deutlich hervortritt.

Besonders zu nennen ist da der Dialog über den Trost in schweren Sorgen (Dialogue of Comfort for Tribulations), ein wahrhaft schönes Buch, das beweist, daß More sich von der Streitsucht und Hysterie erholt hatte. Wie sein erstes Buch steht auch dieses letzte im Rahmen eines fiktiven Gespräches, aber es ist auf englisch geschrieben, in einem Stil, der alles, was More bis dahin erreicht hatte, übertrifft. Das Gespräch findet zwischen zwei Ungarn (Onkel und Neffe) statt, die nach der Schlacht von Mohacs auf die Rückkehr der Türken und damit auf das Ende eines christlichen Lebens warten. Der Neffe sucht den Trost, den ihm der Onkel niemals vorenthält. Diesen Trost fand More in der

Meditation über das Leiden Christi und in einem großartigen Stoizismus von christlicher Art: da nach Gottes Befehl das irdische Leben ein Gefängnis für die Seele ist und das Leben nur zum Tod führen kann, macht es ja nichts aus, wenn ein Mensch dem anderen auch noch ein wenig Gefangenschaft und Tod auferlegt. Das Buch strahlt Souveränität aus und sogar Heiterkeit. Hier hatte der Glaube endlich die Theologie beiseite geschoben.

Es wäre am vernünftigsten gewesen, More im Kerker sterben zu lassen. Es konnte nicht lange dauern, denn er war 57 und nicht mehr gesund. Cromwell, der seine alte Achtung für More nicht vergessen hatte, wollte dies; aber das hätte nicht Heinrichs Rachsucht befriedigt. Im Herbst 1534 erklärte ein neues Gesetz es zum Hochverrat, den königlichen Supremat in der nun schismatischen Kirche auch nur mündlich zu verneinen, und im Mai 1535 entschloß sich der König in einem der für ihn charakteristischen Wutanfälle, dieses Gesetz gegen seinen ehemaligen Kanzler anzuwenden. Mehrere Verhöre, während derer Cromwell versuchte, More zur Rettung seines Lebens zu überreden, brachten nichts Inkriminierendes hervor, da More einen perfekten Ausweg entdeckt hatte: Er weigerte sich einfach, irgendeine Frage über die Rolle des Königs in der Kirche zu beantworten. Das Gesetz bestrafte das Verneinen, nicht aber das Schweigen. Doch in einer Privatunterhaltung mit dem königlichen Anwalt Richard Rich scheint More etwas gesagt zu haben, das sich in eine Hochverratsanklage umdeuten ließ – trotz der Tradition, Rich habe bei seiner Aussage einen Meineid geschworen, handelte es sich wahrscheinlich nicht um eine reine Erfindung. Der Prozeß fand am 1. Juli 1535 statt. Sein Ausgang stand nie in Frage, doch wurde er zu einer Art Triumph für den Angeklagten, weil sein juristisches Geschick der anderen Seite große Schwierigkeiten bereitete. Nach dem Todesurteil ergriff More die vom Gesetz vorgeschriebene Gelegenheit zu einer letzten Ansprache mit beiden Händen: In einer freimütigen und leidenschaftlichen Rede gab er seinen Widerstand gegen die Revolution in der Kirche und seinen Glauben an die Einheit der Ecclesia Christi rückhaltlos bekannt. Am 6. Juli stieg er heiter und ruhig auf das Schafott. Der Fall seines Kopfes deutete das Ende der alten Kirche in England an, aber ebenso seinen persönlichen und dauerhaften Sieg über Heinrich VIII.

Was soll man von More denken? Was für eine Art Mensch war er? Zeigen die verschiedenen Stadien seines Lebens einen sich wandelnden

Mann? Warum brach seine Karriere zusammen und für welche Überzeugung erlitt er den Märtyrertod? Ich muß betonen, daß wohl alle Fragen über More nur unsichere Antworten erhalten können, so lange nicht genug Arbeiten vorliegen, die nicht unter dem Zeichen des frommen Vorurteils stehen. 400 Jahre der Anbetung haben ein scheinbar unzerstörbares Bild geschaffen, auf das dann die Kanonisierung 1935 das Siegel setzte. Danach war More einer der größten und wunderbarsten Menschen des 16. oder irgendeines Jahrhunderts: stets liebenswürdig, zuvorkommend und freundlich, intellektuell und moralisch ein Riese, allen Schicksalsschlägen gewachsen, immer wahrheitsgetreu, niemals verstimmt, von vollkommen reinem Gewissen und schließlich das Opfer seiner Reinheit – kurz gesagt, ein wahrer Heiliger und dadurch noch besonders anziehend, daß selbst seine Heiligkeit so viel Menschliches an sich hatte. Wenn man auch nur leise Zweifel äußert, erweckt man die Donner der katholischen Kirche, besonders in den Vereinigten Staaten, wo jede zweite Stadt ihre Hl.-Thomas-More-Schule hat. Daß More, entgegen der damaligen Gewohnheit (so heißt es, obwohl sich weitere Beispiele finden lassen), auch seine Töchter humanistisch erziehen ließ, hat zwei sehr verschiedene Gruppen stark beeindruckt: weibliche Lehrorden und rabiate Feministinnen. Nur Gutes will man von ihm hören, und selbst die Kritiker bezeugen ihre Ehrfurcht. Als z. B. Gerhard Ritter seine Anglophobie auch auf More ausdehnte, indem er ihn als Prototypen der angeblich typisch englischen Heuchelei hinstellte, die die brutalen Nationalinteressen mit moralischen Phrasen zu verkleiden pflegt, nahm er gleichwohl an, daß More dabei persönlich unschuldig gewesen sei (Die Dämonie der Macht, 1947). Bei manchen Historikern kommt noch hinzu, daß More ein Denker und Schriftsteller war, der es zu Wirksamkeit und Einfluß im öffentlichen Leben gebracht hat – also manche Wunschträume des Schreibtisches erfüllte. Über wenige Menschen in der Geschichte ist ein so einstimmig positives Urteil gefällt worden.

Natürlich könnte all dies richtig sein und es wäre gewiß unverantwortlich, nur aus Lust am Widerspruch und sogenannter Originalität daran zu zweifeln. Schaut man sich die Sache aber weniger befangen an, sieht sie doch anders aus. Zunächst einmal muß man fragen, aus welchen Quellen das übliche Bild Mores geschöpft worden ist. Die Beweismittel für die Biographie Mores sind zahlreicher, als dies im 16. Jahrhundert gewöhnlich ist. Wir besitzen mehrere frühe Biographien, die allerdings in der Hauptsache von derjenigen abhängig sind, die William Roper,

Mores Schwiegersohn, zwanzig Jahre nach der Hinrichtung verfaßt hat. Die anderen tun meist nur bisweilen fragwürdige Familientraditionen hinzu. Weiterhin haben wir die Briefe von Mores Freunden, besonders von Erasmus, die Einzelheiten über sein Leben und seine Persönlichkeit belegen. Drittens stehen Mores eigene Werke da, einschließlich seiner erhaltenen Briefe, und viertens wären die Archive seiner Ämter zu nennen, besonders die Unmenge an Prozeßakten während seiner Tätigkeit in den Kanzleien des Herzogtums Lancaster und des Staates. Die letzten, die am unpersönlichsten sind, werden erst neuerdings langsam untersucht, so daß bisher seine Rolle als Lordkanzler nur anhand einiger Anekdoten von Roper beschrieben worden ist.[1] Ropers Biographie, die man übrigens noch nie kritisch untersucht hat, obwohl sie manche unwahrscheinliche Einzelheiten enthält, war von vornherein bewußt im Hinblick auf eine Kanonisierung geschrieben. Trotzdem hat man sie immer willig als normale Historie beurteilt, so daß selbst heutige Biographien dieser Vorlage stets noch in der Anlage und der Auslegung folgen, selbst wenn sie weitere Quellen heranziehen. Die Zeugnisse der Freunde stammen alle aus den Jugendjahren, aus der Zeit vor dem Kampf mit dem Protestantismus. Es sei bemerkt, daß sich More und Erasmus nach 1521 nie mehr getroffen haben. Was Mores eigene Werke angeht, so macht man im allgemeinen einen raschen Sprung von der Utopia zu den Briefen und Schriften aus dem Gefängnis. So ergibt es sich, daß die übliche Interpretation über die 15 Jahre von Mores öffentlicher Tätigkeit recht flüchtig hinweggeht. Natürlich erwähnt man seine Ketzerjagd, aber nur, um sie voller Verlegenheit zu entschuldigen: Ein so makelloser Mensch könne dergleichen nur widerwillig unternommen und milde durchgeführt haben. Seine Streitschriften hat man meist nur für zufällige biographische Fakten ausgewertet. Im wesentlichen besteht der More der Tradition also aus dem relativ jugendlichen Humanisten, der die Utopia geschrieben hat und der Freund des Erasmus gewesen ist, und aus dem im Kerker auf den Märtyrertod wartenden Helden, der sich alles Weltlichen entledigt hatte. Daß es beide Figuren gab, darf man nicht leugnen; aber ist das Ergebnis die ganze Figur?

Sobald man die Frage stellt, entstehen Schwierigkeiten. More soll immer heiter, generös und höflich gewesen sein, selbst gegenüber

---

[1] [But see J. A. Guy, *The Public Career of Sir Thomas More* (Brighton, 1980), which appeared two years after this was written.]

Opponenten, mit einem echten Genie für die Freundschaft. Gewiß, doch verstrickte sich der in so vieler Beziehung leidenschaftliche Mann bereits in jüngeren Jahren leicht in Zwistigkeiten mit anderen Gelehrten, die Erasmus peinlich wurden. Er hatte Nachsicht mit den vom Glauben Abfallenden, so daß er sich z. B. geduldig Mühe gab mit seinem Schwiegersohn, als dieser zeitweise einer Neigung zum Luthertum nachgab. Gewiß, aber in seinem Kampf gegen die Häresie in England war er ungewöhnlich wild und rücksichtslos – viel mehr als andere gute Katholiken in seinem Kreise. Seine Töchter behandelte er mit besonderer Liebe – seine zweite Frau jedoch verspottete er oft, auch im Druck, und in den 'fröhlichen Geschichtchen' treten die Frauen meist als verführerisch oder keifend auf. Sein berühmter Witz war oft unangenehm scharf und ziemlich herablassend, wodurch er sich manche Feinde gemacht hat. Warum sich der treue Diener seines Königs, der es verstand, in öffentlichen Angelegenheiten eine kompromißlose Haltung zu vermeiden, ohne das geringste Zögern gegen den Scheidungsprozeß wandte, hat noch niemand erklärt; und doch hing der Rest seines Lebens von diesem Entschluß ab. Kurz gesagt: More war kein einfacher Mensch, sondern außerordentlich kompliziert. Das wahrzunehmen bedeutet keine Herabsetzung. Es handelt sich nicht um Wandlungen und Verschiebungen während seines Lebens, wie sie bei jedem Menschen vorkommen, sondern um eine immer wieder auftretende, geradezu konsequente Zweideutigkeit. Wo man ihn auch anpackt, entweicht er einem, sowohl im Großen wie im Kleinen. Selbst sein Geburtsjahr könnte (es wurde beim Eintrag ein Fehler gemacht) 1477 sein und es hat sich herausgestellt, daß hinter dem berühmten Bild Mores von Holbein ein weniger schönes steckt, das übermalt worden ist! Der zweite Versuch war zweifellos erfolgreich, doch selbst da steht etwas Zweideutiges im Gesicht. Das leichte Lächeln, das gar nicht vergnügt ist, die Augen, die scharf doch verhüllt am Beobachter vorbeischauen: dieser Mann zieht sich von der Umwelt zurück. Das Bild wurde 1527 gemalt. Nicht ohne Grund spielte More immer mit der Ironie. Stets war er bemüht, seine Meinung hinter mehreren Schleiern zu verbergen. Der simple durchsichtige Herr des frommen Öldrucks ist er nicht gewesen. Die Frage liegt nahe, warum er die Schleier und die Zweideutigkeit vorzog.

Die Tradition hat, wie gesagt, nur den heiteren Humanisten und den abgeklärten Heiligen kennen wollen. Deshalb muß er als lebensbejahend, als humorvoller Optimist, als Freund der ganzen Welt dargestellt werden. Damit jedoch hat man ihm Unrecht getan. Er sah tiefer und war ernster. Selbst in der Utopia, einem Buch, das so viel Amüsantes und Spielerisches enthält, ging More von einem recht pessimistischen Begriff der Menschheit aus. Die Welt, so sagt er, kann der Sünde nicht entgehen. Der gefallene Mensch hat keine eigene Macht, ein Gott gefälliges Leben zu führen; er braucht dazu Gottes Gnade. Mores Grundbegriffe haben erstaunlich viel mit denen Luthers gemeinsam, obwohl die beiden dann genau entgegengesetzte Schlüsse aus ihnen zogen. In der Gesellschaft ist die verderblichste Sünde die Begierde; alle Unzulänglichkeiten des Daseins lassen sich von ihr ableiten. Weil der Mensch also nicht im Stande ist, von Natur aus ein anständiges Leben ohne Gier zu führen, muß ihm von außen her eine strikte Sozialordnung auferlegt werden. Diese findet man daher in dem Staate 'Nirgendwo', dessen strenges System fast keine Möglichkeit der Veränderung enthält – oder braucht. Das Leben ist dort recht angenehm für diejenigen, die sich gehorsam der Ordnung fügen: Darin besteht die Freiheit, wie bei Mönchen. Das Individuum verschwindet in der Gemeinschaft und in der effektiven Unterdrückung des Einzelmenschen läßt sich schwer das Prinzip 'homo mensura' wiederfinden, das doch den echten Humanisten kennzeichnete. More war eben in erster Linie Christ und zwar einer, der sich der Tradition des Paulus und Augustin angeschlossen hatte. Gewiß waren auch seine Kommilitonen Christen, doch trifft man bei keinem anderen auf ein so deutliches Bewußtsein der Sünde und des Bösen. Die Religion des Erasmus, wie er sie z. B. in seinem Handbuch eines christlichen Ritters erklärte, hatte etwas Oberflächliches an sich: Der Mensch könne zu seiner eigenen Rettung beitragen, wenn er sich nur die Mühe macht, die moralischen Gebote der Bibel zu beobachten. More verstand offenbar viel besser, wie schwarz es im Menschenherzen aussehen kann, und an die Möglichkeit eines anständigen Lebens glaubte er jedenfalls nur im Rahmen einer strengen Ordnung. Man erinnere sich, daß er von Beruf Jurist und Richter war.

Dieses Bewußtsein von der Dunkelheit des Menschenherzens erklärt auch Mores ungewöhnlich hysterische Reaktion auf die Reformation, die für ihn nur sündhafte Ketzerei sein konnte. Wie andere humanistische Kritiker hatte er in der Zeit von Luther die Mängel und Fehler der Kirche angegriffen, aber sowie die alte Ordnung in Gefahr geriet, konnte er im Luthertum keinen Verbündeten, sondern nur noch den Feind sehen. Erasmus kam später zu einer ähnlichen Einsicht, ohne es eigentlich ganz zu wollen; More hingegen, der immer mehr zum Kämpfen geneigt war, wußte von keinem Grund zur Zurückhaltung. Die Leidenschaft seines Ausbruches beweist seine Überzeugung, daß es dem Menschen nicht erlaubt sein darf, die von Gott der gefallenen Welt auferlegte Ordnung in Zweifel zu ziehen. Obwohl an dem System gleichfalls der Makel der Sünde haftet, verstellt jeder Versuch, es zu untergraben, den Weg zum Heil. Er vertrat also den Standpunkt, daß dem Menschen das eigene Urteil verboten ist, weil er als Kind der Sünde nur des Verderbens fähig ist. In diesem Punkte ging er stark von der in der Utopia angedeuteten Linie ab. Ehe Luther klargemacht hatte, was ein freies Gewissen zu tun vermag, gestattete More in seinem Idealstaat die Glaubensfreiheit unter der einzigen Bedingung, daß niemand einem anderen seinen Glauben aufzwingen darf. Damit war es nun vorbei: Glaubensverschiedenheiten waren zu unerträglichen Häresien geworden, und der wahre Glaube (die Tradition) mußte anderen mit Gewalt aufgezwungen werden. Es wird deutlich, daß für More das Ketzertum mehr enthüllte als nur ein politisches oder sogar theologisches Problem. Indem es dem sündigen Menschen ein Privaturteil über die göttliche Weltordnung erlaubte, stellte es Mores tiefste psychologische Überzeugungen in Frage. An sich war diese Stellungnahme nicht außergewöhnlich, aber er empfand sie so persönlich, daß sich seine Gedankenwelt und Lebensart schlagartig veränderten. Warum geschah das?

Wenn es um die Psychologie der Verstorbenen geht, muß man sich in acht nehmen, aber More hat wirklich genug Schlüsselpunkte hinterlassen. Das vierjährige Ringen um den Eintritt ins Kloster hat seine Bedeutung, wie auch die Ursache, die die Absicht fehlschlagen ließ. Wie bereits oft erkannt worden ist, bezog Mores Leidenschaftlichkeit auch das Sexuelle ein. Er brauchte den Geschlechtsverkehr und gab dies auch zu. Andererseits deutet die Suche nach der Kartause an, daß ein Hauptpunkt der mittelalterlichen Religion für ihn besonderes Gewicht hatte. Offensichtlich bestand für More die wahre Frömmigkeit – Gottes strengste Forderung an den Menschen – in der Abkehr von der Welt und zumal in der Keuschheit. Aus verchiedenen Gründen, wobei sowohl der Druck der Familie zu einer juristischen Karriere als auch seine eigene Natur ihre Rollen gespielt hatten, war es ihm unmöglich gewesen, der Berufung zu folgen, so daß er am eigenen Körper die Erfahrung der Erbsünde gemacht hatte. Manches Erstaunliche in seinem Leben erklärt sich daraus, z. B. das Büßerhemd, das er heimlich trug, doch auch der Entschluß, zwischen der Welt und seinem

Inneren mehrere Schleier aufzuhängen. Nun versteht man seine schönen Züge: die Barmherzigkeit gegenüber dem einzelnen Sünder, die Schaffung eines erbaulichen und Gott befriedigenden Familienlebens, die Gewissenhaftigkeit in jeder Tätigkeit, die ironische Ergebenheit, wenn es zum Leiden kam, besonders aber die Abgeklärtheit der letzten Monate. Für More war eben der Kerker die Mönchszelle, die er in der Jugend nicht hatte ertragen können – und das ist keine Theorie, denn fast ebenso erklärte er es seiner Tochter. Aber auch die dunkle Seite – z. B. die Ungeduld mit jedem Widerstand oder die Verstimmung gegenüber dem Weiblichen, die beide in seinen Schriften zutage treten – erklären sich aus der frühen Erfahrung. Dieser seiner Sünde bewußte Sünder, der wohl zeit seines Lebens mit Dämonen kämpfte, brauchte die Unterstützung der Überlieferung, die er in der Kirche fand, und konnte der ihm so deutlich erkennbaren Gefahr des allgemeinen Chaos nur mit Haß und Verzweiflung begegnen. Die Grundlage dieser Einstellung kommt doch immer wieder zum Vorschein. Die Utopier vergleichen den Geschlechtsverkehr mit dem Kratzen beim Jucken und mit dem Stuhlgang. In einem der 'Geschichtchen' rettet Gott eine junge Dame vor dem Ehebruch, indem er mittels eines Fiebers ihre Schönheit zerstört. Das Leitmotiv der endlosen Kontroverse mit Tyndale – jenes Verbrechen, das More nicht aus dem Kopf geht – ist die Sünde der Ketzer, die durch die Heirat ihren Keuschheitseid gebrochen haben. Auch Mores drastische Reaktion auf Heinrich VIII. Ehescheidung ist wohl damit erklärt. Da er der Bibel folgend den ursprünglichen Sündenfall mit 'dem Fleische' verband und ihn an sich selbst erfahren hatte, mußte ihm das Sakrament der Ehe, durch das allein das Geschlechtliche Gott gefällig wird, besonders heilig sein.

More besaß also nicht die muntere Leichtigkeit des traditionellen Heiligen, der (wie Roper sagte) nie in Wut geriet. Er war nicht einfach der Gerechte, den die böse Welt umgebracht hat, weil sein Gewissen ihre Bosheit zu klar ans Licht stellte. Im Gegenteil, More war oft zornig, über sich und über andere; die äußere Ruhe kostete Anstrengung. Und wenn es um die Ketzer ging, gab er jeden Versuch auf, seine Leidenschaft zu zügeln. Fast kann man dankbar sein, daß es ihm vergönnt war, am Ende seines Lebens die Ruhe und Abgeklärtheit zu finden, die ihm in der Jugend verlorengegangen waren. Das heißt nicht, daß man für Heinrich VIII. dankbar sein soll, sondern nur, daß selbst die unerfreulichsten Menschen manchmal wider ihren Willen Gutes tun.

Zu untersuchen bleibt noch die Frage, aus welchen Gründen dem König die Chance geboten wurde, More diesen Dienst zu leisten. Warum starb More eigentlich? Oder besser gesagt — denn sein Tod war direkt nur die Folge des verbissenen Hasses seines Landesherrn — welche Stellung nahm More zu den Problemen ein, die die Reformation und die königliche Politik aufgeworfen hatten? Wie stand er zu Kirche und Papsttum?

Als Theologe war More geflissentlich unoriginell. Das trifft übrigens auch (was erstaunen mag) auf seine anderen geistigen Tätigkeiten zu: Weder als Humanist noch als Jurist hat er nach dem Neuen gesucht. Die Utopia enthält eine glänzende Idee, aber es ist die Idee eines Dichters, der seiner Einbildung freien Lauf läßt, nicht die eines Philosophen, der eine Gedankenwelt revolutionieren will. Auch als Richter (so weit wir das bisher wissen) verhielt er sich konservativ und versuchte sogar, die Neuerungen seines Vorgängers Wolsey einzuschränken. Der ganze erstaunliche Drang nach Reform, der im englischen Leben und Recht der Zeit anzutreffen ist, verdankte ihm wenig oder nichts; selbst die ungewöhnlichen und zumeist ironischen Vorschläge in der Utopia übten zu Hause, wo dreißig Jahre lang niemand das Buch gelesen hat, keinen Einfluß aus. Als Theologe war More noch konservativer, zum Teil wohl deshalb, weil er erst in der Zeit seiner Streitschriften, also im Alter von 45 Jahren, ernstlich an das notwendige Studium ging. Er erwarb sich eine eindrucksvolle Kenntnis der Bibel und der Kirchenväter (er bevorzugte Augustin und Origenes), als auch eine bescheidenere der späteren Scholastik, wenngleich seine theologische Bildung nie der eines Erasmus oder Luther gleichkam. Sein Glaube war in mancher Beziehung sehr einfacher Art: Er glaubte positiv an die konkreten Einzelheiten der mittelalterlichen Lehre — Himmel, Hölle und Fegefeuer waren für ihn physische Orte. Wie Richard Marius gesagt hat, war seine Welt 'die des ausgehenden Mittelalters, in der nicht nur er, sondern auch Hieronymus Bosch und Girolamo Savonarola lebten, mit ihren seltsamen und erschreckenden Visionen vom Gottesurteil, mit schauerlichen Teufeln, die der Erde ihre gespaltenen Hufe aufprägten, und mit den verklärten himmlischen Gestalten, die ihr Licht durch die Luft ausbreiteten'. Man muß dies betonen, um endlich den unwahrscheinlichen Thomas More, der als eine Art moderner Liberaler erscheint, loszuwerden.

Irdisch gesprochen war diese Welt wesenhaft unsicher; nur zu leicht konnte man durch einen Fehltritt die Hoffnung auf die Gnade verlieren.

Was More theologisch so sehr von Luther abgestoßen hat, war gerade, daß sie beide dies erkannt hatten und zwar in sehr ähnlicher Art; daß aber Luther sich angemaßt hatte, der Gnade Gottes sicher sein zu können ohne die institutionelle Hilfe und Führung, die für More – den Juristen und verfehlten Mönch – unumgänglich blieben. Für diese Hilfe und Führung, davon war More im wachsenden Maß überzeugt, hatte Gott die Kirche erschaffen als Bewahrerin und Erklärerin der Überlieferung. Für More bedeutete die Kirche eine lebendige Gegenwart, in der der Heilige Geist ständig wirkte, so daß ihre Autorität der der Schrift allein (Gottes Wort, aber nicht Gottes letztes Wort) überlegen sein mußte. Dies überstieg alle einzelnen Probleme im Klerus. Obwohl More wußte, daß die Priester auch Menschen sind und daher der Sünde fähig, verteidigte er sie in seiner Polemik unermüdlich gegen die berechtigsten Beschwerden. Gegen Ende seines Lebens bedauerte er einmal, daß er und Erasmus in früherer Zeit Kritik an der Kirche veröffentlicht hatten: Er bedauerte die Veröffentlichung, nicht die Kritik! Selbst über die Wahrheit hieß es schweigen, wenn es um die Pflicht ging, der lebendigen Stimme Gottes Gehorsam zu leisten.

Die Kirche war von Gott verordnet und daher vollkommen unanfechtbar. Von diesem Begriff ging More jedoch nicht direkt zur Anerkennung aller päpstlichen Ansprüche über. Gewiß konnte es für More nur eine einzige Kirche geben, die eine einheitliche Organisation und eine oberste Führung benötigte. Wie sein Widerstand gegen Heinrich VIII. klarmacht, war er auch vollkommen überzeugt davon, daß kein Laie Herrscher der Kirche sein konnte – vermutlich weil nur die Weihe es dem gefallenen Menschen möglich machte, seinen Mitmenschen den Willen Gottes zu vermitteln. Doch seine Stellung zum Papsttum ist so unklar, daß sogar Versuche gemacht worden sind, ihn als Anhänger der Konzilsbewegung des 15. Jahrhunderts anzusehen. Das trifft wohl nicht zu, schon deshalb nicht, weil ja die Autorität der Kirche solche Ideen offiziell verworfen hatte, aber vielleicht auch deshalb nicht, weil der König daran dachte, das Konzilsprinzip für den eigenen Zweck auszubeuten. Da blieb wohl nur die päpstliche Herrschaft in der Kirche übrig. Was aber More davon zu sagen hatte, war keineswegs eindeutig oder bewunderungsvoll. Laut seines eigenen Zeugnisses hatte er 1521 versucht, den König zu überreden, im Kampf mit Luther dem Papst nicht zu viel Autorität zuzuschreiben; 1534 konnte er Cromwell daran erinnern und ironisch betonen, daß er seine nun höhere Meinung von Heinrich selbst gelernt hätte. Am wahrscheinlichsten scheint, daß er dem Papst praktisch die Kirchenherrschaft zugestand, ohne den Primat als ein religiöses Grundprinzip anzuerkennen.

Man muß verklausuliert reden, weil wir von More keine eindeutige Aussage besitzen; daß seine Familie im späteren Rückblick seine angebliche Papsttreue betonte, ist kein Beweis. In seiner letzten Rede erklärte More, daß er die Autorität der einen Kirche (den Papst scheint er nicht erwähnt zu haben) nur davon ableitete, daß sie seit Jahrhunderten 'vom ganzen Körper des Christentums' angenommen gewesen sei. Das ist eine sehr pragmatische Einstellung, die zu manchem anderen in Mores Leben paßt. Sie enthält ebenfalls Schwierigkeiten, die More bewußt oder unbewußt unterdrückt hat, z. B. das Problem der griechischen Kirche. Vielleicht hätte er seine Meinung deutlicher gemacht, wenn das freie Sprechen über diese Fragen ohne die Androhung des Hochverratsprozesses möglich gewesen wäre. Wegen dieser Gefahr mußte er schweigen, nicht aus Feigheit, sondern aus der Überzeugung, daß eine ehrliche Antwort der Suche nach dem Märtyrertod und daher dem unerlaubten Selbstmord gleich sei.

More starb also gewiß für die eine katholische Kirche, außerhalb derer kein Heil sein kann, weil für ihn diese Kirche nur in der sichtbaren und allgemeinen Organisation bestehen konnte. Ob er damit auch für das Papsttum starb, scheint mir viel weniger sicher zu sein. 1935 bestätigte der Papst durch die Kanonisierung, daß das seiner Ansicht nach der Fall gewesen sei; aber in Mores eigenen Schriften und Reden läßt sich der Beweis dafür nicht leicht finden.

More starb für das, was er sein Gewissen (conscience) nannte, doch bedeutete das in keiner Weise die Gewissensfreiheit. Im Gegenteil: Zeit seines Lebens verneinte er die Freiheit des menschlichen Selbstbewußtseins und bestand auf dem Gehorsam gegenüber der Behörde. Das Gewissen, von dem er sprach, bedeutete das Bewußtsein einer von Gott offenbarten Wahrheit. Diese Wahrheit war die historisch bewiesene Existenz der Kirche, deren Einheit mit jedem Mittel der legitimen Macht zu verteidigen war. In dieser – und wirklich in jeder – Hinsicht war More ein Mensch seines Zeitalters: vielleicht liberal und sicher katholisch im Sinne des frühen 16. Jahrhunderts; weder als Liberaler noch als Katholik würde er jedoch in das 20. Jahrhundert passen. Wie jeder Heilige wäre er gewiß entsetzt zu entdecken, für welche Ideen er heute oft verantwortlich gemacht wird. Wenn sich die Geschichte anders entwickelt und Heinrich VIII. nicht aus persönlichen Gründen

alle seine Richtlinien verändert hätte, wäre More wohl ein einfluß-
reicher Staatsmann und ein erfolgreicher Vertreter der totalitären Idee
gegen die Gewissensfreiheit geworden. In dem Zusammenstoß mit der
politischen und kirchlichen Revolution, die in England in den 1530er
Jahren ablief, und in der zwei echte Prinzipien (das Neue und das Alte)
miteinander rangen, vertrat Thomas Cromwell, die mißverstandenste
Gestalt seiner Zeit, eine bessere Hoffnung auf die zukünftige Freiheit als
Thomas More. Das vermindert aber nicht die geschichtliche Bedeutung
des in diesem Kampf Besiegten. Als Märtyrer und Glaubenszeugen
sollen und können nur die Bekehrten und Gläubigen ihn ansehen.
Jedermann jedoch kann die Anziehungskraft seiner Persönlichkeit
anerkennen und die Größe dieses Mannes, der, dazu verurteilt, am Ende
seiner Welt zu stehen, durch seine innere Stärke über sein Schicksal
triumphierte.

46

THOMAS CROMWELL REDIVIVUS*

'The lord Cromwell', said Foxe, was 'a man whose worthy fame and deeds are worthy to live in perpetual memory,'[1] and his eloquence moved Michael Drayton to assist in a long and tedious poem on 'great Cromwell'. By and large, the memory of Foxe's hero remained alive into the nineteenth century when a combination of king-worship and hatred of the Reformation reduced Cromwell's stature and allowed the voices of his enemies, especially that of Reginald Pole, to dictate historians' assessment of him. He became at best the servile instrument of his master's policy, at worst a ruthlessly unscrupulous promoter of a secular despotism; and it is particularly noticeable that his lowly origins, aggravated by the fact that he actually went into trade and – horror of horrors – lent money, came to be used against him even by American scholars supposedly free of such snobberies. In general accounts he virtually vanished from sight as the history of the reign was increasingly seen as the history of the king, a development sealed for two generations by A. F. Pollard's biography of Henry VIII. Then came the revaluations of the last twenty-five years, the rediscovery of Thomas Cromwell. I think now that in *England under the Tudors* (1955), attempting to restore him to view and show him in a truer light, I made some rather extravagant claims for him, though I stand by the essence of my opinions there. I still think that Cromwell was the most remarkable English statesman of the sixteenth century and one of the most remarkable in the country's history. I still think that he instigated and in part accomplished a major and enduring transformation in virtually every aspect of the nation's public life. And I still think that he was largely responsible for the fact that the medieval heritage of common law and representative institutions remained at the heart of England's

---

* [*Archiv für Reformationsgeschichte* 68 (1977), 192–208.]

[1] John Foxe, *Acts and Monuments*, ed. J. Pratt (1870), v, 362.

modern government, until very recent times. However, neither the supposition that Cromwell rather than Henry guided government in the 1530s, nor the view that he planned a constitutional rather than an absolute monarchy for his reformed state, has found universal acceptance, so that his figure remains uncertain and disputed. It therefore seems not unnecessary to draw his portrait here once more, though it will have to be a firm sketch rather than a full presentation picture.[2]

Thomas Cromwell was born about the year 1485, the son of a clothworker of Putney in Surrey who, like others of his trade, also kept an ale house. His early life remains obscure, and the stories later told of it offer little illumination.[3] However, it would appear that in his teens he got into sufficient trouble to leave the country for a while, and he made his way through the Netherlands into Italy where he allegedly served as a soldier, possibly taking part in the battle of the Garigliano (1503). He then turned to trade, serving a Venetian merchant but travelling back to the Netherlands: he was active at Antwerp in 1514.[4] He had probably come straight from Rome where earlier that year he stayed at the English Hospice.[5] Shortly after this date he must have returned to England, to marry and settle down. He married money, in a modest way, but also acquired a mother-in-law for whom he provided in his house even after his wife had died. There were some daughters; the only son, Gregory, on whom he lavished great care, proved a dull disappointment though in the end he recovered his father's peerage and some of his lands. The real heir of Cromwell's greatness was his nephew Richard Williams who adopted his uncle's name and passed it to the Huntingdon branch of the family which produced Oliver.

There has been some doubt about the date of Cromwell's entry into Wolsey's service, but it is now known that he picked up the rising star much earlier than Merriman supposed: he was in the cardinal's household by about 1516 and described as of his council by 1519.[6] Thus he served Wolsey for at least fourteen years – fourteen years in what

---

[2] In this article I naturally rely on what I have written about Cromwell in works which I do not propose to cite here at every point: *Tudor Revolution; Policy and Police; Reform and Renewal*; some of the essays in these *Studies*. [For my latest and fullest account of Cromwell's career I may now refer to *Reform and Reformation: England 1509–1558* (1977).]

[3] The account given by Merriman, i, 5 ff., can be corrected and modified by a few facts discovered since.

[4] PRO, Early Chancery Proceedings (C 1), 482/33.

[5] G. Parks, *The English Traveller in Italy* (1954), 366, 376.

[6] BL, Egerton MS 2886; PRO, Star Chamber Proceedings, Henry VIII (Stac 2), 2/274.

was throughout that time the real centre of government and power – though throughout that time he never played any part on the national stage. At the request of a personal friend from Boston (Lincs.), he paid a second visit to Italy in 1517–18, in order to help the town get a bull of indulgence from Pope Leo X.[7] He is said to have eased the journey by learning the New Testament by heart, in Erasmus's recently published translation; certainly he knew the Bible well for the rest of his days. Somehow he acquired a good knowledge of the law of England and built up a successful private practice for which much evidence survives, the earliest from about 1518 or 1519; he was also soon in demand as an out-of-court arbitrator.[8] In 1524 he was admitted to Gray's Inn, more a testimony to his standing among London attorneys than evidence of any formal training in the law. This combination of commercial and legal experience came increasingly to be at Wolsey's disposal, though private practice did not cease till about 1532, and in the 1520s Cromwell occupied the place of the cardinal's man of all work, his leading lay councillor.

Cromwell's riotous and unusual early career – he once said later that he had been 'a ruffian' in his youth – left very definite marks upon the man. Wherever one touches him one finds originality and the unconventional, and his most persistent trait was a manifest dissatisfaction with things as they were. He seems to have lacked those natural ties to the past which most people acquire in childhood, despise in adolescence, and submit to as they grow older; growing up outside the conventional lines of his day, he remained all his life a questioner and a radical reformer. At the same time, the hard road he had to tread to worldly success and especially to power – so much more hazardous than that open to the bright child of poor parents who found his way into the Church – had evidently taught him the limits of the possible and the need for patience and adjustment. His life had made him a very political animal, but one equipped with lasting principles. His acquaintance was as varied as his experience. He had ties with the city of London and especially the Merchants Adventurers, and he knew the cloth trade at first hand. His connection with Gray's Inn, augmenting the effects of his legal practice, brought personal contacts with many common lawyers and especially the friendship of Edward Hall, the

---

[7] W. E. Lunt, *Financial Relations of the Papacy with England 1327–1534* (Cambridge, Mass., 1962), 510–11. John Foxe garbled the story, ascribing it to the first visit and making Julius II the pope whom Cromwell solicited.

[8] PRO, Stac 2, 13/139–41; Court of Requests Proceedings (Req 2), 4/45.

historian. In the 1520s he played bowls at John Rastell's house, and he was well acquainted with Thomas More; they shared a common friend in the intellectual Italian merchant Antonio Bonvisi, long settled in England. Wolsey's household provided an introduction to a large mixed group of men, the middle-rank administrators who ran affairs in England under the cardinal and many of whom Cromwell was to use in the king's service thereafter; it also provided contacts with an important group of Cambridge-bred radicals who influenced Cromwell's thinking on Church and state, and who were to become the backbone of his planning staff. In the Parliament of 1523 he learned the ways and the minds of the House of Commons. Work for Wolsey brought many other experiences and contacts, especially with the realities of monastic lives and economies. Bishops and archdeacons, noblemen and gentry, merchants and lawyers, thinkers and writers, Englishmen and Italians and Flemings, these and more formed the setting of his life; but so did poor men and women, or at least the many people in difficulties who sought his aid. The only area of public life that was unfamiliar to him was the king's Court which he did not penetrate until he made his way to power. Acquaintance and experience had made this inwardly exceptionally determined man outwardly flexible and almost invariably affable. He never refused to listen to any petitioner, however dubious; he devoted an inordinate amount of his time to the importunities of those in need of help; and as he climbed ever higher he acquired a justified reputation for never forgetting old friends.

Cromwell was a solidly built man, given to stoutness; his large face with its small eyes, long upper lip and jutting chin concealed more than it revealed. Unlike Wolsey, he ignored pomp and cultivated a plain accessibility which reflected his genuine interest in other people. An exceptionally lively mind hid behind the formidable façade and expressed itself in vigorous and witty speech; his conversation charmed even enemies, and he had great natural gifts as an orator. Words, in fact, meant much to him, and he took his part in the maturing of the English language which was going forward in his day. Fluent in Italian and probably in French, he knew Latin and possibly some Greek, all self-taught. His tastes were those of the intellectual rather than the aesthete; though he seems to have laboured to display a conventional appreciation for attractive buildings and artefacts, he never emulated Wolsey's natural love or eye for such things. Cromwell's major intellectual interest would seem to have lain in political philosophy – the analysis and understanding of political structures. For a man actively engaged in manipulating and transforming such a structure, he was exceptionally concerned to grasp the meaning of what he handled: exceptionally but advantageously, for his desire to elucidate and act upon principle saved him from the excessive pragmatism and mere opportunism to which both his necessary concern with the immediate task and the self-centredness of the king he served were bound to drive him.

Cromwell was once thought to have been a conscious disciple of Machiavelli, whatever that may mean, but it is more likely than not that he did not read Machiavelli until the later 1530s. So far as one can give a name-label to his political philosophy, it could be called Aristotelian. It was Aristotle's analysis that he asked Thomas Starkey to expound, and he certainly knew that striking Aristotelian, Marsiglio of Padua, whose fourteenth-century writings were to prove so relevant and useful to the architect of the break with Rome. The influence of the common law and a clear grasp of the role of Parliament certainly helped to shape his mind; his administration was to witness the recovery of both from the threat posed by Wolsey's devotion to equity and autocracy.

Above all, Cromwell shared the anticlerical feelings which in the reign of Henry VIII dominated so much of public life: he hated the 'snuffing pride of prelates' (as Hall put it), objected to the elevated claims of a ritualistic priesthood, and had conceived a deep dislike of the regular orders. Contrary to older opinion, it is now manifest that his anticlericalism stemmed from more positive feelings than lay resentment or envy; it stood rooted in his religion. Exactly what he believed remains a debatable point. In 1530, he lamented the existence of Luther, but that remark was addressed to Wolsey and meant to please. At his death he claimed to have ever adhered to the Catholic faith, but that was meant only to rebut the charges of sectarian extremism which had brought him down. He probably grew more Protestant as the decade advanced. To some Lutheran envoys, who had said that 'Christ owed much to him, even as he owed everything to Christ', he admitted in 1538 that on the whole he was of their persuasion but would 'as the world stood, believe even as his master the King believed'. That mixture of cool conviction and canny care probably comes nearest to the truth. He had in effect become convinced that only a form of protestantism could serve the kind of polity he was building. Though as a rule his faith remained restrained by his awareness of the political possibilities, it was strong enough to make him drive faster than Henry liked and to play an important part in his downfall.

Cromwell's sober faith took its shape from a genuine devotion to the Bible, a devotion he shared with such passionate reformers as Latimer, such genuine Protestants as Cranmer, and such Christian humanists as Erasmus and the Erasmians.[9] Bible-worship could take very different forms in the many people whom it alone united. In Cromwell's case it supplied one of the driving forces to an essentially political temperament, the principled undertone and transcendental justification of labours that concentrated upon reforming the earthly existence of men by reconstructing the state and using the dynamic thus released (rendered active in the legislative potential of parliamentary statute) to remedy the abuses and deficiencies for so long debated and identified. It was Cromwell's purpose to remake and renew the body politic of England, a purpose which because of the comprehensiveness of his intentions amounted to a revolution but which proceeded by using the means inherited from the past. Not only did the practical statesman in him grasp the political advantages of introducing major change so far as possible under the guise of continuity, but Cromwell the thinker also comprehended the roots and long established realities of the polity he wished to transform. These realities lay in a general order embodied in the common law and in the making of new law by discussion and consent, not by edict. In a very real sense, Cromwell had a vision – a vision of order, improvement, the active removal of all that was bad, corrupt or merely inefficient, and the creation of a better life here and now in preparation for the life to come. To Cromwell, the reformed Church was to serve the purposes of the reformed commonwealth, whereas more definitely religious minds would have wished to reverse that order of priorities.

In Cromwell, therefore, the movement for reform which grew to strength throughout the 1520s found a man attuned to its call but also singularly able to translate talk into action; and the prophets of reform naturally flocked to him. Humanists, Protestants and economic thinkers, ardent men and self-seekers and cranks, genuine idealists and men disgruntled by failure or envy, all presented themselves, wrote letters, sent tracts or memorials or bad encomical poems. Often they

---

[9] Cromwell, no Erasmian himself, nevertheless respected Erasmus; he just did not find the humanism of that previous generation, with its acceptance of a universal papal Church, particularly useful to his task.

also sent information and denunciations which, there is no doubt, he needed and valued as much as ideas of reform. Some he took into his service, some he advanced in the king's, for some he secured gifts or pensions, some few he ignored. With the best of them – with a Thomas Starkey or Richard Morison – his relations were more those of intellectual equals and friends than those of master and servant. He certainly wanted to employ suitable pens in the writing of books and pamphlets intended to defend the revolution on which he was engaged: the campaign of propaganda, exploiting the potential of the printing press first revealed by Erasmus and Luther and (nearer home) Tyndale's group, was deliberate, designed and competent. But it is clear that he also hoped for intellectual exchanges and especially for positive ideas and proposals of reform: and he got them. However, it would be wrong to suppose that Cromwell acted simply as the agent of these thinkers. Most of the reforms deemed necessary had in any case been long apparent; what was needed now was their redaction to legislative proposals – the drafting of particular bills for Parliament. Cromwell's office included men engaged in this work; he himself took a very active share in it; his chief assistants came not from the ranks of the reforming scholars but from the real experts, the common lawyers. Cromwell's people were demonstrably busy in this activity from 1531 onwards, years before the best known and most original writers joined his staff. The lead in this age of reform came from the top.

Cromwell the thinker – friend and mentor to a group of university-bred intellectuals – is probably the most surprising Cromwell to have emerged from the investigations of the last twenty-five years. Earlier scholars, even those most hostile to him, allowed him practical ability and emphasized his determined skill at getting things done; and in this they were right even when they misinterpreted his purpose. In studying his work one soon comes to recognize the recurrence of certain striking features. Once Cromwell identified the existence of a problem requiring solution he formulated it precisely (often, of course, with the aid of others), devised a solution which went to the root of the issue, converted this solution into practical politics by framing a specific measure of reform (usually distinguished by its thorough exploration of the details), and lastly endeavoured to apply it with tireless persistence. These are the familiar hallmarks of successful action, and one expects statesmen to possess such qualities. Few, however, in that age or any other, have evinced them at all consistently, and fewer still with the regularity of insight, speed of execution and relentless followthrough which distinguished Cromwell. Not without reason was he, who performed his promises, compared favourably with Wolsey who was forever promising without hope or intention of performing.

Cromwell worked in ways that became almost schematical. The first stage of action – the theoretical solution of the problem – involved memoranda to himself, the gathering of basic information, the drafting of papers by himself and his assistants, no doubt also many unrecorded discussions (sometimes with the king). Next came the embodiment of the answer in an authoritative document designed to produce action, and here Cromwell throughout his career displayed a predilection for the most authoritative of all, parliamentary statute, even when no constitutional convention demanded it, and even though he had much experience of the way in which Parliament could frustrate him. He meant to go to the heart of things, and statute alone could transform the law upon which action had to rest and which action had to employ to become effective. The act of Parliament was very much Cromwell's deliberately chosen instrument of action. His administration produced the largest and most remarkable body of statutes ever seen before the nineteenth century (apart from the revolutionary measures of the Long Parliament which signified not the activity of the state but its collapse); and the great political fact of the Reformation was only in part responsible for an outburst that reached into all the alleys of law and society. Both before and after Cromwell, the bulk of public legislation derived from sectional or individual inspiration; in his day, exceptionally, it derived from government initiative. But he was never content with the mere making of new law: what stands out as fully is his determination to make the law actually work. He seems almost never to have given up, often at risk to himself; setbacks were occasions for trying again; and once a point of policy had been achieved, the minister continuously and even stridently pursued its application in the reality of enforcement.

Examples abound to demonstrate these qualities. The most familiar (as well, no doubt, as the most important) are found in Cromwell's work on the Church. The creation of the royal supremacy – the political revolution which subjected the spirituality to the rule of the laity embodied in king and Parliament – began with the putting together of a coherent theory upon which to justify it. This involved the collection of evidence in support of a doctrine of national autonomy, evidence which was used both in the preambles of statutes and in a barrage of propaganda tracts. The principle once established, Cromwell worked out the consequences in a long series of legislative enactments and steered them through a Parliament which contained in both Lords and Commons sizable bodies of opponents and doubters. Turning law into actuality meant using the powers of the supremacy to force both submission and reform on the Church, seeking out and suppressing opposition, and urging dynamic transformation on clergy and laity alike, a continuous activity which was pursued in a stream of injunctions, circulars, private letters, interrogations, instructions, protests, threats and cajolings. The dissolution of the monasteries displays the same attitudes and qualities, from the erection of a principle (monastic seclusion is a false retreat from social duty, and the wealth thus locked up should be employed for social reform, especially education), through the collection of statistical data (the *Valor Ecclesiasticus*), to the first steps which tackled a manageable number of institutions, the carrying through of the vast programme in a mere four years, and the solution of the many administrative problems raised. I am not forgetting the part played by lay demand for monastic lands in easing the exercise; but I am here describing Cromwell's manner of proceeding.

The subjection of the Church was only part of Cromwell's great political programme, the creation of a genuinely unitary realm; another of its pillars, Cromwell's handling of the outlying parts of the king's dominions, evinces the same characteristics. In his few years of power he thoroughly overhauled the administration of Calais, reorganized Wales and the marches, transformed the government of the north, and terminated the existence of territories exempt from the royal administration of justice. Even in Ireland, where predictably he fell furthest short of success, he proved his principled pertinacity: he ended the feudal independence of the great families, established rule by an English lord deputy with a permanent garrison (the shape of the future), and brought at least the accessible parts of the island within his unitary structure; and he achieved this unswervingly through setbacks which included a major rebellion and much opposition from the very people in the Dublin Pale upon whose advice and co-operation he normally relied.[10]

[10] For the best assessment of Cromwell's Irish policy see Brendan Bradshaw, *The Irish Constitutional Revolution of the Sixteenth Century* (Cambridge, 1979), part II. [For a somewhat different view, cf. S. G. Ellis, 'Thomas Cromwell and Ireland, 1532–40', *HJ* 23 (1980), 497–519.]

In small matters as in large he testified to this relentless energy. For years after what doctrine called a service to the commonwealth had proved to be unworkable in the face of little understood economic conditions, he kept up his attempt to control prices by regulation; he devised a reform of the royal Household which it took three years of pushing at Court and in Council to get accepted; against repeated delay by opposition in and out of Parliament, he promoted for eight years the abolition of sanctuaries, which he regarded as an obstacle to proper law enforcement, until he won. And so on, through all the branches of his furiously omnipresent activity.

I do not, of course, mean to suggest that Cromwell worked out every bit of policy for himself, that he could operate consistently as though in a vacuum free of political and personal considerations, that he was invariably successful — least of all, that he was invariably right. His chief contribution did not lie in a striking universal originality; it is doubtful whether there was anything totally new about any of the ideas that became operative in the 1530s; what was new was just that for once they were taken seriously and made to work. Where others had dreamed or tinkered, Cromwell acted and consolidated. His Welsh and Irish policies, for instance, rested upon advice received from the locality and debated there for decades before; his economic measures took account of suggestions worked out in divers quarters; his political doctrine of Church and state owed something to long-standing common-law attitudes, more to the researches and theories of various divines and lawyers, but something substantial also to his own contributions for which he found confirmation in Marsiglio. He always had to steer reform and transformation through the shoals of politics — past king, bishops, nobility, through Parliament, in and around the dangerous cross-currents of Court faction. He was no King Utopus but a working politician intent upon a coherent and all-embracing policy which in practice could be got through only by accepting compromises in which the coherent impetus at times looked like getting lost. As is the fate of politicians, Cromwell sometimes failed to get anywhere at all. Yet through the obfuscation of political and social confusion one unmistakably discerns the fixed purpose of a directing mind, tackling just about every long defined problem of the body politic and several not previously thought of, and producing a really astonishing number of working solutions. Considering that Cromwell had at best eight years during which he really dominated the king's government, it is amazing

382

how much fundamental reform he managed to introduce, nor is it any wonder that the upheaval caused by his bursting upon the scene should have reverberated for generations of further developments as well as occasional retreats.

Three different charges have been levelled against Cromwell's achievement: one, that it was not really his because he acted simply as the king's executive agent; two, that his real purpose was to create a royal despotism to which every sort of worthy tradition and liberty was to be sacrificed; and three, that what he did was marred by a coldblooded and unscrupulous ruthlessness which defied justice and relied on terror. Even though there are particles of truth in all three of them, we now know with some confidence that they are all essentially false; but they are not yet dead.

I have so often argued the case for regarding Cromwell as the real inspiration behind the work of the 1530s that I shall not do so here at length.[11] Of course, he neither could nor would ignore Henry VIII whose interventions, when they came, were always sovereign and decisive, but the evidence that Cromwell took most of the initiatives is by now overwhelming. One need only regard the occasions on which he was clearly doing things unknown to Henry, or pursuing policies about which Henry had plainly shown himself doubtful. In the drafting of the important Act of Appeals (1533), the King's ill-considered contributions were discarded at the next stage of Cromwell's revising.[12] The Dispensations Act (1534), central in several ways to the complex of Reformation statutes, emerged as a draft from Cromwell's hand, was by him promoted in the Commons before the king saw it, at Henry's belated insistence was hurriedly amended with a delaying clause, and yet a week later was made effective when Cromwell overbore Henry's reluctance.[13] Cromwell's Irish policy differed profoundly from that favoured by Henry before 1534 and after 1540 when dreams of reducing the whole island to obedience were readily entertained, and it is not even certain that Cromwell kept Henry continuously informed of what he was doing.[14] This last question arises in a good many of his activities, major and minor. Above all, it is hard to deny that Cromwell throughout tried (and until 1539 with some success) to push on with the

[11] Most recently in 'The King of Hearts', a review of J.J. Scarisbrick's *Henry VIII*, for which see above, no. 5.

[12] Above, no. 24.

[13] Discussed in *Reform and Reformation*.

[14] For this see Bradshaw's *Irish Const. Revolution*, passim.

reform of religion much faster and further than Henry approved. It was he, not the king, who promoted the vernacular Bible, going so far as to use versions derived from the translation of Tyndale whom Henry abominated. Cromwell's sympathies for Lutheranism, muted though they remain, are too well attested to ignore, and they were never shared by the king. The reaction of 1539, which unquestionably resulted from Henry's intervention, neatly confirms that the drift towards protestantism which it arrested had been Cromwell's policy, not Henry's. No one can now say with confidence exactly how much each man contributed to the work of the decade, but it is simply not possible to accept that the powerful revolutionary impulse of those years should have come from the king since there is no sign of it at all in the other parts of the reign. It came from the minister whose clear sight and willingness to take risks throughout contrasted with his master's habitual preference for caution and procrastination in the face of all major issues.

How exactly one judges Cromwell's achievement – which injured so many entrenched interests and convictions – may have to remain a matter for debate, especially as his sudden and premature end left many things uncompleted and many plans unfulfilled. He himself (as he naturally would) regarded himself as a builder and not a destroyer, and it is true that everything he did was designed to produce a structure, not a desert. On the other hand, no one can build so much on ground already occupied without also destroying a good many things, and the losses of the decade (especially in the abolition of the monastic orders) were considerable. To me it seems that what was achieved in laying foundations for a reformed polity – a reform long since demanded on various sides – greatly exceeded the value of what was lost; especially, though I share the regret for the disappearance of magnificent buildings and libraries, I cannot see that the going of the monks themselves, in the state they were in, was much loss to anyone. Yet even those who might share this view include some who nevertheless question Cromwell's ends. It is agreed that he aimed at the final consolidation of England into a unitary and centralized state, but it is not agreed how he saw that state's constitutional structure: did he plan what actually came – a unified realm which preserved the limiting machinery of law, Parliament and a prerogative controlled by law – or did he mean to erect a royal autocracy which only later events prevented from flowering?

Old surviving prejudices ought to give way to the evidence, and the evidence accumulating says that Cromwell and his associates really believed in strengthening law and statute rather than mere monarchic rule: the fact that in an age of increasing absolutisms England retained the constitutionalism which proved so irksome to the Stuarts was intended by those who recast the polity in the 1530s. Again, I have argued the case before, but let me add new points. The royal supremacy inherited from despotic Rome could have been a weapon of domestic despotism: yet we know that even at the height of the drive for it the Cromwell circle believed in using parliamentary statute for the protection of the laity's rights against abuses by divine-right enthusiasts (among whom the king should really be counted).[15] Some have held, as one or two perhaps still hold, that in 1539 Cromwell hoped to endow royal proclamations with a legislative power that would have rendered Parliament as superfluous as the Cortes of Castile became the year before; the latest investigation, going much deeper than anyone ever had before, has firmly buried this ancient *canard* by demonstrating the precise and limited function which proclamations exercised in the Cromwellian concept of government.[16] We have often been told that Cromwell's formidable enlargement of the king's ordinary revenue could have made the monarchy independent of parliamentary taxation and was thus intended to remove the best possible protection for constitutional rule and liberties, and yet no one has ever looked at what happened at the time. It does not seem as though that opinion was shared by Cromwell who in 1540, when the Crown's income stood at its highest, thought it necessary to seek a grant of supply, even though he had to face the obvious objection that a king so recently enriched should leave his subjects' pockets alone. Furthermore, those who have argued this false case ought to have noticed that no absolutist monarchy in Europe was ever able to exist without taxation: the real issue always was whether a king could gain power to tax without consent, an ambition that not even those most suspicious of Cromwell have discovered in his work. Wolsey's practice had been more ominous in this respect. I repeat: Cromwell's political concepts rested upon a high regard for the common law and a recognition of the function of Parliament both of which were mobilized for the reform of the realm.

Thus Cromwell built rather than destroyed, on ancient foundations

---

[15] See Gardiner's recollections of what Lord Chancellor Audley, Cromwell's chief legal adviser, told him: *The Letters of Stephen Gardiner*, ed. J. A. Muller (Cambridge, 1923), 392.

[16] R. W. Heinze, *The Proclamations of the Tudor Kings* (Cambridge, 1976), esp. ch. 6.

which he consciously and conscientiously respected; he always preferred to ground change, even revolution, upon tradition. Much of the secret of his success lay in this ability to present transformation as the mere realization of established truths, a skill which is still capable of deceiving some historians who cannot see that the age of Cromwell did anything very drastic to the body politic.[17] That view would have greatly astonished Thomas More who thought that he was dying for the preservation of an eternal truth suddenly threatened by the powers of darkness. On the other hand, the historian who thinks it apposite to recall Hitler's employment of the *Reichstag* in order to cast doubt upon Cromwell's use of Parliament[18] would have bewildered both the lord privy seal and his king who were accustomed to so much successful opposition from Lords and Commons alike that until Cromwell took over Henry had rather shared Wolsey's preference for few Parliaments or none. It is really clear by now that Cromwell treated Parliament as the only instrument available, and usable despite the difficulties involved, for the carrying out of a major reform programme, and it is also clear that however much he succeeded in managing and occasionally dominating it (in the fashion of later chief ministers) he never reduced it, or even tried to reduce it, to impotence or subjection. It was left to a later Cromwell to teach possible lessons to the likes of Hitler.

That leaves the third charge, the accusation of a peculiarly revolting ruthlessness, sometimes enlarged further into a conviction that Cromwell's willingness to proceed by the law depended on the making of laws which themselves offended against justice. Cromwell could certainly be ruthless, and his revolution, like any revolution, had its victims. Despite his well attested capacity for kindness and generosity in personal relations,[19] he never hesitated in enforcing the rigour of the law upon those who broke it, and it would be astonishing to hear that he ever lost any sleep over the deaths of men he sent to execution. Yet it must surely be considered that he was also always anxious to make sure that the law had really been broken; we now know that being denounced to Cromwell meant not automatic execution but a thorough investigation, and that more such cases were dropped than pursued.[20] At times Cromwell even tried to temper the law's fury, and Henry's, to

[17] Esp. G. L. Harriss and P. H. Williams, 'A revolution in Tudor history?', *PP* 25 (1963), 3 ff.
[18] J. Hurstfield in his attack on my view of Cromwell: 'Was there a Tudor despotism after all?', *TRHS* 5th ser. 17 (1967), 83 ff.
[19] See Paul Van Dyke, *Renascence Portraits* (New York, 1905), 164 ff.
[20] For this see the whole argument deployed in *Policy and Police*.

help people who excited his sympathies in despite of his normal prejudices, as when he endeavoured to assist the last Carthusians in London.[21] The victims of his revolution were in the main people involved in politics and public life, people moreover who had provoked the king's wrath and not the minister's. The Nun of Kent who prophesied Henry's early death, More and Fisher whom Henry furiously regarded as ingrates deserving the worst fate possible, the disaffected courtiers who took charge of the Pilgrimage of Grace, the disloyal nobility gathered round the families of Pole and Courtenay — all these died because Henry wanted them dead, even though loyal opinion (assisted by the king's instinctive skill in finding scapegoats for his worst deeds) liked to blame the plebeian upstart for the fate of so many people of distinction. Cromwell's own enemies — men like the dukes of Norfolk and Suffolk, the earls of Derby and Shrewsbury, or Bishop Gardiner — not only survived but were never even threatened with disaster throughout his rule, a mistaken abstention from personal vendettas which they in their turn did not emulate when they got their chance of bringing Cromwell down.

On only one occasion in his career did Cromwell play the part of unscrupulous intriguer for which much tradition has cast him. That was in the spring and summer of 1536 when he allied with conservative Court factions to destroy the Boleyns and then used the problem of the succession to defeat his temporary allies. The outcome of this hidden battle was to establish his unchallenged ascendancy in the king's government, and he used the really dirty means employed because too much was at stake, not only power but also policy. His reforming programme was doubly threatened: the decline of the Boleyns (supporters of reform) raised the spectre of reaction, while the reactionary factions would obviously have put an end to reform if they had been allowed to enjoy the fruits of victory. In a way this episode reveals a lot about the inner reality of Thomas Cromwell: on the one occasion when he used false charges and true lack of scruple to gain his ends he did so because there was no other way of saving the cause of reform and renewal to which he had dedicated himself. But the murder of Anne Boleyn and her friends must nevertheless remain the one bad deed of Henry VIII in which Cromwell takes an almost equal share of responsibility. His own death on the scaffold, occasioned by the virulent hatred of men he had cast down but refrained from destroying, as well

---

[21] Ibid. 423, n. 3.

as by his attachment to a reform of the faith, was thus no unjust nemesis and in measure an expiation. But it did untold harm to the nation and the polity to which he had given his life.

Thus Cromwell, inevitably involved in politics in which (thanks to the nature of the king) blood flowed too often and too readily, should be seen as a man of principle, willing if no other way existed to use the worst methods of the day, but not himself by nature either a killer or a lover of terror. But was his legalism mere sham? Is it true that though he stayed firmly within the law he managed to do this by first creating laws contrary to justice and forced through despotically? Since the answer to this question will in measure depend on historians' moral beliefs, it cannot ever perhaps be definite. For myself I share the revulsion of any remotely liberal mind at the deeds which disfigure that age, and I cannot ever read Thomas Wyatt's *Circa regna tonat* – his lament over the victims of the Boleyn disaster – without being moved to anguish and indignation. But the historian's task is to understand before he approves or condemns, and understanding requires a grasp of how things looked to those we study. True, even at the time there were those who lamented the violence of the 1530s, and they included not only opponents of the regime but even Thomas Starkey who supported it. But before we decide that Cromwell's handling of the law amounted to a cynical manufacture of convenient rules, against the proper standards of the day and in the teeth of opinion, we need to consider those standards and that opinion. I do not underestimate the difficulties of doing so, but two points may help to clarify things.

In the first place, there is no evidence at all that the laws in question – more particularly the treason laws of 1534 and 1536 – were forced through against the will of Parliament or by corruptly coercing it. By now we know enough about the willingness of those Parliaments to oppose, modify and even defeat government bills to remain at least sceptical in the face of unsupported charges which reduce Commons and Lords to mere rubber-stamping machines when all the extant evidence indicates that they were no such thing. And in the second place, the general reaction may be judged more reliably than by citing the protests of those who, opposed to Cromwell's policies, thought him and his doings evil enough to be called any name. Rather it would seem to have been generally accepted that the king's rule needed to be protected by a fearsome law of treason and that traitors, convicted by the course of the law, died justly. The very fact that at the death of the duke of Somerset in 1552 the populace expressed their horror highlights the absence of any such demonstrations from all the other executions of the age. After all, when people thought that victims died innocently and, though under the law, contrary to justice, they knew how to make their feelings plain, as they did in the burnings of Queen Mary's reign. Her father could hang, draw and quarter dozens without ever being given to understand that an injustice was thought to have been committed.

The fact is that the age agreed generally to the law under which it lived and accepted the severities thought necessary for the protection of a revolution. Nothing has yet been said to prove otherwise, and our own revulsion is irrelevant. Among the convictions of the age and of its law the belief that death by execution in its more horrible forms was a proper reward for those who denied the ultimate and basic loyalties stood firmly entrenched. Cromwell shared it, but so did Thomas More who showed no aversion to the burning of heretics and actively assisted in bringing them to their death. When examining the fallen lord chancellor in the Tower in 1535, Cromwell pointed out that the king had as much right to enforce the law of his supremacy with the axe as the pope had to enforce the law of his supremacy with the stake, and More could only reply that the second law enjoyed a wider acceptance throughout Christendom than the first, an answer convincing neither in logic nor in fact.[22] Of course, one may hold various views of the truth of Christ's Church on earth, and people did. But one needs to recognize that all the representatives of those various views agreed upon the need for an ultimate sanction. Judicial killing for a principle of state constituted part of the sixteenth century's view of its world; Cromwell's treason laws, rendered severe by the revolutionary circumstances of the day but fully in accord with legal precedent, were in tune with the standards of his time, however vile they may be by ours, and it needed no chicanery to get them made. The standards that the age demanded related to enforcement, and here Cromwell behaved with exemplary propriety, to the point of being ultimately accused of culpable negligence in protecting the king.

What remains at issue, as it always has been and perhaps always will be, is the principle of state for which Cromwell set up these safeguards. Perhaps, if it were true that he aimed at nothing better than the elevation of untrammelled secular power at the expense of possibly eternal truths,

[22] *St Thomas More: Selected Letters*, ed. Elizabeth Frances Rogers (New Haven, 1961), 251.

his actions would lose all justification, though such terms themselves introduce personal, even emotional, elements into the discussion which tend to render the dialogue pointless. Still, for a long time his policy was regarded in that light, even by one who approved of the Reformation. A. F. Pollard thought that where the interests of king and state were concerned Cromwell 'had no heart and no conscience and no religious faith; no man was more completely blighted by the sixteenth century's worship of the state'.[23] He was completely wrong, even though Cromwell would be an easier man to understand if he had been right. Whether we approve or deplore the English Reformation, we assuredly must correctly apprehend the mind of its first promoter. Cromwell's heart and conscience compelled him to act as he did because he served a genuine vision of a new polity, a commonwealth reformed in body and soul; the state that to Pollard he seemed to worship was a state devoted to true religion as well as to secular renewal; all of which he proved when he allowed his faith to carry him into actions and positions that enabled his enemies to persuade the king to take his life. Realist and statesman though he was, he had enough idealism in him to surrender to the dangerous temptation of doing ill for righteousness' sake, and in any case, serving Henry VIII, his hands were tied. Perhaps those who condemn him for his uses of power because they think him irreligious and cynical will be willing to overlook those same deeds once they are persuaded that Cromwell committed them in the service of a spiritual cause. For myself, recognizing his complexity and his passion for that cause, I prefer to regret that he, too, suffered idealism to drive him into outrage and would rather give him his well deserved due for the work he did in a cool political spirit for the betterment of the realm.

[23] In his article on Cromwell in *Encyclopaedia Britannica*, 11th edition.

47

J. A. FROUDE AND HIS HISTORY
OF ENGLAND*

Froude's long life spanned an interesting age in the history of historical studies during which one kind of professionalism was replaced by another. The tradition which he inherited treated historians as the writers of a specialized form of literature, as men of learning and art who occupied themselves with composing predominantly political narratives based on wide reading in mainly printed sources, and who were likely to depend on their pens for their income. Such historians were thus professional men in the sense that they spent their working days on history and earned their living by it, but not in the sense that they had a necessary and salaried connection with any institution of learning. During Froude's life this tradition died in Germany where serious history became the preserve of university teachers, and this new principle invaded England when William Stubbs, who had made his scholarly name in the vicarage of Navestock in Essex but was by nature a new-style professional, became Regius professor of modern history at Oxford in 1866. Froude, who succeeded Stubbs at one remove in 1892, thus ended his career among those new-style ranks, after a lifetime of professionalism of the old kind. This transit admittedly had more of the symbolic than the real about it, if only because Froude held the chair for only two years, but in one somewhat surprising respect Froude was a suitable figure to advertise the transformation. Though his historical work sprang unmistakably from the tradition which went back from Macaulay through Lingard, Hallam and Gibbon to Hume and Robertson, and though he never showed any signs of even knowing about the things going on in the historical seminars of Berlin and

---

* [Written in 1979 as an introduction for a proposed reprint of Froude's *History of England from the Fall of Wolsey to the Armada* by AMS Press Inc. of New York. The publishers, having so far been unable to undertake this reprint, have kindly permitted me to include the piece in this collection. References to the *History* are to the standard 12-volume edition.]

Göttingen, he grasped by some instinct the significance of the unexplored archives on the opening of which the German revolution had depended. Froude, a professional historian of the old kind who wrote history designed to be read as literature and wrote because he needed an income, was also a proto-professional of the new kind who sought out hitherto unused manuscripts and in the end came to teach the subject. In this last stage, standing somewhat incongruously in a world already dominated by F. W. Maitland, the prophet of the future of English historiography, he also shared the discovery that this new and formal professionalism had its disadvantages. The older historians could spend all their time on studying and writing history; they taught and examined no one, administered no departments, made no appointments, sat on no academic committees.[1] In retrospect they would seem to have led paradisal lives, though very likely they would not have agreed that this was so; it is no wonder that they managed to write those many and large volumes.

James Anthony Froude was born in 1818, younger son to Robert Hurrell Froude, rector of Dartington in Devon and later archdeacon of Totnes.[2] His mother died when he was only two and a half years old, and his childhood was ruined by a sternly repressive father, by his eldest brother Hurrell in whom consciousness of inescapable superiority fed on a manifestly sadistic temperament, and by the horrors of Westminster School where Anthony, a natural victim, spent nearly five years among quite appalling bullies whom their teachers left alone to torture weaker children. A weak and sickly child, much given to fearful imaginings, Froude might easily have died and rather expected to, especially as the family inclined to consumption. He certainly should have emerged incurably neurotic. But though this very unhappy youth left its mark, he somehow became reasonably normal: a tall, thin, tough, quite well balanced young man, given to fishing, swimming and strenuous exercise, who (as he never ceased to regret) wasted his years at Oxford in trying to keep up with the sons of the gentry. Nevertheless,

---

[1] The discovery that the security of a salaried post has its drawbacks for the scholar was made at the time by other men of learning: R. Porter, 'Gentlemen and geology: the emergence of a scientific career, 1600–1920', *HJ* 21 (1978), 809–36.

[2] For Froude's life see A. F. Pollard in *DNB (First Supplement)*, and especially Waldo Hilary Dunn, *James Anthony Froude: a Biography* (2 vols., 1961 and 1963). Dunn, for whom Froude was a lifelong passion, is too much the partisan to be reliable in all his assessments, but since his book consists in great part of Froude's own autobiographical fragments and hundreds of his letters it throws much light and makes interesting reading.

he was elected to a fellowship at Exeter College in 1842 and in 1846 took deacon's orders: he seemed set for a conventional university career which at that time would have involved little enough work. At this ill-timed moment he began to have doubts about the Christian religion. This was the age of the Oxford Movement, that powerful, seemingly irresistible reaction against evangelical protestantism; its leaders were Froude's brother Hurrell (who had died in 1839, thereby enabling Froude to see his impossible brother in the rosy glow cast by tragedy) and John Henry Newman (later a cardinal of the Church of Rome) who had tried his hand at converting young Anthony. But despite his admiration for both men Froude came deeply to resent the violent disapproval of the Reformation, the bigoted worship of all things medieval, and the self-satisfied ritualism of the Tractarians. Personal experience of the simple protestant faith at its best in the household of an Anglo-Irish parson (where he served as a tutor) showed him how false the prevalent convictions at Oxford were; and in his late twenties he came to quarrel with everybody there. The European revolutions of 1848 attracted him during a brief phase of political radicalism, and he published a book (*Nemesis of Faith*) which in the form of fiction but with accuracy exposed his experiences with family and school. Outraged, Exeter College burned the book and made him resign his fellowship. However, his holy orders (which he could not shed until 1872 when the law was changed to permit this) stood in the way of any other career, and at the age of thirty-one he seemed doomed to failure.

So far his life had been miserable as well as aimless, but the next phase, which opened with his marriage in 1849 to Charlotte Maria Grenfell, sister-in-law to his friend Charles Kingsley, brought him fame as well as, after a penurious start, a reasonable fortune. After his first wife died (1860) he remarried almost at once, choosing her friend Henrietta Elizabeth Warre, and though in 1874 he lost his second wife also he throughout lived in a happy family setting: he loved children in general and his own in particular. It was during these years that he became an historian. The twelve volumes of his *History of England from the Fall of Wolsey to the Defeat of the Spanish Armada* appeared in pairs between 1856 and 1870, but their production was accompanied by much else; Froude was a most prolific writer of essays, reviews, comments and books.[3] From 1860 to 1874 he edited a monthly journal, *Fraser's*

---

[3] A full bibliography would be as cumbersome as it would here be out of place. Froude wrote to order, especially biographies, but his lives of Bunyan (1878), Caesar (1879) and Luther (1883) are

Magazine, with notable success, and the *History of England* was no sooner off his hands than he settled down to a four-volume work on *The English in Ireland in the Eighteenth Century*.

Since his purpose in writing this last was at least in part to attack the conciliatory Irish policies of the Gladstone administration, it is no wonder that he provoked some very violent reactions, but in fact the book signalled the start of yet another new phase in his life, one in which he became something of a public figure. He had laid the foundations a little earlier when he visited the United States for a short lecture tour dedicated to the hopeless task of dissuading Americans from supporting rebellion in Ireland; he had also already established contacts with various prominent conservative politicians in England, usually through their wives. So in 1874, partly to escape the depression caused by his second wife's death, he accepted an invitation from Lord Clarendon, foreign secretary in Disraeli's government, to visit South Africa and report on the situation there, in an effort to support the federal schemes then being prepared for that distracted part of the world. Quickly persuaded of the virtues of a forward English policy designed to annex the independent Boer republics to the north and east of the Cape Colony, he went a second time in 1875 in a more private capacity, but his activities caused only trouble. In Africa his recommendations offended local interests who regarded him as an intruder, while at home his views were thought to be simplistic and effectively ignored. Froude, in fact, made a poor politician.

However, he had now acquired a taste for travelling, and his sixties saw him, with energies undiminished despite occasional ailments, en route to Australia, New Zealand and the West Indies, as well as on two yachting and fishing holidays in Norway. Meanwhile the books continued to pour forth, most of them unimportant but one of them a major work which again drew much fire. In 1881–4 there appeared the two volumes of his *Thomas Carlyle: a History of his Life in London, 1834–1881*, a memoir of his old friend and mentor who had appointed him his literary executor and commissioned the biography himself. Nevertheless, Froude's frankness in revealing the agonies of Carlyle's marriage caused much offence, while Carlyle's niece tried hard to get her uncle's papers – and the profits to be made from their use – for

journalistic exercises based on no serious research and devoid of originality. The three books produced out of his Oxford lectures (*Erasmus, English Seamen of the 16th Century, The Council of Trent*) reflect the honest labour he put into them and are better worth reading – but still rather minor works.

herself. Froude was much distressed by the furore, to the point of coming briefly to regret his long association with the man who had been the chief intellectual influence on his life. Still, his contacts in high places remained loyal, a state of affairs which even survived an indifferent biography of Disraeli (1890), and when in 1892 the Regius professor of modern history at Oxford (Froude's devoted enemy Edward Augustus Freeman) unexpectedly died, the prime minister, the marquess of Salisbury, offered the chair to Froude, seventy-four years old. He accepted, with some qualms, and proved to be a popular lecturer, though he found it difficult to make contact with undergraduates so far removed from him in age and sympathies, but he died, after a prolonged illness, in October 1894.

Froude's was truly a complicated character, despite an outward pretence of straightforward simplicity. His pleasures indeed were simple, and he much enjoyed all sorts of physical exercise. His conversation, reserved for his friends, delighted them; on his day, he counted as one of the most brilliant talkers around, and we can still get a taste of this from his letters of which he produced an endless and very entertaining stream. His wit varied from the acidulous to the playful, but he was at heart too earnest a man to display much humour, and he took most things seriously. His deepest admiration he reserved for that very Victorian quality, manliness. He deplored anything that smacked of weakness and therefore hated the liberalism prevalent in his day which he regarded as a betrayal of the mission divinely entrusted to England. It might be thought no accident that his birthday fell on 23 April – St George's Day – and his patriotism was always unrestrained, commonly aggressive, though never really chauvinist. Absolutely no liberal, he cannot be called a proper tory either, being at heart a radical who had learned (both from experience and from Carlyle) to despise industrial democracy, parliamentary institutions and the inadequacies of lesser breeds, such as the Negroes he met in America and South Africa, or the Irish whom he knew well from frequent visits. Yet direct contact produced also very different reactions: he always scrupulously emphasized the things he admired even about people he wrote off as a group, the only exception being the Manchester business community among whom he spent his first married years and for whose philistine bigotry he always maintained his hatred. Whether his worship of the heroic owed more to the contrary conditioning of his childhood or to the lessons taught by Carlyle is not material; in any case, it dominated all his thinking, and it mattered that he was the sort of romantic who can find heroes only in the past. By the same token, he peopled the past with the sort of heroes he dreamed of. In some ways the child that knew how every thicket held a giant and every brook a malignant sprite never died in him, and all his life he girded his loins to play St George to every sort of dragon.

It is therefore no wonder that his closest friends were men equally conscious of the threats posed by the meanness of their own age, such as the demonic figure of Carlyle, or that obsessive activist, Charles Kingsley, ever restless and ever troubling. To the former he talked, and with the latter he walked – dozens of miles a day sometimes. However, his circle of good friends was very large and included many men of peace. It also included many highly intelligent women, for Froude absolutely lacked the Victorian predilection for relegating women either to the kitchen or a pedestal; he was never more relaxed or attractive than in his relations with the opposite sex. Among men one finds, not surprisingly, few philosophers or theologians but rather men of action and some good scholars, especially that outstanding anthropologist, Max Müller, one of Germany's gifts to Oxford. Throughout his life Froude retained his love for the classics, especially the Greeks, on whom he was raised. He spoke Spanish but does not seem to have read much in it; and though he spoke little German he worshipped Goethe whom he read in the original and cited (usually with grammatical mistakes) on frequent occasions. His close acquaintance in fact extended beyond the shores of Britain to embrace several Irishmen of the ascendancy, Ralph Waldo Emerson and John Motley in the United States, and a relay of friends in the other parts of the British Empire that he visited. Froude had a gift for friendship and readily developed unquestioning loyalties which were rarely misplaced. In Europe, on the other hand, he seems to have had very little interest, visiting Spain only for purposes of research and Italy once under family pressure for a holiday. Open though he remained to experience – he had an excellent eye for scenery as well as people – it must be admitted that the outward appearance of a confident champion of the Anglo-Saxon virtues, which he paraded on occasions suitable and unsuitable, represented a persistent inner reality.

One aspect of his associations must strike one as surprising. Carlyle and (if he can be so classified) Kingsley apart, he seems never to have mixed with other historians. He occasionally mentioned Macaulay (whom he never met and never liked), but that he should have written so much history in the half-century from 1850 onwards without ever apparently becoming aware of Leopold von Ranke, the foremost influence on that age's historical studies, is startling and revealing. Professional historian though he might be (in the sense already defined), he really remained a man of letters and affairs who happened in the main to write historical works. He also, by the way, remained some sort of Christian, largely on the grounds that the world would be even more horrible if human instincts were not restrained by Christian precepts. Many of his attitudes and reflections suggest that, despite the good humour and courtesy that he showed even in his most slashing moods, he lived through many an inner struggle with black despair and irrational hatreds of which he told the world almost nothing. After what father and brother and fellow schoolboys had done to him, it would have been no wonder. With a perfectly genuine and humble generosity he nevertheless always professed high admiration at least for the first two members of that baleful trinity, even when they most crushingly rejected him.

The complexity of this superficially transparent man comes out quite plainly in the fact that his whole life – his scholarly and public life – really consisted of a chain of controversies whose occurrence always seemed to surprise him. His break with the Church, a common enough event among the offspring of clerical fathers, made an exceptional amount of noise, partly because he was Hurrell's brother and Newman's protégé, partly because the authorities at Oxford reacted with quite excessive indignation, but partly also because he chose to advertise the circumstances in a novel which exposed the miseries of his childhood and touched, delicately, on sexual problems. (Throughout his life, Froude was singularly free of the age's addiction to primness and prudery.) His great work, the *History of England*, caused widespread offence because he chose to praise the Reformation when its reputation stood at its lowest ebb, and to rehabilitate Henry VIII, then regarded as the classical tyrant of English history who had destroyed the marvels of medieval religion and monasticism. True, the reaction he provoked expressed bigoted prejudice and a quite spectacular ignorance of history, but Froude should not have been so surprised, seeing that he went continually out of his way to disparage Roman Catholicism and indeed all forms of priesthood. Moreover, he worked so fast and often so carelessly that he gave enough opportunities to those who wished to call him a liar and a cheat, opportunities enthusiastically taken by Freeman who for reasons that have never been properly understood elected himself Froude's nemesis. (Freeman himself, of course, believed that he was called by History to demolish the enemy to the truth: but to pursue the question involves studying Freeman's personality, which lacks interest.) The hunt was carried on for years, mostly anonymously in the pages of the *Saturday Review*, and that despite the fact – of which Freeman was not only aware but proud – that he himself knew very little about the sixteenth century. It must satisfy a sense of justice that in the long run this violence did the hunter far more harm than the prey.

Froude so regularly stirred up passions that his professions of innocence have been hard to accept, genuine though they almost certainly were. He himself might regard his views on Ireland as no more than sensible deductions from observation. But he disseminated them widely when English policy in Ireland was a major public issue; he wrote four volumes on eighteenth-century Ireland which were not only opinionated but backed by quite insufficient research – thus provoking the contemporary expert, W. H. E. Lecky, who happened to be a supporter of Gladstone's policy; and his lectures in the States seemed calculated to rouse the maximum fury by both provoking the enormously powerful Irish-American lobby and annoying those in England who deplored unpatriotic attacks on English statesmen delivered among foreigners (two separate sets of bigots, in fact). He committed himself too readily and rashly to imperialist factions in South Africa and Australia, to white ascendancy in Jamaica, to contempt for both Turks and Russians at the time of the Crimean War: he ought to have understood that his own preference for passionate attachments would result in predictable counter-attacks. Even the lucidity of his style, which made the violence of his opinions so very obvious, worked against him. The fury roused by his *Life of Carlyle*, with its unfashionably open revelations, again greatly exceeded any measure to be called just, but though Froude claimed to be merely obeying Carlyle's own call for less hypocrisy in biographers he should not have been surprised at the reaction he met. Repeatedly at the centre of violent controversies, he usually gave the impression of being quite innocent in the matter. One may suppose that he saved himself – his sanity and his work – by that honest though mistaken opinion. Froude rarely responded to attacks and more rarely still went into battle against his detractors because so far as he was concerned there were no controversies. After a while, therefore, all those nameless frothings-at-the-mouth came to look unconvincing and rather distasteful.

Nevertheless, in one respect his silence did him harm. The world, especially of scholarship, came to believe that Froude was really not to be trusted: the charges of congenital inaccuracy and deliberate distortion stuck because he virtually never troubled to refute them. Some of this apparent indifference arose from an essentially stoical and equable temperament, surprising in one so combative when he took pen in hand, but it owed much too to a pervasive superficiality in judgment. He seems never to have understood his own complex nature and motives, or the springs of his own passions, and he expected others to accept his own conviction of humble righteousness. Some such psychological superficiality also imbued his writings: he was always liable to see things too simply in black and white, in terms of heroes and villains, and he was quite capable of uncritically using dubious evidence when it suited his book, while acutely criticizing any that needed to be removed from the path. But such things do not necessarily support the not uncommon conviction of his day that Froude was a fraud, a conviction confirmed by the manner in which the historian, pouring out his work at a most extraordinary rate, slid from controversy to controversy without ever admitting that there might be grounds for questioning his confident assertions or attempting to demolish the arguments used against him.[4]

However, at this late date those agonies and upheavals of Froude's day, much as they agitated his contemporaries even as they tended to leave the man himself barely touched, matter little unless there is still cause to read Froude; if there is, they help us to understand why he wrote as he did. Several pieces in that enormous output still repay attention: some of the essays, perhaps the late Oxford lectures, the biography of Carlyle. Above all, however, Froude deserves to be judged by his *History of England*, the work into which he poured most of himself and to which he devoted quite extraordinary labours. Some preliminary articles apart it was also his first foray into historical research and writing, begun when he was barely thirty and completed (despite frequent forebodings that he would not live to see the end) in twenty long years. Its enthusiastic reception by a general readership was

---

[4] Even the great F. W. Maitland, a man not given to malice, could once express a hope (only half in jest) that an interesting document he had found had not been forged by Froude (*The Letters of Frederick William Maitland*, ed. C. H. S. Fifoot [1965], no. 265).

from the first matched by the sour reaction of the reviewers, very few of whom knew anything about the subject but most of whom disliked the Reformation; and a hundred years of studying it have provided much support for the hostile opinion that charged him with excessive inaccuracy and undue bias. Freeman's often ignorant attacks have stuck, and so have the more particular criticisms of three generations of Tudor historians. These criticisms go beyond the obvious fact that all works of history become out of date as knowledge accumulates. Froude's *History* has come to be thought of as a splendid piece of literature with no claim to professional attention.

Not that everybody has written it off. Thus Conyers Read, an American historian who happened to share Froude's hatred of popery, called it 'the classic for the period from the fall of Wolsey to the defeat of the Armada and one of the great masterpieces of English historical literature';[5] he always did his best to have the book maintained in use. If it is indeed still worth reading today that favourable opinion must at least in part be correct: which means that we need to take a closer look at it in order to judge its virtues and faults. Its enormous length precludes a full analysis here, but the essential items in praise and dispraise of it are not many and can be investigated by a study of some parts. I propose in the main to confine myself to the first three volumes (which deal with the second half of Henry VIII's reign), a manageable sector which contains all the issues raised by Froude's manner of proceeding. It is also the part most freshly conceived and written, done before the inevitable weariness of going on for so long began to overtake him. Those who still like Froude think him at his best there.

Froude originally planned to write a history of Elizabeth I's reign but soon decided that he needed to start with the beginnings of the English Reformation in 1529; exhaustion of interest rather than a more deliberate decision induced him to stop at 1588 instead of carrying on to 1603. He expressly stated his purpose in undertaking the task: he had been infuriated by the fashionable denunciation of the Reformation and protestantism current in Oxford circles and widely accepted in the Church and laity of England, a denunciation which he believed represented a falsification of history.[6] To that extent he certainly

[5] Conyers Read, *Bibliography of British History: Tudor Period, 1485–1603* (2nd edn, Oxford, 1959), no. 340.

[6] The attack on the Reformation combined various strands. John Lingard's very influential *History of England from the First Invasion by the Romans to the Revolution of 1688* (8 vols., 1819–30) had presented a sober but strictly papist view of it, and in the 1830s this received support from the

fulfilled his purpose: in his pages the Reformation emerged once more as the formative period of English greatness, the seed-bed of all that was admirable and profitable in the subsequent experience of the English nation. He also explained that he began reading in the conviction that Henry VIII, though he presided over the beginnings of good things, was himself a deplorable bloodstained despot of whom nothing favourable could be said, whereas Elizabeth was a wise and noble statesman herself responsible for the successes of her glorious reign. In the upshot he came to think that the king was really the statesman of destiny and a true father of his people, while the daughter lacked all the necessary qualities of mind or character, the successes of her reign being the work of her great ministers, especially William Cecil, Lord Burghley. The second claim – that he had had to change his mind – was meant to support the first – that the Reformation was the triumph of virtue. If he had shown himself so open to persuasion by the evidence, surely his verdict, dissent though it might from current convictions on the character of sixteenth-century history, could be trusted to be free of bias, be reliable. The question is: was it? Or rather, insofar as bias can be proved in the historian, does it really destroy the reliability of his history?

The charges against Froude amount to two: that he wrote history under the guidance of overwhelming prejudices, and that he doctored his research to support those violently distorted conclusions. As to prejudices, he certainly had them, but the ones that have caused the most affront are so obvious as to minimize the problem. Froude hated the Church of Rome and believed that the protestant Reformation was the source of all right developments. In actual fact, his championship of the Reformation did not follow the conventional lines: unlike John Foxe in the sixteenth century, or Gilbert Burnet in the seventeenth, he did not regard protestantism as the absolute truth of all religion. His own religious experience inclined him against all doctrinal exclusiveness, and he favoured the transformations of the Reformation era not because they brought in the only true faith but because they initiated (as he saw it) the political developments which made England great, free and

learned attacks of S. R. Maitland on John Foxe's praise of the early reformers. Maitland collected his notes in 1849, in *Essays on Subjects connected with the Reformation in England*: their effect was the greater because he appeared to have no denominational grounds for demolishing favourable views of the Reformation. All this was grist to the mill of romantic medievalists – descended in part from Walter Scott and in part from William Blake, and sentimentally moved by their distaste for industrial capitalism to believe that the sixteenth century had destroyed all that was beautiful and holy. These attitudes helped to produce the Oxford Movement with its ambition to undo the Reformation, and it was this climate that Froude encountered at Oxford.

imperially dominant. His regard for the reformed religion derived from his aggressive patriotism. But if his approval of protestantism lacked religious fervour, his attitude to Roman Catholicism fed on little except passion. Certainly his sources and predecessors gave him plenty of guidance in the dialectic of anti-popery, but he added a special powerful conviction of the sheer wickedness that seemed to him to be the sole distinguishing mark of the pope's religion and its political consequences. Rome (and its satellites) meant tyranny to him – tyranny, oppression, torture and the enslaving of the human mind in darkest superstition. These convictions run right through the book, so that their constantly and often crudely repeated assertion can become very wearisome; however, since they are so freely expressed they are easily discounted. No one need believe Froude's view of the great religious confrontation of the Reformation era, but no one need really allow it to interfere with a reading and even an enjoyment of the book.

In any case, the later twentieth century is likely to find the second of Froude's ingrained fervours more troublesome. If his treatment of the warring religions owed little to any deeply religious feelings of his own, whence sprang his consistent attitude? The answer is that he held firmly to a racial view of mankind; he really believed that humanity consisted of various races among which some were superior to others. This faith came out occasionally in his correspondence in mildly anti-Semitic remarks, though on the whole Froude was indifferent to the Jews and such problems as they might pose – much more indifferent than was common at the time. It came out much more throughout his life in his attitude to African Blacks: accepting the Boer view of South African 'kaffirs', or the West Indian planters' view of emancipated slaves, he regarded Negroes as inferior and as necessarily in tutelage to white guidance and control. It should be added that his remarks on these delicate matters were never vicious; what he felt sprang from a paternal regard for those who could not be expected to come up to the high standards of the Anglo-Saxon race and therefore merited help – the help of a stern father or schoolmaster. In all this Froude proved himself highly conventional; he simply shared the beliefs current among most Englishmen of his day and was quite unselfconscious about them. He thought in this way before the impact of Charles Darwin elaborated racist prejudice into a faith by seeming to give the authority of science to notions of inborn superiorities and inferiorities, but when he began to be acquainted with it he naturally found Darwinism acceptable both to his undogmatic Christianity and to his social concepts.

In any case, his views on race must be understood not only in the setting of his own day but also in the sense in which he used the term. The nineteenth century regularly used the word race when it meant nation, and Froude's racism derived from his assurance of the greatness of the English nation – then, of course, at the height of its world-wide power. He shared what were, once again, highly conventional views about the superiority of the 'Teutonic' north of Europe over the 'Latin' south, and amongst the Teutons he readily awarded the palm to the so-called Anglo-Saxons both in their homeland and in the offshoots that they had spread across the world. His beliefs about the Irish – composed of much pity, some respect, and not infrequent abomination – differed little from his views about Caribbean Negroes, and he sympathized with the growing number of Americans who lamented the dilution of the allegedly original Anglo-Saxon 'stock' by European and Irish immigration.

None of this need be sympathetic to the present-day reader, but neither should he allow it to trouble him unless it affects the tone and tenor of Froude's *History* – which it does. Right from the start we get that insistence on the special manliness, heroism and military valour of the English – rosycheeked Englishmen, as most unnervingly he can call them – which then runs through the book. Froude really believed that the 'true' English were morally and physically superior to all other nations, and he thus came to judge individuals and periods very simply by the criterion whether they assisted or hampered the aggressive greatness of the English people and their liberty. Again it is quite easy to discount these frequent intrusions of elevated patriotic nonsense, but it has to be admitted that tenets of this sort could seriously affect the story as he told it. He convinced himself that in the sixteenth century the English experienced a heroic age in which their true qualities were given full and free rein, and not surprisingly he came to think that everything he saw around him – an urbanized, industrialized England which was moving towards democracy (mob rule) and the collapse of aristocratic values – represented a decline from those truly marvellous days. Here Carlyle's influence played its part, but so did natural inclination. It is quite fascinating to read Froude's outpourings on the horror of democracy, the absurdities of constitutional reform, the contemptability of Parliament and parties, which almost to a word could be matched with similar pronouncements from despairing conservatives a hundred years later. What, however, matters here is that because of these notions touching heroism and decline Froude's *History* was in part written as a tract for the times: his picture of Henrician and Elizabethan England was conceived – unconsciously conceived, I incline to think – as a lesson and corrective for present discontents. This sort of thing does affect the lasting value of any historian's work. Not only did Froude write about the Reformation under the teleological banner of a future greatness to be explained from its beginnings in an heroic age, but he made the age look specially heroic because in his mind he was for ever contrasting it with the despicable era in which he was condemned to live.[7]

Thus unquestionably Froude's private passions affected and distorted his historical description, but always in ways so open and straightforward that they permit the reader to apply the necessary correction. We know better, for instance, than to accept his static and hostile view of 'the middle ages' (all 1200 years of them?) as an era of popish darkness redeemed only by English battle honours, or on a smaller point his curious conviction that the really very minor conflict called the Wars of the Roses was the worst and bloodiest event in history (all things English, even civil wars, always being more gigantic than anyone else's). When we read about a manly horror at the novel crime of murder by poison which upright Englishmen, accustomed to leading with the left (and the chin), could only abominate, we need only think of England's history as related by Shakespeare (of whose history Froude spoke highly) to realize what nonsense such passages are. Oddly enough, more trouble is caused by a third and quite minor set of prejudices which unconsciously caused Froude to do the subtlest injustice to the age he was studying. He knew it for an article of faith that state intervention in the nation's economy was almost a sin and certainly always an error; very far from well versed in matters economic, he accepted the currently dominant teaching of the classical economists and frequently blamed Tudor governments for one of the few things for which they can fairly claim credit, namely their efforts at social control designed to

---

[7] Froude's remarks about Parliament offer an instructive example of his tactics. He could never find words bad enough for the Parliament of his own day, whereas he automatically assumed that the Tudor assemblies were full of highminded and worthy patriots. Thus where a liberal or whig historian would have condemned the sixteenth century but rejoiced to find early traces there of the later triumphant institution (the Mother of Parliaments), Froude's conservatism led him to emphasize the great start made under the Tudors in order to highlight the miserable state the Parliament had reached in the age of Gladstone and Disraeli.

protect the people against the vicissitudes of fortune and the excesses of
the strong. Froude tried to recognize the good intentions but regarded
them as so misguided and surprisingly foolish that he felt obliged to
treat them as blameworthy. This prejudice caused him to miss more of
the social and even political truth about the century than his other
prejudices caused him to invent, but the damage done is subtle – mostly
by omission, so that for instance we never even hear of the great
inflation which set its mark on the whole century – and perhaps lessened
by the fact that, like most historians in his time, he had in any case little
interest in economic history.

I have said that in reading Froude we can make allowance for his
protestant and patriotic fervour and, provided that we do not react with
a passionate distaste to his passionate preferences, still read him with
much interest and some profit. However, it obviously matters whether
we can trust him to give us history, not fiction. Whether those fervours
can really be abstracted from the story as told and leave us with
historical truth depends on whether they governed his selection and
interpretation of the evidence. Obviously Froude did not ask many of
the questions we might ask today, nor could he anticipate a century's
research. We must read him as a nineteenth-century historian, not a
present-day one. But can we read him as an historian at all? Was Froude
the fraud of an early hostile tradition? Did his alleged research rest on
pretence, on falsification, and even on invention, as his enemies maintained? Since they knew little of the sources he used there is no point in
retracing their steps, but we must come to understand Froude the
working historian.

In the first place, we must grasp how very hard he worked, a fact of
which he was rightly proud. He really explored the archives, at a time
when there were no lists or calendars to guide him. He had one piece of
good fortune, in that the foundation of the Public Record Office in 1839
brought together collections hitherto scattered and sometimes hard of
access, but when he worked in those collections they had not begun to
be ordered or properly listed. He had to read all those materials in
manuscript, and so far as correspondence and state papers are concerned
he read most of what is extant. In addition he worked at the British
Museum, among the Cecil papers at Hatfield House, and in the Spanish
archives at Simancas,[8] reading and transcribing with his own hand

---

[8] Lingard had gone to Simancas, but it was Froude who opened historians' eyes to the importance
of that magnificent archive.

thousands of Tudor documents. Where I have myself had occasion to use materials available to him I can testify to the commendable thoroughness of his search. Of course he omitted large categories of sources, such as the financial and legal records which no one at the time had got around to studying: he was concerned to write political history, and he concentrated on its usual materials.

All this work on manuscript merits real respect. Neither Froude's enemy Freeman nor his successor A. F. Pollard faced the challenge of the archives in whose dust and confusion Froude spent innumerable hours, deciphering with difficulty and without assistance, and scribbling at speed until his hand was ready to drop off. In all that labour he certainly made mistakes. His transcripts were usually shot through with minor inaccuracies, and (like his successors) he often erred in dating undated documents. When he translated a Latin, French or Spanish paper he could be quite cavalier in his determination to employ a vivid version of near-Tudor usage. But I cannot say that I have found him improperly perverting his documents; his errors are on the whole venial and do not affect the argument. While one may well disagree with his interpretation of a letter, a despatch or a deposition, one cannot convict him of deliberately falsifying the document in question; his judgment, like that of any historian, may well be disputed, but it is not the case that he invented or constructed the materials he used. In the basic essentials he was honest, and he unquestionably looked very much further for his sources than any of his predecessors had done and most of his successors were to do. Nor, by and large, would I accuse him of habitually misjudging the evidence for partisan purposes. Where those letters are concerned, he tried with some success (and occasional failure) to get their meaning right. In any case, since (and I may as well say this outright) his interpretation of the age was in general much sounder than that offered by his opponents, he really lacked the temptation to commit all those sins against the truth of which he has been accused.

There is one serious exception to this essentially favourable verdict. Froude opened his campaign by reading the parliamentary statutes of the time and to the end of his days remained perversely proud of the fact that he rested his general interpretation on them. Inasmuch as he thus started work from genuine records instead of just regurgitating earlier chronicles and histories, he did indeed do well and produced something like a revolution in method, but he comprehensively spoiled the effect of his virtue by believing all that he read in the statute book. As he always explained, he found there what he regarded as a true description of the condition of England and a true account, moreover, of the love the realm bore to that good and great monarch, King Henry VIII. It never seems to have occurred to him that talk of that mighty lord and father of his people was put into preambles drafted by the king's servants, that acts concerned to remedy some deficiency in the body politic need to be checked against the ascertainable facts of reality before the picture they paint can be assessed, or that there may be a very large gap between the intentions expressed in reforming statutes and their practical effect. When challenged, he simply asserted that the Parliament of England – of sixteenth-century England – was too worthy a body to tell lies; he also assumed that what was proclaimed was as good as done. He could not have been more wrong on either count. In addition he put implicit trust in Henry's own letters and despatches: others might be capable of pretence or prevarication, but when a statement carried the king's signature it was true. Thus there lies at the heart of Froude's method a very serious fault not untypical, again, of historians of that age: he applied intelligent criticism to only one side of the evidence before him.

So firmly did Froude become wedded to his trusting reliance on statutes and royal despatches that even the appearance of new materials could not shake him. When late in life he looked at the newly discovered despatches of the imperial ambassador to England (from the archives at Brussels and Vienna of which he had known nothing in his youth) – those very documents which were to form the main source for later and in their way equally uncritical historians hostile to Henry VIII and the early Reformation – he refused to admit that they in any way altered the story he had drawn from his limited material, even though they are in fact almost totally incompatible with central parts of it. His essay on *The Divorce of Catherine of Aragon* (1891) is a sad book, testifying as it does only to the possession of well-adjusted blinkers. Of all Froude's faults as an historian his blind reliance on the statutes is the worst – perhaps the only serious one because it makes him present an England and a Henry VIII that really sheer widely from the truth; and whenever he cites an act of Parliament in support of an interpretative point he should be disbelieved. Here, at the start of his research, he showed himself to be the amateur that most of his later research shows him not to have been, and it is distressing that increasing experience did not make him go back over those tyro efforts. In this rooted error we may see some of the consequences of his essential isolation. If he had gone to school with Mommsen or Ranke, or even Stubbs, to learn something about the systematic criticism of sources, he would probably have found no reason much to alter his major conclusions – his preconceived notions would have seen to that – but he would not have rested some crucial points on so naive an assessment of the evidence.

Still, whatever may be true of the setting provided, his detailed narrative depends very little on that evidence or that error. It too, of course, contains its quota of mistakes or mis-statements; no history of such length, written at such speed, could be free of them. Some were the sort of errors that derive from the relatively early state of research, the sort that later research corrects. Some sprang from Froude's inability to analyse social and economic issues, an inability which he shared with other historians whom he emulated in professing to have paid due heed to such matters. His much praised first chapter, possibly inspired by Macaulay's famous third, which describes the realm from those misused statutes, is a tissue of error and mere imagination. Yet when all Froude's mistakes are added up, even those that were clearly tendentious, he survives very well by the side of some one could name, especially the later defenders of a papalist view of the era, such as the unconscionable Cardinal Gasquet. Nevertheless, some of Froude's errors might possibly support the charge of deliberate falsification in relatively small points, designed to create highly misleading conclusions by accumulation. A few examples will show that Froude was certainly capable of purposive misrepresentation, but that these more than slips matter very little in the creation of the totality he presents.

Froude said that Henry VIII himself composed the poor law of 1536 (vol. i, 80). He did not, in fact, know the very remarkable proposal which the king presented to Parliament and which would have offered better grounds for the sort of encomium Froude pronounced than did the far from impressive bill which actually passed, but in any case all that his evidence entitled him to say was that Henry brought in the bill, not that he wrote it.[9] Here he overstates, in order to endow the king with the obligatory paternal glory.

Froude deliberately read far more precision, purpose and nobility into an alleged early organization of protestant reformers (ibid. 170) in order to show how morally superior they were to their opponents. That organization did not exist, nor do the sources cited by him support the

---

[9] Cf. G. R. Elton, *Reform and Reformation: England 1509–1558* (1977), 226–7.

terms he used of it. This may be called tendentious distortion, far from unknown in any historian's work: unfortunate, unnecessary, but unimportant.

Froude wished to make all the opponents of the Reformation appear as worshippers of superstition, for which reason he accused Catherine of Aragon and Sir Thomas More of believing in the pretensions of the so-called Nun of Kent (ibid. 312). Yet he cannot have found any evidence that the queen adhered to the Nun because none exists, and he must have seen More's careful account of his reactions which shows his scepticism. Here, where he alleged no sources, he is really not playing fair.

Intent on making Henry VIII a reformer, he credits the king with a desire to provide a vernacular Bible for his people and with being prevented by 'the bishops' (ibid. 516). Yet he could not possibly have offered evidence for the statement that the king 'had himself long desired an authorized English version' because on that point all such evidence as exists clearly points the other way. This is a tendentious invention.

Froude hated monasticism: therefore the supporters of the Nun of Kent must all have been monks (vol. ii, 55), even though one of those named, Henry Gold, was even in the act of attainder identified as a secular priest. Here prejudice caused a casual reading of his favourite source.

Anxious to think only good of the king, Froude automatically had the Nun and her followers condemned in a formal trial when yet he must have known that none such occurred (ibid. 65): they were dealt with unheard by parliamentary act of attainder. This looks like a tendentious lie.

Sion Monastery was a house of Bridgettines; by calling it Carthusian (ibid. 316) Froude may have been trying to insinuate that even the strictest monastic order was corrupted by superstition: a casual error which may be a Freudian slip.

On a different level, when Froude spoke of the House of Lords as purely ornamental (ibid. 348) he talked absurd nonsense, as he mostly did when he turned to Parliament and 'party', regularly spoken of as though institutionally identical with their nineteenth-century manifestations. This anachronism has a touch of the tendentious because Froude liked to see 'the people' (his rosycheeked Englishmen) as the agents of greater glory, and it has produced consequences among historians worse .

than anything his championship of the Reformation did: later historians have followed him in improperly ignoring the Lords. But the tendentiousness here was not deliberate.

When Froude came to the death of Thomas Cromwell he faced a dilemma. Cromwell, promoter and agent of reform, was to him a worthy man, but he was destroyed by Henry VIII who could do no wrong. So we get a description of Cromwell's alleged misdeeds which says of the unprovable and highly improbable charges raised against him that they carried 'probability on their front' (vol. iii, 310): poor old Henry, much distressed, could not help himself.[10] Here the demands of the tendentious interpretation forced the historian into public contortion.

This selection will suffice. Froude was indeed capable of misusing evidence or resting a case rhetorically on no evidence at all. He is not to be trusted throughout, and the untutored reader can at times be misled by his sophistry. But the sum of tendentious errors of this sort (or deliberate, or accidental, lies) does not remotely equal the horrors alleged against him. I am inclined to think that he was more inaccurate in tiny matters (especially transcripts) than his respectable contemporaries, but that in important issues his errors and mis-statements were certainly no worse than those of Macaulay, Freeman or even the pedantic S. R. Gardiner. Where he deliberately misleads, only those who read him for gospel truth will suffer: and are there any such today? Nor must we overlook his positive qualities, his skills and insights. It is too easily forgotten that often Froude saw something clearly that others at the time and since have been anxious to obfuscate. Himself the victim of a minor heresy hunt, he could nevertheless assess persecution soberly and justly, without the false note of indignation which he permits himself too often in his narrative (vol. i, 172). Contrary to some opinions still current today, he evaluated the real importance of the Reformation Parliament with much precision (ibid. 189). His appreciation of Thomas More is a deal more sensible and balanced than that most commonly found today, among the worshippers and acolytes with their wide influence (ibid. 361). Much tendentious misunderstanding could have been avoided if his sound scepticism concerning an internal spy-system had been heeded by later historians (ibid. 365, n. 2). Again, the examples could be multiplied. If Froude occasionally introduced error and more occasionally still misused evidence, he also on occasion

[10] Cf. above, vol. i, 271–6.

410

introduced truth where lies had been; and on balance he did markedly more of the second than the first.

One particular facet of Froude's labours calls for a special word. As we have seen, he reversed the common judgment of the day on the two foremost members of the House of Tudor, elevating Henry VIII and depressing Elizabeth. Since his day these assessments have once more much altered. Henry VIII remained a hero to his next biographer, A. F. Pollard, who prudently discarded some of Froude's extravagant praise but concurred in the general view that here was a great king personally building a nation's greatness and behaving as morally as a statesman, constrained by circumstances, might. This opinion stood until I ventured to reject it: arguing that the king was far from masterfully competent or invariably in charge, I drew attention to the much more important creative role of his great ministers. This remains my view of the matter, even though a recent pair of biographies, one outstanding and the other very interesting, have once more given us a Henry VIII who himself, in statesmanlike fashion, ruled his own and his people's fate.[11] However, even these modern biographers have not returned wholly to Pollard and Froude: they are more critical of his work than the former and firmly deny him the virtues discerned by the latter. The king's personality and achievement thus remain in dispute, but no one now would endorse Froude's opinion without very severe reservations.

The fortunes of Queen Elizabeth in the hands of historians have been less complicated. An early effort to retrieve her reputation from Froude's attack was made by Mandell Creighton, but it was the publication of J. E. Neale's biography which decreed that she should once more be regarded as the foremost statesman of her day. Policy, it is now most commonly held, owed everything to the queen: Burghley and the rest have retreated to the position of influential advisers. The grumbles which so impressed Froude are now seen as an unjustified letting off of steam by politicians who did not have the good sense to accept that Elizabeth was more brilliant than any of them.[12] Even though some dissent is beginning to make itself heard from scholars less bemused by Gloriana,[13] the dominant voice remains that of her worshippers, especially as Neale has been joined by A. L. Rowse; the latest

[11] A. F. Pollard, *Henry VIII* (1905); G. R. Elton, *Henry VIII: an Essay in Revision* (1962); J. J. Scarisbrick, *Henry VIII* (1968); Lacey Baldwin Smith, *Henry VIII: the Mask of Royalty* (1971).

[12] M. Creighton, *Queen Elizabeth* (1899); J. E. Neale, *Queen Elizabeth* (1934).

[13] J. Hurstfield, *Elizabeth I and the Unity of England* (1960); C. H. Wilson, *Queen Elizabeth and the Revolt of the Netherlands* (1970).

Papers

biography of serious weight is adulatory.[14] My own view is that Elizabeth was as lucky in her modern historians as she was in the events of her reign. Although Froude certainly far too readily decried one whose dislike of war and uncertainty in the face of drastic decisions did not measure up to his concept of heroism, he was right to emphasize Burghley's role and to cast doubt on the queen's invariable excellence. A new and independent study is rather urgently needed.

James Anthony Froude gave a solid and enduring framework to a crucial sixty years of English history, telling their story with great verve and often fascinating detail. He identified the serious main-line of Reformation and reform, endowing it – in the face of the ignorant disapprobation and meanminded anguish so current in his day – with that positive, creative and edifying air that in truth belongs to it. He clothed his construction in a language that for many has made the work endure; there appear to be those who would be willing to read it as literature without wanting to learn history from it. This, I think, is rather unkind to Froude who was very much concerned whether what he wrote was history or not and on the whole rightly believed that it was. It is also a judgment which I find it difficult to accept. I agree that his much praised style combines speed and lucidity, is often excellent and sometimes beautiful, and handles the swift narrative exceptionally well, though it is much less well suited to the patient analysis of problems; but I find it a little wearisome because its pace varies so little. Froude, I feel, tends to march on stilts: though one should remember, of course, that no one was supposed to read those twelve volumes through in one go. To me the more relaxed, even less artificial style of his splendid letters seems much more attractive than his public prose, but that is a matter of taste. What matters is that the history in the work, all cautions and qualifications allowed for, still remains well worthy of attention. Froude's *History of England* is two things, neither negligible: a remarkable achievement of historical story-telling, and in itself a striking memorial to Victorian attitudes. It can profitably be read for both these reasons.

[14] A. L. Rowse, *The England of Elizabeth* (1950); P. Johnson, *Elizabeth: a Study in Power and Intellect* (1974).

48

THE HISTORIAN'S SOCIAL FUNCTION*

There is said to be a crisis in historical studies whose collapse some predict. I think myself that the word crisis gets over-used, and I am convinced that history as a subject of study and instruction will survive. We may find fewer students of it in schools and universities, but we shall stop well short of the retreat (itself, it seems to me, now halted) that has befallen the classical languages. People will continue to read history, even serious history, and people will continue to write history, even good history. Still, there are enemies, some lurking in thickets, some boldly skirmishing across the plain, and while their peashooters cannot kill they can and do hurt. Those sufficiently out of date still to think that what gets the customers is relevance continue to proclaim that history is irrelevant to a forward-looking – indeed, a progressive – society; and since their numbers include a good many who decide what happens in colleges of education, in schools, and (worst of all) in the Department of Education and Science, their obscurantism is not to be ignored. I do not here, in this company, need to defend or justify the study of history, but I feel urged to warn historians that they would be well advised to consider and state their case: at the very least we cannot any longer take it for granted that society will as a matter of course accept us at our own valuation and therefore support us. Today, therefore, on this last occasion that I address this body as President, I should like to consider the grounds on which I would argue that no healthy society can afford to abandon the professional study of the past at its highest, most intensive, and to all appearances least practical level. I cannot now also attend to the history that is told to the generality: one thing at a time.

There are a number of traditionally used justifications which I have come to regard as either insufficient or untrue. Historians have been said to serve society in a variety of ways. They record the actions of men and

* [Presidential address, 1976: *TRHS* 5th ser. 27 (1977), 197–211.]

preserve their memory for posterity. Some people like to be preserved for posterity (to the point of failing to destroy incriminating tapes) and some do not; but unfortunately this preservation of the past is just what the philistines regard as the dangerous effect of a concern with history. Thus there can be little point in emphasizing this function, however well we may think of it. Historians, as Charles Beard put it, are themselves the memory of mankind, and he was right in thinking that without memory man is mindless and inhuman: unable to remember, he cannot look forward, he lacks a third dimension, he is paper-thin. True indeed, but our critics not only are paper-thin but content to be so. These are therefore insufficient justifications because they rest on claims, true enough in themselves and attractive to those so inclined, which only underscore the objections used by others to attack the continued use and usefulness of historical studies.

As for the commonest defence employed in our behalf, it is unfortunately my belief that it will not stand up to inspection. This is the illusion that, to quote Bacon, history makes men wise. Is it not very widely held that a knowledge of past events and developments forms the best foundation for assessing the present and perhaps even the future: that historians are the teachers of mankind? A nice thought, if only it were true. The chief purpose of historical studies lies, it is believed, precisely there: we should study history in order to understand the present. In a desperate attempt to gain social approval, historians themselves have done much to give currency to such beliefs, to the point where some will offer themselves as persons able to look into the roots of present discontents and discern the shape of things to come. Present-directed history is on the increase; even ancient historians and medievalists have been known to proclaim to the world that the twentieth century cannot understand itself unless it attends to the effects of the Peloponnesian War or the coronation of Charlemagne upon (I suppose) the policy of the Kremlin or the balance-of-payments crisis. Perhaps I exaggerate, but not by much. Those less assured than they should be of the justice of their cause are always liable to pin the hostile slogan over their hearts with a slightly sickly smile.

Still, though I deplore them I can understand these aspirations which place the study of the past under the guiding star of the present, but I must point out that they rest on assumptions which experience all the time denies to be true. What proof is there that an understanding of the past improves a man's understanding of his present? The many excellent historians of nineteenth-century Germany who put their learning at the service of nation and politics made ghastly mistakes, displayed appalling misconceptions, caused disastrously false convictions to settle in the public mind, but anyone who for that reason would deny their quality as historians would be guilty of an equal misjudgment. I vividly remember that good man and excellent historian, Alfred Cobban, rubbing his hands in glee when Labour won the 1964 election, ecstatically convinced that a new dawn had risen for the universities of this country, a day of glorious, government-supported expansion and virtue. Twelve years later, facing the consequences of an egalitarian contempt for 'elitism' and 'excellence', we know him for a poor prophet, but we do not need to think him a worse historian for all that. Sometimes I think that only historians of a naturally pessimistic turn of mind ever manage to forecast things correctly, but even a consistent expectation that things will get worse can be sadly disappointed. Even what might appear to be obvious links between a man's experience in the study and the needs of his active calling seem far from sure to offer beneficial instruction: I remain to be persuaded that a minister of foreign affairs is better able to discharge his office because he once investigated the career of Metternich.

Of course, I agree that history, by enlarging a man's acquaintance, enlarges his experience and thus can improve his judgment and his vision, but I find no grounds for thinking that this happens necessarily and good grounds for fearing that a conscious preoccupation with wishing it to happen works the other way. Knowing history does not make you a better prophet, but trying to serve as adviser and prophet can spoil your work as an historian. It matters little what political allegiance may have stirred the scholar into wanting to use his learning about the past in order to assist and explain the present: both Seeley and Tawney would have been better historians if they had not so firmly fixed their purpose on being immediately serviceable to their own society. By allowing their history to serve their politics they reduced the worth of their contribution to both. In fact, I believe that there are fundamental reasons why historians cannot make better prophets than might be the practitioners of other forms of learning – reasons closely connected with the manner in which history must be investigated. I shall come back to this.

I have thrown down the claims which most of us make when challenged to justify our labours: have I left us naked to our enemies? I propose now to construct a covering garment of much superior quality, to be worn not so much with pride as with arrogance. And I propose to do so by going to the roots of our existence as historians. If there is a claim to be entered on behalf of history, it must start by demonstrating that history exists as an intellectual enterprise and discipline distinguishable from other pursuits and not to be replaced by them, for that is just what the adversary denies; and I would maintain that that demonstration depends on showing that history operates by a method peculiar to itself. History has often been denied disciplinary status because there is said to be no such thing as historical method: historians, it is alleged, employ no more than a form of common sense, sharpened and directed by the borrowing of methods from real disciplines. I disagree. Certainly we borrow techniques of all kinds first developed by other scholars – by linguists, bibliographers, philosophers, mathematicians, anthropologists, psychologists and so forth. Dealing with the whole experience of mankind, the historian cannot but use whatever technical devices mankind has developed for understanding itself. But being concerned with his proper task, the study of the past, the historian would not be discharging it faithfully unless he subjected all these techniques, chosen for their usefulness in solving this problem or that, to the general rules of his own method, developed to solve the universal problems of investigating that which has gone beyond recall.

The historian's task is to discover, reconstruct and explain what has happened in the past from such survivals of the past as are found in the present. The pervasive problems facing him are two: the extant evidence is always incomplete and usually highly ambiguous, and in trying to understand and explain that evidence he inescapably introduces the (possibly distorting) subjectivity of his own mind. These barriers stand squarely in the way of every effort to produce an account of the past which comes as close as possible to a truthful reconstruction, independent of the observer, of past situations and events. They are universals and arise no matter what particular type of event is being investigated, what historical age or region is studied, or what line of approach (political, economic, intellectual and so forth) is employed. All historians face these special difficulties, the condition of their calling. And since the difficulties are universal, so is their solution: historical method is the method deliberately devised for use by all historians so that they can minimize the effects of incompleteness, ambiguity and subjectivity in the treatment of extant evidence. It is therefore on the treatment of evidence that the method concentrates, and it does so in three respects: discovery, comprehension and interpretation.

The first task of the historian is to find such evidence as may be available to answer his questions, and in doing so he at once confronts the worst hazard of the whole enterprise. Since it must be he who decides what is relevant to his enquiry, how can he avoid the danger of allowing the terms of the enquiry to dictate the discovery, with the result that he will come to do no more than document an answer at which he had already arrived on the basis of little evidence or none? We all know how frequently this happens in practice, especially when the historian finds himself proving a case in which he is emotionally involved. But there is an answer, and it lies in three categorical imperatives of the method. One: the first approach to the evidence must be void of specific questions directing the search which should rather at this stage be an open investigation looking to the evidence to suggest questions. Two: all the available and potentially relevant evidence must be seen. Three: no evidence must be constructed additional to that which is found extant in its own right. These are hard demands. But let it be noted at once that they clearly distinguish the historical method from that of the experimental sciences (which construct experiments – artificial occurrences – in order .to test conjectured consequences), of the social sciences with their preliminary instruments (models and questionnaires) and their manipulation by quantification, or of the philosophical sciences which employ logic in order to draw out the implications of propositions set up as the start of the enquiry. The historian starts by not knowing where he is going; all that he knows is that there is an area of history to be investigated, and that there are historical materials to be worked through from which he will learn the particular questions he should pursue.

Of course, I know that this analysis contradicts the advice usually given to beginners, namely that they must formulate questions before reading. Both experience and reflection have taught me that, on the contrary, one must in the first instance read solely to open the mind to questions arising from the evidence – a mind kept clear of all but the most general questions (such as: I wonder what is in these documents which I have chosen to read because I want to know what the people living in that place and time were doing about governing themselves, or earning a living, or dealing with crime). 'Real' – that is, pointed – questions will soon rise up like an exhalation, at which point the mind, hitherto relatively passive, becomes dominant in the purposeful pursuit of the problems thus established as interesting and valid. Only if the historian works in this way can he be sure that his answers were not put there from the first by himself; only thus can he avoid the dangers of what J. H. Hexter has called 'source-mining', the search for convenient evidence to support a conclusion already arrived at. It follows, secondly, as I have said, that in order to eliminate accident and bias so far as he may he must investigate all the possibly relevant evidence, a prescription which in English history, for instance, becomes very difficult in the twelfth century and soon thereafter impossible. It nevertheless remains the only sound rule, and where it cannot be followed (except at the cost of eternal silence) the historian is obliged to devise ways for reducing the mass without prejudging the results of the enquiry. Briefly, I hold that this again is best done by interpolating a stage at which the choice of what is studied is not governed by the ultimate questions to be answered but perhaps by an archival criterion: one may choose to work through a given sector of the mass – as it might be the files of an institution or the correspondence of a certain person – with no limit to the issues thought relevant, before selectively investigating the remainder under the direction of the questions which the first reading has brought forward. Much, naturally will depend on the soundness of the choice made in identifying a dominant archive. These again are hard rules, but I know from experience that they can be observed at least with that approximation to precision that is the best that we as historians, operating in the imprecisions of men's fortunes, can ever hope to achieve.

Perhaps I need not say much on the third point, that which prohibits the creation of evidence. It may seem obvious and trite. However, a good deal especially of the more ambitious history one reads derives from such constructed evidence, put in where natural evidence deserts us, and those who advocate the use of theory – for instance psychological or economic theory – are particularly prone to that practice. Erikson's notorious book on Luther presents a picture of the man which owes almost everything to the author's (rather particular and limited) psychoanalytical doctrine and almost nothing to the evidence which the sixteenth century has left behind. An emphasis on technical statistics, insofar as it involves extrapolation rather than calculation, or on anthropological analogies, can have similar effects. I am not, of course, decrying the usefulness of such techniques; I am only asserting that they need to be applied under the continuous and careful control of the strict historical method if they are to help the enterprise rather than pervert it. Any historian will use speculation and conjecture in order to fill gaps in the knowledge based on evidence, and the more sophisticated his mind and his understanding of the technique become the more intelligent and possibly persuasive his gap-filling will be. But it remains conjecture, and in erecting arguments upon figures, analogies and theories the historian must himself remain aware of a difference which also he should not allow the reader to forget.

Discovery is followed by comprehension, by which I mean understanding what the details of evidence brought to light really mean. I do not need here to repeat familiar points about the criticism of sources, but I should like to remind you that it depends upon the rigorous observation of one principle: the material must be evaluated in its own terms and in relation to what surrounds it, that is with reference to the meaning it had at the time it was deposited in the record and not with reference to the historian's own present. Lawyers, for instance, whose training efficiently creates an ahistorical cast of mind, notoriously read old law under the guidance of present significance, a habit proper to themselves but so wrong for the historian that large parts of our constitutional history still need rescuing from the consequences of historians' humble prostration before the shrine of legal mystery. Or take the literature of protest, a recurring phenomenon in history and therefore too readily divorced from its historical context. Whether they are inclined to protest themselves or to the repression of protest, historians have too often managed to read such writings as though they bore only some eternal, politico-philosophical, meaning. The social thought of the sixteenth century, for instance, has been ill-treated by instinctive defenders of an existing order who concentrate upon its hierarchic concepts without realizing that the prevalence of these really reflects their absence in the politics of the day; it has been worse treated by radicals who describe its moral outrage against oppression while forgetting that the men giving voice to that outrage denounce just those practices of resistance and rebellion which the radical historians regard as the proper reply to oppression. Either way we do not get what the sixteenth century thought and wrote. However, when I assert that we have a duty to understand the past for its own sake and in its own terms, I had better, to prevent misunderstanding, add that I do not wish us to ignore the past's relationship with the present, perhaps with eternity.

We must fulfil that duty so that the past which we relate to the present shall be, as far as possible, the real past.

Lastly, in this brief sweep over historical method, I turn to the problem of interpretation – of making sense of what we have found out. In practice, most historical interpretation comes down to discovering and describing various forms of causal relationships – the ways in which various phenomena acted upon one another so as to produce the discovered result. (I know we are not supposed to talk of causes, but despite the philosophers no other concept in fact so comprehensively describes historians' main analytical preoccupation.) Here again the historical method is peculiar in two ways. The historian never argues from cause to effect, always from effect to cause; and he operates by multiplying causes. He argues from effect to cause because he is always trying to explain an event (or complex of events) known to him, by reference to its antecedents which he needs to disentangle if he is to understand what he already knows. Although we may write that the arms race before 1914 helped to bring about the outbreak of war, we really arrived at that statement the other way round: we argue that the war (which we happen to know took place) derived in part from the arms race. This manner of reasoning is necessarily true of all historical enquiry because until one knows what happened one has no occasion to seek causes and influences. It is this peculiarity of the historical method – its inability to argue forward, to predict – that deprives the historian of any professional claims to play the prophet. Nothing in his method, and (if he is honest) nothing in his experience, entitles him to say that from a given set of circumstances he can forecast what will happen. On the contrary, all his experience has taught him how powerful the contributions are of the unexpected, the unforeseen, the contingent, the accidental and the unknowable, in shaping the fates of men and the course of events. Trained, and rightly trained, to hindsight – to working from effect from cause – the historian, confronted with the question, 'what will come of this?', can only humbly answer, 'your guess is as good as mine' – an answer which more usually he hides behind his favourite phrase, 'well, it all depends'.

Secondly, in seeking to discover his causes the historian works by multiplication and cumulation. Two sound philosophic precepts are anathema to him: the injunction to look for the essence of a problem, and the injunction to avoid multiplying entities beyond necessity. His necessity knows no end: he throws away Ockham's razor and grows his epistemological beard, sprouting in all directions. Reduction to essence is wrong because it has been found that historical phenomena cannot be different from what they are, namely a particular manifestation which is the product of all antecedents, discovered or as yet undiscovered. You may really not take away any element in the complex, however trivial it may appear, without altering the phenomenon itself from the shape which the process of investigation has shown it to possess. This, of course, is one reason why history throws up so many controversies which often circle around rival emphases in the vast mish-mash of relevant contributory and explanatory detail; but it is also why historical knowledge progresses through such controversies which operate by adding rather than reducing. It is very rare in history for what one man has said about an event to be altogether discarded in the progress of better knowledge; rather it gets subsumed into an ever growing agglomerate of interpretation in which it continues to occupy a place.

It will have become clear in this analysis of method that I am confining the term history to one of the two disciplines that lay claim to it. These two I may call empirical or thesis-free, and determinist or thesis-dominated. By thesis I here mean a general scheme of interpretation, regarded as universally applicable, as derived from laws discoverable in the historical process, and as possessed of powers of prediction. The most important current example, of course, is Marxist-Leninist history (in its various forms), but other such universal schemes – as the Toynbean, the Islamic or the Christian – have or have had large vogues. I am not for one moment suggesting that the empirical discipline is free of all forms of thesis: it involves the production of generalizations which can set up an interpretative thesis. This, however, is limited to the single problem for which it is constructed and has no power to predict. Insofar as it employs alleged general laws, these are loose and large views of human behaviour derived from experience and devoid of that normative power which a law must possess to deserve the name. In empirical history, universals form the beginning of understanding; in determinist history, the end of it. My reason for treating history as though it were necessarily of the former kind is simple enough: thesis-free history is fully concerned with the proper subject matter of history, namely the past, whereas thesis-dominated history is not. Men adopt thesis-dominated historical schemes not because they want to understand the past – the ease with which they accommodate or eliminate awkward facts in order to preserve the thesis proves this — but because they want to gain information about the future. It is the predictive power of the thesis, supposedly proved from earlier predicting successes, which attracts: prophecy, not history, is the proper concern of thesis-dominated history, from Joachim da Fiore to the Russian sextet who so informed their audience at the San Francisco Congress of 1975. It is therefore not really history at all.

Let me sum up my definition of the method peculiar to history proper, a definition which, as I am well aware, has had to be a crudely compressed account of possibly controversial views. The historical method consists of an approach to the material to be studied which involves broadfronted attacks without preconceptions, and not linear forays determined by specific enquiry; it involves an understanding of things in terms of the time when the material was created; and it involves interpretation proceeding from effect to cause and by means of the multiplication of causes rather than by distinguishing between essentials and accidentals. If it is objected that this method is also used by people who are not historians, I reply that in that case they miscall themselves. Much present-day sociology uses historical method (of a sort), but that is because it is really social history; empirically inclined economists sometimes operate like historians, but that is because they are in fact practising economic history. Not surprisingly the results sometimes suggest that these fish have slipped from water into an element not altogether familiar to them. In particular they are likely not to realize — even more than genuine historians are found not to realize — the consequences which for the historian flow from the nature of his materials and method: consequences which to some may seem like limitations that call the whole enterprise in question, but which to me constitute the foundations of the historian's claims upon his society.

In the first place, historians have to accept that not everything they would wish to know can be known. There are prefectly good historical questions which we cannot answer. Thanks to the expansion of the profession, the growing number of sharp intelligences in it, the accumulation of knowledge, the fructifying effects of new questions, and also occasionally the usefulness of newly adopted techniques, the tally of unanswered questions once thought unanswerable shrinks all the time; but a residue of truly unanswerable questions will remain. This should worry only those who seek in history a universal bible, and they would be well advised to turn to its thesis-dominated version. Secondly, we must resign ourselves to the fact that even where we know we shall never know completely; our best understanding of any remotely complex historical situation will always be imperfect. But this again need trouble no historian who stops short of wishing to have his views and reconstructions treated as holy writ, the more so because it leads to the third important consequence which is that in history there are in effect no closed issues. Any answer we may give to historical questions is always liable to be at least altered by new knowledge and new thought, quite often in adjacent territory rather than in work on the question itself; the progress of historical learning is as endless and as ever in flux as is history itself; there is never an end and always more to learn. The historian's intellectual life terminates only with his physical existence. When we remember that this is very far from true for colleagues in other disciplines, especially in the natural sciences where problems can get finally solved, we ought to thank our Muse for saving us from such disaster by the characteristically ironic device of a built-in and inescapable uncertainty in everything we do.

However: I think that the true significance of that uncertainty remains insufficiently recognized, a fact for which we historians are in measure to blame. History being an unending double dialogue – a dialogue between the scholar and his sources, and a dialogue between scholars – and historians being men of passion, it follows that to the innocent eye of the by-stander historical debate looks like the battles of theologians: as though the disputants were defending rival certainties when in reality they are advancing various hypothetical interpretations from whose collisions better knowledge and clearer understanding may (and usually do) emerge. These idiosyncrasies of the profession, which, I regret to say, sometimes deceive even its members, have disguised the basic truth about historical study which derives directly from the nature of its materials, the methods used to work on them, and the ultimate open-ended uncertainty that is our fate. Because there are no certainties there can be no authorities: history is free. There is, indeed, only one authority whose word is law, and that is the historical evidence: but it is typically an ambiguous authority whose word sounds differently in different ears and whose law disconcertingly changes shape as various obedient subjects endeavour to abide by it. I do not wish to be misunderstood: I do not subscribe to the frivolous, even nihilist, notion of relativism which thinks that historical understanding is only what happens in the observer's mind and varies casually from historian to historian. I think that there is a historical reality which we seek to grasp and can come closer and closer to grasping; and I think that the willingness of historians to agree on so much, as well as the special unwillingness of the relativists to have their own interpretations doubted, support my belief. But that is another large question which here I must put aside.

In history there are no authorities: history is a free study in which no man can claim rule, or credence for his mere *ipse dixit*, and in which the only true sin is to deny a hearing to views with which one happens to disagree. This truth, too, eliminates those forms of history which suppose that to cite Scripture or Zarathustra or Engels on a disputed point of historical truth is to settle the issue. I have always regretted that common parlance calls works of history 'the authorities', for that is exactly what they are not. I may believe what Professor X has written and doubt what Dr Y has replied, but my faith owes nothing to any submission to authority or even to any choice between rival authorities. If Professor X is to be believed it is only because his management of the evidence is more convincing; and when a still more convincing interpretation comes along all his apparent authority will avail him nothing. When, far too many years ago, I was examined on my dissertation, one of my examiners, apropos of some statement of mine, said very courteously, 'But that is not what Pollard says.' Rather taken aback I replied, somewhat rudely, 'But that is only what Pollard says.' In retrospect, I confess, I am less shocked by my rudeness than by the examiner's attitude which supposed that the issue was not what the evidence meant but how one could possibly dissent from authority. None of us hold authority; none of us have any right to pronounce upon problems *ex cathedra*; all of us have the right to argue freely and to be judged solely by the quality of our argument; all of us live under the single obligation faithfully to heed the one authority there is, the historical record.

History, then, is by its inmost nature a free study in which nothing is solved by citing edicts or rules. Does this exhilarating truth tell us anything of the function the historian must discharge in his social capacity? It does indeed, but in order to make my meaning plain I must briefly digress to consider the nature of other intellectual disciplines. And here I am guided by Thomas Kuhn whose views, I am sure, are by now familiar enough. Kuhn, you will remember, argues that a science becomes 'mature' (that is, worthy of the name) when it achieves what he calls a paradigmatic structure. By this he means a generally agreed framework of theoretic interpretation – a structured view of that world which the science in question studies – within which the process of research (called by him accurately, though a little irreverently, puzzle-solving) is carried out. The paradigm not only determines the lines of research but distinguishes between successful and unsuccessful research; it becomes an authoritative structure which separates orthodoxy from heresy by calling things true and false; and it can be removed only by a revolution when it will be replaced by another paradigm. This, of course, is a crude summary of subtle enough ideas but it is accurate; and I think Kuhn is right partly because observation confirms his analysis, and partly because scientists have told me that indeed this is how they operate.

The paradigmatic principle and method are general throughout both the natural and the social sciences, varied only by the occasional coexistence of more than one paradigm in temporary rivalry one with another (during a pre-revolutionary stage); 'maturing' tends to reduce the several to one. Indeed, it is the stated aspiration of both kinds of science to build such structures: their express ambition is to find a framework which will explain every phenomenon found within it. Sociologists are quite as eager to elevate their science to that kind of maturity as are physicists. Revealingly enough, the main intellectual assault upon history from social scientists concentrates on denying us the status of a science because we do not operate with such compelling frameworks. I have read social scientists so caught up in the paradigmatic predicament that they cannot at all understand how any non-paradigmatic science can claim to exist; they simply have no means of grasping that there are valid forms of knowledge which achieve their ends in other ways. Again, I do not wish to be misunderstood: all disciplines are fully entitled to employ whatever to them seem the right methods for their kind of enquiry, provided they grant the same right to others. Developed interpretative frameworks are a dominant feature in practically every intellectual enterprise; but they are, or they should be, totally absent from history. As I have already hinted, the interpretative structures we build explain nothing except the particular set of circumstances from which they are inferred; each piece of history as treated by every historian has a scheme applicable only to itself and not transferable to any other set of historical questions. The only use of such transfers consists in applying apparent analogies in order to open questions: they are the beginning of study, not the end of it, and no historical problem is solved by being subsumed under a general paradigm. Thus, for instance, an understanding of the prehistory of the Russian revolution may suggest to the student of seventeenth-century England questions and lines of research that may be worth exploring; but only disaster results if he instead assumes that a 'theory of revolutions' worked out from what happened in 1917, or 1848, or 1789, will provide usable answers for his own investigations. We may be stimulated into a particular enquiry by somebody else's mini-paradigm, but we are not obliged to come up with answers that fit it nor should we be wise to treat the paradigm as guide or crutch. If our results fit it, this is by accident – because for once empirical study supported rather than refuted the initial theory. (Of course, it is better to have no initial theory: but let that pass.) The only large paradigmatic structure to which historians adhere consists of a world-view which says that human beings are rational, irrational, divers, like-minded, wise, foolish, brave, timid, moderate, violent, ambitious, submissive, kindly and vicious – a structure so fluid and unauthoritative that it eliminates no answers and can create no heresies. Even the historian who confounds the probabilities of nature and of men's minds by claiming that all civilization derives from the teaching of visitors from Venus is no heretic, though we may think him ill-advised and ask in vain for his proof.

Thus the historian's freedom from authority is not confined to his relations with other historians; it is the very inward essence of his craft and distinguishes him singularly from practitioners in adjacent intellectual enterprises. To this freedom he has surrendered the very human desire to discover great schemes, large answers, words that may save or damn mankind: he will be limited, particular – and free. And it is this freedom that he contributes to society and with which he repays society's willingness to support him. Paradigmatic sciences are fascinating, valuable, inescapable – and dangerous. As a method of research the use of world-views, frameworks and models may be entirely unexceptionable. But these things do not stay within the region to which they belong; they escape into the political and social lives of men. The social scientists who seek to discover the true structure of society rapidly transform an instrument of research into a norm for the society studied; what is thought to be the reality of social relationships discovered by enquiry becomes reality by being imposed (with the authority of science) upon those relationships – a happy instance of self-legitimation – or alternatively is set up as a supposedly real bogeyman for political attack. It is here that the historian's proper function and true service enter: possessed of intellectual freedom he must resist the imposition of intellectual dictatorship and its social consequences. As all the disciplines rush after paradigms, there are not many such free men left around; and among those left free only the historian – still possessed of influence, capable of just the sort of questions to which paradigm-mongers are vulnerable, and available in sufficient numbers – can successfully stand up to the claims and pressures of developed science. Our peculiar method of working, which renders us incapable of seeking 'maturity' in the production of a universal law or system, enables us, and our social duty obliges us, to subject the paradigmatic structures of others to criticism and if necessary to demolition by applying our own unhindered, unauthoritative, pragmatic and sometimes simplistic doubts to their claims to authority – especially when that authority moves from intellectual concerns (where after all it constrains only other practitioners of the same discipline) to political, where it constrains us all. History is sceptical – sceptical of anything that cannot be demonstrated by rational proof; universal structures in human existence, which assuredly cannot be demonstrated, can as certainly be asserted and imposed; historians are – or rather, should be – continually sceptical of them. And since universal structures are by their nature enemies to freedom – the freedom of the mind and ultimately of the body – the survival of liberty in thought, in speech, in speculation, in every aspect of life, comes to depend on the continued existence of historians, questioning all authoritative statements and alleged laws of existence by asking their simple question: what actually happened?

But if historians are to discharge this function they need to take care. They can do so only if they follow their own trade honestly and faithfully, without regard to favour, without fear of consequences, above all without respect to the supposed needs and calls of the passing day. Only if they obey the legitimate demands of their own science can they successfully undertake to criticize the sciences of others. Those who would wish to make history acceptable and socially serviceable by directing its thoughts to the present day and the alleged demands of contemporary society unfortunately, with the best of intentions, lead it straight to destruction and damnation. The more we turn from studying the past for the sake of understanding that past to the use of the past for the purposes of the present, the more we abandon our proper role and the less useful and justified do our labours, do our lives, become. It is not our task to produce panaceas: the world is full of people – from scientists through pundits to gurus – willing to do that. What society has a right to expect from us is that we should act as mankind's intellectual conscience, helping in our sceptical way to sort the true from the untrue, the useful from the pernicious, the valid from the pretentious, and teaching others (especially our students) those proper standards of sceptical questioning which alone can protect freedom. It is our task to undermine self-appointed certainties and to break the shackles of structures, whether they dominate the mind or all of life. If the world of the mind contained nothing but historians it would be a wild anarchy; but it does not contain only historians, and without them it would become a collection of despotisms. The balance between order and freedom, especially in an age which finds the first easier to preserve than the second, depends, I suggest to you, on the continued practice of conventional, empirical historical study. The nations are today much beset by the claims of absolutist system-builders, whether they be political dictators or social equalizers or fanatics for any cause from the sole usefulness of wheat-germ to that enslavement which has stolen the name of liberation. To those still willing to listen the historian, trained to freedom, offers the gift of sceptical criticism, which is liberty. How can any society afford to lose its historians?

II

REVIEWS

REVIEWS

(a) JOEL HURSTFIELD, *Freedom, Corruption and Government in Elizabethan England.* Cambridge, Mass.; Harvard University Press, 1973.*

Professor Hurstfield has collected the main part of his articles and essays in a volume which offers an opportunity to assess his important contribution to Tudor history. He tells us that his interests have been focussing increasingly on the theme of liberty and authority in Tudor England and that this collection represents a preliminary report. What the real relationship was between the government's powers and the nation's right to live and think as it pleased is assuredly a large question; as Dr Hurstfield says, it poses one of the historian's gravest difficulties, that of understanding from the inside the conventions of a past society while at the same time discovering some suitable absolute standard by which to assess them. Dr Hurstfield raises fundamental questions of great interest; how far do his answers carry conviction?

The collection is not quite as coherent as its author suggests. If one looks for relevance to the central theme announced, the last four pieces seem to bear only marginally. The pleasant essay on 'Tradition and change in the English Renaissance' is a convenient summary of reasonably familiar generalizations about the part played by humanism in the making of the intellectual character of Elizabethan England. By contrast, 'County government: Wiltshire c. 1530 – c. 1600' uses original sources to describe the structure of shire organization and throws some light on local reactions to the centre; the problem of liberty and authority may lurk there somewhere but is not brought out. 'Office-holding and government mainly in England and France' (originally a chapter in the third volume of the *New Cambridge Modern*

* [*Reviews in European History*, 1/2; Sept. 1974.]

History) tries to summarize too much and falls back on an overdrawn picture of monarchic collapse which leaves the political realities of the day unexplained. The concluding chapter on 'Gunpowder Plot and the politics of dissent' is mainly a suitable attack on the absurdities of Catholic propaganda-history, with the second half of the title uneasily tacked on to the *jeu d'esprit* of the first. The two pieces placed together under the title 'Religion and the Succession' discuss the ecclesiastical policies of the two Cecils and the succession debates of the 1590s; these are straight pieces of historical analysis whose contribution to the larger purpose eludes me. That still leaves five articles revolving around the questions of freedom, royal power and the distorting effect of corruption, the core of the book.

The book is also divided between what may be called learned articles, based on serious research, and essays exploiting the author's own well-stocked mind as well as the work of others. The former includes the familiar article on corruption in the mid-sixteenth century which first (in 1953) introduced historians to some of the less public realities of Tudor administration, the 'Religion and Succession' pair which contributes permanently to our understanding of Elizabethan politics, and the article on Wiltshire. These are all admirable examples of the historian's basic craft, very well written and carefully based on the sources. Among these learned pieces one may also include the perceptive review of Menna Prestwich's *Cranfield*.

The remaining five entries belong to the second category and pose more serious problems. The essays on the English Renaissance and European governments were intended to be summaries of received knowledge and discharge their purpose well enough. One may question whether Dr Hurstfield has correctly interpreted the system of fees which paid for these early-modern bureaucracies; his language (pp. 314, 319) suggests that he sees no difference between fees and gifts. Improper gifts and bribes certainly passed, but fees were fixed and known charges levied automatically for every government transaction on behalf of a private party (issuing or registering documents, making copies, etc.). There was no element of corruption in them, and it is misleading to hint that there may have been. Dr Hurstfield is also less than perfectly clear on the difficult subject of grants of offices in reversion (p. 316). One must distinguish between offices held in freehold and disposable at the possessor's will (as in seventeenth-century France), and offices of which the possessor could try to convey the succession by private treaty subject to the Crown's willingness to authorize the reversion by letters patent (as in England). The latter practice retained more royal control than Dr Hurstfield allows; seekers after reversions could be disappointed, and the 'purchase' money they had paid to the sitting tenant could be lost. The general air of disorganized misery which Dr Hurstfield sees hanging over these governments owes at least something to these failures to distinguish.

The reviewer's real problems arise with the remaining essays – those in which the central theme of liberty and authority is mainly argued. I refer in particular to three: 'Was there a Tudor despotism after all?', 'The paradox of liberty in Shakespeare's England', and 'Political corruption in modern England: the historian's problem'. None of these is based on intensive new research, and all rest on a rather thin foundation of evidential material. This is not to condemn them but to identify their character and purpose. They are by way of reflections upon the general nature of the age as it has come to look in the author's mind after years of reading and teaching Tudor history. I have already had occasion to take issue with the first, and most important, of the three and shall not repeat my discussion;[1] in any case, in a prefatory note Dr Hurstfield says that he proposes to comment on my article, and further argument must await that comment. Nor should it be thought by those always anxious to scent scandal that these arguments between friends are really a battle of enemies. The disagreement between us concerning certain vital issues of the century and the interpretation of its mind is both legitimate and compatible with mutual regard. The importance of the problems, and the misunderstandings already current among those not so familiar with them, suggest that I should nevertheless use this opportunity to bring out the grounds of our disagreement.

Dr Hurstfield's argument is this: Tudor government was autocratic and planned to create a legislative despotism by substituting royal edicts (proclamations) for the slow and uncertain processes of parliamentary statute-making. Even though this attempt failed, the regime did not change character; the outward appearance of a restrained constitutionalism does not hide a reality dominated by absence of free speech, many constraints on opinion, and arbitrary executive action. Pervasive uses of patronage and the prevalence of corruption are used to fill in the interpretation, but they are not essential to it – which is just as well because neither phenomenon is peculiar to any particular form of

[1] [See no. 14 in vol. 1 above.]

government. Articulation by patronage came naturally to a hierarchic society based on personal relationships, and in the Tudor system it did much good; corruption is a moral failing encountered in every system yet tried. What matters is the picture of a government ambitious to rule despotically and in great part enabled to do so by its apparatus of control over opinion.

I, on the contrary, hold that the Tudor system, especially after the Reformation, embodied an effort to transform government and society by means universally at the time recognized as legitimate and depending upon the consent of the 'political nation' which it was quite capable of withholding in and out of Parliament. Tudor government insisted on testing all powers, including its own, against the law, this being regarded as independent of executive action and in practice treated as such. The debates and resistance encountered so frequently disprove the notion that this outward constitutionalism was but window-dressing.

These summaries, much too concise, demonstrate the existence of legitimate differences of opinion. But it needs to be shown whence these differences arise. Dr Hurstfield says (p. 12) that he wishes to discover the roots of Tudor society, 'the assumptions they lived by', and that failure to do so 'has led to a great deal of historical controversy, not all of it fruitful'. My dispute with him really rests on my conviction that he has not fulfilled this entirely proper ambition. The background to his paper on the paradox of liberty is his own concept of liberty (twentieth century, and strictly English at that) against which he attempts to measure what meanings of the term he can find in the age of Elizabeth. This method strikes me as mistaken because it begins by assuming the points yet to be established. The method produces Dr Hurstfield's frequent resort to modern analogies and parallels which he expressly distrusts and yet feels urged to employ – the use of Hitler's enabling law to interpret the function of statute in Tudor England, for instance, or the enlightenment he gets from modern 'mass media' when considering Tudor manipulation of opinion.

Thus the disagreement between us arises not from personal attitudes (we equally hate oppression, deplore corruption, dislike hypocrisy) but from differences in historical method. Dr Hurstfield in effect starts with a 'model' of a free society by means of which he tests several events in the sixteenth century. I believe that understanding must come from inside the period studied whose definition of a free society must be worked out from all the evidence available; only after this has been done can one usefully measure the time-bound against more absolute standards. In the last resort, my doubts about Dr Hurstfield's reconstruction arise from his use of the evidence. I do not think that he has cast his net anything like widely enough; the paper on despotism, especially, in which he says that he has (deliberately?) looked for no new evidence, rests on much too slender foundations. And the evidence produced is alleged without sufficient analytical discussion. It is strange that in an article published in 1967 which turns in great part upon Henry VIII's act of proclamations there should be no mention of another article exclusively concerned with the act and published in 1960.[2] Virtually all the material deployed here against Henry VIII's government had over the years received critical attention to which Dr Hurstfield makes no reference. Perhaps he was being kind: rather than saying that he failed to be convinced by sophistical reasoning, he passed in silence over the offending scholars. But such kindness frustrates any fruitful debate because it forces the respondent (as in this case it has forced me) into reluctant repetition of himself, and also because it leaves the supposedly conclusive facts without substance.

Lastly, I sometimes cannot accept such analysis of the evidence as Dr Hurstfield undertakes. His opinion of the act of proclamations seems to have convinced many but cannot, I maintain, be derived from the documents. It is common ground that the act as passed created no new despotic powers in the Crown. Dr Hurstfield, however, believes that the government-sponsored bill, replaced in the course of debate by the one that received the royal assent, intended to give to proclamations the full powers of statutes and thus to enable the Crown to legislate by mere edict. This view he rests mainly on his interpretation of the preamble, for he argues (rightly, I think) that the existing preamble is that which introduced the abortive bill. He discerns here the government's original intention, namely to substitute proclamations for acts of Parliament. But there is nothing remotely hinting at such intentions in that preamble which rehearses (correctly) the existing prerogative powers in issuing proclamations, deplores the frequent breaches of them, calls for an enforcing statute, and declares the purpose of the act to be (1) to confirm the royal power to issue proclamations as hitherto, and (2) to secure obedience to them as though they were made by Parliament. Indeed, the preamble explicitly asserts that the statute is necessary because otherwise constant disobedience might drive the king into an

[2] [Cf. above, vol. 1, no. 19.]

435

Reviews

arbitrary extension of his powers. Between this preamble and what Dr Hurstfield recognizes to be a mild enactment there is no conflict, only consonance.

The view of Tudor rule so eloquently expounded in this book is derived, I think, from a just conviction that the century was full of political savagery and dubious public morality. Where it goes wrong is in confusing justified disapproval with historical analysis and in restricting the enquiry to too narrow a range of sources and questions. In the outcome, this approach distorts the realities of Tudor government and life under it. The debate, no doubt, will continue, but what is required now is a far more exhaustive discovery and analysis of the evidence in our sources.

(b) *The Lisle Letters.* Edited by MURIEL ST CLARE BYRNE. Chicago and London; The University of Chicago Press. 1981. 6 vols.*

In the reign of Henry VIII, when a man was arrested for treason (an arrest which among the eminent tended to be equal to a conviction with the usual consequences) his papers were confiscated and disappeared into the royal archives in the Tower. Considering the number of people who suffered this fate, the amount of surviving material is distressingly small. What happened to Cardinal Wolsey's unquestionably massive, and unquestionably confiscated, correspondence a remnant of which was acquired by Sir Robert Cotton? Where are the papers of Bishop Fisher and Sir Thomas More? Perhaps the former kept none; the latter, practising his famous discretion, very likely destroyed his in the months during which, still free, he could confidently look forward to his arrest. Of course, there are scattered items from his and other people's correspondence which have accidentally survived here and there, but – apart from Thomas Lord Darcy's small collection – only two private archives now exist among the Henrician state papers at the Public Record Office: those of Henry VIII's lord privy seal and vicegerent, Thomas Cromwell, and those of his lord deputy at Calais, Arthur Plantagenet, Viscount Lisle.

Most people have heard of the first and few (until now) of the second, though the lives of the two men were closely intertwined. In fact, Lisle was in several respects more fortunate than Cromwell. Imprisoned on a

* [*London Review of Books*, 16 July 1981.]

436

charge of treason, he was never tried and in the end set at liberty, only to die almost at once of ripe old age. More important in the present context, his papers still form a separate collection, having escaped the disastrous attentions of nineteenth-century archivists who felt disgustingly free to break up and rearrange collections – 'to make sense' – without keeping a record of what they found. (Even less excusably, such vandalism still at times occurs today.) Cromwell's papers were so mistreated to form the mainstay of the artificial class called 'State Papers, Henry VIII (SP 1)', with the result that it is nowadays often impossible to say whether a given document came from his files or not. Froude was the last historian to read the Cromwell correspondence in its original state in which it survived from 1540 to the 1860s. Though the editors of that famous calendar, *The Letters and Papers of Henry VIII*, included the Lisle papers they left them undisturbed, and it is this remarkable collection, familiar enough to students of Henry VIII's reign, which forms the basis, in judicious selection, of this monumental edition of close on 1700 letters (with additional material thrown in). The nineteenth century thought that the Lisle papers contained little material bearing on their own limited, 'high politics', attitude to history; finding in Cromwell's archives the main strain of events, Brewer, Gairdner and the rest (destroyers of archives) made it the heart of their edition, whereas the personal and family affairs of the Lisles could be interspersed in the calendar without being incorporated in SP 1.

So there they lay (available and mostly used in their calendared form), till one day . . . One day in the early 1930s, a young student of Tudor England, interested especially in its language, literature and social life, came upon them and decided to do something about them. The something in question has now seen the light of day, fifty years later and in six very large volumes. Newcomers to the Public Record Office in the late 1940s soon heard of the mini-factory established in a cubicle off the Rolls Room upstairs where Miss Muriel St Clare Byrne, author of that well known and affectionate little book, *Elizabethan Life in Town and Country* (1925), and editor of Henry VIII's love letters to Anne Boleyn (1936), was beavering away, sorting, transcribing, annotating thousands of letters exchanged between Lord Lisle, his wife Honor, their agents in London, and leading members of the Henrician court and political circles. If it seemed that there was something less than professional about the operation at times – something in the nature of a vacuum cleaner sucking up everything in sight – it was also plain that the little room housed an enterprise driven forward by relentless persistence, utter commitment and loving involvement. After a time, rumour reported that the work of decades, though completed, could find no publisher willing to risk bankruptcy by actually putting it into print. Meanwhile, Miss Byrne grew no younger. Now at last, however, the faith which moves mountains has moved even a publisher, and, whatever one may think of the edition, everybody who has any sort of justice and kindness in his heart must rejoice at the courage of the University of Chicago Press who have taken this half-century's enterprise under their wing, as well as at the courage of Miss Byrne who stuck it out against all disappointments for so long.

Whatever one may think of the edition: the verdict has in measure been already preempted by several magisterially enthusiastic reviews by eminent persons (not all of them expertly acquainted with the era). Perhaps, therefore, the time has come at even so early a date to attempt a more judicious appraisal. Miss Byrne's dedicated labours deserve to be treated as worthy of criticism as well as praise. Thus the exceedingly long time taken to do the work has left its mark. The frequent citation of long discarded authors (especially Trevelyan who knew nothing at first hand about the sixteenth century) gives the book at times an old-fashioned air, while important recent studies of direct relevance – for instance Michael Bush's analysis of the dispute between Lisle and Edward Seymour (1966)[1] – are overlooked. In fact, to judge from the bibliography, the editor closed her reading list well over a decade ago, a decade full of very important contributions. This has led to error. Miss Byrne's description of early-Tudor society as one in which 'a great political Plan' tried everything 'by the simple standard of what was expedient for the consolidation of power' reads oddly by now when we have come to understand the haphazardness of much of this plan, the crucial importance of the law and its institutions, and the powerful drive for a reform in faith and morals which animated so much activity. Indeed, it reads a bit oddly in the light she herself later throws on so many of the realities of the age's politics, and thus comes to look like a premature generalization, derived from elderly 'authorities', with which she must have come to disagree as the work went on. She confuses the king's Chamber with his Privy Chamber, a point of importance in the tracking of so many careers to which she devotes such

1. [*HJ* 9 (1966), 255–74.]

labours. Henry VII's mythical treasure reappears; Anne Boleyn is called marquise of Pembroke when in fact, and most significantly, she was created marquess in her own right. Much time is taken up with fighting R. B. Merriman who in 1902 had the influential temerity to call Lisle a person of no account; but Merriman no longer has any influence – and his verdict on Lisle may not have been so crassly mistaken as Miss Byrne maintains. Some of the detail is wrong: thus 'obolus' means farthing, not penny, an error which quadruples a tax assessment.[2] And the editor's Latin is disconcertingly shaky. Her treatment of case-endings suggests that she would have done better to copy medieval clerks who in their equal uncertainty preferred to use abbreviation marks. A three-line passage from some letters patent contains three elementary mistakes and moreover sees special significance in a very common formula; and this sort of thing recurs more than once.

Pedantry, no doubt, and in so vast a compilation one may well expect more and worse slips than do occur. A more serious criticism must be directed at the whole plan of the work which unfortunately will operate counter to the effect that it deserves to have. For one thing, the editor not only left no stone unturned; she has also taken care that absolutely everything found beneath those stones shall be put into print. Thus the reader is overwhelmed with masses of antiquarian detail which indeed testifies to laudable industry and persistence but also makes large parts of the book unreadable. Every section carries appendices where further research proliferates. Documents of all sorts are printed in all sorts of places. These six volumes may well provide a large reservoir of materials to be further exploited by others – letters, legal documents, statements of accounts – but such selections (which at times simply burden the edition) can be dangerous too because they suggest that the much vaster quantity of like material not in print does not need to be searched for. The selection is idiosyncratic, being guided by the desire to know every last thing about the characters in the Lisle circle, and it is somewhat sentimentalized by a determination to convey the affection which those characters have instilled in Miss Byrne after such long years of close acquaintance.

Above all, the heart of the matter, the Lisle Correspondence itself, is presented in a way which makes reading and digesting it more difficult than it need have been. Miss Byrne carefully explains her editorial procedures (which are indeed pretty much exemplary and do not need

[2][A silly slip: obolus of course means halfpenny.]

439

her slightly nervous defence – a defence which seems to be addressed to the long defunct ghost of A. F. Pollard) and wisely modernizes spelling and so forth: the letters themselves are easy reading. Corrected decipherings of messy hands and revised datings nearly always carry perfect conviction. But the letters are embedded in a continuous narrative plus analysis, arranged in chapters; this breaks up the chronological sequence and attempts to compel the reader to accept a story with interpretation at the editor's hands. Nor are the letters at all easy to find, often interspersed as they are within the commentary and (in view of costs, understandably) not differentiated in the printing. Miss Byrne would have done better if she had followed more conventional practice by producing her edition and then separately writing her book about its revelations. Her decision to do both things in one, and to do them at inordinate length in inordinate detail, makes the edition so enormous and so charged with digressions that no one can really be expected to read through it.

So much for curmudgeonly reservations; now to the admission that in many ways this is a marvellous work. Miss Byrne claims many things for the Lisle correspondence which are absolutely true and absolutely important. Here there is room only to hint at them. The papers illumine early-Tudor English in ways that will surprise those unfamilar with its easy, flexible, colloquial vigour, and especially those who have thought Thomas More's laboured prose typical. They provide a splendid picture of life in a noble household and family; especially they help to knock two familiar and false generalizations on the head. Honor Lady Lisle – downright, businesslike, self-centred and sensible – would have been astonished to hear that sixteenth-century women lived a life of helpless slavery, and the loving relations between herself and her much older husband hammer yet another nail in the coffin housing the strange thesis that marital affection was unknown in England before the eighteenth century. Above all, the correspondence gives an extensive and splendidly clear view of what the facts of place-hunting, favour-hunting and royal patronage – those desires and ambitions by now widely recognized as the essential elements in Tudor social and political life – really meant. Since the correspondence covers in the main only the years during which the Lisles were at Calais and thus out of direct contact with the king's court, that centre of the governing order's existence, it is no wonder that so much of it turns upon efforts to keep in touch, to keep track of the see-saw of royal favour, and to seek advantage at a distance. Well served by his agents, especially the invaluable John Husee whose letters would alone make the collection worth having, Lisle heard everything: his correspondence is stuffed with what must in Henrician terms be called political inside information. It is not gossip that gets recounted in these mentions of Henry's smiles or frowns, Cromwell's forthcomingness or warnings, the ups and downs of fortunes, but the true substance of those events that produced policy at the highest level. How the king received a New Year's gift (a moment when the barometer was studied with special care by the experts) showed who stood where, who might be able to help, who was out or on the way to disaster – and it therefore showed the relationships at the heart of 'high politics'. This is front-page stuff and to be treated as such. To have so much of it collected together, not in abstracts but in that fullness which alone reveals meaning, and more particularly to have very often what in early-Tudor correspondence tends to be hard to get – both sides to an exchange of letters – is an enormous boon and should quickly assist historians to penetrate to facts of life which have too often been ignored or treated in fleshless generalizations. That it will also attract non-specialists is certain because the life is here; that they will regularly mistake much meaning is a minor problem to which we can attend in time.

The people who crowd these pages vary in quality and weight but become real enough; here Miss Byrne's passion for every bit of detail, hunted for through the public records, pays off handsomely. She obviously became very much involved with them all, and in many cases one finds it easy to agree with her affectionate assessment of them. Lady Lisle was all she says, even if she is inclined to discount the evident signs that her ladyship could be ruthless and noisy. Her children (by her first husband, Sir John Basset) offer more material for understanding the attitudes of stern but loving parents than for judging their own still undeveloped personalities; however, they too come across as quite interesting in themselves. So do many of the Lisles' correspondents, pursuing their own ends while loyally serving their master's interests. What, however, of Lord Lisle himself? An illegitimate son of Edward IV, he began a courtier's career under Henry VII and continued it under Henry VIII, serving in the royal household and in war, and accumulating a modest fortune. He was never very prominent – as good a reason as any for his untroubled survival at a time when royal blood in one's veins constituted a major personal risk. As Miss Byrne emphasizes, he was evidently a man of kindness and sweet temper. She makes a strong but even so surprising case for a birth-date in about 1462, which would mean that when he got his first, and only, office of public importance, as governor of Calais, he was in his early seventies. The case is strong but also circumstantial, and it may be mistaken. As Miss Byrne says, we often forget how long-lived sixteenth-century people could be. However, a man of fifty as one of young King Henry VIII's household companions seems as unlikely as that a man of about seventy-five should have been thought capable of causing his wife's mistaken impression that she was pregnant with a Plantagenet child. Too much depends on the supposition that after his marriage to Elizabeth Woodville Edward IV would have sired no more bastards: that king's reputation runs another way.

As deputy of Calais Lisle was evidently conscientious and reasonably thorough – not by any means the ninny that recent tradition had made him – but Miss Byrne's praise for his administration goes beyond the acceptable. Her defence of him skips rather too swiftly over the great investigating commission of 1535 and its statutory aftermath, events at least in part occasioned by the government's dissatisfaction with their representative. Calais, it is true, would have been a very difficult charge for anybody; an inexperienced and possibly old man, however honest and concerned, must have found it an impossible task. There was never enough money; the wool staple was in precipitate decline; members of the garrison and the civil administration maintained running feuds of great virulence; above all, England's outpost on the continent, ever threatened by the likelihood of French attacks, stood exposed to the two political movements most feared by Henry VIII – extreme religious radicalism infiltrating from the Netherlands, and the possibility of treasonable dealings with the king's enemies in Catholic Europe, especially Cardinal Pole. A mixture of these two threats in the end landed Lisle in disgrace, the Tower, and peril of his life. Miss Byrne argues that he was innocent of all charges and fell victim to Cromwell's manoeuvres in early 1540 against his own personal enemies: despite years of genuine friendship, Cromwell at the last betrayed him because he needed a fall guy for his last desperate intrigues. This reconstruction of the events leading up to Cromwell's fall is on the whole convincing; it fits well with what has so far been thought of that crisis and constitutes the book's major contribution to general history. On the other hand, it is not possible to accept that Lisle did not offer Cromwell a chance by taking some very dubious steps; his kindness, frankness and essential decency need not be doubted, but that there was a touch – quite a notable touch – of helpless dimwittedness about him is also clear. At moments thoughts obtrude of Lord Emsworth, as there are moments when Lady Lisle reminds one of P. G. Wodehouse's formidable aunts.

The man who in the end comes to dominate these volumes is indeed Thomas Cromwell. The king is there, threatening or friendly, frequently spoken of, a dangerous and incalculable particle. But the minister provides the real structure of the Lisles' relations with the world of Court, Council, politics and patronage. The fact has its esoteric importance to the historian. Ever since Cromwell was 'rediscovered' there have been doubts whether the survival of his correspondence did not distort the picture in his favour. Well, here we have another extant correspondence, centring upon a man who tried to keep in touch with all the influential figures: and yet the predominant importance of Cromwell, his crucial role, come across quite as startlingly as in what remains of his own archive. Miss Byrne's reaction to the lord privy seal is very interesting. She evidently started with the conventional dislike of him, enlarged by her justified contempt for Cromwell's biographer, Merriman; when first she looked at the letters she expected to find the ruthless, bloodthirsty and inhuman servant of royal whims – the king's hired assassin – whom a hostile tradition had so carefully constructed. But unlike some others she preserved an open and honest mind, with the result that Cromwell soon grew for her into the person he actually was: a statesman with real and even elevated purposes, a man of genuine understanding and affability, a tower of strength to those who sought his help. If both the Lisles were capable of exasperating him by their mixture of innocence and importunity, he seems to have remained patient and at their service – not a service which would bring him much substantial reward or political advantage. And if in 1540 he used Lisle in that desperate attempt to keep his own footing and head, he cannot, on the conclusive evidence of earlier relations, have done so without regret. Moreover, he manoeuvred in such a way that if he won he could easily rescue Lisle who would inevitably be saved if he lost. Appropriately though in a manner unusual for that reign, the intriguer went under while the victim escaped. A good moral ending which should not make one forget that, England, disastrously deprived of Thomas Cromwell, would hardly have missed old Arthur Plantagenet.

No review can do full justice to all that these six volumes contain, but a word must be said about the contribution of the publisher. These are beautiful volumes enhanced by handsome printing, elegant binding, imaginative endpapers, well reproduced illustrations and many expensive facsimiles. The Chicago University Press has indeed done Miss Byrne proud, and Miss Byrne deserves to see the results of those endless and painful labours come forth, in her eighty-sixty year, in such splendid guise. Despite such criticisms as this review has ventured to offer, it is to be hoped that all students of Tudor history, Tudor language and literature, and indeed Tudor life will do the little work required to overcome the handicaps of the arrangement. All, one hopes, will acquaint themselves with the world of the Lisles, and some (one trusts) will think the money well spent that acquires a private copy. The excellent index will give all of them every assistance, but a healthy bank balance will not come amiss.

(c) The Complete Works of St Thomas More. Vol. 8: *The Confutation of Tyndale's Answer*, ed. LOUIS A. SCHUSTER, RICHARD C. MARIUS, JAMES P. LUSARDI, RICHARD J. SCHOECK. – Vol. 9: *The Apology*, ed. J. B. TRAPP. – The Tower Works: Vol. 12: *The Dialogue of Comfort against Tribulation*, ed. LOUIS L. MARTZ AND FRANK MANLEY; vol. 13: *Treatise on the Passion etc.*, ed. GARRY E. HAUPT; vol. 14: *De Tristitia Christi*, ed. CLARENCE E. MILLER. New Haven/London; Yale University Press, 1973, 1979, 1976.*

The Yale edition of More's works progresses at a rate which does great credit, above all, to the general editor (Richard Sylvester) but also to the particular editors and the gallant Press which bears so much of the burden. The present work is well up to the standard we have come to expect, a fact rendered the more remarkable by the devastating size of the book. More's text fills 1,034 pages which have been edited (from the printed versions of 1532/3 and 1557) with exceptional care and printed most handsomely. Four appendices deal with bibliographical matters of much complexity; in particular, Anthea Hume's important list of 'English Protestant books printed abroad, 1525–1535' merits attention. The Introduction, which charmingly appears in vol. iii, consists of a long essay by Louis A. Schuster on 'Thomas More's polemical career, 1523–1533', a really brilliant paper by Richard C. Marius on 'Thomas More's view of the Church', and a useful investigation of 'The career of

* [*EHR* 89 (1974), 382–7; 95 (1980), 367–9; 93 (1978), 399–404.]

Robert Barnes' by James P. Lusardi (More appended an attack on
Barnes to his war with Tyndale, finding Barnes much easier meat).
Lusardi adds a long note on the texts used. The notes of the
Commentary are extensive and generally satisfactory, the glossary is
sensible, and the index is truly commendable. The vast enterprise marks
a triumph of editorial competence and devotion.

However, the contents of the editorial contributions as well as of
More's original work require rather more critical assessment. There is a
marked contrast between the essays of Schuster and Marius, and if one
easily comes to prefer the latter it is not because he is a professor of
History while the former is a professor of English. It is because Marius
can write and think, whereas Schuster blusters and reacts. Again and
again, Marius formulates true insights in a memorable way. He refuses
to bow the knee before More (a refreshing attitude in the Yale Edition),
recognizing that Sir Thomas simply failed to understand what the
reformers were talking about especially when they spoke of the faith
that saves, and that he was invariably unfair and crude in his
interpretation of them. At the same time he fully brings out More's
conscientious, reasoned and integral beliefs, especially his mature
concept of the Church Universal. Marius can accept, without excuses,
More's determination to persecute heretics, and at the same time can
make plain the core of humanity in the man. This is an unusual example
of true impartiality, persuasively and beautifully written, and accurate
in detail.

By contrast Schuster stands firmly in the shadows of idolatry,
excusing everything and determinedly refusing ever to see anything
wrong in More – More, we must remember, the polemicist. There are
too many errors. The proclamation of March 1530 is still dated a year
too early. A. W. Pollard invariably appears as A. F. The story of
Stephen Vaughan's attempt to recruit Tyndale is garbled, and the
influence of Christopher St German assumed without proof. James
Bainham, we are told, was 'sobered by detention in prison' (p. 1251);
Bainham was burned, which may indeed have sobered him. The 1531
praemunire is described as a threat imposed by Parliament; not so. The
whole essay seems misplaced in the edition of a text – discursive, full of
commonplace detail, and seriously deficient in historical perspective. Of
its 132 pages, only twelve deal with the *Confutation* itself. And a
professor of English who confuses flaunting and flouting, who calls the
printing press 'this iron Goliath', who can describe the introduction of a

superfluous (and dubious) atrocity story as 'shocking photography', who can speak of More's 'classified' knowledge of the English reformers, of 'this process of centrifugal association which becomes a characteristic gestalt of More's polemic structure', and of approaching More's polemical writings 'from this perspective of audience-orientation' – such a writer needed either better teaching years ago or a more severe editor now. He seems to accept it as axiomatic that More always spoke the truth; at least, he never discusses his wilder statements. Schuster's most remarkable contribution touches on More's obsession with Luther's alleged lechery in marrying a nun. This Schuster calls an 'example of comic abuse'. Notions of what is comic do differ, but it beats me how one can find anything funny in the effect or humorous in the intention of that oft-repeated scream. Here Marius (as usual) is a better guide when he says that More 'could not tolerate his opponents because he believed they were malicious and obstinate' (p. 1335). Nothing funny in this for Sir Thomas.

However, there is an excuse for Schuster. Anyone who is committed to the More of tradition must find More the controversialist, the writer of polemics, a very difficult thing to accept and expound; and the difficulty is probably greatest in the context of the *Confutation*. In the reading of the endless tome there are only two adjectives that come readily to mind: tedious and hysterical. What did More think he was doing? Did he really expect anyone to wade through this interminable repetition of barely varied matter, this voluble and detailed dissection of every passage cited, this constant reliance on mere assertion – for authorities are cited rarely, nearly always Scripture, with a small admixture of the Fathers? I know, in fact, of no evidence that the book was read. The tone, too, virtually never varies. More attempts few of his famous merry tales and hardly any jokes, and those he does insert all fall pretty flat, except the delightful tale of Origen's horror at the thought of another confrontation with Tyndale. Very occasionally only does the taut string relax from which a single shrill note of disgust, horror, revulsion and contempt resounds for page after page. It was not tactically wise of More (though, of course, it was his preferred polemic method) to cite so much from Tyndale, for on this evidence Tyndale was much the better writer of English (as indeed I think he was). Certainly there are good moments in this welter. Even at his most obsessional More could not entirely suppress his brilliant wit. 'Mark,' says Tyndale, rather ponderously. 'Tyndale', says More, 'is a great marker: there is nothing with him now but mark, mark, mark. It is a pity that the man were not made a marker of chases in some tennis play.' One wishes that More had more often employed this highly effective tone of superior banter. He betrays some pride in his lord chancellorship; why, then, does he prefer to play the fishwife? Good sense appears in a defence of the 'holy war' against the Turks and in a very interesting disquisition on the problems of translating. But these are oases, and the reader dies of thirst long before he reaches them. The only remark of Schuster's that I find it easy to agree with is to the effect 'that a consecutive reading of any few pages selected at random would acquaint the reader with a representative cross section of More's prevailing themes'. Yes indeed. But there are here over one thousand pages.

It is important to remember, despite some convictions to the contrary, that not all controversialists of the time were so exhaustingly tedious. There is nothing exceptional about More's unfairness, violence, abusiveness and anger: these can readily be matched. But who else of even moderately comparable stature bored so consistently when he came to involve himself in polemics? It is not a matter of writing in the vernacular; More's Latin reply to Luther's attack on Henry VIII has all the same hallmarks. In this mood More is a markedly less interesting and effective writer than Tyndale himself, or such a lesser figure as Richard Morison; any comparison with Luther would be quite unfair. It is not easy to see why this should have been so. Some of the trouble lay in More's method which he defended as being exceptionally scrupulous – his virtual transcription (in chunks) of the opponent, with detailed answers point by point. His selection of what to quote does indeed seem fair, though it is still selection, but as a polemical technique this is death. His very determination to point out every slip, error, prevarication and ambiguity in the opponent – which one may regard again as proving an innate honesty and which certainly demonstrates his deep seriousness in the battle – helps to render him diffuse, ill-organized, repetitive and dull – and endless. But the real cause of his failure to write effective controversy seems to inhere in the very compulsion to engage in it. More was, so to speak, too serious about the issues and too committed. Because he knew so utterly that he was confronted with the devil and his disciples he lost all sense of proportion and therefore all ability to structure his attack; because he could not bring himself first to understand his opponents before demolishing them he fired vast volleys of anguished verbiage very little of which damaged the target. Not that a high seriousness and a deep commitment necessarily make a man a bad advocate; they did in More's case because he was in despair. The world he knew and thought necessary was falling apart. Unable to rise to a level of resignation which might seem cynical, unable to discover even a scintilla of virtue in what was happening, he could only scream his agony. One feels for the man, but one cannot read his book.

The issue which More debated deserved better than he managed to give to it, and the position he defended was much more persuasive than he made it appear. In the *Confutation* More is essentially concerned with one matter only, the nature of the true Church. Following Tyndale's every twist, he discusses the sacraments, the claims of the moral law, the nature of faith, the problems of sin, and so forth, but what is constantly at issue is the Church, the Church as the keeper of Christ's religion, as the true teacher and the true authority. More's deepest concerns spring from his powerful sense of man's sin of disobedience. He knows how thin the crust is of order and civilization beneath which lurk anarchy and chaos, and in the face of this peril he can fall back only on authority in every tradition-hallowed form. Interestingly enough, though careful (in 1533) to avoid any discussion of the papal claims, he yet allows one to see that he accepted the pope's universal supremacy. Naturally, he discovers proof in Scripture and in the customs and canons of 1,500 years, naturally he cites likeminded men of earlier days. But the hard core of his position is personal: a personal reaction to a personally experienced disaster. Any concept of the Church (such as he discerns in Luther and Tyndale) which would restrict it to God's elect destroyed the external and visible authority which alone restrained men from working out the implications of their sinful nature; and by a comprehensible twist, the reformers' emphasis on predestination to More submerged man's ability to choose grace, thus opening the door to *anomia* and the end of order. More rises to real eloquence only when he comes to defend free will, and he does so because he has to show that free will is the opposite to wilfulness. To him it is the first condition of man's moral potential and striving. More was a true conservative who despaired of what men did to alter their condition but retained his faith in men's power for good, not a radical who sees only human corruption and seeks the way out in the revolutionary effects of transformation imposed from outside. The pity of it was that when confronted by Tyndale and Barnes, and overwhelmed by his horror at their teaching,

More gave way to his despair and jettisoned the power of hope. Before he died he was to rediscover it, but the More of 1532–3 was not the More of 1534–5.

There are two lesser points embedded in the *Confutation* which similarly warn the historian that the conventional More needs serious reconsideration. One I have already touched upon. More's endless repetition of the charge of lust and lechery against Luther and the other priests who had taken wives cannot really be written off either as a device to sell his polemics or as some sort of joke. It is deeply entrenched in the matter and manner of the book, and he cannot leave the point alone. I have before this raised the question of More's attitude to matters sexual: this relentless harping on the vileness of copulation between a priest and a nun bears on the problem. So do the passages specially chosen by Schuster from More's *Dialogue* (1529) to illustrate his horror of heresy (pp. 1186–7). More there used reports about the Sack of Rome to beat the Lutherans, but the atrocity stories that particularly drew his attention had powerful sexual elements in them. Schuster thinks he meant to 'jab at the apathy of his countrymen'; perhaps, at least, he meant to arouse their attention. The point is that unlike many other reports from Rome these stories are of the 'strong meat' kind and are certainly quite unprovable; they carry the air of tales that usually attach themselves to stories of savage events, and I do not believe them to be true. Schuster rightly says that we do not know where More got his information about the Sack; he might have added that that information was so inadequate that he ascribed the worst personal atrocities to German heretics when in fact they were committed by Catholic Spaniards. More used these stories because he thought them effective, but More remembered them and told them at length because – it seems to me – a preoccupation with the problems of men's sexual nature came readily to him. After all, this was the man who abandoned the life monastic because he found 'the flesh' too powerful within himself, the man who created a family in which the flesh was not to much tamed as made pleasing to God. Unless we come to grips with this side of More's thinking we do an injustice both to his humanity and to his revulsion against those who had vowed chastity and yet deserted it. In the present state of More studies, it is difficult to get this matter into perspective; one needs to beware both of those who will not have a saint preoccupied with sex and those who would love to psychoanalyse a man for all seasons.

And lastly, More the persecutor. The *Confutation* leaves no doubt that More was very serious about the killing of heretics and regarded his part in such activities as his proper service to God, Church and Commonweal. He would burn Erasmus's *Praise of Folly* and some of his own earlier works, if only he could, not because they were really bad in themselves but because neither he nor Erasmus realized at the time how men would 'take harm of that that is good' (p. 179). A persistent preacher of heresy was, by God's grace, taken with the proofs of his crime upon him and burned 'with more profit unto his soul than had been haply to have lived longer and after died in his bed' (p. 359). In relating his examination of poor bewildered Richard Webbe, More grows positively smug (pp. 813–16). We may remember the one time during his final troubles that Cromwell managed to upset his equanimity: the time when Cromwell asked what difference there was between the discovery of heretics that More had encouraged and the seeking out of traitors he seemed to object to. More really had no answer to that. Neither the history of the 1530s nor the history of Thomas More can be rightly understood as long as we adhere to R. W. Chambers's endeavour to 'free' More of the charge of heresy-hunting. More not only hunted heretics but believed it was his spiritual duty to do so, and in the *Confutation* at least he shows not one touch of pity for misguided men. Venom governs all. 'Cankered minds' (his phrase – p. 172 – not, as is often alleged, an invention of Thomas Cromwell's) required surgery; real heretics were well burned.

The *Confutation* is not a major work, and even in the More canon it must come fairly low. Nevertheless, it contributes in very important ways to our understanding of the man and of his times, and no one can really pretend to have said anything very significant about More who has not confronted the challenge it presents to the conventional image of the man or sought the light it throws on his innermost convictions. Above all it helps to give a historical dimension to More, a man who changed as all men do in the course of time and under the pressure of circumstances, but is too commonly treated as though he was somehow a finished piece of marble from the start. We owe a real debt of gratitude to the devoted labours of those who have by herculean efforts provided this important aid in the penetration of More's mystery, and nothing critical said in this review must be allowed to obscure that debt.

More wrote the *Apology* a few months after he resigned the great seal;

evidently, withdrawal from office did not immediately mean withdrawal from the affairs of this world. The book belongs entirely to his
role as hammer of heretics. It forms a hinge: in it he engaged Tyndale for
the last time and opened his campaign against Christopher St German, a
battle terminated only by his arrest which finally turned his mind to
other things. As the reason for thus continuing the argument he gave the
need to refute certain charges against himself made by the 'brethren', the
heretical organization which, obsessed by conspiracy theories, he
believed to be after his blood because almost alone he stood out against
the triumph of heresy. And so, employing his familiar controversial
style and methods, he tried to dispose of the accusation that he wrote too
much and too tediously, that his treatment of Tyndale and Barnes
lacked common courtesy, that he showed an undue bias towards the
clergy, and that he picked bits from his adversaries' writings to refute
rather than deal fairly with the whole of their position. This last charge
he rebutted successfully: as he claimed, he had always cited by stages
almost all of any book he was combating. But that practice was itself a
cause of his tedious prolixity, and in the *Apology* he remained lengthy,
tedious and rude about Tyndale and Barnes. More had recovered a
touch of sovereignty, and the *Apology* is markedly less hysterical than
the earlier *Confutation*. Nevertheless it stands firmly in line with that
repulsive work – savage and authoritarian (to quote Mr Trapp), full of
contemptuous sneers, and quite unwilling to see opponents as fallible
human beings deserving of at least some compassion. Once again, More
labours the 'incestuous sacrilege and very beastly bitchery' of renegade
friars breaking their vows by marrying, and once again he expresses his
conviction that heretics are to be 'well and worthily burned'.

However, what seems to have particularly provoked More was the
charge that his polemics lacked 'the charitable mild manner' employed
by the anonymous author (that is, St German) of a treatise on the
division between the spiritualty and temporalty. St German's short
book lamented that strife and ascribed the general unpopularity of the
Church to various shortcomings and unsound practices among the
clergy. In defence of the spiritualty against one whom he sarcastically
called 'the pacifier', More really went to town. Here he certainly proved
the truth of the charge that he showed himself unduly partial towards
the clergy, for he would admit not a breath of criticism against an
institution and an order which emerge even more lily-white than they
looked black to anticlericals. (Alas for Erasmus's *Praise of Folly*.) More

had much excellent fun at the expense of arguments which relied rather vaguely on supposed general opinions ('some say . . .'): here More really is at his wittiest. Unfortunately, despite some sneers at opponents who pompously blamed him for frivolity in solemn matters, More was in this work generally far from frivolous and himself pretty pompous. In effect he demonstrated the truth of the charges he set himself to refute: he showed himself long, tedious and violent. This passionate assault on a new adversary reveals much about the man. Nothing in St German's treatise compelled More to take up the cudgels. The old common lawyer was no Lutheran or Tyndalian: if More's deep convictions about heresy are to be used to excuse his passion in controversy, why was that passion roused by this non-heretical critique of the clergy? At this stage of his life More evidently saw challenges everywhere which he found himself unable to resist. Though a better managed treatise than the *Confutation*, the *Apology* confirms the conclusion that More the polemicist was really a disaster, especially to himself. Even his style and language came off second best against St German's whose prose is simpler, clearer and more persuasive, though somewhat beset with a lifetime's experience of the language of the law.

Needless to say, this is not the view of the present editor. Professor Trapp's labours on this volume fully reach the high standards of excellence we have come to expect in this series. He faced one unusual problem in that he was dealing with the only work of More's which had already been edited in modern times – by A. I. Taft in 1930 – and he scrupulously cites Taft's notes in his own. More surprisingly, he copies Taft by reprinting St German's treatise as an appendix: being attacked by More evidently best guarantees an author this kind of immortality. Mr Trapp's edition is notably superior – a better text and much better apparatus. Occasional minor mistakes are inevitable and forgivable. Thus I doubt that More, referring to fees received from the king, had lands held in fee in mind rather than those profits of office which throughout the 1520s formed the bulk of his income (p. 334). As chancellor of the Duchy More certainly did not deal mostly with 'cases of civil disobedience' (p. 379); in fact in that office he cannot have tried anybody on indictment, as Mr Trapp seems to suppose he regularly did. But the notes are in general full, useful and very learned, and the introduction contains some excellent matter both of bibliographical information and of assessment. Against the misplaced efforts at exculpation of such as R. W. Chambers, Mr Trapp acknowledges

More's role as an active persecutor of heretics and does not hide his regret. He is also right in holding that some of the specific horror stories spread about More were inventions which More successfully refuted in the *Apology*. Yet in the end he cannot really free himself from More-idolatry. He will not concede that More's bitter passion in the enterprise must be accepted, certainly understood, but also accounted for in any evaluation of the man. It just is not enough to conclude that simply because he did not regard his persecuting duty as a pleasure his actions and motives stand justified (p. lxix). Perhaps More 'can face the worst that can be thought or said with the clearest of consciences', but if so then only because his conscience permitted him to contemplate the burning of deluded fellow-men with express approval. Nor is More always to be trusted, on the grounds that we know him to have been honourable: his treatment of Hunne's case, for instance (on which J. D. M. Derrett contributes a very disappointing essay) remains unconvincing and disingenuous despite all that piety can say for him.

The fact is that so long as More's writings are regarded as in manner partaking of the nature of holy writ we shall get no nearer to an understanding of his personality and of the events in which he was involved. Mr Trapp refers to his character as a non-variable *datum* usable in proving a case: we know it, and it therefore enables us to cleanse him from obloquy. But this character that allegedly we know is something put together from the plaudits of his friends (recorded many years before), from the hagiographical labours of his son-in-law, and from the marvellous letters and writings produced (later) during his imprisonment. The More of the *Confutation* and the *Apology* can be judged gentle, generous and wise only by an act of voluntary deafness. His writings against the heretics do not display the saint – not even the plaster saint – and it serves no purpose to shut one's eyes to the fact. What is more, they do not even display him as a man successful in controversy. Of course, as all such debaters do, he scores points, but he uses far too much plain rudeness, too much superior arrogance, too much blind bigotry, and far too relentless a tone of voice to be really persuasive; throughout, one never loses the uneasy feeling that persuasion to him comes second to extermination. In manner at least – matter being a problem of the faith – his adversaries regularly surpass him. Let us remember, as it is never admitted in those devoted circles, that More lost his polemical battles, both at the time and by any dispassionate later assessment. Arguing this away does harm to history and even more harm to Thomas More whose astonishing transformation in the last fifteen months of his life thus ceases to be the human miracle it was.

Here is one successful series. A further four fat volumes testify to the remarkable energies of the editorial team directed by R. S. Sylvester, as well as to the indefatigable pen of Sir Thomas More. The format is by now familiar. A lengthy introduction discusses the text and provides various essays on the contents; the text itself is presented in so scrupulously scholarly a fashion that surely this must become the *editio ultima*; then follows a very long commentary keyed to lines in the text, which is a repository of often recondite and occasionally superfluous learning; next comes a glossary of difficult words which demonstrates that More's vocabulary baffles Americans even more often than Englishmen; lastly, the excellent index covers all parts. The editors of these present volumes have done their work with the devoted excellence which we have come to expect from this undertaking and are fully entitled to the same sort of acclaim and admiration as has greeted their predecessors. They have also followed precedent by refusing to submerge themselves in a grey anonymity, for in the prefatory essays they appear very much in their own persons and rights. Martz's disquisition on More's 'Tower Works' elaborates his contribution to the well known meeting held in 1970 at St John's University, New York.[1] Manley very nearly succeeds in imposing upon the *Dialogue of Comfort* the sort of thematic structure that its author rather signally failed to achieve. Haupt is interesting on the exegetical tradition within which More's *Treatise on the Passion* must be placed. One member of the team had a specially onerous and specially rewarding assignment. The recent discovery, at Valencia, of More's original manuscript of the *Tristitia Christi* has enabled Miller to reproduce the text in facsimile, faced on opposing pages with a transcription and a translation (the translation is exceptionally felicitous). Out of his labours he has distilled a fascinating analysis of More as a writer — writing very fast without deteriorating into a scribble, correcting as he went, producing (like the experienced author he was) good clean copy for the printer even after much deleting, interlining and amending.

The materials here presented comprise the works traditionally

[1] [L. L. Martz, 'Thomas More: the Tower Works,' *St Thomas More: Action and Contemplation*, ed. R. S. Sylvester (New Haven, 1972), 57–83.]

ascribed to More's time in the Tower, written, this is, in the fourteen months of his imprisonment, and even though Haupt shows that *The Treatise on the Passion* was well advanced while the author was yet at liberty that traditional description retains its value. In sheer amount it is an astonishing production, poured out in circumstances which, however leisured, would hardly be considered as well suited to works of learning. Evidently More saved not only his soul but also his sanity by this furious activity. However, from a reader's point of view it has to be said that he wrote too much. The editors of the Yale project are committed to believing in their subject's unfailing excellence, but the less committed mind must confess to finding More's English style less attractive than they do. I can see some point in C. S. Lewis's sour comments on this accumulation of rambling sentences, strung together rather than structured into an edifice. One has to remember that More was confronting the task of expressing in an underdeveloped vernacular what was usually said only in a learned language. It is also true that his choice of a colloquial and demotic style has its pleasing aspects. Nevertheless, his pace lacks variety, his vocabulary lacks excitement, and his syntax lacks inventive form; among his contemporaries, Tyndale, Cranmer and especially Richard Morison manifestly surpass him. Oddly enough, his Latin style displays just those characteristics of nervous energy and concentrated craftsmanship which appear so rarely when he is using his mother tongue. What carries one through his writings is matter not manner, thought not ornament.

Of course, he could do much better at times. More has a habit of flashing out: the blade, or more commonly the sledgehammer, suddenly strikes out of the general mumble. Taking my courage in both hands, I must say that I remain unimpressed by the famous 'merry tales'. Some are moderately amusing, but too many harp embarrassingly on the shortcomings of women: on this evidence, More was a notable male chauvinist. Admittedly he stood in an established tradition of such anecdotes in which wives are always shrews and husbands always hen-pecked: but could he not have found at least one story that shows a woman in a good light? We are instructed to delight in the tale of the carpenter's wife who nagged her husband into cutting off her head, and in Mother Maud's tale of the fox as confessor. The first strikes me as exceptionally nasty, and the second rambles on in a very self-indulgent manner, labouring its simple point and again turning on attitudes which are neither gentle nor compassionate. The best of More is not in these stories but in the seemingly casual asides which show how well he understood the minds and manners of men: 'we find that our Saviour himself wept twice or thrice, but never find we that he laughed so much as once'; 'to counsel a man never to think on that case is in my mind as much reason as the medicine that I have heard taught one for the toothache, to go thrice about a churchyard and never think on a foxtail'; 'marry, I never saw fool yet that thought himself other than wise'.

The crudenesses of the 'merry tales' matter because they remind us of the many ambiguities at the core of More's personality, an ambiguity still disconcertingly present even in these last works which concentrate so singlemindedly on the prospect of death and the search for salvation. After he had cast off the burdens of office and public life, he determined 'to remember the immortality of the life to come', and in these writings we learn what he meant by that. Once immured in the Tower, he knew that he faced the overwhelming ordeal of remaining steadfast in the face of dreadful tribulations – deprivations, possible torture, the likelihood of a painful and dishonourable death – but the evidence of *The Treatise on the Passion* shows that he did not need prison to bring the prospect home to him. These matters occupied his mind from mid-1532 to the end, and the works before us fully demonstrate how he came to terms with fate. It is important to remember that More had no doubts at all concerning the traditional Christian scheme: after death he would experience either the bliss of heaven or the torments of hell, and he believed in the physical reality of both in the best medieval manner. Nothing so well illustrates the distance between his age and ours – a distance too often forgotten by those who prefer to treat him as some kind of well-meaning liberal humanist – than his vivid and horrified descriptions of hell, the more realistic because so matter of fact. There is far less sensationalism in More's vision of the damned than in his report of the Sack of Rome in the *Dialogue concerning Heresies* (one of the many signs of the sovereign maturity that he had gained from his sufferings), but there is no mistaking the strictly physical notion of what hell was like which he entertained.

With this kind of hell as the alternative, he naturally had only one way open to him: he had to adhere to his faith and be saved, and he had to last out till the release brought by death. The first would appear to have posed no problem. By this time, More thought the truths of the faith quite plain and requiring no argument, so that there is virtually no theological debate in these writings. The More who could temper his regret at the spread of Lutheran heresy with memories of the common ground on which all Christians stood had come a long way from the hysterical author of *The Confutation of Tyndale* and the determined persecutor of heretics. Even at his most impassioned – for instance in the lengthy sermon on the sin of covetousness which fills much of Book Two of the *Dialogue of Comfort* – he retains his serenity; the combativeness which had been so marked a facet of his character from his young days down to 1532 has gone entirely. And he had gained this peace of mind and soul without acquiring a trace of cynicism or even resignation: he remained deeply involved and concerned, for others as well as himself. Flat and stark as much of his exegesis and his moralizing are in these writings, a superiority of spirit shines through which can only be called saintly.

Though More was certain that the most serious temptation – to doubt God's love and grace as revealed in the teaching of the Church – could not trouble him, he was nevertheless very apprehensive that circumstances might cause him to lose his way long enough for disaster to strike. That, at least, is the usual opinion, supported in the main by our editors. Is it correct? It assumes that his meditations represent his own search for assurance and remedy, but that is not what he says. Throughout, and especially in the *Dialogue of Comfort*, he is offering advice to others; he explains rather than discusses how a man should face such ordeals. There are really no unresolved questions seeking a resolution. The pretence of a genuine argument between two friends in that *Dialogue* wears so thin that More himself is forced to introduce several rather clumsy attempts to present more of an exchange of contrasting attitudes. Vincent, the young man seeking assurance, is not quite reduced to the 'yea verily, Socrates' of More's Platonic model, but his questions too rarely interrupt the flow of his uncle's discourse, and when he does get a longer speech of his own he tends to continue rather than oppose the older man's line of argument. In short, in these last writings More offers the result and not the process of his struggle for assurance; he had found the way before he wrote, and he now describes it so that others may learn from him. Genuine meditation never came very naturally to one ever inclined to instruct and exhort. The difference appears when More is set beside such as Thomas à Kempis or Marguerite d'Angoulême who also endeavoured to resolve the human condition in the face of God's mystery: they contemplate the needs of their own souls, while More addresses himself to the souls of others. Deeply concerned with matters which moved others to exalted outpourings, More proved conclusively that he was never a mystic.

Yet his answer to the problem with which his fate had confronted him was nevertheless very much in line with the thought of mystics and contemplatives whom this downright and active man so little resembled. He held that man's only hope of comfort and victory in time of tribulation lay in meditation upon the example of the Saviour. Thus, as his friend Erasmus had also done in his different way, he called for an *imitatio Christi*. But now this no longer meant following the ethical imperatives of the Founder's life: it meant following the Son of Man in his last agony. The one theme that runs through all these writings is the passion of Christ: his suffering, voluntarily undergone, is described again and again with a vivid concreteness which is both touching and frightening. Even the *Tristitia* which, left unfinished, does not actually get there was plainly going to reach a climax with yet another meditation on the Passion. Though the purpose of that suffering – the redemption of mankind – is not forgotten, it gets far less attention than the agony of the Passion itself, for what More is seeking is not an assurance of salvation but the support that thinking upon the death upon the cross will bring to those facing their own dissolution. God the Father, Christ the Saviour, put in far less of an appearance than one might have supposed; it is Christ's suffering humanity that ultimately dominates all More's last thoughts. In those footsteps he sees himself walking and expects others to be called to walk also; and having placed himself firmly, though humbly, in that succession, he means to convey his realization and his comfort to all who need it. The mode of these works is therefore neither philosophical nor theological nor truly meditative but powerfully homiletic.

The other writings are interesting, and the *Tristitia*, being in Latin, has a positive beauty of its own, but only the *Dialogue of Comfort* can be considered a major work – despite its unevenness of style and lack of taut structure one of More's greatest works. He returns in it to the device first used in *Utopia*. Once again we are listening to a conversation placed in a fictional but also very real setting – Hungary in the lull that intervened between the battle of Mohacz and the siege of Vienna, when people there, pitifully aware of their helplessness, were looking every day for the irresistible return of the Turks, bringing with them killing, destruction and the devastation of the Christian faith. Terror and despair encompass everybody. It has, of course, been taken for granted (though Manley rightly warns against overdoing the subtlety) that More was really thinking about England and his own predicament: the Turk stands for the onslaught of heresy and schism, and the tribulations in question were those facing More and anyone else determined to resist Henry VIII. Very occasionally, it is true, an English reality emerges from behind the Turkish fiction, but most of the time the surface story also commands the inner meaning of the book; attempts to reduce everything to More's personal experience and position in effect trivialize his purpose. He does not use a contrived setting simply to represent another particular setting which it would be unwise to identify more precisely; on the contrary, he employs it for a universal attack on the universal problem of human suffering in the cause of faith and conscience, and for a universal demonstration of the consolation which grasping God's will and Christ's example can bring. The long disquisition on suicide has relevance to himself inasmuch as he evidently regarded any courting of martyrdom (in which he included failure to avoid it, so far as conscience permitted) as a form of unlawful suicide, but true suicide he never contemplated, and the disquisition bears far more directly on Hungary and other lands where self-destruction might become a desirable alternative to the heathen enslavement threatened by Islam.

More quite frequently neglects the fiction of the *Dialogue*: thus Book Two runs right away from his setting which has to be brought back at the start of Book Three, with a touch of embarrassment. But when he does so stray he enlarges the discourse: he does not perhaps direct it towards the Tower of London. For myself, I should be careful of treating the *Dialogue* as containing quite as much autobiography as the editors see in it; and it would be agreeable to think that the unconscionable Archdeacon Harpsfield also erred when he regularly identified the women in More's anti-feminist stories with Dame Alice. Do we really want to suppose that More gave to his family and to posterity a work designed to strengthen their fortitude in adversity in which light relief is provided by sly hints that his second wife was a fool and a philistine, that he rather dreaded her tantrums, and that he liked to laugh at her behind his hand? That is what the family tradition alleges and what here finds acceptance. Well, it may be so.

Quite apart from his main purpose, More clearly enjoyed writing the *Dialogue of Comfort*. Vincent and Anthony, especially the latter, are well realized individuals provided with personal histories of participation in wars, court acquaintances, business visits to Germany, and so forth. The playfulness that produced *Utopia* was not quite extinct, even in the Tower, even on the eve of death. How this work (or indeed any of these writings) got out of the Tower, to be preserved and then printed in the reign of Mary or abroad, remains mysterious; their fortunate fate says something about the nature of imprisonment in the Tower. To More prison lacked terror, but he knew that he had to persuade others to see the loss of liberty in the right light. Of all the trumpet calls in the *Dialogue* none rings out more triumphantly than his great demonstration that, since God has decreed death at the end of life and permanent confinement as its condition, there is no cause to regard the death and imprisonment inflicted by other men as any form of tribulation. He would have been horrified to hear it thus put: but the man who died on the scaffold on 6 July 1535 had won a victory not only over his own fearful humanity, not only over Henry VIII, but also over God.

(d) M. L. BUSH, *The Government Policy of Protector Somerset.* London; Edward Arnold, 1975.*

One by one, the fixed stars of the Tudor firmament, once one of the most cosily familiar sectors of the national cosmos, are falling from their places. Henry VII the money-grubbing miser has gone, taking Henry VII the sagacious moderate with him. Henry VIII, the architect of reform and master of his fate, is clinging on by a bare toehold. Thomas More has lost his invariable saintliness, and Thomas Cromwell his comprehensive villainy. True, only small voices have so far dared hint that all is not well with Gloriana herself, and Lord Burghley resists the closer look because Conyers Read's two large and unreadable volumes stand as an impassable barrier between student and subject. But surely the wave of rethinking will not for ever retreat before the year 1558. Meanwhile, however, it is now the turn of the Protector Somerset, uncle and guardian to young Edward VI.

The general view of Edward Seymour, earl of Hertford and duke of Somerset, was established long ago. Firmly and fondly delineated in 1900 by A. F. Pollard, in his first and worst book, he still appeared

* [*Times Literary Supplement*, 6 January 1976.]

bearing the same visage (only more so) in W. K. Jordan's 500 pages of adjectival praise (1968).[1] As everybody knows, Somerset was 'the good duke', a man of high and worthy ideals, eager promoter of religious reform, father of the commonwealth and passionate defender of the unregarded poor. If some people, to whom nothing was sacred, set themselves to point out that this shining knight seemed to be unusually keen on adding to his extensive properties, could not live at peace with his wife (her fault, perhaps), and was possessed of a singularly arrogant and uncivil temper, the duke's defenders had little difficulty in sweeping aside these foibles in their endeavour to present a liberal and far-sighted statesman, precursor out of his time of so much progress, who was cruelly struck down by the selfish hatred of the possessing classes.

Dr Bush will have none of this. He sees Somerset's actions and purposes dominated by one overriding concern – the war with Scotland which he had inherited from the previous reign but which in fact he had made his own even before Henry VIII died. (That king always regarded Scotland as a sideshow in his quarrel with France.) Somerset meant to win that war by making effective the marriage treaty between Edward VI and the infant Mary Queen of Scots, and he resolved to hold the country down by means of permanent garrisons planted along the border and up the east coast. Even when it became apparent that he could not maintain or supply his forces, and even after his aggression had led to the direct intervention of 10,000 French troops which guaranteed his failure, he blindly persisted with his obsession. The war dictated his other policy decisions. By 1548, inflation had become so severe that the government had to take action, as indeed it was pressed to do by a motley crowd of preachers, advisers and lobbyists to whom Dr Bush, showing cause, denies the familiar title of commonwealth-men. Unquestionably those amongst them that blamed the debasement of the coinage were on the right track, but reform of the coinage would have cut off the immediate supply of cash needed for the dreadfully expensive war, for which reason the Protector would not contemplate it. Thus he listened the more readily to those who maintained that sheep-farming, enclosing and the engrossing of farms lay at the heart of the problem, an economically mistaken view which precipitated politically perilous steps. It was the attraction of an action that did not interfere with the war, and which was moreover advertised as likely to solve England's manpower problems, that made

[1] [Cf. above, vol. i, no. 11.]

Somerset the seeming friend of the rural poor. In the country-wide risings of 1549, which at least in part sprang from the official attack on agrarian grievances as well as from the official neglect of the real roots of inflation, Somerset shared to the full the feelings of the ruling order and supported the drastic action called for by the gentry and the Privy Council. The religious settlement of 1549, in which for once the Protector compromised with his own protestant sympathies, reflected mainly a desire to keep Charles V, then at the height of his power, from intervening while England was fighting the Scots. Nor did Somerset either devise or back a general programme of reform, though he has been frequently credited with doing just that. Most of the statutes touching social or economic problems sprang from privately promoted bills. The Protector's exceptionally intensive use of royal proclamations is explained as arising from circumstances (especially, again, the war) and not from any design to rule energetically and clearsightedly in the teeth of a class opposition entrenched in Parliament. And ambitions to improve the machinery, badly needed at the time and entertained for instance by Somerset's backer William Paget, met no response from the Protector.

Thus, according to Dr Bush, there was absolutely nothing about this regime that justifies the traditional ascription of an idealistic, though possibly unpractical, vision. The Protector's ideas and attitudes were those of his time and order. His difficulties arose from circumstances some of which (the war, the risings) he helped to create, while the pressures of inflation and religious divisions were passed on from the previous reign. The duke's obsessive and abrasive personality complicated all political problems, and his conventional desire to be thought virtuous accounts for what others have seen as idealism. His mind was never out of step with those of his colleagues in government, though he had an unfailing knack for alienating people by his harsh manners and inflexible ways. 'Somerset failed because he was prone to *idées fixes*, not because he was an idealist or too magnanimous.'

An important revision: does it stand up? There are times when Dr Bush appears to press his argument a bit too relentlessly; occasionally he gives the impression that he is working out a preconceived thesis rather than establishing truths derived from the evidence. But this is merely a defect of manner, reinforced by an arrangement which begins and ends by stating conclusions worked out in analytical chapters that are designed to prove the point. What matters is that the point is proved, and a reader would be poorly advised to suppose otherwise. Some readers, possibly less instructed in the history of these issues, may even be left with a feeling that there was no need to argue a case: Dr Bush frames his criticisms of others (mainly of Pollard and Jordan, but occasionally also of R. B. Wernham or this reviewer) so gently in decorous footnotes that the uninitiated may not become aware how much he is altering and overturning accepted interpretations. In truth, the new assessment carries powerful conviction, with one single exception. Apparently Dr Bush has not used the important dissertation by D. E. Hoak on Edward VI's Council, now in process of becoming a book.[2] If he had done so, he would probably have altered his view that Somerset consistently had the agreement of his fellow-councillors in all he did, for it now appears that the duke ruled effectively without the aid of the Council whose alleged decisions were his alone. As Dr Hoak demonstrates, this was one man's regime, and a self-willed autocrat's at that. Recognition of this fact does not affect Dr Bush's general and particular conclusions concerning the policy pursued, but it compels some change in one's view of the man and in one's assessment of his relation to what came after. Although I agree that suspicions I once expressed of Somerset's authoritarian tendencies were probably unjustified, I am not persuaded that he did not wish to rule as quasi-king and without either rivals or companions. He was not only bad-tempered but also ruthlessly ambitious, a side of him that seems to be underplayed here. Furthermore, his manner of rule played its part in making his policies differ more from those of the duke of Northumberland than Dr Bush would seem prepared to accept.

These, however, are relatively minor points. The main thing is the demolition of the good duke. How was it achieved? There are those, some respectable scholars among them, who hold that historical revisions reflect little more than changing attitudes in historians; and when in addition the revision attacks a liberal view (indeed, a liberal legend), suspicions that an essentially immoral stance (subservience to an existing order, siding with government) is being expressed rise readily in certain minds. Dr Bush runs the risk of being accused of various sins – from 'being an administrative historian' through belonging to a certain school to possibly even countenancing a Tory conspiracy. No one can prevent such manifestations of a mild paranoia, and in the interests of the larger amusement one would not even wish to try. But,

[2] [D. E. Hoak, *The King's Council in the Reign of Edward VI* (Cambridge, 1976).]

in truth, what Dr Bush has done rests on nothing more esoteric than a proper study and use of the evidence. He has employed no new techniques, asked no fashionably new questions, adopted no political or psychological thesis; instead he has thoroughly applied himself to reading and understanding the extant materials in their own proper right. By such means, infused with a highly intelligent insight, he has created a new and better view of things. That is how historical knowledge should advance, and that is how as a rule it does.

(e) ARTHUR B. FERGUSON, *Clio Unbound. Perception of the Social and Cultural Past in Renaissance England.* Durham, N.C.; Duke University Press, 1979.*

There are times when work on the history of history must appear distinctly narcissistic, especially when it deals with ages which did not regard history very highly. Why should there be so much interest in what the sixteenth century thought about history when, by comparison with its theological, political, and philosophical preoccupations, it thought rarely and practised intermittently? Yet we have already had three major works on these themes – Smith Fussner's high-flown discovery of a revolution in historical thought, Fritz Levy's elegant survey of the age's historical theorizing, and May McKisack's devoted pursuit of Tudor antiquaries.[1] Now Arthur B. Ferguson adds himself to these ranks, with a study of much complexity which, however, throws light less on Tudor historiography than on the occasional virtues and more frequent deficiencies of a whole genre.

As an admirer of Ferguson's earlier book on the social thought of the English humanists,[2] I find myself doubtful about the wisdom of this switch to historiography. Still, it was his choice to make. He correctly maintains that in the sixteenth century history meant in the main political history (what he keeps calling *res gestae*); yet he asks that his writers should discover an interest in the history of social and cultural affairs and he attempts to demonstrate that such an interest gradually pushed to the fore as the century advanced. The argument starts with an

* [*History and Theory* 20 (1981), 92–100.]

[1] F. Smith Fussner, *The Historical Revolution: English Historical Writing and Thought 1580–1640* (1962); F. J. Levy, *Tudor Historical Thought* (San Marino, Cal., 1967); May McKisack, *Medieval History in the Tudor Age* (Oxford, 1971).

[2] Arthur B. Ferguson, *The Articulate Citizen and the English Renaissance* (Durham, N.C., 1965).

analysis of the two kinds of historians allegedly to be found: this turns out to be the familiar distinction between narrative historians (chroniclers) and the seekers after 'relics' (antiquaries). The supposed interaction of the two is then traced in their treatment of the Church, the law and the language, with two final chapters on 'the course of civilization' in which the Tudor writers are classed as being concerned with the linear history of the ascent of man, and with the double problem of change – decay and improvement. If Fussner's hero was Bacon, Levy's probably Camden, and McKisack's Agarde, Ferguson elects Daniel and Hooker as the most successful practitioners of the sort of history he favours.

This choice of a poet and a theologian defines his intellectual preferences and underscores a confusion springing from his failure to distinguish between the practice of history and its use for nonhistorical purposes; if that distinction had been kept firmly in mind, the argument of the book would have been clearer. Ferguson sometimes overstates the difference between historians and antiquarians. Thus it is true that Camden was more of a chronicler in his *Annals* and more of an antiquary in his *Britannia*; yet he could insert his interest in 'relics' into his narrative, which, for instance, stops to say things about the effects of exploration on trade and science, or analyses Irish tax systems in the course of describing the Elizabethan conquest of the island. Like most historians of ideas, Ferguson prefers to fit people rather than ideas into categories, a process which to me seems to reverse the natural order of things: ideas of necessity get themselves defined, while people can happily hold contradictory ones in unexpected conjunction. Nevertheless, the age itself made a distinction between historians and antiquaries, thus roughly justifying the main structure of the book.

The theme of the book is the triumph, in historical studies, of the antiquaries' social and cultural concerns over the historians' purely political ones. So bald a summary must be unfair – too simple and too crude. The book in fact resists any simple summary, partly because the general theme announced at the beginning gets lost several times as Ferguson is tempted into by-ways not readily visible from the historical high road. Pecock and Fortescue, introduced to provide a baseline from which change can be measured, become the subjects of extensive essays only partly linked to that role – interesting essays, but confusing in this place. An excursus on St German's views on sovereignty, perceptive in itself, very quickly leaves St German's historical thinking behind. These recurring moves sideways are often in themselves illuminating, but together with the tenuousness of the supposed subject they account for the difficulty one has in following the discourse. Ferguson states (p. 79) that he has been concerned 'to highlight only those aspects more relevant to the emergence of a historical attitude toward the social and cultural past', which must imply the search for an ascending line in this welter of writings. In practice this line turns out to waver about, up and down, to and fro; it throws out sideshoots into apparent irrelevancies; in the end the question must arise whether the transformation posited by Ferguson actually took place.

In spite of its many scattered new insights, its several competent analyses, and its interesting discussion of progress ideas (in which Ferguson, confronted with doubts about improvement derived from the doctrine of original sin, proves rather uncomprehending in the face of his sources), the book has several weaknesses which in part arise from this whole style of writing intellectual history, but in part are particular to itself.

In the first place, it is much too long: things are said over and over again, usually in rather solemn fashion. There is a tendency to make the same point differently in consecutive sentences. Though Ferguson writes sensible English and on the whole avoids jargon, he likes to sort out his arguments in the hearing of the reader, and he assuredly suffers from one of the most tiresome afflictions that beset the history of ideas: he takes everything, however absurdly risible, very seriously. His style insists on an importance which the matter often lacks; the reader is subdued by a stately pomposity of superfluous elaboration. What, for instance, do we learn from so tautologous a statement as that 'the quality of the resulting history thus depended largely on the degree to which Renaissance antiquaries were able to elevate mere topics of historical interest to the level of historical problems' (p. 82)? It would help if so many geese had been spared transformation into swans – and far from mute swans at that.

Against this excessive respect for the writers discussed stands Ferguson's constant awareness of twentieth-century expectations which gives the book an astonishingly anachronistic air. In fact the twentieth century keeps sticking its superfluous nose into the discourse. Tudor writers, it seems, are to be judged by their willingness to fulfil demands they had never heard of. 'Sixteenth-century thinkers', we learn (p. 79), 'did not have a frame of reference such as would permit them to ask the kind of questions the present-day social scientist would ask; and the answers he would ordinarily look for are therefore not likely to be forthcoming.' And why, pray, should those sixteenth-century thinkers conform to the 'paradigm' (a word here once again over-used) set up by what, on any reckoning, must be some of the daftest operators in the intellectual history of mankind? What sort of criticism of John Stow is represented by the remark that he did not 'possess a frame of theoretical reference such as would suggest the kind of questions the modern social historian would ask' (p. 101)? At least we can be grateful to learn that 'Elizabethan England produced no Spenglerean analysis of Western culture' (p. 389). A small cheer for such unexpected mercies. Elsewhere (p. 79) Ferguson kindly concedes that his writers should not be condemned for not asking those famous questions, but he does so in terms of such patient and patent superiority that the concession loses all force. His real stance is better illustrated by his final verdict on the narrative historians under review, judged inadequate because they stuck 'to past politics devoid of the social and cultural dimensions essential to what a modern mind would consider a realistic perception even of political history' (p. 421). A history of ideas so firmly directed by the faiths of the historian's own age does not promise well. The reason for this surprising lack of historical empathy is also plain: Ferguson is in pursuit of a theme unknown to the sixteenth century and artificially imposed upon it by the twentieth.

There may be some who do not object to such a method: they may hold that in this way the modern historian may free himself from conventional notions about a past age, see novel import and connections, and thus refresh his own understanding of the age studied. Perhaps, if he remembers in time that the dead have a right to be judged by their own aspirations, he may successfully work that way, though I deeply distrust a method which is much more likely to invent a past age than to discover it. In any case, Ferguson does best when he forgets his social scientists and social historians. He is illuminating on those fifteenth-century predecessors of the humanist renovation, on the historical assessments implicit in the concept of *adiaphora*, and on Tyndale's attitude to biblical study; and the concluding chapters on the course of civilization contain points of bright light as well as a good deal of occluding vapour given off by the present day. However, even if the general approach were to be accepted as safer than it is, the investigation still falters, often to the point of collapse, for three other reasons. The author deals with substantive issues on which he is insufficiently informed and he therefore tends to follow supposedly authoritative opinion rather blindly; he limits his area of investigation too much and thus creates schemes which the introduction of additional material must destroy; and he divorces his writers from the world within which they wrote. That last flaw, so characteristic of the history of ideas, is subtly brought out in his remark that 'the years of apparent doubt and disenchantment [that is, the last decade of the century] were also years of intellectual achievement' (p. 388), this rather banal observation being supported by a reference to Hooker, engaged in 'laying a philosophical foundation for the Anglican Church'. Does it not matter to this assessment that for forty years hardly anyone can be shown to have read Hooker?

The other two shortcomings – insufficient understanding of certain historical problems and too narrow a choice of sample – require more demonstration, a task not rendered easier by the fact that they are usually linked.[3] However, let me illustrate the first by looking at Ferguson's treatment of the Church and the law. Both, indeed, ought to be central to the argument because both depended for their self-justification on a tangle of partly dogmatic and partly historical tenets, and because both were professionally concerned with those social and cultural issues which the book pursues. Ferguson was therefore right to give them extended attention: his use of them should have proved

[3] A number of misleading or confusing statements may be noted. To speak still of the 'peculiarly secular character of the English Reformation' is to express views superseded by much recent work (p. xiii). Higden's *Polychronicon* is not a good example of 'the best of medieval chronicles', compared with William of Malmesbury or even Matthew Paris (p. 7). Camden's *Annals* should be used in a proper edition, not in the abbreviated form edited by W. T. MacCaffrey (p. 53). *Contempus* for *contemptum* unhappily looks like more than an uncorrected printer's error (p. 148). What evidence is there that More, at least by 1530, 'was not opposed in principle to translating the Bible into English' (p. 154)? Linking Huizinga and Maynard Smith as equals in historical insight argues a high degree of egalitarian nondiscrimination (p. 166). Thomas Smith's allocation of 'virtually unlimited legislative authority to the king and parliament when acting as one' (that is, to the king-in-Parliament) was a commonplace of Tudor political thinking and experience, and was certainly, despite doubts stated in 1906, equal to a notion of legislative sovereignty (p. 243). If Fortescue supposed that statute could not touch property rights, he must have overlooked the many acts of resumption of his day (p. 244). The fact that the sixteenth century gave a wrong date to the *Modus Tenendi Parliamentum* does not entitle one to call that treatise spurious (p. 272). Anyone who can say that Lambarde's defence of the Star Chamber places him 'with the Stuart defenders of the royal prerogative' has failed to notice fifty years of work on Tudor constitutional history (p. 287). Thomas More's was so far from being the characteristic English response to 'the troubled years of the early sixteenth century' that he became one of the victimized minority (p. 419); the common intellectual reaction was welcoming, as again much recent work has made clear.

highly instructive in advancing his argument. That they do not fulfil this role with anything like the force and conviction possible derives from the historical maltreatment meted out to them. The whole discussion of puritanism (pp. 195 ff.) is rendered null by the fact that Ferguson, in a breathtaking oversimplification, identifies puritanism with Thomas Cartwright. The unquestioning employment of the term is itself incomprehensible nowadays when those best learned in the field do not use it without reluctance and apprehension; the explanation lies no doubt in the absence of all the massive recent work from the footnotes of this book. But if the term is to be used at all, it must include such diverse writers as John Ponet, William Fulke, Laurence Chaderton or William Perkins, and it must include William Harrison, perhaps the most historically aware of all that breed. What is more, we get here nothing new on Cartwright (or Whitgift); a rehash of their exchanges, even though it succeeds in identifying historical issues contained in them, should not be allowed to do duty for the complex patterns of thought on the Church and its history which proliferated from the 1530s onwards.

The law, in a way, gets worse treatment. We start inauspiciously with an assertion that justice is a social value, true enough for the present day but not so obvious to sixteenth-century lawyers usually convinced that it was an eternal value. We soon discover that, true to his habit of obedience to 'authority', Ferguson has swallowed whole the Pocock/Kelley thesis of English lawyers' insularity and ahistoricity. The whole section is dominated by the conviction that in order to be truly good they should have been like the French legists in whom pressing problems of conflicting laws produced some fascinating historical insights. (Kelley, I fear, would regard the last sentence – a not unnatural reaction to French chauvinism – as a typically English piece of anti-French chauvinism.) A better historical approach would have taken into account the reasons why English lawyers felt no need for such exertions, would have emphasized the occasions on which, moved by intellectual curiosity, they nevertheless looked abroad, and might have criticized them for identifying their famous 'custom' (of which much is here said though nothing of consequence) with that of the whole realm when yet they encountered different local customs in many manors and municipalities of the land. Instead – and in the teeth of some of Ferguson's own discoveries – we get the by now conventional Pocock-inspired learning on immemorial notions, learning which everybody (including its original author) now agrees simply does not cover all the ground. Ferguson achieves his result by effectively reducing the body of English lawyers to three people – Fortescue, St German and Coke, in the end whittling them down to the last one only. This unhappy reductionism is aggravated by a conventional misreading of Coke's emphasis on the immemorial existence of the law as totally antihistorical.

By such means it becomes possible to underestimate, for instance, St German's strong sense of an historical element in the law, or Thomas Smith's powerful interest in comparative studies: Coke is the culmination of the genus, and his fond belief that he alone knew what the law was is trustingly accepted. The game is given away in the remark that Coke 'came to personify the common law . . . and spoke for what was no doubt the majority of his colleagues' (pp. 265–6); 'Coke and those of the legal profession for whom he apparently spoke' (p. 267); 'the presumably considerable body of lawyers for whom he spoke' (p. 268). No doubt, apparently, presumably: the words shamefacedly beg the question and allow Ferguson to slide over his own admission that there were other lawyers who continued to think the immemoriality of the law open to question. As is indeed well enough known by now, Coke's determination to become the pope of the common law was by no means generally accepted until after the Restoration. Making him the 'paradigm' thus perverts the argument *ab initio* by shutting out a mass of evidence to the contrary. Besides, even Coke, however much he thumped the tub of immemoriality, frequently, and of necessity, recognized the facts of historical change in the law. His bigotry notwithstanding, he was far from being the blind idiot that some historians of ideas have tried to make him. In the end, his immemorial law boils down to general principles and maxims, while he knew that the positive law itself was capable of change and development. How could any judge of so many years' standing have failed to know this?

To discover the realities of lawyers' attitudes requires a study of the law, not of a few treatises and *obiter dicta* – though even treatises, if more had been drawn on, would have altered the burden of the argument. What of John Parkyns, whose introduction to his highly popular *Profitable Book Treating of the Laws of England* (first published in 1528) displays an understanding of the socially and historically conditioned relativism of the positive law almost worthy of the French? Even by Ferguson's own admission, Thomas Smith and John Davies are seen to have looked to the civil law for comparison (as indeed, though Ferguson does not say so, Coke did when it suited him);[4] the antiquaries' search for 'origins' is shown to have paid heed to historical development; Spelman and Selden, worthy men though they were – the second a towering scholar – did not come so much out of nowhere as his 'authorities' have misled Ferguson into believing. If some lawyers really believed in the immemorial existence of Parliament, others were well aware of its quite recent history. For what reason are all those devotees to the historical study of the law less 'paradigmatic' than Coke? The most splendidly antihistorical remark cited comes not from a common lawyer but from the civilian, Alberico Gentili: 'I therefore tell you that there is no reason why any lawyer or teacher of the law should read or know any history' (p. 279, my translation). The contrast with Lambarde the common lawyer could not be greater and should have been pursued; yet Ferguson can only comment that English civilians (Gentili was English?) had no more interest in the relationship of history and law than their common-law colleagues. I am afraid that here the scheme presented derives not so much from a study of the thinkers – for Ferguson is quite good on Smith and Lambarde – as from an externally imposed conviction which rests upon already outdated scholarship.

Perhaps it was to be expected that a line of argument as single minded as Ferguson's should be vulnerable to the objection that he has not looked at enough examples, but in this case the objection becomes really formidable. His catchment area is much too small, a fact disguised by a wordiness which extends the book to over 400 pages. In the first place, he sticks exclusively to what is in print, a limitation perhaps excusable in one who has to work such a long way from the archives but a limitation nevertheless. Gordon Zeeveld demonstrated a generation ago, in his *Foundations of Tudor Policy* (Cambridge, Mass., 1948), how much would be missed in Tudor intellectual history if manuscripts were left out. The accident of nineteenth-century printing thus admits Thomas Starkey's *Dialogue of Pole and Lupset* (though the publications of the Parker Society, equally accessible and full of relevant matter, are not used) but eliminates some of Thomas Smith's interesting studies of Roman coinage and of war. The understanding and use of history which lay behind the Henrician Reformation have been much illumined by

---

[4] See a forthcoming article by Hans Pawlish in the *Historical Journal* ['Sir John Davies, the Ancient Constitution, and civil law', *HJ* 23 (1980), 689–702] for a proper statement of the revisionary truth – though that Pocock's analysis is not quite enough is not news.

Reviews

Graham D. Nicholson's Cambridge dissertation, which employed
unprinted sources; this could have been seen on microfilm. No blame
attaches to Ferguson for being unaware of current research, especially
that of Glyn Parry (also at Cambridge) on William Harrison; yet
unfortunately this matters because Parry's identification of Harrison as
the author of a vast chronology must profoundly alter the views
advanced by Ferguson on the interrelation of historical, topographical
and antiquarian studies. Harrison, I think, will come to look rather
important in these historiographical enterprises.

But alas, even print has been used selectively, with results that must
unhappily be called tendentious. We hear much of Thomas Starkey,
whose interest in history limped well behind his theological and political
concerns; yet we have but a few lines on his associate Richard Morison,
who, influenced by Machiavelli, contributed a thoroughly historical
analysis to the events of the 1530s. That fascinating encyclopaedia called
Holinshed's Chronicle, central to our understanding of the history the
age wanted to know, absolutely cries out for a very careful analysis; it is
passed over in silence. In consequence, for instance, Richard Stanyhurst's sociopolitical treatment of Irish history makes one brief and
uninformative appearance only, whereas it could have been used to
demonstrate just those interests which engage Ferguson's attention.
Plowden's *Reports* contain comments on matters elsewhere in this book
regarded as relevant (for instance, sovereignty), and it has already been
remarked that most of the available literature of the law puts in no
appearance. If we are to be told about spelling reform, why is Thomas
Whythorn's scheme, full of historical notions and readily available in
James Osborn's book, ignored?[5] Most disquieting is the treatment
accorded to Thomas More. Guided by Richard Marius, Ferguson
presents a sound analysis of More's views on the Church as an historical
phenomenon, but the author of a seminal history (*Richard III*) and a
sociocultural construct with historical underpinnings (*Utopia*) is effectively left out. Of *Utopia* we are told only that by providing a single
original legislator More displayed a static view of social origins (p. 368).
Considering how full that book is of historical concerns and allusions,
this is really not good enough. Since Ferguson in effect confines himself
to the controversy over the Church, he can naturally conclude that
'More's historical insights were . . . limited by his appeal to the divine
efflatus [sic] as the ultimate authority' (pp. 156–7); and this conclusion in

5 *The Autobiography of Thomas Whythorn*, ed. James M. Osborn (Oxford, 1961).

turn gives aid and comfort to the theory of a later discovery of a 'social and cultural past.'[6]

I repeat that the book contains quite a few sound and pointed particular essays: nothing that Ferguson writes could ever be without some really valuable contributions. In this case, however, the whole is worse than its parts. The thesis developed is maintained only by an unjustified limitation of the enquiry in various ways, and by substantive distortions arising from misunderstandings and an inadequate study of the facts of the age. Ferguson started from the thesis that in the sixteenth century history for too long lived under the restraint of political concerns exemplified in the chronicle tradition as reformed by Polydore Vergil. It was only with Daniel, Hooker and ultimately Bacon that the history he regards as more serious achieved some sort of maturity. Thomas More, Richard Morison, Christopher St German and Thomas Smith, properly understood, destroy the chronological scheme; William Harrison, William Lambarde and even William Camden gravely undermine the fundamental dichotomy posited. And this is to name only the more obvious writers in a crowd.

The first error of this book lies in its original conception, which sprang from a schema devised on twentieth-century premises. If sixteenth-century historical understanding is worth investigation, it must be because it arose out of that century's own experience framed conceptually in its own terms. We need to find out what they wanted from history and to ascertain how they went about satisfying that desire, and we must not set them up against an anachronistic standard of *desiderabilia*. If the enquiry had proceeded in that manner it would probably have fruitfully enlarged the insights which Ferguson provided in his earlier book, for occasionally those make an appearance here – especially in his recognition of the role played by Tudor humanism. Unfortunately he does not seem so well at home with that other overwhelming cause of thought, the Protestant Reformation. What defined and directed historical perception in Renaissance England had nothing to do with notions of a social or cultural past; rather it arose from a view of God, man and society present and past rooted in an ideology compounded of humanism and protestantism. This compound was responsible for the mixture of optimism and pessimism

---

[6] The effects of all that selectivity are further aggravated by an extensive reliance on secondary works, many of them pretty elderly, too many of them by practitioners of English literature rather than historians, and most of them (*observata refero*) by American scholars. Ferguson attaches himself to a particular tradition of intellectual history with possibly unwise docility.

about the human condition which Ferguson rightly identifies as a very
noticeable feature of the age but tries to explain in terms improper to it.
The true relationship between that ideology and the sixteenth century's
view of history remains still to be comprehensively expounded – which
at least means that the doubts expressed at the start of this review about
the intensity of the current interest in the sixteenth-century historians
were misconceived.

(f) LAWRENCE STONE, *The Causes of the English Revolution*. London;
Routledge and Kegan Paul, 1972.*

Professor Stone is certainly a brave man. To undertake an explanation
of that notoriously unexplained event, the revolution in seventeenth-
century England, in 168 pages (twenty-five of them filled with
bibliographical references and the index) takes courage. Actually even
fewer than 143 pages are specifically devoted to the task, for we first get
twenty pages on the theory of revolutions and fifteen reviewing the
majestic gentry controversy. Only the third essay (108 pp.) analyses the
'preconditions', 'precipitants' and 'triggers' of the first civil war. The
book's title misleads somewhat: the real revolution after 1646 is
expressly kept in the wings.

It would appear that this essay grew out of Mr Stone's teaching at
Princeton, and one can well understand the enthusiasm which his firm,
lucid and sweeping analysis must have evoked. It contains many of those
brilliant flashes which we are accustomed to find in his work: concise
summaries of complex problems which convey a sudden understanding
and open the mind to striking speculations. When a man of Mr Stone's
repute and skill produces a magisterial summary of this kind, acceptance
(even unquestioning acceptance) is likely to extend well beyond his
immediate audience, and it is therefore desirable to subject his claim to
have laid bare the causes of the revolution to a degree of critical
assessment which at first sight might seem excessive for so short a book.

For myself, I do not find much enlightenment in the slightly modish
discussion of theories of revolution, and the fact that hardly any of this
reappears in the essay on the actual history of the event suggests that Mr
Stone, too, got less from this theoretical framework than he had hoped.
He greatly admires the typology provided by Chalmers Johnson which

* [*HJ* 16 (1973), 205–18.]

strikes me as simplistic, unsubtle and buttressed by unconvincing examples. Since Mr Stone himself accepts the view that the English revolution fell well short of the truly revolutionary aims and achievements which Johnson's types demand it is hard to see how that theory could have been linked to fact. Much the same applies to the other writers discussed whose notions vary between the fairly obvious and the obviously contrived. No amassing of such models gets us nearer to understanding what happened in Stuart England. The discussion of the gentry controversy, on the other hand, is very good; coming from one of the contestants most deeply involved, it is strikingly fair and thoughtful. But it, too, at best contributes obliquely and modestly to the major preoccupation of the book, and least so when it attempts to produce a generalized interpretation.

When he comes to concern himself with the English revolution, Mr Stone reverts to the facts of the case, and at once a breath of agreeable familiarity pervades the air. His 'preconditions' and 'precipitants' are our old friends, circumstances and long-term causes, his 'triggers' the immediate causal events of tradition. He sees the civil war as the end-product of a century's developments which included social change consequent upon economic pressures (especially the proliferation of middling estates to which the 'rise of the gentry' has long since been reduced in the vocabulary of historians), the uncertainties of Tudor government which put power into the hands of the locality at the expense of the centre, the decline of threats from abroad which permitted the growth of internal divisions, the Reformation, and the alienation of a large part of the governing classes from an increasingly distant and disconcerting court. All this is well set out, with sufficient detail and with remarkable achievements of learned compression. The 1630s are once again seen as sealing the 'crisis of confidence' as Laudian policies completed the destruction of the uneasy unity which had marked the reign of Elizabeth. Finally, the events of 1640–2 are neatly brought together to show how the triumph of opposition collapsed into the formation of parties. Mr Stone emphasizes the king's determination to recover power even at the risk of war and lays sound stress on the Irish rebellion as the main precipitator of the ultimate confrontation in England.

Thus – notwithstanding new theories of revolution and the current concern with social analysis – we end up with an account so traditional as to deserve the name whiggish. There is nothing in this analysis of the causes of the war that would have surprised S. R. Gardiner or A. F. Pollard. Of course, old-established may simply equal true, and if this is so this comprehensive and yet compact modern summary will serve an admirable purpose. Perhaps we should still treat the civil war as the outcome of a full century's events, of growing strains in the body politic in which the opposing poles of Crown and Parliament, Court and Country, episcopalianism and puritanism, prerogative and common law increasingly drifted apart as shifts in power failed to be reflected in the political adjustments required, and as personal folly and incompetence closed doors to better solutions. By stretching its lines across the decades, concentrating attention upon selected features, and in effect displaying the drastic end as necessarily derived from somewhat generalized antecedents, the explanation here provided achieves that satisfactorily coherent framework which has given the traditional explanation such long life.

But is it true? Surely it is possible to treat every single one of Mr Stone's preconditions, and some of his precipitants too, in historically accurate ways which would do little to guide the explaining mind to the crisis of 1640. Parliament can be shown to be constantly involved in political argument, often with the Crown, without producing that breakdown demanded by the thesis, until 1628. Prerogative can rightly be shown to be part of the common law, not in alleged opposition to it. Puritanism can be described as never revolutionary until after Laud attacked it. Such analyses might be as insufficient as the traditional ones adopted by Mr Stone, but they are as valid: evidently the story of all these phenomena is much more complex, much less predictable and predicting, than the treatment accorded to them here would suggest. In addition, there are some points made in this book which are simply wrong. A few minor errors can be ignored,[1] but on occasion Mr Stone preserves the traditional picture by evading recent fundamental revisions. He still adheres to a view of early-Tudor despotism which very few people would endorse because it seriously misconceives the purposes, possibilities and practice of Henrician government: but that issue may here be treated as marginal. It matters more that he should still call the medieval parish priest 'little more than a semi-literate dirt farmer of dubious morals' (despite P. Heath and M. Bowker), that he should

[1] The book on Elizabeth Sussex (p. 156, n. 98) is by R. B. Manning, not by R. A. Marchant; the author of the work on the *Articulate Citizen* (n. 106) is A. B. Ferguson, not W. K. What was not restored in 1660 were feudal incidents; feudal tenures continued. Elizabeth would indeed have done well if she had obeyed a demand that she 'beget an heir'.

still see constitutional significance in the badly overstated 'rivalries' of prerogative and common-law courts (despite W. J. Jones), or that the classes of the 1570s should still be described as a model for 'ideological party organization' (despite P. Collinson). For the Tudor Parliament, Mr Stone relies, understandably, on Neale, but he seems to have missed the growing realization that Neale was wrong in concentrating so much on conflict and in ignoring the ability to oppose and interfere which marked pre-Elizabethan Parliaments. There is less excuse for his not admitting that Neale's own account disposes of the old notion that opposition grew in a straight line through the reign.

Altogether, the account is shot through with tradition-hallowed but doubtful statements. We are told that 'at the first hint of war the Crown [under Elizabeth] was obliged to go cap in hand to Parliament for funds', and this, as always, is used to underline the inherent weakness of government. But the Crown needed and got peace-time taxation quite regularly from 1534 onwards, while in the whole century Parliament only once, in 1566, showed any sign of wishing to use its alleged 'power of the purse' for political purposes. The most hotly contested tax of the century was that of 1523, a fact which again works against loose notions of increasing independence or power. Nearly all Tudor subsidy grants were made at the start of sessions, and Elizabeth's unprecedented practice of asking for supply in [nearly] every session of all the Parliaments she called produced no political reaction or action from the Commons. Or again, we are told that by the early seventeenth century (that is, in James I's first Parliament) there was 'the beginning of a formal opposition', a statement for which Mr Stone cites four very elderly authorities embedded in unquestioned traditions, W. M. Mitchell's book which he must have known cannot be relied on at all, and P. Zagorin who in fact refutes this particular interpretation. Thanks to Mr Ruigh we now know that even in 1624 there was nothing resembling organized faction or formed opposition. The description (very necessary to the explanation) of governmental weakness under the later Tudors is heavily overdrawn. Of course, it was necessary to conciliate men of weight, and local worthies could be both powerful and independent, but the notion that government lay at their mercy would have greatly surprised them. Elizabeth and her Council pressed heavily upon all office-holders and dignitaries; they achieved remarkable success in improving the administration of the law or the raising of armies; the conventional picture of a ramshackle system is wildly out of true. Historians who most readily deplore the power of modern governments over their citizens are curiously reluctant to allow vitality and powers of survival to earlier governments that were less strictly structured. It should be said that Elizabethan government worked – and that this meant neither regular imposition of the central will nor regular submission to peripheral independence.

Altogether, the generalizations of tradition upon which this book's modernized version builds are much less secure than they are made to appear. The whole business needs reordering from the ground upwards. We need to see the sixteenth century in terms of its own experience, not as the prehistory of a later revolution. We need to regard even the reigns of the early Stuarts without the conviction that the only thing of moment in their history is the ultimate breakdown of government which we know was to come. If thereafter we want to investigate the causes of the civil war, we need to remember that no revolution of the size claimed for this one ever so readily stopped short and reversed itself. Mr Stone's analysis proceeds on the assumption that in mid-century not only government failed but society fell apart. What evidence is there for this – what evidence of fact, the wilder talk of minorities apart? In any case, it should by now be realized that the work of the last twenty years or so, endeavouring to understand situations rather than track 'trends', has in general found that in that century people lived and agreed and quarrelled with one another, fighting for power and favour and rights and religion (and many of them doing none of these things) without ever undermining their conviction that they lived in a cohesive society and under a working government. It is only by directing all developments towards the distant end of 1640 that the debates and dissatisfactions which are the experience of any live society assume the guise of necessary causes; what is more, by so directing their efforts historians of the causes of the civil war have repeatedly misjudged the reality of attitudes and convictions and actions by imposing false polarities upon them.

Mr Stone's essay is a handsome restatement of these traditional explanations. He has proved that there is plenty of life yet in the tradition. To an historian who time and again finds reason to doubt generalizations about such things as the power of government, the role of the common law, the theory of obedience, the existence of puritanism and party, and especially perhaps the operations in and of Parliament, this is a disquieting situation. If we are to get further, we need at this present no essays on the causes of the civil war, but studies of the political behaviour of all sorts of men in all sorts of institutions, unaffected by the historian's foreknowledge of the later event. In that way we may ultimately perhaps arrive at an explanation of the mid-seventeenth-century breakdown, but it will be less well tailored, less readily reduced to a list of preconditions, precipitants and triggers, less satisfactory to theorists of revolution. On the other hand, it might be real.[2]

(g) ANTONIA FRASER, *Cromwell, Our Chief of Men*. London; Weidenfeld & Nicolson, 1973.*

S. R. Gardiner called Cromwell the greatest of Englishmen, but when he came to write his little book on Oliver's place in English history the phrase acquired no substance. More recent studies also never achieve anything much better than adequacy; in many ways the best of them remains Sir Charles Firth's sober volume first published in 1907. R. S. Paul has laboured to do justice to the man's religion; Maurice Ashley has seen him variously as the prototype of a fascist dictator and the spiritual ancestor of Sir Winston Churchill; Christopher Hill, calling him God's Englishman, seems really to think of him as the Englishman's dubious god. Oliver, in the end, defeated them all. He has now defeated Lady Antonia Fraser who, drowning in the morass, drags the reader after her.

This is certainly the biggest book on Cromwell — well over 700 pages of it. It rests on honest and hard work; it embodies solid reading in printed materials and some acquaintance with unpublished manuscripts; its prose, never meretricious, varies from the competent to the unexciting. Reading this interminable book is made no easier by occasional lapses in grammatical structure and a cavalier attitude to commas which help to confuse. The author is not always certain of her words: unexceptional for unexceptionable contrasts with inimicable for inimical. We find Cromwell incurring the focus of public attention and

[2] [For the works cited in this review see: P. Heath, *The English Parish Clergy on the Eve of the Reformation* (1969); Margaret Bowker, *The Secular Clergy in the Diocese of Lincoln 1495–1520* (Cambridge, 1968); W. J. Jones, *The Elizabethan Court of Chancery* (Oxford, 1967); P. Collinson, *The Elizabethan Puritan Movement* (1967); W. M. Mitchell, *The Rise of the Revolutionary Party in the English House of Commons* (New York, 1957); R. E. Ruigh, *The Parliament of 1624: Politics and Foreign Policy* (Cambridge, Mass., 1971).]

* [*Spectator*, 9 June 1973. I have restored some cuts made by the journal.]

settlers called upon to upstake themselves: both sound obscurely painful experiences. The elderly story about Richard Cromwell's good luck with Henry VIII is no more convincing than the novel assignment of Mark Antony to a triumvirate of conspirators also including Brutus and Cassius. Of all things, the Protector's motto should have been accurately translated: what he meant was that 'in war peace is sought', as his experiences had taught him, not 'let peace be sought in war', which suggests a preference for doing things by aggression which would not seem to have been at all his normal attitude. An excellent chapter on the Protector's court and family suggests that the author's best abilities lie in social history of the more discursive kind; the poor first chapter on family antecedents suggests that she swallows legends with excessive ease and likes to ascribe mystical qualities to blood, provided it is either Celtic or Norman. The battles are handled well and the constitutional problems not well at all. In the end that disturbing figure eludes this biographer as he has eluded all others.

The book's chief faults are two – poor organization and a lack of psychological penetration. The first accounts for its inordinate length. This is not really a biography of Oliver Cromwell but a relentless history of his times written around him. Of course, we cannot understand Cromwell without understanding what happened in his life-time, and a person so much the cause of action in himself and others calls for the inclusion of much general history. But in obeying these demands Lady Antonia keeps losing the thread: where she should summarize, allude or adumbrate, she recites, expounds and comments. This book lacks intellectual discipline, and even its virtues of sense, modesty and care cannot in consequence make it readable.

The problem of psychological insight is never easy in historical biography, but in Oliver's case it is crucial because he has a way of appearing to each searching student as a reflection of his own bundle of predilections. The extraordinary difficulty of depicting a man so manifestly demonic is assuredly an excuse for ultimate failure in explaining him, but this biographer does worse than she need have done. She is much too honest to play about with dubious psychologizing, though now and again she uses terms which she does not seem to grasp with precision. An author who can say that a person suffered from what 'in modern language' would be called a nervous breakdown cannot at least be accused of modishness, but when a tiresome journey to Russia is called traumatic that taint begins to appear. 'Paranoic' (*sic*) and 'psychosomatic' are flashed about a bit too readily. Lady Antonia is, of course, aware that Cromwell's personality was very unstable and she rightly draws attention to his frequent terrifying rages; but, despite talk of 'the dark night of the soul', she never persuades me that, being evidently nice, sensible and a bit downright, she comprehends the violence and frustration at the heart of the man which, failing too frequently, he strove to control. As for his religion, the conscious core of him, we get a valiant attempt to expound it, but the understanding of puritanism here displayed is from the outside — is that of an earnest and not very perceptive student. Where is the sense of God battering the soul of Oliver Cromwell as well as pouring occasional balm? Lady Antonia makes no attempts to exculpate the man and especially permits a combination of sympathy for the Irish and a critical attitude to the sources unusual in her to dominate the most repulsive phase of the great man's public life; but with all her piling of detail and painting of shadows she still fails to lay bare his inner reality.

Why should Oliver have proved so universally elusive? Well, in the first place he is in fact an exceptionally difficult person to do justice to: the stage he occupied gets in the way. Very few historians can free themselves from firm convictions about the English revolution and the civil wars, and Cromwell is therefore always liable to lose his humanity and appear as superhuman — a hero or a villain larger than life. Yet he cannot be accepted as superhuman until he is treated and understood as a public man, a politician and labourer in affairs, proceeding by methods and upon grounds which apply also to others. Secondly, he is very well — at any rate, very plentifully — recorded; we know a lot about his words and moods as well as his actions, and the sum total often bewilders quite rightly because this highly emotional man bewildered not only contemporaries but himself too. Some consistency in thought, some regular pattern of behaviour and reaction, such things help to bring understanding of an historical figure: Oliver, stuttering and thrashing about, resists such aids to portraiture. Then there is the extraordinary achievement to account for, against a background formed of manifestly often very modest abilities and excruciatingly conventional attitudes (and just as it is clear that here we have that figure beloved by English historians, the typical backwoods squire, the confusing fellow gives birth to thundering and radical particularity). Cromwell's one unquestioned greatness as a military organizer and commander in battle appeared only in middle age, urgently asking to be explained in terms of his personality but too late in manifesting itself to assist in understanding his formation. Doubts have been expressed about this, but though he achieved his victories in the face of general ineptitude amongst those he knocked down, I am persuaded (by Lady Antonia, among others) that he had genius in war.

Was Oliver sane – or at any rate capable of sanity and balance? Lady Antonia rightly draws attention to the boisterous good spirits he showed in battle. He loved fighting and seems to have relished killing: never did he feel so much at ease as among the flashing swords. Nor would it be wise to ascribe this kind of reaction solely to convictions about fighting the battles of the Lord: the physical exhilaration of combat seems to have helped by itself to banish the brooding doubts and stammering hesitancies which so often beset him. The only other times that he displayed a like freedom from care were apparently those moments of tedious horseplay and crude jesting that he could indulge in at the expense of others. A simple soldier-man and rather nasty with it? Certainly not, as the frequent flashes of reflective insight, the thoughts cherished for others, the sense of personal destiny subordinated to the spiritual regeneration of a nation show well enough. Above all there was his ability to tolerate bloodyminded troublemakers (the age abounded with them, all claiming mandates from God and the people), an ability quite astounding in a man of his power who at other times so readily destroyed opposition with brutal efficiency. His religion itself was not typical but peculiar: it was by the standards of his own time, not those of ours, that he manifested a strange mixture of faith and doubt, simplicity and deviousness, wild spiritual exhilaration and institutionalized decorum. Wherever one touches Cromwell simplicities in fact writhe into marvellously opaque complexities. The often incomprehensible muddle of his speeches, shot through with those famous, drastically clear, sentences that strike like lighting, may owe something to poor reporting; but it is too much at one with the confused, confusing, primitive, subtle, furious, considerate man and mind to be ignored as an accident of the evidence. Certainly, a man who believed that all his doings were the work of God and who received his instructions direct from on high was bound to hesitate and dither so long as the orders failed to come through, even as he was bound to act without a moment's doubt once the message had been delivered – commonly in prayer. The behaviour which disconcerted so many at the time and gave him the reputation of a cynic and hypocrite did assuredly arise from these more respectable difficulties. But yet there remain too many fundamental and irreconcilable contradictions; but yet we confront a man whose God invariably advised him in the manner most conducive to his worldly advance. Who really created both hesitations and actions? Who in fact was the creator – God of Oliver, or Oliver of his God? And does that make this energetic, usually competent politician, this highly successful general, this solid ruler in an exceptionally difficult situation – the only leader of a revolution who did not have to escape personal disaster by pursuing ever more radical ends – once again into a superhuman being? The one thing Oliver never became was a statesman: the compassing of lasting achievements in the body politic was beyond him.

In the end it remains uncertain whether Cromwell possessed greatness, intellectual power, insight and foresight, the ability to define tasks precisely – or whether he really rose so high because he did not know where he was going and never matched inner force to the situation into which events and the animal drive of his being catapulted him. This biography brings us no nearer to solving the puzzle.

(h) BLAIR WORDEN, *The Rump Parliament 1648–1653*. Cambridge University Press, 1974.*

The wave of precise historical scholarship, devoted to an exhaustive use of the sources and unfettered by preliminary interpretative theories, which some twenty-five years ago burst out of the medieval reservoir to flood the sixteenth century, is now engulfing the seventeenth. This is good news. Too many historians of the 'century of revolution' had been content to fight the ideological battles of that age or indeed of their own day, getting us no further in understanding. With the arrival of scholars like Gerald Aylmer, Valerie Pearl and David Underdown, new light began to dawn. Dr Worden's first book proves him to be a worthy member of that company.

He has shown some courage in choosing his subject. After the heroic days of resistance to tyranny, civil war and the execution of the king, the years during which a truncated remnant of the Long Parliament ruled England have always seemed at least an anticlimax, perhaps even the satyr-play needed to relieve the tragedy. Concentration was apt to be

* [*Spectator*, 9 March 1974.]

diverted to Dunbar and Drogheda, pursuing Cromwell around the islands, while what went on at Westminster was written off as a pointless display of inefficient selfishness rightly in the end terminated by the returning warrior. Little or nothing of this survives Dr Worden's vigorous examination.

The book comprises three sections: an analysis of the Rump's membership, an analytical discussion of attempts at reform, and a narrative account of the Parliament's history especially in its conflict with the victorious Army. Dr Worden completes the process begun by J. H. Hexter thirty years ago when he puts to sleep all talk of 'presbyterian' and 'independent' parties, or indeed of anything resembling party, and shows how diverse and in manner unpredictable so many Rumpers were. Not all can even be categorized as republicans by conviction, especially as so many of those excluded in Pride's Purge returned after a while, and most of them were willing to accept whatever settlement could be arrived at. Despite its origins the Rump was conservative rather than revolutionary, those favouring change being generally unable to specify the changes they wanted. However, though it achieved little, this Parliament did make some stabs at reform and was not unserious about it. Evidently the bad reputation of the Rump has for too long reflected only the bitterness of its enemies, especially of Levellers and the Army. The Rump had to govern three kingdoms shattered by war and for about half its life further disturbed by the struggle to suppress royalism in Scotland and Ireland. At least these troubles held the members together: after Worcester, facing the insoluble problem of an Army determined upon idealistic reform and eager for its backpay, they fell apart.

The quarrel with the Army destroyed the Rump, but not until Cromwell decided that he could no longer work with this civil government and had indeed been cheated by it. In the most striking piece of revision in the book, Dr Worden demonstrates that the outburst of fury with which the lord general sent the House packing was not, as he was afterwards to claim, justified by its alleged conspiracy to perpetuate itself. The bill that so enraged Cromwell was one for a dissolution followed by new elections, not for an enlargement of the existing body by 'recruiting'. Cromwell may have been genuinely in error until it was too late, after which (probably realizing his mistake) he allowed the fateful bill to vanish and false stories to be put about; or he may have been seeking an excuse to substitute the rule of the saints which did follow the expulsion of the Rump. At any rate, the man who had effectively created the system of 1649 was also the man who four years later threw it out. The Rump was only the first of the suits of clothes tried on it in an endeavour to cover the nakedness of the sword, but it set the pattern of failure. Cromwell tired of it because it would not undertake the reforms in law and religion for which the Army was pressing, but since (as Dr Worden says) he meant it to provide a conservative bastion against social revolution it shows a significant lack of sense on his part that he should have expected it to prove conveniently reformist on such matters as he wished to see reformed.

The main concern of this book is with the parliamentary and national history of the period, and notwithstanding the serious deficiencies of the evidence Dr Worden succeeds in telling a full and satisfying tale. But his outstanding contribution lies perhaps in what he has to say about Oliver Cromwell. No more than anyone else can he make 'sense' of the man, but that is because sense in that simple form was absent from Cromwell's character and actions. Those constant inner cross-purposes, those best intentions shattered by political incompetence and frequent impatience, that entirely idiosyncratic mixture of idealism and practical ruthlessness, all this comes through convincingly; and so, rendered three-dimensional, comes the truth of the man's greatness. Dr Worden, who knows that history is about real people, supplies many memorable portraits, but though none is really attempted of Oliver the whole book stands in the shadow of a personality here better realized than in most biographies.

This, then, is political history at its best – anchored in reality, fascinated by men's motives and doings in affairs, marching steadily through the events to bring out the issues and confusions without surrender to either antiquarianism or pattern-making. To his other virtues as an historian Dr Worden adds high skill as a writer. He can even jest without destroying the atmosphere of the scene, a rare gift. If the book owes its enduring virtues to the author's determination to tell it as it was and to his willingness to abide by the limitations of the evidence, it should also be recognized that without the deployment of a powerful and disciplined historical imagination Dr Worden would, on such a subject, have written the kind of worthy dull book with which readers of history are only too familiar. As it is, he has written one to fascinate and captivate.

Reviews

(i) *The Formation of National States in Western Europe*, ed. CHARLES
TILLY. Princeton University Press, 1975.*

It would appear that for quite a few years now a number of scholars
have been engaged, under the auspices of the Committee on
Comparative Politics of the Social Science Research Council, on an
investigation of the state-building activities of European nations, with
an eye to offering illumination to those who want to understand and
assist the emergence of organized independent countries in the so-called
Third World. A large amount of money has been spent (which the
committee, we are told, was 'inspired' to get from the Ford
Foundation); there have been conferences, workshops and pleasant
gatherings at Palo Alto and Bellagio. The present vast tome is one major
product of the enterprise, apparently the most expensive of them all. It
merits consideration both as a collection of studies and as a symptom of
the sort of corporate organization which to some is the ultimate in
learned enterprise.

The volume consists of seven substantive and substantial chapters,
surrounded by two commentaries by Charles Tilly ('Reflections on the
history of European state-making' and 'Western state-making and
theories of political transformation'). The individual contributors are
Samuel E. Finer ('State- and nation-building in Europe: The role of the
military'), Gabriel Ardant ('Financial policy and economic infrastruc-
ture of modern states and nations'), Rudolf Braun ('Taxation,
sociopolitical structure, and state-building: Great Britain and Brandenburg-Prussia'), David H. Bayley ('The police and political development
in Europe'), Charles Tilly ('Food supply and public order in modern
Europe'), Wolfram Fischer and Peter Lundgreen ('The recruitment and
training of administrative and technical personnel'), and Stein Rokkan
('Dimensions of state-formation and nation-building: a possible paradigm for research on variations within Europe'). Getting all this
together and bringing out the book must have been an astounding
labour, so formidable that perhaps it should silence captious criticism.
Nevertheless, captious criticism must regret the ignorant spelling of
'Habsburg' with a 'p' and several lapses in the rendering of non-English
terms, must wonder at a proof-reading which left in a large number of
errors and omissions ('Hardenburg' and 'Scharnost' on p. 153 rightly
became 'Hardenberg' and 'Scharnhorst' in the index; 'the little port riot'

* [*Journal of Modern History* 49 (1977), 294–8.]

of p. 387 was earlier rendered correctly as 'the Littleport riot'), and must wonder at a strangely mixed bibliography which unhappily adopts the practice of dating books by the year of a reprint rather than that of the original publication. One absurd result is that the present reviewer gets in twice, with the same book and identical texts. The demands of translation have been met with varying success, but Ardant suffers: the *memoirs* drawn up by *intendants* are memorials, not memoirs (p. 176); the 'emission of currency' (p. 190) looks likely to provoke ribaldry; the 'reticence' with which the French provinces accepted unification was presumably reluctance. The editorial team do not always seem to have worked one with another.

However, what of the contents? The contributions vary considerably in quality and style: some of the writing is very opaque, while a few participants value lucidity and elegance of writing. Finer is characteristically vigorous and direct as well as illuminating: but then the role of war and armies in developing organized states is both manifest and well established. Bayley's analysis of police systems provides the best example of clear description and exposition: we really learn a good deal about the subject discussed, though Bayley, in his honesty, recognizes that police forces (and the differences among them) are a product of organized states, not a means toward them. Fischer's discussion of the English civil service benefits from the good research available but also contributes real insights and is exceptionally well written; though Lundgreen's sections of the same chapter lack his colleague's beautiful clarity, they still succeed very well in bringing out the facts about the French and Prussian bureaucracies. That, alas, is the end of unstinted praise. It is very hard to discern any firm purpose in Ardant's ramblings around the French taxation system (no other country receives any useful attention from him); while Tilly's discussion of food supply, elegant and wide-ranging though it is, fails to persuade the reader that the topic contributes to the theme of the collection. Braun's analysis is vitiated by massive errors about England, the less surprising perhaps because he thought it sufficient to rest his case on D. L. Keir's never very impressive textbook: this is like judging Shakespeare from Mary Lamb's *Tales*. As for Rokkan's devoted building of models, one reader must confess himself comprehensively baffled. There may be students to whom those complex drawings and painful tabulations offer enlightenment, but the parts of the essay presented in ordinary language turn up only conventional and rather loose generalizations – just the sort of thing, the editor tells us, that it was the purpose of the exercise to control and improve by detailed historical study. Indeed, in an introduction full of warnings and reservations, Tilly hints clearly enough at his doubts about Rokkan's achievement, though in his conclusion he in his turn sinks into a morass of theories – developmental, functional, historical – which seem to gyrate in an empty empyrean and do not get one any nearer that comprehensive schema demanded by the sponsors – and indeed aspired to by the participants.

Controlling theories by historical study involves more than historical accuracy, but it assuredly demands that. In this volume, too many details call up doubts. It may be only because this is where my own knowledge concentrates that England seems to suffer most from ignorance, though experience over the years suggests that comparative historians tend usually to be weakest on that country, mainly because they have a knack for picking the wrong guides. Finer drastically postdates the disappearance of a multiplicity of authorities (which he regards as characteristically medieval) for England, thereby preserving his general time scale. His account of Tudor armies is also very confusing, in that he seems both to deny and to assert the continued existence of private retinues on consecutive pages (he is right the second time). When Tilly says that English regulations meant to encourage the profitable export of corn rather than protect the population from starvation, he ignores centuries of export prohibition designed to keep grain at home. As for Braun, an account of taxation which relies on Kennedy (1913) and Dietz (1920), both long since known to be unsatisfactory, cannot help being wildly inaccurate; it would be tedious to list the errors which mar page after page, but it must be emphasized that no reader should accept any statement of his without checking the sort of recent literature which he has used for his analysis of Brandenburg-Prussia. And what does Ardant mean by saying that the Stuart kings tried to avoid taxes from political motives? It is a notable relief to read Fischer's thoroughly competent pages which mark a true contribution to knowledge and should especially terminate the description of English civil servants in the early modern period as amateurs. Even he has been ill served by a proof-reader who lets him call the Royal Society by its right name and by the name of Royal Academy on one and the same page.

This sort of thing is discouraging but not, of course, the ultimate point of criticism. Two major questions hang about the enterprise –

questions touching, respectively, its immediate and its secondary purposes. There was certainly nothing wrong with the idea of studying European states of the state-building era comprehensively, with an eye to establishing both common and diverse experiences: much illumination can lie that way. But precision apart, any hope of success depends largely on whether the right territories and themes are covered, and on both counts this collection (as Tilly inclines to admit) can too readily be faulted. In effect, the only countries studied are France, Prussia and Great Britain, sufficiently differing entities but still not enough by themselves. Only Bayley seriously uses Italy; only Tilly, pursuing food, really looks at the Mediterranean; only Rokkan, sweeping around Europe and the centuries, includes Scandinavia. The omission of Russia is a pity, that of Austria-Hungary bewildering, that of Spain very serious. The Eastern empires would have yielded results markedly different from those obtained from the West, and the Iberian peninsula should have offered opportunities for checking on the conclusions got from French data. One feels that France was chosen as the paradigm, England by way of an obvious control, and Prussia because good work had been done on it: understandable but unsatisfactory grounds for the delimitation of territory. As for themes, the selection proves even more confining and distorting. Both Bayley and Tilly concede that they have very little to contribute to the main question asked; enjoyable though their essays are, they should surely have been spared to make room for studies that absolutely demand to be included. Three topics in particular ruin the investigation by their absence: the law, the Church and the ideology of nationalism. Tilly regrets the omission of the first two, whose importance, he says, came to be recognized too late – in the course of the work – but it must baffle understanding how they could ever have been overlooked at the start.

All the states here analysed grew very much out of the peace-keeping and justice-providing activities of monarchies, and even though that fact occasionally occurs to this or that author we nowhere find any specific, detailed discussion (however brief) of this central element in state building. Unification and the assertion of central authority everywhere depended upon the absorption into central hands of precisely those functions which had previously been much diffused; the inmost nature of the polities that emerged owed most to the kind of law they used and the kind of courts they created for its administration. All these states in one way or another looked back to the Roman empire and remembered and used its law. The only reason why the theme was left out would seem to be the authors' decision to treat states simply as engines of exploitation; bewildered by their concentration on the 'extraction of resources' (mobilization of men and money), they entirely overlooked the fact that among the formative influences were other purposes quite as important to the inhabitants as to the rulers. In trying to avoid supposedly out-of-date concepts that played with 'organic structures' and consent, the bias of the enquiry leans heavily toward the control and monopolizing of the means of violence, certainly a part of the story but by no means the foremost or the most revealing.

Leaving out the Church would come naturally to this group of social scientists and historians anxious to be at home in the social sciences, but it tends to make nonsense of the whole enquiry. For one thing, the Church was itself a polity, the first to achieve thorough organization and therefore often a model for state-building agencies. For another, it regularly became an instrument in the unification of realms and the concentration of power in monarchic hands. For a third, both its active role and its response to pressures varied significantly from territory to territory, as a result of which it provides one of the more convenient tools for comparative analysis. Furthermore, religion formed one of the major components of nationalist ideology, the third major theme inexcusably neglected here. How can one consider the building of France without regarding both *la gloire* and *l'Eglise*, the emergence of Prussia without specifically analysing the functions of its peculiar Lutheranism and its peculiar ethos of *bürgerliche Pflicht*, the making of England without a word about the elect nation and God's Englishman? It is a common error in Anglo-Saxon historiography, rightly suspicious of Hegelian excesses, to forget that people have deeply entrenched and ideologically defined loyalties to the political structure within which they live and that these cannot be built without creating, exploiting and satisfying such basically non-material and often ill-defined convictions. Perhaps, however, these things are missing here simply because they resist quantification?

The omission is the more serious when the supposed further purpose of these studies is taken into account. Tilly in effect allows that investigating the making of Europe's states has thrown little or no light on the likely processes by which states may emerge in Africa and Asia, and I must simply state my belief that no one is going to gain enlightenment from the models and tables with which Rokkan attempts to universalize commonplace generalizations. This failure to offer the sponsoring committee the bone they had hoped to get is aggravated by the omission of ideological problems, for the new states look quite as likely to be created by conflicts between Marxist and nationalist passions as by the organizing of taxes or police systems. Of course, it may well be held that the sponsors ought not have expected to get any useful answers to their question. In his rather sorrowful foreword, Lucien W. Pye, chairman of the committee, nobly accepts the fact; he also, astonishingly, records his regret at finding how large a part war had played in the making of European states. Yes indeed, though the initial definitions of the task made sure that war should loom even larger than in any case it must; and war will very probably dominate the fate of Africa and Asia, too. Whether all this endeavour and all this money were worth expending on the discovery of facts as obvious as that history establishes only particulars and generalizations applicable to the events studied, that it offers no guidance for an assessment of the future or an analysis of very differing circumstances, and that it demonstrates the profound effects of war in human affairs is something that everybody may judge for himself. At any rate, both by what they did and by what they failed to do the authors of this volume have saved themselves and their discipline from the corruption which afflicts the social sciences when they profess to build paradigms and enunciate prophecies. Mr Pye is to be congratulated on a generosity which welcomes this misbegotten offspring of honest purposes in the hope that it may lead to debate and the advance of knowledge. So be it.

(j) *National Consciousness, History, and Political Culture in Early-Modern Europe*, ed. OREST RANUM. Baltimore and London; The Johns Hopkins University Press, 1975.*

This volume contains the Schouler Lectures for 1973, delivered at the Johns Hopkins University, and unlike most such collections it is interesting, both in its successes and its failures. The editor tells us that the lecturers 'were asked to consider the relationship of national consciousness, history, and political culture in one of six nation-states during the early-modern era', and we thus have essays on Italy (Felix Gilbert), France (W. F. Church), Germany (Leonard Krieger), England (John

* [*HJ* 18 (1975), 884–7.]

Pocock), Russia (Michael Cherniavsky) and Spain (Helmut Koenigsberger), in which this awesome assignment is tackled. The contributors
manifestly appreciated their problem, especially the fact that of all the
terms employed in Professor Ranum's definition only 'history' and
'nation-states' seem to have a precise and agreed meaning; and the
agreed meaning of the second surely casts doubt on the inclusion of Italy
and Germany. They are even able to differ over the era under review:
Gilbert regards himself as charged with tackling the years (approximately) 1530–50, while Krieger ranges over the 300 years after 1500.
Cherniavsky takes in even the fifteenth century, and Pocock, by
contrast, barely steps outside the middle years of the seventeenth
century. No one really attempts to define 'political culture', and only
Cherniavsky provides what looks like a description of it in his account
of the political use to which the tsars' involvement in religion was put.
As for national consciousness, they all try to make sense of the term but
nearly all fall back on briefly outlining examples of self-conscious
nationalism they find in writers (mostly of history); only Koenigsberger, in the best written piece, remembers that a nation is not equal to
a few of its publicists, and that historical evidence need not be confined
to printed books.

The firmest impression left is of great diversity, and the editor's
attempt to pull the whole thing together does not in fact achieve much
more than a mild state of bewilderment, aggravated by his honest doubt
about the validity of the terms in which the discussion is conducted. To
some extent this diversity simply reflects differences in treatment.
Church, for instance, confines himself to a review of historical writings
which tracks the theme of patriotism attached to the monarchy as the
embodiment of the *patrie*. This essay has the merit of perfect clarity, but
it offers nothing new in insight or interpretation, nor can Church
disguise the low quality of most of the writers and ideas he chronicles so
faithfully. Pocock, on the other hand, offers another instalment of his
interior dialogue with himself (the number of references to his own
earlier writings is impressive); there is, however, real progress when he
allows the Ancient Constitution to retreat before the Elect Nation, thus
recognizing by implication that the historical myths which gave coherence to nationhood had to do more with religion than law and that they
long preceded the seventeenth-century manifestations upon which he
has so far concentrated. True, we are still in rather a rarefied atmosphere:
the propaganda of the English Reformation, of which Foxe was an

outgrowth not a founder, needs to be pursued more in occasional tracts (like those of Richard Morison), in the doctrine of statutes and proclamations, and in the rhetoric of sermons than in the works of a few historians and lawyers if we are to understand the commonplaces of national consciousness and their extraordinarily early and powerful hold. Krieger's paper, certainly the one in which a systematic argument is best set out and followed through, suffers from the fact that (as he knows) he has to study the absence of both a cohesive national self-consciousness and an indigenous political culture. Nevertheless, he really contributes to knowledge: his analysis of the two kinds of history (antiquarian and philosophical) as specially defined in the German distinction of *gelehrt* and *pragmatisch* is fascinating, and so is the well-described interplay of abstract national dreams (empire) with actual national loyalties (attached to particularist territories). Gilbert confesses himself handicapped by the fact that his assignment precipitates him into the dead ground of Italian historiography, between Guicciardini and Muratori; even his elegance cannot quite cover the whole theme's inappropriateness to the Italy of those confused years. One really welcomes Koenigsberger's cool sanity on the subject of Castilian national consciousness, that very real thing; here at last we meet history – the events of the past – instead of the mostly rather indifferent historical writing upon which the other contributors concentrate.

What perhaps one misses most urgently (Koenigsberger apart) is a recognition that national consciousness belongs to a nation, not just its self-appointed opinion-makers. Of course, this is an exceptionally difficult thing to study: where, except among the writers, do we look for evidence of opinion? Cherniavsky does find an answer of unusual interest by stepping well outside his brief and considering symbolism – the symbols of the Orthodox faith as presented by ceremonial, ecclesiastical architecture and the nomenclature of princes. (Admittedly something seems to have gone wrong here, perhaps because the author unhappily died before the book went to press: although we are given four illustrations the text refers to only one of them, and we are told only that the symbol had meaning, not what that was.) Only he and Krieger really advance beyond familiar and well-established positions into interpretations which need to be pondered and incorporated in the general history of the countries they deal with; only here, what happened really looks new in the light of what can be said about the ideas manifested by actors and commentators. Church tells us nothing that makes the French arrogance of Louis XIV's reign more comprehensible or more profound than it was before we read his essay, and Pocock's continued refusal to take the sixteenth century seriously deprives his paper of innovatory force; Cherniavsky, on the other hand, really does show how and why the intense, inward-looking and xenophobic nationalism of the Russian ruling caste came to create the despotism of the tsars and the Orthodox Church, and Krieger really enables one to understand how the nationalism of the humanists and the early reformers came to be the property of university professors of history – that most German of phenomena.

The organizers of the lectures were probably wise to avoid strictly comparative contributions and allow each author to explore his own particular country; any other method would no doubt have softened the intellectual rigour of the discussion and could easily have produced waffle, a quality happily absent throughout. But by rights the reader should have been led to the making of comparisons, to the seeking of enlightenment by setting country over against country. This, of course, is what Ranum tries to do in his introduction, but without success. The trouble lies in the main in the contributors' failure to agree on the questions to be asked, so that points of contact between them are too few. This trouble itself derives from the excess of ambition which linked three such diverse and difficult themes under one umbrella. Naturally enough every author tends to find his centre of gravity in one or the other of them; only Krieger manages a true balance, and that largely because in Germany, exceptionally, the writers of history constituted the true bearers of such national consciousness as did exist and prepared the only road found towards a native political culture. In France they were no more than government hacks, even if some of them wrote good history; in England they have been consistently over-regarded, at the expense of divines, journalists, politicians and philosophers who contributed far more to either national consciousness or political culture; in Spain they play no part remotely as significant as that of soldiers and legists; in Italy they were temporarily insignificant; and in Russia they did not really exist at all.

Nevertheless, certain themes emerge which could fruitfully be studied in the historians and which are central to the themes embraced. For instance, every country here included derived its consciousness of nationhood from historical ideas – often myths – which developed mainly in the Renaissance, though most of them had a much longer existence at least in embryo. It might be profitable to set them side by side: Britain's Brutus, the Frankish myth, Arminius and his like in Germany, the Byzantine ancestry of Russia's Orthodox nationhood, the real Romanism of Italy and Spain – these are powerful unifying stories which occupied the minds of many that have left no formal writings behind. The effects of various national attitudes upon different traditions of historical writing might repay comparative investigation. Another theme worth pursuing across the board would be the constant interaction of the larger and the smaller – the dialectic of nationhood and localism which so often seems to deny a national consciousness yet starkly apparent at other times. The brave endeavours here recorded, even in their often manifest failure to advance the discussion, could form a foundation for further exploration: and that is achievement enough.

GENERAL INDEX

General index

Cromwell, Thomas (*cont.*)
205, 223–4, 229, 234, 236, 253, 280,
283–6, 315, 317, 322–4, 327, 329–31;
religion of, 377–8, reputation of, 373,
383; resentment against, 24–5, 186,
193, 199–200, 204, 206–7, 210–11;
working methods of, 379–81; *also* 10,
48, 88n, 91, 109n, 308, 319–20, 361,
410, 450.—And: Council, 18–20, 23,
27, 30, 32–4, 36; Court, 42–4, 45–6,
51–2; faction, 50, 54–5, 210–11; More,
346, 362, 370; Parliament, 9, 14–15, 17,
67, 152–3, 376; taxation, 218–25,
229–30, 232
Cromwell, Thomas (diarist), 257, 265
Crowley, Robert, 237–8, 245–9, 251
Crown, *see* Dispensing power, Kingship,
Supremacy; clerk of the, 103; title to,
106, 146
Cumberland, 189; earl of, *see* Clifford

Dacre, Thomas lord, 208
Daniel, Samuel, 465, 473
Darcy, Arthur, 196
Darcy, Thomas lord, 50, 54, 192, 194–8,
201, 204, 206–14, 436
Darwin, Charles, 402
Daubeney, Harry, earl of Bridgewater, 13
Davies, John, 309, 470–1
de Brie, Germain, 354
Debts, 285
Defamation, 292
de la Pole, William, duke of Suffolk, 60
Demurrers, 179
Denmark, *see* Scandinavia
Denys, Thomas, 27
Derby, earl of, *see* Stanley
Dethick, William, 59–60
Devereux, Richard, 10
Devereux, Robert, 2nd earl of Essex, 34,
40, 46–7, 53–4
Devereux, Walter, viscount Hereford and
1st earl of Essex, 31
Devon, earl of, *see* Courtenay, Mountjoy
D'Ewes, Simonds, 62, 66, 72, 75, 166–8
Disease, 333–6
Dispensations act, 383

Dispensing power, 124
Disraeli, Benjamin, earl of Beaconsfield,
394–5, 404n
Docwra, Thomas (prior of St John's), 74
Doncaster (Yorks), 201
Donne, John, 338
Dorset, marquess of, *see* Grey
Dortrecht, synod of, 314
Dover (Kent), 147, 219, 222, 226
Drayton, Michael, 373
Drury, Robert, 17
Dublin, 204
Dudley, Ambrose, earl of Warwick, 34
Dudley, Edmund, 17, 75, 278–9, 281
Dudley, John, earl of Warwick and duke
of Northumberland, 30–2, 38, 51, 54,
237, 327
Dudley, Robert, earl of Leicester, 20,
34–5, 40, 43, 53–5, 261–2
Durham, 189–90, 199, 202, 239–40

Economic problems, 238–40, 243, 246–7,
250–3, 282, 331; *and see* Enclosure
Education, 239–40, 247, 312–13
Edward I, 119n
Edward II, 24
Edward III, 268, 306
Edward IV, 13, 39, 131, 216, 441–2;
Parliaments of the reign of, 61, 64,
113–18, 122–4, 133, 141
Edward VI, 35, 111n, 135, 234, 281,
460–1; Council under, 29, 32; faction
under, 51; Parliaments of the reign of,
9, 15, 140, 153, 165–6, 286; preaching
before, 237, 242; reform under, 315,
325, 330; taxation under, 230
Edward the Confessor, 270n
Egerton, Thomas, lord Ellesmere (lord
chancellor), 19
Eliot, John, 20
Elizabeth I, and Church, 317–18, 326; and
Council, 24, 33–8; and faction, 45–6,
52–3, 56; and Parliament, 9, 20, 159;
and reform, 281–2, 286; and taxation,
8, 230–2; Court of, 39, 42, 45, 47;
Froude on, 400–1, 407; marriage and
succession, 174, 261–2; Parliaments of

500

Gibbon, Edward, 391
Gladstone, William Ewart, 394, 398, 404n
Gold, Henry, 409
Gondomar, Diego Sarmiento, count, 23
Goodrich, Thomas (bp of Ely), 31
Grafton, Richard, 176
Grantham (Lincs), 254, 265
Gray's Inn, 375
Great Wardrobe, 130n
Grenfell, Charlotte Maria, 393
Grey, Thomas, marquess of Dorset, 89–90, 197
Grindal, Edmund (abp of Canterbury), 178
Grocyn, William, 311
Grotius, Hugo, 314
Guevara, Antonio de, 40–1
Guildford, Henry, 18
Guildford, Richard, 17
Gunthorpe, John (clerk of Parliaments), 113, 116–17

Hale, Matthew, 288
Hales, Christopher, 200
Hales, Edward, 111n
Hales, John, 234–5, 237, 249–51
Hall, Arthur, 160, 172, 254–73
Hall, Edward, 357, 377
Hallam, Henry, 391
Hallom, John, 192
Hamerton, Stephen, 191
Handguns, 205
Hanseatic League, 355
Harcourt (family), 66
Harleian Library, 63
Harpsfield, Nicholas, 459
Harrison, William, 469, 472–3
Hastings, Brian, 192
Hastings, Francis, earl of Huntingdon, 31
Hatton, Christopher, 19, 42, 256–7, 260–1
Hatton, Richard (clerk of Parliaments), 84, 124, 129–33
Hengham, Ralph de, 119n
Henry III, 269, 271
Henry IV, 232n

Henry V, 39, 306
Henry VI, 39, 59, 113, 118–19
Henry VII, and reform, 278–9; Council of, 17, 25, 32; Court of, 40, 42, 52, 441; Parliaments of the reign of, 14–15, 63–4, 96–9, 104, 106, 124–5, 128, 131–3, 268–70; taxation under, 216, 228; *also* 242, 439, 460
Henry VIII, and Cromwell, 383–4; and More, 354–5, 359–61, 368, 370–2, 447, 460; and Parliament, 9; and reform, 274, 280, 286–8; and Reformation, 319, 323–5, 327, 329–30; and taxation, 216, 228–30; Council of, 18–19, 23–4, 30–1; Court of, 39–40, 42, 45–52, 441–2; dry stamp of, 51; faction under, 50–1, 54; Froude on, 397, 400–1, 408–10; Parliaments of the reign of, 9–10, 13, 15, 62, 65–78, 82, 84–92, 93–6, 100–3, 107–8, 125–6, 130, 133–40, 151–3; religion of, 316–17, 323; reputation of, 411; resistance to, 185–7, 196, 206, 212–13, 346, 386–7, 459; *also* 37, 390, 437, 460–1
Herbert, William, earl of Pembroke, 31
Hereford, viscount, *see* Devereux
Heresy, 26, 202, 204–5, 318, 410; *and see* More
Hertford, earl of, *see* Seymour
Hesse, 322
Hexham (Northumberland), 190
Hext, Edward, 302–3
Higden, Ranulf, 468n
Hilsey, John, 204
Historiography, 183–5, 268–73, 309–10, 399–412, 413–28, 464–74, 494
Hoby, Philip, 19
Holbein, Hans, 344, 365
Holinshed, Ralph, 472
Hooker, John, 270n
Hooker, Richard, 316, 465, 468, 473
Hooper, John, 237, 327
Horses, export of, 152
Hotman, Jean, 314
Household, royal, members of, 26–9, 34–5, 41–3
Howard, Catherine, 51, 103, 107

Leo X (pope), 375
Lessees, 285
letters patent, acts concerning, 147, 150, 179, 286
Levellers, 484
Lever, Thomas, 235, 237–8, 242–5, 249, 251
Linacre, Thomas, 311
Lincoln, 196, 198; earl of, *see* Clinton
Lincolnshire, rebellion in, 185, 189–91, 193–5, 197–201, 204, 211, 214
Lincoln's Inn, 355
Lingard, John, 391, 405n
Lisle, Honor lady, 437, 440–1
Lisle, lord, *see* Plantagenet
Litton, Robert, 17
Lollardy, 306, 313–14, 316–17, 322
London, 197–8, 239, 247, 259, 280, 299, 314, 325; and Parliament, 163–4; lord mayor of, 26–7
Longland, John (bp of Lincoln), 27, 199–201
Lords, House of, 9, 29, 162, 164, 170, 174, 176, 179–80, 221, 409; clerk of, *see* Parliament, clerk of; Journals of, 58–92, 138, 160, 164–5; presence in, 61–3, 69, 71–3, 75, 81–2, 88–90; proxies in 70, 76–7
Louth (Lincs), 190–1, 214
Louvain, 357
Lovell, Thomas, 17
Lübeck, 323
Lucian, 357
Lucius (king), 271
Luther, Martin (and Lutheranism), 55, 204, 279, 313–17, 321–4, 328–31, 348, 350, 352, 359, 367, 370, 377, 379, 447–8

Macaulay, Thomas Babington, 391, 396–7, 408, 410
Machiavelli, Niccolò, 309, 312, 377, 472
Machlinia, William de, 93, 97
Madrid, 306
Magna Carta, 272
Magnus, Thomas, 26
Maitland, Frederick William, 392
Mallory, Melchisedek, 254–5, 259n, 267

Manchester (Lancs), 102
Manners, Thomas, earl of Rutland, 210
Marguerite d'Angoulême, 457
Marriage, clerical, 323, 325; law of, 285
Marshall, William, 204, 310n
Marsiglio of Padua, 310n, 377
Martyr, Peter (Vermigli), 325
Mary I, 23, 46, 111n, 340; and Reformation, 134, 327; and taxation, 230; as princess, 185–6, 205–6, 210–11; Council of, 29, 32–3, 35, 38; factions under, 49, 51–2; Parliaments of the reign of, 9, 15, 153–4, 164
Mary (queen of Scots), 46, 159, 169–70, 180n, 461
Maryland, 341
Mason, John, 19
Massachusetts, 342
Matthew Paris, 468n
Melanchthon, Philip, 204, 324–5, 327
Merchants, 340; Italian, 106, 131
Merchant Taylors Company, 75
Merton, statute of, 271
Metternich, prince Clemens, 415
Middle March, 189
Middlesex, 286
Mildmay, Walter, 19, 34, 255–6, 258–61, 267, 270–2
Miller, Thomas (Lancaster herald), 194
Milton, John, 337
Modus Tenendi Parliamentum, 68–9, 84–5, 232n, 270n, 468n
Mohacz, battle of, 361, 458
Moigne, Thomas, 197–8, 206
Mommsen, Theodor, 408
Monasteries, dissolution of, 13, 107, 186, 199–201, 203, 211–12, 287, 384
Montague, Edward, 30
Moon capsule, 339
More, dame Alice, *see* Myddleton
More, John, 73–4, 355
More, Thomas, ambiguity of, 345–7, 364–5; and Cromwell, 376; and heresy, 316, 322, 346, 348–50, 359–61, 365–7, 389, 446–53, 457; anti-feminism in, 345–6; as polemicist, 446–8; Augustinian, 350; biography of, 355–62;

General index

Smith, Thomas (*cont.*)
43, 177–8, 312–13, 473; on the constitution, 5–6, 159–60, 468n, 470–1; on the economy, 249, 252–3, 281
Social sciences, 422, 425–6
Somerset, duke of, *see* Seymour
Soulemont, Thomas, 88, 139
South Africa, 394–5, 398, 402
Southampton, earl of, *see* Fitzwilliam, Wriothesley
Southwark (Surrey), 150
Spain, 23, 339, 396, 492–5
Spilman, Francis (clerk of Parliaments), 112, 133, 135, 137
Stafford, Edward, duke of Buckingham, 40, 89–90, 125–6
Stafford, Henry lord, 111
Stanley, Edward, earl of Derby, 210, 387
Stanyhurst, Richard, 472
Staple, merchants of, 115
Star Chamber, 126n, 207, 275, 292, 295, 298, 300, 302
Starkey, Ralph, 62, 72
Starkey, Thomas, 280, 309, 312, 330, 377, 379, 388, 471–2
Stationers Company, 260
Statute, authority of, 109, 264, 380, 385; commonwealth mentioned in, 236–7; confirming acts, 148, 150; enacting clauses, 144–55; printing of, 92–109, 141, 144, 161, in separates 102–3; private, 14–16, 86, 106, 117, 126–8, 137–8, 149–50, 162; public, 86–7, 103–7, 119–22, 126, 128–31, 135–7, *and see Communes peticiones*; [particular acts are listed under their subject]
Stones, George, 199–200
Stow, John, 467
Strafford, earl of, *see* Wentworth
Strassburg, 321, 326–7, 330
Stubbs, William, 391
Succession, 153, 205–6, 210, 212, 249, 361, 432
Suffolk, duke of, *see* Brandon, de la Pole; earl of, *see* Howard
Supply acts, 94, 100, 102, 125, 131, 139–40, 144, 160, 216–17, 219–21, 228, 231–2, 477
Supremacy, royal, 146, 202–3, 380–1, 385
Sussex, earl of, *see* Radcliffe
Sweden, *see* Scandinavia

Talbot, Francis, 14th earl of Shrewsbury, 31
Talbot, George, 7th earl of Shrewsbury, 196, 210, 213, 387
Talbot, Gilbert, 17
Talbot, Gilbert, 10th earl of Shrewsbury, 35
Tate, Francis, 270n
Taxation, 10–11, 216–33, 307, 385, 477; *and see* Parliament, Supply
Taylor, John (clerk of Parliaments), 67–71, 74–5, 83–7, 90–2, 100, 124, 127, 130, 133, 135, 141
Tempest, Nicholas, 191
Tempest, Thomas, 207, 211
Textiles, 103
Theft, 293–4
Throckmorton, Elizabeth, 46
Throckmorton, George, 48
Tournai, 10
Tower of London, as archive, 111–13, 122, 133, 160, 436; as prison, 254, 256, 262, 265, 278, 354–5, 361, 389, 442, 460
Treason, 103, 146–7, 149, 151, 205, 212, 214, 292, 297, 361–2, 388–9, 436–7
Tudor, Edmund, earl of Richmond, 115
Tudor government, nature of, 433–6, 475–8; *and see* Kingship
Tuke, Brian (clerk of Parliaments), 68, 103, 124
Tunstall, Cuthbert (bp of London and Durham), 26, 28, 30–1, 202
Turks, 361, 458–9
Tyndale, William, 204, 313, 315, 317, 322, 324, 331, 348, 359, 368, 379, 384, 445, 448, 451, 467

Udall, Nicholas, 312
Ulnagers, 179n
Universities, 150, 240, 245, 253, 280, 312, 325, 355

508

General index

INDEX OF AUTHORS CITED

Includes only passages in which writers' views are discussed or assessed; writers contemporary with the events with which they deal are listed in the General Index.

Index of authors cited

Haupt, G.E., 454–5
Hay, D., 302n
Hexter, J.H., 184n, 418, 484
Hill, J.E.C., 479
Hoak, D.E., 29, 463
Howe, B., 59n
Hume, A., 444
Hurstfield, J., 8n, 53, 386, 411, 431–6

Ingram, M., 291, 299, 300n
Ives, E.W., 54

James, M.E., 194, 196, 207, 208n
Jenkins, A.L., 141n
Jenkinson, H., 98n
Johnson, C., 474–5
Johnson, P., 412
Jones, N.L., 176–6
Jones, W.J., 477
Jones, W.R.D., 237, 251–2
Jordan, W.K., 234, 461

Kelley, D., 469
Koenigsberger, H.E., 492–3
Krieger, L., 491–4
Kuhn, T., 424–5

Langbein, J.H., 297
Lemasters, G., 29, 32
Levy, F.J., 464–5
Lewis, C.S., 455
Lingard, J., 400n
Loach, J., 158
Loades, D.M., 313, 317
Lundgreen, P., 486–7
Lusardi, J.P., 445

MacCaffrey, W.T., 52
Macfarlane, A., 29, 300
McKisack, M., 464–5
Maitland, F.W., 309, 399n
Maitland, S.R., 400n
Manley, F., 454, 459
Marius, R.C., 444–6, 472
Martz, L.L., 454
Mattingly, G., 187, 208–9
Merriman, R.B., 439, 443

Meyjes, G.H.M.P., 314
Miller, C.E., 454
Miller, H., 12
Mitchell, W.M., 477
Munsche, P., 299
Myers, A.R., 59–60

Neale, J.E., 7, 10, 12, 16, 156, 158, 160,
    164, 167–8, 170–2, 174–80, 182, 257,
    260, 266, 272, 411, 477
Nicholson, G.D., 472
Nicolas, N.H., 59n
Nijenhuis, W., 314
Notestein, W., 156–7, 172, 182
Nuttall, G., 314

Oberman, H.A., 329

Pantzer, K., 93n, 94n, 96n
Parry, G., 472
Paul, R.S., 479
Pawlish, H.P., 309n
Pearl, V., 483
Platt, J., 314
Pocock, J.G.A., 469–70, 492, 494
Pollard, A.F., 58, 64–5, 68, 71–2, 75, 87,
    164, 235–8, 282, 373, 390, 406, 411,
    424, 440, 460, 476
Prestwich, M., 432
Procter, R., 93

Radzinowicz, L., 296n, 302
Ranum, O., 491–2, 494
Read, C., 53, 186, 400, 460
Ritter, G., 363
Rokkan, S., 486–91
Roskell, J.S., 156–7
Rowse, A.L., 411
Ruigh, R.E., 477

Samaha, J., 301
Scarisbrick, J.J., 188, 208n, 411
Schofield, R.S., 217n
Schuster, L.A., 444–7, 449
Seeley, J.R., 415
Sharpe, I., 290–1, 303
Smith, L.B., 411

511